THE SECOND WORLD WAR

VOLUME V
CLOSING THE RING

WINSTON S. CHURCHILL

THE
SECOND WORLD WAR

VOLUME V

CLOSING THE RING

CASSELL & CO. LTD

LONDON · TORONTO · MELBOURNE · SYDNEY

WELLINGTON

Composed by Ebenezer Baylis and Son,
Ltd., The Trinity Press, Worcester, and
London. Printed in Great Britain by
Ebenezer Baylis and Son, Ltd.; Wyman
and Sons, Ltd., London, Reading, and
Fakenham; The Chapel River Press,
Andover, Hants; Hazell Watson and
Viney, Ltd., Aylesbury and London;
and Greycaines (Taylor Garnett Evans
and Co. Ltd.), Watford, Herts. Bound
by Webb, Son & Co. Ltd., London,
E.C.1; G. & J. Kitcat Ltd., London,
S.E.1; and The Leighton-Straker Book-
binding Co. Ltd., London, N.W.10

First published 1952

Moral of the Work

—————— ❧❧❧ ——————

IN WAR: RESOLUTION

IN DEFEAT: DEFIANCE

IN VICTORY: MAGNANIMITY

IN PEACE: GOODWILL

ACKNOWLEDGMENTS

I MUST again acknowledge the assistance of those who helped me with the previous volumes, namely, Lieutenant-General Sir Henry Pownall, Commodore G. R. G. Allen, Colonel F. W. Deakin, Mr. Denis Kelly, and Mr. C. C. Wood. I have also to thank the very large number of others who have kindly read these pages and commented upon them.

I am obliged to Air Chief Marshal Sir Guy Garrod for his help in presenting the Air aspect.

Lord Ismay has continued to give me his aid, as have my other friends.

I record my obligation to His Majesty's Government for permission to reproduce the text of certain official documents of which the Crown Copyright is legally vested in the Controller of His Majesty's Stationery Office. At the request of His Majesty's Government, on security grounds, I have paraphrased some of the telegrams published in this volume. These changes have not altered in any way the sense or substance of the telegrams.

I am indebted to the Roosevelt Trust for the use they have permitted of the President's telegrams quoted here, and also to others who have allowed their private letters to be published.

PREFACE

IN *The Hinge of Fate* I described the decisive change for the better in our fortunes which lighted the winter of 1942 and the spring of 1943. *Closing the Ring* sets forth the year of conflict from June 1943 to June 1944. Aided by the command of the oceans, the mastery of the U-boats, and our ever-growing superiority in the air, the Western Allies were able to conquer Sicily and invade Italy, with the result that Mussolini was overthrown and the Italian nation came over to our side. Hitler and the circle of countries he had occupied was isolated, and, with the immense onslaught of Russia from the east, was completely surrounded. At the same time Japan had been forced on to the defensive and was vainly trying to hold the vast territories she had overrun.

The danger which faced the United Nations was no longer Defeat, but Stalemate. Before them lay the formidable task of invading the two aggressors in their homelands and liberating from their grip the peoples they had struck down. This world-wide problem was faced at the Conferences between Great Britain and the United States at Quebec and Washington in the summer, and at the triple meeting of the main Allies at Teheran in November. There was no difference between us of aim or of resolve to give all to the common cause. Grave divergences of method and of emphasis were inevitable because of the various angles from which the three partners naturally approached the decisions which were required. How agreement was reached upon all the supreme issues is the tale I now have to tell. It carries us to the liberation of Rome and to the eve of the British and American crossing of the Channel and entry into Normandy.

I have followed the method I used in earlier volumes. I do not seek to do more than make a contribution to history from the standpoint of the British Prime Minister and Minister of Defence. In this my directives, telegrams, and minutes, written at the time and not in the after-light, are my stepping-stones. It has been suggested that the answers to many of these documents should also be included. I, on the other hand, have found it necessary in this volume to practise compression and selection in an increasing degree. A final volume is already needed to record and complete the story. I can therefore only make my excuses to any who may feel that their point of view is not fully set forth.

More than seven years have passed since the events here recorded happened. Many international relationships have changed. Deep rifts have opened between former comrades. New and perhaps darker clouds have gathered. Old foes have become friends, and even allies. In this setting some of the sentiments and expressions contained in telegrams, minutes, and reports of Conferences may jar upon the readers in other countries. I can only remind them that these documents have an historical value and that we were then engaged in a fierce and terrible war. When men are fighting for their lives they are not often disposed to be complimentary to those who are trying to kill them. On the other hand, to soften all harsh expressions about the enemy nations of those days would prevent a true picture being presented. Time and Truth are healers.

WINSTON S. CHURCHILL

Chartwell,
   Westerham,
      Kent

September 1, 1951

Theme of the Volume

HOW

NAZI GERMANY WAS ISOLATED

AND

ASSAILED ON ALL SIDES

CLOSING THE RING

—— ·{◇}· ——

TABLE OF CONTENTS

BOOK I

ITALY WON

TABLE OF CONTENTS

BOOK II

TEHERAN TO ROME

MAPS AND DIAGRAMS

TABLE OF CONTENTS

BOOK I

ITALY WON

CHAPTER I

THE COMMAND OF THE SEAS

GUADALCANAL AND NEW GUINEA

Maritime Power – The Mediterranean Freed – The Mortal Struggle with the U-Boats – The Battle of the Atlantic the Dominating Factor in the War – An Atlantic Convoy Conference Meets – The Decisive Battle with the U-Boats Fought and Won – Air Cover Protects Our Convoys – The Climax of April 1943 – A Welcome Respite – New Weapons – The Schnorkel – Retrospect on the Pacific War – The Struggle for New Guinea – The Solomon Islands – Guadalcanal – A Noble Feat of Arms – Our Efforts to Help the United States – The End of the Japanese Offensive – The Japanese Defeat in New Guinea – The Turn of the Tide.

*E*ARLIER volumes have led us to the point where the aggressors, both in Europe and Asia, had been driven to the defensive. Stalingrad in February 1943 marked the turn of the tide in Russia. By May all German and Italian forces in the African continent had been killed or captured. The American victories in the Coral Sea and at Midway Island a year before had stopped Japanese expansion in the Pacific Ocean. Australia and New Zealand were freed from the threat of invasion. Henceforward in Europe the Axis must expect and await the Anglo-American assault which had so long been purposed. The tremendous armies of the United States were growing in strength and quality with every month that passed. But the Western Allies could never strike home at Hitler's Europe, and thus bring the war to a decisive end, unless another major favourable change came to pass. Anglo-American "maritime power", a modern term expressing the combined strength of naval and air forces

3

properly woven together, became supreme on and under the surface of the seas and the oceans during 1943. It was not until April and May that the U-boats were beaten and the mastery of the life-lines across the Atlantic was finally won. Without this no amphibious operations on the enormous scale required to liberate Europe would have been possible. Soviet Russia would have been left to face Hitler's whole remaining strength while most of Europe lay in his grip.

In the Mediterranean also the U-boats were mastered. Our armies for the Sicilian and Italian campaigns were assembling and could now be launched across the sea against the under-belly of Hitler's Europe. Besides this the Mediterranean was the main artery in the communications of the British Empire. The extirpation of Axis power in North Africa opened to our convoys the direct route to Egypt, India, and Australia, protected from Gibraltar to Suez by sea and air forces working from the newly won bases along the route. The long haul round the Cape, which had cost us so dear in time, effort, and tonnage, would soon be ended. The saving of an average of forty-five days for each convoy to the Middle East increased magnificently at one stroke the fertility of our shipping.

*   *   *   *   *

The single-handed British struggle against the U-boats, the magnetic mines, and the surface raiders in the first two and a half years of the war has already been described. The long-awaited supreme event of the American alliance which arose from the Japanese attack on Pearl Harbour seemed at first to have increased our perils at sea. In 1940 four million tons of merchant shipping were lost, and more than four million tons in 1941. In 1942, after the United States was our Ally, nearly eight million tons of the augmented mass of Allied shipping had been sunk. Until the end of 1942 the U-boats sank ships faster than the Allies could build them. The foundation of all our hopes and schemes was the immense shipbuilding programme of the United States. During 1943 the curve of new tonnage rose sharply and losses fell. Before the end of that year new tonnage at last surpassed losses at sea from all causes, and the second quarter saw, for the first time, U-boat losses exceed their rate of replacement. The time was presently to come when more U-boats would be

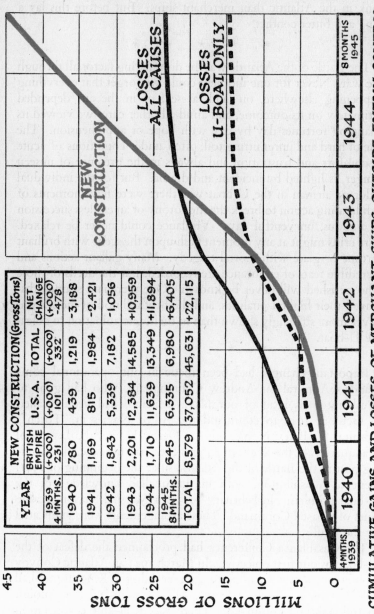

YEAR	NEW CONSTRUCTION (Gross Tons)			
	BRITISH EMPIRE (+000)	U.S.A. (+000)	TOTAL (+000)	NET CHANGE (+000)
1939 4 MNTHS.	231	101	332	-478
1940	780	439	1,219	-3,188
1941	1,169	815	1,984	-2,421
1942	1,843	5,339	7,182	-1,056
1943	2,201	12,384	14,585	+10,959
1944	1,710	11,639	13,349	+11,894
1945 8 MNTHS.	645	6,335	6,980	+6,405
TOTAL	8,579	37,052	45,631	+22,115

CUMULATIVE GAINS AND LOSSES OF MERCHANT SHIPS OUTSIDE ENEMY CONTROL (1600 GROSS TONS AND OVER), 1939-45

MILLIONS OF GROSS TONS

5

sunk in the Atlantic than merchant ships. But before this lay a long and bitter conflict.

*   *   *   *   *

The Battle of the Atlantic was the dominating factor all through the war. Never for one moment could we forget that everything happening elsewhere, on land, at sea, or in the air, depended ultimately on its outcome, and amid all other cares we viewed its changing fortunes day by day with hope or apprehension. The tale of hard and unremitting toil, often under conditions of acute discomfort and frustration and always in the presence of unseen danger, is lighted by incident and drama. But for the individual sailor or airman in the U-boat war there were few moments of exhilarating action to break the monotony of an endless succession of anxious, uneventful days. Vigilance could never be relaxed. Dire crisis might at any moment flash upon the scene with brilliant fortune or glare with mortal tragedy. Many gallant actions and incredible feats of endurance are recorded, but the deeds of those who perished will never be known. Our merchant seamen displayed their highest qualities, and the brotherhood of the sea was never more strikingly shown than in their determination to defeat the U-boat.

*   *   *   *   *

Important changes had been made in our operational commands. Admiral Sir Andrew Cunningham, who had gone to Washington as head of our Naval Mission, had been recalled in October 1942 to command the Allied Navies in "Torch". Admiral Sir Percy Noble, who at Derby House, the Liverpool headquarters of the Western Approaches, had held the commanding post in the Battle of the Atlantic since the beginning of 1941, went to Washington, with his unequalled knowledge of the U-boat problem. In February 1943 Air Marshal Slessor became chief of Coastal Command. These arrangements were vindicated by the results.

The Casablanca Conference had proclaimed the defeat of the U-boats as our first objective. In March 1943 an Atlantic Convoy Conference met in Washington, under Admiral King, to pool all Allied resources in the Atlantic. This system did not amount to full unity of command. There was well-knit co-operation at all levels and complete accord at the top, but the two

Allies approached the problem with differences of method. The United States had no organisation like our Coastal Command, through which on the British or reception side of the ocean air operations were controlled by a single authority. A high degree of flexibility had been attained. Formations could be rapidly switched from quiet to dangerous areas, and the command was being reinforced largely from American sources. In Washington control was exerted through a number of autonomous subordinate commands called "sea frontiers", each with its allotment of aircraft.

*   *   *   *   *

After the winter gales, which caused much damage to our escorts, but also checked the U-boat attack, the month of February 1943 had shown an ugly increase in the hostile concentrations in the North Atlantic. In spite of heavy losses, the number of operational U-boats at Admiral Doenitz's disposal at the beginning of the year rose to two hundred and twelve. In March there were over a hundred of them constantly at sea, and the packs in which they hunted could no longer be evaded by skilful routeing. The issue had to be fought out by combined sea and air forces round the convoys themselves. Sinkings throughout the world rose to nearly 700,000 tons in that month.

Amid these stresses a new agreement was reached in Washington whereby Britain and Canada assumed entire responsibility for convoys on the main North Atlantic route to Britain. The decisive battle with the U-boats was now fought and won. Control was vested in two joint naval and air headquarters, one at Liverpool under a British and the other at Halifax under a Canadian admiral. Naval protection in the North Atlantic was henceforward provided by British and Canadian ships, the United States remaining responsible for their convoys to the Mediterranean and their own troop transports. In the air British, Canadian, and United States forces all complied with the day-to-day requirements of the joint commanders at Liverpool and Halifax.

The air gap in the North Atlantic south-east of Greenland was now closed by means of the very-long-range (V.L.R.) Liberator squadrons based in Newfoundland and Iceland. By April a shuttle service provided daylight air-cover along the whole route. The U-boat packs were kept underwater and harried continually,

7

while the air and surface escort of the convoys coped with the attackers. We were now strong enough to form independent flotilla groups to act like cavalry divisions, apart from all escort duties. This I had long desired to see.

* * * * *

It was at this time that the H$_2$S apparatus, described in Volume IV,* of which a number had been handed over somewhat reluctantly by our Bomber Command to Coastal Command, played a notable part. The Germans had learnt how to detect the comparatively long waves used in our earlier Radar, and to dive before our flyers could attack them. It was many months before they discovered how to detect the very short wave used in our new method. Hitler complained that this single invention was the ruin of the U-boat campaign. This was an exaggeration.

In the Bay of Biscay however the Anglo-American air offensive was soon to make the life of U-boats in transit almost unbearable. The rocket now fired from aircraft was so damaging that the enemy started sending the U-boats through in groups on the surface, fighting off the aircraft with gunfire in daylight. This desperate experiment was vain. In March and April 1943 twenty-seven U-boats were destroyed in the Atlantic alone, more than half by air attack.

In April 1943 we could see the balance turn. Two hundred and thirty-five U-boats, the greatest number the Germans ever achieved, were in action. But their crews were beginning to waver. They could never feel safe. Their attacks, even when conditions were favourable, were no longer pressed home, and during this month our shipping losses in the Atlantic fell by nearly 300,000 tons. In May alone forty U-boats perished in the Atlantic. The German Admiralty watched their charts with strained attention, and at the end of the month Admiral Doenitz recalled the remnants of his fleet from the North Atlantic to rest or to fight in less hazardous waters. By June 1943 the shipping losses fell to the lowest figure since the United States had entered the war. The convoys came through intact, and the Atlantic supply line was safe.

The struggle in these critical months is shown by the table on page 10.

* See Vol. IV, p. 251

8

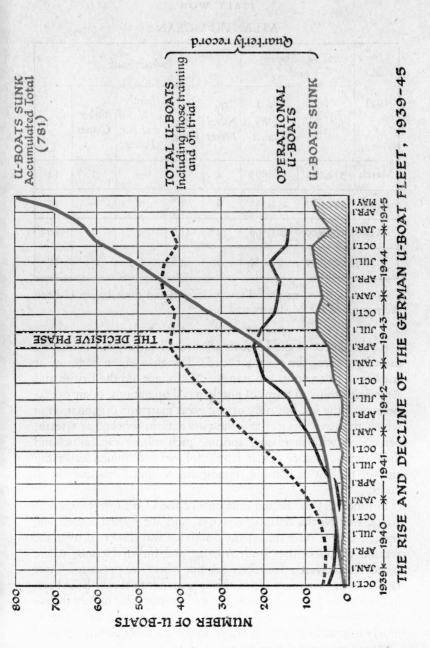

THE RISE AND DECLINE OF THE GERMAN U-BOAT FLEET, 1939-45

U-BOATS SUNK
Accumulated Total
(781)

Quarterly record

TOTAL U-BOATS
Including those training
and on trial

OPERATIONAL
U-BOATS

U-BOATS SUNK

THE DECISIVE PHASE

NUMBER OF U-BOATS

9

ATLANTIC OCEAN

1943	Allied Shipping sunk		U-boats sunk				
	By U-boat	Total. All Causes	By Naval Forces	By Air Forces	Jointly by Naval and Air Forces	Other Causes	Total
March	514,744	538,695	4	7	—	1	12
April	241,687	252,533	6	8*	1	—	15
May	199,409	205,598	12*	18*	7	3	40
June	21,759	28,269	6	9*	2	—	17

Note.—In the same period seven German and three Italian U-boats were sunk in the Mediterranean.

★ ★ ★ ★ ★

As the defeat of the U-boats affected all subsequent events we must here carry the story forward. The air weapon had now at last begun to attain its full stature. No longer did the British and Americans think in terms of purely naval operations, or air operations over the sea, but only of one great maritime organisation in which the two Services and the two nations worked as a team, perceiving with increasing aptitude each other's capabilities and limitations. Victory demanded skilful and determined leadership and the highest standard of training and technical efficiency in all ranks.

In June 1943 the beaten remnants of the U-boat fleet ceased to attack our North Atlantic convoys, and we gained a welcome respite. For a time the enemy's activity was dispersed over the remote wastes of the South Atlantic and Indian Oceans, where our defences were relatively weak but where we presented fewer targets. Our air offensive in the approaches to the U-boat bases in the Bay of Biscay continued to gather strength. In July thirty-seven U-boats were sunk, thirty-one by air attack, and of these nearly half were sunk in the Bay. In the last three months of 1943

* These figures each include one Italian.

fifty-three U-boats were destroyed, while we lost only forty-seven merchant ships.

Throughout a stormy autumn the U-boats struggled vainly to regain the ascendancy in the North Atlantic. Our combined sea and air defence was by that time so strong that they suffered heavy losses for small results in every convoy battle. In anti-U-boat warfare the air weapon was now an equal partner with the surface ship. Our convoys were guarded by more numerous and formidable surface escorts than ever before, reinforced with escort carriers giving close and advanced air protection. More than this, we had the means to seek out and destroy the U-boats wherever we could find them. The combination of support groups of carriers and escort vessels, aided by long-range aircraft of Coastal Command, which now included American squadrons, proved decisive. One such group, commanded by Captain F. J. Walker, R.N., our most outstanding U-boat killer, was responsible for the destruction of six U-boats in a single cruise.

The so-called merchant aircraft-carrier, or M.A.C. ship, which came out at this time was an entirely British conception. An ordinary cargo ship or tanker was fitted with a flying deck for naval aircraft. While preserving its mercantile status and carrying cargo it helped to defend the convoy in which it sailed. There were nineteen of these vessels in all, two wearing the Dutch flag, working in the North Atlantic. Together with the catapult-aircraft merchant ships (C.A.M.S.), which had preceded them with a rather different technique, they marked a new departure in naval warfare. The merchant ship had now taken the offensive against the enemy instead of merely defending itself when attacked. The line between the combatant and non-combatant ship, already indistinct, had almost vanished.

The immense United States war production was now reaching its peak. Long-range aircraft and ships of many types, including the escort carriers we so greatly needed, were flowing from American yards and workshops. Many of these, and much special equipment, especially Radar, were placed at our disposal to help our own industry, and American naval and air forces joined in the battle everywhere.

Although in the face of the harsh facts Admiral Doenitz was forced to recoil, he continued to maintain as many U-boats at sea as ever. But their attack was blunted and they seldom attempted

THE CRISIS OF THE
BATTLE
August 1st, 1942,
to May 21st, 1943

Summary of Losses
Gross Tons
British   1,974,384
Others   1,786,338
Total   3,760,722

THE BATTLE OF THE ATLANTIC
MERCHANT SHIPS SUNK BY U-BOAT IN THE ATLANTIC

12

THE BATTLE OF THE ATLANTIC
MERCHANT SHIPS SUNK BY U-BOAT IN THE ATLANTIC

THE THIRD ATTACK ON
THE CONVOY ROUTES
Sept. 19th, 1943, to
May 15th, 1944

Summary of Losses	
	Gross Tons
British	119,854
Others	194,936
Total	314,790

THE BATTLE OF THE ATLANTIC
MERCHANT SHIPS SUNK BY U-BOAT IN THE ATLANTIC

to cut through our defences. He did not however despair. On January 20, 1944, he said, "The enemy has succeeded in gaining the advantage in defence. The day will come when I shall offer Churchill a first-rate submarine war. The submarine weapon has not been broken by the setbacks of 1943. On the contrary, it has become stronger. In 1944, which will be a successful but a hard year, we shall smash Britain's supply [line] with a new submarine weapon."

This confidence was not wholly unfounded. At the beginning of 1944 a gigantic effort was being made in Germany to develop a new type of U-boat which could move more quickly underwater and travel much farther. At the same time many of the older boats were withdrawn so that they could be fitted with the "Schnorkel" and work in British coastal waters. This new device enabled them to recharge their batteries while submerged with only a small tube for the intake of air remaining above the surface. Their chances of eluding detection from the air were thus improved, and it soon became evident that the Schnorkel-fitted boats were intended to dispute the passage of the English Channel whenever the Allied invasion was launched.

* * * * *

A retrospect is necessary here to remind the reader of the stirring far-flung operations which had changed the whole scene in the Far East in 1942.

While British sea-power was deployed mainly in the Atlantic and the Mediterranean, the United States was bearing almost alone the whole burden of the war against Japan. In the immense ocean spaces from India to the western coast of America itself we could give little support except with slender Australian and New Zealand naval forces. Our depleted Eastern Fleet, now based in East Africa, could do no more for a time than protect our convoys. In the Pacific however the balance had turned. The naval superiority of the United States was re-established, and the Japanese, while trying to consolidate their gains in the East Indies, had nothing to spare for incursions into the Indian Ocean. Much had happened in the Pacific since the Battles of the Coral Sea and Midway Island in the summer of 1942. Admiral Nimitz, with his headquarters at Pearl Harbour, controlled the North, Central, and South Pacific. General MacArthur, who had reached

Australia from the Philippines in March 1942, commanded the South-West Pacific, extending from the China coast to Australia, and including the Philippines, the Bismarck Archipelago, New Guinea, all the east coast of Australia, and the Solomon Islands.

The Imperial Japanese Navy, deeply conscious of defeat in the Central Pacific, turned once more to the South-West. Here, more remote from the main sources of American power, they hoped to renew their triumphant advance. Their first thrust, towards Port Moresby, in New Guinea, having been foiled by the Battle of the Coral Sea, the enemy resolved to attack by land across the Owen Stanley Mountains. Thus began the struggle for New Guinea. Simultaneously they determined to seize the Solomon Islands. They already held the small island of Tulagi, and could quickly set about the construction of an air base in the neighbouring island of Guadalcanal. With both Port Moresby and Guadalcanal in their possession they hoped the Coral Sea would become a Japanese lake, bordering upon North-Eastern Australia. From Guadalcanal Japanese airmen could reach out towards other and still more distant island groups along the main line of sea communications between America and New Zealand. American and Australian resistance to these two assaults form an admirable example of bold inter-Service action resting on maritime power.

The Solomon Islands became the objective of both sides, and Admiral King in Washington had long planned their occupation. On July 4, 1942, air reconnaissance disclosed that the enemy were already constructing an airfield on Guadalcanal. Admiral Ghormley, commanding the South Pacific area, without waiting to perfect his plans, struck on August 7 with the 1st Marine Division, already in New Zealand. The uncompleted Japanese air base was quickly captured and the battle for Guadalcanal began. It was to last six months.

* * * * *

From their main Fleet base in the Carolines and from Rabaul the Japanese could maintain greatly superior naval and air forces in these waters. The Japanese commander in Rabaul at once sent a strong force of cruisers and destroyers to Guadalcanal. In the early hours of August 9, aided by heavy rain squalls, the Japanese surprised the Allied naval forces guarding the approach to the landing-place and almost annihilated them. In about forty

minutes they sank three American heavy cruisers and the Australian cruiser *Canberra*, while receiving themselves only minor
damage. Had the Japanese admiral followed up this remarkable
success he could have swept through the strait to the eastward
and destroyed the American transports, which were still discharging their troops and stores. Like other Japanese commanders before and after him in this war, he missed his opportunity and withdrew.

The American commander could however no longer support
the landing. After unloading all that he could he retired, leaving
his 17,000 Marines ashore alone on a hostile island without air
cover and exposed to reinforced land attack. This was indeed a
grim moment. But the United States Marines were undaunted.
In spite of ceaseless air attack they held and improved their position, while a supply service by sea was improvised and the captured airfield was brought into use. From this moment fighters
and dive-bombers manned by the Marines worked from Guadalcanal itself and gave instant relief.

The Japanese now sought a decision at sea. On August 24 an
inconclusive action was fought to the north of the Solomons.
Enemy transports approaching Guadalcanal were driven off by
air attack. On August 31 the aircraft-carrier *Saratoga* was
damaged by a submarine, and a fortnight later the carrier *Wasp*,
of Mediterranean repute, was sunk. Both sides built up their
strength. Early in October, in another night engagement, a strong
force of Japanese cruisers was beaten off, one being sunk; but two
enemy battleships bombarded the airfield, and presently landed
4,500 reinforcements at a stroke. Another crisis was at hand.

★   ★   ★   ★   ★

Admiral Nimitz and General MacArthur urged, not un-
naturally, that priority should be given to the Pacific theatre at
the expense of European operations. They were powerfully
supported at Washington by Admiral King. But the descent in
North-West Africa ("Torch") was now dominant, and major
strategy prevailed. The climax of the battle on land now came.
For ten days from October 19, 1942, the Marines in close jungle
fighting held all their positions and beat the Japanese to a stand-
still. In another fleet action, mainly fought by aircraft north of the
Solomons, the carrier *Hornet*, which had replaced the *Wasp*, was

sunk. The carrier *Enterprise*, the battleship *South Dakota*, and two cruisers were damaged. The Japanese had two carriers disabled.

Admiral Halsey, who had succeeded Admiral Ghormley, and who found himself for the moment without any carriers, now appealed through Admiral Nimitz for one or more British carriers. Although we had little knowledge of American Pacific plans, we realised that an intense crisis had arisen in the Solomons. It was obvious that no carriers could reach the scene for many weeks. I earnestly desired to help in this heroic struggle, but with the main naval responsibility for landing the Anglo-American Army in North-West Africa upon us we could make no immediate proposal. It was not until December that the strain and climax of "Torch" lessened. I then sent the President a full account of our carrier position and made the best offer in our power.

Former Naval Person to President Roosevelt   2 Dec 42

Ever since we received a request for carrier reinforcement for your Pacific Fleet we have been earnestly seeking to meet your wishes. We did not feel able to come to a decision about these very few vital units until we knew how our carriers had fared in the restricted and dangerous waters in which they had to operate for "Torch". The hazards of "Torch" are not yet ended, as our build-up of shore-based aircraft will not enable the withdrawal for some time of the two carriers now employed on "Torch". Knowing however how urgently you require a reinforcement of carriers in the Pacific, we are prepared to take a risk now and come to a decision as to what we can give you.

Our carrier strength consists of four long-endurance armoured fleet carriers. We are prepared to withdraw *Illustrious* from the Eastern Fleet, and give Admiral Somerville the *Unicorn* and an auxiliary carrier. We are also prepared to withdraw *Victorious* from the Home Fleet and to send you both *Victorious* and *Illustrious* if you can allow [your] *Ranger* [a smaller carrier] to join the Home Fleet. In view of the vital importance of the Atlantic communications, the necessity of supporting the North Russian convoys, the possible appearance of *Graf Zeppelin* at the end of the year, and the present condition of *Indomitable* and *Formidable*, we could not release both *Victorious* and *Illustrious* without the addition of *Ranger* to the Home Fleet.

I am much in favour of sending you two carriers rather than one if this can be managed, as this will not only give you increased strength, but would allow the two ships to work as a tactical unit, which would appear to be necessary, as neither ship carries sufficient aircraft to

THE SOUTH-WEST PACIFIC

500 SEA MILES

Luzon
PHILIPPINE
ISLANDS
Leyte Gulf
Mindanao
Yap
Palau Is.
Morotai
Halmahera
Celebes
Timor
Hollandia
Wewak
NEW GUINEA
Lae
Manus I.
Admiralty Is.
Emirau
Kavieng
Rabaul
New Britain
Green I.
Bougainville
New Georgia
Solomon Is.
Guadalcanal
Truk
Caroline Islands
Mariana Is.
Tinian
Saipan
Guam
Eniwetok
Kwajalein
Marshall Is.
Gilbert Is.
Tarawa
AUSTRALIA

19

operate singly. I would propose to send Admiral Lyster, who is known to a good many of your officers, in command. Both ships should proceed to Pearl Harbour, arriving about the end of December, to adjust their complement of aircraft. If you are in favour of this exchange Pound will settle details with King.

Admiral King was however unwilling to spare the *Ranger*, and in consequence we could only send the *Victorious*. She left the Home Fleet for Pearl Harbour in December.

★　★　★　★　★

Meanwhile in November a series of sea and air fights which eventually proved decisive began around the Solomons, with heavy losses on both sides. On the night of November 13, in a fierce action, two United States cruisers and four destroyers were lost, with both the American admirals engaged. On the Japanese side a battleship and two destroyers were sunk. Eleven Japanese transports, with strong supporting forces, were at the same time moving towards Guadalcanal. In the thirty-six hours of ceaseless fighting which followed a second Japanese battleship, a cruiser, and three destroyers, and above all seven transports filled with troops, were sunk, at the cost to the Americans of only one more destroyer. The Japanese at this point lost confidence in the venture. Ever-increasing American reinforcements began to arrive, and the glorious Marines were relieved by the Army. The conflict continued without pause, but the enemy made no further bid for victory. On January 4, 1943, Imperial Headquarters in Tokyo ordered the evacuation of Guadalcanal, which was accomplished without serious loss. On February 9 Admiral Halsey was able at last to report that the island had been conquered.

This episode marked the end of the Japanese offensive surge. In six major naval engagements and many lesser encounters two American carriers, seven cruisers, and fourteen destroyers had been sunk, besides the Australian cruiser *Canberra*. The Japanese losses were one carrier, two battleships, four cruisers, and eleven destroyers. The loss of life on both sides was severe, on land, at sea, and in the air. "For us who were there," writes an American eye-witness, whose moving account I have followed, "Guadalcanal is not a name but an emotion, recalling desperate fights in the air, furious night naval battles, frantic work at supply or construction, savage fighting in the sodden jungle, nights broken

by screaming bombs and deafening explosions of naval shells."*
Long may the tale be told in the great Republic.

*   *   *   *   *

The tide of war had also turned in New Guinea.† The Japanese
overland advance began on July 22, 1942, from the north coast
towards Port Moresby, which was guarded by two brigades of
the 7th Australian Division back from the Middle East. The
Owen Stanley Mountains, rising to over thirteen thousand feet,
form the spine of the New Guinea land mass. Through these a
foot-track traverses the passes and the virgin jungle. A single
Australian Militia battalion fought a stubborn delaying action,
and it was not until the second week of September that the five
Japanese battalions employed approached Port Moresby. Here,
at the Imita Ridge, the enemy advance was stayed.

While all this was in progress 2,000 Japanese Marines landed
from the sea and tried on August 26 to take the three air-strips
being built near Milne Bay, at the southernmost tip of the great
island. After a fortnight's intense fighting along the seashore
more than half of the invaders were killed and the rest dispersed.
The Japanese were thenceforth thrown on to the defensive in New
Guinea. By trying to take both New Guinea and Guadalcanal
they had lost their chance of winning either. They now had to
retreat over the mountain track under close Australian ground and
air pursuit. Disease and hunger took a heavy toll. The American-
Australian air-power grew constantly. The United States 32nd
Division was flown in. The Japanese convoys carrying reinforcements suffered enormous losses. Ten thousand desperate fighting
men, with their backs to the sea, held the final perimeter at Buna.
It was not till the third week of January 1943 that the last resistance
was overcome. Only a few hundred Japanese survived. More
than fifteen thousand had been killed or perished from starvation
and disease. By February the south-eastern end of New Guinea,
as well as Guadalcanal, was firmly in Allied hands. A Japanese
convoy of twelve transports, escorted by ten warships, on its way
to reinforce their important outpost at Lae was detected in the
Bismarck Sea. It was attacked from the air on March 2 and 3, and
both transports and escort, carrying about fifteen thousand men,
were destroyed.

*   *   *   *   *

* *The Struggle for Guadalcanal*, by S. E. Morison.   † See map, p. 491.

By June 1943, when this volume opens, the prospect in the Pacific was encouraging. The last Japanese thrusts had been hurled back and the enemy was now everywhere on the defensive. They were compelled to reinforce by costly processes the positions they still held in New Guinea, especially the garrisons of Salamaua and Lae, and to build a series of supporting airfields along the coast. The American movement towards the Philippines began to be defined. General MacArthur was working westward along the north coast of New Guinea, and Admiral Halsey was slowly advancing along the island chain of the Solomons towards Rabaul. Behind all towered up the now rapidly rising strength of the United States. The eighteen months which had passed since Pearl Harbour had revealed to the rulers of Japan some of the facts and proportions they had ignored.

CHAPTER II

THE CONQUEST OF SICILY

July and August 1943

Preparations for Invading Sicily – General Alexander's Final Plan – Order of Battle – Concentration of Widespread Forces – Hitler's Conference of May 20 – Our Seizure of Pantelleria Island – Effective Cover Plans – The Appointed Day, July 10 – An Ugly Turn in the Weather – Serious Air Losses – Successful Seaborne Landings – Steady Advance of the British and American Armies – Our Next Strategic Move – My Telegram to Smuts of July 16 – Progress of the Campaign – Eisenhower Declares for the Invasion of Italy – Discussions Between the British and American Chiefs of Staff – General Patton's Fine Advance – Centuripe, Catania, and Messina – Alexander's Report – Sicily Liberated in Thirty-eight Days.

CASABLANCA Conference in January decided to invade Sicily after the capture of Tunis. This great enterprise, known by the code-name "Husky", presented new and formidable problems. Severe resistance had not been expected in the North African landings, but now the still numerous Italian Army might fight desperately in defence of its homeland. In any case it would be stiffened by strong German ground and air forces. The Italian Fleet still possessed six effective modern battleships and might join in the battle.

General Eisenhower considered that Sicily should only be attacked if our purpose was to clear the Mediterranean sea-route. If our real purpose was to invade and defeat Italy he thought that our proper initial objectives were Sardinia and Corsica, "since these islands lie on the flank of the long Italian boot and would force a very much greater dispersion of enemy strength in Italy than the mere occupation of Sicily, which lies off the mountainous

B*

toe of the peninsula."* This was no doubt a military opinion of high authority, though one I could not share. But political forces play their part, and the capture of Sicily and the direct invasion of Italy were to bring about results of a far more swift and far-reaching character.

The capture of Sicily was an undertaking of the first magnitude. Although eclipsed by events in Normandy, its importance and its difficulties should not be underrated. The landing was based on the experience gained in North Africa, and those who planned "Overlord" learned much from "Husky". In the initial assault nearly 3,000 ships and landing-craft took part, carrying between them 160,000 men, 14,000 vehicles, 600 tanks, and 1,800 guns. These forces had to be collected, trained, equipped, and eventually embarked, with all the vast impedimenta of amphibious warfare, at widely dispersed bases in the Mediterranean, in Great Britain, and in the United States. Detailed planning was required from subordinate commanders whose headquarters were separated by thousands of miles. All these plans had to be welded together by the Supreme Commander at Algiers. Here a special Allied Staff controlled and co-ordinated all preparations. As the plan developed many problems arose which could only be solved by the Combined Chiefs of Staff. Finally the convoys had to be assembled, escorted across the oceans and through the narrow seas, and concentrated in the battle area at the right time.

* * * * *

Planning at General Eisenhower's headquarters had begun in February. It now became necessary to appoint his principal subordinates.

In all wars where allies are fighting together the control of strategy usually rests in the main with whoever holds the larger forces. This may be modified by political considerations or the relative war effort in other theatres, but the principle that the more powerful army must rule is sound. For reasons of policy we had hitherto yielded the command and direction of the campaign in North-West Africa to the United States. At the beginning they were preponderant in numbers and influence. In the months that had passed since "Torch" began the arrival of the victorious Eighth Army from the Desert and the building up in Tunisia of

---

* *Crusade in Europe*, p. 176.

the British First Army had given us the proportion there of eleven British divisions to four American. Nevertheless I strictly adhered to the theme that "Torch" was an American expedition, and in every way supported General Eisenhower's position as Supreme Commander. It was however understood in practice that General Alexander as Eisenhower's Deputy had the full operational command. It was in these circumstances that the victory of Tunis was gained and the general picture presented to the American public and to the world as an overriding United States enterprise.

But now we had entered upon a new stage—the invasion of Sicily, and what should follow from it. It was agreed that action against Italy should be decided in the light of the fighting in Sicily. As the Americans became more attracted to this larger adventure, instead of being content for the rest of the year with Sardinia, and while the prospects of another joint campaign unfolded, I felt it necessary that the British should at least be equal partners with our Allies. The proportions of the armies available in July were: British, eight divisions; United States, six. Air: the United States, 55 per cent.; British, 45 per cent. Naval, 80 per cent. British. Besides all this there remained the considerable British armies in the Middle East and in the Eastern Mediterranean, including Libya, which were independently commanded by General Maitland Wilson, from the British headquarters at Cairo. It did not seem too much in these circumstances that we should have at least an equal share of the High Command. And this was willingly conceded by our loyal comrades. We were moreover given the direct conduct of the fighting. Alexander was to command the Fifteenth Army Group, consisting of the Seventh United States and the Eighth British Armies. Air Chief Marshal Tedder commanded the Allied Air Force, and Admiral Cunningham the Allied naval forces. The whole was under the overall command of General Eisenhower.

The British assault was entrusted to General Montgomery and his Eighth Army, while General Patton was nominated to command the United States Seventh Army. The naval collaborators were Admiral Ramsay, who had planned the British landings in "Torch", and Admiral Hewitt, U.S.N., who with General Patton had carried out the Casablanca landing. In the air the chief commanders under Air Chief Marshal Tedder were General

Spaatz, U.S. Army Air Force, and Air Marshal Coningham, while the air operations in conjunction with the Eighth Army were in the hands of Air Vice-Marshal Broadhurst, who had recently added to the fame of the Western Desert Air Force.

The plan and the troops were at first considered only on a tentative basis, as the fighting in Tunisia was still absorbing the attention of commanders and staffs, and it was not until April that we could tell what troops would be fit to take part. The major need was the early capture of ports and airfields to maintain the armies after the landings. Palermo, Catania, and Syracuse were suitable, but Messina, the best port of all, was beyond our reach. There were three main groups of airfields, at the south-east corner of the island, in the Catania plain, and in the western portion of the island.

Air Chief Marshal Tedder argued that we must narrow the attack, capture the south-eastern group of airfields, and seize Catania and Palermo later on. This meant that for some time only the small ports of Syracuse, Augusta, and Licata were likely to be available, and the armies would have to be supplied over the open beaches. This was successful largely because of the new amphibious load-carrier, the American D.U.K.W., and even more the "landing-ship, tank" (L.S.T.). This type of vessel had first been conceived and developed in Britain in 1940. A new design, based on British experience, was thereafter built in large numbers in the United States, and was first used in Sicily. It became the foundation of all our future amphibious operations, and was often their limiting factor.

* * * * *

General Alexander's final plan prescribed a week's preliminary bombardment to neutralise the enemy's Navy and Air. The British Eighth Army, under General Montgomery, was to assault between Cape Murro di Porco and Pozzallo and capture Syracuse and the Pachino airfield. Having established a firm bridgehead and gained touch with the U.S. forces on its left, it was to thrust northwards to Augusta, Catania, and the Gerbini airfields. The U.S. Seventh Army, under General Patton, was to land between Cape Scaramia and Licata, and to capture the latter port and a group of airfields north and east of Gela. It was to protect the flank of the Eighth Army at Ragusa in its forward drive. Strong of an aircraft who had been compelled to land by lack of fuel. No enemy outpost now remained south of Sicily.

* * * * *

Intense air attack upon Sicily began on July 3 with the bombing of airfields both there and in Sardinia, which made many unusable. The enemy fighters were thrown on to the defensive, and their long-range bombers forced to withdraw their bases to the Italian mainland. Four of the five train ferries operating across the Straits of Messina were sunk. By the time our convoys were approaching the island air superiority was firmly established, and Axis warships and aircraft made no serious effort to interfere with the seaborne assault. By our cover plans the enemy were kept in doubt until the last moment where our stroke would fall. Our naval movements and military preparations in Egypt suggested an expedition to Greece. Since the fall of Tunis they had sent more planes to the Mediterranean, but the additional squadrons had gone, not to Sicily, but to the Eastern Mediterranean, North-West Italy, and Sardinia. In the critical period while the convoys were approaching their target General Eisenhower established his headquarters in Malta, where communications were excellent. Here he was joined by General Alexander and Admiral Cunningham. Air Marshal Tedder remained near Carthage to control the combined air operations.

July 10 was the appointed day. On the morning of July 9 the great armadas from east and west were converging south of Malta, and it was time for all to steam for the beaches of Sicily. Admiral Cunningham says in his dispatch: "The only incidents which occurred to mar the precision of this remarkable concentration were the loss by U-boat attack of three ships in convoy.* The passage of the convoys was covered most effectively; the majority were not sighted by enemy aircraft."

On my way to Chequers, where I was to await the result, I spent an hour in the Admiralty War Room. The map covered an entire wall, and showed the enormous convoys, escorts, and supporting detachments moving towards their assault beaches. This was the greatest amphibious operation so far attempted in history. But all depended on the weather.

* * * * *

* A fourth ship was sunk in a convoy from Egypt.

The morning of the 9th was fine, but by noon a fresh and unseasonable north-west wind sprang up. During the afternoon the wind increased, and by evening there was a heavy swell, which would make landings hazardous, particularly on the western beaches in the American sector. The landing-craft convoys plunging northward from Malta and from many African ports between Bizerta and Benghazi were having a rough voyage.

Arrangements had been made for postponing the landing in case of necessity, but a decision would have to be taken not later than noon. Watching anxiously from the Admiralty, the First Sea Lord inquired by signal about the weather conditions. Admiral Cunningham replied at 8 p.m., "Weather not favourable, but operation proceeding." "It was," he says, "manifestly too late for postponement, but considerable anxiety was felt, particularly for the small-craft convoys making up against the sea." They were indeed much delayed and became scattered. Many ships arrived late, but fortunately no great harm resulted. "The wind," says Cunningham, "mercifully eased during the night, and by the morning of the 10th had ceased, leaving only a tiresome swell and surf on the western beaches."

The bad weather helped to give us surprise. Admiral Cunningham continues: "The very efficient cover plan and the deceptive routeing of convoys played their part. In addition the vigilance of the enemy was undoubtedly relaxed owing to the unfavourable phase of the moon. Finally came this wind, dangerously close at the time to making some, if not all, the landings impracticable. These apparently unfavourable factors had actually the effect of making the weary Italians, who had been alert for many nights, turn thankfully in their beds, saying, 'To-night at any rate they can't come.' BUT THEY CAME."

The airborne forces met hard fortune. More than one-third of the gliders carrying our 1st Air Landing Brigade were cast off too early by their American towing aircraft and many of the men they carried were drowned. The rest were scattered over south-eastern Sicily, and only twelve gliders arrived at the important bridge which was their aim. Out of eight officers and sixty-five men who seized and held it until help came twelve hours later only nineteen survived. This was a forlorn feat of arms. On the American front the air landings were also too widely dispersed, but the many small parties creating damage and confusion inland worried the Italian coastal divisions.

The seaborne landings, under continuous fighter protection, were everywhere highly successful. Syracuse and Pachino on the British front, Licata and Gela on the American, were captured. The Eighth Army took Augusta on the 12th. On the American front very heavy counter-attacks were made on the U.S. 1st Division by part of a German armoured division. For a time the position was critical, but after a stiff fight the enemy were beaten off and our Allies pressed on to capture the important airfields east of Gela.

The major effort of the Eighth Army was now directed against the airfields at Catania and Gerbini. Aided by more airborne and seaborne landings of parachute and Commando troops, which captured vital bridges, the Army crossed the river Simeto. But now German troops from farther west reinforced the Italians and progress beyond the river was stopped. On the 16th the left flank of the Eighth Army reached Caltagirone, in close touch with the Americans, who were also pressing westwards along the coast and had taken Porto Empedocle.

Twelve airfields were now in our hands, and by July 18 there were only twenty-five serviceable German aircraft in the island. Eleven hundred planes, more than half of them German, were left behind destroyed or damaged. Our air forces tried hard to stop the passage of troops from the mainland to Messina. They were only partly successful against the heavy anti-aircraft fire.

On July 16 General Alexander ordered the Eighth Army to attack the western side of Mount Etna, and the Seventh Army to seize the roads around Enna and cut the west-east highway at Petralia. The 50th Division could make little progress, and the Germans had brought reinforcements, including six battalions of the redoubtable 1st Parachute Division, from the mainland. On its left we made some ground, but it was clear that a new plan and more troops were needed. There was a lull on the British front till the 78th Division arrived from Tunisia.

★   ★   ★   ★   ★

Our next strategic move was still in suspense. Should we cross the Straits of Messina and seize the toe of Italy, should we seize the heel at Taranto, or should we land higher up the west coast, in the Gulf of Salerno, and capture Naples? Or, again, must we restrict ourselves to the occupation of Sardinia? In June General Eisenhower had been asked for his opinion. The problem was a difficult one. At the Washington Conference in May ("Trident") we had decided to transfer to India about August much of the assault shipping and certain air forces then allotted to the Sicily attack. Eisenhower had also been warned that after November 1 four American and three British divisions would have to be withdrawn to Britain for the cross-Channel invasion in 1944. On June 30 he proposed that when the capture of Sicily had been completed we should attack either the toe of Italy or Sardinia. If Sardinia were chosen he could probably be ready by October, but he did not expect to be able to invade the mainland of Italy before November, and by then the weather might be too bad for amphibious landings. To justify so late a descent upon Italy there had to be a good prospect of a speedy advance.

The progress made in Sicily clarified the scene. The contrast may be judged from the telegram in which I set the whole position before Smuts on July 16.

16 July 43

In our May talks at Washington we found serious American misgivings lest we should become deeply involved in the Mediterranean, and a hankering for winding up the campaign there with the capture of Sardinia. This we combated, and as our forces in the Mediterranean far outnumber the American we were able to have the matter left open till after the capture of Sicily. Not being satisfied with this, I requested the President to send General Marshall with me to North Africa, and there upon the spot to convince Eisenhower and others that nothing less than Rome could satisfy the requirements of this year's campaign. We agreed that the decision should be taken when it was seen how the fighting in Sicily went. If it was severe and prolonged, then only Sardinia might be possible. If however our enterprise prospered and Italian resistance was seen not to be formidable, then we were immediately to invade the Italian mainland.

2. The moment is now approaching when this choice must be made, and I need not tell you I shall make it a capital issue. I believe the President is with me; Eisenhower in his heart is naturally for it. I will in no circumstances allow the powerful British and British-controlled armies in the Mediterranean to stand idle. I am bringing the very fine Polish army from Persia into Syria, where it can also participate.

3. The situation in the Balkans is also most hopeful, and I am sending you a report from the Middle East Headquarters showing the

Italian forces on the verge of collapse. Not only must we take Rome and march as far north as possible in Italy, but our right hand must give succour to the Balkan Patriots. In all this there is great hope provided action is taken worthy of the opportunity. I am confident of a good result, and I shall go all lengths to procure the agreement of our Allies. If not, we have ample forces to act by ourselves.

4. When are you coming over here? You know what a warm welcome awaits you and how close is our community of ideas on war. All the above is for your eye alone and of operational secrecy.

★   ★   ★   ★   ★

Meanwhile Allied Air Forces were harrying the enemy communications and airfields in Southern Italy and the port of Naples. On July 19 a strong force of American bombers attacked the railway yards and airport at Rome. Havoc was wrought, and the shock was severe. In Sicily itself the Americans were advancing steadily under the spirited leadership of General Patton. Their 3rd Infantry and 2nd Armoured Divisions were given the task of reducing the western end, where only Italians now remained, while their IInd Corps, comprising the 1st and 45th Divisions, was directed to gain the northern coast and then to thrust eastward along the two main roads towards Messina. Palermo was taken on July 22, and by the end of the month the Americans had reached the line Nicosia–S. Stefano. Their 3rd Division, its task in Western Sicily completed, had been brought in to support the coastal drive, while the 9th Division was brought over from Africa, where, like our 78th, it had been in reserve.

The field was thus disposed for the final battles. These were certain to be severe, since, apart from what remained of the Italian garrison, more than three German divisions were now in action, under a well-tried German commander, General Hube. But the speedy collapse of Italy became probable. There was a marked change of feeling in our circles in Whitehall, and we decided on the bolder plan of a direct attack on the west coast of Italy to seize Naples. Washington agreed, but insisted that no more forces could be provided than those agreed upon at the "Trident" Conference. The Americans held that none of the operations elsewhere, especially "Overlord", should be prejudiced by more vigorous action in the Mediterranean. This reservation was to cause keen anxiety during the landing at Salerno.

General Eisenhower and his principal commanders now agreed that Italy should be the next and immediate target. They still preferred to land first on the toe, because they were short of landing-craft and planes, but for the first time they too began to favour the direct attack on Naples. This was so far from our newly won air bases in Sicily that it would much reduce the fighter cover for the landing. None the less Naples soon became the centre of all thoughts. The chance of quickly crushing Italy seemed to justify delaying operations against Burma, and the Admiralty stopped the assault shipping for India from leaving the Mediterranean.

On July 22 the British Chiefs of Staff urged their American colleagues to plan the direct attack on Naples on the assumption that extra shipping and aircraft-carriers would be available. The Americans took a different view. While agreeing to the attack, they adhered to their original decision that no reinforcements from America should be sent to General Eisenhower for this or any other purpose. He should do the best he could with what he had. Moreover, they insisted that three of his heavy bomber groups should be withdrawn to Britain. Conflict thus arose. The American Chiefs of Staff did not believe that the conquest of Italy would threaten Germany, and they also feared that the Germans would withdraw and that we should find ourselves hitting the air. They did not think there was much to be gained by bombing Southern Germany from airfields in Southern Italy, and they wanted all efforts against Germany to be concentrated on the shortest route across the English Channel, although nothing could happen there for ten months.

The British Chiefs of Staff pointed out that the Washington Conference had expressly stated that the elimination of Italy from the war was one of the prime Allied objects. The attack on Naples, now given the code-name of "Avalanche", was the best means of accomplishing this, and the collapse of Italy would increase enormously the chances of the cross-Channel invasion being not only successful but decisive. Portal, Chief of the Air Staff, emphasised that the full-scale attack on German industry, particularly on factories producing fighters, could only be effective with the help of the Italian airfields. Their possession would therefore be a great contribution to a successful invasion of France. The Americans remained unmoved. However, most of the forces to be employed in "Avalanche" were British, and we resolved to do everything in our power to ensure its success. To overcome the weakness in long-range fighters the Admiralty allotted four escort carriers and a light fleet carrier to support the landing, and the Air Ministry gave General Eisenhower three of our bomber squadrons which had been due for early withdrawal.

While these somewhat sharp discussions were in progress the scene was completely transformed by the fall of Mussolini on July 25. The argument for invading Italy seemed overwhelming. As will be seen, the Germans reacted very quickly, and our invasion, and particularly the attack on Naples, was not greatly eased. "Avalanche" only just succeeded, and it was fortunate that we had provided additional British sea- and air-power. The risks would have been further reduced if the extra shipping which we considered essential to accelerate the build-up after landing there had been accorded. In this we could not carry American opinion with us, and before the operation began many American ships were withdrawn, and some of the British assault shipping was also released to India.

* * * * *

We must now return to the Sicilian battlefield. On August 3 Alexander telegraphed:

The offensive has opened well. . . . I have just returned from a visit to General Patton, who is in great heart. The Seventh American Army have done a grand job of work and are fighting really well. The Canadians have made a very satisfactory début and are fighting well. Progress may be slow, but the country must be seen to be believed. Only a few mountain roads, which pass through gorges and round cliffs, which are easily defended and more easily demolished.

The brilliant capture of Centuripe by our newly arrived 78th Division marked the last phase. Catania fell on the 5th, and thereafter the whole British line swung forward to the southern and western slopes of Mount Etna. The U.S. 1st Division took Troina on August 6 after a stiff fight, and their 9th Division, passing through the 1st, entered Cesaro on the 8th. Along the north coast the U.S. 45th Division, followed by their 3rd Division, reached Cape Orlando on August 10, with the aid of two small but skilful outflanking amphibious operations. After the capture of Randazzo on the 13th the enemy broke contact all along the front, and, under cover of their strong anti-aircraft defences of the Messina Straits, escaped during the following nights to the mainland. Our armies raced for Messina. Enemy demolitions on the coastal road from Catania slowed up the Eighth Army, and by a narrow margin the prize fell to the Americans, who entered the town on August 16.

General Alexander to Prime Minister   17 Aug 43
    The following facts are of interest:
    Sicily invaded July 10. Messina entered August 16. Island taken in thirty-eight days. Sicily has coastline 600 miles and area 10,000 square miles. Island is heavily fortified with concrete pill-boxes and wire. Axis garrison: Italian, 9 divisions; German, 4 divisions, equalling 13 divisions. Total forces: Italian, 315,000; German, 90,000, making total 405,000 soldiers. Our forces: Seventh Army, 6 divisions, including airborne division; Eighth Army, 7 divisions, including airborne and armoured brigades, making Allied total 13 divisions. . . .
    It can be assumed that all Italian forces in island on July 10 have been destroyed, though a few battered units may have escaped to mainland. It is impossible yet to estimate booty and war material captured. Guns, tanks, rifles, and machine-guns are lying scattered about all over island.
    During whole operation the Air Forces have maintained domination throughout, and their tactical air forces have in consequence concentrated a record proportion of their efforts on support of our armies in the field. Over 1,000 enemy aircraft have been taken on airfields. The Royal Navy have kept our sea-lanes open and supplied us with everything we needed.

And later:

General Alexander to Prime Minister   17 Aug 43
    By 10 a.m. this morning, August 17, 1943, the last German soldier was flung out of Sicily and the whole island is now in our hands.

★   ★   ★   ★   ★

    So ended a successful and skilful campaign of thirty-eight days. The enemy, once they had recovered from the initial surprise, had fought stubbornly. The difficulties of the ground were great. The roads were narrow, and cross-country movement was often impossible except for men on foot. On the Eighth Army front the towering mass of Mount Etna blocked the way, and enabled the enemy to watch our moves. As they lay on the low ground of the Catania plain malaria ran riot among our men. Nevertheless, once we were safely ashore and our Air Forces were operating from captured airfields the issue was never in doubt. The enemy, according to General Marshall's report, lost 167,000 men, of whom 37,000 were Germans. The Allies lost 31,158 killed, wounded, and missing.

CHAPTER III

THE FALL OF MUSSOLINI

Mussolini in the Toils – A Joint Proclamation to the Italian People – Mussolini Confers with Hitler near Rimini – Arrival of Grandi on the Scene – The Fascist Grand Council Meets, July 24 – Grandi's Motion for the Deposition of Mussolini Carried – The Arrest of Mussolini, July 25 – The End of Twenty-one Years' Dictatorship – Hitler's Unwise Dispersion of Forces – He Receives the News from Italy – My Forecast of November 25, 1942 – Correspondence with Roosevelt on Impending Italian Peace Proposals – My Thoughts on the Fall of Mussolini – The Fate of British Prisoners in Italy – Anglo-American Discussion of Armistice Terms.

MUSSOLINI now had to bear the brunt of the military disasters into which he had, after so many years of rule, led his country. He had exercised almost absolute control and could not cast the burden on the Monarchy, Parliamentary institutions, the Fascist Party, or the General Staff. All fell on him. Now that the feeling that the war was lost spread throughout well-informed circles in Italy the blame fell upon the man who had so imperiously thrust the nation on to the wrong and the losing side. These convictions formed and spread widely during the early months of 1943. The lonely dictator sat at the summit of power, while military defeat and Italian slaughter in Russia, Tunis, and Sicily were the evident prelude to direct invasion.

In vain he made changes among the politicians and generals. In February General Ambrosio had succeeded Cavallero as Chief of the Italian General Staff. Ambrosio, together with the Duke of Acquarone, the Minister of Court, were personal advisers of the King and had the confidence of the Royal circle. For months they had been hoping to overthrow the Duce and put an end to the Fascist régime. But Mussolini still dwelt in the European scene as if he were a principal factor. He was affronted when his new military chief proposed the immediate withdrawal of the Italian divisions from the Balkans. He regarded these forces as the counterpoise to German predominance in Europe. He did not realise that defeats abroad and internal demoralisation had robbed him of his status as Hitler's ally. He cherished the illusion of power and consequence when the reality had gone. Thus he resisted Ambrosio's formidable request. So durable however was the impression of his authority and the fear of his personal action in extremity that there was prolonged hesitation throughout all the forces of Italian society about how to oust him. Who would "bell the cat"? Thus the spring had passed with invasion by a mighty foe, possessing superior power by land, sea, and air, drawing ever nearer.

During July the climax came. Since February the taciturn, cautious-minded, constitutional King had been in contact with Marshal Badoglio, who had been dismissed after the Greek disasters in 1940. He found in him at length a figure to whom he might entrust the conduct of the State. A definite plan was made. It was resolved that Mussolini should be arrested on July 26, and General Ambrosio agreed to find the agents and create the situation for this stroke. The General was aided unwittingly by elements in the Fascist Old Guard, who sought a new revival of the party, by which, in many cases, they would not be the losers. They saw in the summoning of the highest party organ, the Fascist Grand Council, which had not met since 1939, the means of confronting the Duce with an ultimatum. On July 13 they called on Mussolini and induced him to convene a formal session of the Council on July 24. The two movements appear to have been separate and independent, but their close coincidence in date is significant.

*　　*　　*　　*　　*

We had at the time no definite knowledge of the inner stresses of Italian politics, but reports of growing demoralisation and unrest had for some time reached Allied headquarters. Strikes and rioting in the Northern Italian cities had followed on our bombing raids. We knew that the food situation in Italy had worsened as rail traffic was disrupted. It seemed that the time had come to launch an appeal to the Italian people upon the Sicily landing. President Roosevelt had proposed a proclamation which seemed to us to assume for the United States a position which was not fair to the British share in the Italian war. On July 5 I cabled him as follows:

The War Cabinet had contemplated a joint declaration to the Italian people in the name of both our countries. Whereas "Torch" was by agreement planned as an American expedition with a British contingent and I have acted as your lieutenant throughout, we consider "Husky" [Sicily] and post-"Husky" as joint undertakings in which we are equal partners. This would certainly seem justified by the proportion of troops, naval forces, shipping, and aircraft involved. I fully accept your dictum that "there should be no senior partner".

2. However, since we have been longer in quarrel or war with Italy than you, and also since a document of this character written by one man in its integrity is better than a joint production, we are ready that you should speak at this juncture to the Italian people on behalf of both our countries and in the interests of the common cause.

3. There are a few amendments which I venture to suggest to you in all the frankness of our friendship. They are of importance, because without them untoward reactions might grow among the British people and their forces that their contribution had not received equal or sufficient recognition. In fact, they are only mentioned once, and all else is either United States or United Nations.

4. The amendments are as follows:

(*a*) After the words "against whom on December 11, 1941, your Government declared war" insert, "I speak also on behalf of His Britannic Majesty's Government and in their name."

(*b*) After the words "under the command of General Eisenhower" insert, "and his Deputy General Alexander."

(*c*) The end of the sentence "The skies over Italy are dominated by the vast air armadas of the United Nations" should read, "of the United States and Great Britain. Italy's sea-coasts are threatened by the greatest accumulation of British and Allied sea-power ever concentrated in the Mediterranean." (I am sure you will see the justice of this, as after all it is the United States and Great Britain who are doing virtually the whole thing.)

5. Finally, we think that the message to the Italian people would seem to come better after an initial success in Sicily has been achieved, because a repulse would make it somewhat inappropriate. It would anyhow be lost to the world in the cannonade, and will hardly get through to the Axis fighting troops in time to influence the crunch.

Roosevelt recognised the justice of our case, and I sent him a revised draft which we felt would be appropriate.

This is a message to the Italian people from the President of the United States of America and the Prime Minister of Great Britain.

At this moment the combined armed forces of the United States and Great Britain, under the command of General Eisenhower and his Deputy General Alexander, are carrying the war deep into the territory of your country. This is the direct consequence of the shameful leadership to which you have been subjected by Mussolini and his Fascist régime. Mussolini carried you into this war as the satellite of a brutal destroyer of peoples and liberties. Mussolini plunged you into a war which he thought Hitler had already won. In spite of Italy's great vulnerability to attack by air and sea, your Fascist leaders sent your sons, your ships, your air forces, to distant battlefields to aid Germany in her attempt to conquer England, Russia, and the world. This association with the designs of Nazi-controlled Germany was unworthy of Italy's ancient traditions of freedom and culture—traditions to which the peoples of America and Great Britain owe so much. Your soldiers have fought, not in the interests of Italy, but for Nazi Germany. They have fought courageously, but they have been betrayed and abandoned by the Germans on the Russian front and on every battlefield in Africa from El Alamein to Cape Bon.

To-day Germany's hopes for world conquest have been blasted on all fronts. The skies over Italy are dominated by the vast air armadas of the United States and Great Britain. Italy's sea-coasts are threatened by the greatest accumulation of British and Allied sea-power ever concentrated in the Mediterranean. The forces now opposed to you are pledged to destroy the power of Nazi Germany, which has ruthlessly been used to inflict slavery, destruction, and death on all those who refuse to recognise the Germans as the master race.

The sole hope for Italy's survival lies in honourable capitulation to the overwhelming power of the military forces of the United Nations. If you continue to tolerate the Fascist régime, which serves the evil power of the Nazis, you must suffer the consequences of your own choice. We take no satisfaction in invading Italian soil and bringing the tragic devastation of war home to the Italian people; but we are determined to destroy the false leaders and their doctrines which have brought Italy to her present position. Every moment that you resist the combined forces of the United Nations—every drop of blood that you sacrifice—can serve only one purpose: to give the Fascist and Nazi leaders a little more time to escape from the inevitable consequences of their own crimes. All your interests and all your traditions have been betrayed by Germany and your own false and corrupt leaders;

it is only by disavowing both that a reconstituted Italy can hope to occupy a respected place in the family of European nations.

The time has now come for you, the Italian people, to consult your own self-respect and your own interests and your own desire for a restoration of national dignity, security, and peace. The time has come for you to decide whether Italians shall die for Mussolini and Hitler—or live for Italy, and for civilisation.

ROOSEVELT
CHURCHILL

Allied aircraft dropped leaflets of this proclamation over Rome and other Italian cities on July 17.

★   ★   ★   ★   ★

Two days later the Duce, accompanied by General Ambrosio, left by air to meet Hitler at a villa at Feltre, near Rimini. "There was a most beautiful cool and shady park," writes Mussolini in his memoirs, "and a labyrinthine building which some people found almost uncanny. It was like a crossword puzzle frozen into a house." All preparations had been made to entertain the Fuehrer for at least two days, but he left the same afternoon. "The meeting," says Mussolini, "was, as usual, cordial, but the entourage and the attitude of the higher Air Force officers and of the troops was chilly."★

The Fuehrer held forth lengthily upon the need for a supreme effort. The new secret weapons, he said, would be ready for use against England by the winter. Italy must be defended, "so that Sicily may become for the enemy what Stalingrad was for us." †
The Italians must produce both the man-power and the organisation. Germany could not provide the reinforcements and equipment asked for by Italy owing to the pressure on the Russian front.

Ambrosio urged his chief to tell Hitler plainly that Italy could not continue in the war. It is not clear what advantage would have come from this, but the fact that Mussolini seemed almost dumbstruck finally decided Ambrosio and the other Italian generals present that no further leadership could be expected from him.

In the midst of Hitler's discourse on the situation an agitated Italian official entered the room with the news, "At this moment

★ Mussolini, *Memoirs, 1942–43* (English edition), p. 50.
† Rizzoli, *Hitler e Mussolini: Lettere e Documenti*, p. 173.

44

Rome is undergoing a violent enemy air bombardment." Apart from a promise of further German reinforcements for Sicily, Mussolini returned to Rome without anything to show. As he approached he flew into a huge black cloud of smoke rising from hundreds of wagons on fire in the Littorio railway station. He had an audience of the King, whom he found "frowning and nervous". "A tense situation," said the King. "We cannot go on much longer. Sicily has gone west now. The Germans will double-cross us. The discipline of the troops has broken down. . . ." Mussolini answered, according to the records, that he hoped to disengage Italy from the Axis alliance by September 15. The date shows how far he was out of contact with reality.

The chief actor in the final drama now appeared on the scene. Dino Grandi, veteran Fascist, former Foreign Minister and Ambassador to Britain, a man of strong personal determination, who had hated the Italian declaration of war upon Britain, but had hitherto submitted to the force of events, arrived in Rome to take the lead at the meeting of the Grand Council. He called on his old leader on July 22, and told him brutally that he intended to propose the formation of a National Government and the restoration to the King of the supreme command of the armed forces.

*　　*　　*　　*　　*

At 5 p.m. on the 24th the Grand Council met. Care appears to have been taken by the Chief of Police that they should not be disturbed by violence. Mussolini's musketeers, his personal body-guard, were relieved of their duty to guard the Palazzo Venezia, which was also filled with armed police. The Duce unfolded his case, and the Council, who were all dressed in their black Fascist uniform, took up the discussion. Mussolini ended: "War is always a party war—a war of the party which desires it; it is always one man's war—the war of the man who declared it. If to-day this is called Mussolini's war, the war in 1859 could have been called Cavour's war. This is the moment to tighten the reins and assume the necessary responsibility. I shall have no difficulty in replacing men, in turning the screw, in bringing forces to bear not yet engaged, in the name of our country, whose territorial integrity is to-day being violated."

Grandi then moved a resolution calling upon the Crown to assume more power and upon the King to emerge from obscurity and assume his responsibilities. He delivered what Mussolini describes as "a violent philippic", "the speech of a man who was at last giving vent to a long-cherished rancour." The contacts between members of the Grand Council and the Court became evident. Mussolini's son-in-law, Ciano, supported Grandi. Everyone present was now conscious that a political convulsion impended. The debate continued till midnight, when Scorza, secretary of the Fascist Party, proposed adjourning till next day. But Grandi leaped to his feet, shouting, "No, I am against the proposal. We have started this business and we must finish it this very night!" It was after two o'clock in the morning when the voting took place. "The position of each member of the Grand Council," writes Mussolini, "could be discerned even before the voting. There was a group of traitors who had already negotiated with the Crown, a group of accomplices, and a group of uninformed who probably did not realise the seriousness of the vote, but they voted just the same." Nineteen replied "Yes" to Grandi's motion and seven "No". Two abstained. Mussolini rose. "You have provoked a crisis of the régime. So much the worse. The session is closed." The party secretary was about to give the salute to the Duce when Mussolini checked him with a gesture, saying, "No, you are excused." They all went away in silence. None slept at home.

Meanwhile the arrest of Mussolini was being quietly arranged. The Duke of Acquarone, the Court Minister, sent instructions to Ambrosio, whose deputies and trusted agents in the police and the Carabinieri acted forthwith. The key telephone exchanges, the police headquarters, and the offices of the Ministry of the Interior were quietly and unobtrusively taken over. A small force of military police was posted out of sight near the Royal villa.

Mussolini spent the morning of Sunday, July 25, in his office, and visited some quarters in Rome which had suffered by bombing. He asked to see the King, and was granted an audience at five o'clock. "I thought the King would withdraw his delegation of authority of June 10, 1940, concerning the command of the armed forces, a command which I had for some time past been thinking of relinquishing. I entered the villa therefore with a mind completely free from any forebodings, in a state which, looking back on it, might really be called utterly unsuspecting."

On reaching the Royal abode he noticed that there were everywhere reinforcements of Carabinieri. The King, in Marshal's uniform, stood in the doorway. The two men entered the drawing-room. The King said, "My dear Duce, it's no longer any good. Italy has gone to bits. Army morale is at rock-bottom. The soldiers don't want to fight any more. . . . The Grand Council's vote is terrific—nineteen votes for Grandi's motion, and among them four holders of the Order of the Annunciation! . . . At this moment you are the most hated man in Italy. You can no longer count on more than one friend. You have one friend left, and I am he. That is why I tell you that you need have no fears for your personal safety, for which I will ensure protection. I have been thinking that the man for the job now is Marshal Badoglio. . . ."

Mussolini replied, "You are taking an extremely grave decision. A crisis at this moment would mean making the people think that peace was in sight, once the man who declared war had been dismissed. The blow to the Army's morale would be serious. The crisis would be considered as a triumph for the Churchill-Stalin set-up, especially for Stalin. I re lise the people's hatred. I had no difficulty in recognising it last night in the midst of the Grand Council. One can't govern for such a long time and impose so many sacrifices without provoking resentments. In any case, I wish good luck to the man who takes the situation in hand." The King accompanied Mussolini to the door. "His face," says Mussolini, "was livid and he looked smaller than ever, almost dwarfish. He shook my hand and went in again. I descended the few steps and went towards my car. Suddenly a Carabinieri captain stopped me and said, 'His Majesty has charged me with the protection of your person.' I was continuing towards my car when the captain said to me, pointing to a motor-ambulance standing near by, 'No. We must get in there.' I got into the ambulance, together with my secretary. A lieutenant, three Carabinieri, and two police agents in plain clothes got in as well as the captain, and placed themselves by the door armed with machine-guns. When the door was closed the ambulance drove off at top speed. I still thought that all this was being done, as the King had said, in order to protect my person."

Later that afternoon Badoglio was charged by the King to form a new Cabinet of Service chiefs and civil servants, and in the evening the Marshal broadcast the news to the world. Two days later the Duce was taken on Marshal Badoglio's order to be interned on the island of Ponza.

* * * * *

Thus ended Mussolini's twenty-one years' dictatorship in Italy, during which he had raised the Italian people from the Bolshevism into which they might have sunk in 1919 to a position in Europe such as Italy had never held before. A new impulse had been given to the national life. The Italian Empire in North Africa was built. Many important public works in Italy were completed. In 1935 the Duce had by his will-power overcome the League of Nations—"Fifty nations led by one"—and was able to complete his conquest of Abyssinia. His régime was far too costly for the Italian people to bear, but there is no doubt that it appealed during its period of success to very great numbers of Italians. He was, as I had addressed him at the time of the fall of France, "the Italian lawgiver." The alternative to his rule might well have been a Communist Italy, which would have brought perils and misfortunes of a different character both upon the Italian people and Europe. His fatal mistake was the declaration of war on France and Great Britain following Hitler's victories in June 1940. Had he not done this he could well have maintained Italy in a balancing position, courted and rewarded by both sides and deriving an unusual wealth and prosperity from the struggles of other countries. Even when the issue of the war became certain Mussolini would have been welcomed by the Allies. He had much to give to shorten its course. He could have timed his moment to declare war on Hitler with art and care. Instead he took the wrong turning. He never understood the strength of Britain, nor the long-enduring qualities of Island resistance and sea-power. Thus he marched to ruin. His great roads will remain a monument to his personal power and long reign.

* * * * *

At this time Hitler made a crowning error in strategy and war direction. The defection of Italy, the victorious advance of Russia, and the evident preparations for a cross-Channel attack by Britain and the United States should have led him to concentrate and develop the most powerful German army as a central reserve. In this way only could he use the high qualities of the German

48

command and fighting troops, and at the same time take full advantage of the central position which he occupied, with its interior lines and remarkable communications. As General von Thoma said while a prisoner of war in our charge, "Our only chance is to create a situation where we can use the Army." Hitler, as I have pointed out in an earlier volume, had in fact made a spider's web and forgotten the spider. He tried to hold everything he had won. Enormous forces were squandered in the Balkans and in Italy which could play no part in the main decisions. A central reserve of thirty or forty divisions of the highest quality and mobility would have enabled him to strike at any one of his opponents advancing upon him and fight a major battle with good prospects of success. He could, for instance, have met the British and Americans at the fortieth or fiftieth day after their landing in Normandy a year later with fresh and greatly superior forces. There was no need to consume his strength in Italy and the Balkans, and the fact that he was induced to do so must be taken as the waste of his last opportunity.

Knowing that these choices were open to him, I wished also to have the options of pressing right-handed in Italy or left-handed across the Channel, or both. The wrong dispositions which he made enabled us to undertake the main direct assault under conditions which offered good prospects and achieved success.

*　*　*　*　*

Hitler had returned from the Feltre meeting convinced that Italy could only be kept in the war by purges in the Fascist Party and increasing pressure by the Germans on the Fascist leaders. Mussolini's sixtieth birthday fell on July 29, and Goering was chosen to pay him an official visit on this occasion. But during the course of July 25 alarming reports from Rome began to come in to Hitler's headquarters. By the evening it was clear that Mussolini had resigned or had been removed, and that Badoglio had been nominated by the King as his successor. It was finally decided that any major operation against the new Italian Government would require withdrawals of more divisions than could be spared from the Eastern Front in the event of the expected Russian offensive. Plans were made to rescue Mussolini, to occupy Rome, and to support Italian Fascism wherever possible. If Badoglio signed an armistice with the Allies, further plans were drawn up

for seizing the Italian Fleet and occupying key positions throughout Italy, and for overawing Italian garrisons in the Balkans and
in the Ægean.

"We must act," Hitler told his advisers on July 26. "Otherwise
the Anglo-Saxons will steal a march on us by occupying the airports. The Fascist Party is at present only stunned, and will
recover behind our lines. The Fascist Party is the only one that
has the will to fight on our side. We must therefore restore it.
All reasons advocating further delays are wrong; thereby we run
the danger of losing Italy to the Anglo-Saxons. These are matters
which a soldier cannot comprehend. Only a man with political
insight can see his way clear."

* * * * *

We had long pondered over the consequences of an Italian
collapse. Eight months before I had written:

POSITION OF ITALY

NOTE FOR THE WAR CABINET BY THE PRIME MINISTER

November 25, 1942

It is in my opinion premature to assume that no internal convulsion
in Italy could produce a Government which would make a separate
peace. If we increase the severity of our pressure upon Italy . . . the
desire, and indeed the imperative need, of getting out of the war will
come home to all the Italians, including the rank and file of the Fascist
Party. Should Italy feel unable to endure the continued attacks which
will be made upon her from the air, and presently, I trust, by amphibious operations, the Italian people will have to choose between, on
the one hand, setting up a Government under someone like Grandi to
sue for a separate peace, or, on the other, submitting to a German
occupation, which would merely aggravate the severity of the war.

2. I do not share the view that it is in our interest that the Germans
should occupy and take over Italy. We may not be able to prevent it.
It is still my hope that the Italians themselves will prevent it, and we
should certainly do what we can to further this move. If there were
a revolution in Italy and an Armistice Government came into power
it is at least arguable that the German interests would be as well served
by standing on the Brenner as by undertaking the detailed defence of
Italy against the wishes of its people, and possibly of a Provisional
Government.

3. When a nation is thoroughly beaten in war it does all sorts of
things which no one would imagine beforehand. The sudden, sullen,
universal, simultaneous way in which Bulgaria—Government, Army,

and people alike—cut out in 1918 remains in my memory. Without caring to make any arrangements for their future or for their safety, the troops simply marched out of the lines and dispersed to their homes, and King Ferdinand fled. A Government headed by a peasant leader remained to await the judgment of the victors.

4. Therefore I would not rule out the possibilities of a sudden peace demand being made by Italy, and I agree with the United States policy of trying to separate the Italian people from their Government. The fall of Mussolini, even though precautions may have been taken against it beforehand, might well have a decisive effect upon Italian opinion. The Fascist chapter would be closed. One tale would be finished and another would begin. I consider it would be well to drop leaflets over all Italian towns that are bombed, on the theme, "One man alone is the cause of your sufferings—Mussolini."

5. It is to be observed that we are under no obligations to offer any terms to the vanquished, should they sue for them. That decision must be taken when and if we are offered their surrender, and in the meanwhile we certainly ought not to make promises, as some of the American propaganda leaflets have seemed to do.

The news from Rome now raised these issues, and prompted me to telegraph to the President.

Former Naval Person to President Roosevelt　　　　26 July 43

Changes announced in Italy probably portend peace proposals. Let us consult together so as to take joint action. The present stage may only be transition. But anyhow Hitler will feel very lonely when Mussolini is down and out. No one can be quite sure this may not go further.

The President's message to me crossed this telegram.

President Roosevelt to Prime Minister　　　　26 July 43

By coincidence I was again at Shangri-La this afternoon when the news from Rome came, but this time it seems to be true. If any overtures come we must be certain of the use of all Italian territory and transportation against the Germans in the north *and against the whole Balkan peninsula,** as well as use of airfields of all kinds. It is my thought that we should come as close as possible to unconditional surrender, followed by good treatment of the Italian populace. But I think also that the Head Devil should be surrendered, together with his chief partners in crime. In no event should our officers in the field fix on any general terms without your approval and mine. Let me have your thoughts.

＊　　＊　　＊　　＊　　＊

* Author's italics.

The results of our joint action would dominate the future course of the war. I spent part of the same day in setting down on paper my reactions to the Italian drama. In the afternoon the War Cabinet met to discuss the new situation, and to consider the draft which I had composed. That evening I sent a copy to the President for his comments.

Former Naval Person to President Roosevelt   26 July 43

I send you my thoughts in the form in which I submitted them to the War Cabinet, obtaining their full approval.

2. I don't think myself that we should be too particular in dealing with any non-Fascist Government, even if it is not all we should like. Now Mussolini is gone I would deal with any non-Fascist Italian Government which can deliver the goods. The goods are set out in my memo. herewith. My colleagues also agreed with this.

THOUGHTS ON THE FALL OF MUSSOLINI
By the Prime Minister

It seems highly probable that the fall of Mussolini will involve the overthrow of the Fascist régime, and that the new Government of the King and Badoglio will seek to negotiate a separate arrangement with the Allies for an armistice. Should this prove to be the case it will be necessary for us to make up our minds first of all upon what we want, and secondly upon the measures and conditions required to gain it for us.

2. At this moment above all others our thoughts must be concentrated upon the supreme aim, namely, the destruction of Hitler, Hitlerism, and Nazi Germany. Every military advantage arising out of the surrender of Italy, should that occur, must be sought for this purpose.

3. The first of these is, in the President's words, "the use of all Italian territory and transportation against the Germans in the north and against the whole Balkan peninsula, as well as use of airfields of all kinds." This must include the surrender to our garrisons of Sardinia, the Dodecanese, and Corfu, as well as of all the naval and air bases on the Italian mainland as soon as they can be taken over.

4. Secondly, and of equal importance, the immediate surrender to the Allies of the Italian Fleet, or at least its effective demobilisation and paralysis, and the disarmament of the Italian air and ground forces to whatever extent we find needful and useful. The surrender of the Fleet will liberate powerful British naval forces for service in the Indian Ocean against Japan, and will be most agreeable to the United States.

5. Also, of equal consequence, the immediate withdrawal from, or surrender of, all Italian forces in Corsica, the Riviera, including Toulon, and the Balkan peninsula—to wit, in Yugoslavia, Albania, and Greece.

6. Another objective of the highest importance, about which there will be passionate feeling in this country, is the immediate liberation of all British prisoners of war in Italian hands, and the prevention, which can in the first instance only be by the Italians, of their being transported northwards to Germany. I regard it as a matter of honour and humanity to get our own flesh and blood back as soon as possible and spare them the measureless horrors of incarceration in Germany during the final stages of the war.

7. The fate of the German troops in Italy, and particularly of those south of Rome, will probably lead to fighting between the Germans and the Italian Army and population. We should demand their surrender, and that any Italian Government with whom we can reach a settlement shall do their utmost to procure this. It may be however that the German divisions will cut their way northwards in spite of anything that the Italian armed forces are capable of doing. We should provoke this conflict as much as possible, and should not hesitate to send troops and air support to assist the Italians in procuring the surrender of the Germans south of Rome.

8. When we see how this process goes we can take a further view about action to be taken north of Rome. We should however try to get possession of points on both the west coast and east coast railways of Italy as far north as we dare. And this is a time to dare.

9. In our struggle with Hitler and the German Army we cannot afford to deny ourselves any assistance that will kill Germans. The fury of the Italian population will now be turned against the German intruders, who have, as they will feel, brought all these miseries upon Italy and then come so scantily and grudgingly to her aid. We should stimulate this process in order that the new, liberated, anti-Fascist Italy shall afford us at the earliest moment a safe and friendly area on which we can base the whole forward air attack upon South and Central Germany.

10. This air attack is a new advantage of the first order, as it brings the whole of the Mediterranean air forces into action from a direction which turns the entire line of air defences in the West, and which furthermore exposes all those centres of war production which have been increasingly developed so as to escape air attack from Great Britain. It will become urgent in the highest degree to get agents, Commandos, and supplies by sea across the Adriatic into Greece, Albania, and Yugoslavia. It must be remembered that there are fifteen German divisions in the Balkan peninsula, of which ten are mobile.

Nevertheless, once we have control of the Italian peninsula and of the Adriatic, and the Italian armies in the Balkans withdraw or lay down their arms, it is by no means unlikely that the Germans will be forced to withdraw northwards to the line of the Save and Danube, thus liberating Greece and other tortured countries.

11. We cannot yet measure the effects of Mussolini's fall and of an Italian capitulation upon Bulgaria, Roumania, and Hungary. They may be profound. In connection with this situation the collapse of Italy should fix the moment for putting the strongest pressure on Turkey to act in accordance with the spirit of the Alliance, and in this Britain and the United States, acting jointly or severally, should if possible be joined or at least supported by Russia.

12. The surrender of, to quote the President, "the Head Devil, together with his chief partners in crime," must be considered an eminent object, and one for which we should strive by all means in our power short of wrecking the immense prospects which have been outlined in earlier paragraphs. It may be however that these criminals will flee into Germany or escape into Switzerland. On the other hand, they may surrender themselves or be surrendered by the Italian Government. Should they fall into our hands, we ought now to decide, in consultation with the United States, and, after agreement with them, with the U.S.S.R., what treatment should be meted out to them. Some may prefer prompt execution without trial except for identification purposes. Others may prefer that they be kept in confinement till the end of the war in Europe and their fate decided together with that of other war criminals. Personally I am fairly indifferent on this matter, provided always that no solid military advantages are sacrificed for the sake of immediate vengeance.

"Your message," replied the President to me on July 30, "expresses generally my thoughts of to-day on the prospects and methods of handling the Italian situation with which we are now confronted." He suggested certain minor changes. These in no way altered the substance of the document, and were readily adjusted. "I have not had time to consult my colleagues," I replied on the 31st, "but I have no doubt whatever that our joint draft as amended expresses in perfect harmony the minds of our two Governments on the broad policy to be pursued. It seems to be a case of 'two hearts that beat as one'."

My paper in a slightly amended form was placed before the War Cabinet on August 2, and approved by them as a draft joint directive from both Governments to the Combined Chiefs of Staff. I took it with me when I went to Quebec for a final discussion with the President. Its main interest however lies in showing our joint reactions to the news of Mussolini's fall.

★   ★   ★   ★   ★

Complex problems now lay before us. We had to consider how to treat the new Italian Government. We had to expect the imminent collapse of Italy as an Axis partner, and to draft in detail the terms of surrender, bearing in mind not only the reactions in Italy itself, but also in Germany. We had to take into account the strategic implications of these events, to plan what to do in areas outside Italy, in the Ægean and in the Balkans, which were still held by Italian forces.

On July 27 the President sent me the draft of a broadcast for General Eisenhower to make to the Italian people. This had been approved by the Joint United States Chiefs of Staff, and contained the following sentence: "Your men will return to their normal life and their productive avocations, and hundreds of thousands of Italian prisoners now in our hands will return to the countless Italian homes who long for them. The ancient liberties and traditions of your country will be restored."

I was not only concerned about the draft of this joint message, but about the fate of our prisoners of war in Italian hands.

Former Naval Person to President Roosevelt   28 July 43

There are 74,000 British prisoners in Italy, and there are also about 30,000 Yugoslavs and Greeks. We cannot agree to any promise to release "hundreds of thousands of Italian prisoners now in our hands" unless our men and Allied men are saved from the horrors of German captivity and restored to us.

2. Moreover, apart from Italian prisoners taken in Tunis and Sicily, we have at least a quarter of a million Italians captured by Wavell two years ago and parked about the world. We think it is too much to offer the return of such a large plurality of prisoners arising from earlier phases of the war, nor do we think it necessary. We are ready however to agree to all Italian prisoners taken in Tunis and taken or to be taken in Sicily being traded against the British and Allied prisoners mentioned above.

3. Accordingly we suggest that Eisenhower's message at this point should read as follows:

"Your men will return to their normal life and to their productive avocations, and, provided all British and Allied prisoners now in your hands are restored safely to us and not taken away to Germany, the

55   c*

hundreds of thousands of Italian prisoners captured by us in Tunisia and Sicily will return to the countless Italian homes who long for them," etc.

The following day I telegraphed to General Eisenhower:

Prime Minister to General Eisenhower (Algiers)   29 July 43

There are obvious dangers in trying to state armistice terms in an attractive, popular form to the enemy nation. It is far better that all should be cut and dried and that their Government should know our full demands and their maximum expectations. We are sending our alternative draft to your Government, and will no doubt reach agreement with them in plenty of time for any negotiations which you may have to conduct or which we shall be handling.

All our thoughts are now concentrated upon the great battle which Alexander is about to begin under your supreme direction in Eastern Sicily. The destruction of the three German divisions now facing the Fifteenth Army Group, happening at this time of all others, may well produce decisive effects in every quarter.

And to the President:

Former Naval Person to President Roosevelt   29 July 43

I was so glad to hear your voice again [on the telephone] and that you were in such good spirits.

2. I have told Eisenhower that we fully agree to his releasing the proclamation with our amendment inserted about British and Allied prisoners.

3. Discarding etiquette, I have sent a direct message to the King of Italy through Switzerland emphasising our vehement and savage interest in this matter. I am most grateful for your promise to put the screw on through the Pope or any other convenient channel. If the King and Badoglio allow our prisoners and key men to be carried off by the Huns without doing their utmost to stop it, by which I mean using physical force, the feeling here would be such that no negotiations with that Government would stand a chance in public opinion.

4. *Armistice Terms.* The War Cabinet are quite clear that we ought not to broadcast armistice terms to the enemy. It is for their responsible Government to ask formally for an armistice on the basis of our principle of unconditional surrender. Then I suppose envoys would be appointed and a rendezvous fixed. Our version is already in your hands. As you will see, it follows the main lines of Eisenhower's draft, but is more precise and is cast in a form suited to discussion between plenipotentiaries rather than a popular appeal. There are great dangers in trying to dish this sort of dose up with jam for the patient.

5. We also think that the terms should cover civil as well as military requirements, and that it would be much better for them to be settled by envoys appointed by our two Governments than by the general commanding in the field. He can of course deal with any proposals coming from the troops on his immediate front for a local surrender.

6. Finally, all our thoughts are concentrated upon the great battle about to be fought by the British Eighth and United States Seventh Armies against the 65,000 Germans cornered in the Eastern Sicilian tip. The destruction of these men could not come at a better time to influence events, not only in Italy but throughout the world. It is grand to think of our soldiers advancing side by side like brothers and with good prospects of victory ahead.

The President agreed with us that Eisenhower should not broadcast terms for an armistice with the enemy, but urged that in order to avoid unnecessary and possibly costly military action against Italy he should be authorised to state conditions when and if the Italian Government asked him for them. I did not see why such a proposal should necessarily be made to Eisenhower, none of whose forces were in contact with the enemy except in Sicily, and then only with the Germans. It seemed to me more likely that the Italian Government would negotiate through the Vatican, the Turks, or the Swiss. I agreed however that if Eisenhower were suddenly approached by an envoy he should have precise terms, embodying the principle of unconditional surrender, which he could immediately use as the basis for granting an armistice, and after much discussion the following articles were agreed:

1. Immediate cessation of all hostile activity by the Italian armed forces.

2. Italy will use her best endeavours to deny to the Germans facilities that might be used against the United Nations.

3. All prisoners or internees of the United Nations to be immediately turned over to the Allied Commander-in-Chief, and none of these may from the beginning of these negotiations be evacuated to Germany.

4. Immediate transfer of the Italian Fleet and Italian aircraft to such points as may be designated by the Allied Commander-in-Chief, with details of disarmament to be prescribed by him.

5. Agreement that Italian merchant shipping may be requisitioned by the Allied Commander-in-Chief to meet the needs of his military-naval programme.

6. Immediate surrender of Corsica and of all Italian territory, both

islands and mainland, to the Allies, for such use as operational bases and other purposes as the Allies may see fit.

7. Immediate guarantee of the free use by the Allies of all airfields and naval ports in Italian territory, regardless of the rate of evacuation of the Italian territory by the German forces. These ports and fields to be protected by Italian armed forces until this function is taken over by the Allies.

8. Immediate withdrawal to Italy of Italian armed forces from all participation in the current war, from whatever areas in which they may now be engaged.

9. Guarantee by the Italian Government that if necessary it will employ all its available armed forces to ensure prompt and exact compliance with all the provisions of this armistice.

10. The Commander-in-Chief of the Allied forces reserves to himself the right to take any measure which in his opinion may be necessary for the protection of the interests of the Allied forces or for the prosecution of the war, and the Italian Government binds itself to take such administrative or other action as the Commander-in-Chief may require, and in particular the Commander-in-Chief will establish Allied military government over such parts of Italian territory as he may deem necessary in the military interests of the Allied nations.

11. The Commander-in-Chief of the Allied forces will have a full right to impose measures of disarmament, demobilisation, and demilitarisation.

On July 31 I telegraphed to the President:

. . . So much for the immediate emergency. We hope however that you will also urgently have our Instrument of Surrender* examined, so that we reach full agreement on it. There are several points in this not dealt with in the emergency terms, and it is couched in a precise, formal, and legal vein, on which much thought has been bestowed here. We are rather puzzled to know why you never refer to this document, as it seems to us to be in fact only a more careful and comprehensive version of the emergency armistice terms. We should be very grateful if you would let us know how you feel about it. We ought certainly to have it, or something like it, ready as soon as possible.

The President agreed, but said that he needed further advice from the American Chiefs of Staff and the State Department. We thought it was essential that any statement made to the Italian people should be agreed formally both by the Americans and our-

* Not printed.

58

selves and not merely put out by Allied Headquarters at Algiers, and anyhow it was very much better for the generals to go on with the military operations and to keep the armistice terms till they were asked for.

★ ★ ★ ★ ★

Upon our attitude to the new Italian Government of Badoglio depended the speed with which the Italians would probably approach us for peace terms.

We gave much thought to this matter, which was already being observed in the Press on both sides of the Atlantic.

President Roosevelt to Prime Minister   30 July 43

There are some contentious people here who are getting ready to make a row if we seem to recognise the House of Savoy or Badoglio. They are the same element which made such a fuss over North Africa.

I told the Press to-day that we have to treat with any person or persons in Italy who can best give us, first, disarmament, and, second, assurance against chaos, and I think also that you and I after an armistice comes could say something about self-determination in Italy at the proper time.

Former Naval Person to President Roosevelt   31 July 43

My position is that once Mussolini and the Fascists are gone I will deal with any Italian authority which can deliver the goods. I am not in the least afraid for this purpose of seeming to recognise the House of Savoy or Badoglio, provided they are the ones who can make the Italians do what we need for our war purposes. Those purposes would certainly be hindered by chaos, Bolshevisation, or civil war. We have no right to lay undue burdens on our troops. It may well be that after the armistice terms have been accepted both the King and Badoglio will sink under the odium of surrender and that the Crown Prince and a new Prime Minister may be chosen.

I should deprecate any pronouncement about self-determination at the present time, beyond what is implicit in the Atlantic Charter. I agree with you that we must be very careful not to throw everything into the melting-pot.

Prime Minister to Foreign Secretary   31 July 43

Many things in life are settled by the two-stage method. For instance, a man is not prevented from saying, "Will you marry me, darling?" because he has not got the marriage contract, drawn up by the family solicitors, in his pocket. Personally I think the terms which Eisenhower may now offer are much more likely to be understood by an envoy, and thus be capable of immediate acceptance, than the legal verbiage of the Instrument of Surrender, and they will look much better if published. If we get emergency terms it means that the Italians will have given themselves up to us, lock, stock, and barrel. There would be nothing improper in our requiring them to hand over the pull-through and other cleaning materials afterwards.

President Roosevelt to Prime Minister   3 Aug 43
I have read Instrument of Surrender, and while the language seems on the whole good I seriously doubt advisability of using it at all. After all, the terms of surrender already approved and sent to Eisenhower ought to be all that is necessary. Why tie his hands by an instrument that may be over-sufficient or insufficient? Why not let him act to meet situations as they arise?

All this awaited our impending Conference at Quebec.

CHAPTER IV

WESTWARD HO!

SYNTHETIC HARBOURS

On Board the "Queen Mary" – Brigadier Wingate – The Plan for "Overlord" – The Combined Operations Organisation – The Work of "Cossac" – Where to Strike? – The Need of Harbours and Piers – The Birth of the "Mulberries" – The Plan is Unfolded – A Majestic Project – Floating Breakwaters – Vision of a Floating Airfield – Three Dominating Assumptions About "Overlord" – Mountbatten Given the Supreme Command in Burma – My Note of August 7 on Operations in the Far Eastern Theatre.

PROSPECTS of victory in Sicily, the Italian situation, and the progress of the war made me feel the need in July for a new meeting with the President and for another Anglo-American Conference. It was Roosevelt who suggested that Quebec should be the scene. Mr. Mackenzie King welcomed the proposal, and nothing could have been more agreeable to us. No more fitting or splendid setting for a meeting of those who guided the war policy of the Western world could have been chosen at this cardinal moment than the ancient citadel of Quebec, at the gateway of Canada, overlooking the mighty St. Lawrence River. The President, while gladly accepting Canadian hospitality, did not feel it possible that Canada should be formally a member of the Conference, as he apprehended similar demands by Brazil and other American partners in the United Nations. We also had to think of the claims of Australia and the other Dominions. This delicate question was solved and surmounted by the broad-minded outlook of the Canadian Prime Minister and Government. I for my part was determined that we and the United States should have the Conference to ourselves, in view of all the vital business we had in common. A triple meeting of the heads of the three major Powers was a main object of the future; now it must be for Britain and the United States alone. We assigned to it the name "Quadrant".

I left London for the Clyde, where the *Queen Mary* awaited us, on the night of August 4, in a train which carried the very heavy staffs we needed. We were, I suppose, over two hundred, besides about fifty Royal Marine orderlies. The scope of the Conference comprised not only the Mediterranean campaign, now at its first climax, but even more the preparations for the cross-Channel design of 1944, the whole conduct of the war in the Indian theatre, and our share in the struggle against Japan. For the Channel crossing we took with us three officers sent by Lieut.-General F. E. Morgan, Chief of Staff to the Supreme Allied Commander, yet to be finally chosen, who with his combined Anglo-American staff had completed our joint outline plan. As the whole of our affairs in the Indian and Far Eastern theatres were under examination I brought with me General Wavell's Director of Military Operations, who had flown specially from India.

I took also with me a young Brigadier named Wingate, who had already made his mark as a leader of irregulars in Abyssinia, and had greatly distinguished himself in the jungle fighting in Burma. These new brilliant exploits won him in some circles of the Army in which he served the title of "the Clive of Burma". I had heard much of all this, and knew also how the Zionists had sought him as a future Commander-in-Chief of any Israelite army that might be formed. I had him summoned home in order that I might have a look at him before I left for Quebec. I was about to dine alone on the night of August 4 at Downing Street when the news that he had arrived by air and was actually in the house was brought me. I immediately asked him to join me at dinner. We had not talked for half an hour before I felt myself in the presence of a man of the highest quality. He plunged at once into his theme of how the Japanese could be mastered in jungle warfare by long-range penetration groups landed by air behind the enemy lines. This interested me greatly. I wished to hear much more about it, and also to let him tell his tale to the Chiefs of Staff.

I decided at once to take him with me on the voyage. I told

him our train would leave at ten. It was then nearly nine. Wingate had arrived just as he was after three days' flight from the actual front, and with no clothes but what he stood up in. He was of course quite ready to go, but expressed regret that he would not be able to see his wife, who was in Scotland and had not even heard of his arrival. However, the resources of my Private Office were equal to the occasion. Mrs. Wingate was aroused at her home by the police and taken to Edinburgh in order to join our train on its way through and to go with us to Quebec. She had no idea of what it was all about until, in the early hours of the morning, she actually met her husband on a platform at Waverley Station. They had a very happy voyage together.

As I knew how much the President liked meeting young, heroic figures, I had also invited Wing-Commander Guy Gibson, fresh from leading the attack which had destroyed the Möhne and Eder Dams. These supplied the industries of the Ruhr, and fed a wide area of fields, rivers, and canals. A special type of mine had been invented for their destruction, but it had to be dropped at night from a height of no more than sixty feet. After months of continuous and concentrated practice sixteen Lancasters of No. 617 Squadron of the Royal Air Force attacked on the night of May 16. Half were lost, but Gibson had stayed to the end, circling under fierce fire over the target to direct his squadron. He now wore a remarkable set of decorations—the Victoria Cross, a Distinguished Service Order and bar, and a Distinguished Flying Cross and bar—but no other ribbons. This was unique.

My wife came with me, and my daughter Mary, now a subaltern in an anti-aircraft battery, was my aide-de-camp. We sailed on August 5, this time for Halifax, in Nova Scotia, instead of New York.

*   *   *   *   *

The *Queen Mary* drove on through the waves, and we lived in the utmost comfort on board her, with a diet of pre-war times. As usual on these voyages, we worked all day long. Our large cipher staff, with attendant cruisers to dispatch outgoing messages, kept us in touch with events from hour to hour. Each day I studied with the Chiefs of Staff the various aspects of the problems we were to discuss with our American friends. The most important of these was of course "Overlord".

I had reserved the interlude which a five days' voyage presented for the consideration of our long-wrought plans for this supreme operation of crossing the Channel. Study on an ever-expanding scale had gone forward since the struggles on the coasts of Norway and France in 1940, and we had learned much about amphibious war. The Combined Operations Organisation, which I had then set up under my friend Admiral of the Fleet Sir Roger Keyes, had played an all-important part and created a new technique. Small-scale raids by the Commandos paved the way for greater things, and not only gave us confidence and experience, but showed the world that although beset on all sides we were not content with passive defence. The Americans, still neutral, had observed this new trend, and later developed it in their own way on a vast scale.

In October 1941 Admiral Keyes was succeeded by Captain Lord Louis Mountbatten. We were still hard-pressed, and our only ally, Russia, seemed near to defeat. Nevertheless I had resolved to prepare for an invasion of the Continent when the tide should turn. First we had to increase the intensity and scope of our raids, and then translate all this experience into something much more massive. To mount a successful invasion from the United Kingdom new engines of war must be contrived and developed, the three fighting Services must be trained to plan and fight as one team, supported by the industry of the nation, and the whole island converted into an armed camp for launching the greatest seaborne assault of all time.

When Mountbatten visited me at Chequers before taking up his new duties I told him, according to his account, "You are to plan for the offensive. In your headquarters you will never think defensively." This governed his actions. To provide him with the necessary authority for his task he had been made a member of the Chiefs of Staff Committee, with the acting rank of Vice-Admiral and equivalent honorary rank in the other Services. As Minister of Defence I retained personal responsibility for his head-quarters, and thus he reported direct to me whenever necessary. At Vaagsö in Norway, at Bruneval, at St. Nazaire and elsewhere, the Commandos played a steadily increasing part in our affairs. Our raids culminated in the costly attack on Dieppe in August 1942. When thereafter we passed to major Anglo-American offensives we applied our lessons to the North African landings and to our amphibious descents in the Mediterranean. In all these Mountbatten's organisation took a prominent and indispensable part.

In May 1942 a body known as "the Combined Commanders" had been appointed to grip the problem. It included the Commanders-in-Chief at home, Mountbatten, and later General Eisenhower, commanding the United States forces in Britain. At the Casablanca Conference in January 1943 it was decided to set up an Allied Inter-Service Staff under a British officer to prepare a definite plan for "Overlord". This group began its task in London, under Lieut.-General F. E. Morgan, with the short title of "Cossac".*

The first question was where a landing in force could best be made. There were several options: the Dutch or Belgian coast; the Pas de Calais; between the mouths of the Somme and the Seine; Normandy; Brittany. Each of these had its own advantages and disadvantages, which had to be weighed up under a whole set of different headings and varying, sometimes uncertain, factors. Of these the principal were beaches; weather and tides; sites for constructing airfields; length of voyage; near-by ports that could be captured; the nature of the hinterland for subsequent operations; provision of cover by home-based aircraft; enemy dispositions, their minefields and defences.

The choice narrowed to the Pas de Calais or Normandy. The former gave us the best air cover, but here the defences were the most formidable, and although it promised a shorter sea voyage this advantage was only apparent. While Dover and Folkestone are much closer to Calais and Boulogne than the Isle of Wight is to Normandy, their harbours were far too small to support an invasion. Most of our ships would have had to sail from ports along the whole south coast of England and from the Thames estuary, and so cross a lot of salt water in any case. General Morgan and his advisers recommended the Normandy coast, which from the first had been advocated by Mountbatten. There can be no doubt now that this decision was sound. Normandy gave us the greatest hope. The defences were not so strong as in the Pas de Calais. The seas and the beaches were on the whole suitable, and were to some extent sheltered from the westerly gales by the Cotentin peninsula. The hinterland favoured the

* Chief of Staff, Supreme Allied Commander.

rapid deployment of large forces, and was sufficiently remote from the main strength of the enemy. The port of Cherbourg could be isolated and captured early in the operation. Brest could be outflanked and taken later.

All the coast between Havre and Cherbourg was of course defended with concrete forts and pill-boxes, but as there was no harbour capable of sustaining a large army in this fifty-mile half-moon of sandy beaches it was thought that the Germans would not assemble large forces in immediate support of the sea-front. Their High Command had no doubt said to themselves, "This is a good sector for raids up to ten or twenty thousand men, but unless Cherbourg is taken in working order no army in any way equal to the task of an invasion can be landed or supplied. It is a coast for a raid, but not for wider operations." If only there were harbours which could nourish great armies, here was the front on which to strike.

* * * * *

Of course, as the reader will have seen, I was well abreast of all the thought about landing-craft and tank landing-craft. I had also long been a partisan of piers with their heads floating out in the sea. Much work had since been done on them, following a minute which in the course of our discussions I had issued as long ago as May 30, 1942.

Prime Minister to Chief of Combined Operations
They *must* float up and down with the tide. The anchor problem must be mastered. The ships must have a side-flap cut in them, and a drawbridge long enough to overreach the moorings of the piers. Let me have the best solution worked out. Don't argue the matter. The difficulties will argue for themselves.*

Thought later moved to the creation of a large area of sheltered water protected by a breakwater based on blockships brought to the scene by their own power and then sunk in a prearranged position. This idea originated with Commodore J. Hughes-Hallett in June 1943, while he was serving as Naval Chief of Staff in General Morgan's organisation. Imagination, contrivance, and experiment had been ceaseless, and now in August 1943 there was a complete project for making two full-scale temporary harbours.

* See facsimile, facing p. 78.

which could be towed over and brought into action within a few days of the original landing. These synthetic harbours were called "Mulberries", a code-name which certainly did not reveal their character or purpose.

*   *   *   *   *

One morning on our voyage, at my request, Brigadier K. G. McLean, with two other officers from General Morgan's staff, came to me as I lay in my bed in the spacious cabin, and, after they had set up a large-scale map, explained in a tense and cogent tale the plan which had been prepared for the cross-Channel descent upon France. The reader is perhaps familiar with all the arguments of 1941 and 1942 upon this burning question in all its variants, but this was the first time that I had heard the whole coherent plan presented in precise detail both of numbers and tonnage as the result of prolonged study by officers of both nations.

Further discussions on succeeding days led into more technical detail. The Channel tides have a play of more than twenty feet, with corresponding scours along the beaches. The weather is always uncertain, and winds and gales may whip up in a few hours irresistible forces against frail human structures. The fools or knaves who had chalked "Second Front Now" on our walls for the past two years had not had their minds burdened by such problems. I had long pondered upon them.

It must be remembered that in the "Mulberry" harbours we had a multiple problem to face. The whole project involved the construction in Britain of great masses of special equipment, amounting in the aggregate to over a million tons of steel and concrete. This work, undertaken with the highest priority, would impinge heavily on our already hard-pressed engineering and ship-repairing industries. All this equipment would have to be transported by sea to the scene of action, and there erected with the utmost expedition in the face of enemy attack and the vagaries of the weather.

The whole project was majestic. On the beaches themselves would be the great piers, with their seaward ends afloat and sheltered. At these piers coasters and landing-craft would be able to discharge at all states of the tide. To protect them against the wanton winds and waves breakwaters would be spread in a great arc to seaward, enclosing a large area of sheltered water. Thus sheltered, deep-draught ships could lie at anchor and discharge, and all types of landing-craft could ply freely to and from the beaches. These breakwaters would be composed of sunken concrete structures known as "Phoenix" and blockships known as "Gooseberries". In my second volume I have described the similar structures which I thought might in the First World War have been used to create artificial harbours in the Heligoland Bight.* Now they were to form a principal part of the great plan.

* * * * *

This was the scheme of the "Mulberry" harbour, but even so it was not enough. There would not be room for all the ships we needed. Many would have to discharge outside. To shield these and the very numerous naval vessels engaged an additional scheme of *floating* breakwaters was proposed. For this purpose several devices were being considered, among them one to create a barrier to wave action by means of a continuous screen of air bubbles discharged from pipes laid on the sea-bed. It was hoped that this screen would break up and absorb the rhythm of the waves. Another device, known as a "Lilo", consisted of partially inflated air bags carrying submerged curtains of concrete. These would be moored in line to seaward of the "Phoenix" and enclose a considerable additional area of water. Neither of these ideas reached fruition, but eventually a device called the "Bombardon" was adopted, embodying some of the features of the "Lilo". It was a cruciform steel structure about 200 feet long and 25 feet high, with all but the top arm of the cross submerged. In the event this device was of doubtful value, as we shall see in due course.

I was very well satisfied with the prospect of having the whole of this story presented to the President with my full support. At least it would convince the American authorities that we were not insincere about "Overlord" and had not grudged thought or time in preparation. I arranged to assemble in Quebec the best experts in such matters from London and Washington. Together they could pool resources and find the best answers to the many technical problems.

I was now convinced of the enormous advantages of attacking the Havre-Cherbourg sector, provided these unexpected harbours

* See Vol. II, Chapter XII.

could be brought into being from the first and thus render possible the landing and sustained advance of armies of a million rising to two million men, with all their immense modern equipment and impedimenta. This would mean being able to unload at least 12,000 tons a day.

* * * * *

There was another associated problem on which my mind dwelt, namely, the maintenance of fighting air superiority over the battle area. If we could create a floating airfield we could refuel our fighter aircraft within striking distance of the landing points, and thus multiply our air-power on the spot at the decisive moment. Among the numerous devices discussed during this busy voyage was one called "Habakkuk". This project was conceived by a Mr. Pyke on Mountbatten's staff. His idea was to form a structure of ice, large enough to serve as a runway for aircraft. It would be of ship-like construction, displacing a million tons, self-propelled at slow speed, with its own anti-aircraft defence, with workshops and repair facilities, and with a surprisingly small refrigerating plant for preserving its own existence. It had been found that by adding a proportion of wood pulp in various forms to ordinary sea ice the mixture lost the brittle qualities associated with ice and became extremely tough. This substance, called Pykrete, after its inventor, seemed to offer great possibilities not only for our needs in North-West Europe, but also elsewhere. It was found that as the ice melted the fibrous content quickly formed a furry outer surface which acted as an insulator and greatly retarded the melting process. Much development work was eventually done on this idea, particularly in Canada, but for various reasons it never had any success.

* * * * *

Three dominating assumptions were made both by the framers of the plan and the British Chiefs of Staff. With these I was in entire agreement, and, as will be seen later, they were approved by the Americans and accepted by the Russians.

1. That there must be a substantial reduction in the strength of the German fighter aircraft in North-West Europe before the assault took place.
2. That there should be not more than twelve mobile German

divisions in Northern France at the time the operation was launched, and that it must not be possible for the Germans to build up more than fifteen divisions in the succeeding two months.

3. That the problem of beach maintenance of large forces in the tidal waters of the English Channel over a prolonged period must be overcome. To ensure this it was essential that we should be able to construct at least two effective synthetic harbours.

*   *   *   *   *

I also had many discussions with the Chiefs of Staff on our affairs in the Indian and Far Eastern theatres. We had none too good a tale to tell. A division had advanced at the end of 1942 down the Arakan coast of Burma to recapture the port of Akyab. Though strengthened until a complete corps was engaged, under the command of General Irwin, the operation had failed, and our troops were forced back over the Indian frontier.

Although there was much to be said in explanation, I felt that the whole question of the British High Command against Japan must come under review. New methods and new men were needed. I had long felt that it was a bad arrangement for the Commander-in-Chief India to command the operations in Burma in addition to his other far-reaching responsibilities. It seemed to me that the vigorous prosecution of large-scale operations against the Japanese in South-East Asia necessitated the creation of a separate Supreme Allied Command. The Chiefs of Staff were in complete agreement, and prepared a memorandum on these lines for discussion with their American colleagues in Quebec. There remained the question of the commander of this new theatre, and we were in no doubt that he should be British. Of the various names that were put forward, I was sure in my own mind that Admiral Mountbatten had superior qualifications for this great command, and I determined to make this proposal to the President at the first opportunity. The appointment of an officer of the substantive rank of Captain R.N. to the Supreme Command of one of the main theatres of the war was an unusual step; but, having carefully prepared the ground beforehand, I was not surprised when the President cordially agreed.

*   *   *   *   *

I produced for the Chiefs of Staff Committee a note on plans and policies, from which the following is an extract:

7 Aug 43

Before we meet the Americans we must settle upon:

(a) The general plan for the South-East Asia Command and the Supreme Commander, and

(b) Positive proposals for attacking the enemy, and proving our zeal in this theatre of war, which by its failures and sluggishness is in a measure under reasonable reproach.

I feel that we ought to let Brigadier Wingate tell his story and furnish the United States Chiefs of Staff with copies of his report, and thus convince them that we mean business in this sector of the South-East Asia front. Obviously the Arakan force should lie up against the enemy and engage him. But the amphibious operations against Akyab ought to be stopped now, not only in the interests of the Mediterranean campaign, which should be paramount, but also because it is in itself a faulty and unsound operation. It seeks to strike the enemy where he is best prepared. It lays itself open to serious counter-measures by him. It achieves no major strategic purpose.

*　　*　　*　　*　　*

It is astonishing how quickly a voyage can pass if one has enough to do to occupy every waking minute. I had looked forward to an interval of rest and a change from the perpetual clatter of the war. But as we approached our destination the holiday seemed to be over before it had begun.

CHAPTER V

THE QUEBEC CONFERENCE: "QUADRANT"

Arrival at Halifax – My Telegram to the King, August 11 – Visit to Hyde Park – My Memorandum of August 17 – The "Quadrant" Conference Opens, August 19 – The Chiefs of Staff Report Upon "Overlord" – I Propose an American Commander – Strategy in Italy – A Supreme Commander for South-East Asia – Major Strategy Against Japan – Proposed British Contribution Against Sumatra – My Telegram to Mr. Attlee, August 22 – British Claims to Share in the Main Attack on Japan – An Amusing Incident – Mountbatten Appointed to S.E. Asia – My Telegram to Mr. Attlee of August 25 – My Liaison Officers with General MacArthur and Generalissimo Chiang Kai-shek – Eisenhower Prepares for the Invasion of Italy – Need to Take Naples – Disquieting Estimates of British Reinforcements – I Give Instructions for a Large Increase.

HALIFAX was reached on August 9. The great ship drew in to the landing jetty and we went straight to our train. In spite of all precautions about secrecy, large crowds were assembled. As my wife and I sat in our saloon at the end of the train the people gathered round and gave us welcome. Before we started I made them sing *The Maple Leaf* and *O Canada!* I feared they did not know *Rule, Britannia*, though I am sure they would have enjoyed it if we had had a band. After about twenty minutes of hand-shakings, photographs, and autographs we left for Quebec.

Two days later I telegraphed to the King:

Prime Minister to His Majesty the King   11 Aug 43
　　With humble duty.

　　1. The Citadel is in every way delightful, and ideally suited to the purpose. Arrangements for the President are perfect. He has the

upper floor, and ramps are fitted everywhere for his convenience. I am most grateful to Your Majesty for arranging this. I have telegraphed to the Governor-General thanking him for the trouble he has taken and for his kindly welcome.

2. The holding of this Conference in Canada, and especially at Quebec, is most timely, as there is a lot of fretfulness here, which I believe will soon be removed. I meet the Canadian Cabinet this morning and the Quebec Cabinet this afternoon, and start thereafter for Hyde Park.

3. I presume Your Majesty will already have seen the question that I put to the Deputy Prime Minister and Foreign Secretary about Mountbatten. I have not yet heard from them, but I am increasingly inclined to suggest this solution to the President. Brigadier Wingate made a deep impression on all during the voyage, and I look for a new turn being given to the campaign in Upper Burma.

4. Your Majesty will also have noticed that I have heard from the Great Bear, and that we are on speaking, or at least growling, terms again.

I also telegraphed to the President.

Former Naval Person to President Roosevelt　　　　　11 Aug 43
I have just arrived, after a most swift and agreeable journey, on which it has been possible to work continuously. The Warden family* are looking forward keenly to their visit to Hyde Park, where we propose to arrive the afternoon of the 12th. Are we right in thinking we should all bring our thinnest clothes?

My wife was forced to rest in the Citadel, but next day Mary and I travelled to Hyde Park. We visited Niagara Falls on the way. The reporters asked me what I thought of them, and gave the following account of our talk: " 'I saw them before you were born. I came here first in 1900.' 'Do they look the same?' 'Well,' I replied, 'the principle seems the same. The water still keeps falling over.' " We were the President's guests till August 14. It was so hot that I got up one night because I was unable to sleep and hardly to breathe, and went outside to sit on a bluff overlooking the Hudson River. Here I watched the dawn.

★　　★　　★　　★　　★

In these same August days I prepared a general statement upon the whole of our war policy. The greater part of it concerned operations in Burma and the Indian Ocean and their reactions

* My code-name was "Colonel Warden".

upon the war against Japan. These will be described later. The paper is dated August 17. The immediate point on which my mind was focused was to procure the invasion of Italy as the natural consequence and exploitation of our victory in Sicily and Mussolini's fall.

Should Naples be captured [Operation "Avalanche"] in the near future we shall have a first-rate port in Italy, and other harbours, like Brindisi and Taranto, will fall into our possession thereafter. If by November our front can be established as far north as the Leghorn–Ancona line the landing-craft in the Mediterranean will have played their part. A detachment would be required from the landing fleet for amphibious turning movements such as we have seen in Sicily, for minor descents across the Adriatic, and for operations such as "Accolade" [the capture of Rhodes and other islands in the Ægean]. The disappearance of the Italian Fleet as a factor should enable a great diminution in naval strength in the Mediterranean to be made, just as the use of first-class harbours supersedes the need of landing-craft. There should therefore be during the late autumn the power to move landing-craft and assault ships back for "Overlord", and also to send a sufficient detachment through the Suez Canal to the Indian theatre. I repeat however that the *maximum* number for which landing-craft should be supplied in a single flight is 30,000 men.

Although I have frequently spoken of the line of the Po or of the Alps as being desirable objectives for us this year in Italy, it is not possible to see so far at present. A very great advantage will have been gained if we stop at the Leghorn–Ancona line. We should thus avoid the danger which General Wilson has pointed out of the immense broadening of the front which will take place as soon as that line has been passed. The estimate which has been given me of twenty-two divisions was presumably formed for this broad front. What is the estimate needed to hold the Leghorn–Ancona line? If we cannot have the best there are very good second bests. From such a position we could by air supply a fomented rising in Savoy and the French Alps, to which the young men of France would be able to rally, and at the same time with our right hand we could act across the Adriatic to stimulate the Patriot activities in the Balkan peninsula. It may be necessary for us to accept these limitations in order that the integrity of Operation "Overlord" shall not be marred.

* * * * *

On August 17 the President and Harry Hopkins reached Quebec, and Eden and Brendan Bracken flew in from England. As the delegations gathered further news of Italian peace moves came out to us, and it was under the impression of Italy's approaching surrender that our talks were held. The Chiefs of Staff had been at work with their American colleagues in the Citadel since August 14, and had drafted a comprehensive progress report on the future strategy of the war for 1943–44. In fact "Quadrant" was a series of technical Staff conferences, the results of which were surveyed in two meetings between the President and myself and our Service chiefs.

The first plenary session was held on August 19. Highest strategic priority "as a prerequisite to 'Overlord'" was given to the combined bomber offensive against Germany. The lengthy discussions upon Operation "Overlord" were then summarised in the light of the combined planning in London by General Morgan. The Chiefs of Staff now reported as follows:

OPERATION "OVERLORD"

(a) This operation will be the primary United States-British ground and air effort against the Axis in Europe. (Target date, May 1, 1944.) After securing adequate Channel ports, exploitation will be directed towards securing areas that will facilitate both ground and air operations against the enemy. Following the establishment of strong Allied forces in France, operations designed to strike at the heart of Germany and to destroy her military forces will be undertaken.

(b) Balanced ground and air force to be built up for "Overlord", and there will be continuous planning for and maintenance of those forces available in the United Kingdom in readiness to take advantage of any situation permitting an opportunistic cross-Channel move into France.

(c) As between Operation "Overlord" and operations in the Mediterranean, where there is a shortage of resources available resources will be distributed and employed with the main object of ensuring the success of "Overlord". Operations in the Mediterranean theatre will be carried out with the forces allotted at "Trident" [the previous Conference at Washington in May], except in so far as these may be varied by decision of the Combined Chiefs of Staff.

We have approved the outline plan of General Morgan for Operation "Overlord", and have authorised him to proceed with the detailed planning and with full preparations.

These paragraphs produced some discussion at our meeting. I pointed out that the success of "Overlord" depended on certain conditions being fulfilled in regard to relative strength. I emphasised that I strongly favoured "Overlord" in 1944, though I had not been in favour of "Sledgehammer" in 1942 or "Round-up" in 1943. The objections which I had to the cross-Channel operation were however now removed. I thought that every effort should be made to add at least 25 per cent. to the first assault. This would mean finding more landing-craft. There were still nine months to go, and much could be done in that time. The beaches selected were good, and it would be better if at the same time a landing were to be made on the inside beaches of the Cotentin peninsula. "Above all," I said, "the initial lodgment must be strong."

As the United States had the African command, it had been earlier agreed between the President and me that the commander of "Overlord" should be British, and I proposed for this purpose, with the President's agreement, General Brooke, the Chief of the Imperial General Staff, who, it may be remembered, had commanded a corps in the decisive battle on the road to Dunkirk, with both Alexander and Montgomery as his subordinates. I had informed General Brooke of this intention *early in 1943*. This operation was to begin with equal British and American forces, and as it was to be based on Great Britain it seemed right to make such an arrangement. However, as the year advanced and the immense plan of the invasion began to take shape I became increasingly impressed with the very great preponderance of American troops that would be employed after the original landing with equal numbers had been successful, and now at Quebec I myself took the initiative of proposing to the President that an American commander should be appointed for the expedition to France. He was gratified at this suggestion, and I dare say his mind had been moving that way. We therefore agreed that an American officer should command "Overlord" and that the Mediterranean should be entrusted to a British commander, the actual date of the change being dependent upon the progress of the war. In August 1943 I informed General Brooke, who had my entire confidence, of this change, and of the reasons for it. He bore the great disappointment with soldierly dignity.

*   *   *   *   *

As to Italy, the Chiefs of Staff proposed that there should be three phases in our future operations. First, we should drive Italy out of the war and establish airfields near Rome, and if possible farther north. I pointed out that I wanted it definitely understood that I was not committed to an advance beyond the Ancona–Pisa line. Second, we should seize Sardinia and Corsica, and then press hard against the Germans in the north of the peninsula to stop them joining in the fight against "Overlord". There was also "Anvil", a projected landing in Southern France in the neighbourhood of Toulon and Marseilles and an advance northwards up the Rhone valley. This was to lead to much controversy later on. Recommendations were made about supplying Balkan and French guerrillas by air, intensifying the war against the U-boats, and making more use of the Azores as a naval and air base.

* * * * *

On the major question of the South-East Asia Command the original proposals of the British Chiefs of Staff had been considered. The plan of a Supreme Commander found favour, and the following recommendations were made:

(*a*) That the Combined Chiefs of Staff will exercise a general jurisdiction over strategy for the South-East theatre and the allocation of American and British resources of all kinds between the China theatre and the South-East Asia Command.

(*b*) That the British Chiefs of Staff will exercise jurisdiction over all matters pertaining to operations, and will be the channel through which all instructions to the Supreme Commander are passed.

* * * * *

There was a spirited argument at our first plenary meeting on the whole question of Far Eastern strategy, on which the work of the Chiefs of Staff was to centre in the following days. Japan's island empire must be crushed mainly by the application of maritime power. No army could be engaged without first winning control of Japanese waters. How could the air weapon be used? Opinions diverged sharply. There were some close to the President who advocated making the main assault through Burma into China. They argued that ports and air bases in China would be indispensable for intensive and sustained air attacks against the mainland of Japan. Although politically attractive in American eyes, this idea ignored the impossibility of deploying large armies, most of which would have to be found by Britain, in the jungles of Burma, and also the presence of very strong Japanese forces in China operating on interior lines of communication, and above all the relatively minor contribution which could be made to such an undertaking by the expanding sea-power of the United States.

Alternatively we could make a direct attack by sea against Japan's island barrier in the Central and South Pacific. The burden of this would fall mainly on the Navy and the maritime air forces. Such a thrust would be aimed first at the Philippines, which to all Americans offered an attractive goal. With the Philippines once more in American hands Japan would be isolated from many of her chief sources of supply and the garrisons in the outlying islands of the Dutch East Indies would be cut off from all hope of rescue. They would eventually wither and die without the need for costly fighting.

From the Philippines the encirclement of the Japanese homeland could begin. New bases on the China coast, in Formosa, and in the small islands south of Japan might all be necessary, but once these were obtained the full-scale invasion of Japan became practicable. The bold sweep of this conception was the more attractive in that it rested squarely on the might of American sea-power. Very large naval forces would be needed, but only in the final phase would great armies be required, and by then Hitler would be overthrown and the main strength of Britain and the United States could be hurled against Japan.

I was anxious to state my views on this occasion before the remaining meetings of the Chiefs of Staff. The British planners were proposing in the coming winter to extend the operations of Wingate's forces into Northern Burma, and I was convinced that this should be supplemented by the seizure of the tip of Sumatra. I said at the meeting that I was convinced that "the attack on Sumatra was a great strategic blow which should be struck in 1944. This operation, 'Culverin,' would be the 'Torch' of the Indian Ocean. In my opinion it would not be beyond the compass of our resources. We should be striking and seizing a point of our own against which the Japanese would have to beat themselves if they wished to end the severe drain which would be imposed on their shipping by our air action from Sumatra." The President seemed to think that such an operation would be heading away from the main direction of our advance towards Japan. I pointed out that the alternative would be to waste the entire year, with nothing to show for it but the minor port of Akyab and the future right to toil through the swamps and jungles of Burma, about the suggested reconquest of which I was very dubious. I emphasised the value of the Sumatra project, which I compared, in its promise of decisive consequences, with the Dardanelles operation of 1915. The idea of trying to tie up all our amphibious resources in the Indian Ocean in 1943–44 in order to retake Akyab seemed to me not to be right.

The next day I minuted:

Prime Minister to General Ismay, for C.O.S. Committee   20 Aug 43

We are not yet agreed among ourselves about the policy to be pursued in Akyab, "Culverin," etc., and in my opinion the whole matter has been insufficiently studied. I am still studying it myself. In the meanwhile it is not possible to come to any decision with the Americans in the matter. I hope the Chiefs of Staff will beware of creating a situation where I shall certainly have to refuse to bear any responsibility for a decision which is taken on their level. This would entail the whole matter being referred to the War Cabinet at home after our return. I remain absolutely where I was at the last Conference, and where we all were, that a campaign through Rangoon up the Irrawaddy to Mandalay and beyond would be most detrimental and disadvantageous to us. The capture of Akyab without such a campaign is only an act of waste and folly. . . .

The situation I wish to have at this time next year is that we are masters of "Culverin", that Wingate is in touch with the Chinese in Yunnan, that the communications in Upper Burma have been improved as far as possible, and that we have a free option where to strike next amphibiously, having regard to the reactions from the enemy, which by then will have been apparent.

Two days later I telegraphed home:

Prime Minister (Quebec) to Deputy Prime Minister   22 Aug 43

The President and General Marshall are very keen on Mountbatten's appointment, which it is certain the United States Government will cordially accept. Our Chiefs of Staff concur. There is no doubt of the need of a young and vigorous mind in this lethargic and stagnant Indian scene. I have no doubts whatsoever that it is my duty to make this proposal formally and to submit Mountbatten's name to the King. Mountbatten and Wingate, working together, have thrown a great deal of new light upon future plans. It is essential that, following upon this Conference, an announcement should be made in a few days. I hope my colleagues will feel this is the best course to take.

2. We have also cleared up to our satisfaction the difficulties about

the South-East Asia Command. Broad strategic plans and major assignments of forces and supplies will be decided by the Combined Chiefs of Staff, subject to the approval of their respective Governments. But all operational control will be vested in the British Chiefs of Staff, acting under His Majesty's Government, and all orders will go through them.

3. We have not been able to reach a final conclusion about the extent to which the floods will have delayed the proposed operations in North Burma, nor have we yet given sufficient detailed study to the first stage of Operation "Culverin" to decide whether that should be given priority in amphibious operations during 1944. At least another month's intense study is required. The discussions however have been most friendly, and there is no doubt that the United States Chiefs of Staff are gratified at the constructive interest which we have shown in war plans against Japan in 1944. Soong arrives on Monday, but will in principle be told no more than what is contained in my immediately following.

4. General Marshall has consented to my being represented on General MacArthur's staff by a British liaison officer of General's rank. This will enable us to follow much more closely than hitherto what is happening in that theatre. I discussed this matter with Dr. Evatt when he was in London. He said he was all for it, and I am now telegraphing to Curtin about it, pointing out that this will bring us more closely into touch with the war in the Pacific.

5. Eden and Hull are locked in lengthy discussions. Hull remains completely obdurate about not using the word "recognition" in respect of the French Committee. We have therefore agreed that they shall publish their document, and we ours and the Canadians theirs, after communicating with Russia and others concerned. Eden has this matter in hand. I have pointed out in the plainest terms to the President that they will certainly have a bad Press, but he says he would rather have a sheet anchor out against the machinations of de Gaulle. Our position is of course different, for we are doing no more for the Committee by our formula than we did for de Gaulle when he was alone and quite uncontrolled by others.

* * * * *

The Staff discussion upon the share we were to have in the major assault upon Japan became heated and led to an amusing incident. Each of the joint Staffs had behind them a considerable group of twelve to twenty high Staff officers, a quivering audience, silent, with gleaming eyes. Presently the chairman said, "I think we had better discuss this without our Staffs being present," upon which the group of high Staff officers filed out into a waiting-room. The quarrel was duly settled, as usual, and Mountbatten, whose position as Chief of Combined Operations gave him a seat on the British Chiefs of Staff Committee, seized this opportunity to ask the chairman if he might give a demonstration of the special mixture of ice which his scientists had found. This was called Pykrete.* On receiving permission one of his Staff wheeled in on a large dumb-waiter two blocks of ice about three feet high, one common or garden ice, the other Pykrete. He invited the strongest man present to chop each block of ice in half with a special chopper he had brought. All present voted General Arnold into the job of "strong man". He took off his coat, rolled up his sleeves, and swung the chopper, splitting the ordinary ice with one blow. He turned round, smiling, and, clasping his hands, seized the chopper again and advanced upon the block of Pykrete. He swung the chopper, and as he brought it down let go with a cry of pain, for the Pykrete had suffered little damage and his elbows had been badly jarred.

Mountbatten then capped matters by drawing a pistol from his pocket to demonstrate the strength of Pykrete against gunfire. He first fired at the ordinary ice, which was shattered. He then fired at the Pykrete, which was so strong that the bullet ricochetted, narrowly missing Portal.

The waiting officers outside, who had been worried enough by the sound of the blows and the scream of pain from General Arnold, were horrified at the revolver shots, one of them crying out, "My God! They've now started shooting!"

But who in war will not have his laugh amid the skulls?—and here was one.

* * * * *

Actually the dispute between the British and American Chiefs of Staff was on the issue that Britain demanded a full and fair place in the war against Japan from the moment when Germany was beaten. She demanded a share of the airfields, a share of the bases for the Royal Navy, a proper assignment of duties to whatever divisions she could transport to the Far East after the Hitler business was finished. In the end the Americans gave way. My friends on the Chiefs of Staff Committee had been pressed by me

---

* The special substance for use in the Habakkuk project, and named after its inventor, Mr. Pyke. See p. 69.

to fight this point, not indeed to pistols, but to the utmost limit, because at this stage in the war what I most feared was that American critics would say, "England, having taken all she could from us to help her beat Hitler, stands out of the war against Japan and will leave us in the lurch." However, at the Quebec Conference this impression was effectively removed.

* * * * *

On the late afternoon of August 23 we had our second plenary meeting to discuss the draft of the final report of the Combined Chiefs of Staff. This document reiterated the points raised in their first report as amended after our discussion on them, and in addition set out in detail proposed operational arrangements in the Far East. No decision was reached in the report on the actual operations to be undertaken, though it was decided that the main effort should be put into offensive operations with the object of "establishing land communications with China and improving and securing the air route". In the "overall strategic concept" of the Japan war plans were to be made to bring about the defeat of Japan within twelve months after the collapse of Germany. I said I was glad to see that this was to be our target rather than planning on the basis of a prolonged war of attrition.

Finally, the general principle of a separate South-East Asia Command, which I had proposed to the President before the Conference, was accepted. I said that I was anxious to make a public announcement about this as soon as possible. This would also help to show how much of the discussions at "Quadrant" had been concerned with the war against Japan, and thus set forth sufficient reasons why Russia had not been included in the deliberations. It was generally agreed by those present that we should do this.

* * * * *

I now told the Viceroy of the decision to set up a South-East Asia Command, with Mountbatten as Supreme Commander.

Prime Minister to Viceroy of India   24 Aug 43

We have now formed and set up the South-East Asia Command, separate from the command in India, which was foreshadowed by me at the time of Field-Marshal Wavell's appointment to the Viceroyalty. There are great advantages in having under a British commander a combined command similar to that which exists in North Africa. We have had some discussions with the Americans in the weeks that have passed upon the person of the commander. After a great deal of consideration I decided to propose Lord Louis Mountbatten, now Chief of Combined Operations, for this very important post. Mountbatten has unique qualifications, in that he is intimately acquainted with all three branches of the Services, and also with amphibious operations. He has served for nearly a year and a half on the Chiefs of Staff Committee, and thus knows the whole of our war story from the centre. I regard this as of great importance on account of the extremely varied character of the South-East Asia front by land and sea. Mountbatten is a fine organiser and a man of great energy and daring. His appointment has been cordially welcomed by the President and by the American Chiefs of Staff, and was hailed with delight by Soong on behalf of the Generalissimo. I am therefore, with the approval of the Cabinet, making the necessary submissions to the King, and send this message to you for your information, as it is important that the announcement should emerge out of the present Conference. It will be made public to-morrow, August 25.

Next day I sent the following telegram to my colleagues at home:

Prime Minister to Deputy Prime Minister and   25 Aug 43
War Cabinet only

Everything here has gone off well. We have secured a settlement of a number of hitherto intractable questions—*e.g.*, the South-East Asia Command, "Tube Alloys," and French Committee recognition. On this last we all had an awful time with Hull, who has at last gone off in a pretty sulky mood, especially with the Foreign Secretary, who bore the brunt. Unanimous agreement is expressed in a masterly report by the Combined Chiefs of Staff, which the President and I have both approved. All differences have been smoothed away, except that the question of the exact form of our amphibious activities in the Bay of Bengal has been left over for further study. I think however it is settling itself as I wished. There is no doubt that Mackenzie King and the Canadian Government are delighted and feel themselves thoroughly "on the map".

2. The black spot at the present time is the increasing bearishness of Soviet Russia. You will have seen the telegram received from Stalin about the Italian overtures. He has absolutely no ground for complaint, as we have done no more than hand the Italian representative the severe directions expressing unconditional surrender which had already received the cordial approval of the Soviet Government, and have immediately reported all these matters to him.

3. The President was very much offended at the tone of this message.

He gave directions to the effect that the new Soviet Chargé d'Affaires was to be told he was away in the country and would not be back for some days. Stalin has of course studiously ignored our offer to make a further long and hazardous journey in order to bring about a tripartite meeting. In spite of all this I do not think his manifestations of ill-temper and bad manners are preparatory to a separate peace with Germany, as the hatreds between the two races have now become a sanitary cordon in themselves. It is disheartening to make so little progress with these people, but I am sure my colleagues will not feel that I myself or our Government as a whole have been wanting in any way in patience and in loyalty.

4. I am feeling rather tired, as the work at the Conference has been very heavy and many large and difficult questions have weighed upon us. I hope my colleagues will think it proper for me to take two or three days' rest at one of these mountain camps before I broadcast on Sunday and proceed to Washington. I am also planning to broadcast when taking a degree at Harvard University on September 3, and to return home immediately thereafter. It is only in the event of some unexpected development in Italy or elsewhere which would make it desirable for me and the President to be close together that I should prolong my stay. In any case, I shall be back in good time before the meeting of Parliament. The Foreign Secretary returns by air on Saturday, and is sending Cadogan with me to Washington.

I decided to have two liaison officers, one with MacArthur and the other with Chiang Kai-shek. When I got home I sent for Generals Lumsden and Carton de Wiart to come to Chequers, and offered them these appointments, to the great delight of both. Lumsden was one of our most distinguished and accomplished officers, who at the very beginning of the war, in the first contact with the enemy, had brought the armoured car back into popularity. He soon gained General MacArthur's confidence, and proved a valuable liaison officer. He was killed in January 1945. A Japanese suicide bomber attacked the battleship *New Mexico* during the bombardment of Lingayen Gulf. On the bridge stood Admiral Fraser, the British commander, and General Lumsden. By pure chance the first moved to the opposite side to get a better view. A minute later the suicide bomber struck. All at Lumsden's end of the bridge were killed. His death was a loss to his country and to me personally.

* * * * *

We must now return to the Italian scene. Contrary to our

earlier hopes, the bulk of the Germans successfully withdrew across the Straits of Messina. On August 10 General Eisenhower had held a meeting of his commanders to select from a variety of proposals the means by which the campaign should be carried into Italy. He had to take special account of the enemy dispositions of that time. Eight of the sixteen German divisions in Italy were in the north under Rommel, two were near Rome, and six were farther south under Kesselring. These powerful forces might be reinforced from twenty German divisions which had been withdrawn from the Russian front to refit in France. Nothing we might gather for a long time could equal the strength which the Germans could put in the field, but the British and Americans had command of sea and air, and also the initiative. The assault upon which all minds were now set was a daring enterprise. It was hoped to gain the ports of Naples and Taranto, whose combined facilities were proportioned to the scale of the armies we must use. The early capture of airfields was a prime aim. Those near Rome were as yet beyond our reach, but there was an important group at Foggia adaptable for heavy bombers, and our tactical air forces sought others in the heel of Italy and at Montecorvino, near Salerno.

General Eisenhower decided to begin the assault in early September by an attack across the Straits of Messina, with subsidiary descents on the Calabrian coast. This would be the prelude to the capture of Naples (Operation "Avalanche") by a British and an American army corps landing on the good beaches in the Gulf of Salerno. This was at the extreme range of fighter cover from the captured Sicilian airfields. As soon as possible after the landings the Allied forces would drive north to capture Naples.

The Combined Chiefs of Staff advised the President and me to accept this plan, and to authorise the seizure of Sardinia and Corsica in second priority. We did so with alacrity; indeed, it was exactly what I had hoped and striven for. Later it was proposed to land an airborne division to capture the airfields south of Rome. This also we accepted. The circumstances in which this feature was cancelled are recounted in a later chapter.

*   *   *   *   *

What I regarded as highly satisfactory decisions had thus been obtained and all was moving forward. But towards the end of

August a British officer arrived at Quebec from General Eisenhower's headquarters with very disconcerting news. He stated that by December 1 six divisions would have crossed the Straits of Messina and passed through Calabria, and another six would have landed at Salerno. I at once protested against this alarming under-estimate of our resources.

Prime Minister to General Alexander 26 Aug 43

General Whiteley, who has been here, has told us the dates and scales of "Baytown" and "Avalanche" respectively.* This has filled me with the greatest concern, and I hope you will be able to reassure me. Assuming that our landings are successful and that we are not defeated in the subsequent battles, I cannot understand why two and a half months or more will be required to get ashore, or why it should be necessary, once we have obtained an effective port and bridgehead at "Avalanche", to march all the "Baytown" divisions through Calabria instead of sending some at least of them round by sea.

2. Moreover, the rate of build-up to twelve divisions on the mainland by December 1 seems to me to open dangers of the gravest kind. First, no effective help can come to enable the Italians in Rome to turn against the Germans, and the dangers of a German Quisling Government being installed, or alternatively sheer anarchy supervening, will be aggravated and prolonged. Secondly, if your rate of build-up is no more than twelve divisions by December 1, and these only in the Naples area, what is to prevent the Germans in the same time from bringing far larger forces against them? They are at present said to have sixteen divisions in the Italian peninsula. I am not myself convinced that these are in fact complete divisions. On the contrary, it would seem likely that they are the leading elements and headquarters in several cases. But if the liberation of Rome and the gaining of the important political and military advantages following therefrom are to be delayed for more than three months from now no one can measure the consequences.

3. I am most anxious to hear from you before I leave America, as the President was also much distressed by the date mentioned, and if it is really the kind of time-table that is being worked to it would be better for us to face the worst in consultation. I hope however that you will chase these clouds away.

I addressed myself to this administrative failure as soon as I got home. The measures to re-form our armoured divisions which I had asked for on August 2, and which had been pursued

* "Baytown": the attack across the Straits of Messina. "Avalanche": the attack on Naples (Salerno).

by General Brooke, were already producing results, and the pessimistic estimates of which General Whiteley had been the bearer were soon overcome. The British 1st Armoured Division was re-equipped and became again a magnificent fighting force. Two Polish divisions, the New Zealand Division, and the 4th British-Indian Division were brought to the highest pitch and transported to Italy. The extraordinary prowess of the United States engineers transformed the port of Naples from ruin into a first-class harbour. In the early days of October a hundred thousand men were added to General Alexander's army. Had this not been achieved a disaster might easily have occurred, for the Germans were arriving in strength.

CHAPTER VI

ITALY: THE ARMISTICE

Italian Peace Overtures – My Telegram to the President of August 5 – Final Meeting between Italian and German Chiefs – Badoglio's Problem – My Telegrams to Mr. Eden of August 7 and 9 – And His Reply – Italian Plenipotentiary from Badoglio Arrives in Spain – I Report to the President, August 16 – Our Joint Telegram to General Eisenhower – Discussions in Lisbon between General Castellano and General Bedell Smith – Congratulations to General Alexander – General Zanussi Arrives – An Ultimatum to the Italian Envoys – Joint Report by the President and Me to Stalin – Signature of the Armistice Terms by General Castellano near Syracuse – The British Eighth Army Crosses the Straits of Messina, September 3 – Italian Fears of German Occupation of Rome – Eisenhower Resolves to Launch "Avalanche" as Planned – Announcement of the Armistice at 6 p.m., September 8 – The Germans Encircle Rome – The King Escapes to Brindisi – Imperative Need to Occupy the Italian Bases in the Eastern Mediterranean – The Italian Fleet Fights its Way Through to Surrender at Malta – Mussolini Rescued by Hitler's Orders, September 12 – The Hundred Days – Italy Becomes a Main Battleground.

DETAILED plans had already been made between the British and United States Governments about the probable surrender by Italy. The drafting of armistice terms was begun before the end of July, and on August 3 I circulated the documents to the War Cabinet "in case of an approach being made to us by Italy". We wished to have time to deal by political or diplomatic channels rather than through Allied Force Headquarters. On this same day the first peace overtures from Rome were made. Our Ambassador in Lisbon informed the Foreign Office that the new Counsellor of the Italian Legation there, who had just arrived from Rome, wished to see him, and hinted that

88

he bore a message from the Badoglio Government. This Italian diplomat was Ciano's former *chef de cabinet*, the Marquis D'Ayeta. He had American relations, and was an acquaintance of Sumner Welles. His mission to Lisbon had been planned under Badoglio's instructions by the new Italian Foreign Secretary, Guariglia. On the following day D'Ayeta was invited to the British Embassy. He made no reference to an armistice, but explained that, although the King and Badoglio wanted peace, they had to make a pretence of continuing the fight in order to avoid a German *coup d'état* in Italy. It was clear from what he said that Guariglia was particularly concerned to explain away to the Allies a meeting in Northern Italy with Ribbentrop which he was about to fulfil in order to soften German suspicions.

I immediately informed the President of this Italian approach.

Former Naval Person to President Roosevelt   5 Aug 43

The following story has been told to British Ambassador Campbell at Lisbon by a newly arrived Italian Counsellor. . . . I send it to you for what it is worth, which is substantial. Ambassador Campbell was instructed to make no comment. It certainly seems to give inside information. Though I am starting now for Quebec, Anthony will be here, and you can communicate both with him and me.

The King and the Army leaders had been preparing a *coup d'état*, but this was precipitated, probably by a few days only, by the action of the Fascist Grand Council. Fascism in Italy is extinct. Every vestige has been swept away. Italy turned Red overnight. In Turin and Milan there were Communist demonstrations which had to be put down by armed force. Twenty years of Fascism has obliterated the middle class. There is nothing between the King, with the Patriots who have rallied round him, who have complete control, and rampant Bolshevism. The Germans have an armoured division just outside Rome, and will march in if there is any sign of Italian weakening. There are ten thousand scattered about inside Rome, mostly with machine-guns. If we bomb Rome again there will be a popular rising, and the Germans will then march in and slaughter everybody. They have actually threatened the use of gas. As many Italian troops as possible have been concentrated round Rome, but they have no stomach for fighting. They have practically no weapons, and are no match for even one well-equipped German division.

In these circumstances the King and Badoglio, whose first thought was to make peace, have no alternative but to put up a show of going on with the fight. Guariglia is to meet Ribbentrop perhaps to-morrow, as a result of which there will be a communiqué stating in plainer terms than hitherto that Italy is still the active ally of Germany. But this will be only pretence. The whole country is only longing for peace, and above all to be rid of the Germans, who are universally execrated.

If we cannot attack Germany immediately through the Balkans, thus causing German withdrawal from Italy, the sooner we land in Italy the better. The Germans however are resolved to defend it line by line. When we land in Italy we shall find little opposition, and perhaps even active co-operation, on the part of the Italians.

D'Ayeta never from start to finish made any mention of peace terms, and his whole story, as you will have observed, was no more than a plea that we should save Italy from the Germans as well as from herself, and do it as quickly as possible.

He expressed the hope that we would not heap abuse on the King and Badoglio, which would precipitate the blood-bath, although a little of this would help them to keep up the pretence *vis-à-vis* the Germans.

* * * * *

The desire of all the Italian personalities involved was for peace with the Allies, and the Italian High Command were already eager to fight against the Germans. Guariglia and the Italian Foreign Office hoped by time and caution to achieve the turn-over without incurring German wrath and revenge. Thus, although we could not measure the forces at work, we came in contact with two Italian representatives. So did the Germans. On August 6 Guariglia and General Ambrosio met Ribbentrop and Keitel on the frontier. The military discussions were acri-monious. Ambrosio requested the return home of the Italian divisions in France and the Balkans. Keitel, on the contrary, during the meeting ordered the German units poised at the border posts to enter Italy. Meanwhile Foreign Secretary Guariglia con-ducted a bland and meaningless conversation with Ribbentrop in the hopes of postponing a German onslaught.

* * * * *

On August 6 another Italian diplomat, Signor Berio, approached our diplomatic representative in Tangier. His instructions were direct from Badoglio. Again a plea for time was made, but on this occasion a genuine desire to treat was expressed, and Berio was authorised to open negotiations.

I was on my way by sea to the Quebec Conference when this news reached me, together with Mr. Eden's comments. The

Foreign Secretary wrote: "We are entitled to regard it as an offer by the Badoglio Government to negotiate on terms. . . . Should we not then reply that, as is well known, we insist on unconditional surrender, and the Badoglio Government must as a first step notify us that Italy surrenders unconditionally? Subsequently, at a later stage, if the Badoglio Government was to do this, we should then inform them of the terms on which we should be prepared to cease hostilities against Italy."

On receiving this message I minuted in red ink in the margin, "Don't miss the bus"; and again, "If they surrender immediately we should be prepared to accord conditions as acts of grace and not as a bargain." I then sent the following reply, dated August 7, to the Foreign Secretary:

Prime Minister to Foreign Secretary   7 Aug 43

We agree with the course you have taken. Badoglio admits he is going to double-cross someone, but his interests and the mood of the Italian people make it more likely Hitler will be the one to be tricked. Allowance should be made for the difficulties of his position. Meanwhile the war should be carried forward against Italy in every way that the Americans will allow.

And again, on the day of my arrival in Canada:

Prime Minister to Foreign Secretary   9 Aug 43

Badoglio must state that he is prepared to place himself unreservedly in the hands of the Allied Governments, who have already made it plain that they desire Italy to have a respectable place in the New Europe.

Reference should also be made to General Eisenhower's offer of the return of Italian prisoners of war taken in Tunisia and Sicily, provided Allied prisoners are speedily set free.

2. The object of the above is to convey to the Italian Government the feeling that, while they have to make the formal act of submission, our desire is to treat them with consideration, so far as military exigencies allow. Merely harping on "unconditional surrender" with no prospect of mercy held out even as an act of grace may well lead to no surrender at all. The expression "honourable capitulation" has also been officially used by the President, and I do not think it should be omitted from the language we are now to use.

3. We have just arrived [at Halifax], after a most pleasant voyage filled with fruitful discussions.

I passed to the President Mr. Eden's reply.

Former Naval Person (Quebec) to President Roosevelt　　　12 Aug 43

Eden suggests that our Tangier representative replies to Badoglio's emissary Berio as follows:

Badoglio must understand that we cannot negotiate, but require unconditional surrender, which means that Italian Government should place themselves in hands of Allied Governments, who will then state their terms. These will provide for an honourable capitulation.

The instructions will continue:

Badoglio's emissary should be reminded at the same time that the Prime Minister and President have already stated that we desire that in due course Italy should occupy a respected place in New Europe, when peace has been re-established, and that General Eisenhower has announced that Italian prisoners taken in Tunisia and Sicily will be released provided all British and Allied prisoners now in Italian hands are released.

This is simply made up of our existing declarations. If you approve it in principle please cable at once direct to Eden at the Foreign Office, as I shall be on the move. If text does not meet your view we can discuss it on arrival. I think the Italian envoy ought to have an answer as soon as possible.

The President telegraphed to Mr. Eden approving this language, and the Italian envoy at Tangier was so informed.

These tentative approaches by the Italian Government were now superseded by the appearance in Spain of a plenipotentiary from the Italian High Command. On August 15 General Castellano, Chief of Staff to General Ambrosio, called on Sir Samuel Hoare at the British Embassy in Madrid. Castellano said that he was instructed by Marshal Badoglio to say that as soon as the Allies landed on the Italian mainland the Italian Government was prepared to join them against Germany. If the Allies accepted the proposal Castellano would immediately give detailed information about German troop dispositions. I at once passed this new information to the President.

Former Naval Person (Quebec) to President Roosevelt　　　16 Aug 43

I send you herewith four telegrams I have received from London about a renewed approach by Badoglio. The following is the kind of answer which I suggest should be made:

"We note the statement of Italian envoy: 'We are not in a position to make any terms. We will accept unconditional surrender provided we can join as allies in fighting the Germans.' We, the Allies, for our part cannot make any bargain about Italy changing sides, nor can we make plans in common at this stage. If however serious fighting breaks out between the Italian Army and German intruders a new situation would be created. The Italians know quite well that British and United States Governments do not seek to deny Italy her respected place in Europe. The Italian Government should therefore resist the Germans to the best of their ability as soon as possible, pending arrival of Anglo-American armies. In particular they should stop further invasion of Italy by German troops by blowing up bridges and tunnels and tearing up railway lines and roads in north of Italy, and thus cutting communications of German troops in south of Italy. Effective action of this kind would be regarded by victorious Allies as valuable service, and would render further co-operation possible against the common foe. There is no doubt of the ability of Italian Government and people to destroy and paralyse the German communications, and action of this kind would be proof of their sincerity. Another proof would be the safeguarding of British and Allied prisoners from being taken away to Germany. In any case where this is attempted by Germans, and Italian Government have not the power to resist, the prisoners should be set free and succoured by Italian people. A further vital service which Italian Government certainly has it in its power to render to the Allies is to sail Italian warships to any ports in Allied occupation.

"Fourthly, the furnishing by the Italian Government of any information of German dispositions, and any assistance given by Italian troops and people to the disembarkations of Allies when they take place, especially if accompanied by fighting between Italians and Germans, would be favourably recognised. Fifthly, any co-operation between Italian troops in the Balkan peninsula and the various Patriot forces in the field, taking the form of resistance to the Germans and leading to bloodshed, would be favourably viewed.

"Thus, by taking action against the common enemy, the Italian Government, Army, and people could without any bargain facilitate a more friendly relationship with United Nations. In particular we state that if Allied troops arrive at any point where they find Italians fighting Germans we shall aid Italians to our utmost."

Eden should be here to-morrow, and we can discuss the whole position together. I send you this budget in order that you may see way my mind is working.

The Chiefs of Staff are considering the practical steps and timings required to make an Italian turn-over effective.

★　　★　　★　　★　　★

The President and I agreed that Eisenhower should send General Bedell Smith and the British General Strong, head of his Intelligence Staff, to Lisbon to open negotiations there with the Italian emissary. They took with them the final military terms of surrender, which had now been thrashed out in our "Quadrant" Conference at Quebec.

The President and Prime Minister to General Eisenhower   18 Aug 43

The President and the Prime Minister having approved, the Combined Chiefs of Staff direct you to send at once to Lisbon two Staff officers, one United States and one British. They should report upon arrival to the British Ambassador. They should take with them the agreed armistice terms, which have already been sent to you. Acting on instructions, the British Ambassador in Lisbon will have arranged a meeting with General Castellano. Your Staff officers will be present at this meeting.

2. At this meeting a communication to General Castellano will be made on the following lines:

The unconditional surrender of Italy is accepted on the terms stated in the document to be handed to him. (He should then be given the armistice terms for Italy already agreed and previously sent to you. He should be told that these do *not* include political, economic, or financial terms, which will be communicated later by other means.)

These terms do *not* visualise the active assistance of Italy in fighting the Germans. The extent to which the terms will be modified in favour of Italy will depend on how far the Italian Government and people do in fact aid the United Nations against Germany during the remainder of the war. The United Nations however state without reservation that wherever Italian forces or Italians fight Germans or destroy German property or hamper German movement they will be given all possible support by the forces of the United Nations. Meanwhile, provided information about the enemy is immediately and regularly supplied, Allied bombing will so far as possible be directed upon targets which affect the movements and operations of German forces.

The cessation of hostilities between the United Nations and Italy will take effect from a date and hour to be notified by General Eisenhower.

Italian Government must undertake to proclaim the armistice immediately it is announced by General Eisenhower, and to order their forces and people from that hour to collaborate with the Allies and to resist the Germans.

The Italian Government must, at the hour of the armistice, order that all United Nations prisoners in danger of capture by the Germans shall be immediately released.

The Italian Government must, at the hour of the armistice, order the Italian Fleet and as much of their merchant shipping as possible to put to sea for Allied ports. As many military aircraft as possible shall fly to Allied bases. Any ships or aircraft in danger of capture by the Germans must be destroyed.

3. General Castellano should be told that meanwhile there is a good deal that Badoglio can do without the Germans becoming aware of what is afoot. The precise character and extent of his action must be left to his judgment, but the following are the general lines which should be suggested to him:

General passive resistance throughout the country, if this order can be conveyed to local authorities without the Germans knowing. . . .

Germans must not be allowed to take over Italian coast defences.

Make arrangements to be put in force at the proper time for Italian formations in the Balkans to march to the coast, with a view to their being taken off to Italy by United Nations.

On August 19 the parties met at the British Embassy in the Portuguese capital. Castellano was told that General Eisenhower would accept the Italian Government's unconditional surrender on the terms now handed to him. It is difficult to make hard-cut military negotiations fit in with flexible diplomacy. The Italian envoy general at Lisbon was placed in a hopeless position. The purpose of his visit, as he emphasised, was to discuss how Italy could take the field against Germany. Bedell Smith had to reply that he could only discuss unconditional surrender.

These talks coincided with the final conquest of Sicily. On the same day I telegraphed to General Alexander:

Prime Minister (*Quebec*) *to General Alexander* 19 Aug 43
(*Middle East*)

I am overjoyed at this new, brilliantly executed achievement. I congratulate you most heartily upon all you have done. I will shortly send you a telegram for publication to your troops of the Fifteenth Army Group, but I think it better that the President and the King should send their compliments to Eisenhower first, and I am so advising.

2. You are no doubt informed of General Castellano's approaches to us and the answer we have sent from here. Our greatest danger is that the Germans should enter Rome and set up a Quisling-Fascist Government under, say, Farinacci. Scarcely less unpleasant would be the whole of Italy sliding into anarchy. I doubt if the Badoglio Government can hold their double-faced position until the present date fixed for "Avalanche", so that anything that can be done to shorten this period without endangering military success will be most helpful.

General Alexander to Prime Minister (Quebec)   20 Aug 43
Many thanks for your kind message, which I value very highly.
Everything possible is being done to put on "Avalanche" at the earliest
possible date. We realise here very clearly that every hour gives enemy
more time to prepare and organise against us.

*   *   *   *   *

The discussions in Lisbon with General Castellano continued
throughout the night of August 19. The Italian general drew out
on a map the dispositions of both the German and Italian forces in
Italy after he had realised that there would be no yielding by
Bedell Smith upon the question of terms. After a suitable delay
in order to cover up his visit to Portugal, Castellano returned to
Rome bearing the military terms of surrender, and also a wireless
set and Allied codes in order to remain in contact with Allied
Force Headquarters in Algiers.

Yet another Italian emissary, General Zanussi, appeared on
August 26 in Lisbon. He was the principal assistant to the chief of
the Italian General Staff, and was accompanied by General Carton
de Wiart, V.C., who had been released from a British prisoner-of-
war camp to act as intermediary to this mission. The purpose of
this latest visitor was far from clear. Perhaps Badoglio feared that
Castellano had given too much away and wanted to be clear what
he was doing. Carton de Wiart had been told that "one dove had
been sent out, but as it had not returned another was being dispatched". Zanussi had instructions from Badoglio to try to reach
London and press for an Allied landing north of Rome.

As discussions had already begun with Castellano, it was
decided to send Zanussi to General Eisenhower's headquarters.
Before he left however an incident of chivalry took place. The
Italian general wished to return to Rome to report on the failure
of his mission. He discussed the matter with his English companion, who quietly said that he was of course prepared to
accompany him. Zanussi describes in his own words Carton de
Wiart's remarks. "I am a prisoner of war. I have been released to
accompany you on a mission to London. Since the mission has
not taken place and you are returning to Italy I shall take my
place again at the side of my comrades." The Italian replied that
he would not hear of such a plan. He knew that all had been done
that was possible to get him to England, and he would go and
see General Eisenhower as suggested. Carton de Wiart should

therefore consider himself free. It was an Anglo-Italian episode which may well be remembered by both nations.

The latest Italian emissary was therefore sent to Algiers, where he gave further information about the movements of the Germans in Italy.

On August 31 General Bedell Smith, accompanied by General Zanussi, met Castellano in Sicily, as had been arranged. Castellano explained that if the Italian Government were a free agent they would accept and announce the armistice terms as the Allies desired. They were however under the control of the Germans. Since the Lisbon meeting the Germans had sent more troops into Italy, and the whole country was virtually under German occupation. It was therefore impossible for the armistice to be announced at the time required by the Allies—*i.e.*, before the main Allied landing in Italy, details of which Castellano was most anxious to learn. The Italians wanted to be quite sure that these landings would be strong enough to guarantee the security of the King and Government in Rome.

It was clear that the Italian Government were particularly anxious that we should make a landing north of Rome to protect them against the German divisions near the city. Castellano talked in terms of fifteen Allied divisions taking part in such an operation. General Bedell Smith made it clear that he was not prepared to continue the talks on the basis that the armistice should be announced *after* the main Allied landings, and refused to give him any information on the strength of the impending Allied operations. Castellano thereupon asked to be allowed to consult his Government again. He was told that the terms were final and the time-limit had already expired, but that in view of the present discussion the Allies were willing to wait until midnight of September 1–2, by which time a firm acceptance or refusal must be given. That evening Castellano returned to Rome.

The Allied High Command perceived that the Italian Government was rapidly losing its nerve and would not have the courage to sign an armistice unless convinced of the overwhelming strength of the Anglo-American attack upon the mainland of Italy. General Eisenhower therefore proposed to General Castellano that an airborne force should be landed near Rome. This would depend upon a guarantee by Badoglio's Government that "the armistice is signed and announced as desired by the Allies; that the Italians will seize and hold the necessary airfields and stop all anti-aircraft fire; that the Italian divisions in the Rome area will take action against the Germans".

The President and I, now together in the White House, sent the following telegram to Eisenhower: "We highly approve your decision to go on with 'Avalanche' and to land an airborne division near Rome on the conditions indicated. We fully recognise military considerations must be dominant at this juncture." The War Cabinet met in London on the same day and endorsed this view.

* * * * *

We reported to Stalin the development of the Italian situation.

Prime Minister and President Roosevelt to Premier Stalin   2 Sept 43
We have received from General Castellano statement that the Italians accept and that he is coming to sign, but we do not know for certain whether this refers to short military terms, which you have already seen, or to more comprehensive and complete terms in regard to which your readiness to sign was specifically indicated.

2. The military situation there is at once critical and hopeful. Our invasion of the mainland is beginning almost immediately, and the heavy blow called "Avalanche" will be struck in the next week or so. The difficulty of the Italian Government and people in extricating themselves from Hitler's clutches may make a still more daring enterprise necessary, for General Eisenhower will need as much Italian help as he can get. The Italian acceptance of the terms is largely based on the fact that we shall send an airborne division to Rome to enable them to hold off the Germans, who have gathered Panzer strength in that vicinity, and who may replace the Badoglio Government with a Quisling Administration, probably under Farinacci. Matters are moving so fast there that we think General Eisenhower should have discretion not to delay settlement with the Italians for the sake of the difference between the short and long terms. It is clear that short terms are included in long terms, that they proceed on basis of unconditional surrender, placing the interpretation in hands of Allied C.-in-C.

3. We are therefore assuming that you expect General Eisenhower to sign short terms on your behalf if that be necessary to avoid the further journeying of General Castellano to Rome and consequent delay and uncertainty affecting military operations. We are of course anxious that Italian unconditional surrender be to Soviet as well as to

Great Britain and United States. The date of surrender announcement must of course be fitted in with the military stroke.

＊　＊　＊　＊　＊

General Castellano returned to Sicily, formally authorised by his Government to sign the military terms of surrender. On September 3 in an olive grove near Syracuse the act was performed. I received this news in a telegram from General Alexander.

General Alexander to Prime Minister   3 Sept 43
The short armistice terms were signed this afternoon, on the fourth anniversary of the war, between General Bedell Smith, representing General Eisenhower, and General Castellano, representing Marshal Badoglio, duly authorised to do so.

Castellano is remaining here near my headquarters, and we are starting military talks this evening to arrange best assistance which Italian forces can contribute to our operations.

Before dawn on September 3 the British Eighth Army had crossed the Straits of Messina to enter the Italian mainland.

Prime Minister to Premier Stalin   5 Sept 43
General Castellano, after a long struggle, signed the short terms on September 3, and he is now working out with Generals Eisenhower and Alexander the best way to bring them into force. This will certainly lead to immediate fighting between Italian and German forces, and we are going to help the Italians at every possible point as effectively and speedily as we can. The next week will show a startling development. The invasion of the toe has been successful and is being pressed, and Operation "Avalanche" and the airborne venture are both imminent. Though I believe we shall get ashore at "Avalanche" in strong force, I cannot foresee what will happen in Rome or throughout Italy. The dominant aim should be to kill Germans and make Italians kill Germans on the largest scale possible in this theatre.

I am staying over this side of the Atlantic till this business clears itself. Meanwhile accept my warmest congratulations on your new set of victories and penetrations on your main front.

It now remained to co-ordinate the terms of the Italian surrender with our military strategy. The American General Taylor, of the 82nd Airborne Division, was sent to Rome on September 7. His secret mission was to arrange with the Italian General Staff for the airfields around the capital to be seized during the night of the 9th. But the situation had radically changed since Castellano had asked for Allied protection. The Germans had powerful forces at hand, and appeared to be in possession of the airfields. The Italian Army was demoralised and short of ammunition. Divided counsels seethed round Badoglio. Taylor demanded to see him. Everything hung in the balance. The Italian leaders now feared that any announcement of the surrender, which had already been signed, would lead to the immediate German occupation of Rome and the end of the Badoglio Government. At two o'clock on the morning of September 8 General Taylor saw Badoglio, who, since the airfields were lost, begged for delay in broadcasting the armistice terms. He had in fact already telegraphed to Algiers that the security of the Rome airfields could not be guaranteed. The air descent was therefore cancelled.

Eisenhower now had to make a quick decision. The attack on Salerno was due to be launched within less than twenty-four hours. He therefore telegraphed to the Combined Chiefs of Staff:

8 Sept 43

I have just completed a conference with the principal commanders, and have determined *not* to accept the Italian change of attitude. We intend to proceed in accordance with plan for the announcement of the armistice, and with subsequent propaganda and other measures. Marshal Badoglio is being informed through our direct link that this instrument entered into by his accredited representative with presumed good faith on both sides is considered valid and binding, and that we will *not* recognise any deviation from our original agreement.

After consultation the President and I sent the following reply:

8 Sept 43

It is the view of the President and the Prime Minister that, the agreement having been signed, you should make such public announcement regarding it as would facilitate your military operations.

Accordingly at 6 p.m. General Eisenhower broadcast the announcement of the armistice, followed by the text of the declaration, which Marshal Badoglio himself announced about an hour later from Rome. The surrender of Italy had been completed.

*   *   *   *   *

During the night of September 8-9 German forces began the encirclement of Rome. Badoglio and the Royal Family installed themselves in a state of siege in the building of the Ministry of War. There were hasty discussions in an atmosphere of mounting tension and panic. In the small hours a convoy of five vehicles passed through the eastern gates of Rome on the road to the Adriatic port of Pescara. Here two corvettes took on board the party, which contained the Italian Royal Family, together with Badoglio and his Government and senior officials. They reached Brindisi in the early morning of September 10, when the essential services of an anti-Fascist Italian Government were rapidly set up on territory occupied by Allied forces.

After the departure of the fugitives the veteran Marshal Caviglia, the victor of Vittorio Veneto in the First World War, arrived in Rome to take upon himself the responsibility of negotiating with the German forces closing in round the city. Scattered fighting was already taking place at the gates. Certain regular units of the Italian Army and Partisan bands of Roman citizens engaged the Germans on the outskirts.

On September 11 opposition ceased with the signature of a military truce, and the Nazi divisions were free to move through the city.

*   *   *   *   *

The surrender had been pressed on Marshal Badoglio in order not to upset the timing of the Allied landings in the heel and in the Rome area. The essential steps were completed in the formal signature of the armistice terms, but there were other fruits to be gathered in this dread harvest: the Italian Fleet must be safely transferred to Allied ports; there were many Italian divisions in South-Eastern Europe whose equipment would be valuable to the Allies in the continued struggle against Nazi Germany; there were still more important Italian bases in the Eastern Mediterranean. It was essential that these islands should not fall into hostile hands.

I was acutely aware of this particular danger.

Prime Minister to General Wilson (Middle East)   13 Sept 43
The capture of Rhodes by you at this time with Italian aid would be a fine contribution to the general war. Let me know what are your plans for this. Can you not improvise the necessary garrison out of the forces in the Middle East? What is your total ration strength?

This is a time to think of Clive and Peterborough and of Rooke's men taking Gibraltar.

Lest it should be thought that I pressed this mood unduly, I cite the final summary of the Combined Chiefs of Staff of our decisions recorded at Washington.

EASTERN MEDITERRANEAN

The Combined Chiefs of Staff have taken note of the action which the Commander-in-Chief Middle East is taking in respect of Rhodes and other islands in the Dodecanese. They approve this action, and are considering what further can be done.

I was soon to revert to these matters.

* * * * *

Meanwhile, after dark on September 8, in accordance with Allied instructions, the main body of the Italian Fleet left Genoa and Spezia on a daring voyage of surrender to Malta, unprotected either by Allied or Italian aircraft. Next morning when steaming down the west coast of Sardinia it was attacked by German aircraft from bases in France. The flagship *Roma* was hit, and blew up with heavy loss of life, including the Commander-in-Chief, Admiral Bergamini. The battleship *Italia* was also damaged. Leaving some light craft to rescue survivors, the rest of the Fleet continued its painful journey. On the morning of the 10th they were met at sea by British forces, including the *Warspite* and *Valiant*, which had so often sought them before under different circumstances, and were escorted to Malta. A squadron from Taranto, including two battleships, had also sailed on the 9th, and, after passing at sea the British force on its way to occupy that port, reached Malta the following day without incident.

On the morning of the 11th Admiral Cunningham informed the Admiralty that "the Italian battle fleet now lies at anchor under the guns of the fortress of Malta".

* * * * *

I was anxious that we should treat the Italian Navy well. To Cunningham I cabled on September 10: "Should the Italian Fleet arrive in our ports after having scrupulously fulfilled armistice conditions and sustained the revengeful attack of German bombers, I hope you will consult General Eisenhower in order that they shall be received in kindly and generous manner. I feel sure this will be in accordance with your sentiments." And later in the day: "Films should be taken if possible of surrender of

Italian Fleet, their courteous reception by the British, and kindly treatment of wounded, etc."

The splendid prize of the whole Fleet of what had been a victorious Power of the first rank thus fell into our hands. It must be made to play its part on our side.

Prime Minister to Admiral Cunningham (Algiers)   12 Sept 43

At the earliest possible moment you should report on the ammunition of all natures of guns and torpedoes in the Italian Fleet, beginning with the most important units, showing how much on board, any taken at Taranto, etc., and estimates of quantities and exact specifications for manufacture. Without waiting for the whole story to be complete, send at once to Admiralty for transmission to United States through proper channels requirements for the principal and most modern units. I can probably arrange for speedy manufacture here.

With the collapse of the Fascist régime every region of Italy was in a ferment of political speculation. The organisation of resistance to the Germans fell by default into the hands of an underground Committee of Liberation in Rome, and linked with the mounting activity of Partisan bands which now began activities throughout the peninsula. The members of this committee were politicians driven from power by Mussolini in the early 1920s or representatives of groups hostile to Fascist rule. Over all hung the menace of a recrudescence of the hard core of Fascism in the hour of defeat. The Germans certainly did their best to promote it.

★　　★　　★　　★　　★

Mussolini had been interned after July 26 on the island of Ponza, and later at La Maddalena, off the coast of Sardinia. Fearing a German *coup de main*, Badoglio had at the end of August moved his former master to a small mountain resort high in the Abruzzi, in Central Italy. In the haste of the flight from Rome no precise instructions were given to the police agents and Carabinieri guarding the fallen Dictator. On the morning of Sunday, September 12, ninety German parachutists landed by glider near the hotel where Mussolini was confined. He was removed, without casualties, in a light German aircraft, and carried to yet another meeting in Munich with Hitler.

The rescue of Mussolini enabled the Germans to set up in the north a rival Government to Badoglio's. A skeleton Fascist régime was established on the shores of Lake Garda, and it was here that was played out the drama of Mussolini's Hundred Days. The Germans clamped down their military occupation upon the regions lying north of Rome; a skeleton Administration of uncertain allegiance sat in Rome, now open to the movements of the German Army; at Brindisi the King and Badoglio set up a rump Government under the eyes of an Allied Commission and with no effective authority beyond the boundaries of the administrative building of the town. As our armies advanced from the toe of the peninsula Allied military government took over the task of controlling the liberated regions.

Italy was now to pass through the most tragic time in her history and to become the battle-ground of some of the fiercest fighting in the war.

CHAPTER VII

THE INVASION OF ITALY

AT THE WHITE HOUSE AGAIN

Angling in the Lake of the Snows – My Broadcast from Quebec –
Growing Canadian Share in the War – The Second and Third Fronts
– The Campaign in Africa and Italy – Mountbatten, a "Complete Tri-
phibian" – I Join the President in Washington – A Degree at Harvard
– Importance of the Combined Chiefs of Staff Committee – General
Smuts' Criticisms of the Plans and Progress of the War – He Offers an
Alternative Plan – My Reply – He Suggests Postponing "Overlord"
– I Dismiss this Idea – Invasion of the Toe of Italy – Resignation of
Admiral Pound through Ill-health – Our Conference of September 9 at
the White House – My Memorandum to the President – Wide Agree-
ment in Principle Between Us All – I Preside at Another Plenary
Meeting in the White House – An Event in Anglo-American History.

THE Quebec Conference ended on August 24, and our notable
colleagues departed and dispersed. They flew off in every
direction like the fragments of a shell. After all the study and
argument there was a general desire for a few days' rest. One of
my Canadian friends, Colonel Clarke, who had been attached to
me by the Dominion Government during the proceedings, owned
a ranch about seventy-five miles away amid the mountains and
pine forests from which the newspapers get their pulp to guide us
on life's journey. Here lay the Lake of the Snows, an enormous
dammed-up expanse of water reported to be full of the largest
trout. Brooke and Portal were ardent and expert anglers, and a
plan had been made among other plans at the Conference for them
to see what they could do. I promised to join them later if I could,
but I had undertaken to deliver a broadcast on the 31st, and this

hung overhead like a vulture in the sky. I remained for a few days in the Citadel, pacing the ramparts for an hour each afternoon, and brooding over the glorious panorama of the St. Lawrence and all the tales of Wolfe and Quebec. I had promised to drive through the city, and I had a lovely welcome from all its people. I attended a meeting of the Canadian Cabinet, and told them all that they did not already know about the Conference and the war. I had the honour to be sworn a Privy Counsellor of the Dominion Cabinet. This compliment was paid me at the instance of my old friend of forty years' standing and trusted colleague, Mr. Mackenzie King.

There was so much to say and not to say in the broadcast that I could not think of anything, so my mind turned constantly to the Lake of the Snows, of which glittering reports had already come in from those who were there. I thought I might combine fishing by day with preparing the broadcast after dark. I resolved to take Colonel Clarke at his word, and set out with my wife by car. I had noticed that Admiral Pound had not gone with the other two Chiefs of Staff to the lake, and I suggested that he should come with us now. His Staff officer said that he had a lot of cleaning up to do after the Conference. I had been surprised by the subdued part he had taken in the far-ranging naval discussions, but when he said he could not come fishing I had a fear that all was not well. We had worked together in the closest comradeship from the first days of the war. I knew his worth and courage. I also knew that at home he would get up at four or five in the morning for a few hours' fishing before returning to the Admiralty whenever he saw the slightest chance. However, he kept to his quarters and I did not see him before starting.

We had a wonderful all-day drive up the river valley, and after sleeping at a rest-house on the way my wife and I reached the spacious log cabin on the lake. Brooke and Portal were leaving the next day. It was just as well. They had caught a hundred fish apiece each day, and had only to continue at this rate to lower the level of the lake appreciably. My wife and I sallied forth in separate boats for several hours, and though we are neither of us experts we certainly caught a lot of fine fish. We were sometimes given rods with three separate hooks, and once I caught three fish at the same time. I do not know whether this was fair. We did not run at all short of fresh trout at the excellent meals. The President had wanted to come himself, but other duties claimed him. My aide-de-camp, Mary, had been invited to address an important gathering of American W.A.C.s at Ogle-thorpe, and was flown off accordingly. The President sent me the following:

President to Colonel Warden   27 Aug 43
Wednesday the first is all right in every way [for Washington]. If Subaltern [Mary] wants to go to Oglethorpe it would give her more time in Washington if she were to come down a day or two ahead. I hope Lady Warden is getting a real rest, and that you are also. Also I hope you have gone to One Lake.* Be sure to have big ones weighed and verified by Mackenzie King.

I sent the biggest fish I caught to him at Hyde Park. The broadcast made progress, but original composition is more exhausting than either arguing or fishing.

*   *   *   *   *

We returned to Quebec for the night of the 29th. I attended another meeting of the Canadian Cabinet, and at the right time on the 31st, before leaving for Washington, I spoke to the Canadian people and to the Allied world. A few quotations are pertinent to this account.

The contribution which Canada has made to the combined effort of the British Commonwealth and Empire in these tremendous times has deeply touched the heart of the Mother Country and of all the other members of our widespread family of States and races.

From the darkest days the Canadian Army, growing stronger year by year, has played an indispensable part in guarding our British home-land from invasion. Now it is fighting with distinction in wider and ever-widening fields. The Empire Air Training Organisation, which has been a wonderful success, has found its seat in Canada, and has welcomed the flower of the manhood of Great Britain, of Australia, and New Zealand to her spacious flying-fields and to comradeship with her own gallant sons.

Canada has become in the course of this war an important seafaring nation, building many scores of warships and merchant ships, some of them thousands of miles from salt water, and sending them forth

* During the Quebec Conference the President invited me to come for an afternoon's fishing with him in a lake to which he had been recommended. We had a very pleasant luncheon, but I only caught one small fish and he none. He therefore called the lake "One Lake".

manned by hardy Canadian seamen to guard the Atlantic convoys and our vital life-line across the ocean. The munitions industries of Canada have played a most important part in our war economy. Last, but not least, Canada has relieved Great Britain of what would otherwise have been a debt for these munitions of no less than two thousand million dollars.

All this of course was dictated by no law. It came from no treaty or formal obligation. It sprang in perfect freedom from sentiment and tradition and a generous resolve to serve the future of mankind. I am glad to pay my tribute on behalf of the people of Great Britain to the great Dominion, and to pay it from Canadian soil. I only wish indeed that my other duties, which are exacting, allowed me to travel still farther afield and tell Australians, New Zealanders, and South Africans to their faces how we feel towards them for all they have done, and are resolved to do. . . .

We have heard a lot of talk in the last two years about establishing what is called a Second Front in Northern France against Germany. Anyone can see how desirable that immense operation of war would be. It is quite natural that the Russians, bearing the main weight of the German armies on their front, should urge us ceaselessly to undertake this task, and should in no way conceal their complaints, and even reproaches, that we have not done it before. I do not blame them at all for what they say. They fight so well, and they have inflicted such enormous injury upon the military strength of Germany, that nothing they could say in honest criticism of our strategy or the part we have so far been able to take in the war would be taken amiss by us, or weaken our admiration for their own martial prowess and achievement. We once had a fine front in France, but it was torn to pieces by the concentrated might of Hitler; and it is easier to have a front pulled down than it is to build it up again. I look forward to the day when British and American liberating armies will cross the Channel in full force and come to close quarters with the German invaders of France. . . . Personally, I always think of the Third Front as well as the Second Front. I have always thought that the Western democracies should be like a boxer who fights with two hands and not one.

I believe that the great flanking movement into North Africa, made under the authority of President Roosevelt and of His Majesty's Government, for whom I am a principal agent, will be regarded in the after-time as quite a good thing to do in all the circumstances. Certainly it has reaped rich and substantial results. Africa is cleared. All German and Italian armies in Africa have been annihilated, and at least half a million prisoners are in our hands. In a brilliant campaign of thirty-eight days Sicily, which was defended by over 400,000 Axis troops, has been conquered. Mussolini has been overthrown. The war impulse of Italy has been destroyed, and that unhappy country is paying a terrible penalty for allowing itself to be misled by false and criminal guides. How much easier it is to join bad companions than to shake them off! A large number of German troops have lately been drawn away from France in order to hold down the Italian people, in order to make Italy a battleground, and to keep the war as distant and as long as possible from German soil. By far the greater part of the German Air Force has been drawn off from the Russian front, and indeed is being engaged and worn down with ever-growing intensity, by night and day, by British and American and Canadian airmen. More than all this, we have established a strategic initiative and potential, both from the Atlantic and from the Mediterranean, of which the enemy can neither measure the weight nor foresee the hour of application.

To judge by the latest news from the Russian battle-fronts, Marshal Stalin is certainly not wasting his time. The entire British Empire sends him our salutes in this brilliant summer campaign, and on the victories of Orel, Kharkov, and Taganrog, by which so much Russian soil has been redeemed and so many hundreds of thousands of its invaders wiped out.

I gave the fullest prominence to Mountbatten's appointment.

A Supreme Commander of the South-East Asia front has been chosen, and his name has been acclaimed by British, American, and Chinese opinion. He will act in constant association with Generalissimo Chiang Kai-shek. It is true that Lord Louis Mountbatten is only forty-three. It is not often under modern conditions and in established military professions that a man gets so great a chance so early. But if an officer, having devoted his life to the military art, does not know about war at forty-three he is not likely to learn much more about it later on. As Chief of Combined Operations Lord Louis has shown rare powers of organisation and resourcefulness. He is what—pedants notwithstanding—I will venture to call a "complete triphibian"—that is to say, a creature equally at home in three elements, earth, air, and water, and also well accustomed to fire. We all wish the new command and its commander full success in their novel, varied, and certainly most difficult task.

*   *   *   *   *

I left Quebec by train, and arrived at the White House on September 1. Throughout the talks at Quebec events had been marching forward in Italy. The President and I, as has been recorded elsewhere, had directed during these critical days the course of the secret armistice talks with the Badoglio Government, and had also been following anxiously and closely the military arrangement for a landing on Italian soil. I deliberately prolonged my stay in the United States in order to be in close contact with our American friends at this critical moment in Italian affairs. On the day of my arrival in Washington the first definite and official news was received that Badoglio had agreed to accept the surrender terms proposed by the Allies. The strategic arrangements debated at "Quadrant" had of course been considered in the light of the possible Italian collapse, and this aspect was our main concern in these days.

While in Washington I attended several American Cabinets or their equivalent and was in close touch with leading American personalities. Poor Hopkins at this time was very ill and had to retire for a complete rest to the naval hospital. The President was very anxious for me to keep a longstanding appointment and receive an honorary degree at Harvard. It was to be an occasion for a public declaration to the world of Anglo-American unity and amity. On September 6 I delivered my speech. The following extract may be printed here.

To the youth of America, as to the youth of Britain, I say, "You cannot stop." There is no halting-place at this point. We have now reached a stage in the journey where there can be no pause. We must go on. It must be world anarchy or world order. Throughout all this ordeal and struggle which is characteristic of our age you will find in the British Commonwealth and Empire good comrades to whom you are united by other ties besides those of State policy and public need. To a large extent they are the ties of blood and history. Naturally I, a child of both worlds, am conscious of these.

Law, language, literature—these are considerable factors. Common conceptions of what is right and decent, a marked regard for fair play, especially to the weak and poor, a stern sentiment of impartial justice, and above all the love of personal freedom, or, as Kipling put it, "Leave to live by no man's leave underneath the law"—these are common conceptions on both sides of the ocean among the English-speaking peoples. We hold to these conceptions as strongly as you do.

We do not war primarily with races as such. Tyranny is our foe. Whatever trappings or disguise it wears, whatever language it speaks, be it external or internal, we must for ever be on our guard, ever mobilised, ever vigilant, always ready to spring at its throat. In all this we march together. Not only do we march and strive shoulder to shoulder at this moment under the fire of the enemy on the fields of war or in the air, but also in those realms of thought which are consecrated to the rights and the dignity of man.

I spoke about our Combined Staffs.

At the present time we have in continual vigorous action the British and United States Combined Chiefs of Staff Committee, which works immediately under the President and myself as representative of the British War Cabinet. This Committee, with its elaborate organisation of Staff officers of every grade, disposes of all our resources, and in practice uses British and American troops, ships, aircraft, and munitions just as if they were the resources of a single State or nation. I would not say there are never divergences of view among these high professional authorities. It would be unnatural if there were not. That is why it is necessary to have plenary meetings of principals every two or three months. All these men now know each other. They trust each other. They like each other, and most of them have been at work together for a long time. When they meet they thrash things out with great candour and plain, blunt speech, but after a few days the President and I find ourselves furnished with sincere and united advice.

This is a wonderful system. There was nothing like it in the last war. There never has been anything like it between two allies. It is reproduced in an even more tightly knit form at General Eisenhower's headquarters in the Mediterranean, where everything is completely intermingled and soldiers are ordered into battle by the Supreme Commander or his Deputy, General Alexander, without the slightest regard to whether they are British, American, or Canadian, but simply in accordance with the fighting need.

Now in my opinion it would be a most foolish and improvident act on the part of our two Governments, or either of them, to break up this smooth-running and immensely powerful machinery the moment the war is over. For our own safety, as well as for the security of the rest of the world, we are bound to keep it working and in running order after the war—probably for a good many years, not only until we have set up some world arrangement to keep the peace, but until we know that it is an arrangement which will really give us that protection we must have from danger and aggression, a protection we have already had to seek across two vast world wars.

Alas, unwisdom has already prevailed!

★   ★   ★   ★   ★

I had, as usual, had an official summary of the Conference sent to the Dominion Prime Ministers. Field-Marshal Smuts was disappointed by the scale on which our plans were based, and also by their apparent leisurely time-table. I always, as the reader knows, found great comfort in feeling that our minds were in step. The cables that passed between us throw a true and intimate light upon the main issues of the war at this milestone. It was no burden to me but a relief to dictate from my general body of knowledge acquired at the summit full explanations to one I knew so well.

General Smuts to Prime Minister   31 Aug 43

For your private ear I should like to voice my personal misgivings about the progress of the war. If you don't agree with me please forget my grouse. But if in any way you share my feeling you will take your own initiative in the matter.

While our Middle East campaign was conducted with conspicuous vigour from El Alamein to the end in Tunisia, I sense a slackening and tardiness in operations since then. It took us several months between Tunisia and the Sicilian landing, and there is now another strange pause after Sicily at a stage in our affairs when the urgency is very great. To compare the Anglo-American effort, with all our vast resources, with that of Russia during the same period is to raise uncomfortable questions which must occur to many others. Our comparative performance on land is insignificant and its speed very unsatisfactory. There is much and constant boasting of our production effort, especially of the colossal American production. And after almost two years of war the American fighting forces must be enormous. But still, the Russians account for the vast bulk of the German Army on land. Shipping and other troubles account for this difference in part, but that is not the whole story. I have the uncomfortable feeling that the scale and speed of our land operations leaves much to be desired. Our Navy is acting up to its usual high standard, and our Air Force is magnificent. But almost all the honours on land go to the Russians, and deservedly so, considering the scale and speed of their fighting and the magnificence of their strategy on a vast front.

Surely our performance can be bettered and the comparison with Russia rendered less unflattering to us. To the ordinary man it must appear that it is Russia who is winning the war. If this impression continues what will be our post-war world position compared with that of Russia? A tremendous shift in our world status may follow, and will leave Russia the diplomatic master of the world. This is both unnecessary and undesirable, and would have especially bad reactions for the British Commonwealth. Unless we emerge from the war on terms of equality our position will be both uncomfortable and dangerous. . . . I do not yet know what was being planned at Quebec, and assume the best programmes have been worked out and approved. But what about the rate of their execution? There is grave danger in delay, in tardiness of performance on our part.

General Smuts to Prime Minister   3 Sept 43
After sending my previous message criticising our war progress I must frankly express my disappointment with this Quebec plan as being an inadequate programme for the fifth year of the war, and especially after the enormous change that has taken place in our war fortunes recently. This plan has only added to my misgivings and fears for the future. It does no justice to the real strength of our position, and may gravely affect public morale as well as future relations with Russia. We are capable of a much greater effort, and should face the position with greater boldness.

In effect, the plan merely proposes to continue and increase the present bombing and anti-U-boat campaigns, to take Sardinia and Corsica and the South of Italy and bomb northwards from there. We are then to fight our way northwards through Italy over difficult mountainous terrain in a campaign which may take much time before we reach Northern Italy and the main German defence position. Next spring we shall cross the Channel in force if the air and military situation in France is favourable, and we may invade France from the south if only as a diversion. We leave the Balkans to the guerrillas, with air encouragement from us.

So much for the West. In the East we do some island-hopping which may bring us up against the enemy's main base in the Carolines some time towards the end of next year. The resources of the Dutch East Indies we leave meanwhile to the enemy while we make efforts to open the Burma route and assist China as much as possible by air. Some undefined amphibious operations against Burma are also indicated.

Bombing appears to me the only serious part of this plan. All the rest is still on a small scale, similar to what we have been doing for the last couple of years. Surely this would not be a serious effort for this stage of the war nor a proper use of our greatly improved war position. If by the end of 1944 we have done no better than merely nibble at the enemy's main positions we may experience a dangerous revulsion of opinion, and rightly so. It would compare most unfavourably with the grand effort and achievement of Russia, who may conclude that her suspicions of us are justified.

In the absence of inner Staff information, it is difficult for me to suggest alternative plans, but I feel convinced that we can and should do much more and better than the Quebec plan, which would unduly drag out and prolong the war, with all the attendant risks and possibilities I have indicated in my former message. The bombing policy, the anti-U-boat campaign, and the large-scale attack across the Channel I approve. But in the Mediterranean we should take Sardinia and Corsica and immediately attack in North Italy without fighting our way all up the peninsula. We should immediately take Southern Italy and move on to the Adriatic, and from a suitable point there launch a real attack on the Balkans and set its resurgent forces going. This will bring Turkey into the picture and carry our Fleet into the Black Sea, where we shall join hands with Russia, supply her, and enable her to attack Hitler's fortress itself from the east and south-east. With the vast change in the war situation on the Russian front I do not think this too ambitious a programme to work to. . . .

After consideration I replied to Smuts.

Prime Minister to Field-Marshal Smuts   5 Sept 43

Your two telegrams.

1. The invasion of the toe of Italy now begun is of course only the prelude to a far heavier attack which is imminent, and will, if successful, produce consequences of a far-reaching character. We hope presently to open a heavy front across Italy as far north as we can get. Such a front will absorb about twenty divisions from the Mediterranean, and may require reinforcement if selected for counter-attack by the enemy.

2. I have always been most anxious to come into the Balkans, which are already doing so well.* We shall have to see how the fighting in Italy develops before committing ourselves beyond Commandos, agents, and supplies, but the whole place is aflame, and with the defection of the twenty-four Italian divisions scattered in the Balkans, who have ceased to fight and now only try to get home, it may well be that the Germans will be forced to retire to the line of the Save and the Danube. . . .

3. I think it better not to demand entry into the war by Turkey at this present time, as the forces with which we should have to fight are more usefully employed in the Central Mediterranean. The question may be put to Turkey later in the year.

4. In spite of these serious needs and projects in the Mediterranean, which strain our resources to the full, we have to find seven divisions from that theatre from November on for the build-up of Operation

---

* This sentence appears inconsistent with my general policy as so often expressed in these volumes. I did not mean "come into the Balkans" with an army.

"Overlord" in the spring of 1944. For this purpose every personnel ship which can be gathered, apart from those used by the United States in the Pacific, is being employed in the ceaseless transportation of American troops and air forces. None of our ships have been idle this year, and yet there are so far only two American divisions in England. It is not physically possible to make a larger concentration by the date mentioned. We shall be able to match the American expedition with a nearly equal force of British divisions, but after the initial assault the build-up must be entirely American, as I am completely at the end of man-power resources, and even now have to ask the Americans to interrupt the movement of field troops in order to send over some thousands of engineers to help make the installations and establishments required for the gathering of their transatlantic army.

5. These projects in Europe, together with the air offensive and the sea war, completely absorb all our resources of man-power and of ship-power. This fact must be faced. There is no comparison between our conditions and those prevailing in Russia, where the whole strength of a nation of nearly two hundred millions, less war losses, long organised into a vast national army, is deployed on a two-thousand-miles land front. This again is a fact which must be faced.

6. I think it inevitable that Russia will be the greatest land Power in the world after this war, which will have rid her of the two military Powers, Japan and Germany, who in our lifetime have inflicted upon her such heavy defeats. I hope however that the "fraternal association" of the British Commonwealth and the United States, together with sea- and air-power, may put us on good terms and in a friendly balance with Russia at least for the period of rebuilding. Farther than that I cannot see with mortal eye, and I am not as yet fully informed about the celestial telescopes.

7. In the East we British have no shortage of forces, but the same difficulty of coming into action as the United States in the Atlantic and also in the Pacific. The shipping stringency rules all oversea and amphibious action, and, for the rest, in Burma there are the jungles, the mountains, and the fact that more than half the year is swamped by the monsoon. However, a vigorous campaign has been set on foot. I brought young Wingate to Quebec, and he is being raised from a Brigadier to a Corps Commander, with powerful jungle forces adapted to the purpose being formed with the utmost speed for an attack in the first month of next year. The appointment of Mountbatten heralds an amphibious operation of novelty and far-reaching scope which I am pressing with all possible energy, the details of which I will unfold to you when we meet.

8. Believe me, my dear friend, I am not at all vexed at your two

telegrams of criticism. I am confident that if we were together for two or three days I could remove such of your anxieties as are not inherent inexorable facts. Night and day I press for greater speed in action and less cumbrousness in organisation. I am waiting this side of the Atlantic pending the Italian *coup* and its repercussions, but I expect to be home when Parliament meets, and hope to find you at least approaching our shores.

Smuts was to some extent reassured by this full statement. "Your telegram," he said, "has come as a great relief. It makes clear that Italian expedition of twenty divisions would cover whole peninsula and constitute another real front." But he added a day later:

9 Sept 43

I suggest that our victories in Mediterranean should be followed up in Italy and Balkans instead of our now adopting a cross-Channel plan, which means switching on to a new theatre requiring very large forces and involving grave risks unless much more air softening has taken place. Preparations for Channel plan should be slowed down or put into temporary cold storage while bombing campaign is intensified to prepare for eventual military knock-out.

This last suggestion required immediate correction from me if our two minds were to continue to work harmoniously on the problem from independent angles. Smuts alone and far from Washington could not know the atmosphere and proportions which governed our collective thought.

Prime Minister to Field-Marshal Smuts　　　　　11 Sept 43

There can be no question whatever of breaking arrangements we have made with United States for "Overlord". The extra shipping available in consequence of U-boat warfare slackening and of Italian windfalls will probably enable us to increase build-up of "Avalanche" [the expedition to Italy]. I hope you will realise that British loyalty to "Overlord" is keystone of arch of Anglo-American co-operation. Personally I think enough forces exist for both hands to be played, and I believe this to be the right strategy.

★　　★　　★　　★　　★

Meanwhile the invasion of Italy had begun. At dawn on September 3 the 5th British and 1st Canadian Divisions of the Eighth Army crossed the Straits of Messina.★ Practically no opposition was encountered. Reggio was speedily taken, and the

★ See map, p. 217.

advance began along the narrow and hilly roads of Calabria. "The Germans," cabled Alexander on September 6, "are fighting their rearguard action more by demolitions than by fire. . . . While in Reggio this morning there was not a warning sound to be heard or a hostile plane to be seen. On the contrary, on this lovely summer day naval craft of all types were plying backwards and forwards between Sicily and the mainland, carrying men, stores, and munitions. In its lively setting it was more like a regatta in peace-time than a serious operation of war."

In a few days the divisions of the Eighth Army had reached Locri and Rosarno, while an infantry brigade, landed by sea at Pizzo, found only the tail of the retreating Germans. There was little fighting, but the advance was severely delayed by the physical difficulties of the country, demolitions carried out by the enemy, and his small but skilfully handled rearguards.

Prime Minister to General Alexander   7 Sept 43

Many thanks for your telegrams about operations in the toe of Italy. Please tell me exactly what the move of airborne division to seize Rome involves, and where it fits into your programme. We are all fully in favour of the bold policy proposed, although we have to take details on trust.

2. I am also deeply interested in your mention of Taranto. About when do you propose doing this?

3. I am still very much concerned about build-up after "Avalanche". Surely if you can get the port of Naples into working order you should be able to push in two divisions a week. Let me know the order in which you propose to bring our army into Italy. When do the New Zealanders, Poles, 4th Indian and 1st Armoured and other really high-class divisions come into action? It seems you will have to hold a front at least as large as that in final stages of Tunis—*i.e.*, about a hundred and seventy miles—and one never can tell if, given time, Germans may not bring a real punch to bear upon that front.

4. I am waiting here with the President to judge results of "Avalanche", and thereafter returning home. I hope however to come out to you in the first half of October, and General Marshall will come from America. I shall have some important things to tell you then.

Alexander replied that the Italian Government's being unable to announce the armistice had forced him to make certain changes. The 82nd U.S. Airborne Division could not be flown in to the Rome area, as no arrangement for its reception had been made by the Italians and the Germans were thought to be in occupation

117

of the airfields. "Avalanche" would go in as planned, except that no airborne forces would take part. About 3,000 soldiers of the 1st Airborne Division had sailed in naval ships for Taranto, and should arrive there on September 9. It was impossible to say what reception they would receive. By opening the port of Taranto early he hoped to increase the build-up into Italy.

At the same time our efforts to seize Rhodes and other islands in the Ægean began. Later chapters will tell the tale.

* * * * *

In the White House the President and I sat talking after dinner in his study, and Admiral Pound came to see us upon a naval point. The President asked him several questions about the general aspects of the war, and I was pained to see that my trusted naval friend had lost the outstanding matter-of-fact precision which characterised him. Both the President and I were sure he was very ill. Next morning Pound came to see me in my big bed-sitting-room and said abruptly, "Prime Minister, I have come to resign. I have had a stroke and my right side is largely paralysed. I thought it would pass off, but it gets worse every day and I am no longer fit for duty." I at once accepted the First Sea Lord's resignation, and expressed my profound sympathy for his breakdown in health. I told him he was relieved at that moment from all responsibility, and urged him to rest for a few days and then come home with me in the *Renown*. He was completely master of himself, and his whole manner was instinct with dignity. As soon as he left the room I cabled to the Admiralty placing Vice-Admiral Syfret in responsible charge from that moment pending the appointment of a new First Sea Lord.

* * * * *

On September 9 we held a formal conference with the President at the White House. The C.I.G.S. and the C.A.S. had flown back to London some days before, and I was accompanied by Field-Marshal Dill, Ismay, and the three representatives of the British Chiefs of Staff in Washington. The President brought with him Leahy, Marshall, King, and Arnold. A number of telegrams about the Italian Fleet coming over to us made an agreeable introduction. I expressed the hope that the Italian Fleet would be treated with respect by the Allies wherever it might arrive.

In preparation for this meeting I had prepared a memorandum to the President, which I had submitted to him earlier in the day. He asked me to read it out, and thought it would make a basis for our discussion.

9 Sept 43

It would surely be convenient before we separate to have a plenary meeting of the Combined Chiefs of Staff in order to take stock of the new world situation which will arise on the assumption that the present battle for Naples and Rome is successful and that the Germans retreat to the line of the Apennines or the Po.

2. Assuming we get the Italian Fleet, we gain not only that Fleet, but the British Fleet, which has hitherto contained it. This very heavy addition to our naval power should be used at the earliest possible moment to intensify the war against Japan. I have asked the First Sea Lord to discuss with Admiral King the movement of a powerful British battle squadron, with cruisers and ancillaries, to the Indian Ocean via the Panama Canal and the Pacific. We need a strong Eastern Fleet based on Colombo during the amphibious operations next year. I should be very glad if it were found possible for this fleet to serve under the American Pacific Command and put in at least four months of useful fighting in the Pacific before taking up its Indian Ocean station. We cannot afford to have idle ships. I do not know however how the arrival of such reinforcements would enable the various tasks assigned to United States forces in the Pacific to be augmented. Apart from strategy, from the standpoint of high policy His Majesty's Government would desire to participate in the Pacific war in order to give such measure of assistance as is in their power not only to their American Allies, but on account of the obligations to Australia and New Zealand. Such a movement of our ships to and through the Pacific would undoubtedly exercise a demoralising effect upon Japan, who must now be conscious of the very great addition of naval weight thrust against her, and besides this it would surely give satisfaction in the United States as being a proof positive of British resolve to take an active and vigorous part to the end in the war against Japan.

3. The public must be gradually led to realise what we and our Combined Staffs have so fully in mind, namely, the conversion of Italy into an active agent against Germany. Although we could not recognise Italy as an ally in the full sense, we have agreed she is to be allowed to work her passage, and that useful service against the enemy will not only be aided but recompensed. Should fighting break out between Italians and Germans the public prejudices will very rapidly depart, and in a fortnight or so matters may be ripe, if we can so

direct events, for an Italian declaration of war against Germany. The question of the Italian flag flying from Italian ships, and even some arrangement of Italians manning those vessels under British or American control, requires consideration. The whole problem of handling and getting the utmost use out of the Italian Navy requires review now on a high level.

4. On the overall assumption of a decisive victory in the Naples area, we are, I presume, agreed to march northwards up the Italian peninsula until we come up against the main German positions. If the Italians are everywhere favourable and their Army comes over to help, the deployment of at least a dozen Italian divisions will be of great advantage in holding the front across Italy and in permitting relief of Allied forces. If, after the Battle of Naples is over, we are not seriously resisted south of the main German line, we ought not to be long getting up against it with light forces, and I should hope that by the end of the year at the latest we should be confronting it in full strength. If sooner, then better. There can be no question of whittling down "Overlord". We must not forget at this juncture our agreement to begin moving the seven divisions away in succession from the beginning of November. All the more important is it to bring Italian divisions into the line, and our State policy should be adapted to procure this end.

5. I have been contemplating the 1944 campaign in the light of these new possibilities, and I remain strongly convinced that we should be very chary of advancing northward beyond the narrow part of the Italian peninsula. Of course, if the Germans retreat to the Alps another situation is presented, but, failing that, it would seem beyond our strength, having regard to the requirements of "Overlord", to broaden out into the plains of Lombardy. We have also to consider that the Germans, working on interior lines, may perhaps bring a heavier force to bear upon our front in Italy than we shall have there at the end of the year. The possibility of a strong German counter-attack cannot be excluded. I should like it to be considered whether we should not, when we come up against the main German position, construct a strong fortified line of our own, properly sited in depth. Italian military labour could be used on a large scale for this purpose. Italian troops could naturally take part in defending the line. Thus by the spring we should be able in this theatre either to make an offensive if the enemy were weak, and anyhow to threaten one, or, on the other hand, stand on the defensive, using our air-power, which will in the meanwhile have been built up, from behind our fortified line, and divert a portion of our troops for action elsewhere, either to the west or to the east. I hope this may be studied.

6. We are both of us acutely conscious of the great importance of the Balkan situation. We should make sure that the Mediterranean High Command, absorbed in its present battle, does not overlook the needs of the Patriot forces there. The problem of the Italian forces requires immediate study. The orders of the C.-in-C. Middle East, General Wilson, published to-day, are well conceived for the moment, but we require to see more clearly exactly what is intended. On the assumption that the Italians can be drawn into the war against Germany, far-reaching possibilities seem to be open. There is surely no need for us to work from the bottom of the Balkans upwards. If we can get an agreement between the Patriots and the Italian troops it should be possible to open quite soon one or more good ports on the Dalmatian coast, enabling munitions and supplies to be sent in by ship and all forces that will obey our orders to be raised to good fighting condition. The German situation in all this theatre will become most precarious, especially from the point of view of supplies. When the defensive line across Northern Italy has been completed it may be possible to spare some of our own forces assigned to the Mediterranean theatre to emphasise a movement north and north-eastward from the Dalmatian ports. For the moment the utmost efforts should be put forth to organise the attack upon the Germans throughout the Balkan peninsula and to supply agents, arms, and good direction.

7. Lastly, the question of islands is now ripe for consideration. Sardinia, I imagine, will come over immediately, though we may have to send some help to the Italians in procuring the disarmament of any German units there. In Corsica the Germans have perhaps already been overcome, but surely here is the place for a French expedition. Even if only one division could be sent by the French National Committee, the island could probably be quickly liberated, and there is little doubt that its manhood would enable at least another division or two to be raised locally. General Wilson's telegram about the operations against Rhodes and other islands in the Dodecanese is all right so far as it goes, but I am not satisfied that sufficient use is being made under the present conditions of the forces in the Middle East. I am making an immediate inquiry into the exact location of all troops above battalion strength, hoping that improvised expeditionary forces and garrisons may be provided for various minor ventures.

8. We must expect far-reaching reactions in Bulgaria, Roumania, and Hungary, and these again may produce a movement from the Turk without our having to make any request or incur any obligation. All this again requires military and political consideration on the high level, and I feel that we should do well to take a preliminary survey this afternoon if you are agreeable.

There was wide agreement in principle between us all along the lines set forth in the above note, and the Staffs concerted the necessary action in the days that followed.

* * * * *

The next day the President left Washington for his home at Hyde Park. He asked me to use the White House not only as a residence but for any conference I might wish to hold, either with the British Empire representatives who had gathered in Washington or with the United States war chiefs, and not to hesitate to call another plenary meeting should I deem it necessary. I availed myself fully of these generous facilities. Accordingly, as there was a general desire to take stock of the rapid movement of events in Italy and of the progress of the fierce and critical battle for Naples, I convened another meeting at the White House on September 11, at which I presided myself. The United States were represented by Admiral Leahy, General Marshall, Admiral King, General Arnold, Harry Hopkins, Averell Harriman, and Lew Douglas. I brought with me Dill and Ismay, and our three representatives on the Combined Chiefs of Staff.

All current matters were discussed. General Marshall reported the conditions in the Naples area, and the rapid reinforcement of the German divisions. General Arnold mentioned that we had now nearly three thousand operative aircraft engaged over Italy, which, he said, was more than the whole German Air Force on all fronts. I directed attention to the lamentable proposals for building up our forces on the mainland. I had been, I said, horrified to see the figure of only twelve divisions to be achieved by December 1. It was vitally important to accelerate the growth of the army in Italy by every possible division. Even the arrival of one division a fortnight earlier might make a serious difference. General Marshall entirely agreed and said that everything should be done.

He then told us about the brilliantly successful air landings by the United States Air Force in the South Pacific theatre. As a result of their descent in the Markham valley, combined with seaborne attack, the garrison of eight to ten thousand Japanese had been virtually isolated. American troops were pounding Salamaua and were close to Lae. Airfields should soon be in our possession from which the enemy airfields could be made untenable. This in turn would change the whole sea situation. The Japanese position in New Britain might soon be desperate. There were also signs of Japanese evacuation from the Solomons.

It was an honour to me to preside over this conference of the Combined Chiefs of Staff and of American and British authorities in the Council Room of the White House, and it seemed to be an event in Anglo-American history.

CHAPTER VIII

THE BATTLE OF SALERNO
A HOMEWARD VOYAGE

Anglo-American Descent Upon Salerno – Stubborn German Re-sistance – Taranto Seized – Alexander on the Spot – The Navy Lends a Hand – Congratulations from Stalin – We Embark on the "Renown" – Progress of the Battle: Alexander's Reports – The Victory Gained – My Message to Eisenhower – Mary's Adventure – Naples Taken – My Telegram to Eisenhower of September 25, and His Reply – Interchanges with the Commanders – A Pause to Con-solidate.

O N the night of September 8 Alexander sent me his "Zip" message. As the Allied armada approached the Salerno beaches that evening they heard the announcement from the British broadcast of the Italian surrender. To men keyed up for battle the news came as a shock, which for the moment relaxed the tension and had an unfortunate psychological effect. Many thought that on the morrow their task would be a walk-over. Officers at once strove to correct any such impression, pointing out that whatever the Italians might do there would certainly be strong resistance from German forces. There was a sense of anticlimax. Nevertheless, as Admiral Cunningham remarked, to have withheld the existence of the armistice would have been a breach of faith with the Italian people.

Covered by a strong British fleet, the assault convoys entered the Gulf of Salerno with only minor air attack. The enemy was aware of their approach, but he could not tell until the last moment where the blow would fall.

The landing of the Fifth Army, commanded by General Clark, began before dawn. The assault was delivered by the VIth U.S.

Corps and the British Xth Corps, with British Commandos and U.S. Rangers on the northern flank. The convoys had been sighted at sea, and General Eisenhower's broadcast of the previous evening caused the German troops in the neighbourhood to act immediately. Disarming the Italians, they took over the whole defence themselves, and made good use of the advantage which modern weapons give to the defence in the early stages of a landing. Our men were met by well-aimed fire as they waded ashore, and they suffered heavily. It was difficult to provide proper air cover for them, as many of our fighters were operating at extreme range from Sicily, but these were reinforced by carrier-borne aircraft.

Once across the beaches the VIth U.S. Corps made good progress, and by the night of the 11th had advanced as much as ten miles, with their right flank bent back to the sea. The British corps met stiffer opposition. They succeeded in taking Salerno and Battipaglia. The Montecorvino airfield also fell into our hands, but as it remained under enemy fire it could not provide the sorely needed refuelling ground for our fighters. The Germans reacted very quickly. Their troops opposing the Eighth Army, which was toiling its way up the toe of Italy, were brought at all speed to the new battle. From the north came the greater part of three divisions, from the east a regiment of parachutists.* Our own reinforcement was much slower, as shipping, especially small craft, was scarce. The German Air Force, though weakened by their losses in Sicily, made an intense effort, and their new radio-controlled and glider bombs caused losses to our shipping. All the resources of the Allied Air were turned on to hamper the approach of enemy reinforcements and blast their concentrations. Warships steamed into Salerno Bay to give the support of their heaviest guns. The Eighth Army was spurred on by Montgomery to gain contact with the hard-pressed Fifth. All this helped, and in the opinion of a highly placed German officer the eclipse of the Luftwaffe and the lack of any defence against naval bombardment were decisive.

*　　*　　*　　*　　*

While the Salerno battle was raging a remarkable stroke was made upon Taranto, for which not only Alexander, but Admiral

* The order of battle of the German and Italian divisions on September 8 is set out in Appendix E (p. 632).

Cunningham, on whom fell the brunt of execution, deserve the highest credit for well-run risks. This first-class port was capable of serving a whole army. The Italian surrender which now broke upon us seemed to Alexander to justify daring. There were no transport aircraft to lift the British 1st Airborne Division, nor any ordinary shipping to carry it by sea. Six thousand of these picked men were embarked on British warships, and on September 9, the day of the landing on Salerno beaches, the Royal Navy steamed boldly into Taranto harbour and deposited the troops ashore, unopposed. One of our cruisers which struck a mine and sank was our only naval loss.*

* * * * *

It had been planned that I and those of our party who had not already flown to England should go home by sea, and the *Renown* awaited us at Halifax. I broke the train journey to say good-bye to the President, and was thus with him at Hyde Park when the Battle of Salerno began. I resumed my train journey on the night of the 12th, to reach Halifax on the morning of the 14th. The various reports which reached me on the journey, as well as the newspapers, made me deeply anxious. Evidently a most critical and protracted struggle was in progress. My concern was all the greater because I had always strongly pressed for this seaborne landing, and felt a special responsibility for its success. Surprise, violence, and speed are the essence of all amphibious landings. After the first twenty-four hours the advantage of sea-power in striking where you will may well have vanished. Where there were ten men there are soon ten thousand. My mind travelled back over the years. I thought of General Stopford waiting nearly three days on the beach at Suvla Bay in 1915 while Mustafa Kemal marched two Turkish divisions from the lines at Bulair to the hitherto undefended battlefield. I had had a more recent experience when General Auchinleck had remained at his headquarters in Cairo surveying orthodoxly from the summit and centre the wide and varied sphere of his command, while the battle, on which everything turned, was being decided against him in the desert. I had the greatest confidence in Alexander, but all the same I passed a painful day while our train rumbled for-

---

* I have in my home the Union Jack, the gift of General Alexander, that was hoisted at Taranto, and was the first Allied flag to be flown in Europe since our expulsion from France.

THE SALERNO LANDING

ward through the pleasant lands of Nova Scotia. At length I wrote out the following message for Alexander, feeling sure he would not resent it. It was not sent till after I had sailed.

Prime Minister to General Alexander   14 Sept 43

I hope you are watching above all the Battle of "Avalanche", which dominates everything. None of the commanders engaged has fought a large-scale battle before. The Battle of Suvla Bay was lost because Ian Hamilton was advised by his C.G.S. to remain at a remote central point where he would know everything. Had he been on the spot he could have saved the show. At this distance and with time-lags I cannot pretend to judge, but I feel it my duty to set before you this experience of mine from the past.

2. *Nothing* should be denied which will nourish the decisive battle for Naples.

3. Ask for anything you want, and I will make allocation of necessary supplies, with highest priority irrespective of every other consideration.

His answer was prompt and comforting.

General Alexander (Salerno) to Prime Minister (at sea)   15 Sept 43

I feel sure you will be glad to know that I have already anticipated your wise advice and am now here with Fifth Army. Many thanks for your offer of help. Everything possible is being done to make "Avalanche" a success. Its fate will be decided in the next few days.

I was also relieved to learn that Admiral Cunningham had not hesitated to hazard his battleships close inshore in support of the Army. On the 14th he sent up the *Warspite* and *Valiant*, which had just arrived at Malta conducting to surrender the main body of the Italian Fleet. Next day they were in action, and their accurate air-directed bombardment with heavy guns impressed both friend and foe and greatly contributed to the defeat of the enemy. Unhappily, on the afternoon of the 16th the *Warspite* was disabled by a new type of glider bomb, about which we had heard something, and were to learn more.

Prime Minister (at sea) to Admiral Cunningham (Algiers)   15 Sept 43

I am very glad you have put in the *Warspite* and *Valiant*, as importance of battle fully justifies exceptional action.

Please give them my best wishes.

The following also came in:

Premier Stalin to President Franklin D. Roosevelt   14 Sept 43
and to Prime Minister Churchill

I congratulate you on new successes, and especially on the landing at Naples. There is no doubt that the successful landing at Naples and break between Italy and Germany will deal one more blow upon Hitlerite Germany and will considerably facilitate the actions of the Soviet armies at the Soviet-German front. For the time being the offensive of the Soviet troops is successfully developing. I think that we shall be in a position to achieve more successes within the next two-three weeks. It is possible that we shall have recaptured Novorossisk within the next few days.

It was a relief to board the *Renown*. The splendid ship lay alongside the quay. Admiral Pound was already on board, having come through direct from Washington. He bore himself as erect as ever, and no one looking at him would have dreamed that he was stricken. I invited him to join us at my table on the homeward voyage, but he said he would prefer to take his meals in his cabin with his staff officer. Within half an hour we sailed, and for the next six days we zigzagged our way across the ocean.

★   ★   ★   ★   ★

All the time the Battle at Salerno went on. The telegrams flowed in. Alexander was kind enough to keep me fully informed, and his vivid messages can be read in their relation to the whole event.

General Alexander to Prime Minister (at sea)   16 Sept 43

I have just returned from an extensive tour of the Fifth Army front. I saw both corps commanders, all division commanders, and several front line brigades. Although I am not entirely happy about the situation, I am happier than I was twenty-four hours ago, for following reasons:

The Germans have not put in a serious attack since night 13th. This has given us time to improve our position somewhat, rest for very exhausted troops, and get some reinforcements of men and material in. Eighth Army are also drawing nearer. I have also been able to cheer them up and issue certain directions, of which the following are most important. Hold what we have gained, at all costs consolidating key positions by digging, wiring, and mining. Reorganise scattered and mixed units and formations. Form local reserves and as strong a mobile reserve as possible. Inform troops of rapid approach of Eighth Army and flow of reinforcements now arriving day and night. Present weakness is [due to] following. Germans have been able concentrate strong forces quicker than we have been able to build up sufficient forces to hold what had been gained in first rush. Germans hold most of the dominating features and overlook us on to the beach. Our troops are tired. There is very little depth anywhere; we have temporarily lost the initiative. Last night our Air dropped a parachute battalion behind enemy lines in Avellino area. Air flew in 1,600 men of the 82nd Division last night. I have arranged with the Navy to bring 1,500 British infantry reinforcements from Philippeville in cruisers; these should be here in under forty-eight hours. I have speeded up arrival 3rd U.S. Division, which will start landing on 18th.

First elements of 7th Armoured Division arrive to-night, but will take few days to disembark and concentrate. One infantry brigade also arrives to-night. We have just completed three landing strips, and Spitfires are now operating from Salerno and neighbourhood.

The whole of the air forces are concentrated on this battle area. We shall regain the initiative and start to gain key points as soon as we are strong enough to do so. God's blessing on our enterprise and a little luck will ensure success to our arms.

129

Prime Minister (at sea) to General Alexander   16 Sept 43

My feeling about "Avalanche" is expressed in Foch's maxim, *Cramponnez partout*. The Navy are quite right to throw their heavy ships in, for this is a battle of far-reaching significance. My feeling is you are going to win.

Prime Minister to General Alexander   17 Sept 43

I am very glad to feel you have taken a personal grip of "Avalanche" position. I had, as you know, been worried about rate of "Avalanche" build-up. It is great news that Montgomery expects to bring Eighth Army into action on 17th.

2. It is right to use the battleships in the inshore squadron in view of favourable naval balances.

3. Every good wish. Please continue to keep me informed. I am in mid-ocean, but can receive fully at all hours.

For three critical days the issue hung in the balance. Battipaglia was lost, but the 56th Division, though weakened by heavy losses, succeeded in stopping a further drive from there to the sea. On the front of the VIth U.S. Corps the enemy, taking advantage of the thinly held gap between that corps and the British, turned in from the north, crossed the river Sele, and threatened to reach the landing beaches behind the Americans. They were stopped only just in time by the defence of the American batteries. The Allied line was held by the narrowest of margins. The 45th U.S. Division, which had been held in reserve on board their ships, was now in full action on the VIth Corps front. Reinforcements were beginning to arrive. Our 7th Armoured Division and the 82nd U.S. Airborne Division came in by sea and air. After six days of bitter fighting, in which we suffered moments of grave hazard, the Germans failed to throw us back into the sea. On the 15th Kesselring realised he could not succeed. Pivoting his right on the high ground above Salerno, he began to swing his whole line back. Next day the Fifth and Eighth Armies joined hands. We had won.

★　★　★　★　★

General Alexander to Prime Minister (at sea)   18 Sept 43

The general situation continues to improve, and the initiative is passing to us. There have been several strongish attacks against Xth British Corps in north, but all these have been repulsed. On VIth Corps front Americans are on offensive, and fighting is still going on in Altavilla. As you know, Fifth Army and Eighth Army patrols have joined hands. 7th Armoured Division are getting ashore well. 1,500 infantry reinforcements for Xth Corps arrived last night. American reinforcement of about 1,600 due to arrive in a day or two. 3rd U.S. Division starts disembarking to-morrow evening. The build-up of ammunition and supplies is satisfactory. Eighth Army are advancing on Aluetta and Potenza, but up to writing I have not received [any] report as to the location of their spearheads. 1st British Airborne Division, in Taranto area, are active, and have joined hands with the Canadians, but are too weak to do more than harass the Germans. 78th Infantry Division is due to start unloading at Taranto on September 22, and 8th Indian Division at Brindisi on September 23. My immediate aim is to build up three strong fighting groups: Fifth U.S. Army in Salerno area, Eighth Army in centre, British Vth Corps under Eighth Army in Taranto area. From these firm bases we shall advance northwards, and I have issued a directive to the following effect. Fifth Army to pivot on hills north-west of Salerno and secure the heights about Avellino. Eighth Army to secure Potenza area. Next objectives will be Fifth Army to secure port Naples, Eighth Army the airfields in Foggia area. I do not wish to mislead you by being over-optimistic, but I am satisfied that we now have the situation in hand, and will be able to carry out our future operations according to plan.

As we reached the Clyde decisive news arrived from Alexander.

General Alexander to Prime Minister   19 Sept 43

I can say with full confidence that the whole situation has changed in our favour and that the initiative has passed to us. . . .

I am rejoining my main H.Q. at Syracuse to-morrow.

On September 21 I sent my congratulations to General Eisenhower, and asked him to convey my compliments to General Clark.

Prime Minister to General Eisenhower (Algiers)   21 Sept 43

I congratulate you on the victorious landing and deployment northwards of our armies. As the Duke of Wellington said of the Battle of Waterloo, "It was a damned close-run thing," but your policy of running risks has been vindicated. If you think fit, send a message from me on to Clark, who from all I hear has done wonders. We certainly do work together in a way never before seen among allies.

2. It does seem to me most desirable, if you could manage it, to push more French troops into Corsica and to put a substantial detachment of British or American troops into Sardinia. As we now have good harbours for disembarkation they need not be combat-loaded, but their presence will animate the Italian troops and the French and local Patriots.

3. We are backing you up all we can about working with the Italian Government, and I am pretty sure all will go as you wish it.

4. Field-Marshal Smuts will be in Cairo Monday, September 27, staying with Casey, and will be in your theatre about four days later on his way here. He possesses my entire confidence, and everything can be discussed with him with the utmost freedom. He will stay some months in London, taking up his full duties as a member of the British War Cabinet. He will carry great weight here with public opinion. I shall be grateful if he is treated with the utmost consideration. He is a magnificent man and one of my most cherished friends.

* * * * *

Our six-day voyage would have been less pleasant if I had known what was happening to some of my children. Randolph had been in Malta recruiting volunteers for the 2nd Special Air Service Regiment in the early days of September. Here he met Brigadier Laycock, who was a great friend of his and mine. Laycock, who knew what was going to happen, said, "There is going to be a show for the Commandos. Would you like to come?" So Randolph went with him, and was closely engaged throughout the battle.

Mary had an adventure of a different kind. The *Renown* was slanting across a fairly rough sea when one of the officers suggested a walk on the quarterdeck. This, as he should have known, was forbidden on account of the zigzags, which made it impossible to calculate how waves would come aboard. Mary was leaning over the taffrail with her companion when the ship changed course. "Oh, look," she said, "there's a lovely wave coming towards us!" "Cling on!" cried the officer, who realised the danger. In one second the deluge swept them both head over heels across the deck to the starboard scuppers, and but for the fact that Mary came against an upright of the rails she would have gone overboard. The commander saw what had happened from behind the after-turret, and was about to order a "Man overboard" buoy to be dropped, when the recovery heel of the ship sent most of the water that had come on board pouring back the other way, and Mary on the return journey managed to clutch the anchor cables. The poor officer went to and fro in the same excursion. They were dragged, dripping, into safety. The officer was much scolded. Mary changed her clothes, and all this was concealed from me until we landed.

Another event of a more agreeable character also occurred in my personal circle. Among the party of a dozen Wrens who had come with us was a most beautiful girl. Leslie Rowan, my private secretary, wooed and won her in these few days at sea. But this was kept hidden from all by the parties concerned. They are now happily married.

On our arrival I received the following:

President Roosevelt to Prime Minister   20 Sept 43

Delighted you are all safely home, and I hope you had a smooth run. All is quiet here. Congress has been here for a week, and it is still quiet. My best to all three of you.

★　　★　　★　　★　　★

Once the Battle of Salerno had been won Naples and the Foggia airfields lay before us. The British Xth Corps, with the United States VIth Corps on their right, drove back the enemy's rearguards around Vesuvius, marched past the ruins of Pompeii and Herculaneum, and entered Naples. An immense effort was now concentrated upon opening the harbour, which had been subjected to every form of destruction at experienced hands. Nevertheless this work, in which the Americans excelled, was so effective that within a fortnight 5,000 tons of supplies a day could be handled. The two airfields near the city were soon brought into use, and gave welcome relief to our fighter squadrons, hitherto acting from improvised landing strips. Meanwhile on the east coast the 1st Airborne Division had patrolled as far as Gioja and Bari by September 15. The 78th Division and an armoured brigade landed behind them, and, with the Vth Corps headquarters, joined the Eighth Army. Six Royal Air Force squadrons began to act from the Gioja airfield at the same time. The enemy evacuated the Foggia airfields on September 25. Termoli was taken by Commandos landed from the sea, who, with the help of reinforcements, held out against fierce counter-attacks.

★　　★　　★　　★　　★

A few days after my return I sent General Eisenhower a telegram which should be borne in mind in reading all my messages and memoranda of the autumn and winter. The second paragraph sought to establish the proportion of effort, especially where bottle-necks were concerned, which should be devoted to our various enterprises. These proportions should not be overlooked by those who wish to understand the controversies with which a later chapter deals. War presents the problem of the correct employment of available means, and cannot often be epitomised as "One thing at a time".

Prime Minister to General Eisenhower (Algiers)   25 Sept 43

As I have been pressing for action in several directions, I feel I ought to place before you the priorities which I assign in my own mind to these several desirable objectives.

2. Four-fifths of our effort should be the build-up of Italy. One-tenth should be our making sure of Corsica (which will soon finish) and in the Adriatic. The remaining tenth should be concentrated on Rhodes. This of course applies to the limiting factors only. These, I presume, are mainly landing-craft and assault shipping, with light naval craft.

3. I send this as a rough guide to my thought only because I do not want you to feel I am pressing for everything in all directions without understanding how grim are your limitations.

General Eisenhower to Prime Minister   26 Sept 43

We are examining resources carefully to give Mid-East necessary support in this project, and feel sure that we can meet minimum requirements of Mid-East.

When Montgomery can get the bulk of his forces forward to support the right of the Fifth Army things will begin to move more rapidly on the Naples front. As is always the case following the early stages of a combined operation, we have been badly stretched both tactically and administratively. We are working hard to improve the situation and you will have good news before long.

Eisenhower's answer did not refer as specifically as I had hoped to what I deemed the all-important part of my message, namely, the small proportion of troops required for subsidiary enterprises.

*   *   *   *   *

I continued my interchanges with Alexander and Montgomery.

Prime Minister to General Alexander   25 Sept 43

I quite understand that the Eighth Army has to pull up its tail.

2. I like the idea of an advance on a broad front which the enemy will have difficulty in stemming, but I suppose you will also help yourself forward with minor amphibious scoops.

3. You will see that I have announced in Parliament that the Italian campaign is the "Third Front". The Second Front is here in Great Britain, in potential but not yet engaged. This form of statement

should be adhered to, as it is less disagreeable to the Russians and avoids arguing with them as to whether the Italian campaign is the Second Front or not.

Naples was entered by the Anglo-American Fifth Army on October 1.

Prime Minister to General Eisenhower (Algiers) 2 Oct 43

I rejoice with you at the brilliant turn our affairs in the Mediterranean have taken, and that Sardinia and Corsica have fallen as mere incidents in the campaign. Every good wish for the future.

Prime Minister to General Alexander (Italy) 2 Oct 43

I consider that the advance of the Eighth Army on the eastern flank is of enormous value.

I note that Montgomery will soon have to halt to bring up supplies, but I trust this does not mean that his patrols and light forces will not keep in touch with the enemy's rearguards. Everything in our Intelligence goes to show that the enemy's object is to gain time and retire northwards without serious losses. He has not in any case the strength to make a front against the forces you are now deploying. I consider that this favourable position is due to your master-stroke in seizing Taranto, with its unequalled harbour facilities, and beg you to accept my most sincere compliments upon it.

I have studied the plan you have sent home by your officer, and note that you have already accomplished the first and second phases of it. I hope the third phase will be accomplished by the end of the month or thereabouts, and that we shall meet in Rome.

General Alexander to Prime Minister 3 Oct 43

I am most grateful for your kind message, and I appreciate your praise so much. . . . Once I can get R.A.F. properly established and our administrative set-up working as it should, then all will be straight sailing.

I have now established my headquarters at Bari, where I am near the battle-front and within easy reach of my two Army Commanders and my main bases. Air Marshal Coningham is of course with me.

To sum up, all will be well, and the German will be harassed and continuous pressure applied to his rearguards all the time by light mobile forces and air forces when we cannot reach him with our main bodies.

Prime Minister to General Montgomery (Italy) 2 Oct 43

I am delighted to see the Eighth Army striding on so splendidly. Many congratulations on all you have done. I daresay you remember what I said to you that day in Tripoli about where we might meet.

General Montgomery to Prime Minister   5 Oct 43

Thank you for your kind message. We have advanced a long way and very quickly. It had to be done in order to come to the help of Fifth Army, but it has been a very great strain on my administration, which had to be switched from the toe to the heel during the operations and which is now stretched to the limit. When I have got the lateral Termoli–Campobasso I will have to halt my main bodies for a short period and operate in advance of that lateral only with light forces while I get my administration on a sound basis during the period of the halt. But light forces directed in sensitive areas can be very effective, and by this means I will retain the initiative and gain ground. After the halt I will advance with my whole strength on Pescara and Ancona. I shall look forward to meeting you in Rome.

★   ★   ★   ★   ★

A pause was now enforced upon both our armies. North of Naples the Fifth Army met strong resistance along the river Volturno, which needed time and supplies to overcome. In the Eighth Army's advance up the toe of Italy General Montgomery had deliberately taken every administrative risk in order to reach the Salerno battlefield. His base had now to be moved from the toe at Reggio to the heel at Taranto and Bari. Until this was accomplished the Eighth Army had reached the end of its tether. Moreover, the capture of Foggia enabled a start to be made in occupying its airfields with heavy bombers. This was a massive task, requiring the carriage of many thousand tons of stores, and could be effected only by degrees. In mid-October the Germans had nineteen divisions in Italy, and the Allies the equivalent of thirteen. Large reinforcements and much consolidation were required to hold our rapid and brilliant conquests. All this put a strain on our shipping.

September had been indeed a fruitful month. Anglo-American inter-Service co-operation by land, sea, and air had reached a new record. The commander of the German Tenth Army in Italy has since stated that the harmonious co-operation between our Army, Air, and Naval forces under one supreme command was regarded by the Germans with envy. The Italian Fleet was in our hands; their Air Force and Army, though prevented by the Germans from joining us in useful numbers, were no longer ranged against us. The enemy had been defeated in pitched battle and our armies had bitten three hundred miles off Italy's boot. Behind them lay captured airfields and ports, ample, when developed, for our needs. Sardinia, so long thrust forward in Staff argument as the alternative to the assault on Italy, fell into our hands for nothing, as a mere bonus, on September 19, and Corsica was taken by French troops a fortnight later. The Italian enterprise, to launch which we had struggled so hard, had been vindicated beyond the hopes even of its most ardent and persistent advocates.

Great credit is due to General Eisenhower for his support of this brief and spirited campaign. Although the execution fell to Alexander, the Supreme Commander had really taken the British view of the strategy, and had been prepared to accept the ultimate responsibility for an enterprise the risks of which had been needlessly sharpened by his own military chiefs in their rigid adherence to the plans for Burma, and by their stern and strict priorities for "Overlord", which were carried in the secondary ranks to a veritable pedantry. There can be no doubt at all that Italy was the greatest prize open to us at this stage, and that a more generous provision for it could have been made without causing any delay to the main cross-Channel plan of 1944.

CHAPTER IX

A SPELL AT HOME

Report on the War to Parliament – Complaints of Delay – Agitations for a Second Front – Appraisal of the Action of the Italian Government – Application of Similar Principles to Germany – Nazi Tyranny and Prussian Militarism the Target – Warning about the Pilotless Aircraft Bombardment – Need to Rally the Italian Nation – Death of the Chancellor of the Exchequer, Sir Kingsley Wood – Sir John Anderson Succeeds Him – Death of Admiral Pound – The Anglo-Portuguese Treaty of 1373 and the Azores – Position in the Coal-mining Industry – The Rebuilding of the House of Commons – Two Essential Features of an Effective Chamber – My Memorandum on the Transition from War to Peace – Plans for the Transition Period – Appointment of Lord Woolton as Minister of Reconstruction.

DURING the homeward voyage I prepared a speech for Parliament upon my return. I was well aware of the criticism I should have to meet, and that the increasing success of the war would only make the disaffected elements in the House and in the Press feel more free to speak their minds.

On September 21, two days after landing, I accordingly made a report to the House of Commons, which occupied no less than two and a half hours. To avoid the Members tailing off for luncheon I asked for an hour's adjournment, which was accorded.

* * * * *

The first complaint was that much time had been lost in making the attack upon Naples by futile negotiations with the Italian Government. To this I could see I had a good answer.

I have seen it said that forty days of precious time were lost in these negotiations, and that in consequence British and American blood was needlessly shed around Salerno. This criticism is as ill-founded in fact as it is wounding to those who are bereaved. The time of our main attack upon Italy was fixed without the slightest reference to the attitude of the Italian Government, and the actual provisional date of the operation was settled long before any negotiations with them had taken place, and even before the fall of Mussolini. That date depended upon the time necessary to disengage our landing-craft from the beaches of Southern Sicily, across which up to the first week in August the major part of our armies actually engaged there had to be supplied from day to day. These landing-craft had then to be taken back to Africa. Those that had been damaged—and they were many—had to be repaired, and then reloaded with all their ammunition, etc., in the most exact and complex order before there could be any question of carrying out another amphibious operation.

I suppose it is realised that these matters have to be arranged in the most extraordinary detail. Every landing vessel or combat ship is packed in the exact order in which the troops landing from it will require the supplies when they land, so far as can be foreseen. Every lorry indeed is packed with precisely the articles which each unit will require when that lorry comes. Some of the lorries swim out to the ships and swim back. They are all packed exactly in series, with the things which have priority at the top and so on, so that nothing is left to chance that can be helped. Only in this way can these extraordinary operations be carried out in the face of the vast modern fire-power which a few men can bring to bear. The condition and preparation of the landing-craft were the sole but decisive limiting factors. It had nothing to do with "wasting time over the negotiations", nothing to do with the Foreign Office holding back the generals while they worried about this clause or that clause and so forth. There was never one moment's pause in the process of carrying out the military operations, and everything else had to fit in with that main-line traffic.

When I hear people talking in an airy way of throwing modern armies ashore here and there as if they were bales of goods to be dumped on a beach and forgotten I really marvel at the lack of knowledge which still prevails of the conditions of modern war. . . .

I must say, if I may make a momentary digression, that this class of criticism which I read in the newspapers when I arrived on Sunday morning reminds me of the simple tale about the sailor who jumped into a dock, I think it was at Plymouth, to rescue a small boy from drowning. About a week later this sailor was accosted by a woman, who asked, "Are you the man who picked my son out of the dock the other night?" The sailor replied modestly, "That is true, ma'am." "Ah," said the woman, "you are the man I am looking for. Where is his cap?"   *   *   *   *   *

The second complaint was about the Second Front, for which the Communist elements and some others were steadily pressing.

I now tried to speak to the German High Command as well as the House of Commons, and at the same time to mislead the first and instruct the second.

I call this front we have opened, first in Africa, next in Sicily, and now in Italy, the Third Front. The Second Front, which already exists potentially and which is rapidly gathering weight, has not yet been engaged, but it is here, holding forces on its line. No one can tell—and certainly I am not going to hint—the moment when it will be engaged. But the Second Front exists, and is a main preoccupation already of the enemy. It has not yet opened or been thrown into play, but the time will come. At the right time this front will be thrown open, and the mass invasion from the West, in combination with the invasion from the South, will begin.

It is quite impossible for those who do not know the facts and figures of the American assembly in Britain, or of our own powerful expeditionary armies now preparing here, who do not know the dispositions of the enemy on the various fronts, who cannot measure his reserves and resources and his power to transfer large forces from one front to another over the vast railway system of Europe, who do not know the state and dimensions of our Fleet and landing-craft of all kinds, to pronounce a useful opinion upon this operation.

[Here one of our two Communist Members interjected, "Does that apply to Marshal Stalin?"]

We should not in a matter of this kind take advice from British Communists, because we know that they stood aside and cared nothing for our fortunes in our time of mortal peril. Any advice that we take will be from friends and Allies who are all joined together in the common cause of winning the victory. The House may be absolutely certain that His Majesty's present Government will never be swayed or overborne by any uninstructed agitation, however natural, or any pressure, however well-meant, in matters of this kind. We shall not be forced or cajoled into undertaking vast operations of war against our better judgment in order to gain political unanimity or a cheer from any quarter. The bloodiest portion—make no mistake about it —of this war for Great Britain and the United States lies ahead of us. Neither the House nor the Government will shrink from that ordeal. We shall not grudge any sacrifice for the common cause.

★   ★   ★   ★   ★

The most difficult issue was the decision the President and I had taken, of which I was, as the reader has seen, a strong partisan, to deal with the King and Marshal Badoglio and recognise and treat them as co-belligerents. The same passions were aroused on this occasion in the same kind of people as on the Admiral Darlan affair the year before. I felt however on even stronger ground in this case.

We may pause for a moment to survey and appraise the act of the Italian Government, endorsed and acclaimed as it was by the Italian nation. Herr Hitler has left us in no doubt that he considers the conduct of Italy treacherous and base in the extreme—and he is a good judge in such matters. Others may hold that the act of treachery and in-gratitude took place when the Fascist confederacy, headed by Musso-lini, used its arbitrary power to strike for material gain at falling France and so became the enemy of the British Empire, which had for so many years cherished the cause of Italian liberty. There was the crime. Though it cannot be undone, and though nations which allow their rights and liberties to be subverted by tyrants must suffer heavy penalties for those tyrants' crimes, yet I cannot view the Italian action at this juncture as other than natural and human. May it prove to be the first of a series of acts of self-redemption.

The Italian people have already suffered terribly. Their manhood has been cast away in Africa and Russia, their soldiers have been deserted in the field, their wealth has been squandered, their empire has been irretrievably lost. Now their own beautiful homeland must become a battlefield for German rearguards. Even more suffering lies ahead. They are to be pillaged and terrorised in Hitler's fury and revenge. Nevertheless, as the armies of the British Empire and the United States march forward in Italy the Italian people will be rescued from their state of servitude and degradation, and be enabled in due course to regain their rightful place among the free democracies of the modern world.

I cannot touch upon this matter of Italy without exposing myself to the question, which I shall be most properly asked, "Would you apply this line of argument to the German people?" I say, "The case is different." Twice within our lifetime, and three times counting that of our fathers, they have plunged the world into their wars of expansion and aggression. They combine in the most deadly manner the qualities of the warrior and the slave. They do not value freedom themselves, and the spectacle of it in others is hateful to them. When-ever they become strong they seek their prey, and they will follow with an iron discipline anyone who will lead them to it. The core of Germany is Prussia. There is the source of the recurring pestilence. But we do not war with races as such. We war against tyranny, and we seek to preserve ourselves from destruction. I am convinced that the British, American, and Russian peoples, who have suffered measureless waste, peril, and bloodshed twice in a quarter of a century through the Teutonic urge for domination, will this time take steps to put it beyond the power of Prussia or of all Germany to come at them again with pent-up vengeance and long-nurtured plans. Nazi tyranny and Prussian militarism are the two main elements in German life which must be absolutely destroyed. They must be rooted out if Europe and the world are to be spared a third and still more frightful conflict.

The controversies about whether Burke was right or wrong when he said "I do not know the method of drawing up an indictment against a whole people" seem to me to be sterile and academic. Here are two obvious and practical targets for us to fire at—Nazi tyranny and Prussian militarism. Let us aim every gun and let us set every man who will march in motion against them. We must not add needlessly to the weight of our task or the burden that our soldiers bear. Satellite States, suborned or overawed, may perhaps, if they can help to shorten the war, be allowed to work their passage home. But the twin root of all our evils, Nazi tyranny and Prussian militarism, must be extirpated. Until this is achieved there are no sacrifices that we will not make and no lengths in violence to which we will not go. I will add this. Having, at the end of my life, acquired some influence on affairs, I wish to make it clear that I would not needlessly prolong this war for a single day; and my hope is that if and when British people are called by victory to share in the august responsibilities of shaping the future we shall show the same poise and temper as we did in the hour of our mortal peril.

★　　★　　★　　★　　★

I had thought it right in the course of my speech to give at this time a serious and precise warning about the attack which was impending upon us by pilotless aircraft or rockets. It is always prudent to be on record publicly as having given warning long before the event. This is more particularly true when its scale and gravity cannot be measured.

We must not in any circumstances allow these favourable tendencies to weaken our efforts or lead us to suppose that our dangers are past or that the war is coming to an end. On the contrary, we must expect that the terrible foe we are smiting so heavily will make frenzied efforts to retaliate. The speeches of the German leaders, from Hitler downwards, contain mysterious allusions to new methods and new weapons which will presently be tried against us. It would of course be natural for the enemy to spread such rumours in order to encourage his own people, but there is probably more in it than that. For example, we now have experience of a new type of aerial bomb which the enemy has begun to use in attacks on our shipping, when at close quarters with the coast. This bomb, which may be described as a sort of rocket-assisted glider, is released from a considerable height, and is then apparently guided towards its target by the parent aircraft. It may be that the Germans are developing other weapons on novel lines with which they may hope to do us damage and to compensate to some extent for the injury which they are daily receiving from us. I can only assure the House that unceasing vigilance and the most intense study of which we are capable are given to the possibilities.

★　★　★　★　★

I also outlined my thought upon the political state of Italy, and upon the now cruel reality of civil war spreading in that unhappy country.

The escape of Mussolini to Germany, his rescue by paratroops, and his attempts to form a Quisling Government which, with German bayonets, will try to re-fix the Fascist yoke on the necks of the Italian people, raise of course the issue of Italian civil war. It is necessary in the general interest as well as in that of Italy that all surviving forces of Italian national life should be rallied together around their lawful Government, and that the King and Marshal Badoglio should be supported by whatever Liberal and Left Wing elements are capable of making head against the Fascist-Quisling combination, and thus of creating conditions which will help to drive this villainous combination from Italian soil, or, better still, annihilate it on the spot. We are coming to the rescue and liberation of Italy. [A Member interjected, "You will not get the Italian people to rise behind the banner of turn-coats."] I think the hon. gentleman may be not thinking quite sufficiently of the importance of diminishing the burden which our soldiers have to bear. . . . The Government certainly intend to pursue a policy of engaging all the forces they can to make head against the Germans and drive them out of Italy. We are not going to be put off that action by any fear that perhaps we should not have complete unanimity on the subject. Parliament does not rest on unanimity; democratic assemblies do not act on unanimity. They act by majorities. That is the way they act. I wish to make it perfectly clear that we are endeavouring to rally the strongest forces together in Italy to make head against the Germans and the Mussolini-Quisling-Fascist combination.

My final words were somewhat unceremonious, but true:

The best method of acquiring flexibility is to have three or four plans for all the probable contingencies, all worked out with the utmost detail. Then it is much easier to switch from one to the other as and where the cat jumps.

These arguments convinced the House and there was no effective challenge.   *   *   *   *   *

On the same day that I finished this lengthy speech I and my colleagues suffered a very heavy and unexpected loss in the sudden death of the Chancellor of the Exchequer. I did not hear the news till I awoke on the morning of the 22nd. Kingsley Wood had become in later years a close personal friend of mine. After he went to the Air Ministry in 1938 we worked for the same objects. I gave him my full support, and undoubtedly he made an invaluable contribution to the readiness of the Royal Air Force to meet the mortal trial of 1940. He had been Chancellor of the Exchequer from the time I was called upon to form the National Government, and his record was a very fine one. His third Budget, balanced at five and three-quarter thousand millions, conformed to all the soundest principles of war-time finance. Half was raised by taxation. Our rate of borrowing was incredibly low. Instead of the slogan "Security and 6 per cent." of the First World War, we succeeded in borrowing enormous sums in the fifth year of this war at an average rate of 2 per cent. The cost of living had not risen by more than 30 per cent. over the pre-war level. The "Pay as you earn" principle had occupied the closing weeks of Kingsley Wood's life, and on the very day that he died he was looking forward to making a statement to the House on the subject. He had given effect, with high efficiency, to the request I made to him in 1940 to provide compensation for those whose homes and businesses were destroyed in the Blitz, by the elaborate insurance scheme which he devised. I spent the few hours that remained before the House met in preparing a tribute to him, which is on record.

In Sir John Anderson, at this time Lord President of the Council and chairman of our most important Cabinet Committee, and our chief representative on "Tube Alloys",* I found a worthy successor. John Anderson had been Chairman of the Board of Inland Revenue, and also head of the Home Office for

* Atom Bomb Research and Development.

ten years, but he had a far wider outlook than can be gained from any department. In the Irish troubles he had risked his life continually with the utmost composure, and this bearing was repeated when as Governor of Bengal an attempt was made to assassinate him. He had an acute and powerful mind, a firm spirit, and long experience of widely varied responsibilities. His appointment was announced on September 24.

*   *   *   *   *

Except for a few chats on the deck, I had seen little of Sir Dudley Pound on our homeward voyage, as he kept to his cabin. On the train journey to London he sent me a letter formally resigning his office of First Sea Lord, of the burden of which I had relieved him when his illness became pronounced in Washington. The question of his successor required careful consideration. Admiral Sir Andrew Cunningham was an obvious choice, proposed by the First Lord, Mr. Alexander, on account of the reputation which he had won in all the fighting in the Mediterranean. Could he, on the other hand, be spared from this scene at a time when so much was going forward and all operations expanding? In Admiral Fraser, then commanding the Home Fleet, we had an officer of the highest seagoing reputation, who had also long experience of Admiralty administration and staff work. It was to him I first offered the post. The Admiral said that of course he would serve wherever he was sent, but that he thought Andrew Cunningham was the right man. "I believe I have the confidence of my own fleet," he said. "Cunningham has that of the whole Navy." He asked me to weigh the matter longer. I replied that his attitude was most becoming, and after further thought and consultation I took him at his word and decided to face the serious change in the Mediterranean fighting command. Admiral Andrew Cunningham was therefore chosen. His second-in-command, Admiral John Cunningham, took his place. The changes were announced to the public and the Service, who knew nothing of Pound's illness, on October 4, when I published the following letter to Sir Dudley Pound:

I am sorry indeed that you have felt it necessary to lay down your charge on account of your health, and that our four years' work together in this war must come to an end. No one knows better than I the quality of your contribution at the Admiralty and on the Chiefs of Staff Committee to the safety of the country and the success of our arms. Your vast and precise knowledge of the sea war in all its aspects, your fortitude in times of anxiety and misfortune, your resourcefulness and readiness to run the risks without which victory can never be won, have combined to make your tenure as First Sea Lord memorable in the records of the Royal Navy.

You leave us at a moment when the control of the Mediterranean is virtually within our grasp, when the Italian Fleet has made its surrender in Malta harbour, and when, above all, the U-boat peril has been broken in a degree never before seen in this war. These results have been of measureless value to your country, and your notable share in them sheds lustre on your name.

Pound lived for little more than a fortnight. He became completely paralysed by another more severe stroke. The last time I saw him, though his mind was as good as ever, he could neither speak nor move the greater part of his body. When I shook his left hand on parting he gripped me with a most surprising strength. He had been a true comrade to me, both at the Admiralty and on the Chiefs of Staff Committee. He died on October 21, Trafalgar Day.

Admiral Fraser went back to his fleet at Scapa. At the end of the year he had the distinction of fighting in his own flagship and sinking the *Scharnhorst* in a direct encounter. This was a naval episode of high honour and importance. When I next saw him in London I reminded him of the famous lines:

> Not once or twice in our rough island-story
> The path of duty was the way to glory.

The Admiral seemed all the more pleased because, as I judged, he had never heard the quotation before. I hoped he thought I had made it up myself on purpose.

★　★　★　★　★

I have not burdened this account with the lengthy correspondence with the United States and Portugal which led to our agreement about the use by British and American flotillas and air forces of the extremely important key islands of the Azores. Everything was settled in a satisfactory manner, so that on October 12 I could report our conclusions to Parliament. "I have an announcement," I said, "to make to the House arising out of the treaty signed between this country and Portugal in the year

1373 between His Majesty King Edward III and King Ferdinand and Queen Eleanor of Portugal." I spoke in a level voice, and made a pause to allow the House to take in the date, 1373. As this soaked in there was something like a gasp. I do not suppose any such continuity of relations between two Powers has ever been, or will ever be, set forth in the ordinary day-to-day work of British diplomacy.

"This treaty," I went on,

was reinforced in various forms by treaties of 1386, 1643, 1654, 1660, 1661, 1703, and 1815, and in a secret declaration of 1899. In more modern times the validity of the Old Treaties was recognised in the Treaties of Arbitration concluded with Portugal in 1904 and 1914. Article I of the treaty of 1373 runs as follows:

"In the first place we settle and covenant that there shall be from this day forward . . . true, faithful, constant, mutual, and perpetual friend-ships, unions, alliances, and deeds of sincere affection, and that as true and faithful friends we shall henceforth, reciprocally, be friends to friends and enemies to enemies, and shall assist, maintain, and uphold each other mutually, by sea and by land, against all men that may live or die."

This engagement has lasted now for nearly six hundred years, and is without parallel in world history. I have now to announce its latest application. At the outset of the war the Portuguese Government, in full agreement with His Majesty's Government in the United King-dom, adopted a policy of neutrality with a view to preventing the war spreading into the Iberian peninsula. The Portuguese Govern-ment have repeatedly stated, most recently in Dr. Salazar's speech of April 27, that the above policy is in no way inconsistent with the Anglo-Portuguese Alliance, which was reaffirmed by the Portuguese Government in the early days of the war.

His Majesty's Government in the United Kingdom, basing them-selves upon this ancient alliance, have now requested the Portuguese Government to accord them certain facilities in the Azores which will enable better protection to be provided for merchant shipping in the Atlantic. The Portuguese Government have agreed to grant this request, and arrangements, which enter into force immediately, have been concluded between the two Governments regarding (1) the conditions governing the use of the above facilities by His Majesty's Government in the United Kingdom and (2) British assistance in furnishing essential material and supplies to the Portuguese armed forces and the maintenance of the Portuguese national economy. The agreement concerning the use of facilities in the Azores is of a temporary nature only, and in no way prejudices the maintenance of Portuguese sovereignty over Portuguese territory.

★ ★ ★ ★ ★

The next day I had to make a long speech to the House on the coal-mining situation, which was affected by the vital need of coal and the claims of the fighting forces for man-power, and also by the underlying threat of the nationalisation of the coal-mines, which was a suspended issue between the parties. There had been a lot of rumblings on this point, and I was concerned only with the maintenance of national unity.

I thought it might help if I reminded the House at the outset of this discussion of the general foundations upon which we stand at the present time. We have a National Coalition Government, which came together to try to pull the nation out of the forlorn and sombre plight into which the action, or inaction, of all political parties over a long period of years had landed it. I stand very well placed in that matter, having been out for eleven years. What holds us together is the prosecution of the war. No Socialist or Liberal or Labour man has been in any way asked to give up his convictions. That would be indecent and improper. We are held together by something outside, which rivets all our attention. The principle that we work on is, "Everything for the war, whether controversial or not, and nothing controversial that is not *bona fide* needed for the war." That is our position.

We must also be careful that a pretext is not made of war needs to introduce far-reaching social or political changes by a side-wind. Take the question of nationalising the coal-mines. Those words do not terrify me at all. I advocated nationalisation of the railways after the last war, but I am bound to say that I was a bit affected by the experience of the national control of the railways after the war, which led to the public getting a very bad service, to the shareholders having very unsatisfactory returns, and to one of the most vicious and hazardous strikes with which I have ever been concerned. However, as I say, the principle of nationalisation is accepted by all, provided proper compensation is paid. The argument proceeds not on moral grounds, but on whether in fact we could make a more fertile business for the nation as a whole by nationalisation than by relying on private enterprise and competition. It would raise a lot of difference of opinion and be a tremendous business to nationalise the coal-mines, and unless it could be proved to the conviction of the House and of the country and to the satisfaction of the responsible Ministers that that was the only way in which we could win the war we should not be justified in embarking upon it without a General Election. It would be very difficult to have a General Election at the present time. . . .

I am told and can well realise that anxiety exists among the miners about what is to happen to them and their industry after the war. They had a very grim experience after the last war, which went on biting away at them for a long period and greatly affected the whole conception that they had of mining as a means of getting their living. I know that there is anxiety. We can all lie awake thinking of the nightmares that we are going to suffer after the war is over, and everyone has his perplexities and anxieties about that time. But I for one, being an optimist, do not think peace is going to be so bad as war, and I hope we shall not try to make it as bad. After the last war, which I lived through in a responsible position, nearly everyone behaved as badly as they could, and the country was at times almost uncontrollable. We have profited a great deal in this war by the experience of the last. We make war much better than we did, owing to previous experience. We are also going to try to profit to the full by the hard experience of what happened in the last peace. I am casting no reflection on the Government of that day when I say that, armed with their dear-bought experience, we shall make the transition from war to peace in a more orderly and disciplined fashion than we did last time.

But the miners are worried about their future. His Majesty's Government give the assurance to them that the present system of control, plus any improvements that may be made to it, will be continued after the war until Parliament shall decide upon the future structure of the industry. That means either that there will be a settlement by agreement between the great parties, or that there will be a General Election at which the people will be free to choose between political doctrines and political leaders. But anyhow, until all that is over there will be no decisive change in the present structure of the coal industry, or any removal of the many guarantees for the continuity of employment and wages and limitation of profits which are embodied in it. I am so anxious that we should all be together in this.

This statement eased the tension which existed, and I am glad to-day to read it over again.

* * * * *

Finally, on October 28 there was the rebuilding of the House of Commons to consider. One unlucky bomb had blown to fragments the Chamber in which I had passed so much of my life. I was determined to have it rebuilt at the earliest moment that our struggle would allow. I had the power at this moment to shape things in a way that would last. Supported by my colleagues, mostly old Parliamentarians, and with Mr. Attlee's cordial aid, I sought to re-establish for what may well be a long period the two great principles on which the British House of Commons stands in its physical aspect. The first is that it must be oblong, and not semicircular, and the second that it must only be big enough to give seats to about two-thirds of its Members. As this argument has long surprised foreigners, I record it here.

There are two main characteristics of the House of Commons which will command the approval and the support of reflective and experienced Members. The first is that its shape should be oblong and not semicircular. Here is a very potent factor in our political life. The semicircular assembly, which appeals to political theorists, enables every individual or every group to move round the centre, adopting various shades of pink according as the weather changes. I am a convinced supporter of the party system in preference to the group system. I have seen many earnest and ardent Parliaments destroyed by the group system. The party system is much favoured by the oblong form of chamber. It is easy for an individual to move through those insensible gradations from Left to Right, but the act of crossing the Floor is one which requires serious consideration. I am well informed on this matter, for I have accomplished that difficult process, not only once, but twice. Logic is a poor guide compared with custom. Logic, which has created in so many countries semicircular assemblies with buildings that give to every member not only a seat to sit in, but often a desk to write at, with a lid to bang, has proved fatal to Parliamentary government as we know it here in its home and in the land of its birth.

The second characteristic of a chamber formed on the lines of the House of Commons is that it should *not* be big enough to contain all its members at once without overcrowding, and that there should be no question of every member having a separate seat reserved for him. The reason for this has long been a puzzle to uninstructed outsiders, and has frequently excited the curiosity and even the criticism of new Members. Yet it is not so difficult to understand if you look at it from a practical point of view. If the House is big enough to contain all its members nine-tenths of its debates will be conducted in the depressing atmosphere of an almost empty or half-empty chamber. The essence of good House of Commons speaking is the conversational style, the facility for quick, informal interruptions and interchanges. Harangues from a rostrum would be a bad substitute for the conversational style in which so much of our business is done. But the conversational style requires a fairly small space, and there should be on great occasions a sense of crowd and urgency. There should be a sense of the importance of much that is said, and a sense that great matters are being decided, there and then, by the House.

This anyhow was settled as I wished.

★　★　★　★　★

During these busy days I thought it right, now that our ultimate victory appeared certain, to dwell upon what would descend upon us at the same time as victory. This chapter may well close with the two notes I wrote to my colleagues upon these problems, already looming ahead.

WAR—TRANSITION—PEACE

MEMORANDUM BY THE PRIME MINISTER AND MINISTER OF DEFENCE

19 Oct 43

It is the duty of His Majesty's Government to prepare for the tasks which will fall upon us at the end of the war. The urgent needs are:

(a) A sound scheme of demobilisation, having regard to the un-doubted need of our keeping considerable garrisons in enemy-occupied territory.

(b) The provision of food for our island on a scale better than the war-time rations.

(c) The resumption of the export trade and the restoration of our Mercantile Marine.

(d) The general turn-over of industry from war to peace.

And, above all,

(e) The provision during a transition period of employment for all able-bodied persons seeking it, and especially for the ex-Service-men.

Any decisions which are needed for the supreme objects of *food* and *employment* in the years immediately after the war must be taken now, whether they involve legislation and whether they are controversial or not.

2. Much work has already been done on these lines by the depart-ments and committees concerned. We must be careful not to have these urgent practical duties confused and overlaid by party politics or held up by endless discussions about long-term schemes for building a new world order, etc.

3. There are in fact three stages, namely,

(i) War,
(ii) Transition, and
(iii) Peace and freedom.

The present Government and Parliament are fully entitled to make all necessary preparations for the transition period, and we should be held severely accountable if found in default. As early as possible in the transition period (for which all preparations will have been made) a General Election must be held, in order that the electors may express their will upon the form that is to be given to our post-war and post-transition society.

4. We do not know whether this election will be fought on an agreed programme by the parties now composing the Coalition Government or whether the leader of the majority in the present House of Commons will be forced to place his own programme before the electors. In either case it is probable that a Four Years Plan will be announced, which, apart from carrying out the enormous administrative measures required in the transition period, will also comprise a series of large decisions on progress and reform which will, from one angle or the other, shape the post-war and post-transition period. There will therefore be no lack of work for the new Parliament.

5. In the meanwhile there are a number of important policies, such as education, social insurance, the rebuilding of our shattered dwellings and cities, on which there is or may be found a wide measure of general agreement. These steps must be brought to a high degree of preparation now during the war, any necessary preliminary legislation being passed, so that they are ready to come into force in the early days of the transition period.

6. It is impossible to tell how long the war against Japan will outlast the war against Germany. It would perhaps be safe, as a working basis, to make the transition period last for two years after the defeat of Germany, or four years from January 1, 1944, whichever period shall end the sooner.

* * * * *

A month later I decided upon the appointment of a Minister of Reconstruction, whose office would be the focal point for all plans for the transitional period. Lord Woolton's conduct of the Food Ministry had gained widespread satisfaction and general confidence. He seemed in every way equipped with the qualities and experience to concert and stimulate the activities of the many departments concerned. He took up his duties on November 12.

CHAPTER X

TENSIONS WITH GENERAL DE GAULLE

Upsurge of the de Gaullist Movement – French Committee of National Liberation Set Up – The Question of Recognition of the Committee – President Roosevelt on the Situation – My Memorandum of July 13 – I Try to Persuade the President to Accord Limited Recognition – He Suggests Instead a Formula of Co-operation – We Debate the Position at Quebec – Qualified Recognition is Given – The Struggle for Power Between de Gaulle and Giraud Continues – Formation of a Free French Consultative Assembly – De Gaulle Becomes Sole President of the French National Committee – Violent Action in Syria – A Year of Disappointing Relationships with the Free French.

D URING the summer of 1943 the relations of the British Government with de Gaulle deteriorated. We had made great efforts to bring together Frenchmen of all parties at Algiers, and I had constantly pressed the Americans to accept General de Gaulle as a leading figure in the political arrangements which we were both trying to facilitate. In the strained atmosphere which pervaded French affairs after the signature of the Clark-Darlan agreements and the appearance of Giraud de Gaulle became more than ever intractable. His position had strengthened in recent weeks. He had many supporters in Tunisia, which was now in Allied hands. News from Metropolitan France, together with the creation of the clandestine Central Committee there, showed the extent of his prestige and an upsurge of the de Gaullist movement. It was in these circumstances that Giraud agreed to meet his rival in North Africa.

On May 30 de Gaulle arrived in Algiers, and sharp and sulky negotiations were begun with the object of setting up a united Provisional Committee to administer the affairs of Fighting France. Wrangling centred round three main issues: Giraud's assumption of supreme civil and military authority; de Gaulle's determination to affirm formally the sovereignty of Fighting France—a step which would violate the letter of the agreements which Darlan had made with General Mark Clark in November 1942; and the question of the former Vichy administrators now in key offices in North Africa, particularly Noguès, Peyrouton, and Boisson. The last-named was a special target. De Gaulle had never forgiven him for the events of 1940 at Dakar.

Tension mounted in Algiers as these bitter discussions were prolonged. On the afternoon of June 3 however agreement was reached, and a French Committee of National Liberation was set up, which included Giraud and de Gaulle, Generals Catroux and Georges, and certain members of the Gaullist Committee from London, which had been dissolved when de Gaulle left for North Africa. The former Vichy governors were excluded from the new body, which was now to be the central provisional administration of Fighting France and her Empire until the end of the war.

* * * * *

The reader will recall that I was in North Africa with General Marshall for conferences with General Eisenhower during these talks on the future of France, and just before my departure I had invited the new Committee to luncheon. When I got back to London I received a telegram from the President voicing his anxiety. "I want to give you," he said on June 5, "the thought that North Africa is in last analysis under British-American military rule, and that for this reason Eisenhower can be used on what you and I want. The bride evidently forgets that there is still a war in progress over here. We receive only the bride's publicity. What is the matter with our British-American information services? Best of luck in getting rid of our mutual headache."

I sent to the President in reply my impressions of Algiers.

Former Naval Person to President Roosevelt   6 June 43

We had the whole French Committee to luncheon on Friday (June 4), and everybody seemed most friendly. General Georges, whom I got out of France a month ago, and who is a personal friend of mine, is a great support to Giraud. If de Gaulle should prove violent or unreasonable he will be in a minority of five to two, and possibly completely isolated. The Committee is therefore a body with collective authority with which in my opinion we can safely work.

2. I consider that the formation of this Committee brings to an end my official connection with de Gaulle as leader of the Fighting French, which was set out in the letters exchanged with him in 1940 and certain other documents of later date, and I propose, in so far as is necessary, to transfer these relationships, financial and otherwise, to the Committee as a whole. While I consider the Committee is a safe repository for arms and supplies, I feel that we should see how they conduct their business and themselves before deciding what degree of recognition we should give them as representing France. Macmillan and Murphy are working in the closest accord, and will keep Eisenhower, with whom the supreme and ultimate power rests, fully informed.

3. I should be strongly opposed to Boisson being dismissed from his post.

★　★　★　★　★

But the wrangling did not cease. De Gaulle would not accept Giraud as Supreme Commander of the French forces. Giraud was anxious to keep the French Army of North Africa intact and clear of Free French influences. This attitude of de Gaulle on the question of military command exacerbated American dislike and distrust of him.

The President again telegraphed to me:

President Roosevelt to Prime Minister　　　　　　　　　　　10 June 43

I have just received the following message from Murphy:

"I was told this afternoon by Giraud that de Gaulle during this morning's session of the French Committee finally brought into the open his wish to act as Commissioner for National Defence, having the attributes of a Minister of War in the ordinary Cabinet set-up. He also demanded the command of French forces not actively engaged in operations, which is contrary to what he has told Eisenhower, Macmillan, and me with respect to his intentions. Giraud absolutely refused to yield command of French forces. He insisted that General Georges be appointed Commissioner for National Defence. A compromise proposal submitted by Catroux very much favoured de Gaulle's proposition. Giraud told me of his determination to retire if the Committee outvoted him on this question, and to inform the British and American Governments and the French people of the injustice caused by de Gaulle's ambition. I have asked Giraud to delay any such action until there has been an opportunity to discuss this question with several members of the Committee."

155

Macmillan had reported to me in the same sense. I was only anxious that a straightforward agreement should be reached.

Prime Minister to Mr. Harold Macmillan (Algiers)   11 June 43

There can be no question of our giving recognition until we know what it is we have to recognise. See St. Matthew, chapter vii, verse 16: "Ye shall know them by their fruits. Do men gather grapes of thorns, or figs of thistles?" Indeed, the whole chapter is instructive.

You are quite right to play for time and let de Gaulle have every chance to come to his senses and realise the forces around him. We play fair with him if he plays fair with us and with France.

The President was less patient.

President Roosevelt to Prime Minister   17 June 43

The following is a paraphrase of a cable I have to-day sent to General Eisenhower:

"The position of this Government is that during our military occupation of North Africa we will not tolerate the control of the French Army by any agency which is not subject to the Allied Supreme Commander's direction. We must have someone whom we completely and wholly trust. We would under no circumstances continue the arming of a force without being completely confident in their willingness to co-operate in our military operations. We are not interested moreover in the formation of any Government or Committee which presumes in any way to indicate that, until such time as the French people select a Government for themselves, it will govern in France. When we get into France the Allies will have a civil Government plan that is completely in consonance with French sovereignty. Lastly, it must be absolutely clear that in North and West Africa we have a military occupation, and therefore without your full approval no independent civil decision can be made. . . ."

*   *   *   *   *

These telegrams from the President revealed such a mounting hostility to de Gaulle's actions in Algiers that I feared for the whole future of Allied relations with the Free French. The Americans reached the point where they might refuse to recognise any provisional administrative body if they thought that de Gaulle would be the dominating influence which would affect the future of France after the war. It was essential to allay American fears on the military question and at the same time to keep in being the new Provisional Committee.

Former Naval Person to President Roosevelt   18 June 43

... I am not in favour at this moment of breaking up the Committee of Seven or forbidding it to meet. I should prefer that General Eisenhower should take your instructions as his directive, and that Murphy and Macmillan should work towards its fulfilment by whatever means they find most appropriate. His Majesty's Government will associate themselves with this policy.

The Committee will then be confronted with a choice of either accepting our decision by a majority or placing themselves in definite opposition to the two rescuing Powers. If, as seems probable, they accept the decision by a majority, it will be for de Gaulle to decide whether he and other dissentients will submit or resign. If de Gaulle resigns he will put himself in the wrong with public opinion, and the necessary measures must be taken to prevent him from creating a disturbance. If he submits we shall probably have further trouble in the future, but this will be better than our sweeping away a Committee on which many hopes are founded among the United Nations as well as in France. We should prescribe the conditions essential for the safety of our forces and place the onus on de Gaulle. At any rate, it would be wise to try this first.

★   ★   ★   ★   ★

The American attitude to the French political scene in North Africa was in part dominated by military necessity. The background to the dispute over de Gaulle was the preparation of the Sicily landings. The quarrels over the French High Command, provoked by de Gaulle, had come at the critical moment. Whatever past arrangements had existed between the British Government and de Gaulle, they could not be allowed to impair our relations with the United States.

On July 13 I had written a paper for my colleagues summarising these developments in American policy towards France, in which I stated:

It has for a good many months past been our object to bring about a union between the French elements cultivated by the Americans in North-West Africa and the French National Committee in London, and particularly between Generals Giraud and de Gaulle. I could, I think, have made a good arrangement at Casablanca, but, as my colleagues know, this was frustrated by the preposterous conduct of General de Gaulle. Since then the President has armed General Giraud's troops in North Africa on a very considerable scale, and he is now much concerned about the demeanour and control of this army.

Meanwhile the de Gaullist organs in London and at Brazzaville, with their backers in the British and American Press, have ceaselessly criticised American policy, and there is no doubt that not only Mr. Hull but the President have become bitterly antagonised thereby.

For all these reasons we have hoped that the personality of de Gaulle should be merged first in the National Committee in London, and, now that juncture has been effected with the Algiers elements, in the Committee of National Liberation. After some crises and spasms this Committee is gradually acquiring a collective character, especially now that the civilian elements are increasing and asserting themselves. The lines of cleavage are no longer defined by the partisans of Giraud or of de Gaulle. These healthy tendencies should be allowed to develop, and if it should become clear in the course of the next few months that de Gaulle and his faction are not the masters of the Liberation Committee, and that he himself has settled down to honest teamwork within its ranks, it might be possible to procure from the President some kind of recognition of the Committee. This result will not however be easily or swiftly obtained, and we have to consider what our course should be in the meanwhile.

When the Liberation Committee was formed I made haste to transfer to it the engagements previously made with General de Gaulle. This process must continue, as otherwise we should have no one to deal with about finance, propaganda, Syria and other French possessions, and the control of the French armed forces. The Foreign Secretary has pointed out to me that we passed an Act of Parliament investing de Gaulle with powers of discipline over the Free French forces in British territory, and certainly these powers must now be vested in the new Committee. There is no objection to dealing with the Committee in its collective capacity as the *de facto* authority. Transacting necessary business with them can only do them good, and, if they are worthy of their responsibilities, will add to their strength.

In a certain sense this implies recognition of the Committee, but it will only be making unnecessary trouble with the United States to emphasise this point or do anything of a *de jure* character at the present stage. We should avoid the use of the word "recognition", and avoid also anything in the nature of a splash or a gesture, while at the same time working with them, for what they are worth, from day to day. It is the duty of the Committee and also in their interest to regain or build up the wounded confidence of the Rescuing Powers, and in particular the estranged United States Government. If we were to take any step of formally recognising the Committee at this juncture, this would give the very greatest offence in Washington. It would draw upon the Administration there the hostile criticism of all who are attempting to oust the President at next year's election. The whole course of the war depends upon our cordial relations with the American Government and President, and we owe it to our troops in the field not to make their task harder by taking any step which would lead to a serious decline in the present very remarkable co-operation. Even if Soviet Russia recognises de Gaulle on account of his recent flirtations with Communist elements, we should still be wise to measure our course by that of the United States. Indeed, in this case it would be still more important not to leave them isolated and give the appearance of working with Russia against them. . . .

I have repeatedly stated that it is in the major interests of Great Britain to have a strong France after the war, and I should not hesitate to sustain this view. I am afraid lest the anti-de Gaullism of the Washington Government may harden into a definite anti-France feeling. If however de Gaulle is gradually merged and submerged into the Committee, and the Committee comports itself in a reasonable and loyal manner, this dangerous tendency on the part of the United States may be deflected and assuaged.

There is no harm in the French Committee coming to feel that we should like to put them into better relations with the United States. It may still be possible to gain for France and the French Empire a recognised place in the councils of the Allies, if the healthy and helpful processes I have noted are allowed to take their course, and if we act with patience, and above all with a sense of proportion, in these vexatious matters.

★   ★   ★   ★   ★

Opinion in our Cabinet circle moved steadily towards some form of recognition, and I sent a further telegram to the President.

Former Naval Person to President Roosevelt   21 July 43

I am under considerable pressure from the Foreign Office, from my Cabinet colleagues, and also from the force of circumstances, to "recognise" the Committee of National Liberation in Algiers. What does recognition mean? One can recognise a man as an Emperor or as a grocer. Recognition is meaningless without a defining formula. Until de Gaulle went to North-West Africa and the new Committee was formed all our relations were with him and his Committee. I stated to Parliament on June 8 that "The formation of this Committee with its collective responsibility supersedes the situation created by the correspondence between General de Gaulle and myself in 1940. Our dealings, financial and otherwise, will henceforward be with the Committee as a whole". I was glad to do this because I would rather deal with the Committee collectively than with de Gaulle alone. I had in fact for many months been working to induce or compel de Gaulle to "Put himself in commission". This seemed to be largely achieved by the new arrangement. Macmillan tells us repeatedly that the Committee is acquiring a collective authority and that de Gaulle is by no means its master. He tells us further that if the Committee breaks down, as it may do if left utterly without support, de Gaulle will become once again the sole personality in control of everything except the powers exercised by Giraud under the armed force of the United States in North-West Africa and Dakar. He strongly recommends a measure of recognition. He reports that Eisenhower and Murphy both agree with this. . . .

I am therefore reaching the point where it may be necessary for me to take this step so far as Great Britain and the Anglo-French interests set out above are concerned. If I do, Russia will certainly recognise [them], and I fear lest this might be embarrassing to you.

I do hope therefore that you will let me know (a) whether you could subscribe to our formula or something like it, or (b) whether you would mind if His Majesty's Government took that step separately themselves. There is no doubt whatever in my mind that the former would be far the better. There are a lot of good men on the Committee—Catroux, Massigli, Monnet, Georges, and of course Giraud, who arrived here yesterday. He will certainly raise all this and bring it to a head.

But it was clear that the Americans were not prepared to recognise the Algiers Committee as now constituted. Giraud was now in the United States negotiating for the supply of arms and equipment for the French army in North Africa. His presence there did not smooth the temper of the de Gaullists.

On July 22 I received a long and important telegram from the President setting forth the considered view of his Government on French affairs.

President Roosevelt to Prime Minister   22 July 43

Various sources continue, though with less pressure, to ask recognition of the existing French Committee of National Liberation. Some people want to recognise it as the organisation acting for French interests in all French territory, including France. Other people want to recognise it as acting for French interests only in former French Empire. Most, not all, are willing to accept the Committee's authority, subject to the military requirements of the British and American forces.

We have been saying, first, that the military requirements are and will be paramount to all civil matters; second, that the French Committee of National Liberation has only begun to function, and should give further and more satisfactory evidence of the complete and genuine unity of the Committee. This unity must eliminate hitherto French political or factional controversies designed to promote either group antagonisms or individual aspirations, and demonstrate a real purpose to unify itself and, behind it, all Frenchmen in support of the co-operative efforts of the United Nations in the prosecution of the war against the Axis Powers, having in mind its single cause of the liberation of France and the success of the United Nations.

The French Committee was supposedly conceived on the principle of collective responsibility of individual Frenchmen for the prosecution of the war, and our relations with it should be kept on this basis, it being understood that as to matters of a military character the two Governments will deal directly with the French Commander-in-Chief of the French forces. French political questions must be left to solution by the people of France when they have been freed from the present domination of the enemy. . . .

This Government is most anxious to join with you and the other United Nations to move along the line of limited acceptance of the Committee, subject always to military requirements, but we should make it clear that the plain conditions of French unity must be properly met.

I do not think we should at any time use the word "recognition", because this would be distorted to imply that we recognise the Committee as the Government of France as soon as we land on French soil. Perhaps the word "acceptance" of the Committee's local civil authority in various colonies on a temporary basis comes nearer to expressing my thought. We must however retain the right and continue the present practice of dealing directly with local French officials in the colonies whenever military advantage to the Allied cause so dictates. Martinique is an illustrative example.

Giraud's visit here was very successful. We kept it on a purely military basis, and we are starting immediately to send additional equipment for his army with every North African convoy. . . .

Roosevelt ended by suggesting a joint formula based on "co-operation with" instead of "recognition of" the French Committee.

I replied to the President's telegram of July 22:

Former Naval Person to President Roosevelt   3 Aug 43

I thought first that your proposed formula was rather chilling and would not end the agitation there is for recognition in both our countries. Meanwhile events have moved in our favour. The

Committee have felt acutely being ignored while the whole Italian problem is open. De Gaulle, I feel, is now more enclosed in the general body of the Committee. The arrangements for command also seem more satisfactory to us than the previous deadlock.

2. I have therefore asked the Foreign Office to suggest a certain modification in your formula designed to bring our two views into harmony. . . . If we cannot agree we will talk it over.

The Quebec Conference already described was now imminent. Meanwhile we had reached a deadlock.

President Roosevelt to Prime Minister   4 Aug 43

I earnestly hope that nothing will be done in the matter of recognition of the Committee of National Liberation until we have an opportunity to talk it over together.

✷   ✷   ✷   ✷   ✷

It was only after stubborn talks that I was able to persuade the Americans to make a declaration in general terms supporting the political arrangements which had already taken shape in North Africa.

Prime Minister (Quebec) to Mr. Macmillan (Algiers)   25 Aug 43

After prolonged discussions of a laborious character we reached what I trust will be considered a series of satisfactory solutions about recognition. We thought it better that we should all express our thought in our own words rather than persevere in a joint declaration by the United States and United Kingdom.

2. In my opinion the President and Mr. Hull have gone a long way to meet our desires. You should tell my friends on the Committee that I am sure the right course for them is to welcome the American declaration in most cordial terms, and not to draw invidious distinctions between any of the forms in which recognition is accorded. On the contrary, the more pleasure they show at the American declaration the more value it will have for them. This is a moment when a friendly attitude towards the United States would be singularly helpful to the interests of France. If, on the other hand, newspaper or radio polemics and reproaches are indulged in the only effect will be to rouse new flames of resentment in the State Department.

✷   ✷   ✷   ✷   ✷

The announcement of the recognition of the French National Committee on the following day marked the end of a period, and though the French leaders were not brought into the armistice negotiations with Italy, nor into the Mediterranean Commission

162

which was subsequently set up to deal with Italian affairs, they were now on formal terms with the Allies as the representatives of France.

*   *   *   *   *

The struggle for power between de Gaulle and Giraud went on unabated as the weeks passed, and frequent clashes took place over both civil and military appointments. The fault did not lie always with de Gaulle, and there were unnecessary incidents over the liberation of Corsica, where Free French elements on the island had occupied Ajaccio on the night of September 9. Giraud ordered a French expedition to Corsica two days later, and the unfortunate disputes between his military commander and the de Gaullist leaders on the spot still further worsened relations. The liberation of the island, from the military point of view, was slowly but successfully accomplished.

Prime Minister to Mr. Harold Macmillan (Algiers)   3 Oct 43
If you think well, you should give the following message from me to Generals Giraud and de Gaulle:
"Many congratulations on the successful progress of your troops in Corsica. I look forward intensely to this famous island soon being liberated and restored to France."

The occupation of the island by French forces was completed on the following day.

*   *   *   *   *

Plans for summoning a provisional Consultative Assembly to broaden the basis of French administration advanced during the month of October. Giraud's position steadily weakened. The only support he possessed lay in certain Army circles who valued American goodwill, and in his rôle of co-President of the National Committee this was fast disappearing. De Gaulle showed himself incomparably the more powerful personality. On November 3 the Assembly met for the first time in Algiers. French political life was crystallising into an embryo Government for the future. On November 8, one year exactly after the North African landings, Giraud resigned from the National Committee, but remained Commander-in-Chief of the French forces. I was disturbed at the possible consequences of these events. It was essential for the future unity of France that some balance of power between these divergent elements should be reached.

I therefore telegraphed to the President:

Prime Minister to President Roosevelt   10 Nov 43

I am not at all content with the changes in the French National Committee which leave de Gaulle sole President. The body we recognised was of a totally different character, the essence being the co-Presidency of Giraud and de Gaulle. I suggest we maintain an attitude of complete reserve until we can discuss the position together.

I hoped on my way through to Cairo to the Teheran Conference to bring the rival Generals together myself at a review of the new French Army.

Prime Minister to Mr. Macmillan (Algiers)   2 Nov 43

In case I am able to find a few days in Africa between now and Christmas, I should like to see something of the new French Army. You might ascertain discreetly from both Generals de Gaulle and Giraud whether this would be agreeable to them. We might have an afternoon parade, spend the night somewhere, and see some exercises in the morning. In these circumstances I should like to be the guest of the French National Committee. It occurred to me they might take this as a compliment, which it is intended to be. I cannot fix dates at the present time, for many obvious reasons.

*   *   *   *   *

My intention was frustrated by the rough and tragic behaviour of the Free French Administration in Syria. The formal independence of Syria and the Lebanon had been proclaimed by the Free French at the end of 1941. We had recognised these republics, and Sir Edward Spears had been sent as British Minister in February 1942. Throughout the year however no progress was made. Changes of Ministry took place in both countries, but no elections were held. Anti-French antagonisms grew. Provisional Governments were appointed in March 1943. The elections in July and August resulted in an overwhelming Nationalist expression in both republics. The majorities demanded the complete revision of the mandatory constitution. The weakness of the Free French Administration led the local politicians, who had little faith in French promises of after-war independence, to strike. On October 7 the Lebanese Government proposed to abolish the French position in the republic. A month later the Free French Committee in Algiers challenged the right of the Lebanese to act in this one-sided manner. M. Helleu, General Catroux's deputy, returned from Algiers to give orders for the arrest of the Lebanese President and most of the Ministers, thereby provoking disturbances, which led to bloodshed, particularly at Beirut. The British Cabinet was disturbed by these events.

The action taken by the French stultified the agreements we had made with the French, and also with the Syrians and Lebanese. It was contrary to the Atlantic Charter and much else that we had declared. It seemed that the situation would be distorted throughout the whole of the Middle East and the Arab world, and also everywhere people would say, "What kind of a France is this which, while itself subjugated by the enemy, seeks to subjugate others?"

Accordingly I felt that the British and United States Governments should react strongly together. Already the character of the body we had recognised at Quebec had been totally altered by de Gaulle's complete assumption of power. But the outbreaks in the Levant were of a different character, and afforded full justification, with the support of world public opinion, for bringing the issue with de Gaulle to a head. I thought that the kidnapped Lebanese President and Ministers should be set at liberty and permitted to resume their full function, and that the Lebanon Assembly should meet again as soon as conditions of law and order could be guaranteed. If de Gaulle refused to do this at once, we should withdraw our recognition from the French National Committee and stop the process of arming the French troops in North Africa.

I was forced to give instructions to General Wilson to be prepared if necessary to take over control of the Lebanon and to re-establish order with British troops. Happily this was not necessary. General Catroux had arrived from Algiers on November 16 to act as mediator, and on November 22 the French authorities released the politicians under arrest, and protracted negotiations began for the ultimate independence of Syria and the Lebanon.

These incidents left their mark upon our relations with the Free French Committee and with General de Gaulle. The result of our year of effort to bring about a united policy founded upon a true sense of comradeship between the United States, Britain, and the Free French leaders had been disappointing.

CHAPTER XI

THE BROKEN AXIS

Autumn 1943

Civil War in Italy – Need to Sustain the King and the Badoglio
Government – I Put the Case to the President – We Agree on Policy –
Mussolini Meets Hitler, September 14 – Hitler on the Duce – The
Republic of Salo – Fate of the Italian Forces in the Balkans and
Ægean – I Explain the Situation to Stalin – Marshal Badoglio Signs
the Long-Term Surrender Agreement at Malta – Declaration about
Italian Co-belligerency by the President, Stalin, and Me – Count
Sforza Comes on the Scene – Use of Italian Man-power and Shipping
– Italy Declares War on Germany, October 13 – A Fragile Situation.

MUSSOLINI'S bid for a Fascist revival plunged Italy
into the horrors of civil war. In the weeks following
the September armistice officers and men of the Italian
Army stationed in German-occupied Northern Italy and Patriots
from the towns and countryside began to form Partisan units and
to operate against the Germans and against their compatriots who
still adhered to the Duce. Contacts were made with the Allied
armies south of Rome and with the Badoglio Government. In
these months the network of Italian resistance to the German
occupation was created in a cruel atmosphere of civil strife,
assassinations, and executions. The insurgent movement in
Central and Northern Italy here as elsewhere in occupied Europe
convulsed all classes of the people.

Not the least of their achievements was the succour and support given to our prisoners of war trapped by the armistice in
camps in Northern Italy. Out of about eighty thousand of these
men, conspicuously clothed in battle dress, and in the main with
little knowledge of the language or geography of the country, at

least ten thousand, mostly helped by the local population with civilian clothes, were guided to safety, thanks to the risks taken by members of the Italian Resistance and the simple people of the countryside.

★　★　★　★　★

From the moment when the armistice was signed and when the Italian Fleet loyally and courageously joined the Allies I felt myself bound to work with the King of Italy and Marshal Badoglio, at least until Rome was occupied by the Allies and we could construct a really broad-based Italian Government for the prosecution of the war jointly with us. I was sure that King Victor Emmanuel and Badoglio would be able to do more for what had now become the common cause than any Italian Government formed from the exiles or opponents of the Fascist régime. The surrender of the Italian Fleet was solid proof of their authority. On the other hand, there were the usual arguments against having anything to do with those who had worked with or helped Mussolini, and immediately there grew up an endless series of intrigues among the six or seven Leftish parties in Rome to get rid of the King and Badoglio and take the power themselves. Considering the critical nature of the battle and the supreme importance of getting Italy to fight with a good heart on our side, I resisted these movements whenever they came to my notice. In this I was supported by Marshal Stalin, who followed the Russian maxim, "You may always walk with the Devil till you get to the end of the bridge."

★　★　★　★　★

After considering proposals from Macmillan at Algiers, and from General Eisenhower, I telegraphed to the President asking for his comments.

Prime Minister to President Roosevelt　　　　　　　　21 Sept 43
. . . I and my colleagues in the War Cabinet have come to the following conclusions:

It is vital to build up the authority of the King and the Brindisi Administration as a Government and have unity of command throughout Italy. . . . Despite Badoglio's broadcast to-night we still feel it is essential that the King should go to the microphone at Bari, tell the Italian people he is there, and proclaim that Badoglio is carrying on the legitimate Government of Italy under his authority. This is needed not only for the Italian people, but for the Italian representatives and garrisons abroad.

The King and Badoglio should be told that they must build up the broadest-based anti-Fascist coalition Government possible. Any healthy elements that can deliver some goods should be rallied in this crisis. These points should be made plain in the King's broadcast. It would be very useful if Count Sforza and the professors who claim to represent the six parties were willing to join in the common effort. It must however be clearly understood that none of these provisional arrangements, dictated by war needs, will stand in the way of the free choice by the Italian people of the form of democratic government which they prefer.

The question of giving the Badoglio Government an Allied status does not come into our immediate programme. Co-belligerency is good enough. On this footing we should work for the gradual conversion of Italy into an effective national force against Germany, but, as we have said, she must work her passage. Useful service against the enemy will be recognised by us in the adjustment and working of the armistice terms. In return we expect Badoglio to continue to work for the Allies on the basis of the armistice. Our principle will be payment by results. Badoglio should be free to declare war on Germany, and by so doing he would at once become, though not an ally, a co-belligerent.

Badoglio can be told that it is no part of our plan to install Allied military government everywhere. If he will co-operate we are ready to hand over territory to his Government as quickly as it is free from the enemy. This offer applies to the historic mainland of Italy, Sicily, and Sardinia. The dealings of the United Nations with the Italian Government in territories which they are allowed to administer will be carried out through a Control Commission.

It would make it much easier for us if the full instrument of surrender, even though somewhat superseded, could now be signed. It is true that many of the clauses could not be operated by the Brindisi Administration in their present situation. But as we go up the peninsula and turn over territory to the Italian Government these questions will become real. We do not want to put ourselves in the position of having to haggle over every requirement with the Government. The longer we leave it the more difficult it becomes to get the instrument signed, so I hope Eisenhower will get Badoglio's signature to it as soon as possible on the basis suggested in the Foreign Secretary's telegrams.

This programme should be put to the King and Badoglio at once. The first essential is that the King should make the public announcement suggested. This should not surely await final refinements of policy.

This crossed the following telegram from the President:

President Roosevelt to Prime Minister   21 Sept 43
I will send the following message to General Eisenhower immediately upon your concurrence:

"In view of the existing situation in Italy the earliest practicable action is important.

"1. You will withhold long-term armistice provisions pending further instructions.

"2. On the basis of military necessity, you are empowered to make recommendations from time to time to lighten the provisions of the military armistice in order to enable the Italians, within the limit of their capacities, to wage war against Germany.

"3. On condition that it declares war on Germany, the present Government of Italy should be permitted, subject to the provisions of paragraph 4 hereunder, to carry on as the Government of Italy, and as such should be treated as a co-belligerent in the war against Germany; such relationship to be based on the clear understanding that it is not in any way to prejudice the untrammelled right of the people of Italy to decide on the form of government they will eventually have, and that no final form of government of Italy will be decided upon until the Germans are evicted from Italian territory.

"4. The Allied Military Government and the appropriate functions contemplated for the Armistice Control Commission will be merged as promptly as practicable into an Allied Commission under the Allied Commander-in-Chief, which shall be empowered to furnish guidance and instructions from time to time to the Badoglio Government on military, political, and administrative matters.

"5. You will encourage in all practicable ways the vigorous use, under your direction, of the Italian armed forces against Germany."

Our two messages did not seem to me to conflict on any important point, except the question of withholding the long terms of surrender. On this I deferred to the President, and we agreed that his telegram should be sent to General Eisenhower as a directive from both of us.

★   ★   ★   ★   ★

On September 14 Mussolini met Hitler for the first time since his "liberation". During the succeeding days the two men debated how to extend the life of Italian Fascism in those parts of

Italy still occupied by the German troops. On the 15th the Duce announced that he had reassumed the leadership of Fascism and that a new Republican-Fascist Party, purged and uplifted from traitorous elements, would rebuild a faithful Government in the North. For a moment it seemed that the old system, now dressed up in a pseudo-revolutionary garb, might flare again into life. But the results disappointed the Germans. Goebbels's comment at this time is revealing.

The Duce has not drawn the moral conclusions from Italy's catastrophe which the Fuehrer had expected. He was naturally overjoyed to see the Fuehrer and to be fully at liberty again. But the Fuehrer expected that the first thing the Duce would do would be to wreak full vengeance on his betrayers. He gave no such indication, however, which showed his real limitations. He is not a revolutionary like the Fuehrer or Stalin. He is so bound to his own Italian people that he lacks the broad qualities of a world-wide revolutionary and insurrectionist.*

But there was to be no turning back. Mussolini's half-hearted "Hundred Days" began. At the end of September he set up his headquarters on the shores of Lake Garda. This pitiful shadow Government is known as the "Republic of Salo". Here the squalid tragedy was played out. The dictator and lawgiver of Italy for more than twenty years dwelt with his mistress in the hands of his German masters, ruled by their will, and cut off from the outside world by carefully chosen German guards and doctors.

The Italian surrender caught their armies in the Balkans completely unawares, and many troops were trapped in desperate positions between local guerrilla forces and the vengeful Germans. There were savage reprisals. The Italian garrison of Corfu, over seven thousand strong, was almost annihilated by their former allies. The Italian troops of the island of Cephalonia held out until September 22. Many of the survivors were shot, and the rest deported. Some of the garrisons of the Ægean islands managed to escape in small parties to Egypt. In Albania, on the Dalmatian coast, and inside Yugoslavia a number of detachments joined the Partisans. More often they were taken off to forced labour and their officers shot. In Montenegro the greater part of two Italian divisions were formed by Tito into the "Garibaldi Divisions", which suffered heavy losses by the end of the war. In the Balkans and Ægean the Italian armies lost nearly forty thousand men after

* The Goebbels Diaries, p. 378.

the announcement of the armistice on September 8, not including those who died in deportation camps.

* * * * *

I explained the situation and our policy to Stalin.

Prime Minister to Premier Stalin 21 Sept 43

Now that Mussolini has been set up by the Germans as the head of a so-called Republican-Fascist Government, it is essential to counter this move by doing all we can to strengthen the authority of the King and Badoglio, who signed the armistice with us, and have since faithfully carried it out to the best of their ability and surrendered the bulk of their Fleet. Besides, for military reasons we must mobilise and concentrate all the forces in Italy which are anxious to fight or at least obstruct the Germans. These are already active.

I propose therefore to advise the King to appeal on the wireless to the Italian people to rally round the Badoglio Government, and to announce his intention to build up a broad-based, anti-Fascist coalition Government, it being understood that nothing shall be done to prevent the Italian people from settling what form of democratic Government they will have after the war.

It should also be said that useful service by the Italian Government, Army, and people against the enemy will be recognised in the adjustment and working of the armistice; but that, while the Italian Government is free to declare war on Germany, this will not make Italy an ally, but only a co-belligerent.

I want at the same time to insist on the signing of the comprehensive armistice terms, which are still outstanding, even though some of those terms cannot be enforced at the present time. Against this Badoglio would be told that the Allied Governments intend to hand over the historic mainland of Italy, Sicily, and Sardinia to the administration of the Italian Government under the Allied Control Commission as they are freed from the enemy.

I am putting these proposals also to President Roosevelt, and I hope that I may count on your approval. As you will readily understand, the matter is vitally urgent for military reasons. For instance, the Italians have already driven the Germans out of Sardinia, and there are many islands and key points which they still hold and which we may get.

He replied as follows:

Premier Stalin to Premier Churchill 22 Sept 43

I received your message of September 21.

I agree with your proposal concerning the appeal by radio of the Italian King to the Italian people; but I consider it entirely necessary that in the appeal of the King it should be clearly stated that Italy, which capitulated to Great Britain, the United States, and the Soviet Union, will fight against Germany together with Great Britain, the United States, and the Soviet Union.

2. I also agree with your proposal about the necessity of signing comprehensive armistice terms. In regard to your reservation that certain of these terms cannot be put into force at the present moment, I understand this reservation only in the sense that these terms cannot be realised now on the territory which so far is held by the Germans. In any case, I should like to receive confirmation or the necessary explanation from you on that point.

I asked the President what he thought of this, and said that I considered that the long-term provisions of surrender might well be dealt with by the Armistice Commission which we were setting up in Italy. I later sent him the following:

Former Naval Person to President Roosevelt　　　　　24 Sept 43

Macmillan now tells me that he is confident that Badoglio's signature can be obtained to the whole set of terms within the next few days, and that the longer we leave it the more haggling there will be. It may be some time before the new Commission can give their views, and I should myself feel happier if we clinched the matter now. This might save us a good deal of trouble later on.

At Eisenhower's suggestion we have made the preamble less harsh. We also provided that the armistice of September 3 will remain operative.

Prime Minister to President Roosevelt　　　　　　　25 Sept 43

I have not answered Uncle Joe's telegram in favour of backing up the King of Italy, and also his remarks about the comprehensive terms, because I do not know what line you are taking with him. You will no doubt have received my telegram. Macmillan reports that there will be no difficulty in getting Badoglio to sign.

The President replied:

President Roosevelt to Prime Minister　　　　　　　25 Sept 43

I go along with your thought about the long set of terms if signature can be obtained quickly, and I am so advising Eisenhower.

★　　★　　★　　★　　★

Other political complications occurred.

Prime Minister to Mr. Macmillan (Algiers)　　　　　25 Sept 43

Astonishment was caused here at a broadcast from the Bari radio in the name of "the King of Italy and Albania and Emperor of Ethiopia".

I need scarcely say that any repetition of follies like that will bring our whole policy into discredit here. How would the King like to be sent back to his Empire in Ethiopia to be crowned?

. . . I presume we are going to see the King's speech before he lets it off, or if there is no time for this that you will anyhow vet it. The reference to the Soviet is of capital importance, as Stalin's support for our policy of using the Italian Government is invaluable.

On September 28 Marshal Badoglio left Brindisi in an Italian cruiser to sign the long-term surrender at Malta. He was received with ceremony on board the battleship *Nelson* by General Eisenhower and his Chief of Staff, General Bedell Smith, Lord Gort, and General Alexander. Badoglio hoped to be spared the clause on unconditional surrender, but the Allied commanders insisted that this was a formal meeting to sign documents presented by the Allied Governments which would admit of no discussion.

After the signatures had been appended Badoglio had a short discussion with General Eisenhower about declaring war on Germany, which the Italian Marshal wished to do. The day ended with a visit to the units of the Italian Fleet anchored in Malta harbour.

Prime Minister to President Roosevelt   28 Sept 43
We agree that the long-term surrender document should be kept secret for the present. I have no doubt U.J. will concur, but it would be well if you told him our views, speaking for both of us.

We think it would be a mistake to talk about making Rome an open city, as it may hamper our forward movement, and will anyway not bind the enemy.

★   ★   ★   ★   ★

The situation was at first bewildering for our troops on the spot. The Italians had been their enemies for more than three years. By joining the United Nations they had in the space of a few weeks acquired a new status, and some of them assumed a new attitude. Requisitioning was no longer possible. Accommodation was denied to British troops, and food refused to officers without Italian ration cards. British military currency was treated with suspicion. Senior officers who had held the rank of Military Governor now became mere liaison officers with the Italians, from whom they could request but no longer compel the facilities which they needed. Much of this was the growing pains of the new régime in Italy, and was presently rectified by high authority, but some Italian civilians were ready to take the fullest advantage of the changes which had occurred. The President and General Eisenhower felt that a public declaration was needed in order to explain "co-belligerent" status to the Italians, and indeed to the world. I welcomed this.

Prime Minister to President Roosevelt   30 Sept 43

I agree that we should make a joint announcement, but would it not be a good chance of getting U.J. in too? It is clear now that he does accept the Italians as co-belligerents. It is true that we may lose a few days in communicating with Moscow, but this delay seems relatively unimportant compared with the value of Russian participation.

If you agree, would you put it to Stalin in the form that we wish an announcement of the kind made; will he join with us in making it, or would he prefer us to go ahead without him? Of course, we should consider any drafting alterations he might wish to propose.

I myself would like to see several changes, and my immediately following telegram embodies these. If you see no objection to them, would you, if you agree to approach Stalin, put the text to him in this form?

The text of the declaration which I drafted read as follows:

"The Governments of Great Britain, the United States, and the Soviet Union acknowledge the position of the Royal Italian Government as stated by Marshal Badoglio, and accept the active co-operation of the Italian nation and armed forces as a co-belligerent in the war against Germany. The military events since September 8 and the brutal maltreatment by the Germans of the Italian population, culminating in the Italian declaration of war against Germany, have in fact made Italy a co-belligerent, and the American, British, and Soviet Governments will continue to work with the Italian Government on that basis. The three Governments acknowledge the Italian Government's pledge to submit to the will of the Italian people after the Germans have been driven from Italy, and it is understood that nothing can detract from the absolute and untrammelled right of the people of Italy by constitutional means to decide on the democratic form of government they will eventually have.

"The relationship of co-belligerency between the Government of Italy and the United Nations Governments cannot of itself affect the terms recently signed, which retain their full force and can only be adjusted by agreement between the Allied Governments in the light of the assistance which the Italian Government may be able to afford to the United Nations' cause."

This was approved by both the President and Stalin.

* * * * *

Count Sforza now entered the Italian scene. Before the Fascist revolution he had been Foreign Minister and Ambassador in Paris. During Mussolini's régime he had been an exile. He had become an outstanding figure among Italians in America. He had declared himself in favour of bringing Italy into the war on the side of the Allies, and had in a letter which he had recently written to a high State Department official expressed his willingness to work with Badoglio. As the situation sharpened he saw his opportunity to gain the chief power in Italy, and was convinced of his right to it. He commanded a good deal of American support, and some of the American-Italian vote. The President hoped it might be possible to bring him into the new system of government without upsetting the King and Badoglio, upon whom our military thought about the Italian campaign was based.

President Roosevelt to Prime Minister   30 Sept 43

Referring to your telegram in regard to Sforza playing with the team, his public speech was, to say the least, not complimentary to the King of Italy. I find however in a recording of his September 26 speech the following extracts, which indicate that he may be useful to our war effort:

"With the present leaders of Italy, if they behave well, if they wage war well, our duty is to go to war, all of us, and to oust the Germans out of Italy.

"I say so out of my only main desire to do a thing which helps victory. We may rally round any Government which enjoys the confidence of the Allies if this Government for the time being proves that it is able to wage a war and to oust the Germans out of Italy.

"If I had to proclaim a republic to-morrow I would say, 'No. First of all we must oust the Germans out of Italy. This is what the Italians want; but when Italy is free the Italians will decide.' "

Former Naval Person to President Roosevelt   1 Oct 43

Your telegram about Sforza. He seems to be saying all sorts of things, many very different to what he wrote in his letter. He really should make up his mind whether he is going to try to help the Royal Badoglio Government or try to discredit it. We ought to know where we are before we build him up. Would it not be a good thing for you to route him to Italy via the United Kingdom and let us give him further friendly treatment here? I don't see much use in having him go to Italy merely to undermine whatever small fighting head against Fascism and the Germans Eisenhower has been able to produce out of the Italians.

President Roosevelt to Prime Minister   2 Oct 43

Your telegram in regard to Sforza. I am informed that he, with his son, expects to arrive by airplane at Prestwick, October 3, en route to Marrakesh.

I hope you can effectively indoctrinate him during his stop in U.K.

I am this date sending the following to Eisenhower:

"Inform Badoglio that it is the view of this Government that Grandi's presence in Badoglio Government at this time would not be acceptable. Even though Grandi was perhaps the chief figure in deposition of Mussolini, he had been so closely associated with Fascism that to place him now in Brindisi Government would cause much adverse comment and misinterpretation. First accretions to Badoglio Government should be men of unequivocal liberal and democratic principle. It is only through the use of such men in responsible positions that this Government can feel justified in supporting the present Italian Government.

"Germany has already taken active belligerent steps against Italy, and the chief strength of Badoglio's Government is its announced determination to rid Italy by force of the German invader. An immediate declaration of war by the Italian Government on Germany is necessary if Italy is to be given the status of a co-belligerent."

I had a long conversation with Count Sforza on his way through London, and believed we had reached an agreement whereby he was to work loyally with the King and Badoglio until we were in a position, following on the capture of Rome at the earliest moment, to form a broad-based non-Fascist Government. I thus steadily held to our charted course. We intended to sustain the monarchy until the liberation of Italy, to bring an Italian Government in on our side in the struggle against Germany, to strengthen that Government by adding representative and resisting elements, and to associate the Russians with our immediate arrangements about Italian affairs.

*   *   *   *   *

While these exchanges went on I pressed for the fullest use of Italian man-power and shipping.

Prime Minister to Foreign Secretary   26 Sept 43

Ought we not to make a convention with the Italian Government in respect of the use of Italian prisoners of war and man-power? We cannot allow these large numbers of Italians to be freed from discipline and control and left at large in Britain or North Africa. There is no means of repatriating them without straining our shipping. Meanwhile we need their man-power. We cannot have the operations in Africa cumbered up with heavy masses of prisoners to guard. Our 1st Armoured Division has been virtually destroyed by being used as mere guards to prisoners.

There is empty shipping coming back from Africa to the United Kingdom. We should ask that the process of shipping prisoners to the United Kingdom should continue pending some new arrangement with the Italian Government. I am quite prepared to consider a change of status for the Italians, provided they continue to do the same work as now and that the discipline is effective.

Prime Minister to First Lord, V.C.N.S., and Admiral   2 Oct 43
Cunningham

We cannot afford to allow units of the Italian Navy to remain idle, whether at Alexandria or elsewhere. My present idea is that we suggest to the Americans that the *Littorios* go to the United States to be fitted for the Pacific warfare and to be used there by them. I would also suggest to the President that after the war these ships be ceded to us, because, first, we have had the main part of the war against them; secondly, we have had heavy losses in capital units; and, thirdly, we have discontinued building capital units in order to further current short-term operations. I am sure such proposals will be received in a most friendly spirit. I should like your advice about all this, and also of course about the structure and value of these ships.

2. With regard to cruisers and other vessels, they must all be put to the highest use. We cannot have valuable ships lolling about in the Mediterranean harbours. The most valuable and modern should be brought into service and our older ones laid up. The older Italian battleships may also have a part to play in the inshore bombarding squadrons, which will certainly be required, though only for short periods, during 1944, both in the Channel and the Indian Ocean.

*   *   *   *   *

Former Naval Person to President Roosevelt   4 Oct 43

Now that U.J. has come in with us about the Italian declaration it appears of the highest importance to compel the King to declare war as soon as possible. This is, as I know, your view. I suggest that instructions be given to Eisenhower to put the fullest pressure upon him. There should be no nonsense about waiting until Rome is taken. It seems to us high time that the Italians began to work their passage. If you are in agreement, pray give the necessary orders without further reference to us.

The President acted promptly.

President Roosevelt to Prime Minister   8 Oct 43
On October 5 I informed Eisenhower as follows:
"The President and Prime Minister are in agreement that the King of Italy declare war on Germany as soon as possible. There appears to be no necessity for waiting until Rome is occupied. You will therefore put pressure on the Italian Government for an early declaration of war without waiting for further successes."

Accordingly on October 13 the Royal Italian Government declared war on Germany.

*   *   *   *   *

Prime Minister to Mr. Macmillan (Algiers)   23 Oct 43
. . . Our policy is to broaden the base and increase the Leftward emphasis of the Italian Government. We have very little information here about the personalities who are already available. You will be watching all this, and should keep me fully informed.
I am clear that any reconstruction of the Italian Government had better wait until we are in Rome. In Rome lie the title-deeds of Italy and of the Roman Catholic Church. Badoglio and the King reinstated there will have a far better chance of rallying such elements of Italian strength as exist. There is the place for us to make our deal and for them to issue their prospectus.
In the meanwhile be careful that nothing is done to make the King and Badoglio weaker than they are. On the contrary, we must hold them up and carry them forward with our armies. Meanwhile all search for strengthening elements can continue.

Prime Minister to President Roosevelt   6 Nov 43
All my information goes to show that we should lose a lot in breaking up the present King-Badoglio show. Victor Emmanuel is nothing to us, but his combination with Badoglio did in fact deliver the Italian Fleet, which is rendering very useful service now, and this same combination is at this moment holding the loyalties of a very large part of the unhappy Italian Army and people, and of course of Italian diplomatic representatives everywhere. Why should we add to the burden of our British and United States soldiers on the march to Rome by weakening any of those aids? We ought not, in my personal opinion,

to countenance a change in the Badoglio-King régime till we are seated in Rome and a really broad-based Italian Government can be formed.

I understand Eisenhower in the main inclines to this view. Surely we should stick to what we have got till we are sure we can get something better, and this can only be ascertained when we have Rome in our possession.

Such was the fragile state of Italian affairs when I set out for Cairo and Teheran.

CHAPTER XII

ISLAND PRIZES LOST

Rhodes, Key to the Eastern Mediterranean – The Command of the Ægean Within Our Reach – General Wilson's Plans Disrupted – Major Lord Jellicoe's Exploit – Seizure of Rhodes, Leros, and Cos Approved by the Combined Chiefs of Staff – The German Grip on Rhodes – Hitler's Concern About the Ægean – The Germans Retake Cos – Imperative Need to Attack Rhodes – My Telegram to the President of October 7 – His Disappointing Reply – My Further Appeals, October 8 – Washington Obdurate – The Question Nevertheless Left Open – News of Hitler's Decision to Fight South of Rome Fatal to the Project – Wilson's Report of October 10 – I Submit with Grief – My Telegram of October 10 to the President – The Fate of Our Leros Garrison – The Germans Attack, November 12 – A Bitter Blow – Pedantic Denials in the Minor Sphere.

THE surrender of Italy gave us the chance of gaining important prizes in the Ægean at very small cost and effort. The Italian garrisons obeyed the orders of the King and Marshal Badoglio, and would come over to our side if we could reach them before they were overawed and disarmed by the Germans in the islands. These were much inferior in numbers, but it is probable that for some time past they had been suspicious of their allies' fidelity and had their plans laid. Rhodes, Leros, and Cos were island fortresses which had long been for us strategic objectives of a high order in the secondary sphere. Rhodes was the key to the group, because it had good airfields from which our own air forces could operate in defence of any other islands we might occupy and complete our naval control of these waters. Moreover, the British air forces in Egypt and Cyrenaica could defend Egypt just as well, or even better, if some of them moved forward to Rhodes. It seemed to me a rebuff to fortune not to pick up these treasures. The command of the Ægean by air and by sea was within our reach. The effect of this might be decisive upon Turkey, at that time deeply moved by the Italian collapse. If we could use the Ægean and the Dardanelles the naval short-cut to Russia was established. There would be no more need for the perilous and costly Arctic convoys, or the long and weari-some supply line through the Persian Gulf.

I felt from the beginning we must be ready to take advantage of any Italian landslide or German round-up.

Prime Minister to General Ismay, for C.O.S. Committee　　　2 Aug 43

Here is a business of great consequence, to be thrust forward by every means. Should the Italian troops in Crete and Rhodes resist the Germans and a deadlock ensue, we must help the Italians at the earliest moment, engaging thereby also the support of the populations.

2. The Middle East should be informed to-day that all supplies to Turkey may be stopped for the emergency, and that they should prepare expeditionary forces, not necessarily in divisional formations, to profit by the chances that may offer.

3. This is no time for conventional establishments, but rather for using whatever fighting elements there are. Can anything be done to find at least a modicum of assault shipping without compromising the main operation against Italy? It does not follow that troops can only be landed from armoured landing-craft. Provided they are to be helped by friends on shore, a different situation arises. Surely caiques and ships' boats can be used between ship and shore?

I hope the Staffs will be able to stimulate action, which may gain immense prizes at little cost, though not at little risk.

Plans and preparations for the capture of Rhodes had been perfected in the Middle East Command over several months. In August the 8th Indian Division had been trained and rehearsed in the operation, and was made ready to sail on September 1. But on August 26, in pursuance of a minor decision at the Washington Conference in the previous May, the command received the orders of the Combined Chiefs of Staff to dispatch to India, for an operation against the coast of Burma, the shipping that could have taken the 8th Indian Division to Rhodes. The division itself was put under orders to join the Allied forces in the Central Mediterranean.

*　＊　＊　＊　＊　＊*

When the tremendous events of the Italian surrender occurred my mind turned to the Ægean islands, so long the object of strategic desire. On September 9 I had cabled from Washington to General Wilson, Commander-in-Chief of the Middle East, "This is the time to play high. Improvise and dare." General Wilson was eager for swift action, but his command had been stripped. He had only available the 234th Brigade, formerly part of the hard-tried garrison of Malta, and no shipping other than what could be scraped up from local resources. The trained assault shipping recently taken from him was not beyond superior control, but the American pressure to disperse our shipping from the Mediterranean, either westwards for the preparations for a still remote "Overlord" or to the Indian theatre, was very strong. Agreements made before the Italian collapse and appropriate to a totally different situation were rigorously invoked, at least at the secondary level. Thus Wilson's well-conceived plans for rapid action in the Dodecanese were harshly upset. Thereafter we were condemned to try our best with insufficient forces to occupy and hold islands of invaluable strategic and political importance.

The Special Air Service Regiment, which had been formed by Lieut.-Colonel David Stirling, D.S.O., and which had already carried out a series of daring and successful raids on enemy airfields, two and three hundred miles behind the enemy lines, had recently been extending its activities beyond the Desert. On the night of September 9 Major Lord Jellicoe, son of the Admiral, who was a leading figure in this daring unit, landed by parachute in Rhodes to try to procure the surrender of the island. If we could gain a port and an airfield the quick dispatch of a few British troops might encourage the Italians to dominate the Germans, whom they far outnumbered. But the Germans were stubborn and stiff, and the Italians yielded themselves to their authority. Jellicoe had to leave hurriedly. Thereafter the capture of Rhodes, held by 6,000 Germans, required forces greater than were available to the Middle East Command.

The occupation of Rhodes, Leros, and Cos was specifically approved by the Combined Chiefs of Staff in their final summary of the Quebec decisions on September 10.* Wilson had sent with great promptitude small parties by sea and air to a number of other islands, and on September 14 reported as follows:

* See Chapter VI, p. 102.

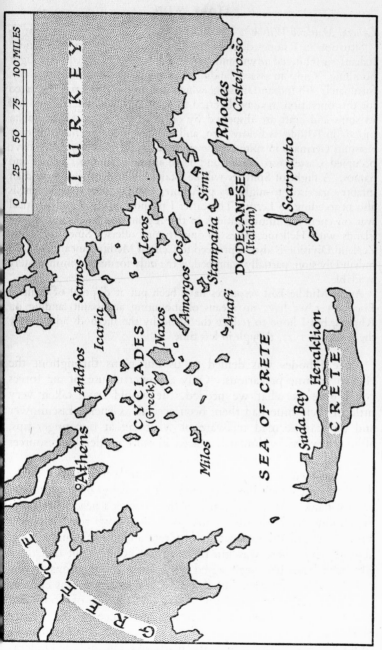

THE SOUTH ÆGEAN SEA

General Maitland Wilson to C.I.G.S.   14 Sept 43

Situation in Rhodes deteriorated too rapidly for us to take action. Italians surrendered town and harbour [to the Germans] after light bombing. Only an assault landing was thereafter practicable, but unfortunately 8th Indian Division, which had been trained and rehearsed for this operation, is now diverted to the Central Mediterranean and its ships and craft are dispersed by order of the Admiralty. Italian morale in Rhodes is below zero, and indicates little intention of ever resisting Germans in spite of asseverations to the contrary. We have occupied Castelrosso island, and have missions in Cos, Leros, and Samos. A flight of Spitfires will be established in Cos to-day, and an infantry garrison to-night by parachute. An infantry detachment is also proceeding to Leros. Thereafter I propose to carry out piratical war on enemy communications in the Ægean and to occupy Greek islands with Hellenic forces as opportunity offers. Since the New Zealand Division is also to proceed to Central Mediterranean, the 10th Indian Division, partially equipped, is the only formation immediately available.

As all Middle East resources have been put at disposal of General Eisenhower we have no means of mounting an assault landing on Rhodes, but I hope to reduce the island by the methods adopted by the Turks in 1522, though in less time.

Once Rhodes was denied to us our gains throughout the Ægean became precarious. Only a powerful use of air forces could give us what we needed. It would have taken very little of their time had there been accord. General Eisenhower and his staff seemed unaware of what lay at our finger-tips, although we had voluntarily placed all our considerable resources entirely in their hands.

We now know how deeply the Germans were alarmed at the deadly threat which they expected us to develop on their south-eastern flank. At a conference at the Fuehrer's headquarters on September 24 both the Army and the Navy representatives strongly urged the evacuation of Crete and other islands in the Ægean while there was still time. They pointed out that these advanced bases had been seized for offensive operations in the Eastern Mediterranean, but that now the situation was entirely changed. They stressed the need to avoid the loss of troops and material which would be of decisive importance for the defence of the continent. Hitler overruled them. He insisted that he could not order evacuation, particularly of Crete and the Dodecanese, because of the political repercussions which would follow. He said, "The attitude of our allies in the south-east and Turkey's attitude is determined solely by their confidence in our strength. Abandonment of the islands would create a most unfavourable impression." In this decision to fight for the Ægean islands he was justified by events. He gained large profits in a subsidiary theatre at small cost to the main strategic position. In the Balkans he was wrong. In the Ægean he was right.

*   *   *   *   *

We rightly made no attempt to occupy Crete, where the considerable German garrison rapidly disarmed the Italians and took charge, but for a time our affairs prospered in the outlying small islands. Troop movements by sea and air began on September 15. The Royal Navy lent a helping hand with destroyers and submarines. For the rest, small coasting vessels, sailing ships, launches, were all pressed into service, and by the end of the month Cos, Leros, and Samos were occupied by a battalion each, and detachments occupied a number of other islands. Italian garrisons, where encountered, were friendly enough, but their vaunted coast and anti-aircraft defences were found to be in poor shape, and the transport of our own heavier weapons and vehicles was hardly possible with the shipping at our disposal.

Apart from Rhodes, the island of Cos was strategically the most important. It alone had an airfield from which our fighter aircraft could operate. This was rapidly brought into use and twenty-four Bofors guns landed for its defence. Naturally it became the objective of the first enemy counter-attack, and from September 18 onwards the target of increasing air raids. Our reconnaissance reported an enemy convoy approaching, and at dawn on October 3 German parachutists descended on the central airfield and overwhelmed the solitary company defending it. The rest of the battalion, in the north of the island, where the enemy landed, was cut off. Clearly a single battalion, all we could spare, could do little on an island thirty miles long to ward off such a double blow. The island fell. The Navy had done their best, without success, to intercept the convoy on its way to Cos, but owing to an unlucky event all but three destroyers had been for the moment drawn away. As part of the main naval concentration at Malta, which was not especially urgent, two of our battleships had been ordered thither at this moment, and needed all the remainder to escort them.

$$\star \quad \star \quad \star \quad \star \quad \star$$

On September 22 Wilson reported his minimum and modest needs for an attack on Rhodes about October 20. Using the 10th Indian Division and part of an armoured brigade, he required only naval escorts and bombarding forces, three L.S.T.s, a few M.T. ships, a hospital ship, and enough transport aircraft to lift one parachute battalion. I was greatly troubled at our inability to support the Ægean operations, and on September 25 I cabled to General Eisenhower:

You will have seen the telegrams from the Commander-in-Chief Middle East about Rhodes. Rhodes is the key both to the Eastern Mediterranean and the Ægean. It will be a great disaster if the Germans are able to consolidate there. The requirements which the Middle East ask for are small. I should be most grateful if you would let me know how the matter stands. I have not yet raised it with Washington.*

The small aids needed seemed very little to ask from our American friends in order to gain the prize of Rhodes and thus retain Leros and retake Cos. The concessions which they had made to my unceasing pressure during the last three months had been rewarded by astounding success. Surely I was entitled to the very small aid which I required to supplement the British forces which were available for action in the Ægean, or had, with the approval of the Combined Chiefs of Staff, already been sent to dangerous positions. The landing-craft for a single division, a few days' assistance from the main Allied Air Force, and Rhodes would be ours. The Germans, who had now regripped the situation, had moved many of their planes to the Ægean to frustrate the very purpose which I had in mind.

$$\star \quad \star \quad \star \quad \star \quad \star$$

I laid the issue before the President in its full scope.

Former Naval Person to President Roosevelt   7 Oct 43
I am much concerned about the situation developing in the Eastern Mediterranean. On the collapse of Italy we pushed small detachments from Egypt into several of the Greek islands, especially Cos, which has a landing ground, and Leros, which is a fortified Italian naval base

* See also my telegram to him of the same date, Chapter VIII, p. 134.

with powerful permanent batteries. We ran this risk in the hope that the Italian garrisons which welcomed us would take part in the defence. This hope appears vain, and Cos has already fallen, except for some of our troops fighting in the mountains. Leros may well share its fate. Our enterprises against Rhodes have not yet succeeded.

2. I believe it will be found that the Italian and Balkan peninsulas are militarily and politically united, and that really it is one theatre with which we have to deal. It may indeed not be possible to conduct a successful Italian campaign ignoring what happens in the Ægean. The Germans evidently attach the utmost importance to this Eastern sphere, and have not hesitated to divert a large part of their straitened Air Force to maintain themselves there. They have to apprehend desertion by Hungary and Roumania and a violent schism in Bulgaria. At any moment Turkey may lean her weight against them. We can all see how adverse to the enemy are the conditions in Greece and Yugoslavia. When we remember what brilliant results have followed from the political reactions in Italy induced by our military efforts should we not be short-sighted to ignore the possibility of a similar and even greater landslide in some or all of the countries I have mentioned? If we were able to provoke such reactions and profit by them our joint task in Italy would be greatly lightened.

3. I have never wished to send an army into the Balkans, but only by agents, supplies, and Commandos to stimulate the intense guerrilla prevailing there. This may yield results measureless in their consequence at very small cost to main operations. What I ask for is the capture of Rhodes and the other islands of the Dodecanese, and the movement northward of our Middle Eastern air forces and their establishment in these islands and possibly on the Turkish shore, which last might well be obtained, thus forcing a diversion on the enemy far greater than that required of us. It would also offer the opportunity of engaging the enemy's waning air-power and wearing it down in a new region. This air-power is all one, and the more continually it can be fought the better.

4. Rhodes is the key to all this. I do not feel the present plan of taking it is good enough. It will require and is worth at least up to a first-class division, which can of course be replaced by static troops once the place is ours. Leros, which for the moment we hold so precariously, is an important naval fortress, and once we are ensconced in this area air and light naval forces would have a most fruitful part to play. The policy should certainly not be pursued unless done with vigour and celerity, requiring the best troops and adequate means. In this way the diversion from the main theatre would only be temporary, while the results may well be of profound and lasting importance.

5. I beg you to consider this and not let it be brushed aside and all these possibilities lost to us in the critical months that lie ahead. Even if landing-craft and assault ships on the scale of a division were withheld from the build-up of "Overlord" for a few weeks without altering the zero date it would be worth while. I feel we may easily throw away an immense but fleeting opportunity. If you think well, would you very kindly let General Marshall see this telegram before any decision is taken by the Combined Chiefs of Staff.

I was pained to receive from the President a telegram which he had sent to Eisenhower which practically amounted to the refusal of all help and left me, already committed, with his and the American Chiefs of Staff's approval, to face the impending blow. The negative forces which hitherto had been so narrowly overcome had indeed resumed their control.

President Roosevelt to Prime Minister   8 Oct 43

I do not want to force on Eisenhower diversions which limit the prospects for the early successful development of the Italian operations to a secure line north of Rome.

I am opposed to any diversion which will in Eisenhower's opinion jeopardise the security of his current situation in Italy, the build-up of which is exceedingly slow, considering the well-known characteristics of his opponent, who enjoys a marked superiority in ground troops and Panzer divisions.

It is my opinion that no diversion of forces or equipment should prejudice "Overlord" as planned.

The American Chiefs of Staff agree.

I am transmitting a copy of this message to Eisenhower.

I noticed in particular the sentence "It is my opinion that no diversion of forces or equipment should prejudice 'Overlord' as planned". To pretend that the delay of six weeks in the return of nine landing-craft for "Overlord" out of over five hundred involved, which would in any case have had six months in hand, would compromise the main operation of May 1944 was to reject all sense of proportion. I therefore resolved to make a further earnest appeal to the President. Looking back upon the far-reaching favourable results which had followed from my journey with General Marshall to Algiers in June, from which the whole of our good fortune had sprung, I thought I might ask for the same procedure, and I made all preparations to fly at once to Tunis.

Prime Minister to President Roosevelt   8 Oct 43

I earnestly pray that my views may receive some consideration from you at this critical juncture, remembering how fruitful our concerted action has been in the past and how important it is for the future.

2. I am sure that the omission to take Rhodes at this stage and the ignoring of the whole position in the Eastern Mediterranean would constitute a cardinal error in strategy. I am convinced also that if we were round the table together this operation could be fitted into our plan without detriment either to the advance in Italy, of which, as you know, I have always been an advocate, or to the build-up of "Overlord", which I am prepared faithfully to support.

3. May I remind you of my anxiety at Quebec when we were informed that the build-up in Italy could not exceed twelve divisions ashore by December 1? There are now by October 9 over fifteen divisions ashore, of which about twelve are in action. We know that the enemy is withdrawing to the north, fighting rearguard actions and carrying off booty; we cannot yet tell whether it is in October or November that we can occupy Rome, but it is certain that we shall not come in contact with the main German forces at the top of the leg of Italy till December, or even later, and we certainly have control of the rate of advance.

4. There is therefore plenty of time to provide a division for the conquest of Rhodes and restore it to the battle-front in Italy before we reach the German fortified line.

5. We must find some means of resolving these difficulties and making sure of what is the right thing to do. I am willing to proceed to Eisenhower's headquarters with the British Chiefs of Staff immediately, if you will send General Marshall, or your personal representative, to meet me there, and we can then submit the results of a searching discussion to you and your Chiefs of Staff. We can be there Sunday afternoon [Oct. 10].

And later in the day:

8 Oct 43

I should have added that my estimate of the effect on "Overlord" to which I referred is limited to a delay of about six weeks in sending home nine landing-craft which were to have started from the Mediterranean this month, nearly six months before they would actually be needed for "Overlord". There ought, I think, to be some elasticity and a reasonable latitude in the handling of our joint affairs.

2. The Quebec decision to send four landing ships with the craft they carry from the Eastern Mediterranean to the Bay of Bengal also for training purposes has turned out ill. This decision should have been reviewed in the light of the new circumstances opened by the

surrender of Italy. Unhappily this was not done, and in consequence the Middle East was stripped bare [of landing-craft] at a moment when great prizes could be cheaply secured.

It is important to note the date of these two telegrams, October 8. On that day our information fully justified the belief that the enemy were withdrawing under cover of rearguards towards or beyond Rome. It was not till a day or two afterwards that we began to apprehend that their intention was to stand and fight south of the city. Though that produced a new situation it did not in itself involve any immediate peril to our forces in Italy.

President Roosevelt to Prime Minister   9 Oct 43

I have received your [telegrams of October 8] and given careful personal consideration to the points you make. I have given careful thought to them, and so has the Staff. I am concerned about the possibility of our armies suffering a reverse by the action of an enemy with superior forces except by air, under a commander of proved audacity and resourcefulness. This applies especially to the absolute safety to the line we hope to gain in Italy.

With a full understanding of your difficulties in the Eastern Mediterranean, my thought in sending [my previous telegram] was that no diversion of force from Italy should be made that would jeopardise the security of the Allied armies in Italy, and that no action toward any minor objective should prejudice the success of "Overlord".

We have almost all the facts now at our disposal on which to judge the commitments probably involved in the Rhodes operation. As I see it, it is not merely the capture of Rhodes, but it must mean of necessity, and it must be apparent to the Germans, that we intend to go farther. Otherwise Rhodes will be under the guns of both Cos and Crete.

I was in accord with obtaining whatever hold we could in the Dodecanese without heavy commitments, but the present picture involves not only a well-organised, determined operation, but a necessary follow-through. This in turn involves the necessity of drawing for the means, largely shipping and air, not ground troops, from some other source, which inevitably must be Italy, "Overlord," or possibly Mountbatten's amphibious operation. The problem then is, are we to enter into a Balkan campaign, starting with the southern tip, or is there more to be gained, and with security, by pushing rapidly to the agreed upon position north of Rome? It appears to me that a greater Allied threat against the Balkans is implied in this than by a necessarily precarious amphibious operation against Rhodes, with a lack evident to the enemy of the necessary means for the follow-through. Strategically, if we get the Ægean islands, I ask myself where do we go from there? and, *vice versa*, where would the Germans go if for some time they retained possession of the islands?

As to the meeting you propose for Sunday [10th] in Africa, this would be in effect another meeting of the Combined Chiefs of Staff, necessarily involving only a partial representation and in which I cannot participate. Frankly, I am not in sympathy with this procedure under the circumstances. It seems to me the issue under discussion can best be adjusted by us through our C.O.S. set-up in better perspective than by the method you propose. We have most of the facts, and will soon have the results of the conference scheduled for to-morrow in Tunis.

*   *   *   *   *

Mr. Roosevelt's reply quenched my last hopes. All I could now do was to ask that the President's original negative message should not prevent a free discussion of the issue at the conference of Commanders-in-Chief. This was accorded for what it was worth.

Prime Minister to General Wilson   9 Oct 43

You should press most strongly at the conference for further support for "Accolade" [Rhodes]. I do not believe the forces at present assigned to it are sufficient, and if you are left to take a setback it would be bad. It is clear that the key to the strategic situation in the next month in the Mediterranean is expressed in the two words "Storm Rhodes". Do not therefore undertake this on the cheap. Demand what is necessary, and consult with Alexander. I am doing all I can.

Prime Minister to President Roosevelt   9 Oct 43

Thank you very much for your kindness in giving so much of your time and thought to the views which I ventured to set before you. At your wish, and as you cannot send General Marshall, I have cancelled my journey, which I told Harry on the telephone I would never undertake without your blessing.

2. I agree with the end of your telegram of to-day, namely, that we should await the result of the conference scheduled for to-day in Tunis, which can then be considered and adjusted by us through the Combined C.O.S. Committee.

3. I am afraid however that your telegram of October 8 to me, a copy of which was sent to Eisenhower, will be taken as an order from you and as closing the subject finally. This I should find it very hard to accept. I hope therefore that you will make it clear that the conference is free to examine the whole question in all its bearings, and should report their conclusions to you and me through Combined Chiefs of Staff. I ask that the conference shall give full, free, patient,

191

and unprejudiced consideration to the whole question after they have heard the Middle East point of view put forward by its representatives.

4. At the present time General Wilson is preparing to attack Rhodes on the 23rd, with forces from his own command, or which have been assigned to him by General Eisenhower. He thinks these forces are sufficient, but I am doubtful whether they are not cut too fine.

The question, to my mind, therefore is whether he should have this modest reinforcement or whether the operation should be cancelled.

5. Cancellation will involve loss of Leros, even if they can hold out so long, and the complete abandonment by us of any foothold in the Ægean, which will become a frozen area, with most unfortunate political and psychological reactions in that part of the world instead of great advantages.

6. I fully agree with all you say about the paramount importance of the build-up in Italy, and I have given every proof of my zeal in this matter by stripping the British Middle Eastern Command of everything which can facilitate General Eisenhower's operations, in which we also have so great a stake.

To this the President replied:

President Roosevelt to Prime Minister   9 Oct 43

The following message has been sent to Eisenhower:

"The Prime Minister in a message to the President expresses the fear that the repetition to you of the President's message of October 8 to the Prime Minister would be taken as an order from the President and as closing the subject finally. The Prime Minister desires that it be made clear to you that the conference scheduled for to-day in Tunis is free to examine the whole question in all its bearings and should report their (your and General Wilson's) conclusions to the President and the Prime Minister through the Combined Chiefs of Staff. The Prime Minister asks that the conference shall give full, free, patient, and unprejudiced consideration to the whole question after having heard the Middle East point of view put forward by its representatives.

"The President directs that the foregoing desire expressed by the Prime Minister be accepted for your guidance."

At the critical moment of the conference information was received that Hitler had decided to reinforce his army in Italy and fight a main battle south of Rome. This tipped the scales against the small reinforcement required for the attack on Rhodes. Wilson reported:

General Wilson to Prime Minister   10 Oct 43

I received your message before conference at Tunis yesterday. I

192

also had a talk with Cunningham and Alexander. I agree that our Rhodes plan as it stood was on such a scale as to incur risk of failure. It might have been worked at the moment of the armistice, but unfortunately some days earlier our shipping resources had been removed and the fleeting opportunity found us powerless to act.

2. Since then conditions have changed to the extent that an assault of a single brigade group followed up by one other brigade four days later would risk having both flights defeated in detail if bad weather intervened. If the forces which at yesterday's conference we all agreed are now necessary were to be made available this would be at the expense of "Overlord" in landing-craft and of Alexander's offensive in ships, landing-craft, and aircraft. The conditions in Italy also having changed materially, according to latest information received yesterday, I could but agree that Alexander's operations ought to have the whole of the available resources.

3. This morning John Cunningham, Linnell, and I reviewed the situation in the Ægean on the assumption that Rhodes would not take place till a later date. We came to the conclusion that the holding of Leros and Samos is not impossible, although their maintenance is going to be difficult, and will depend on continued Turkish co-operation. I am going to talk to Eden about this when he arrives on Tuesday. In any case, the problem of evacuation of the garrison would be one of extreme difficulty, and we hope it may never arise. Our tenancy in the Ægean has hitherto caused the enemy to divert considerable forces in attempts to turn us out.

I replied at once:

Prime Minister to General Wilson   10 Oct 43

Cling on if you possibly can. It will be a splendid achievement. Talk it over with Eden and see what help you can get from the Turk.* If after everything has been done you are forced to quit I will support you, but victory is the prize.

Although I could understand how, in the altered situation, the opinion of the generals engaged in our Italian campaign had been affected, I remained—and remain—in my heart unconvinced that the capture of Rhodes could not have been fitted in. Nevertheless with one of the sharpest pangs I suffered in the war I submitted. If one has to submit it is wasteful not to do so with the best grace possible. When so many grave issues were pending I could not risk any jar in my personal relations with the President. I therefore took advantage of the news from Italy to accept what

---

* Mr. Eden was on his way to the Foreign Secretaries' Conference at Moscow.

I thought, and think, to have been an improvident decision, and sent him the following telegram, which, although the first paragraph is also recorded elsewhere, I now give in full:

Former Naval Person to President Roosevelt   10 Oct 43
I have now read General Eisenhower's report of the meeting. The German intention to reinforce immediately the south of Italy and to fight a battle before Rome is what General Eisenhower rightly calls "a drastic change within the last forty-eight hours". I agree that we must now look forward to very heavy fighting before Rome is reached instead of merely pushing back rearguards. I therefore agree with the conclusions of the conference that we cannot count on any comparative lull in which Rhodes might be taken, and that we must concentrate all important forces available on the battle, leaving the question of Rhodes, etc., to be reconsidered, as General Eisenhower suggests, after the winter line north of Rome has been successfully occupied.

2. I have now to face the situation in the Ægean. Even if we had decided to attack Rhodes on the 23rd, Leros might well have fallen before that date. I have asked Eden to examine with General Wilson and Admiral Cunningham whether with resources still belonging to the Middle East anything can be done to regain Cos, on the basis that Turkey lets us use the landing grounds close by. If nothing can be worked out on these lines, and unless we have luck to-night or to-morrow night in destroying one of the assaulting convoys, the fate of Leros is sealed.

3. I propose therefore to tell General Wilson that he is free, if he judges the position hopeless, to order the garrison to evacuate by night, taking with them all Italian officers and as many other Italians as possible and destroying the guns and defences. The Italians cannot be relied upon to fight, and we have only 1,200 men, quite insufficient to man even a small portion of the necessary batteries, let alone the perimeter. Internment in Turkey is not strict, and may not last long; or they may get out along the Turkish coast.

4. I will not waste words in explaining how painful this decision is to me.

★   ★   ★   ★   ★

To Alexander I said:
                                                               10 Oct 43
You should now try to save what we can from the wreck. . . . If there is no hope and nothing can be done you should consider with General Wilson whether the garrison of Leros should not be evacuated to Turkey, or perhaps wangled along the coast after blowing up the batteries. Efforts must also be made to withdraw the Long-Range

Desert Groups who are on other islands. This would be much better than their being taken prisoners of war and the Italian officers executed.

And to General Wilson:

14 Oct 43

I am very pleased with the way in which you used such poor bits and pieces as were left you. *Nil desperandum.*

★　　★　　★　　★　　★

Nothing was gained by all the over-caution. The capture of Rome proved to be eight months distant. Twenty times the quantity of shipping that would have helped to take Rhodes in a fortnight were employed throughout the autumn and winter to move the Anglo-American heavy bomber bases from Africa to Italy. Rhodes remained a thorn in our side. Turkey, witnessing the extraordinary inertia of the Allies near her shores, became much less forthcoming, and denied us her airfields.

The American Staff had enforced their view; the price had now to be paid by the British. Although we strove to maintain our position in Leros the fate of our small force there was virtually sealed. Having voluntarily placed at Eisenhower's disposal all our best fighting forces, ground and air, far beyond anything agreed at Washington in May or Quebec in August, and having by strenuous exertions strengthened the Army in Italy beyond the plans and expectations of its Supreme Headquarters, we had now to see what could be done with what remained. Severe bombing attacks on Leros and Samos were clearly the prelude to a German enterprise. The Leros garrison was brought up to the strength of a brigade—three fine battalions of British infantry who had undergone the whole siege and famine of Malta★ and were still regaining their physical weight and strength.

On the day that Cos fell the Admiralty had ordered strong naval reinforcements, including five cruisers, to the Ægean from Malta. General Eisenhower also dispatched two groups of long-range fighters to the Middle East as a temporary measure. There they soon made their presence felt. On October 7 an enemy convoy carrying reinforcements to Cos was destroyed by naval and air action. Some days later the Navy sank two more transports. However, on the 11th the long-range fighters were withdrawn. Thereafter the Navy once more faced conditions similar

★ 4th Bn. the Buffs, 2nd Bn. Royal Irish Fusiliers, 1st Bn. King's Own.

to those which had existed in the battle for Crete two years before. The enemy had air mastery, and it was only by night that our ships could operate without crippling loss.

★   ★   ★   ★   ★

The withdrawal of the fighters sealed the fate of Leros. The enemy could continue to build up his forces without serious interference, using dispersed groups of small craft. We now know that the enemy faced a critical situation in shipping. The delay in attacking Leros was due mainly to his fears about an Allied attack in the Adriatic. On October 27 we heard that 4,000 German Alpine troops and many landing-craft had reached the Piræus, apparently destined for Leros, and early in November reports of landing-craft movements portended an attack. Concealed from our destroyers at night amid the islands, moving in small groups by day, under their strong fighter protection, the German troops and aircraft gathered. Our own naval and air forces were unable to interfere with their stealthy approach.

The garrison was alert, but too few. The island of Leros is divided by two narrow necks of land into three hilly sectors, to each of which one of our battalions was allotted. Early on November 12 German troops came ashore at the extreme north-east of the island, and also in the bay south-east of Leros town. The attack on the town was at first repulsed, but that afternoon six hundred parachutists dropped on the neck between Alinda and Gurna Bays and cut the defence in two. Previous reports had stated that the island was unsuited for paratroop landings and the descent was a surprise. Very strong efforts were made to recapture the neck. In the last stages the garrison of Samos, the 2nd Royal West Kents, had been dispatched to Leros, but all was over. They fell themselves a prey. With little air support of their own and heavily attacked by enemy aircraft, the battalions fought on till the evening of November 16, when, exhausted, they could fight no more. Thus this fine brigade of troops fell into enemy power. General Wilson reported:

General Wilson to Prime Minister   17 Nov 43
Leros has fallen, after a very gallant struggle against overwhelming air attack. It was a near thing between success and failure. Very little was needed to turn the scale in our favour and to bring off a triumph. Instead we have suffered a reverse of which the consequences are only

Parteni Bay

Blefuti Bay

MT VEDETTA

MT CLEDI

Alinda Bay

Leros

MT RACHI.

MT APPETICI

Gurna Bay

MT MERAVIGLIA

Pandeli Bay

Portolago Bay

0   1   2 MILES

LEROS

too easy to foresee. . . . When we took the risk in September it was with our eyes open, and all would have been well if we had been able to take Rhodes. Some day I trust it will be our turn to carry out an operation with the scales weighted in our favour from the start.

I had read the telegrams as they came in day after day during my voyage to Cairo with deep feelings.* I now replied:

Prime Minister to General Wilson   18 Nov 43
Thank you for your messages about Leros. I approve your conduct of the operations there. Like you, I feel this is a serious loss and reverse, and like you I feel I have been fighting with my hands tied behind my back. I hope to have better arrangements made as a result of our next Conference.

*   *   *   *   *

With the loss of Leros all our hopes in the Ægean were for the time being ended. We tried at once to evacuate the small garrisons in Samos and other islands, and to rescue survivors from Leros. Over a thousand British and Greek troops were brought off, as well as many friendly Italians and German prisoners, but our naval losses were again severe. Six destroyers and two submarines were sunk by aircraft or mine and four cruisers and four destroyers damaged. These trials were shared by the Greek Navy, which played a gallant part throughout.

*   *   *   *   *

To Anthony Eden, who had now returned home from Moscow, I telegraphed:

Prime Minister (at sea) to Foreign Secretary   21 Nov 43
Leros is a bitter blow to me. Should it be raised in Parliament, I recommend the following line:
One may ask, should such operation ever have been undertaken without the assurance of air superiority? Have we not failed to learn the lessons of Crete, etc.? Have we not restored the Stukas to a fleeting moment of their old triumphs? The answer is that these are very proper questions to ask, but it would not be advisable to answer them in detail. All that can be said at the moment is that there is none of these arguments which was not foreseen before the occupation of these islands was attempted, and if they were disregarded it was because other reasons and other hopes were held to predominate over them.

* I was on my way to the Cairo-Teheran Conference, which is recounted later in this volume.

If we are never going to proceed on anything but certainties we must certainly face the prospect of a prolonged war.

No attempts should be made to minimise the poignancy of the loss of the Dodecanese, which we had a chance of getting so easily and at so little cost and which we have now lost after heavy expenditure. You should also stress the tremendous effort made by the Germans, their withdrawal of almost half their air forces from Italy, where they were already outmatched, and the assistance given to our troops thereby.

3. Don't forget that we probably drowned the best part of two thousand Germans on the way, which, together with those killed in action, is at any rate an offset to our three thousand prisoners. It may well be that the Germans have paid much more than life for life, including prisoners, in this struggle. None the less it is just to say that it is our first really grievous reverse since Tobruk, 1942. I hope however that there will be no need to make heavy weather over this at all.

★   ★   ★   ★   ★

I have recounted the painful episodes of Rhodes and Leros in all their details. They constitute, happily on a small scale, the most acute difference I ever had with General Eisenhower. For many months, in the face of endless resistances, I had cleared the way for his successful campaign in Italy. Instead of only gaining Sardinia, we had established a large group of armies on the Italian mainland. Corsica was a bonus in our hands. We had drawn an important part of the German reserves away from other theatres. The Italian people and Government had come over to our side. Italy had declared war on Germany. Their Fleet was added to our own. Mussolini was a fugitive. The liberation of Rome seemed not far distant. Nineteen German divisions, abandoned by their Italian comrades, lay scattered throughout the Balkans, in which we had not used a thousand officers and men. The date for "Overlord" had not been decisively affected.

I had been instrumental in finding from the British and Imperial forces in Egypt four first-class divisions over and above those which, according to General Whiteley's report, the North-West African Supreme Headquarters had deemed possible. Not only had we aided General Eisenhower's Anglo-American Staff upon their victorious career, but we had furnished them with sub-stantial unexpected resources, without which disaster might well have occurred. I was grieved that the small requests I had made for strategic purposes almost as high as those already achieved should have been so obdurately resisted and rejected. Of course, when you are winning a war almost everything that happens can be claimed to be right and wise. It would however have been easy, but for pedantic denials in the minor sphere, to have added the control of the Ægean, and very likely the accession of Turkey, to all the fruits of the Italian campaign.

CHAPTER XIII

HITLER'S "SECRET WEAPON"

General Ismay's Minute of April 15, 1943 – Mr. Sandys' Appointment – Reports on Peenemünde – Decision of the Defence Committee to Attack Peenemünde – Hitler's Sanguine Hopes – Warning of Rockets and Pilotless Aircraft – Difference of Opinion About Their Relative Importance – Successful Attack on Peenemünde, August 17 – Prolonged Delay Caused to the Germans Thereby – Far-reaching Consequences – Arrival of the Pilotless Aircraft – Report by Dr. R. V. Jones – The "Ski Sites" – My Telegram to President Roosevelt, October 25 – His Reply – Sir Stafford Cripps' Report – Our Timely Measures of Defence.

SEVERAL years before the war the Germans had begun the development of rockets and pilotless aircraft, and had built an experimental station to carry out this work on the Baltic coast at Peenemünde. This activity was of course a closely guarded secret. Nevertheless they were not able entirely to conceal what was going on, and already in the autumn of 1939 references to long-range weapons of various kinds began to appear in our Intelligence reports. During the early years of the war rumours on this subject and scraps of information, often contradictory, reached us from various quarters. In the spring of 1943 the position was reviewed by the Chiefs of Staff, as a result of which on April 15 General Ismay sent me the following minute:

Prime Minister

The Chiefs of Staff feel that you should be made aware of reports of German experiments with long-range rockets. The fact that five reports have been received since the end of 1942 indicates a foundation of fact even if details are inaccurate.

The Chiefs of Staff are of the opinion that no time should be lost in establishing the facts, and, if the evidence proves reliable, in devising counter-measures. They feel this is a case where investigation directed by one man who could call on such scientific and Intelligence advisers as might be appropriate would give the best and quickest results. They therefore suggest that you should appoint an individual who should be charged with the task forthwith. They suggest for your consideration the name of Mr. Duncan Sandys, who, they think, would be very suitable if he could be made available.

In addition, the Chiefs of Staff propose to warn the Minister of Home Security of the possibility of such an attack, and of what is proposed. It is not considered desirable to inform the public at this stage, when the evidence is so intangible.

The Chiefs of Staff ask for your approval to the proposals above.

Mr. Sandys had served in an anti-aircraft unit in Norway in the early days of the war. Later he had suffered crippling disablement to both his feet in a motor accident when commanding the first experimental rocket regiment. He had joined the Government in July 1941 as Financial Secretary at the War Office, and afterwards as Under-Secretary at the Ministry of Supply. In both these offices he had had considerable responsibility for the general direction of weapon development, and had consequently been brought into close contact with the Chiefs of Staff Committee. As he was my son-in-law I was naturally glad that the Chiefs of Staff should wish to give him this important work, though I had in no way suggested it.

A month later he presented his first report, which was circulated to the War Cabinet. The following extract gives the main points.

I have reviewed the evidence regarding German long-range rocket development. In order to supplement this, I asked that an air reconnaissance should be undertaken of the area around Peenemünde, on the Baltic coast of Germany, where, judging from the reports, it seemed probable that rocket development was proceeding. This flight has been made, and the photographs obtained have provided further important information.

It would appear that the Germans have for some time past been trying to develop a heavy rocket capable of bombarding an area from a very long range. This work has probably been proceeding side by side with the development of jet-propelled aircraft and airborne rocket torpedoes. Very little information is available about the progress of this development. However, such scanty evidence as exists suggests that it may be far advanced. London, in view of its size, is much the most likely target.

An intensive effort should be made to obtain further information on this subject from agents on the Continent, from prisoners of war, and by air reconnaissance.

The experimental establishments and factories which appear most likely to be connected with the development and production of this weapon in Germany and German-occupied territory, together with any suspicious works in the coastal region of North-West France, should be subjected to bombing attack. A preliminary list of suggested targets is being sent to the Air Staff.

On June 4 Air Marshal Evill, Vice-Chief of the Air Staff, issued instructions enabling Sandys to deal directly with the Intelligence branches concerned about obtaining further information from agents and prisoners of war, and requested him to make recommendations for air reconnaissance and to notify the Air Staff of the conclusions drawn therefrom. All possible methods of tracing the trajectory of such projectiles and of locating the firing-point were examined. Civil Defence and security measures were set on foot.

On June 11 Mr. Sandys sent a minute to the Air Staff asking that reconnaissance flights should be made at regular intervals over the Peenemünde area and that air photographs should be obtained of all territory in Northern France within 130 miles of London. He also recommended that the experimental station at Peenemünde should be bombed. In his next report he stressed the importance of making the attack without delay.

The latest air reconnaissance photographs provide evidence that the Germans are pressing on as quickly as possible with the development of the long-range rocket at the experimental establishment at Peenemünde, and that frequent firings are taking place. There are also signs that the light anti-aircraft defences at Peenemünde are being further strengthened.

In these circumstances it is desirable that the projected bombing attack upon this establishment should be proceeded with as soon as possible.

On June 28 Sandys reported that aerial photographs of Peenemünde showed large rockets alongside the firing-point. They might have a range of about 90 to 130 miles.

In spite of all efforts to prevent them, the Germans may, without being detected, succeed in emplacing a number of projectors in Northern France and in launching a rocket attack upon London. In that event it would be necessary to locate with the utmost speed the sites from which the rockets were being fired, in order that these might be put out of action by immediate bombing attack.

With the equipment already available at existing Radar stations it should be possible to observe the rockets during flight and to determine the points from which they have been fired, to within a circle of ten miles radius. This performance can be considerably improved by fitting certain ancillary apparatus. The construction of this ancillary apparatus has already been put in hand. The first equipment is now in process of being installed at Rye. The remainder will be completed within two to three months. Special instructions have been issued to the five most suitable stations (Swingate, Rye, Pevensey, Poling, and Ventnor), and the necessary training of operators has begun.

On June 29 the Defence Committee, having been kept fully informed since April, decided:

That the most searching and rigorous examination of the area in Northern France within a radius of 130 miles of London should be organised and maintained, no step being neglected to make this as efficient and thorough as possible.

That the attack on the experimental station at Peenemünde should take the form of the heaviest possible night attack by Bomber Command on the first occasion when conditions are suitable.

That as far as possible plans should be prepared for immediate air attack on rocket firing-points in Northern France as soon as these are located.

      ★   ★   ★   ★   ★

Hitler was meanwhile intent upon the plan. Accompanied by some of his principal adherents of Cabinet level, he inspected Peenemünde about the beginning of June 1943. We were at this time better informed about rocket missiles than about pilotless aircraft. Both methods were in full preparation on a large scale, and Peenemünde was the summit of all research and experiment. No decisive progress had been made by the Germans towards the atomic bomb. "Heavy water" gave little encouragement, but in pilotless aircraft and the rockets Hitler and his advisers saw a means of delivering a new and possibly decisive attack upon England and the rupturing of the Anglo-American plans for a major cross-Channel return to the Continent. The Fuehrer was comforted by all he learned at Peenemünde, and he hurled the utmost German effort into this new and perhaps last hope.

About June 10 he told his assembled military leaders that the Germans had only to hold out. By the end of 1943 London would be levelled to the ground and Britain forced to capitulate. October 20 was fixed as zero day for rocket attacks to begin. It is said that Hitler personally ordered the construction of 30,000 rockets for that day. This, if true, shows the absurd ideas on which he lived. The German Minister of Munitions, Dr. Speer, said that each V2* required about as many man-hours to make as six fighters. Hitler's demand was therefore for the equivalent of 180,000 fighters to be made in four months. This was ridiculous; but the production of both weapons was given first priority and 1,500 skilled workers were transferred from anti-aircraft and artillery production to the task.

On July 9 Mr. Sandys reported that in addition to their plans for a rocket attack on London there was also evidence that the Germans intended to use pilotless aircraft and very long-range guns. Two excavations of a suspicious character had been detected—at Watten, near St. Omer, and at Bruneval, near Fécamp. Special instructions were therefore issued to the selected Radar stations in South-East England to watch for rocket-firing. Plans were also made by the Home Office, not for any wholesale evacuation of London, but for the removal when the time came of a hundred thousand persons in priority classes, such as school-children and pregnant mothers, at the rate of ten thousand a day. Thirty thousand Morrison table shelters were moved into London, bringing the reserve in the Metropolis up to about fifty thousand.

On July 19 our reports stated:

Work of an unexplained nature, including railway sidings, turn-tables, buildings, and concrete erections, is proceeding in North-West France. At most of these places construction is going ahead at a considerable pace, particularly in the case of Watten, where great activity is developing. Some attempt is being made to camouflage this work, and in one case the arrival of anti-aircraft guns has been observed.

When all these facts and reports were brought before the Defence Committee many differences of opinion arose concerning them. Among the scientists and technical officers opinions varied deeply and sharply on the question whether the new form

---

* Our name for the rocket. Pilotless aircraft were called V1.

of attack on the Island would be by rocket bombs or by pilot-less aircraft. At first the rocket was favourite, but its backers weakened their case by what turned out to be vastly exaggerated estimates of the size and destructive power of the missile. Confronted with these, those responsible for home security faced the possibility not only of evacuating children, expectant mothers, and other selected persons from London, but even a wholesale evacuation of the capital itself.

The Minister for Home Security was profoundly disquieted by the reports he studied, and always presented the danger in its most serious aspect. It was certainly his special duty to make sure that the danger was not underrated. Lord Cherwell, on the other hand, did not believe that even if giant rockets could be made it would pay the Germans to make them. As he had maintained from the very beginning, he insisted that they would get far better results at much smaller cost by using pilotless aircraft. Even if they used rockets with warheads of ten or twenty tons, as had been forecast, but which he did not believe was possible, he did not think the destruction in Britain would approach the figures which were produced. Listening to the discussions, which were frequent over many months, between him and Mr. Herbert Morrison, it might have seemed at times that the two protagonists were divided as to whether the attack by self-propelled weapons would be annihilating or comparatively unimportant. Actually the issue, as is usual, was not in the realm of "Yes or No", but in that of "More or Less".

Lord Cherwell's minutes show very clearly that his views on the possible scale of attack were on the whole right and that the most alarmist estimates were wrong.

* * * * *

These discussions caused no delay or indecision in our actions. An attack on Peenemünde was difficult, but imperative, and on the night of August 17 Air Marshal Harris, Chief of Bomber Command, struck with 571 heavy bombers. The buildings were scattered along a narrow strip of coast and protected by a smoke-screen. They could neither be reached by radio-navigation beams from the United Kingdom nor sufficiently identified by the apparatus carried in our planes. It was therefore necessary to bomb by moonlight, although the German night fighters were close at hand and it was too far to send our own. The crews were ordered to bomb from 8,000 feet, much below their usual height, and were told by Air Marshal Harris that if the operation failed on the first night it would have to be repeated on the next night, and on all suitable nights thereafter, regardless of casualties and regardless of the fact that the enemy would obviously do everything possible to increase his defences after the first attack. At the same time everything was done to guide our airmen and deceive the foe. Pathfinders flew ahead to mark the route and the straggling installations, and a master bomber circled the target, assessing results and instructing our planes by radio-telephone. The route taken was almost the same as in previous raids on Berlin, and a small force of Mosquitoes was sent over the capital to mislead the enemy.

The weather was worse than expected and landmarks were difficult to find, but it cleared towards Rügen Island and many crews punctually started their time and distance runs. There was more cloud over the target and the smoke-screen was working, but, says Harris, "the very careful planning of the attack ensured a good concentration of bombs on all the aiming points." The enemy was at first deceived by the feint on Berlin, but not for long enough. Most of our force got away, but the German fighters caught them during their return, and in the bright moonlight forty of our bombers were shot down.

★　★　★　★　★

The results were of capital importance. Although the physical damage was much less than we supposed, the raid had a far-reaching influence on events. All the constructional drawings just completed for issue to the workshops were burned, and the start of large-scale manufacture was considerably delayed. The parent factory at Peenemünde was hit, and the fear of attacks on factories producing the rocket elsewhere led the Germans to concentrate manufacture in underground works in the Hartz Mountains. All these changes caused serious delays in perfecting and producing the weapon. They also decided to shift their experimental activities to an establishment in Poland beyond the range of our bombers. There our Polish agents kept vigilant watch, and in the middle of January 1944 the new weapon was tried. They soon discovered its range and line of fire, but of course the rockets came down many miles apart from each other. German patrols always raced to where they fell and collected the fragments, but one day a rocket fell on the bank of the river Bug and did not explode. The Poles got there first, rolled it into the river, waited till the Germans had given up the search, and then salvaged and dismantled it under cover of darkness. This dangerous task accomplished, a Polish engineer was picked up by a Royal Air Force Dakota on the night of July 25, 1944, and flown to England with many technical documents and more than 100 lb. of essential parts of the new weapon. The gallant man returned to Poland, and was later caught by the Gestapo and executed in Warsaw on August 13, 1944.

* * * * *

The attack on Peenemünde, for which such sacrifices were made, therefore played an important and definite part in the general progress of the war. But for this raid and the subsequent attacks on the launching points in France, Hitler's bombardment of London by rockets might well have started early in 1944. In fact it was delayed until September. By that time the prepared launching sites in Northern France had been overrun by General Montgomery's forces. In consequence the projectiles had to be fired from improvised positions in Holland, nearly twice as far from the target of London, and with much less accuracy. By the autumn German communications became so congested by battle needs that the transport of rockets to the firing-point could no longer secure high priority.

In his book *Crusade in Europe* General Eisenhower expressed his opinion that the development and employment of the "V" weapons were greatly delayed by the bombing of the experimental plants at Peenemünde and other places where they were being manufactured. He goes so far as to say:

It seemed likely that if the German had succeeded in perfecting and using these new weapons six months earlier than he did our invasion of Europe would have proved exceedingly difficult, perhaps impossible. I feel sure that if they had succeeded in using these weapons over a six-months period, and particularly if they had made the Portsmouth–Southampton area one of their principal targets, "Overlord" might have been written off.

This is an overstatement. The average error of both these

weapons was over ten miles. Even if the Germans had been able to maintain a rate of fire of 120 a day and if none whatever had been shot down the effect would have been the equivalent of only two or three one-ton bombs to a square mile per week. However, it shows that the military commanders considered it necessary to eliminate the menace of the "V" weapons, not only to protect civilian life and property, but equally to prevent interference with our offensive operations.

★　　★　　★　　★　　★

In the early autumn it became clear that the Germans were planning to attack us not only with rockets but also with pilotless aircraft. On September 13, 1943, Mr. Sandys reported:

There is evidence that the enemy is considering using pilotless aircraft as a means of delivering bombs on London. Unless the aircraft used are abnormally small or are capable of flying at an exceptional height or speed, it should be possible to deal with them by means of the fighter and anti-aircraft defences of this country. If these pilotless aircraft should be capable of flying at such heights and speeds as to render their interception impossible by air-defence methods they should for all practical purposes be regarded as projectiles.

The counter-measures should be the same as for the long-range rocket, namely, the destruction by bombing of the sources of manufacture and of the sites or airfields from which they are launched.

The state of our knowledge at that time was summed up in a report, dated September 25, by Dr. R. V. Jones, the head of the Air Ministry's Scientific Intelligence Branch:

Much information has been collected. Allowing for the inaccuracies which often occur in individual accounts, they form a coherent picture which despite the bewildering effect of propaganda has but one explanation: the Germans have been conducting an extensive research into long-range rockets at Peenemünde. Their experiments have naturally encountered difficulties, which may still be holding up production. Although Hitler would press the rockets into service at the earliest possible moment, that moment is probably still some months ahead.

It is probable that the German Air Force has also been developing a pilotless aircraft for long-range bombardment in competition with the rocket, and it is very possible that the aircraft will arrive first.

Meanwhile it was observed that in Northern France a large

number of groups of curiously shaped structures were being
erected. All were laid out after the same fashion, and most of
them appeared to be directed on London. Each included one or
more buildings shaped rather like a ski. We later discovered from
air photographs that there were structures similar to these in the
neighbourhood of Peenemünde, and one of the photographs
revealed a minute aircraft close to an inclined ramp. From this
it was deduced that the so-called "ski sites" in Northern France
were probably designed to store, fill, and launch small unmanned
aircraft or flying bombs.

* * * * *

It was not until late in the autumn that I burdened the President with our grave and prolonged preoccupations. The United
States Staffs were kept constantly informed on the technical
level, but at the end of October I cabled by our special personal
contact:

Former Naval Person to President Roosevelt   25 Oct 43
I ought to let you know that during the last six months evidence
has continued to accumulate from many sources that the Germans are
preparing an attack on England, particularly London, by means of
very long-range rockets which may conceivably weigh sixty tons and
carry an explosive charge of ten to twenty tons. For this reason we
raided Peenemünde, which was their main experimental station. We
also demolished Watten, near St. Omer, which was where a construction work was proceeding the purpose of which we could not define.
There are at least seven such points in the Pas de Calais and the
Cherbourg peninsula, and there may be a good many others which
we have not detected.

2. Scientific opinion is divided as to the practicability of making
rockets of this kind, but I am personally as yet unconvinced that they
cannot be made. We are in close touch with your people, who are
ahead of us in rocket impulsion, which they have studied to give aeroplanes a send-off, and all possible work is being done. The expert
committee which is following this business thinks it possible that a
heavy though premature and short-lived attack might be made in the
middle of November, and that the main attack would be attempted in
the New Year. It naturally pays the Germans to spread talk of new
weapons to encourage their troops, their satellites, and neutrals, and it
may well be that their bite will be found less bad than their bark.

3. Hitherto we have watched the unexplained constructions proceeding in the Pas de Calais area without (except at Watten) attacking

them, in the hope of learning more about them. But now we have decided to demolish those we know of, which should be easy, as overwhelming fighter protection can be given to bombers. Your airmen are of course in every way ready to help. This may not however end the menace, as the country is full of woods and quarries, and slanting tunnels can easily be constructed in hillsides.

4. The case of Watten is interesting. We damaged it so severely that the Germans, after a meeting two days later, decided to abandon it altogether. There were 6,000 French workers upon it as forced labour. When they panicked at the attack a body of uniformed young Frenchmen who are used by the Germans to supervise them fired upon their countrymen with such brutality that a German officer actually shot one of these young swine. A week later the Germans seem to have reversed their previous decision and resumed the work. Three thousand more workmen have been brought back. The rest have gone to some of those other suspected places, thus confirming our views. We have an excellent system of Intelligence in this part of Northern France, and it is from these sources as well as from photographs and examination of prisoners that this story has been built up.

5. I am sending you by air courier the latest report upon the subject, as I thought you would like to know about it.

He replied after an interval:

President Roosevelt to Prime Minister   9 Nov 43
We too have received many reports of the German rocket activity. The only information recently coming to me which might be of value to you is a statement that factories manufacturing the rocket bomb are situated in Kaniafried, Richshafen, Miztgennerth, Berlin, Kugellagerwerke, Schweinfurt, Wiener Neustadt, and at an isolated factory on the left side of the road going from Vienna to Baden, just south of Vienna. Production is said to have been delayed owing to the death in the bombing of the experimental station at Peenemünde of Lieut.-General Shemiergembeinski, who was in charge. This came from an informer via Turkey.

*   *   *   *   *

The evidence and conflicting views both among the scientists and my colleagues on the Defence Committee continued to be so evenly balanced and confusing that I asked Sir Stafford Cripps, the Minister of Aircraft Production, with his special knowledge and judicial mind, to review all the information about the German long-range weapons and present a conclusion. On November 17 he made his report.

It would seem that the order of probability from the purely experimental point of view is:

1. Large glider bombs.
2. Pilotless aircraft.
3. Small long-range rockets.
4. Large long-range rockets.

The R.A.F. raid on Peenemünde was undoubtedly of the greatest value, and has set back the developments, whatever they may be, for the long-range offensive weapon.

There is no doubt that the Germans are doing their utmost to perfect some long-range weapon, and the new unexplained structures in Northern France are certainly most suspicious, unless we can assign some other use to them. Under these circumstances I feel we should make all reasonable preparations to cope with the consequences if and when the attack materialises, though there is no evidence of its materialisation before the New Year at the earliest.

We should at the same time maintain photographic cover, and destroy the sites whenever we get the opportunity to do so.

This certainly left much in doubt. On December 14 Air Marshal Bottomley, the Deputy Chief of the Air Staff, reported:

The "Large Sites" in Northern France (including three which have been attacked) are suspected to be connected with long-range rocket attack. One of these sites is protected by as many as fifty-six heavy and seventy-six light anti-aircraft guns.

Evidence is accumulating that the "ski sites" are designed to launch pilotless aircraft. The existence of sixty-nine "ski sites" has been confirmed by photographic reconnaissance, and it is expected that the number will eventually total approximately a hundred. If present rates of construction are maintained the work on some twenty sites should be completed by early January 1944, and the remainder by February. The launching points on the sites in the Pas de Calais and Somme–Seine areas are oriented on London, and those on some of the sites in the Cherbourg area on Bristol.

On December 18 Lord Cherwell, who had been in close touch with Dr. Jones throughout, sent me a report giving his ideas about the date and intensity of the attack which might be expected from the flying bombs. In his view the bombardment would not begin before April, and not more than a hundred a day would be dispatched after the first day or two; of these about twenty-five would get within ten miles of the aiming point. As this would only correspond to fifty to a hundred fatal casualties a day he deprecated large-scale panic measures of evacuation. He still discounted the probability of the use of large rockets. Even if they could be made, which seemed impossible with any existing technique, they would cost twenty or thirty times as many man-hours to produce as the flying bombs, without, in his view, being more efficient.

During the early months of 1944 we developed our plans for meeting the flying bomb attack. It was decided that the defences should be laid out in three zones—a balloon barrage on the out-skirts of London, beyond that a gun belt, and beyond that again an area in which the fighter aircraft would operate. Steps were also taken to hasten the supply from America of the electronic predictors and radio proximity fuzes, which, when the bombard-ment eventually started, made it possible for the gunners to take a heavy toll of the flying bombs.

Meanwhile the British and American Air Forces continued to bomb the hundred or so "ski sites" in Northern France. This was so effective that at the end of April aerial reconnaissance indicated that the enemy was giving up work on them. But our satisfaction was short-lived, for it was discovered that he was building instead modified sites which were much less elaborate and more carefully camouflaged and therefore harder to find and to hit. Wherever found these new sites were bombed. Many were destroyed, but about forty escaped damage or detection. It was from these that the attack was ultimately launched in June.

* * * * *

Nearly fifteen months passed between the minute which the Chiefs of Staff sent me in April 1943 and the actual attack in June 1944. Not a day was wasted. No care was lacking. Preparations involving many months to perfect were set on foot on a large and costly scale in good time. When at length the blow fell upon us we were able, as the next volume will describe, to ward it off, albeit with heavy loss in life and much damage to property, but without any effective hindrance to our war-making capacity or to the operations in France. The whole story may stand as an example of the efficiency of our governing machine, and of the foresight and vigilance of all connected with it.

CHAPTER XIV

DEADLOCK ON THE THIRD FRONT

Hitler Resolves to Fight South of Rome – The German Winter Line – Alexander's Army Weakened – My Telegram to Alexander of October 24, and His Reply – General Eisenhower's Conference of Commanders – He Endorses Alexander's Review of the Battle Situation in Italy – The Withdrawal of Landing-craft Deprives Our Armies of Flexibility – Fall in the Rate of Build-up – Survey of the Changed Situation – My Telegrams to General Marshall and the President – General Marshall's Reply – I Appeal for the Retention of More Landing-craft in the Mediterranean – Eisenhower Authorised to Retain an Extra Sixty-eight until December 15 – My Telegram to Our Ambassador in Moscow, November 9 – I Tell General Brooke of Our Need for the Polish Corps – Undue Demands of the Allied Strategic Air Force – The Eighth Army Crosses the Sangro River – The United States Fifth Army Approaches the German Main Positions at Cassino – Air Fighting – Reduction of German Air Force in Italy – Diversionary Value of the Third Front – A Summary.

EARLY in October, on Kesselring's advice, Hitler changed his mind about his Italian strategy. Till then he had meant to withdraw his forces behind Rome and hold only Northern Italy. Now he ordered them to fight as far south as possible. The line selected, the so-called "Winterstellung", ran behind the river Sangro, on the Adriatic side, across the mountainous spine of Italy, to the mouth of the Garigliano on the west. The natural features of the country, its steep mountains and swift rivers, made this position, several miles in depth, immensely strong. After a year of almost continuous retreat in Africa, Sicily, and Italy the German troops were glad to turn about and fight.

Although the approach of winter would seriously impede our

actions, the main strategic decisions taken at Quebec were helped by the Germans committing themselves so deeply. The primacy accorded to our cross-Channel invasion made Italy henceforward a secondary theatre. That Hitler felt impelled to use so many troops to resist our advance favoured our major objective, but did not justify our making a failure of the Italian campaign.

The Fifth Army resumed their attacks on October 12, and after a ten days' struggle both its corps, the Xth British and VIth American, were well established across the river Volturno and ready to engage the enemy's next delaying position, a series of heights lying south of the river Garigliano. Another week of fighting was needed to eject the enemy from these, but in the first fortnight in November the Army came to grips with the forward defences of the "Winterstellung". On this front the Fifth Army, of six divisions, was faced by an equal number of Germans, who were fighting with their usual stubbornness. The first probing efforts at the German line met with little success. Our men had been fighting hard for two months, the weather was shocking, and the troops needed rest and re-grouping. Nevertheless the plans made at Quebec for a different situation were rigidly enforced and the Mediterranean was to be largely stripped of landing-craft.

Thus the position in Italy was changed greatly to our disadvantage. The Germans were strongly reinforced and ordered to resist instead of to withdraw. The Allies, on the contrary, were sending eight of their best divisions from Italy and the Mediterranean back to England for the cross-Channel attack in 1944. The four extra divisions I was gathering or had sent did not repair the loss. A deadlock supervened, and was not relieved during eight months of severe fighting, which will presently be recounted.

* * * * *

With these facts on my mind I telegraphed to General Alexander on October 24:

Naturally I am made anxious by the departure while your battle is on of our two fine divisions, 50th and 51st, in pursuance of Quebec decisions. I should like to have your feelings about the strength of your army for the tasks which lie immediately ahead. Has the Eighth Army yet pulled its tail up? You mentioned 24th as the date.

2. I am asking for a Combined Staffs Conference somewhere in

Africa about November 15. Anyhow, I shall be along your way about that time. I have much to tell you. Every good wish.

Alexander replied that the number of German divisions in Italy was naturally causing him some anxiety. Their effect would depend on how far the enemy could maintain strong forces south of Rome. Everything was being done to paralyse the German lines of communication by air action, and he was keen to build up our air forces in Italy. All this took time, labour, and material. The Eighth Army had wound up their tail and started their offensive, which was making satisfactory progress in its early stages. "I consider," he said, "that the situation requires very careful watching. I am glad to hear you are visiting us shortly, and will be very glad to see you."

*   *   *   *   *

On the same day General Eisenhower held a Commanders' Conference. He called upon Alexander to review the situation. Alexander's report was so serious that Eisenhower transmitted the entire text to the President and to me. He endorsed all that Alexander had said and described his statement as giving a clear and accurate picture.

PART I

1. (a) On September 9, the date of the launching of "Avalanche" and the announcement of the Italian armistice, the estimate of the general enemy situation was that two divisions were opposing the advance of the Eighth Army in Calabria; one division was in the heel of Italy; three divisions were in a position south of Rome and available to take action against the Allied landing in Salerno Bay; more than two divisions were in the neighbourhood of Rome and nine in the north of Italy. The Germans therefore had a total of some eighteen divisions at their disposal on the mainland. Of these it was considered that some would be engaged in Northern Italy to deal with the internal situation, which was expected to cause them considerable embarrassment.

(b) It was of course realised that our assaults near Salerno would prove hazardous in the face of German opposition, but it was thought that the Italian situation, coupled with the opportunity of landing light forces in the heel and our overwhelming air superiority, weighted the scales sufficiently in our favour, and the risks quite rightly were taken. Further, landing-craft were available in large numbers, and gave us liberty of manoeuvre and flexibility in both build-up and mainten-

SOUTHERN ITALY : OPERATIONS, SEPT.–DEC. 1943

ance by sea. They also afforded the possibility of further amphibious operations to assist the advance by land. This flexibility proved invaluable, and was utilised fully by the Eighth Army in its operations along the coast of Calabria and by the Seventh Army in reinforcing the Salerno area with one division from Sicily in the critical early days of the battle.

(c) Although at that time it was known that craft were to be withdrawn during the winter, the number to be withdrawn and the dates of withdrawal were not established. Our plans then envisaged an estimated build-up of 1,300 vehicles a day from all Mediterranean ports. Such a figure meant that a total of twenty Allied divisions, together with the tactical air forces, could factually have been put into Italy by the end of the year, provided that they could be equipped and their maintenance assured. At the same time, the estimates of craft available for the future allowed sufficient elasticity to assist maintenance and to provide for amphibious operations in conjunction with the land advance to Rome, should such steps be necessary.

PART II

2. (a) To-day the situation has changed greatly. In the south eleven Allied divisions oppose nine German, while farther north there are some fifteen more, a known total of twenty-four divisions, and perhaps as high as twenty-eight divisions. On the basis that there are no unforeseen causes of a still lower rate of build-up, the optimum number of formations at our disposal on the mainland will be: end of November, thirteen divisions; end of December, fourteen to fifteen divisions; end of January, sixteen to seventeen divisions. Our rate of build-up has fallen from the previous estimate of 1,300 vehicles a day to an estimated 2,000 a week, with a consequent delay in the calling forward of air forces and Army formations. The reduction in the build-up of ground forces has also been influenced by the decision to move the Strategic Air Force into the Foggia area as rapidly as possible rather than to wait for the capture of bases in the Rome area. The demands of the air forces should be met by the end of the year.

(b) The reduction in craft, already decreased by wear and tear, has been so serious as to preclude us from taking advantage, other than with minor forces, of the enemy's inherent weakness, which is the exposure of his two flanks to turning movements from the sea. The majority of such craft as are available are required for build-up and for coastwise maintenance on account of demolitions to road and rail facilities, and traffic in the ports, owing to the shortage of lighters and tugs and enemy sabotage to berthing facilities, which will take time to repair.

3. (a) An examination of the enemy position has shown that his

lines of communication enable him to build up in Italy, mainly in the north, to the order of sixty divisions, should they be available, and maintain them there in the winter months, despite our air superiority. The Germans clearly are trying to form a reserve by shortening their lines round the Fortress of Europe. Such a reserve could be employed in reinforcing further their armies in Italy.

(b) In comparison, the Allied position is less favourable. With the resources available no increase in rate of build-up can be made. A stabilised front south of Rome cannot be accepted, for the capital has a significance far greater than its strategic location, and sufficient depth must be gained before the Foggia airfields and the port of Naples can be regarded as secure. This being so, the seizure of a firm defensive base north of Rome becomes imperative. Moreover, we cannot afford to adopt a purely defensive rôle, for this would entail the surrender of the initiative to the Germans.

PART III

4. The obvious present German intention is to hold a line south of Rome, where the country favours defence and allows no scope to the deployment of our superiority in armour or artillery. Coming bad weather will limit the employment of our air forces, as indeed it has done already. Enemy troops may be tired, but they can be relieved by formations from the north. There are indications that this is being done now. We have neither the formations nor the shipping to enable us to do so. It would therefore appear that we are committed to a long and costly advance to Rome, a "slogging match", with our present slight superiority in formations on the battle-front offset by the enemy opportunity for relief; for without sufficient resources in craft no out-flanking amphibious operation of a size sufficient to speed up our rate of advance is possible. There is a danger that a successful conclusion of this "slogging match" might leave us north of Rome in such a state of exhaustion and weakness as not to be able to hold what we have gained, if the Germans bring down from the north fresh divisions for a counter-offensive. An enemy strike of this nature may not be fully neutralised by our air forces during the winter months; other-wise I should feel no concern. The German reinforcement of Italy appears greater than warranted by the internal situation or by purely defensive requirements. If the opportunity for an easy success occurs there is little doubt that it will be seized upon to counter the effects of a year of defeats on all fronts and to raise German morale prior to the campaigns of 1944. The effect in the Balkans and in France might be particularly to our disadvantage.

5. (a) In conclusion, the picture in September looked rosy, pro-vided the initial assault at Salerno was successful. The German divisions

in the north were about to become involved in difficult internal security problems. In the south the rate of build-up was believed to be such that, given no reinforcement by reserve German formations, we should have had twenty divisions opposed to probably his eighteen by the end of December, and our full air force requirements have been on the mainland. It was believed that sufficient craft would be available to turn his sea flanks and maintain forces over the beaches, as might be necessary.

(b) To sum up: To-day the situation is that eleven Allied divisions are fighting a frontal battle in country favouring the defence against an immediate strength of nine German divisions, which can be reinforced at any moment. Our build-up has dwindled to a maximum of sixteen to seventeen divisions by the end of January against a present enemy strength of a certain twenty-four divisions, and our resources are not available for amphibious operations of much more than local character. We may be delayed south of Rome sufficiently long to enable the Germans to clear up the situation in Northern Italy and then reinforce their southern front. In this case the initiative might well pass to them.

This was indeed a masterly document, which touched all the gravest issues of our strategy.

*　　*　　*　　*　　*

I had already raised some of these issues with General Marshall.

Prime Minister to General Marshall (Washington)　　　　24 Oct 43
I hope the President will show you my long telegram to him about our much-needed meeting in Africa. Naturally I feel in my marrow the withdrawal of our 50th and 51st Divisions, our best, from the very edge of the Battle of Rome in the interests of distant "Overlord". We are carrying out our contract, but I pray God it does not cost us dear.

And I now telegraphed the President.

Former Naval Person to President Roosevelt　　　　　　26 Oct 43
You will have seen by now Eisenhower's [report] setting forth the condition into which we are sinking in Italy. We must not let this great Italian battle degenerate into a deadlock. At all costs we must win Rome and the airfields to the north of it. The fact that the enemy have diverted such powerful forces to this theatre vindicates our strategy. No one can doubt that by knocking out Italy we have enormously helped the Russian advance in the only way in which it

could have been helped at this time. I feel that Eisenhower and Alexander must have what they need to win the battle in Italy, no matter what effect is produced on subsequent operations.

I am so grieved to worry you with these matters while you are still suffering from influenza.

General Marshall replied on October 27 that he believed Eisenhower had adequate troops to fight in Italy without taking undue risks. His immediate problem was landing-craft, which would be examined. It seemed to him that in estimating the Italian situation the tremendous advantage of our overwhelming superiority in aircraft was almost ignored. Bad weather could not blot out for certain or for a long period the inevitable result of massed attack on enemy communications.

★ ★ ★ ★ ★

I now appealed to the President about the landing-craft in the Mediterranean.

Prime Minister to President Roosevelt   4 Nov 43

It is with very great regret that I must bring to your notice the increasing anxiety of His Majesty's Government about the withdrawal of landing-craft from the Mediterranean at this critical juncture. We now have before us General Eisenhower's forecast that he will not be able to occupy the line necessary to protect the Rome airfields before the end of January, or even February, if the present programme of withdrawals of landing-craft is rigidly adhered to. He further explains the costly and prolonged frontal attacks that will be necessary in order to achieve this disappointing result. We feel entitled to ask our American Allies to attach weight to our earnest representations in view of the very great preponderance of British troops deployed against the enemy in Italy, with proportionate losses, and also in view of the clear opinions of the United States Commander-in-Chief, under whom we serve.

2. Accordingly, the War Cabinet have formally desired me to ask that consideration shall be given by the United States Chiefs of Staff to the requests put forward by the British Chiefs of Staff. We very much regret that the urgency of the matter does not permit us to wait another three weeks until the next Staff Conference can be convened, as this would entail the departure or immobilisation meanwhile of the landing-craft, with grave injury to the Italian campaign.

3. I may mention that by various intense efforts we have every hope that an additional seventy-five tank landing-craft can be produced in the United Kingdom by the date fixed for "Overlord".

I was relieved to receive his reply.

President Roosevelt to Prime Minister   6 Nov 43

The Combined Chiefs of Staff to-day authorised Eisenhower to retain until December 15 sixty-eight L.S.T.s now scheduled for an early departure for the United Kingdom.

It seems to me that this action ought to meet his essential requirements.

I told Alexander at once. He answered:

General Alexander to Prime Minister   9 Nov 43

The retention of L.S.T.s will do a great deal to help my plans, and am most grateful for them. December 15 will not however allow me to carry out the whole of my plan, and I have explained this in telegram to C.I.G.S.

Prime Minister to General Alexander   9 Nov 43

You should make alternative campaign plans on the basis that the L.S.T.s stay on till January 15. I am pretty certain this will be agreed to at our Conference.

I also sent the following to our Ambassador in Moscow:

Prime Minister to Sir A. Clark Kerr   9 Nov 43

... The exceptionally good weather on the Russian front has carried with it heavy rains in Italy, and the frontal attacks we have had to make with forces which, though not very much stronger than those of the enemy, have been continuously active, have necessarily yielded slow progress.

My wish has always been to sustain and press to the utmost the campaign in Italy and to attract to that front and hold upon it as many divisions as possible. I am glad to say that agreement has been reached by the Combined Staffs that no more landing-craft shall be withdrawn until December 15. This will enable greater power to be put into the whole of our Italian operations. By new intense exertions at home I hope to make up by additional building of landing-craft for the delay in sending home the others.

Half the German strength is in Northern Italy and Istria, separated from our front by some 300 miles. It is from that half that the withdrawals back to South Russia have been made. They have been rendered possible, not by any inactivity on our fighting front, but by a diminution of the risks to internal security due to the passive attitude of the Italians in Northern Italy. We are in no doubt of the correctness of the estimate of German strength given by General Ismay. When he spoke there were six Panzer divisions there, half of them fighting on our front. Deployed south of Rome there are now ten German divisions identified in action, against which we have twelve or thirteen of rather greater strength. This is not much of a preponderance for a continuous frontal attack in mountainous country.

To General Brooke I wrote:

Prime Minister to C.I.G.S. 16 Nov 43

It has now become urgent that Poles should enter the line. They have not done all these years, although an immense amount of preparation and material has been employed. Reinforcements also are urgently needed in Italy, and the Poles are scheduled to go next after the New Zealanders. This is not the time to make changes in their organisation. It is better to take the chance of two divisions becoming under strength. They would still be called the Polish Corps, and we must endeavour to find drafts from other quarters. . . .

Sooner than break up these organisations so laboriously formed in Persia, I would make an inroad on the Polish Armoured Division in Great Britain, which will not be engaged for some time to come. However, I believe that if Polish troops enter the line and are seen to be fighting the Germans it may be possible to obtain a further draft of Poles from Stalin, and I propose to try for this when we meet. The Soviet Government is inclined to be sceptical about this Polish Corps, and suspect that it is being held back and nursed so as to be employed against the Russians in defence of Polish rights. If however the Polish Corps enters the line against the Germans and begins to fight this view will be dissipated. Meanwhile I cannot approve any alteration in the existing unit.

* * * * *

I was increasingly disturbed by the great strain thrown on our limited shipping by the demands of the Allied Heavy Bomber Force, which was being built up on the Foggia airfields in order to attack industrial targets in Eastern Germany beyond the range of our home-based squadrons. It seemed to me that these demands were disproportionate and unrelated to the general situation at that time.

Prime Minister to General Ismay, for C.O.S. Committee 17 Nov 43

It is surely altogether wrong to build up the Strategic Air Force in Italy at the expense of the battle for Rome. The strategic bombing of Germany, however important, cannot take precedence over the battle, which must ever rank first in our thoughts. Major tactical needs must always have priority over strategic policy. I was not aware until recently that the build-up of the Army had been obstructed by the forward move of a mass of strategic air not connected with the battle. This is in fact a departure from all orthodox military doctrine, as well as seeming wrong from the point of view of common sense.

And a week later:

The monstrous block of air, in its eagerness to get ahead, has definitely hampered the operations of the Army.

* * * * *

The Eighth Army meanwhile had moved forward, and after a series of actions closed up to the river Sangro. Here four German divisions were installed. In order to retain the initiative it was General Alexander's intention that the Eighth Army should cross the river, break through the "Winterstellung" on this front, and then advance as far as the road Pescara–Avezzano, whence they would threaten Rome and endanger the communications of the enemy on the western coast. Bridgeheads were thrown across the river, but the main enemy defences lay on high ground beyond. Bad weather, with rain, mud, and swollen rivers, postponed the attack until November 28, but then the 78th, 8th Indian, and New Zealand Divisions, the last recently arrived, attacked and made good progress. After a week of heavy fighting they were established ten miles beyond the Sangro. By December 20 the Canadians had reached the outskirts of Ortone, but it was not until three days after Christmas, after very severe fighting, that the town was cleared of the enemy. This was the first big street-fighting battle, and from it many lessons were learned. But the enemy still held firm, and more reinforcements came to them from Northern Italy. Some more ground was gained during December by the Eighth Army, but no vital objectives were taken, and winter weather brought active operations to a close.

The U.S. Fifth Army, under General Clark, struggled on up the road towards Cassino, and attacked the foremost defences of the German main positions. The enemy were strongly posted on mountains overlooking the road on either side. The formidable Monte Cassino massif to the west was attacked by the Xth British and IInd U.S. Corps on December 2, and finally cleared a week later after a tough struggle. East of the road equally severe operations were carried out by the IInd and VIth U.S. Corps, the latter now including the 2nd Moroccan Division. It was not till the beginning of the New Year that the enemy were ejected and the Fifth Army fully aligned along the river Garigliano and its tributary, the Rapido, where it faced the heights of Cassino and the famous monastery.

In all these land operations the armies had been fully supported by our tactical air forces, while our Strategical Air Force had carried out a number of useful raids behind the enemy lines, notably on Turin, where an important ball-bearing plant was destroyed by American Fortresses. The German Air Force, on the other hand, put forth relatively little effort. By day fighter and fighter-bomber sorties were few. Half a dozen raids by their long-range heavy bombers on Naples had little effect, but a very damaging surprise attack on our crowded harbour of Bari on December 2 blew up an ammunition ship with a chance hit and caused the sinking of sixteen other ships and the loss of 30,000 tons of cargo.

The Germans hardly troubled to contest the mastery of the air that winter over Italy, and greatly reduced their air strength, as the following table shows:

GERMAN AIR FORCE STRENGTH

	July 1, 1943	Oct. 1, 1943	Jan. 1, 1944
Central Mediterranean	975	430	370

Our growing air offensive from England made the enemy withdraw all that could be spared from the Mediterranean and Russia. Every long-range bomber in Italy was taken away for "reprisals" against England, the "Little Blitz" of the following spring.

For reasons which have been explained I had called the Italian campaign the Third Front. It had attracted to itself twenty good German divisions. If the garrisons kept in the Balkans for fear of attack there are added, nearly forty divisions were retained facing the Allies in the Mediterranean. Our Second Front, North-West Europe, had not yet flared into battle, but its existence was real. About thirty enemy divisions was the least number ever opposite it, and this rose to sixty as the invasion loomed closer. Our strategic bombing from Britain forced the enemy to divert great numbers of men and masses of material to defend their homeland. These were not negligible contributions to the Russians on what they had every right to call the First Front.

*   *   *   *   *

I must end this chapter with a summary.

In this period in the war all the great strategic combinations of the Western Powers were restricted and distorted by the shortage of tank landing-craft for the transport, not so much of tanks, but of vehicles of all kinds. The letters "L.S.T." (Landing Ship, Tanks) are burnt in upon the minds of all those who dealt with military affairs in this period. We had invaded Italy in strong force. We had an army there which, if not supported, might be entirely cast away, giving Hitler the greatest triumph he had had since the fall of France. On the other hand, there could be no question of our not making the "Overlord" attack in 1944. The utmost I asked for was an easement, if necessary, of two months—*i.e.*, from some time in May 1944 to some time in July. This would meet the problem of the landing-craft. Instead of their having to return to England in the late autumn of 1943 before the winter gales, they could go in the early spring of 1944. If however the May date were insisted upon pedantically, and interpreted as May 1, the peril to the Allied Army in Italy seemed beyond remedy. If some of the landing-craft earmarked for "Overlord" were allowed to stay in the Mediterranean over the winter there would be no difficulty in making a success of the Italian campaign. There were masses of troops not in action in the Mediterranean: three or four French divisions, two or three American divisions, at least four (including the Poles) British or British-controlled divisions. The one thing that stood between these and effective operation in Italy was the L.S.T.s, and the main thing that stood between us and the L.S.T.s was the insistence upon an early date for their return to Britain.

The reader of the telegrams printed in this chapter must not be misled by a chance phrase here and there into thinking (*a*) that I wanted to abandon "Overlord", (*b*) that I wanted to deprive "Overlord" of vital forces, or (*c*) that I contemplated a campaign by armies operating in the Balkan peninsula. These are legends. Never had such a wish entered my mind. Give me the easement of six weeks or two months from May 1 in the date of "Overlord" and I could for several months use the landing-craft in the Mediterranean in order to bring really effective forces to bear in Italy, and thus not only take Rome, but draw off German divisions from either or both the Russian and Normandy fronts. All these matters had been discussed in Washington without regard to the limited character of the issues with which my argument was concerned.

As we shall see presently, in the end everything that I asked for was done. The landing-craft not only were made available for upkeep in the Mediterranean; they were even allowed a further latitude for the sake of the Anzio operation in January. This in no way prevented the successful launching of "Overlord" on June 6 with adequate forces. What happened however was that the long fight about trying to get these small easements and to prevent the scrapping of one vast front in order to conform to a rigid date upon the other led to prolonged, unsatisfactory operations in Italy.

CHAPTER XV

ARCTIC CONVOYS AGAIN

Suspension of the Convoys in March 1943 – Intense Struggle on the Eastern Front – The Soviet Summer Offensive – Battles of Kursk, Orel, and Kharkov – Retreat of the German Armies – Kiev Regained, November 6 – Molotov Asks for the Convoys to be Resumed – I Press the Admiralty to Comply – The "Tirpitz" Disabled – Hard Treatment of Our Personnel in North Russia – A List of Modest Requests – Mr. Eden Leaves for Moscow – Stalin's Answer to My Letter – I Report its Character to Mr. Eden and the President – I Refuse to Receive Stalin's Message from the Soviet Ambassador – The War Cabinet Endorses My Action – Mr. Eden's Account of His Discussion with Stalin and Molotov on October 21 – The Convoys are Resumed – The "Scharnhorst" Sunk by Admiral Fraser in the "Duke of York", December 25, 1943 – End of the "Tirpitz".

THE year 1942 had closed in Arctic waters with the spirited action by British destroyers escorting a convoy to North Russia. As recorded in a previous volume, this had led to a crisis in the German High Command and the dismissal of Admiral Raeder from control of naval affairs. Between January and March, in the remaining months of almost perpetual darkness, two more convoys, of forty-two ships and six ships sailing independently, set out on this hazardous voyage. Forty arrived. During the same period thirty-six ships were safely brought back from Russian ports and five were lost. The return of daylight made it easier for the enemy to attack the convoys. What was left of the German Fleet, including the *Tirpitz*, was now concentrated in Norwegian waters, and presented a formidable and continuing threat along a large part of the route. Furthermore, the Atlantic, as always, remained the decisive theatre in the war at sea, and in March 1943 the battle with the U-boats was moving to a violent crisis. The strain on our destroyers was more than we could bear. The March convoy had to be postponed, and in April the Admiralty proposed, and I agreed, that supplies to Russia by this route should be suspended till the autumn darkness.

★　★　★　★　★

This decision was taken with deep regret because of the tremendous battles on the Russian front which distinguished the campaign of 1943. After the spring thaw both sides gathered themselves for a momentous struggle. The Russians, both on land and in the air, had now the upper hand, and the Germans can have had few hopes of ultimate victory. Nevertheless they got their blow in first. The Russian salient at Kursk projected dangerously into the German front, and it was decided to pinch it out by simultaneous attacks from north and south. This was foreseen by the Russians, who had had full warning and were ready. In consequence, when the attack started on July 5 the Germans met an enemy strongly installed in well-prepared defences. The northern attack made some ground, but at the end of a fortnight it had been thrown back. In the south success at first was greater and the Germans bit fifteen miles into the Russian lines. Then major counter-attacks began, and by July 23 the Russian line was fully restored. The German offensive had completely failed. They gained no advantages to make up for their heavy losses, and the new "Tiger" tanks, on which they had counted for success, had been mauled by the Russian artillery.

The German Army had already been depleted by its previous campaigns in Russia and diluted by inclusion of its second-rate allies. A great part of its strength had been massed against Kursk at the expense of other sectors of the thousand-mile active front. Now, when the Russian blows began to fall, it was unable to parry them. While the Kursk battle was still raging and the German reserves had been deeply committed the first blow came on July 12 against the German salient around Orel. After intense artillery preparation the main Russian attack fell on the northern face of the salient, with subsidiary onslaughts in the east. Deep penetrations were soon made, and although the defenders fought stoutly their strong-points were in succession outflanked, surrounded, and reduced. Their counter-attacks were repulsed, and under the weight of superior numbers and material they were overborne. Orel fell on August 5, and by the 18th the whole salient to a depth of fifty miles had been cut out.

The second major Russian offensive opened on August 3, while the Orel attack was still at its height. This time it was the German salient around Kharkov that suffered. Kharkov was an important centre of communications, and barred the way to the Ukraine and the Donetz industrial basin. Its defences had been prepared with more than usual thoroughness. Again the major attacks fell on the northern face of the salient, one being directed due south against Kharkov itself, another thrusting south-westwards so as to threaten the whole German rear. Within forty-eight hours both of these had bitten deep, in places up to thirty miles, and Bielgorod had been taken. By August 11 Kharkov was threatened on three sides, a further attack from the east having been launched, while fifty miles to the north-west the Russians were advancing fast. On that day Hitler ordered that Kharkov was to be held at all costs. The German garrison stood to fight it out, and it was not till the 23rd that the whole town was in Russian hands.

These three immense battles of Kursk, Orel, and Kharkov, all within a space of two months, marked the ruin of the German army on the Eastern Front. Everywhere they had been outfought and overwhelmed. The Russian plan, vast though it was, never outran their resources. It was not only on land that the Russians proved their new superiority. In the air about 2,500 German aircraft were opposed by at least twice as many Russian planes, whose efficiency had been much improved. The German Air Force at this period of the war was at the peak of its strength, numbering about 6,000 aircraft in all. That less than half could be spared to support this crucial campaign is proof enough of the value to Russia of our operations in the Mediterranean and of the growing Allied bomber effort based on Britain. In fighter aircraft especially the Germans felt the pinch. Although inferior on the Eastern Front, yet in September they had to weaken it still more in order to defend themselves in the West, where by the winter nearly three-quarters of the total German fighter strength was deployed. The swift and overlapping Russian blows gave the Germans no opportunity to make the best use of their air re-sources. Air units were frequently moved from one battle area to another in order to meet a fresh crisis, and wherever they went, leaving a gap behind them, they found the Russian planes in overmastering strength.

In September the Germans were in retreat along the whole of their southern front, from opposite Moscow to the Black Sea. The Russians swung forward in full pursuit. At the northern hinge a Russian thrust from Viazma took Smolensk on September 25. No doubt the Germans hoped to stand on the Dnieper, the next great river line, but by early October the Russians were across it north of Kiev, and to the south at Pereyaslav and Kremenchug. Farther south again Dniepropetrovsk was taken on October 25. Only near the mouth of the river were the Germans still on the western bank of the Dnieper; all the rest had gone. The land approach to the Crimea, at Perekop, was captured by the Red Army, and the retreat of the strong German garrison in the Crimea was cut off. Kiev, outflanked on either side, fell on November 6, with many prisoners, and the Russians, driving forward, reached Korosten and Jitomir. But a strong armoured counter-attack on their flank drove them back, and the Germans recaptured the two towns. Here the front stabilised for the time being. In the north Gomel was taken at the end of November, and the upper reaches of the Dnieper crossed on each side of Mogilev.

By December, after a three months' pursuit, the German armies in Central and South Russia had been thrust back more than two hundred miles, and, failing to hold the Dnieper river line, lay open and vulnerable to a winter campaign in which, as they knew from bitter experience, their opponents excelled. Such was the grand Russian story of 1943.

*   *   *   *   *

It was natural that the Soviet Government should look reproachfully at the suspension of the convoys, for which their armies hungered. On the evening of September 21 M. Molotov sent for our Ambassador in Moscow and asked for the sailings to be resumed. He pointed out that the Italian Fleet had been eliminated and that the U-boats had abandoned the North Atlantic for the southern route. The Persian railway could not carry enough. For three months the Soviet Union had been undertaking a wide and most strenuous offensive, yet in 1943 they had

FINLAND
L. Ladoga
Gulf of Finland
Leningrad
ESTONIA
L. Peipus
L. Ilmen
LATVIA
Velikie Luki
Viazma
Moscow
Vitebsk
Smolensk
Mogilev
Bryansk
Minsk
Orel
Kursk
Voronezh
Gomel
POLAND (1939)
Pripet
Marshes
Korosten
Bielgorod
R. Don
Kiev
Kharkov
Jitomir
Pereyaslav
U K R A I N E
R. Donetz
Kremenchug
R. Dnieper
Dniepropetrovsk
Krivoi Rog
Taganrog
Rostov
R. Bug
Nikopol
Odessa
Perekop
Sea of Azov
Kerch
ROUMANIA
Sebastopol
B L A C K   S E A

Front July 1, 1943
Front Dec. 31, 1943
German attacks
Russian attacks
Russian pursuit
International frontiers

0   100   200 MILES

OPERATIONS IN RUSSIA, JULY–DEC. 1943

received less than a third of the previous year's supplies. The Soviet Government therefore "insisted" upon the urgent resumption of the convoys, and expected His Majesty's Government to take all necessary measures within the next few days.

Though there was much to be said in answer to all this, I raised the matter with the Admiralty and others on September 25.

Prime Minister to Foreign Secretary, Minister of Production,   25 Sept 43
Minister of War Transport, General Ismay, for C.O.S.
Committee, and Acting First Sea Lord

It is our duty if humanly possible to reopen these Arctic convoys, beginning in the latter part of November in accordance with the moon phase. We should try to run November, December, January, February, and March convoys, total five. Plans should be prepared by the Admiralty and the Ministry of War Transport. I understand that this is feasible.

Now that the Russians have asked for the reopening of these convoys we are entitled to make a very plain request to them for the better treatment of our personnel in North Russia.

The first reply from the Admiralty about the convoys was disappointing to me.

Prime Minister to Foreign Secretary, First Lord, General   27 Sept 43
Ismay, for C.O.S. Committee, and others concerned

CONVOYS TO NORTH RUSSIA

This is not satisfactory. Why cannot the November convoy be a full one? This also applies to the December 8 convoy. We must try to run at least five full convoys before "Overlord" operations start. I do not agree that the situation in the Atlantic or in the Mediterranean will be as strained as it was when we were running these convoys before. Naturally I am not going to make a solemn contract with Marshal Stalin, and we must safeguard ourselves against unforeseeable contingencies, but I consider that November, December, January, February, and March should each see a full-sized convoy dispatched.

I will have a Staff meeting on this subject at 10 p.m. on Tuesday night.

When we met on the night of the 29th to discuss the problem an agreeable new fact was before us. The *Tirpitz* had been disabled by the audacious and heroic attack of our midget submarines. Of six craft which took part two penetrated all the elaborate defences. Their commanding officers, Lieutenant

Cameron, R.N.R., and Lieutenant Place, R.N., rescued by the Germans, survived as prisoners of war, and received the Victoria Cross. Later air reconnaissance showed that the battleship was heavily damaged and would require refit in a dockyard before she could again be ready for action. The *Lützow* had already gone to the Baltic. Thus we had an easement, probably of some months, in the Arctic waters, and I was able to minute to the Foreign Secretary:

> The resumption of the convoys question is practically settled in a favourable sense. Before I send my telegram to Stalin about it let me see your list of grievances about the treatment of our people in North Russia, so that I can combine the two to the best advantage. I should like to do the telegram to-night.

Mr. Eden's complaints were serious, and I accordingly sent the following telegram to Stalin:

Prime Minister to Premier Stalin   1 Oct 43

I have received your request for the reopening of the convoys to North Russia. I and all my colleagues are most anxious to help you and the valiant armies you lead to the utmost of our ability. I do not therefore reply to the various controversial points made in M. Molotov's communication. Since June 22, 1941, we have always done our best in spite of our own heavy burdens to help you defend your country against the cruel invasion of the Hitlerite gang, and we have never ceased to acknowledge and proclaim the great advantages that have come to us from the splendid victories you have won and from the deadly blows you have dealt the German armies.

2. For the last four days I have been working with the Admiralty to make a plan for sending a new series of convoys to North Russia. This entails very great difficulties. First the Battle of the Atlantic has begun again. The U-boats have set about us with a new kind of acoustic torpedo, which has proved effective against the escorting vessels when hunting U-boats. Secondly, we are at very full stretch in the Mediterranean, building up an army in Italy of about 600,000 men by the end of November, and also trying to take full advantage of the Italian collapse in the Ægean islands and the Balkan peninsula. Thirdly, we have to provide for our share of the war against Japan, in which the United States are greatly interested, and whose people would be offended if we were lukewarm.

3. Notwithstanding the above it is a very great pleasure to me to tell you that we are planning to sail a series of four convoys to North Russia in November, December, January, and February, each

of which will consist of approximately thirty-five ships, British and American. Convoys may be sailed in two halves to meet operational requirements. The first convoy will leave the United Kingdom about November 12, arriving North Russia ten days later; subsequent convoys at about twenty-eight-day intervals. We intend to withdraw as many as possible of the merchant vessels now in North Russia towards the end of October, and the remainder with returning convoy escorts.

To avoid new charges of breach of faith from the Soviet, if our efforts to help them proved vain, I inserted a safeguarding paragraph:

4. However, I must put it on record that this is no contract or bargain, but rather a declaration of our solemn and earnest resolve. On this basis I have ordered the necessary measures to be taken for the sending of these four convoys of thirty-five ships.

I then proceeded with our list of grievances about the treatment of our men in North Russia.

5. The Foreign Office and the Admiralty however request me to put before you for your personal attention, hoping indeed that your own eye may look at it, the following representations about the difficulties we have experienced in North Russia.

6. If we are to resume the convoys we shall have to reinforce our establishments in North Russia, which have been reduced in numbers since last March. The present numbers of naval personnel are below what is necessary, even for our present requirements, owing to men having to be sent home without relief. Your civil authorities have refused us all visas for men to go to North Russia, even to relieve those who are seriously overdue for relief. M. Molotov has pressed His Majesty's Government to agree that the number of British Service personnel in North Russia should not exceed that of the Soviet Service personnel and trade delegation in this country. We have been unable to accept this proposal, since their work is quite dissimilar and the number of men needed for war operations cannot be determined in such an unpractical way. Secondly, as we have already informed the Soviet Government, we must ask to be the judges of the personnel required to carry out operations for which we are responsible. Mr. Eden has already given his assurance that the greatest care will be taken to limit the numbers strictly to the minimum.

7. I must therefore ask you to agree to the immediate grant of visas for the additional personnel now required, and for your assurance that you will not in future withhold visas when we find it necessary to ask

for them in connection with the assistance that we are giving you in North Russia. I emphasise that of about one hundred and seventy naval personnel at present in the North over one hundred and fifty should have been relieved some months ago, but Soviet visas have been withheld. The state of health of these men, who are unaccustomed to the climatic and other conditions, makes it very necessary to relieve them without further delay.

8. We should also wish to send the small medical unit for Archangel to which your authorities agreed, but for which the necessary visas have not been granted. Please remember that we may have heavy casualties.

9. I must also ask your help in remedying the conditions under which our Service personnel and seamen at present find themselves in North Russia. These men are of course engaged in operations against the enemy in our joint interest, and chiefly to bring Allied supplies to your country. They are, I am sure you will admit, in a wholly different position from ordinary individuals proceeding to Russian territory. Yet they are subjected by your authorities to the following restrictions, which seem to me inappropriate for men sent by an ally to carry out operations of the greatest interest to the Soviet Union:

(a) No one may land from one of H.M. ships or from a British merchant ship except by a Soviet boat in the presence of a Soviet official and after examination of documents on each occasion.

(b) No one from a British warship is allowed to proceed alongside a British merchantman without the Soviet authorities being informed beforehand. This even applies to the British admiral in charge.

(c) British officers and men are required to obtain special passes before they can go from ship to shore or between two British shore stations. These passes are often much delayed, with consequent dislocation of the work in hand.

(d) No stores, luggage, or mail for this operational force may be landed except in the presence of a Soviet official, and numerous formalities are required for the shipment of all stores and mail.

(e) Private Service mail is subjected to censorship, although for an operational force of this kind censorship should, in our view, be left in the hands of British Service authorities.

10. The imposition of these restrictions makes an impression upon officers and men alike which is bad for Anglo-Soviet relations, and would be deeply injurious if Parliament got to hear of it. The cumulative effect of these formalities has been most hampering to the efficient performance of the men's duties, and on more than one

occasion to urgent and important operations. No such restrictions are placed upon Soviet personnel here.

11. We have already proposed to M. Molotov that as regards offences against Soviet law committed by personnel of the Services and of the ships of the convoys, they should be handed over to the British Service authorities to be dealt with. There have been a few such cases no doubt, partially at any rate due to the rigorous conditions of service in the North.

12. I trust indeed, M. Stalin, that you will find it possible to have these difficulties smoothed out in a friendly spirit, so that we may help each other, and the common cause, to the utmost of our strength.

These were modest requests considering the efforts we were now to make. No answer was received for nearly a fortnight.

* * * * *

As will be described in the next chapter, the Conference of the Foreign Secretaries of the three major Allies, long planned, was now due in Moscow. On October 9 Mr. Eden set out by air. His journey lay through Cairo and Teheran, where he had much business, and he did not reach Moscow till the morning of October 18. During his absence I took charge of the Foreign Office.

Prime Minister to Sir A. Clark Kerr (Moscow)   12 Oct 43

I have received no answer to my long telegram of October 1 about resuming the Arctic convoys. If the cycle of convoys is to begin on November 12 we must have an early reply to our requests about personnel. Several dozens of wireless operators and signals personnel, on whose work the safety of the convoys may well depend, are to leave the United Kingdom, together with about one hundred and fifty reliefs for men due to return home, by destroyers sailing from the United Kingdom on October 21. Pray therefore press for an answer. Meanwhile we are preparing the convoys in the hope that the Soviets still desire them.

Next day I received Stalin's answer.

Premier Stalin to Prime Minister   13 Oct 43

I received your message of October 1 informing me of the intention to send four convoys to the Soviet Union by the Northern route in November, December, January, and February. However, this communication loses its value by your statement that this intention to send Northern convoys to the U.S.S.R. is neither an obligation nor an agreement, but only a statement, which, as it may be understood, is one the British side can at any moment renounce regardless of any influence it may have on the Soviet armies at the front. I must say that I cannot agree with such a posing of the question. Supplies from the British Government to the U.S.S.R., armaments and other military goods, cannot be considered otherwise than as an obligation, which, by special agreement between our countries, the British Government undertook in respect of the U.S.S.R., which bears on its shoulders, already for the third year, the enormous burden of struggle with the common enemy of the Allies—Hitlerite Germany.

It is also impossible to disregard the fact that the Northern route is the shortest way which permits delivery of armaments supplied by the Allies within the shortest period to the Soviet-German front, and the realisation of the plan of supplies to the U.S.S.R. in appropriate volume is impossible without an adequate use of this way. As I already wrote to you earlier, and as experience has shown, delivery of armaments and military supplies to the U.S.S.R. through Persian ports cannot compensate in any way for those supplies which were not delivered by the Northern route.

By the way, for some reason or other there was a very considerable decrease in the delivery of military goods sent by the Northern route this year in comparison with those received last year; and this makes it impossible to fulfil the established [Soviet] plan of military supplies [to the armies] and is in contradiction to the corresponding Anglo-Soviet protocol for military supplies. Therefore, at the present time, when the forces of the Soviet Union are strained to the utmost to secure the needs of the front in the interests of success of the struggle against the main forces of our common enemy, it would be inadmissible to have the supplies of the Soviet armies depend on the arbitrary judgment of the British side. It is impossible to consider this posing of the question to be other than a refusal of the British Government to fulfil the obligations it undertook, and as a kind of threat addressed to the U.S.S.R.

2. Concerning your mention of controversial points allegedly contained in the statement of M. Molotov, I have to say that I do not find any foundation for such a remark. I consider the principle of reciprocity and equality proposed by the Soviet side for settlement of the visa question in respect of personnel of the military missions to be a correct and indeed a just one. The reference to the difference in the functions of the British and Soviet military missions, and that the numbers of the staff of the British military mission must be determined by the British Government only, I consider to be unconvincing. It has already been made clear in detail in the previous *aide-mémoires* of the People's Commissariat for Foreign Affairs on this question.

3. I do not see the necessity for increasing the number of British Service-men in the north of the U.S.S.R., since the great majority of British Service-men who are already there are not adequately employed, and for many months have been doomed to idleness, as has already been pointed out several times by the Soviet side. For example, it can be mentioned that, owing to its non-necessity, the question of the liquidation of the British port base in Archangel was put forward several times, and only now the British side have agreed to liquidate it. There are also regrettable facts of the inadmissible behaviour of individual British Service-men who attempted, in several cases, to recruit, by bribery, certain Soviet citizens for Intelligence purposes. Such instances, offensive to Soviet citizens, naturally gave rise to incidents which led to undesirable complications.

4. Concerning your mention of formalities and certain restrictions existing in Northern ports, it is necessary to have in view that such formalities and restrictions are unavoidable in zones near and at the front, if one does not forget the war situation which exists in the U.S.S.R. I may add that this applies equally to the British and other foreigners as well as to Soviet citizens. Nevertheless the Soviet authorities granted many privileges in this respect to the British Service-men and seamen, about which the British Embassy was informed as long ago as last March. Thus your mention of many formalities and restrictions is based on inaccurate information.

Concerning the question of censorship and prosecution of British Service-men, I have no objection if the censorship of private mail for British personnel in Northern ports would be made by the British authorities themselves, on condition of reciprocity, and also if cases of small violations committed by British Service-men which did not involve court procedure would be given to the consideration of the appropriate military authorities.

★   ★   ★   ★   ★

Mr. Eden had now left Cairo for Teheran, on his way to Moscow, so I sent him the following:

Prime Minister to Foreign Secretary (Teheran)   15 Oct 43

This offensive reply has been received to our telegram about convoys. I send you the reply which I have drafted. As you will be on the spot, I leave it to you to handle as you see fit. I do not think we should give way about the naval reliefs and signalmen. It would be a great relief to be freed from the burden of these convoys and to bring our men home from North Russia. If this is what they really mean and want we ought to oblige them.

Here was my draft:

Prime Minister to Premier Stalin   15 Oct 43

It is impossible for His Majesty's Government to guarantee that the four convoys mentioned can be run irrespective of the military situation on the seas. Every effort and heavy loss and sacrifice would however be made to do so if the Soviet Government attaches importance to the receipt of their cargoes. I cannot undertake to do more than my best, and His Majesty's Government must remain the judge of whether any particular operation of war to be carried out by their forces is in fact practicable or not.

2. The running of these four convoys would be a very great burden to the Royal Navy, and involves the diversion of much-needed flotillas from the anti-U-boat war and from the escorting of troop and other important convoys. It also exposes the main units of the Fleet to serious risks. His Majesty's Government would be very glad to be relieved of the task of running the convoys if the Soviet Government do not attach importance to them.

3. In particular the refusal of the request of the British Government in respect of the reliefs and small increases in the few hundreds of British Service-men in the north of the U.S.S.R., and in particular the signals personnel, on which the safety of these convoys to some extent depends, raises an insuperable obstacle. His Majesty's Government would be very glad to withdraw the handfuls of Service personnel from North Russia, and will do so as soon as they are assured that it is not the desire of the Soviet Government to receive the convoys under the modest and reasonable conditions which the British Government consider necessary.

I commented to the President:

Former Naval Person to President Roosevelt   16 Oct 43

About Russian convoys. I have now received a telegram from U.J. which I think you will feel is not exactly all one might hope for from a gentleman for whose sake we are to make an inconvenient, extreme, and costly exertion. I have sent a suggested answer to Anthony for him to handle as he thinks best.

2. I think, or at least I hope, this message came from the machine rather than from Stalin, as it took twelve days to prepare. The Soviet machine is quite convinced it can get everything by bullying, and I am sure it is a matter of some importance to show that this is not necessarily always true.

Mr. Eden had now reached Moscow.

Prime Minister to Foreign Secretary   18 Oct 43

It is a very good thing you are on the spot to deal with the convoy question. I am seeing the Soviet Ambassador at 3 p.m. to-day, and propose to hand him back the offensive message from Stalin, saying that I do not wish to receive it, as the matter will be settled by you at Moscow. You should not hand in my suggested reply, or take it as anything more than a guide.

Further, the first convoy is assembling and leaves on November 12. The ships are being loaded, and I have not thought it right to interfere with this process, especially as it would involve the United States, who have sent their ships at our suggestion. I hope however that in personal contact with Stalin you may point out, first, the importance of these four convoys, with the 140 cargoes, and the efforts I have had to make to secure the necessary escorts; secondly, the small, petty mitigations we ask in the treatment of our men in North Russia; thirdly, our natural desire to be relieved of the burden of these convoys and to bring our people home from North Russia; fourthly, you could also disabuse his mind of the idea that any threat was intended by my declining to make an absolute contract or bargain; all I wished to do was to reserve the final right of judging whether the operation was militarily practicable or could be attempted, having regard to the general situation in the Atlantic, without being accused, as usual, of a breach of faith, and I must maintain this reservation. . . .

I feel so much for you in the bleak Conference, and wish I were with you. You may have full confidence in the strength of the British position on all these questions, and I have every hope that you will make them feel at once our desire for their friendship and our will-power on essentials. All good luck.

$$\star \quad \star \quad \star \quad \star \quad \star$$

On the same day I asked the Soviet Ambassador to come to see me. As this was the first occasion on which I had met M. Gousev, who had succeeded Maisky, he gave me the greetings of Marshal Stalin and M. Molotov, and I told him of the good reputation he had made for himself with us in Canada. After these compliments we had a short discussion about the Moscow Conference and the Second Front. I explained to him that this kind of operation could not be undertaken on impulse, and that I was always ready to arrange for a meeting between British and Russian military experts, who would go into the facts and figures, upon which everything depended, and without which discussion was futile. I spoke to him earnestly about the great desire we had to work with Russia and to be friends with her, how we saw that she should have a great place in the world after the war, that we should welcome this, and that we would do our best also to make good relations between her and the United States. I further said how much I was looking forward to a meeting with Marshal Stalin if it could be arranged, and how important this meeting of the heads of the British, American, and Soviet Governments was to the future of the world.

I then turned to Stalin's telegram about the convoys. I said very briefly that I did not think this message would help the situation, that it had caused me a good deal of pain, that I feared any reply which I could send would only make things worse, that the Foreign Secretary was in Moscow and I had left it to him to settle the matter on the spot and that therefore I did not wish to receive the message. I then handed back to the Ambassador an envelope. Gousev opened the envelope to see what was inside it, and, recognising the message, said he had been instructed to deliver it to me. I then said, "I am not prepared to receive it," and got up to indicate in a friendly manner that our conversation was at an end. I moved to the door and opened it. We had a little talk in the doorway about his coming to luncheon in the near future and discussing with Mrs. Churchill some questions connected with her Russian fund, which I told him had now reached four million pounds. I did not give M. Gousev a chance of recurring to the question of the convoys or of trying to hand me back the envelope, and bowed him out.

The War Cabinet endorsed my refusal to receive Stalin's telegram. It was certainly an unusual diplomatic incident, and, as I learnt later, it impressed the Soviet Government. In fact, Molotov referred to it several times in conversation. Even before it could be reported to Moscow there were misgivings in Soviet circles. On October 19 Mr. Eden telegraphed that Molotov had called on him at the Embassy and said that his Government greatly valued the convoys and had sadly missed them. The Northern route was the shortest and quickest way of getting supplies to the front, where the Russians were going through a difficult time. The German winter defence line had to be broken. Molotov promised to speak to Stalin about it all and arrange a meeting.

Mr. Eden continued:

My attention has been drawn to the fate of two British merchant seamen recently given severe sentences for an assault in North Russia upon a local Communist leader. I am most reluctant, and the Ambassador agrees with me, to promise resumption of convoys unless these unfortunate British seamen are released and handed over to our naval authorities for removal. . . . I am convinced it would be utterly repugnant to you, as it is to me, to allow these men to languish in a Soviet gaol while we are accepting those risks to British seamen in future convoys. I shall try what I can do by personal appeal to Stalin or Molotov.

The important discussion took place on the 21st. Meanwhile, in order to strengthen Eden's hands, and at his suggestion, I suspended the sailing of the British destroyers, which was the first move in the resumption of the convoys.

Foreign Secretary to Prime Minister   22 Oct 43

I saw Stalin and Molotov last evening. His Majesty's Ambassador was with me, and the conversation, which roamed over a large variety of topics, lasted two and a quarter hours.

2. After some preliminary exchanges of greetings I raised the question of convoys. I said that I must explain how great a strain these convoys placed on the Royal Navy. The passage of each one was a major naval operation, which might require four cruisers and twelve destroyers for its immediate protection, in addition to which the entire Home Fleet would also have to come out to provide cover. To make available the necessary escorts we must reduce our naval strength in the Atlantic. Though it was true that anti-U-boat warfare was going better for us, this struggle was still a closely run thing. At this point I showed Stalin a chart of the number of U-boats in service over the past three years. This proved that the number was now still near its peak. The reason why we were not prepared to promise that we would carry out four convoys was that we did not wish to expose ourselves to reproach if, owing to some sudden development of the war, we could not in fact send all four. But it was our earnest desire to make these convoys available, and I told Stalin that you, who had yourself laboured hard to make the necessary arrangements, had now telegraphed me that you calculated that we should be able to send 130 to 140 cargoes in all, with about 860,000 tons of supplies. If the convoys were to be run we were anxious to start at once. We had made our naval dispositions on this basis, and we wished to avail ourselves of the period during which the *Tirpitz* was out of action. Our requirements in naval personnel had been reduced to what we considered the absolute minimum, and we must insist on that minimum. There were also certain minor requirements which, if general agreement were reached, I wished to put to Molotov.

3. Stalin, who had nodded agreement at my description of the U-boat warfare, said that his difference with you was not about the

difficulties of the operation, but as to whether we were bound to do it. You had implied that if we sailed any one of these convoys it would be as a gift. Stalin did not feel this was a true description of the position. On his understanding of it we were under an obligation to seek to deliver these goods. When he had sent his reply to you however you had been very much offended and would not accept his reply. I replied that we had never suggested that to send these convoys was an act of favour or charity. You had at all times been determined to make every effort to deliver these goods to our Ally, but for the reasons I had explained you could not pledge yourself to a series of operations which you might not be able to carry out. Stalin himself surely must have confidence in the good faith of his Ally, and therefore it was not surprising that you should have been hurt by the message. The Marshal said that this had not been intended.

4. After some further discussion Stalin said that he could not agree to increase the number of men. There were already many of our sailors in North Russian ports with nothing to do, and then they got into trouble with Russian sailors. The Russians might undertake such convoys themselves. I replied that this was not possible. He said that if only our people in North Russia had treated his people as equals none of these difficulties would have arisen, and that if our people would treat his people as equals we could have as much personnel as we liked. After some further argument it was decided that Molotov and I would meet to-morrow, when I would give him a list of our requirements and we would see whether we could reach agreement.

*   *   *   *   *

Thus it was arranged that the convoys should be resumed. The first started in November, and a second followed it in December. Between them they comprised seventy-two ships. All arrived safely, and at the same time return convoys of empty ships were successfully brought out.

The December outward-bound convoy was to bring about a gratifying naval engagement. The disablement of the *Tirpitz* had left the *Scharnhorst* the only heavy enemy ship in Northern Norway. She sallied forth from Alten Fiord with five destroyers on the evening of Christmas Day, 1943, to attack the convoy about fifty miles south of Bear Island. The reinforced convoy escort comprised fourteen destroyers, with a covering force of three cruisers. The Commander-in-Chief, Admiral Fraser, lay to the south-westward in his flagship, the *Duke of York*, with the cruiser *Jamaica* and four destroyers.

Twice the *Scharnhorst* tried to strike at the convoy. Each time she was intercepted and engaged by the escort cruisers and destroyers, and after indecisive fighting, in which both the *Scharnhorst* and the British cruiser *Norfolk* were hit, the Germans broke off the action and withdrew to the southward, shadowed and reported by our cruisers. The German destroyers were never seen and took no part. Meanwhile the Commander-in-Chief was approaching at his utmost speed through heavy seas. At 4.17 p.m., when the last of the Arctic twilight had long since gone, the *Duke of York* detected the enemy by Radar at about twenty-three miles. The *Scharnhorst* remained unaware of her approaching doom, until, at 4.50 p.m., the *Duke of York* opened fire at 12,000 yards with the aid of star-shell. At the same time Admiral Fraser sent his four destroyers in to attack when opportunity offered. One of these, the *Stord*, was manned by the Royal Norwegian Navy. The *Scharnhorst* was surprised, and turned away to the eastward. In a running fight she suffered several hits, but was able with her superior speed gradually to draw ahead. However, by 6.20 p.m. it became apparent that her speed was beginning to fall and our destroyers were able to close in on either flank. At about 7 p.m. they all pressed home their attacks. Four torpedoes struck. Only one destroyer was hit.

The *Scharnhorst* turned to drive off the destroyers, and thus the *Duke of York* was able to close rapidly to about 10,000 yards and reopen fire with crushing effect. In half an hour the unequal battle between a battleship and a wounded battle-cruiser was over, and the *Duke of York* left the cruisers and destroyers to complete the task. The *Scharnhorst* soon sank, and of her company of 1,970 officers and men, including Rear-Admiral Bey, we could only save thirty-six men.

Although the fate of the crippled *Tirpitz* was delayed for nearly a year, the sinking of the *Scharnhorst* not only removed the worst menace to our Arctic convoys, but gave new freedom to our Home Fleet. We no longer had to be prepared at our average moment against German heavy ships breaking out into the Atlantic at their selected moment. This was an important relief

★　　★　　★　　★　　★

When in April 1944 there were signs that the *Tirpitz* had been repaired sufficiently to move for refit to a Baltic port aircraft from the carriers *Victorious* and *Furious* attacked her with heavy bombs, and she was once more immobilised. The Royal Air Force now took up the attack from a base in North Russia. They succeeded in causing further damage, which led to the *Tirpitz* being removed to Tromsö Fiord, which was two hundred miles nearer to Britain and within the extreme range of our home-based heavy bombers. The Germans had now abandoned hope of getting the ship home for repair and had written her off as a seagoing fighting unit. On November 12 twenty-nine specially fitted Lancasters of the Royal Air Force, including those of 617 Squadron, famous for the Möhne Dam exploit, struck the decisive blow, with bombs of twelve thousand pounds weight. They had to fly over 2,000 miles from their bases in Scotland, but the weather was clear and three bombs hit their target. The *Tirpitz* capsized at her moorings, more than half of her crew of 1,900 men being killed, at the cost of one bomber, whose crew survived.

All British heavy ships were now free to move to the Far East.

CHAPTER XVI

FOREIGN SECRETARIES' CONFERENCE IN MOSCOW

Back to the Quebec Conference – Need of a Meeting of the Three Heads of Governments – Correspondence with Stalin – A Preliminary Conference of Foreign Ministers – My Note for Mr. Eden at this Conference, October 11 – The Meeting in Moscow, October 19 – The Soviet Proposals – Stalin Concentrates on the Cross-Channel Invasion – My Private Note to Mr. Eden, October 20 – The Question of Turkey and Sweden Joining in the War – Eisenhower and Alexander's Grave Report on the Battle in Italy – Further Discussion at the Kremlin – The Russians Press the Question of "Overlord" – A Friendly Atmosphere – Mr. Eden's Account – A Russian Share in the Italian Fleet Suggested – My Telegrams of October 29 on This – My Proposed Triple Declaration on German War Criminals Accepted – Important Achievements of the Conference.

RETROSPECT is now necessary to bring the course of diplomatic events into accord with the narrative. Ever since the Quebec Conference we had been making suggestions to Stalin for a triple meeting of the heads of Governments. Already at Quebec I had received the following reply from him:

Premier Stalin to Prime Minister (Quebec)   10 Aug 43
I have just returned from the front, and already had time to become familiar with the message of the British Government dated August 7.

1. I agree that a meeting of the heads of three Governments is absolutely desirable. Such a meeting must be realised at the first opportunity, having arranged with the President the place and the time of this meeting.

At the same time I ought to say that in the existing situation on the Soviet-German front I, to my regret, have no opportunity to absent myself and to leave the front even for one week. Although recently we have had several successes on the front, an extreme strain on the strength and exceptional watchfulness are required in regard to the new possible actions of the enemy from the Soviet troops and from the Soviet Command just now. In connection with this I have to visit the troops on that or other parts of our front more often than usual. In the circumstances at the present time I am not able to visit Scapa Flow or any other distant point for a meeting with you and the President.

Nevertheless, in order not to postpone an examination of the questions which interest our countries, it would be expedient to organise a meeting of the responsible representatives of our States, and we might come to an understanding in the nearest future concerning the place and date of such a meeting.

Moreover, it is necessary beforehand to agree on the scope of the questions to be discussed and the drafts of the proposals which have to be accepted. The meeting will hardly give any tangible result without that.

2. Taking this opportunity, I congratulate the British Government and the Anglo-American troops on the occasion of their most successful operations in Sicily, which have already caused the downfall of Mussolini and the break-up of his gang.

This was the first favourable mention from the Russian side of a meeting between the three Allies at any level. In passing this message to Mr. Eden for transmission to Moscow I said, "I was very glad to hear again from Bruin in the first person. Please forward him my reply, which is in the sense you desire."

After a discussion with the President we framed a joint message to Stalin.

Prime Minister and President (Quebec) to Premier Stalin   19 Aug 43
We have both arrived here with our Staffs, and will probably remain in conference for about ten days. We fully understand strong reasons which lead you to remain on battle-fronts, where your presence has been so fruitful of victory. Nevertheless we wish to emphasise once more importance of a meeting between all three of us. We do not feel that either Archangel or Astrakhan is suitable, but we are prepared ourselves, accompanied by suitable officers, to proceed to Fairbanks [in Alaska] in order to survey whole scene in common with you. The present seems to be a unique opportunity for making a rendezvous, and also a crucial point in the war. We earnestly hope that you will give this matter once more your consideration. The Prime Minister will remain on this side of the Atlantic for as long as may be necessary.

2. Should it prove impossible to arrange the much-needed meeting

of three heads of Governments we agree with you that a meeting on the Foreign Office level should take place in the near future. This meeting would be exploratory in character, as of course final decisions must be reserved to our respective Governments.

Stalin replied:

25 Aug 43

I have received your joint message of August 19.

I entirely share your opinion and that of Mr. Roosevelt about the importance of a meeting between the three of us. In this connection I beg you most earnestly to understand my position at this moment, when our armies are carrying on the struggle against the main forces of Hitler with the utmost strain, and when Hitler not only does not withdraw a single division from our front, but, on the contrary, has already succeeded in transporting, and continues to transport, fresh divisions to the Soviet-German front. At such a moment, in the opinion of all my colleagues, I cannot, without detriment to our military operations, leave the front for so distant a point as Fairbanks, although if the situation on our front were different Fairbanks undoubtedly would be very convenient as a place for our meeting, as I said before.

As regards a meeting of representatives of our States, and in particular of representatives in charge of foreign affairs, I share your opinion about the expediency of such a meeting in the near future. This meeting however ought not to have a purely exploratory character, but a practicable and preparatory character, in order that after that meeting has taken place our Governments are able to take definite decisions, on urgent questions. Therefore I consider it indispensable to revert to my proposal that it is necessary in advance to define the scope of the questions for discussion by the representatives of the three Powers, and to draft the proposals which ought to be discussed by them and presented to our Governments for final decision.

Prime Minister to Premier Stalin   5 Sept 43

The Conference of Foreign Ministers. I was glad to get your message of August 25, in which you agree to an early meeting of Soviet, United States, and British representatives in charge of foreign affairs. If M. Molotov comes we will send Mr. Eden.

2. The Conference even thus constituted could not of course supersede the authority of all Governments concerned. We are most anxious to know what your wishes are about the future, and will tell you our views so far as they are formed. After that the Governments will have to decide, and I hope that we may be able to meet personally somewhere. I would, if necessary, go to Moscow.

3. The political representatives might require to be assisted by military advisers. I would provide a general officer, Sir Hastings Ismay, who is my personal representative on the Chiefs of Staff Committee and conducts the Secretariat of the Ministry of Defence. He could supply the arguments and facts and figures on the military questions involved. I believe the United States would send an officer similarly qualified. This, I think, would be sufficient at this stage for the meeting of Foreign Ministers.

4. If however you wish to go in technical detail into the question of why we have not yet invaded France across the Channel and why we cannot do it sooner or in greater strength than is now proposed, I should welcome a separate technical mission of your generals and admirals coming to London or Washington, or both, when the fullest possible exposition of our thought, resources, and intentions could be laid before them and thrashed out. Indeed, I should be very glad that you should have this explanation, to which you have every right.

5. We are disposed to think that Britain, being a midway point, would be the most convenient place for the meeting, though it might be preferable to hold it outside of London. I have made this proposal to the President, but he has not given me a final decision upon it. If England were agreeable to you I should be glad of your support in the proposal.

6. I hope we can aim at assembling the Conference early in October.

Premier Stalin to Prime Minister   8 Sept 43

The time suggested by you for the meeting of the representatives of the three Governments—the beginning of October—is acceptable. As the meeting-place I propose Moscow. It is important to agree in advance on the agenda, and on the proposals concerning the decisions to be taken on the various questions of the agenda in which our Governments are interested. Now as before I believe that this is necessary for the success of the Conference, which ought to prepare the way for the subsequent agreed decisions of the Governments. I do not foresee any difficulty in coming to terms on other questions concerning the organisation of the meeting.

On the question of the personal meeting between the heads of the three Governments, I have written to the President that I have decided to bring about this meeting as soon as possible, that the time of the meeting suggested by the President—November, December—seems acceptable to me, but that the meeting-place should be selected in a country where all three States have their representatives—for example, in Persia. I made only one reservation—*i.e.*, that the exact moment of the meeting should be fixed in the light of the situation on the Soviet-German front, where more than five hundred divisions on both sides are involved in the struggle.★ This necessitates practically everyday control on the part of the High Command of the U.S.S.R.

On September 10 I answered Premier Stalin's proposal.

With regard to the meeting of Foreign Office representatives, we defer to your wishes that Moscow should be the scene. Accordingly our Foreign Secretary, Mr. Eden, will proceed thither at an early date in October. He will be attended by a suitable staff.

Agenda. His Majesty's Government declares itself willing to discuss any and every subject with its Russian and United States Allies. We will in a few days furnish you with our ideas. But we should particularly like to know what are the main points you have in mind.

This meeting of Foreign Office representatives seems to me a most important and necessary preliminary to the meeting of the three heads of Governments. I am pleased and relieved to feel that there is a good prospect of this taking place between November 15 and December 15. I have for months past informed you that I will come anywhere, at any time, at any risk, for such a meeting. I am therefore prepared to go to Teheran unless you can think of a better place in Persia. I should have preferred Cyprus or Khartoum, but I defer to your wishes. Marshal Stalin, I wish to tell you that on this meeting of the three of us, so greatly desired by all the United Nations, may depend not only the best and shortest method of finishing the war, but also those good arrangements for the future of the world which will enable the British, American, and Russian nations to render a lasting service to humanity.

★   ★   ★   ★   ★

Later, after my return from Quebec to London, I drafted for my colleagues a note upon the general points to be considered at the forthcoming Conference of Foreign Ministers, which had now been arranged.

NOTES BY THE PRIME MINISTER FOR FOREIGN SECRETARY
AT THE FORTHCOMING MEETING
11 Oct 43

Great Britain seeks no territory or special advantage for herself as the outcome of the war, which she entered in pursuance of her obligations and in defence of public law.

2. We hold strongly to a system of a League of Nations, *which will include a Council of Europe, with an International Court and an armed Power capable of enforcing its decisions.*† During the Armistice period, which may be prolonged, we hold that the three Great Powers, the

---

★ A Soviet division was equivalent to about a third of a British or United States division.
† Author's subsequent italics.

British Commonwealth and Empire, the United States, and the Union of Soviet Socialist Republics, with the addition of China, should remain united, well armed, and capable of enforcing the Armistice terms and of building up the permanent structure of peace throughout the globe.

3. We consider that States and nations that have been subjugated by Nazi or Fascist violence during the war should emerge at the Peace Conference with their full sovereign rights, and that all questions of final territorial transference must be settled at the peace table, due regard being paid to the interests of the populations affected.

4. We reaffirm the principles of the Atlantic Charter, noting that Russia's accession thereto is based upon the frontiers of June 22, 1941. We also take note of the historic frontiers of Russia before the two wars of aggression waged by Germany in 1914 and 1939.

5. We should welcome any agreement between Poland and Russia which, while securing a strong and independent Poland, afforded to Russia the security necessary for her western frontier.

6. We are resolved that Nazism and Fascism shall be extirpated in the aggressor countries where they have taken root, and that democratic Governments based upon the free expression of the people's will, obtained under conditions of reasonable tranquillity, shall be set up. This should not exclude measures of military diplomacy or relations with interim Governments which may come into being, so that our main objects may be achieved with the minimum of slaughter, especially to the forces of the Allies.

7. We repudiate all territorial expansion achieved by Germany or Italy during the Nazi or Fascist régimes, and further we consider that the future structure of Germany and the position of Prussia as a unit of the German State should be subject to an agreed policy among the three Great Powers of the West.

8. We are resolved to take all measures necessary to prevent the guilty Powers from becoming an armed menace to the peace of Europe, not only by disarmament, but by prolonged control of every form of warlike apparatus or organisation within their bounds.

9. We have no desire to keep any branch of the European family of nations in a condition of subjection or restriction, except as may be required by the general needs and safety of the world.

10. We proclaim our inflexible resolve to use the authority which victory will confer upon the three Great Powers in order to serve the general good and the cause of human progress.

*　*　*　*　*

The Conference of the three Foreign Ministers in Moscow now played an invaluable part in our complicated affairs. The President had hoped Mr. Hull, at his advanced age, could be spared the full journey to Moscow, and had asked for a rendezvous in London, but Stalin had refused this change. Mr. Hull however would not be deterred. It was a gallant enterprise for this veteran in his frail health to undertake this, his first journey by air.

Before the Conference met in Moscow there had been a considerable interchange of telegrams between the three Foreign Secretaries about the agenda. The Americans put forward four suggestions, including a four-Power declaration, upon the treatment of Germany and other enemy countries in Europe during the Armistice period, and so forth. We, for our part, put forward no less than twelve suggestions, including a common policy towards Turkey, a common policy in Persia, relations between the U.S.S.R. and Poland, and policy in relation to Poland generally. The Russians made one suggestion, and one suggestion only—"the consideration of measures to shorten the duration of the war against Germany and her allies in Europe." Although this was obviously a military rather than a political question, it was clear from the outset that they were not prepared to discuss anything else until it had been fully thrashed out. It was therefore thought advisable to include General Ismay in our delegation.

★　　★　　★　　★　　★

The first formal meeting of the Conference took place on the afternoon of October 19. M. Molotov, after a show of resistance, such as is put up by the Speaker of the House of Commons when he is escorted to the Chair, was elected chairman, to the obvious satisfaction of himself and his delegation. The agenda was then settled. These preliminaries concluded, Molotov handed round the following note of Soviet proposals:

1. That the Governments of Great Britain and the United States take in 1943 such urgent measures as will ensure the invasion of Northern France by Anglo-American armies, and, coupled with powerful blows of Soviet troops on the main German forces on the Soviet-German front, will radically undermine the military-strategical situation of Germany and bring about a decisive shortening of the duration of the war.

In this connection the Soviet Government deem it necessary to ascertain whether the statement made in early June 1943 by Mr. Churchill and Mr. Roosevelt to the effect that Anglo-American forces will undertake the invasion of Northern France in the spring of 1944 remains valid.

2. That the three Powers suggest to the Turkish Government that Turkey should immediately enter the war.

3. That the three Powers suggest to Sweden to place at the disposal of the Allies air bases for the struggle against Germany.

Molotov asked whether Mr. Hull and Mr. Eden would be prepared to discuss these proposals in a closely restricted meeting, after they had had time to study them. This was readily agreed.

Mr. Eden sent me an account of what had passed, and I sent him my views at once.

Prime Minister to Mr. Eden (Moscow)   20 Oct 43

Our present plans for 1944 seem open to very grave defects. We are to put fifteen American and twelve British divisions into France in May, and will have about six American and sixteen British or British-controlled divisions on the Italian front. Unless there is a German collapse, Hitler, lying in the centre of the best communications in the world, can concentrate at least forty to fifty divisions against either of these forces while holding the other. He could obtain all the necessary forces by cutting his losses in the Balkans and withdrawing to the Save and the Danube without necessarily weakening his Russian front. This is one of the most elementary war propositions. The disposition of our forces between the Italian and the Channel theatre has not been settled by strategic needs, but by the march of events, by shipping possibilities, and by arbitrary compromises between the British and Americans. Neither the force built up in Italy nor that which will be ready in May to cross the Channel is adequate for what is required, and only transferences of the order of seven or eight divisions can physically be made between them. I am determined that this situation shall be reviewed.

2. If it lay with me to decide, I would not withdraw any troops from the Mediterranean and would not debouch from the narrow leg of Italy into the valley of the Po, and would engage the enemy strongly on the narrower front while at the same time fomenting Balkan and Southern France disturbances. In the absence of a German collapse, I do not think we should cross the Channel with less than forty divisions available by the sixtieth day, and then only if the Italian front were in strong action with the enemy. I do not accept the American argument that our metropolitan Air Forces can flatten everything out in the battle zone or on its approaches. This has not been our present experience. All this is for your internal consumption, and not for deployment at this stage. It may show you however the

254

dangers of our being committed to a lawyer's bargain for "Overlord" in May, for the sake of which we may have to ruin the Italian front and Balkan possibilities and yet have insufficient forces to maintain ourselves after the thirtieth or fortieth day.

3. You should try to find out what the Russians really feel about the Balkans. Would they be attracted by the idea of our acting through the Ægean, involving Turkey in the war, and opening the Dardanelles and Bosphorus so that British naval forces and shipping could aid the Russian advance and so that we could ultimately give them our right hand along the Danube? How great an interest would they feel in our opening the Black Sea to Allied warships, supplies, and Allied military forces, including Turkish? Have they any interest in this right-handed evolution, or are they still set only on our attacking France?—observing that of course in any circumstances the steady building up of forces in England will hold large German forces in the West. It may be that for political reasons the Russians would not want us to develop a large-scale Balkan strategy. On the other hand, their desire that Turkey should enter the war shows their interest in the South-Eastern theatre.

4. I remain convinced of the great importance of our getting a foothold in the Ægean by taking Rhodes, re-taking Cos, and holding Leros, and building up an effective air and naval superiority in these waters. Do the Russians view with sympathy our effort to hold Leros and desire to take Rhodes? Do they understand the effect this has upon Turkey, and how it opens the possibility of a naval advance into the Black Sea? Again, all the above is simply for your inner thoughts.

* * * * *

On October 21 there was a session in Moscow to consider the Soviet proposals. Mr. Eden, Ambassador Sir Archibald Clark Kerr, Mr. Strang, and General Ismay represented the British, Mr. Hull, Ambassador Harriman, and Major-General Deane the Americans, M. Molotov, Marshal Voroshilov, M. Vyshinsky, and M. Litvinov the Russians. Ismay opened the meeting by a statement on behalf of both the British and American delegations, based on the Quebec decisions, in the course of which he emphasised the limiting conditions which governed the launching of the cross-Channel invasion.

In the discussion that followed our representatives made it absolutely clear that there had in fact been no change of plan on our part and that we intended to go ahead provided the conditions which we had laid down could be fulfilled. With this the Russians seemed content for the moment. Molotov said that the Soviet Government would study Ismay's statement in detail, and would wish to have a further discussion on it later in the Conference.

Mr. Eden then turned to the question of Turkey, and pointed out that we could not at present give the necessary effective support. The question of a joint approach to Turkey was deferred until later. The Russian proposal about Sweden was also mentioned. Sweden would clearly demand guarantees about Finland, a matter which the Russians were reluctant to discuss.

* * * * *

In the evening Eden called upon Stalin and for over two hours discussed a large variety of topics. First in importance, as we have seen, was the question of the Arctic convoys. The conversation then turned to the proposed meeting of the three heads of the Allied Governments. Stalin was insistent that this should take place at Teheran.

On the whole the conversation seemed to go well.

* * * * *

Mr. Eden had now received my telegram of October 20, and sent his comments. He said that the Russians were completely and blindly set on our invasion of Northern France. It was the one decision in which they took an absorbing interest. They asked again and again whether there had been any change in the understanding given to Stalin by the President and myself after the Washington Conference in May that we would invade in the early spring of 1944, and when the operation would start.

On the first point he had assured them that there had been no change, but had emphasised the three conditions which must be present to allow the expedition to be launched with any chance of success.* On the second point it was thought better not to give the actual date, but Mr. Eden assured them that all preparations were going forward to attack in the spring after the weather became favourable.

I replied by return:

Prime Minister to Foreign Secretary (Moscow)   23 Oct 43
If we force Turkey to enter the war she will insist on air support, etc., which could not be provided without detriment to our main operations in Italy. If however Turkey enters on her own initiative,

---
* See p. 69.

perhaps moving through a phase of non-belligerency, we should not have the same obligation, and yet great advantages might be reaped. Obviously timing is vital, and dependent upon what is the aggressive strength of the enemy in Bulgaria and Thrace. *The prize would be to get into the Black Sea with supplies for Russia, warships, and other forces. This is what I call 'giving Russia the right hand'.* Such a movement by Turkey is not impossible, especially if the Germans should begin to cut their losses in the Balkans and withdraw towards the Danube and the Save.

2. *Finland and Sweden.* It would be a great advantage to bring Sweden into the war. We do not think the Germans have the strength to undertake a heavy invasion of Sweden. We should gain a new country and a small but good army. Our gains in Norway would be far-reaching. Valuable facilities would be afforded to Russian air forces. For ourselves, we can do far better bombing of Germany from East Anglia, where we are mounted on a vast scale, than from Sweden, where everything would have to be improvised and imported by air. Our range from England over Germany is just as good as from Sweden. In fact, with present British facilities plus those we hope to acquire north of Rome there is no part of Germany we cannot reach with great weight.

3. Personally I should like to see Turkey come in on her own, and also Sweden. I do not think either of them would be overrun, and every new enemy helps Hitler's ruin. I suggest however that the first step is to find out what we and the Russians want and what will help both of us most in both quarters, and then as a second step go into ways and means immediately thereafter. Try this and let me know.

And two days later I added:

Prime Minister to Foreign Secretary   25 Oct 43
Further reflection confirms my view that we should not discourage the Russian desire that Turkey and Sweden should of their own volition become co-belligerents or actual allies. The Russians should not be put in the position of arguing for this and we of simply making difficulties. We should agree in principle and let the difficulties manifest themselves, as they will certainly do, in the discussion of ways and means. They may well be overcome or put in their proper place and proportion. Anyhow, we ought not to begin by crabbing everything.

★   ★   ★   ★   ★

The serious telegram, recorded in an earlier chapter, from General Eisenhower reporting General Alexander's appreciation

* Author's subsequent italics.

of the battle in Italy had now reached me.* I repeated it to Eden and asked him to show it to Stalin. I added:

26 Oct 43

The reason why we are getting into this jeopardy is because we are moving some of our best divisions and a large proportion of vital landing-craft from the Mediterranean in order to build up for "Overlord", seven months hence. This is what happens when battles are governed by lawyers' agreements made in all good faith months before, and persisted in without regard to the ever-changing fortunes of war. You should let him know, if you think fit, that I will not allow, while I am responsible, the great and fruitful campaign in Italy, which has already drawn heavy German reserves into action, to be cast away and end in a frightful disaster, for the sake of crossing the Channel in May. The battle must be nourished and fought out until it is won. We will do our very best for "Overlord", but it is no use planning for defeat in the field in order to give temporary political satisfaction.

2. It will therefore be necessary for you to make it clear that the assurances you have given about May "Overlord", subject to the specified conditions, must be modified by the exigencies of the battle in Italy. I am taking the matter up with President Roosevelt, but nothing will alter my determination not to throw away the battle in Italy at this juncture, so far as the King's armies are concerned. Eisenhower and Alexander must have what they need to win the battle, no matter what effect is produced on subsequent operations. This may certainly affect the date of "Overlord".

I concluded my comments on this subject three days later.

Prime Minister to Mr. Eden (Moscow)   29 Oct 43

There is of course no question of abandoning "Overlord", which will remain our principal operation for 1944. The retention of landing-craft in the Mediterranean in order not to lose the Battle of Rome may cause a slight delay, perhaps till July, as the smaller class of landing-craft cannot cross the Bay of Biscay in the winter months and would have to make the passage in the spring. The delay would however mean that the blow when struck would be with somewhat heavier forces, and also that the full bombing effort on Germany would not be damped down so soon. We are also ready at any time to push across and profit by a German collapse. These arguments may be of use to you in discussion.

* * * * *

* See pp. 216 ff.

258

In the evening our Ambassador and Ismay accompanied Mr. Eden to the Kremlin. Molotov was with Stalin. Eden opened the proceedings by handing Stalin the Russian text of Eisenhower's telegram about the situation in Italy. Stalin read it aloud to Molotov. When he had finished he showed no trace of disappointment, but said that according to Russian Intelligence there were twelve Anglo-American divisions fighting six German divisions south of Rome, and that there were a further six German divisions on the river Po. He admitted however that General Alexander was likely to have the better information. Mr. Eden said I was anxious that Stalin should have the latest account of the situation in Italy, and should know not only that I was anxious about it, but also that I was insistent that the battle in Italy should be nourished and fought out to victory whatever the implications on "Overlord". He added that the vitally important decisions now confronting the Allies made it all the more necessary that the three heads of Governments should meet as soon as possible.

Stalin observed with a smile that if there were not enough divisions a meeting of the heads of Governments could not create them. He then asked point-blank whether the telegram which he had just read meant a postponement of "Overlord". Eden replied that until it had been fully examined by the Combined Chiefs of Staff and decisions made about improving the position it was impossible to say, but the possibility must be faced. He quoted the passage in my telegram that we were determined to "do our very best for 'Overlord'", but that it was "no use planning for defeat in the field in order to give temporary political satisfaction". There were two difficulties: firstly, landing-craft, and, secondly, moving seven battle-tried divisions to the United Kingdom at the beginning of November for the spearhead of the "Overlord" assault. Perhaps the moving of some or all of them would now have to be postponed, but whether or not this would affect the date of "Overlord", and if so to what extent, it was impossible to say.

Stalin then turned to questions of general strategy. As he saw it, there were two courses open to us: to take up a defensive position north of Rome and use all the rest of our forces for "Overlord", or to push through Italy into Germany.

Mr. Eden said that the first alternative was what we had in

mind. There was no intention, so far as he knew, to go beyond the Pisa–Rimini line. This would give us depth north of Rome and air bases for bombing Southern Europe. Stalin clearly thought we were right, and said that it would be very difficult to get through the Alps, and that it would suit the Germans well to fight us there. After the capture of Rome British prestige would certainly be high enough to permit us to pass over to the defensive in Italy.

The discussion then turned to the other point of attack. Mr. Eden said that we might be able to stage a diversionary attack against Southern France synchronising with "Overlord". If we could secure a bridgehead with a couple of divisions it might be possible to use the French divisions which were being trained and equipped in North Africa. Stalin thought that this was a good idea, since the more we made Hitler disperse the better. These were the tactics he was employing on the Russian front. But would there be enough landing-craft?

He then put the question, "Will the postponement of 'Overlord' be one month or two months?" Mr. Eden said that he could not possibly give an answer. All that he could state definitely was that we would do our very best to launch "Overlord" at the earliest possible moment at which it had a reasonable prospect of success, and that it was most desirable that the three heads of Governments should meet as soon as possible. Stalin entirely agreed, but said that there was some hesitation on the part of the President about going to Teheran. When Eden suggested Habbaniya both he and Molotov firmly refused. Stalin said that he himself could not go far away so long as there was an opportunity of continuing to damage Hitler's armies. The Germans had recently moved some tank divisions from France and Belgium to the Soviet front, but they were short of equipment and raw materials. It was essential to give Hitler no rest, and he volunteered that the Soviet armies would not have had the success that they had won if the Germans had been able to move from the West the forty divisions which were pinned there by the mere threat of our invasion. The Soviet fully understood this contribution to the cause.

Mr. Eden said that the Marshal well knew that the Prime Minister was just as keen on hurting Hitler as he was. Stalin fully acknowledged this, but added with a gust of laughter that

I had a tendency to take the easy road for myself and leave the difficult jobs to the Russians. Eden refused to agree, and mentioned the difficulties of naval operations and our recent heavy losses in destroyers. Stalin became serious again, and said that his people spoke little about naval operations, but realised how difficult they were.

"The whole talk," cabled Mr. Eden, "went off surprisingly well. Stalin seemed in excellent humour, and at no point in the evening was there any recrimination about the past or any disposition to ignore real difficulties that face us. This may only have been a first reaction and second thoughts may not be so good, but it is significant that he should have gone out of his way to acknowledge the contribution we were making by merely pinning forty German divisions in the West, and his sympathetic references to the difficulties of naval operations and to the necessity for landing-craft, etc., seemed to show that he no longer regards an overseas operation as a simple matter. It is clear however that he expects us to make every effort to stage 'Overlord' at the earliest possible moment, and the confidence he is placing in our word is to me most striking."

There had been many signs during the Conference that the Soviet Government sincerely desired permanent friendship with Britain and the United States. They had met us on a number of points, both large and small, about which we foresaw difficulties. Stalin had shown understanding of our problems, and so far there had been no unsatisfactory afterthoughts. "Molotov," said Mr. Eden, "has shown that spirit on many occasions, notably as chairman of our Conference to-day, when we had our final session on military matters. Though he was obviously disappointed at the outcome of what I had told him and Stalin last night, and at our failure wholly to endorse in a manner satisfactory to him Soviet proposals about Turkey and Sweden, he conducted our business with an evident desire to avoid embarrassment to either country. As an indication of goodwill I received a message from him to-night that our two imprisoned sailors have been pardoned.

"Russian representatives have given many other signs of an intention to open a new chapter. Your gesture in respect of convoys has made a deep impression. For the first time for many years Molotov and a number of his colleagues came to dinner at this Embassy to-night. Mikoyan, whose task it is to keep these people informed, was especially eloquent in his tributes to your personal share in the sailing of these convoys.

"In this atmosphere I would give much to be able to close the Conference with some tangible evidence of our goodwill. I am quite sure that if I could give them some encouraging message about their desire to have a small share of the Italian Fleet the psychological effect would be out of all proportion to the value of the ships, whatever that may be. The Ambassador and Harriman fully endorse this view. If it is impossible to give a specific reply before I leave it will be of the greatest help to me if I can at least tell M. Molotov that in principle we agree that the Soviet Government shall have a share of the captured Italian ships and that the proportion for which they ask is reasonable. Details can be worked out subsequently, including dates of delivery. If you can do this to help me I feel sure that the return will more than justify your gesture. I beg your aid."

I at once sent him the Cabinet view about the Italian Fleet.

Prime Minister to Secretary of State   29 Oct 43
 . . . In principle we willingly admit the Russians' right to a share in the Italian Fleet. We had however thought that this Fleet would play its part against Japan, and we had been planning to tropicalise the *Littorios* and some other units for this later phase of the war. If Russia would like to have a squadron in being in the Pacific that would be a very considerable event, and we should like to discuss this project when we meet. . . .

5. At present the only place where Italian ships could be handed over to the Russians would be Archangel and Murmansk. The Italian warships are quite unsuited for working in Arctic waters, and would need several months of dockyard work first. We should also have to be careful lest the immediate transfer to the Russians would have an ill-effect on Italian co-operation. It is important for Italy to have her flag on the sea against Germany. We do not want to provoke a refusal by the Italians to carry on the important work they are doing for us in Taranto dockyard. One cannot be absolutely sure that they would not scuttle some of the ships they brought out from the German clutches if they thought they were to be handed over to foreign crews. They are doing a good deal for us at the present time. Italian submarines are carrying supplies to Leros. Italian destroyers, of which there are only seven good ones, are escorting local convoys. Their cruisers are transporting troops and supplies. We should therefore in

any case have to ensure against publicity until we could take steps to counter these ill-effects. Once distribution of the Italian Fleet begins, the French, the Yugoslavs, and the Greeks would put in their claims, which are pretty good.

6. For all these reasons it would be better to put off this question till "Eureka" [Teheran].

7. It is quite true that we have gained some Italian merchant tonnage, but the amount is actually less than what we have to provide for the minimum requirements of conquered and Italian territory, so that we are actually down on the balance, especially as most of these Italian ships are not fit for anything more than local traffic.

8. Has Mr. Hull referred this request to his Government? It would be essential that we should be agreed. I should like best of all to talk over all this at "Eureka", if that ever comes off.

And later the same day:

Provided the Americans agree, you may tell Molotov that in principle we agree that the Soviet Government shall have a share of the captured Italian ships and that the proportion for which they ask is reasonable. I am presuming the battleship for which they ask is not a *Littorio*. Details and dates of delivery must be settled with regard to operations and not losing Italian aid by precipitate publicity. This is very important. Of course we are looking forward to using the very newest vessels of this Fleet in the war against Japan, and the Russians will surely understand that we ought not to prejudice that. We also feel we [the British] ought to have the two *Littorios* after the war, first, because of the overwhelming share we have had in the whole war against Italy, secondly, because of our heavy naval losses in capital units, and, thirdly, because we have suspended the long-term building of battleships already sanctioned by Parliament in order to concentrate on the current needs of the war.

2. Most especially secret and for your own thought and perhaps fly-throwing: if it were decided that on the defeat of Hitler Russia would play her part against Japan a great design might come into being, as a part of which the fitting out under the Soviet flag and manning with Russian sailors of a substantial naval force at some Pacific base in our possession and the participation of this force of surface ships in the final phase of the war might come into view. However, I hope that the consent I have sent you in the first lines of this telegram will meet your difficulties.

*　　*　　*　　*　　*

I had drafted a proposed declaration on German war criminals as a basis of discussion at the forthcoming meeting of the three heads of Governments.

Prime Minister to President Roosevelt and Premier Stalin   12 Oct 43

Would you very kindly consider whether something like the following might not be issued over our three signatures:

"Great Britain, the United States, and the Soviet Union [in whatever order is thought convenient, we being quite ready to be last] have received from many quarters evidence of the atrocities, massacres, and cold-blooded mass-executions which are being perpetrated by the Hitlerite forces in the many countries they have overrun and from which they are now being steadily expelled. The brutalities of the Nazi domination are no new thing, and all peoples or territories in their grip have suffered from the worst forms of government by terror. What is new is that many of these territories are now being redeemed by the advancing armies of the liberating Powers, and that in their desperation the recoiling Hitlerites and Huns are redoubling their ruthless cruelties.

"Accordingly the aforesaid three Allied Powers, speaking in the interest of the thirty-two United Nations, hereby solemnly declare, and give full warning of their declaration, as follows:

"At the time of the granting of any armistice to any Government which may be set up in Germany those German officers and men and members of the Nazi Party who have been responsible for or have taken a consenting part in the above atrocities, massacres, and executions will be sent back to the countries in which their abominable deeds were done in order that they may be judged and punished according to the laws of these liberated countries and the free Governments which will be erected therein. Lists will be compiled in all possible detail from all these countries, having regard especially to the invaded parts of Russia, to Poland and Czechoslovakia, to Yugoslavia, Greece, including Crete and other islands, to Norway, Denmark, the Netherlands, Belgium, Luxembourg, France, and Italy. Thus Germans who take part in the wholesale shootings of Italian officers or in the execution of French, Dutch, Belgian, or Norwegian hostages, or of Cretan peasants, or who have shared in the slaughters inflicted on the people of Poland or in the territories of the Soviet Republic, which are now being swept clear of the enemy, will know that they will be brought back, regardless of expense, to the scene of their crimes and judged on the spot by the peoples whom they have outraged. Let those who have hitherto not imbrued their hands with innocent blood beware lest they join the ranks of the guilty, for most assuredly the three Allied Powers will pursue them to the uttermost ends of the earth, and will deliver them to their accusers in order that justice may be done.

"The above declaration is without prejudice to the case of the major criminals, whose offences have no particular geographical localisation.

"ROOSEVELT
STALIN
CHURCHILL"

If this, or something like this (and I am not particular about the wording), were put over our three signatures it would, I believe, make some of these villains shy of being mixed up in butcheries now that they know they are going to be beat. We know, for instance, that our threats of reprisals about Poland have brought about a mitigation of the severities being inflicted on the people there. There is no doubt that the use of the terror-weapon by the enemy imposes an additional burden on our armies. Lots of Germans may develop moral scruples if they know they are going to be brought back and judged in the country, and perhaps the very place, where their cruel deeds were done. I strongly commend to you the principle of the localisation of judgment as likely to exert a deterrent effect on enemy terrorism. The British Cabinet endorse this principle and policy.

The declaration was accepted and endorsed, with a few verbal changes.

* * * * *

The three Foreign Ministers had met regularly every day, and covered an immense amount of ground. Their agreements were recorded in a secret protocol, drawn up on November 3. The importance of these lay in the additional machinery of co-opera-tion which was now to be set up. It was agreed to establish a European Advisory Committee in London to begin work on the problems which would arise in Germany and on the Continent when the Hitler régime neared collapse. It was this body which drew up the initial plans for dividing Germany into zones of occupation, an arrangement which caused grave problems later. Of this more in due course. For Italian affairs another Advisory Council was to be constituted, to include a Russian representative. There was to be an exchange of information on any peace-feelers put out by the Axis satellites. The Americans were anxious that a Four-Power Declaration, to include China, pledging themselves to a united conduct of the war "against those Axis Powers with which they are respectively at war", should be signed at this Moscow meeting. This was achieved on October 30. Finally, a protocol agreeing on joint action between Russia and Great Britain in regard to Turkey was drafted by Mr. Eden and signed on November 2.

We had every reason to be content with these results. There had been a smoothing of many points of friction, practical steps for further co-operation had been taken, the way had been prepared for an early meeting of the heads of the three major Allied Governments, and the mounting deadlock in our working with the Soviet Union had in part been removed.

Those who took part in the Conference sensed a far more friendly atmosphere, both on and off duty, than had ever existed before. One of the best-known Russian painters was commissioned by his Government to do a conversation piece of the Conference, and he had made preliminary sketches of various members of the British and American delegations. It is not known whether the picture was ever completed, but it has not yet seen the light of day.

CHAPTER XVII

ADVENT OF THE TRIPLE MEETING

THE HIGH COMMANDS

Urgency of Choosing a Supreme Commander for "Overlord" – We Favour the Choice of Marshall – My Correspondence with Roosevelt – The President's Delay in Deciding – His Desire for a Supreme Commander to Control Both Western Theatres – I Disagree with this Suggestion – Need to Arrange for a Meeting of the Three Powers – My Telegram to Stalin of September 25, and His Reply – Difficulties of Agreement Upon a Suitable Place for the Meeting – Roosevelt's Suggestions – Stalin Will Come Only to Teheran – Roosevelt's Disappointment – Constitutional Difficulties Invoked – I Seek a Preliminary Anglo-American Discussion – My Telegram to the President of October 23 – His Proposal to Invite Generalissimo Chiang Kai-shek – His Suggestion for Including the Russians in the Preliminary Meeting – I Argue Against This – Agreement for a Meeting – The Russians Decline to Confer with the Chinese Government at this Stage.

THE selection of a Supreme Commander for "Overlord", our cross-Channel entry into Europe in 1944, was urgent. This of course affected in the most direct manner the military conduct of the war, and raised a number of personal issues of importance and delicacy. At the Quebec Conference I had agreed with the President that "Overlord" should fall to an American officer, and had so informed General Brooke, to whom I had previously offered the task. I understood from the President that he would choose General Marshall, and this was entirely satisfactory to us. However, in the interval between Quebec and our meeting in Cairo I became conscious that the President had not finally made up his mind about Marshall. None of the other arrangements could of course be made before the main decision had been taken. Meanwhile rumour became rife in the American Press, and there was the prospect of Parliamentary reactions in London. Admiral Leahy in his book* mentions some of the American cross-currents. "The public," he writes, "assumed that Roosevelt would name Marshall as Supreme Commander. There was vehement objection to such a move in the Press. Opponents charged that Marshall was being given 'Dutch promotion'; that Roosevelt planned to take him out of a big job and put him into a small job; that it was a plot against Marshall. At the other extreme there were reports that the American Joint Chiefs considered the post of Supreme Command promotion and were jealous of Marshall."

This question was discussed between us at some length. I was anxious to emphasise the status of General Marshall in every way, provided that the authority of the Joint and Combined Chiefs of Staff was not impaired. I cabled Hopkins in this sense at the end of September.

Prime Minister to Mr. Harry Hopkins   26 Sept 43
There is a lot of talk in the papers about Marshall becoming Supreme Commander-in-Chief over all the forces in the West. What I understood from our talks was that he would command the operation "Overlord". He would not however be only a theatre commander. He might have the same sort of general outlook with us on the whole war against Germany, in addition to his specific command, as Dill has on the Combined Chiefs of Staff Committee in Washington over the whole field. We should be very glad for him to sit with our Chiefs of Staff frequently and to have the whole scene laid before him. But I made it clear that our Chiefs of Staff would more often have to sit together to consider our position from the British point of view, just as your Chiefs of Staff sit together in Washington. It would not fall to him to give decisions outside the sphere of "Overlord". The control of all our combined operations and world strategy must rest with the Combined Chiefs of Staff in Washington, under the final direction of the heads of Governments. Please let me know whether there is anything wrong with this.

A few days later I addressed myself to the President.

1 Oct 43
I am somewhat worried by the way in which our great changes in the High Commands are being broken to the public. So far nothing

* *I Was There* (Gollancz), p. 227.

has been said here, but almost every day some statement is made in the United States about Marshall, and I shall certainly be asked questions when Parliament meets on Tuesday, the 12th. Moreover, it would be difficult for me if Marshall's appointment to the Chief Command in Britain were to be announced apart from Alexander's succession in the Mediterranean. Rumour runs riot, and is fed by carefully balanced and guarded statements, such as that made by Stimson reported in to-day's papers. An impression of mystery and of something to be concealed is given. This is a fine field for malicious people. All this would be blown away by publication of the clear-cut decisions to which we have come. In all the circumstances I hope you will see your way to a simultaneous announcement by us both of the changes, coupled with a statement that they will be brought into effect as soon as convenient to the military situation.

2. Will you also consider my difficulties in the consequential appointments. For instance, I understood that Marshall would like Montgomery for Deputy, or, alternatively, to command under him the British expeditionary armies in "Overlord". This would entail my clearing the Home Command here, now held by General Paget. An opportunity is now open for this, as General Pownall, who was formerly Commander-in-Chief Iraq and Persia, goes with Mountbatten to India as Chief of Staff, and I can post Paget to Iraq and Persia. It is difficult and also harmful to leave these commands vacant for long.

3. Some of the United States papers seem to have begun attacking Mountbatten bitterly, and he has been affected by accounts telegraphed here describing him as "the British princeling and glamour boy who has ousted the proved veteran MacArthur from his rightful sphere", or words to that effect. The prominence given to the Indian Front command by these controversies is of course leading the Japanese to reinforce in that quarter, and intelligence to this effect has already been received. We are told that a large number of correspondents are proceeding or trying to proceed from the United States to Delhi, and that expectation is rife of an early beginning of the campaign. On the other hand, the floods and the monsoon rains will of course prevent any decisive action till the New Year. But this cannot be stated publicly without relieving any anxieties of the Japanese. The prospect of having a formidable band of correspondents champing their bits in Delhi is not a pleasant one, and it would help our fighting chances if everything possible could be done to damp down controversy and publicity in this area.

4. In these circumstances a plain statement of what we have settled for all theatres, including commanders, their Chiefs of Staff, and one

or two of the principal officers, all brought out together, would in my opinion be a great advantage. I could, if you desire, draft such a statement and submit it to you.

The President replied:

President Roosevelt to Prime Minister   5 Oct 43

The newspapers here, beginning with the Hearst-McCormick crowd, had a field day over General Marshall's duties. The drums were beaten rather loudly by the rest of the Press for a few days, but it is pretty much of a dead cat now. It seems to me that if we are forced into making public statements about our military commands we will find ourselves with the newspapers running the war. I therefore hope that nothing will be said about the business until it is actually accomplished. It may be that the situation, other than newspaper criticism by our political enemies, will warrant a joint announcement sooner than I have anticipated, but at the moment I earnestly urge that we say nothing. I agree with you that at the appropriate time we must make an overall statement relative to commands, and I fully appreciate your position at home, but I do not think that the difficulties about secondary commands throughout the world are adequate reasons for making the major announcement in regard to Marshall.

I will do what I can about Mountbatten, because I realise that some of our Press have been treating him very badly, although, on the whole, he has come out of it very well. Certainly American public opinion thoroughly approves of his appointment. I agree with you that we should not permit any undue optimism about this [Burma] campaign either at home or abroad. Nevertheless there is a very proper feeling that Mountbatten will prosecute vigorously anything he is assigned to do.

I hope very much that you will agree that statement about Marshall need not be made at present.

I found the delay in the American decision embarrassing, and on October 17 I cabled to the President, "It seems to me that it is becoming very necessary to have a decision about the High Commands. Unless there is a German collapse, the campaign of 1944 will be far the most dangerous we have undertaken, and personally I am more anxious about its success than I was about 1941, 1942, or 1943."

Nearly a fortnight passed before I received an answer, and then it was indeterminate.

President Roosevelt to Prime Minister   30 Oct 43

Preparations for "Overlord" seem to have reached a stage from which progress is difficult unless and until the Commander is appointed. As you know, I cannot make Marshall available immediately. I am none the less anxious that preparations proceed on schedule agreed at "Quadrant", with target date May 1. I suggest you may care to consider the early appointment of British Deputy Supreme Commander for "Overlord", who, in receipt of precisely the same measure of support as will eventually be accorded to Marshall, could well carry the work forward. If I may make proposal, I suggest appointment of Dill, Portal, or Brooke.

*   *   *   *   *

By the beginning of November we became aware that the President himself and his advisers desired that the Supreme Commander of "Overlord" should also command the Mediterranean, and that the President's idea was that Marshall should command both theatres, and play them in one with another. I presumed that this would be from a headquarters at Gibraltar. I thought it necessary to make the British position clear without delay. As the matter was not suited at this stage for a direct interchange between me and the President, I thought it better to tell Field-Marshal Sir John Dill to talk about it to Admiral Leahy, the chairman of the American Chiefs of Staff Committee.

Prime Minister to Field-Marshal Dill (Washington)   8 Nov 43

You should leave Admiral Leahy in no doubt that we should never be able to agree to the proposal of putting the "Overlord" and Mediterranean commands under an American Commander-in-Chief. Such an arrangement would not be conformable to the principle of equal status which must be maintained among the great Allies. I cannot accept a combination of the two commands under one Commander-in-Chief. This would place him above the Combined Chiefs of Staff, and would also affect the constitutional control of the movements of forces by the President as United States Commander-in-Chief and by the Prime Minister acting on behalf of the War Cabinet. I should certainly never be able to accept responsibility for such an arrangement. Hitherto we have successfully prevented any carping here at the fact that we have been fighting and sustaining casualties in Tunis, Sicily, and Italy on something like a two-and-a-half-to-one basis, although we are serving loyally under a United States general. If I were to attempt to propose anything such as is suggested above there would be an explosion. However, this will not occur while I hold my present office. You may at your discretion impart the above to Mr. Hopkins.

The next day Dill saw Leahy, and made my attitude towards

the unification of the "Overlord" and Mediterranean commands quite clear. Leahy, though personally disappointed, accepted the position, saying, "If that is the opinion of the Prime Minister there is nothing more to be said about it." Dill also saw Hopkins, whom he reported as similarly "disappointed". "At any rate," said Dill, "Hopkins and Leahy know how useless it would be to return to the charge, and I hope they won't."

*　　*　　*　　*　　*

I had hardly got home after my visits to the Citadel, the White House, and Hyde Park during the Quebec Conference, already described, when I turned again to the theme of a meeting of the three heads of Governments which logically followed the Anglo-American conversations. In principle there was general agreement that this was urgent and imperative, but no one who did not live through it can measure the worries and complications which attended the fixing of the time, place, and conditions of this, the first conference of what were then called the Big Three. I give a full account here, because the tale is at least a diplomatic curiosity.

I addressed myself first to Stalin, who, I knew, favoured the idea of a rendezvous at Teheran.

Prime Minister to Premier Stalin　　　　　　　　　　　　　25 Sept 43

I have been pondering about our meeting of heads of Governments at Teheran. Good arrangements must be made for security in this somewhat loosely controlled area. Accordingly I suggest for your consideration that I make preparations at Cairo in regard to accommodation, security, etc., which are bound to be noticed in spite of all praiseworthy efforts to keep them secret. Then perhaps only two or three days before our meeting we should throw a British and a Russian brigade around a suitable area in Teheran, including the airfield, and keep an absolute cordon till we have finished our talks. . . . Thus we shall have an effective blind for the world Press, and also for any unpleasant people who might not be as fond of us as they ought.

2. I suggest also that we use the expression "Cairo Three" instead of Teheran, which should be buried, and also that the code-name for the operation should be "Eureka", which I believe is Ancient Greek. If you have other ideas let me know, and we can then put them to the President. I have not said anything to him about this aspect yet.

Stalin's reply was direct and positive.

Premier Stalin to Premier Churchill   3 Oct 43

I have no objection to the diversionary preparations which you intend to carry out in Cairo. Regarding your proposal to throw British and Russian brigades into the region of "Cairo Three" several days before our meeting in that city, I find this measure inexpedient, as it would cause an unnecessary sensation and would decamouflage the preparations. I suggest that each of us should take with him a sufficient police guard. In my opinion this would be enough to secure our safety. . . .

In fact a complete cordon was established, and the military and police forces used, especially by the Russians, were numbered by thousands.

        ★   ★   ★   ★   ★

As I could not be sure whether the President would be allowed by his security advisers to go to Teheran, I suggested alternatives. One of these was a desert encampment around the Air Force Training School at Habbaniya, which had made so brilliant a defence in 1941. Here we should have been absolutely by ourselves and in perfect security, and the President would have had no difficulty in flying thither in a few hours from Cairo. I therefore telegraphed this proposal to him.

Former Naval Person to President Roosevelt   14 Oct 43

I have a new idea about "Eureka", which I have asked Anthony [then on his way to Moscow] to try on Uncle Joe for subsequent submission to you if U.J. agrees. There is a place in the desert which I now call "Cyprus", but whose real name is Habbaniya. This would be a much easier journey for you from Cairo than "Cairo Three", and very little longer for U.J. We could put up three encampments and live comfortably in perfect seclusion and security. I am going into details on the chance of agreement in the trinity. See also, meanwhile, St. Matthew, chapter xvii, verse 4.

President Roosevelt to Prime Minister   15 Oct 43

I have finally sent the following telegram to Uncle Joe, and I think your idea is an excellent one. St. Peter sometimes had real inspirations. I like the idea of three tabernacles. We can add one later for your old friend Chiang.

"The problem of my going to Teheran is becoming so acute that I feel I should tell you frankly that, for constitutional reasons, I cannot take the risk. The Congress will be in session. New laws and resolutions must be acted on by me after their receipt, and must be returned to the Congress physically before ten days have elapsed. None of this can be done by radio or cable. Teheran is too far to be sure that the requirements are fulfilled. The possibility of delay in getting over the mountains—first east-bound and then west-bound—is insurmountable. We know from experience that planes in either direction are often held up for three or four days. . . .

"In many ways Cairo is attractive, and I understand there are a hotel and some villas out near the Pyramids which could be completely segregated.

"Asmara, the former Italian capital of Eritrea, is said to have excellent buildings, and a landing-field good at all times.

"Then there is the possibility of meeting at some port in the Eastern Mediterranean, each one of us to have a ship. . . . Another suggestion is in the neighbourhood of Baghdad. . . .

"In any event, I think the Press should be entirely banished, and the whole place surrounded by a cordon so that we would not be disturbed in any way.

"I am placing a very great importance on the personal and intimate conversations which you and Churchill and I will have, for on them the hope of the future world will greatly depend.

"Your continuing initiative along your whole front heartens all of us."

Prime Minister to President Roosevelt   16 Oct 43

I entirely agree with the telegram you have sent to U.J. about "Eureka". Let me know what he replies.

Stalin was however adamant on Teheran.

President Roosevelt to Prime Minister   21 Oct 43

Last night I received the following from U.J.:

". . . Unfortunately, not one of the places proposed instead of Teheran by you for the meeting is suitable to me. It became clear during the operations of the Soviet forces in the summer and fall of this year that the summer campaign may overgrow into a winter one and that our troops can continue their offensive operations against the German Army. It is considered by all my colleagues that these operations demand my personal contact with the command and daily guidance on the part of the Supreme Command. Conditions are better in Teheran, because wire telegraph and telephone communications with Moscow exist there. This cannot be said about the other locations. My colleagues insist on Teheran as the place of the meeting for this reason.

"I accept your suggestion of November 20 or 25 as a possible date for the Conference, and I also agree that representatives of the Press should be excluded from the meeting. I hope that a great deal of good will be accomplished by the direct participation in the Moscow meeting of Mr. Hull, who has arrived safely in Moscow."

The President had replied at once:

I am deeply disappointed in your message received to-day in regard to our meeting. I fully understand your reason for requiring daily guidance on the part of the Supreme Command, and your personal contact with the command, which is bringing such outstanding results. . . .

I wish you would realise that there are other vital matters which, in this constitutional American Government, represent fixed obligations on my part which I cannot change. Our Constitution calls for action by the President on legislation within ten days of the passage of such legislation. That means that the President must receive and return to the Congress with his written approval or his veto physical documents in that period. I cannot act by cable or radio, as I have told you before. The trouble with Teheran is the simple fact that the approaches to that city over the mountains often make flying an impossibility for several days at a time. This is a double risk—first, for the plane delivering documents from Washington, and, second, for the plane returning these documents to the Congress. I regret to say that, as head of the nation, it is impossible for me to go to a place where I cannot fulfil my constitutional obligations. I can assume the flying risks for documents up to and including the low country as far as the Persian Gulf, through a relay system of planes, but I cannot assume the delays attending flights in both directions into the saucer over the mountains in which Teheran lies. Therefore, with much regret I must tell you that I cannot go to Teheran, and in this my Cabinet members and the legislative leaders are in complete agreement.

The President suggested Basra.

I am not in any way considering the fact that from United States territory I would have to travel 6,000 miles, and you would only have to travel 600 miles from Russian territory. I would gladly go ten times the distance to meet you were it not for the fact that I must carry on a constitutional Government more than one hundred and fifty years old. . . . I am begging you to remember that I also have a great obligation to the American Government and to maintain the full American war effort.

As I have said to you before, I regard the meeting of the three of us as of the greatest possible importance, not only to our peoples as of to-day, but also to our peoples in relation to a peaceful world for generations to come. It would be regarded as a tragedy by future generations if you and I and Mr. Churchill failed to-day because of a few hundred miles. . . .

Mr. Eden was still in Moscow, and was doing all he could to extract from Stalin an agreed place and time of meeting which would satisfy the President. It was clear that Stalin would insist on Teheran as the place of meeting, and, although it was yet by no means certain that the President would be induced to go there, I began to consider the planning of such a meeting.

* * * * *

Several serious aspects of the impending Conference absorbed my mind. I thought it most important that the British and American Staffs, and above them the President and I, should reach a general agreement on the policy of "Overlord" and its impingement on the Mediterranean. The whole armed strength overseas of our two countries was involved, and the British forces were to be equal at the outset of "Overlord", twice as strong as the Americans in Italy, and three times as numerous in the rest of the Mediterranean. Surely we ought to reach some solid understanding before inviting the Soviet representatives, either political or military, to join us.

I therefore suggested such a plan to the President.

President Roosevelt to Prime Minister　　　　　　　　　22 Oct 43

. . . There should be sufficient time allowed to analyse the results of the current Moscow Conference, and also I think the subsequent Conference we have in mind. For us to stage a meeting while the Moscow Conference is in progress, or at least before its results can be carefully considered, probably would have unfavourable results in Russia.

2. Combined planning teams are now planning an overall plan for the defeat of Japan. It is important that this work be completed and that the respective Chiefs of Staff have an opportunity to study it before a general meeting.

3. Certain outline plans from Eisenhower and commanders in the Pacific covering operations approved at Quebec are to be submitted on November 1, and these should receive some consideration before we arrive at the moment for a combined meeting. . . .

The President thus appeared to favour the idea, but not the timing. There was emerging a strong current of opinion in American Government circles which seemed to wish to win

Russian confidence even at the expense of co-ordinating the Anglo-American war effort. I therefore returned to the charge. I felt it of the utmost importance that we should meet the Russians with a clear and united view both on the outstanding problems of "Overlord" and upon the question of the High Commands.

Former Naval Person to President Roosevelt 23 Oct 43

The Russians ought not to be vexed if the Americans and British closely concert the very great operations they have in hand for 1944 on fronts where no Russian troops will be present. Nor do I think we ought to meet Stalin, if ever the meeting can be arranged, without being agreed about Anglo-American operations as such.

2. I would be content with November 15 if this is the earliest date for your Staffs. I thought the Staffs would work together for a few days before you and I arrive, say 18th or 19th, and we could then go on together to "Eureka". I do not yet know whether it is to be November 20 or 25. I had not imagined that "Eureka" would take more than three or four days or that large technical staffs would take part in it.

3. November 15 would be ninety days from the beginning of our Conference at Quebec. In these ninety days events of first magnitude have occurred. Mussolini has fallen; Italy has surrendered; her Fleet has come over; we have successfully invaded Italy, and are marching on Rome with good prospects of success. The Germans are gathering up to twenty-five or more divisions in Italy and the Po valley. All these are new facts.

4. . . . The date of "Overlord" itself was fixed by splitting the difference between the American and British view. It is arguable that neither the forces building up in Italy nor those available for a May "Overlord" are strong enough for the tasks set them.

5. The British Staffs and my colleagues and I all think this position requires to be reviewed, and that the commanders for both our fronts should be named and should be present. In pursuance of the Quebec decisions we have already prepared two of our best divisions, the 50th and the 51st, now in Sicily, for transfer to England. Thus they can play no part in the Italian battle to which they stood so near, but will not come into action again for seven months, and then only if certain hypothetical conditions are fulfilled. Early in November a decision must be taken about moving landing-craft from the Mediterranean to "Overlord". This will cripple Mediterranean operations without the said craft influencing events elsewhere for many months. We stand by what was agreed at Quebec, but we do not feel that such agreement

should be interpreted rigidly and without review in the swiftly changing situations of war.

6. Personally I feel that if we make serious mistakes in the campaign of 1944 we might give Hitler the chance of a startling come-back. Prisoner German General von Thoma was overheard saying, "Our only hope is that they come where we can use the Army upon them." All this shows the need for the greatest care and foresight in our arrangements, the most accurate timing between the two theatres, and the need to gather the greatest possible forces for both operations, particularly "Overlord". I do not doubt our ability in the conditions laid down to get ashore and deploy. I am however deeply concerned with the build-up and with the situation which may arise between the thirtieth and sixtieth days. I feel sure that the vast movement of **American** personnel into the United Kingdom and the fighting composition of the units requires to be searchingly examined by the commander who will execute "Overlord".

I wish to have both the High Commands settled in a manner agreeable to our two countries, and then the secondary commands, which are of very high importance, can be decided. I repeat I have the greatest confidence in General Marshall, and that if he is in charge of "Overlord" we British will aid him with every scrap of life and strength we have. My dear friend, this is much the greatest thing we have ever attempted, and I am not satisfied that we have yet taken the measures necessary to give it the best chance of success. I feel very much in the dark at present, and unable to think or act in the forward manner which is needed. For these reasons I desire an early conference.

7. All that you say about the plans for Eisenhower and the commanders in the Pacific which are due to be submitted on November 1 would harmonise with a meeting on November 15 at latest. I do not know how long you consider is required for the long-term overall plan for the defeat of Japan to be completed by the combined planners and studied by our respective Chiefs of Staff. I do not consider that the more urgent decisions to which I have referred above ought to be held up for this long-term view of the war against Japan, which nevertheless should be pressed forward with all energy.

8. I hope you will consider that these reasons for [an Anglo-American] meeting are solid. We cannot decide finally until an answer is received from U.J. Should the Teheran meeting not be possible it makes it all the more necessary that we should meet in the light of the information now being received from the Moscow Conference [of Foreign Secretaries]. I am expecting Anthony to start home before the end of the month, and am ready myself to move any day after the first week in November.

9. You will, I am sure, share my relief that Leros has so far managed to hold out. "The dogs eat of the crumbs which fall from their masters' table."

* * * * *

Before the President replied to this proposal he sent me the following message, which showed that he was not yet decided to accept the idea of going to Teheran.

President Roosevelt to Prime Minister 25 Oct 43

It is a nuisenza to have the influenza. McIntire says I need a sea voyage.

No word from Uncle J. yet.

If he is adamant what would you think of you and me meeting with small staffs in North Africa, or even at the Pyramids, and toward the close of our talks getting the Generalissimo [Chiang Kai-shek] to join us for two or three days? At the same time we could ask Uncle J. to send Molotov to the meeting with you and me. Our people propose November 20.

Two days later he sent me his comments on my idea of a preliminary meeting of the Combined Chiefs of Staff.

President Roosevelt to Prime Minister 27 Oct 43

The present Moscow Conference appears to be a genuine beginning of British-Russian-United States collaboration, which should lead to the early defeat of Hitler. . . .

He suggested sending Stalin the following:

Heretofore we have informed you of the results of our combined British-American military Staff Conferences. You may feel that it would be better to have a Russian military representative sit in at such meetings to listen to the discussions regarding British-American operations and take note of the decisions. He would be free to make such comments and proposals as you might desire. This arrangement would afford you and your staff an intimate and prompt report of these meetings. . . .

The suggestion of including the Russians in such a meeting filled me with alarm.

Former Naval Person to President Roosevelt 27 Oct 43

Like you I rejoice in the good progress made at Moscow, and I greatly hope we may arrange "Eureka".

2. I deprecate the idea of inviting a Russian military representative to sit in at the meetings of our Joint Staffs. Unless he understood and

spoke English the delays would be intolerable. I do not know of any really high officer of the Russian Army who can speak English. Such a representative would have no authority or power to speak except as instructed. He would simply bay for an earlier Second Front and block all other discussions. Considering they tell us nothing of their own movements, I do not think we should open this door to them, as it would probably mean that they would want to have observers at all future meetings and all discussions between us would be paralysed. We shall very soon have six or seven hundred thousand British and American troops and airmen in Italy, and we are planning the great operation of "Overlord". There will not be a Russian soldier in any of these. On the other hand, all our fortunes depend upon them.

I regard our right to sit together on the movements of our own two forces as fundamental and vital. Hitherto we have prospered wonderfully, but I now feel that the year 1944 is loaded with danger. Great differences may develop between us and we may take the wrong turning. Or, again, we may make compromises and fall between two stools. The only hope is the intimacy and friendship which has been established between us and between our High Staffs. If that were broken I should despair of the immediate future. . . . I need scarcely say the British Chiefs of Staff fully share these views. I must add that I am more anxious about the campaign of 1944 than about any other in which I have been involved.

* * * * *

The President was still unsure about going to Teheran, and strong pressure was being brought to bear on him in American political circles and his position under the United States Constitution was invoked. I fully appreciated his difficulties.

Prime Minister to President Roosevelt   30 Oct 43

I will meet you in Cairo on the 20th as you suggest, and will, if you will allow me, assume responsibility for making all arrangements for your general security and comfort which would fall upon us as the Occupying Power. Casey has been lent a beautiful villa, which I have seen myself, and am sure would be in every way suitable for you. It is a mile or two from the Pyramids, and surrounded by woods affording complete seclusion. It can be reached from the airfield in twenty minutes without going through any towns. The whole area can be easily cordoned off by British troops. There are some very interesting excursions into the desert which we could make together. I have no doubt Casey would be delighted to place the villa at your disposal. I should probably myself stay at the British Embassy in Cairo, which is perhaps twenty minutes away, but it may be that arrangements could be made for us both to be in the Pyramids area. I believe your Mr. Kirk also has a very fine house. Every facility exists in Cairo for the full Staffs to be accommodated and to meet for business, and they can easily come out to your villa whenever desired. If you like this plan, which, knowing the lay-out, I consider far the best, I will immediately make all preparations, and perhaps you would send an officer to make sure everything is arranged to your liking. . . .

Our plans now began to take shape.

President Roosevelt to Prime Minister   31 Oct 43
Hull's departure from Moscow has meant two days' delay in his getting home. It is essential I see him before I myself leave, as you can readily understand. I had hoped to get three days in North Africa before reaching Cairo. I can however do some of the North African and Italian business on the way back. Therefore I still hope to arrive Cairo by the 20th by flying there directly I reach the harbour. But if wind and weather are bad I might not make Cairo until the 22nd. I think my ship will take me to Oran.

Ever so many thanks for offering to make arrangements at Cairo, which we accept with pleasure. If any hitch develops there we can of course meet in Alexandria, the Staff living ashore and we on our respective ships.

I am wiring Generalissimo [Chiang Kai-shek] to prepare to meet us in the general neighbourhood of Cairo about November 25.

Prime Minister to President   31 Oct 43
Everything will be ready for Operation Sextant ★ from 20th onwards, and Colonel Warden will await Admiral Q and also Celestes†
at rendezvous. No difficulty about accommodation for Staffs.

Eden told me that there was no question of being able to move Stalin from the Teheran proposal. I made therefore every effort to smooth the way.

Prime Minister to General Ismay (Moscow)   1 Nov 43
Reason which prevents triple meeting at "Cairo Three" [Teheran] is said to be possible interruptions of flying over the mountains between Cairo and "Cairo Three", thus putting Admiral Q [President Roosevelt] constitutionally out of touch for transmission of documents. Pray probe the weather facts on the spot, and also let me know whether there is a road from Teheran into Syria, and how long a motor-car would take to travel it with dispatches, which could be brought on by air once south of the mountains. If I could convince Admiral Q

★ Our code-name for the Conference between Britain, the United States, and China.
† "Your humble servant, yourself, and the Generalissimo respectively."

that there would be no interruption in the movement of dispatches our original plan might again be valid.

I now tried a last expedient, namely, that the President and I should meet at Oran in our respective battleships, and that the two Staffs should have a preliminary consultation of four days at Malta. This failed, but the President decided to start in his battleship. He now proposed that the Combined Chiefs of Staff should meet in Cairo before any contact was made with the Russians or the Chinese, whose presence in Cairo had been so strongly urged by him. But the first possible date for a meeting of the Combined Chiefs of Staff would be November 22. The Americans were proposing that the Chinese delegation should arrive on that day, and their presence would inevitably lead to their being drawn into our discussions. I further learned indirectly that the President was simultaneously inviting Molotov to Cairo. I therefore sent the following messages to the President:

Prime Minister to President Roosevelt   11 Nov 43
There seems to have been a most unfortunate misunderstanding. I thought from your telegram that the British and American Staffs would have "many meetings" before being joined by the Russians or Chinese. But now I hear from Ambassador Clark Kerr that on November 9 the United States Ambassador at Moscow delivered a message from you to Stalin inviting Monsieur Molotov to go to Cairo on November 22 with a military representative. November 22 is however the first day on which the Staffs can meet. I ask therefore that the date of the arrival of Molotov and his military representative shall be postponed till November 25 at the earliest.

2. I am very glad to hear also from Ambassador Clark Kerr that you contemplate going on November 26 to Teheran. I rather wish you had been able to let me know direct.

I wished the proceedings to take three stages: first, a broad Anglo-American agreement at Cairo; secondly, a Supreme Conference between the three heads of the Governments of the three major Powers at Teheran; and, thirdly, on returning to Cairo, the discussion of what was purely Anglo-American business about the war in the Indian theatre and the Indian Ocean, which was certainly urgent. I did not want the short time we had at our disposal to be absorbed in what were after all comparatively minor matters, when the decision involving the course of the whole war demanded at least provisional settlement. It seemed also unsuitable that the Soviets should be formally brought into conference with the Chinese Government when they had not declared war against Japan.

"It is very difficult," I wrote to Stalin on the 11th, "to settle things by triangular correspondence, especially when people are moving by sea and air." Some of the difficulties, happily, cancelled each other out.

President Roosevelt to Prime Minister   12 Nov 43

I have just heard that Uncle J. will come to Teheran. . . . I wired him at once that I had arranged the constitutional matter here, and therefore that I could go to Teheran for a short meeting with him, and told him I was very happy. Even then I was in doubt as to whether he would go through with his former offer to go to Teheran. His latest message has clinched the matter, and I think that now there is no question that you and I can meet him there between the 27th and the 30th. Thus endeth a very difficult situation, and I think we can be happy.

In regard to Cairo, I have held all along, as I know you have, that it would be a terrible mistake if Uncle J. thought we had ganged up on him on military action. During the preliminary meetings in Cairo the Combined Staffs will, as you know, be in the planning stage. That is all. It will not hurt you or me if Molotov and a Russian military representative are in Cairo too. They will not feel that they are being given the "run around". They will have no Staff and no Planners. Let us take them in on the high spots.

It is only five hours ago that I received Uncle J.'s telegram confirming Teheran. Undoubtedly Molotov and the military representative will return there with us between the 27th and the 30th, and when and after we have completed our talk with Uncle J. they will return with us to Cairo, possibly adding other military staff to the one representative accompanying Molotov on the first trip.

I think it essential that this schedule be carried out. I can assure you there will be no difficulties.

I am just off. Happy landing to us both.

Prime Minister to President Roosevelt   12 Nov 43

I am very pleased that you have managed to arrange the constitutional matter and that our meeting is now definitely arranged. That is a great step forward.

2. The Chiefs of Staff are however very apprehensive about the arrangements which you have settled for military conversations, and I share their misgivings. I thought from your message that the British and American Staffs would have "many meetings" before being joined

by the Russians or Chinese. I still regard this as absolutely essential in view of the serious questions which have to be settled. There is no objection to you and me seeing Molotov before our meeting with U.J., but the presence of a Soviet military observer so early in the Conference may cause grave embarrassment. His Majesty's Government cannot abandon their rights to full and frank discussions with you and your officers about the vital business of our intermingled armies. A Soviet observer cannot possibly be admitted to the intimate conversations which our own Chiefs of Staff must have, and his exclusion may easily cause offence. None of these objections would have applied to the formal Triple Staff Conference which I suggested should take place in due course.

In the end this danger was removed by the President's invitation to Chiang Kai-shek. Nothing would induce Stalin to compromise his relations with the Japanese by entering a four-Power conference with their three enemies. All question of Soviet representatives coming to Cairo was thus negatived. This was in itself a great relief. It was obtained however at a serious inconvenience and subsequent cost.

Premier Stalin to Premier Churchill   12 Nov 43

Although I wrote to the President that M. Molotov would come to Cairo on November 22, now I must say however that for certain reasons of serious character M. Molotov, to my regret, cannot come to Cairo. He will be able to come to Teheran at the end of November, and will arrive there together with me. Several military men will also accompany me.

It stands to reason that a meeting of the heads of only three Governments must take place at Teheran as it had been agreed. There should be absolutely excluded the participation of the representatives of any other Powers.

I wish success to your meeting with the Chinese concerning the Far Eastern affairs.

It was in this manner that our arrangements took final shape, and we started on our journeys.

BOOK II

TEHERAN TO ROME

CHAPTER XVIII

CAIRO

Voyage in the "Renown" – A Stay at Malta – Khartoum an Impossible Meeting-place – We All Gather Round the Pyramids – The President Arrives – I Meet Chiang Kai-shek and His Wife – My Indictment of Our Mismanagement of Military Operations Since Salerno – Unreal Division of Forces and Responsibilities in the Mediterranean – German Mastery of the Eastern Ægean – The Shadow of "Overlord" – The First Plenary Meeting of the Cairo Conference, November 23 – Chiang Kai-shek's Request for British Naval Support – Our Second Meeting, November 24 – Mr. Eden Joins Us after Conference with the Turks – The Question of the High Command – United States Proposal for One Supreme Commander Against Germany – Adverse Memorandum by the British Chiefs of Staff – I Support Them – Our Allies Remain Silent – A Family Party on Thanksgiving Day, November 25 – Off for Teheran, November 27.

ON the afternoon of November 12 I sailed in the *Renown* from Plymouth with my personal staff on a journey which was to keep me from England for more than two months. With me came Mr. Winant, the American Ambassador, Admiral Cunningham, First Sea Lord, and General Ismay and other members of the Defence Office. I was feeling far from well, as a heavy cold and sore throat were reinforced by the consequences of inoculations against typhoid and cholera. I stayed in bed for several days. My Cabinet colleagues had expressed the kindly wish that my daughter Sarah should come with me, and it gave me pleasure to defer to their request. She was serving in the Air Force, and became my aide-de-camp. We had an uneventful voyage across the Bay, and I was able to go on deck as we passed the Straits of Gibraltar. While we stopped for a few

hours at Algiers on the 16th I had a long talk with General
Georges about the French situation in Africa. As darkness fell
we resumed our course for Malta, which we reached on the 17th.

Here I found Generals Eisenhower and Alexander, and other
important personages. After the conclusion of the Tunisian
campaign I had suggested to the King that General Alexander
should receive the distinction of the North Africa ribbon with the
numerals 1 and 8 upon it, representing the two victorious British
armies of the campaign. I felt that as Eisenhower had been the
Supreme Commander this was also his by right, and I sought and
obtained the King's approval. I had the honour of investing these
two Commanders with this unique decoration. They were both
taken by surprise, and seemed highly gratified when I pinned
the ribbons on their coats. I arrived in Malta quite ill with a
new cold and temperature, but I had sufficient strength to attend
the dinner at the Governor's war-time palace, the real one being
uninhabitable from bombardment.

Although I continued to conduct business without cessation
I had to remain in bed all the time I was in Malta, except for a
Staff conference and a final tour of the frightfully battered dockyard, where the whole of the people and workmen gathered with
great enthusiasm. At midnight on November 19 we sailed again
on our voyage to Alexandria.

A telegram had reached me from the President saying that his
security advisers thought that Cairo was too dangerous for the
Conference. They feared a German air attack from Greece or
Rhodes, and suggested Khartoum instead. Roosevelt of course
had nothing to do with this himself, as he was entirely indifferent
to his personal safety. Khartoum would have been quite unequal
to handling the great staffs we were bringing, amounting altogether to nearly five hundred. I therefore asked Ismay to examine
the resources of Malta. He reported that owing to air damage the
accommodation was not only inadequate for our considerable
gathering, but also extremely primitive. I therefore decided that
we had better stick to Cairo, where all arrangements had been
perfected. The eight squadrons of British aircraft based on
Alexandria would certainly intercept and destroy any German
attack. The enclave near the Pyramids which we were to
occupy was to be guarded by more than a brigade of infantry,
and there were upwards of five hundred anti-aircraft guns hard

by. Accordingly I wirelessed the *Iowa*, which was bringing the President across the ocean:

Prime Minister to President   21 Nov 43
  See St. John, chapter xiv, verses 1 to 4.

On reading this through more carefully after it had gone I was a little concerned lest, apart from a shadow of unintended profanity, it should be thought I was taking too much upon myself and thus giving offence. However, the President brushed all objections aside and our plans continued unchanged. In the event no German aeroplanes ever came within several hundred miles of the Pyramids.

    ★   ★   ★   ★   ★

The *Renown* reached Alexandria on the morning of November 21, and I flew at once to the desert landing-ground near the Pyramids. Here Mr. Casey had placed at my disposal the agreeable villa he was using. We lay in a broad expanse of Kasserine woods, thickly dotted with the luxurious abodes and gardens of the cosmopolitan Cairo magnates. Generalissimo Chiang Kai-shek and Madame had already been ensconced half a mile away. The President was to occupy the spacious villa of the American Ambassador Kirk, about three miles down the road to Cairo. I went to the desert airfield to welcome him when he arrived in the "Sacred Cow" from Oran the next morning, and we drove to his villa together.

The Staffs congregated rapidly. The headquarters of the Conference and the venue of all the British and American Chiefs of Staff was at the Mena House Hotel, opposite the Pyramids, and I was but half a mile away. The whole place bristled with troops and anti-aircraft guns, and the strictest cordons guarded all approaches. Everyone set to work at once at their various levels upon the immense mass of business which had to be decided or adjusted.

What we had apprehended from Chiang Kai-shek's presence now in fact occurred. The talks of the British and American Staffs were sadly distracted by the Chinese story, which was lengthy, complicated, and minor. Moreover, as will be seen, the President, who took an exaggerated view of the Indian-Chinese sphere, was soon closeted in long conferences with the Generalissimo. All hope of persuading Chiang and his wife to go and see the Pyramids and enjoy themselves till we returned from Teheran fell to the ground, with the result that Chinese business occupied first instead of last place at Cairo. The President, in spite of my arguments, gave the Chinese the promise of a considerable amphibious operation across the Bay of Bengal within the next few months. This would have cramped "Overlord" for landing- and tank-landing craft, which had now become the bottle-neck, far more than any of my Turkey and Ægean projects. It would also have hampered grievously the immense operations we were carrying out in Italy. On November 29 I wrote to the Chiefs of Staff: "The Prime Minister wishes to put on record the fact that he specifically refused the Generalissimo's request that we should undertake an amphibious operation simultaneously with the land operations in Burma." It was not until we returned from Teheran to Cairo that I at length prevailed upon the President to retract his promise. Even so, many complications arose. Of this more anon.

I of course took occasion to visit the Generalissimo at his villa, where he and his wife were suitably installed. This was the first time I had met Chiang Kai-shek. I was impressed by his calm, reserved, and efficient personality. At this moment he stood at the height of his power and fame. To American eyes he was one of the dominant forces in the world. He was the champion of "the New Asia". He was certainly a steadfast defender of China against Japanese invasion. He was a strong anti-Communist. The accepted belief in American circles was that he would be the head of the great Fourth Power in the world after the victory had been won. All these views and values have since been cast aside by many of those who held them. I, who did not in those days share the excessive estimates of Chiang Kai-shek's power or of the future helpfulness of China, may record the fact that the Generalissimo is still serving the same causes which at this time had gained him such wide renown. He has however since been beaten by the Communists in his own country, which is a very bad thing to be.

I had a very pleasant conversation with Madame Chiang Kai-shek, and found her a most remarkable and charming personality. I told her how much I had regretted that we could not find an occasion for a meeting at the time when we had both been in America together, and we agreed that no undue formalities should stand in the way of our talks in the future. The President had us all photographed together at one of our meetings at his villa, and although both the Generalissimo and his wife are now regarded as wicked and corrupt reactionaries by many of their former admirers I am glad to keep this as a souvenir.

★　　★　　★　　★　　★

During the outward voyage I had prepared what was in effect an indictment of our mismanagement of operations in the Mediterranean during the two months which had passed since our victory at Salerno. I gave this to the Chiefs of Staff, and they, while agreeing in principle, made a number of comments in detail upon it. The final version read as follows:

For a year from Alamein and the landings in North-West Africa the British and Americans have had virtually unbroken success in every theatre, and there is no doubt that our methods of war direction, through the Combined Chiefs of Staff, working under the heads of the two Governments, have enabled our commanders in the field to gain resounding victories and achieve solid results. In all the history of alliances there never has been such harmony and mutual comprehension not only in the high direction of the war but among the commanders and troops in the field. Our combined operations from the beginning of the Battle of Alamein to the end of the Battle of Naples and the deployment of the Army in Italy may well be regarded as an extremely well-managed and prosperous affair.

2. However, since then there has been a change. We have been overtaken and in a sense outrun by our own successes. Certain divergences of view, of emphasis rather than principle, have opened between the British and American Staffs. We must not allow ourselves to be prevented by victories already gained from subjecting ourselves severally and jointly to searching self-examination with a view to improving our methods and giving an increasingly high standard of service.

3. Since the successful landing and deployment of the Army in Italy in September the war in the Mediterranean has taken an unsatisfactory course. Both the build-up and advance of the Army in Italy, making allowance for bad weather, must be considered extremely slow. There is not a sufficient preponderance over the enemy in the front line. Many of the divisions have been continuously in action since the landing without any spell of relief. At the same time, two of the best British divisions, the 50th and 51st, which stood in Sicily close to the battlefield, were first stripped of their equipment and have since been

withdrawn to the United Kingdom. It has not been found possible to assist the forward movement of the Army to the extent that might have been hoped by making amphibious scoops along either coast. Some of the vitally needed landing-craft have been sent home, losing heavily from the weather on the way. A large number of others have been withdrawn and assembled in preparation for their homeward journey. These orders have now been arrested till December 15, but this is a useless date for Mediterranean purposes. The landing-craft have done nothing in October and November except assist in bringing vehicles ashore. At the same time the build-up of the Strategic Air Force in Italy has hampered the reinforcement of the fighting front. Thus the whole campaign on land has flagged. There is no prospect of Rome being taken in 1943. . . .

5. Side by side with this we have failed to give any real measure of support to the Partisans and Patriots in Yugoslavia and Albania. These guerrilla forces are containing as many [German] divisions as are the British and American Armies put together. Hitherto they have been nourished only by supplies dropped from the air. It is now more than two months since we have had air and naval superiority in the mouth of the Adriatic, yet no ships with supplies have entered the ports taken by the Partisans. On the contrary, the Germans are systematically driving them from these ports and acquiring mastery of the whole Dalmatian coast. It was not possible to prevent the Germans obtaining Corfu and Argostoli, and they actually hold these islands at the moment. Thus the Germans have weathered the difficulties caused by the Italian collapse and desertion, and with great severity are mopping up many of the Patriot forces and cutting them off from the sea.

6. How has it happened? An imaginary line has been drawn down the Mediterranean which relieves General Eisenhower's armies of all responsibility for the Dalmatian coast and the Balkans. These are assigned to General Wilson, of the Middle East Command, but he does not possess the necessary forces. One command has the forces but not the responsibilities, the other the responsibilities but not the forces. This can hardly be considered an ideal arrangement.

7. Most unfortunate of all has been the Dodecanese and the Ægean. Immediately after the fall of Italy a number of islands held by the Italians were occupied by us with Italian consent. Of these the two most important were Cos and Leros. We did not succeed in getting Rhodes, which is of course the master key to the Ægean. Hitler was not slow to recognise the naval and political importance of the fortress of Leros, which had fallen so cheaply into our hands, and with great stubbornness and tenacity he personally set himself to restore the situation in the Ægean. A very large proportion of the German air forces

which would have been available to fight in Italy was moved into the Ægean theatre, and sea transport was improvised.* It was evident early in October that attacks on Leros and Cos were imminent, and on October 4 Cos, where we had only one battalion, was retaken by the Germans. In spite of unexpectedly prolonged defence Leros fell on November 16, the British losses in the whole business being about 5,000 and the enemy scoring his first success since Alamein. All this of course is outside the parish of the High North African Command....

9. The Germans are now complete masters of the Eastern Ægean. Although already outmatched in the air in Italy, they have not hesitated to reduce their air-power there, and have transferred to the Ægean forces sufficient to dominate this theatre. Although the United States and British air forces in the Mediterranean have a first-line strength of over 4,000—*i.e.*, practically equal to the whole of the German Air Force—the Germans have been able to reproduce in the Ægean theatre all the old technique of the days of our air nakedness, and with their Stuka dive-bombers have broken down the resistance of our best troops and sunk or damaged our ships. . . .

11. There are two causes for these misfortunes. The first has been mentioned—the artificial line of division between East and West in the Mediterranean, absolving the Western commanders, who have the forces, of all responsibility for the vital interests at stake in the East. The second cause of course is the shadow of "Overlord". The decisions at Quebec were taken before the consequences of the collapse of Italy were apparent and before the surrender of the Italian Fleet and the successful invasion of the mainland of Europe. Nevertheless they have been maintained until a fortnight ago with inflexible rigidity. It has not been found possible to meet together earlier. We are now faced with the prospect that a fixed target date for "Overlord" will continue to hamper and enfeeble the Mediterranean campaign, that our affairs will deteriorate in the Balkans, and that the Ægean will remain firmly in German hands. All this is to be accepted for the sake of an operation fixed for May upon hypotheses that in all probability will not be realised at that date, and certainly not if the Mediterranean pressure is relaxed.

12. Nor must we overlook the discouraging and enfeebling effect upon the whole of the operations in the Mediterranean of the fact that it is now common knowledge in the Armies that the theatre is to be bled as much as necessary for the sake of an operation elsewhere in the spring. The fact of troops and landing-craft being withdrawn from the very battlefield and of units being put under orders for home is in itself injurious. The intense desire to concentrate upon the enemy

---

* German records show that during this period their Ægean air forces were increased by nearly three hundred aircraft, while those in Italy were reduced by about two hundred.

which carried us from Alamein and sustained us in Tunisia has been impaired. Yet in the Mediterranean alone are we in contact with the enemy and able to bring superior numbers to bear upon him now. It is certainly an odd way of helping the Russians, to slow down the fight in the only theatre where anything can be done for some months.

* * * * *

The first plenary meeting of the Cairo Conference (which was given the code-name "Sextant") was held at the President's villa on Tuesday, November 23. Its purpose was to outline formally to Chiang Kai-shek and the Chinese delegation the proposed operations in South-East Asia, as drawn up by the Combined Chiefs of Staff at Quebec. Admiral Mountbatten, with his officers, had flown from India, and he first gave a description of the military plans he had been given and was executing for 1944 in that theatre. To this I added the general naval picture. Owing to the surrender of the Italian Fleet and other naval events of a favourable character a British fleet would be established soon in the Indian Ocean. There would be ultimately no fewer than five modernised capital ships, four heavy armoured cruisers, and up to twelve auxiliary carriers. Chiang Kai-shek intervened to say that he thought that the success of operations in Burma depended not only on the strength of our naval forces in the Indian Ocean, but on the simultaneous co-ordination of naval action with land operations. I pointed out that there was no necessary connection between the land campaign and fleet action in the Bay of Bengal. Our main fleet base would be able to exercise its influence in sea-power from areas 2,000 to 3,000 miles away from the scene where the armies were operating. There was therefore no comparison between these operations and those carried out in Sicily, where the Fleet had been able to work in close support of the Army.

This meeting was brief, and it was agreed that Chiang Kai-shek should discuss further details with the Combined Chiefs of Staff.

* * * * *

On the following day a second meeting of our Combined Chiefs of Staff was held by the President, without the presence of the Chinese delegation, to discuss operations in Europe and the Mediterranean. We sought to survey the relations of the two theatres and to exchange our views before going on to Teheran. The President opened upon the effect on "Overlord" of any possible action we could take in the meantime in the Mediterranean, including the problem of Turkey's entry into the war.

When I spoke I said "Overlord" remained top of the bill, but this operation should not be such a tyrant as to rule out every other activity in the Mediterranean; for example, a little flexibility in the employment of landing-craft ought to be conceded. General Alexander had asked that the date of their leaving for "Overlord" should be deferred from mid-December to mid-January. Eighty additional L.S.T.s had been ordered to be built in Britain and Canada. We should try to do even better than this. The points which were at issue between the American and British Staffs would probably be found to affect no more than a tenth of our common resources, apart from the Pacific. Surely some degree of elasticity could be arranged. Nevertheless I wished to remove any idea that we had weakened, cooled, or were trying to get out of "Overlord". We were in it up to the hilt. To sum up, I said that the programme I advocated was to try to take Rome in January and Rhodes in February; to renew supplies to the Yugoslavs, settle the Command arrangements, and to open the Ægean, subject to the outcome of an approach to Turkey; all preparations for "Overlord" to go ahead full steam within the framework of the foregoing policy for the Mediterranean.

This is a faithful record of my position on the eve of Teheran.

* * * * *

Mr. Eden had now joined us from England, whither he had flown after his discussions in Moscow. His arrival was a great help to me. On the way back from the Moscow Conference he and General Ismay had met the Turkish Foreign Minister and other Turks at Cairo. At these talks Mr. Eden pointed out that we had urgent need of air bases in the south-west of Anatolia. He explained that our military situation at Leros and Samos was precarious, owing to German air superiority. Both places had since been lost. Mr. Eden also dwelt on the advantages that would be derived from Turkey's entry into the war. In the first place, it would oblige the Bulgarians to concentrate their forces on the frontier, and thus would compel the Germans to replace Bulgarian troops in Greece and Yugoslavia to the extent of some ten divisions. Secondly, it would be possible to attack the one target which might be decisive—Ploesti. Thirdly, Turkish chrome would be cut off from Germany. Finally, there was the moral advantage. Turkey's entry into the war might well hasten the process of disintegration in Germany and among her satellites. By all this argument the Turkish delegation were unmoved. They said, in effect, that the granting of bases in Anatolia would amount to intervention in the war, and that if they intervened in the war there was nothing to prevent a German retaliation on Constantinople, Angora, and Smyrna. They refused to be comforted by the assurances that we would give them sufficient fighters to deal with any air attack that the Germans could launch and that the Germans were so stretched everywhere that they had no divisions available to attack Turkey. The only result of the discussions was that the Turkish delegation promised to report to their Government. Considering what had been happening under their eyes in the Ægean, the Turks can hardly be blamed for their caution.

*   *   *   *   *

As I had heard no more about the plans for the combined command of "Overlord" and the Mediterranean I assumed that the British view had been accepted. But on November 25, during our stay in Cairo, the proposal for one overall Supreme Command was presented to us by the American Chiefs of Staff in a formal memorandum. From this it was apparent that the President and the American High Command felt strongly that a Supreme Commander should be appointed to command all the United Nations' operations against Germany, both from the Mediterranean and the Atlantic. They still wished to see a commander for North-West European operations, a commander of the Allied forces in the Mediterranean, and above both a supreme figure who would not only plan and conduct the war in both theatres, but move the forces from one to the other as he might think best. It must be remembered that we not only had at that time, and were bound to have for many months to come, a very large superiority in all the forces, Army, Navy, and Air, but also that with Alexander's and Montgomery's victories in Tunis and the Desert our reputation stood high.

The American memorandum immediately encountered strong opposition from the British Chiefs of Staff. Both they and I recorded our views in writing. The rejoinder of the British Chiefs of Staff was as follows:

COMMAND OF BRITISH AND UNITED STATES FORCES OPERATING AGAINST GERMANY

MEMORANDUM BY THE BRITISH CHIEFS OF STAFF

25 Nov 43

The British Chiefs of Staff have given careful consideration to the proposal put forward by the United States Chiefs of Staff that "a Supreme Commander be designated at once to command all United Nations operations against Germany from the Mediterranean and the Atlantic". This proposal has immense political implications, and is clearly a matter for the most earnest consideration of the United States and British Governments. Nevertheless the British Chiefs of Staff must say at once that, from the military point of view, they profoundly disagree with the proposal. Their reasons are set out in the paragraphs that follow.

Total war is not an affair of military forces alone, using the word "military" in the widest sense of the term. There are political, economic, industrial, and domestic implications in almost every big war problem. Thus it seems clear that the Supreme Commander for the war against Germany will have to consult both the United States and the British Governments on almost every important question. In fact, it boils down to this, that he will only be able to make a decision without reference to high authority on comparatively minor and strictly military questions, such as the transfer of one or two divisions, or a few squadrons of aircraft, or a few scores of landing-craft, from one of his many fronts to another. He will thus be an extra and unnecessary link in the chain of command.

There is no real analogy between the position of Marshal Foch in the last war and the position now contemplated for the Supreme Commander against Germany. Marshal Foch was responsible only for the Western Front and the Italian Front. His authority did not extend to the Salonika Front, the Palestine Front, or the Mesopotamian Front. Under the arrangements now contemplated the Supreme Commander will have not only "Overlord" and the Italian Front under his authority, but also the Balkan Front and the Turkish Front (if this is opened). There must be some limit to the responsibilities which Allied Governments can delegate to a single soldier, and the sphere now proposed seems to exceed these limits considerably.

The United States Chiefs of Staff propose that the decisions of the Supreme Commander should be "subject to reversal by the Combined Chiefs of Staff". If the main object of this new arrangement is to ensure rapid decisions, it looks as though the above proviso will lead to deplorable consequences. Instances will occur in which the Supreme Commander has issued orders and the troops have marched in accordance with these orders, only to be followed by a reversal of the order by the Combined Chiefs of Staff and consequent confusion. Again, it may happen that the British Chiefs of Staff agree with a decision taken by the Supreme Commander, while the United States Chiefs of Staff totally disagree with it. What happens then? Or, again, the Combined Chiefs of Staff may wholeheartedly support, on military grounds, a decision taken by the Supreme Commander, only to find that one or other of the Governments concerned is not prepared to ratify it. Then what happens?

If the Supreme Commander is going to exercise real control he will need to assemble the whole paraphernalia of Intelligence, Planning, and Administration on an unprecedented scale. This staff will merely be a great pad between the theatre commanders and the Combined Chiefs of Staff. . . .

If the well-tried machinery that has led us safely through the last two years has failed in the smaller problems, it would be better to examine that machinery and see how it can be speeded up and adjusted, rather than to embark upon an entirely novel experiment, which merely makes a cumbrous and unnecessary link in the chain of command, and which will surely lead to disillusionment and disappointment.

*　　*　　*　　*　　*

The American Chiefs of Staff were impressed by the arguments used. They realised that their proposal meant virtually the end of Combined Chiefs of Staff control, since the Super-Supreme Commander would to a large extent take the authority from their hands. They therefore dropped the subject from the Staff discussions on the understanding that it must be settled between the heads of Governments.

*　　*　　*　　*　　*

I warmly approved of the Chiefs of Staff paper, and developed the arguments still further in a note which I wrote the next day.

SUPREME COMMANDER OF ALL OPERATIONS AGAINST GERMANY

NOTE BY THE PRIME MINISTER AND MINISTER OF DEFENCE

26 Nov 43

The difficulties and shortcomings in our conduct of the war since the Battle of Salerno have arisen from divergences of view between our two Staffs and Governments. It is not seen how these divergences would be removed by the appointment of a Supreme Commander working under the Combined Chiefs of Staff and liable to have his decisions reversed by them. The divergences, which are political as much as military, would still have to be adjusted by the present methods of consultation between the Combined Staffs and the heads of the two Governments. Thus the Supreme Commander, after being acclaimed as the World War winner, would in practice find his functions restricted to the narrow ground between the main decisions of policy and strategy, which can only be dealt with by the present methods, and the spheres of the two chief regional commanders.

2. This would certainly not be sufficient to justify arousing all the expectations and setting up all the apparatus inseparable from the announcement of a "Supreme Commander for the defeat of Germany".

3. On the other hand, if the power of decision is in fact accorded to the Supreme Commander the work of the Combined Chiefs of Staff would be virtually superseded, and very great stresses would immediately arise between the Governments and the Supreme Commander. Without going into personalities, it is greatly to be doubted whether any single officer exists who would be capable of giving decisions over the vast range of problems now dealt with by the heads of Governments assisted by the Combined Chiefs of Staff.

4. The principle which should be followed as far as possible between allies of equal status is that the command in any theatre should go to the ally who has the largest forces deployed or about to be deployed there. On this it would be natural that the command in the Mediterranean should be British and that the command of "Overlord" should be American.

5. If the two commands are merged under a Supreme Commander the British would have available against Germany in May [1944] decidedly larger forces than the United States. It would therefore appear that the Supreme Command should go to a British officer. I should be very reluctant, as head of His Majesty's Government, to place such an invidious responsibility upon a British officer. If, on the other hand, disregarding the preponderance of forces involved, the Supreme Command was given to a United States officer and he pronounced in favour of concentrating on "Overlord" irrespective of the injury done to our affairs in the Mediterranean, His Majesty's Government could not possibly agree. The Supreme Commander, British or American, would therefore be placed in an impossible position. Having assumed before the whole world the responsibility of pronouncing and being overruled by one Government or the other, he would have little choice but to resign. This might bring about a most serious crisis in the harmonious and happy relations hitherto maintained between our two Governments.

6. It is not seen why the present arrangement should not continue,

subject to any minor improvements that can be suggested. Under this arrangement an American commander would conduct the immense cross-Channel operation and a British commander would conduct the war in the Mediterranean, their action being concerted and forces assigned by the Combined Chiefs of Staff, working under the heads of the two Governments. . . . More frequent meetings of the Combined Chiefs of Staff should also be arranged, and possibly monthly visits of one week's duration by the chairman of each Chiefs of Staff Committee alternately to London and Washington.

This paper I handed to the President before we left for Teheran, and I was not aware during the Conference at Teheran what his answer would be. I understood from private sources that the American Chiefs of Staff realised fully the clash of authority that might arise between our Combined Staff organisation and the new supreme general, and that after weighing our arguments they were by no means wedded to the plan. Neither the President nor any of his immediate circle referred to the matter in any way on the occasions, formal and informal but always friendly, when we came into contact. I therefore rested under the impression that General Marshall would command "Overlord", that General Eisenhower would succeed him in Washington, and that it would fall to me, representing His Majesty's Government, to choose the Mediterranean commander, who at that time I had no doubt would be Alexander, already waging the war in Italy. Here the issue rested till we returned to Cairo.

* * * * *

Thanksgiving Day, which fell on November 25, is a feature in American life. Every soldier in the American armies is supposed to eat turkey on that date, and most of them did in 1943. Ample supplies of turkeys for all the United States Staffs at Cairo had been brought out in the President's ship. Mr. Roosevelt invited me to join him at dinner in his villa. "Let us make it a family affair," he said. So Sarah was asked too, and also "Tommy" (Commander Thompson), to whom he had taken a great liking. The President's guests included his personal circle, his son, Elliott, his son-in-law, Major Boettiger, and Harry Hopkins and his son Robert. We had a pleasant and peaceful feast. Two enormous turkeys were brought in with all ceremony. The President, propped up high in his chair, carved for all with masterly, indefatigable skill. As we were about twenty, this took a long time, and those who were helped first had finished before the President had cut anything for himself. As I watched the huge platefuls he distributed to the company I feared that he might be left with nothing at all. But he had calculated to a nicety, and I was relieved, when at last the two skeletons were removed, to see him set about his own share. Harry, who had noted my anxiety, said, "We have ample reserves." Speeches were made of warm and intimate friendship. For a couple of hours we cast care aside. I had never seen the President more gay. After the meal was over we returned to the big room in which we had held so many conferences. Dance music—from gramophone records—began to play. Sarah was the only woman present, and she had her work cut out, so I danced with "Pa" Watson (Roosevelt's trusted old friend and aide), to the delight of his chief, who watched us from the sofa. This jolly evening and the spectacle of the President carving up the turkeys stand out in my mind among the most agreeable features of the halt at Cairo.

★   ★   ★   ★   ★

At last all the puzzles had been solved. The difficulties of the American Constitution, Roosevelt's health, and Stalin's obduracy, the complications of a journey to Basra and the Trans-Persian railway, were all swept away by the inexorable need of a triple meeting, and the failure of every other alternative but a flight to Teheran. So we sailed off into the air from Cairo at crack of dawn on November 27 in perfect weather for the long-sought meeting-place, and arrived safely by different routes at different times.*

---

* I have not broken the thread of the narrative to insert a domestic matter which was a this time causing me concern. The question of the release of the Mosleys is dealt with in Appendix F (p. 635).

CHAPTER XIX

TEHERAN: THE OPENING

Security Arrangements – Recapitulation of My Views – Stalin and the President Confer – The First Plenary Meeting, November 28 – The President Opens the Discussion – Stalin's Account of the Situation on the Soviet Front – I State the British View – The Position of Turkey – Thirty-five Divisions for "Overlord" – Stalin Favours the Invasion of Southern France as the Secondary Objective – I Insist upon the Capture of Rome – The President and the Timing of Operations – The Proper Course for Turkey.

I COULD not admire the arrangements which had been made for my reception after landing in Teheran. The British Minister met me in his car, and we drove from the airfield to our Legation. As we approached the city the road was lined with Persian cavalrymen every fifty yards, for at least three miles. It was clearly shown to any evil people that somebody of consequence was coming, and which way. The men on horseback advertised the route, but could provide no protection at all. A police car driving a hundred yards in advance gave warning of our approach. The pace was slow. Presently large crowds stood in the spaces between the Persian cavalry, and as far as I could see there were few, if any, foot police. Towards the centre of Teheran these crowds were four or five deep. The people were friendly but non-committal. They pressed to within a few feet of the car. There was no kind of defence at all against two or three determined men with pistols or a bomb. As we reached the turning which led to the Legation there was a traffic block, and we remained for three or four minutes stationary amid the crowded throng of gaping Persians. If it had been planned out beforehand to run the greatest risks and have neither the security of quiet surprise arrival nor an effective escort the problem could not

have been solved more perfectly. However, nothing happened.
I grinned at the crowd, and on the whole they grinned at me. In
due course we arrived at the British Legation, which lay within a
strong cordon of British-Indian troops.

The Legation and its gardens lay almost adjoining the Soviet
Embassy, and as the Anglo-Indian brigade entrusted with our
safety was in direct contact with the still larger Russian force that
encircled their own domain both soon joined and we became an
isolated area with all the precautions of war. The American
Legation, which was guarded by United States forces, was a mile
or more away, and this meant that either the President or else
Stalin and I would have to traverse the narrow streets of Teheran
two or three times a day, back and forth, during the Conference.
Meanwhile Molotov, who had been in Teheran twenty-four
hours before our arrival, produced a story that the Soviet Secret
Intelligence had unearthed a plot to kill one or more of the "Big
Three", as we were regarded, and the idea of one or other of us
continually going to and fro through the streets filled him with
deep alarm. "If anything like that were to happen," he said, "it
could produce a most unfortunate impression." This could not
be denied. I strongly supported Molotov in his appeals to the
President to move forthwith inside the Soviet Embassy, which
was three or four times as big as the others, and stood in extensive
grounds, now ringed by Soviet troops and police. We prevailed
upon Mr. Roosevelt to take this good advice, and next afternoon
he moved, with his personal staff, including the excellent Filipino
cooks from his yacht, into the Russian domain, where ample
and comfortable quarters were provided for him. Thus we were
all within a circle, and could discuss the problems of the World
War without any chance of annoyance. I was made very comfortable in the British Legation, and had only to walk a couple of
hundred yards to reach the Soviet palace, which might be said
to be for the time being the centre of the world. I continued to
be far from well, and my cold and sore throat were so vicious
that for a time I could hardly speak. However, Lord Moran with
sprays and ceaseless care enabled me to say what I had to say—
which was a lot.

*　　*　　*　　*　　*

There have been many misleading accounts of the line I took,
with the full agreement of the British Chiefs of Staff, at this

Conference. It has become a legend in America that I strove to prevent the cross-Channel enterprise called "Overlord", and that I tried vainly to lure the Allies into some mass invasion of the Balkans, or a large-scale campaign in the Eastern Mediterranean, which would effectively kill it. Much of this nonsense has already in previous chapters been exposed and refuted, but it may be worth while to set forth what it was I actually sought, and what, in a very large measure, I got.

"Overlord," now planned in great detail, should be launched in May or June, or at the latest in the opening days of July 1944. The troops and all the ships to carry them still had first priority. Secondly, the great Anglo-American army in action in Italy must be nourished to achieve the capture of Rome and advance to secure the airfields north of the capital, from which the air attack on Southern Germany became possible. After these were gained there should be no advance in Italy beyond the Pisa–Rimini line— i.e., we should not extend our front into the broader part of the Italian peninsula. These operations, if resisted by the enemy, would attract and hold very large German forces, would give the Italians the chance to "work their passage", and keep the flame of war burning continually upon the hostile front.

I was not opposed at this time to a landing in the south of France, along the Riviera, with Marseilles and Toulon as objectives, and thereafter an Anglo-American advance northwards up the Rhone valley in aid of the main invasion across the Channel. Alternatively, I preferred a right-handed movement from the north of Italy, using the Istrian peninsula and the Ljubljana Gap, towards Vienna. I was delighted when the President suggested this, and tried, as will be seen, to engage him in it. If the Germans resisted we should attract many of their divisions from the Russian or Channel fronts. If we were not resisted we should liberate at little cost enormous and invaluable regions. I was sure we should be resisted, and thus help "Overlord" in a decisive manner.

My third request was that the Eastern Mediterranean, with all the prizes that it afforded, should not be neglected, provided no strength which could be applied across the Channel should be absorbed. In all this I adhered to the proportions which I had mentioned to General Eisenhower two months earlier—namely, four-fifths in Italy, one-tenth in Corsica and the Adriatic, and

one-tenth in the Eastern Mediterranean. From this I never varied
—not an inch in a year.

We were all agreed, British, Russians, and Americans, upon
the first two, involving nine-tenths of our available strength.
All I had to plead was the effective use of one-tenth of our
strength in the Eastern Mediterranean. Simpletons will argue,
"Would it not have been much better to centre all upon the
decisive operation and dismiss all other opportunities as wasteful diversions?" But this ignores the governing facts. All the
available shipping in the Western Hemisphere was already committed to the last ton to the preparation of "Overlord" and the
maintenance of our front in Italy. Even if more shipping had
been found it could not have been used, because the programmes
of disembarkation filled to the utmost limit all the ports and camps
involved. As for the Eastern Mediterranean, nothing was needed
that could be applied elsewhere. The Air Force massed for the
defence of Egypt could equally well or better discharge its duty
if used from a forward frontier. All the troops, two or three
divisions at the outside, were already in that theatre, and there
were no ships, except local vessels, to carry them to the larger
scenes. To get the active, vigorous use of these forces, who otherwise would be mere lookers-on, might inflict grave injury upon
the enemy. If Rhodes were taken the whole Ægean could be
dominated by our Air Force and direct sea contact established with
Turkey. If, on the other hand, Turkey could be persuaded to
enter the war, or to strain her neutrality by lending us the airfields
we had built for her, we could equally dominate the Ægean and
the capture of Rhodes would not be necessary. Either way it
would work.

And of course the prize was Turkey. If we could gain Turkey
it would be possible without the subtraction of a single man, ship,
or aircraft from the main and decisive battles to dominate the
Black Sea with submarines and light naval forces, and to give a
right hand to Russia and carry supplies to her armies by a route
far less costly, far more swift, and far more abundant than either
the Arctic or the Persian Gulf.

This was the triple theme which I pressed upon the President
and Stalin on every occasion, not hesitating to repeat the arguments remorselessly. I could have gained Stalin, but the President was oppressed by the prejudices of his military advisers and

drifted to and fro in the argument, with the result that the whole of these subsidiary but gleaming opportunities were cast aside unused. Our American friends were comforted in their obstinacy by the reflection that "at any rate we have stopped Churchill entangling us in the Balkans". No such idea had ever crossed my mind. I regard the failure to use otherwise unemployable forces to bring Turkey into the war and dominate the Ægean as an error in war direction which cannot be excused by the fact that in spite of it victory was won.

*   *   *   *   *

Shortly after the President's move into his new quarters in the Soviet Embassy Stalin came to greet him, and they had a friendly talk. According to the Hopkins biography the President informed Stalin of his promise to Chiang Kai-shek of active operations in Burma. Stalin expressed a low opinion of the fighting quality of the Chinese troops. The President "referred to one of his favourite topics, the education of the peoples of the Far Eastern colonial areas in the arts of self-government. . . . He cautioned Stalin against bringing up the problems of India with Churchill, and Stalin agreed that this was undoubtedly a sore subject. Roosevelt said that reform in India should begin from the bottom, and Stalin replied that reform from the bottom would mean revolution." I passed the morning peacefully in bed nursing my cold and dealing with many telegrams from London.

*   *   *   *   *

The first plenary meeting was held at the Soviet Embassy on Sunday, November 28, at 4 p.m. The conference room was spacious and handsome, and we seated ourselves at a large, round table. I had with me Eden, Dill, the three Chiefs of Staff, and Ismay. The President had Harry Hopkins, Admiral Leahy, Admiral King, and two other officers. General Marshall and General Arnold were not present: "they had misunderstood the time of the meeting," says Hopkins' biographer, "and had gone off on a sight-seeing tour round Teheran." I had my admirable interpreter of the previous year, Major Birse. Pavlov again performed this service for the Soviets, and Mr. Bohlen, a new figure, for the United States. Molotov and Marshal Voroshilov alone accompanied Stalin. He and I sat almost opposite one another. We had agreed beforehand that the President should preside at this first meeting, and Roosevelt consented to do so. He opened the proceedings in a felicitous speech, saying, according to our record, that the Russians, the British, and the Americans were sitting round the table for the first time as members of the same family, with the single purpose of winning the war. No fixed agenda had been drawn up for the meeting, and it was open to anybody to discuss whatever they liked and to leave undiscussed whatever they did not like. Everyone could speak as freely as he wished on the basis of friendship, and nothing would be published.

In my opening remarks I also stressed the importance of the occasion. This meeting, I said, probably represented the greatest concentration of worldly power that had ever been seen in the history of mankind. In our hands lay perhaps the shortening of the war, almost certainly victory, and, beyond any shadow of doubt, the happiness and fortunes of mankind.

Stalin said that he appreciated our references to the friendship of the three Powers. It was indeed true that a great opportunity had been given to them, and he hoped they would make good use of it.

The President then began the discussion with a brief account of the war situation from the American point of view. He first dealt with the Pacific, which had particular importance for the United States, since American forces there were bearing the main load, assisted by Australia, New Zealand, and China. The United States had concentrated in the Pacific the greater part of their Navy and the best part of a million men. The vast extent of that theatre could be gauged by the fact that a supply ship could do only three trips a year. The United States were pursuing a policy of attrition, which up to the present had been successful. It was certain that Japanese ships, both naval and mercantile, were being sunk more rapidly than new construction could replace them. Mr. Roosevelt then explained the plans for the recapture of Northern Burma. Anglo-American forces would co-operate with the Chinese, and would be under the command of Admiral Lord Louis Mountbatten. Plans were also being discussed for an amphibious operation against the Japanese lines of communication from Bangkok. Considerable forces were to be employed, although every effort had been made to keep them down to the minimum required to achieve our essential objectives. Those objectives were to keep China actively in the war, to open the Burma Road, and to establish positions from which Japan could be vanquished with the greatest possible speed, once Germany had collapsed. It was hoped to secure bases in China which would enable Tokyo to be attacked in the coming year.

The President then turned to Europe. There had been many Anglo-American conferences and many plans. A year and a half ago it had been decided to launch an expedition across the English Channel, but owing to transportation and other difficulties it was still impossible to decide a definite date for the operation. An adequate force must be assembled in England, not only for the actual landing, but also for marching inland. The English Channel had proved such a disagreeable body of water that it was impossible to stage an expedition before May 1, 1944. This was the date decided upon at Quebec. He explained that landing-craft were the limiting factor in all landings, and if it were decided to mount a very big expedition in the Mediterranean we should have to give up the cross-Channel operation altogether. If a lesser operation in the Mediterranean were decided upon the delay would amount to one, two, or perhaps three months. Consequently both he and I wished in this military conference to hear from Marshal Stalin and Marshal Voroshilov what action would be of the greatest service to the Soviets. Many plans had been mooted—increasing the strength of our attack in Italy, the Balkans, the Ægean, Turkey, and so forth. The most important task of the Conference would be to decide which of these to adopt. The governing object would be for the Anglo-American armies to draw the greatest weight off the Soviet forces.

* * * * *

Stalin, speaking next, welcomed the successes of the United States in the Pacific, but said that the Soviets could not join in the struggle against Japan at the present time, since practically all their forces were required against Germany. The Soviet forces in the Far East were more or less sufficient for defence, but they would have to be at least trebled in order to attack. The moment for joining their friends in this theatre would be the moment of Germany's collapse: then they would march together.

As for Europe, Stalin said that he would like to begin with a few words about the Soviet experiences in the conduct of the war. Their attack in July had been anticipated by the Germans; but when sufficient troops and equipment had been collected the Soviets had found it comparatively easy to pass to the offensive. He frankly admitted that they had not expected the successes which were gained in July, August, and September. The Germans had proved weaker than had been thought.

He then gave details of the latest situation on the Soviet front. On some of the sectors they had been slowed down, on others they had stopped altogether, while in the Ukraine, west and south of Kiev, the initiative had passed to the Germans within the last three weeks. The Germans had recaptured Jitomir, and would probably recapture Korosten. Their objective was the recapture of Kiev. Nevertheless in the main the initiative still rested with the Soviet armies.

He had been asked, he said, how the Anglo-American forces could best help Russia. The Soviet Government had always felt that the Italian campaign had been of great value to the Allied cause in that it opened the Mediterranean. But Italy was not a suitable jumping-off ground for the invasion of Germany. The Alps stood between. Therefore nothing was to be gained by concentrating large numbers of troops in Italy for the invasion of Germany. Turkey would be a better point of entry than Italy; but it was a long way from the heart of Germany. He believed that North or North-West France was the place for Anglo-American forces to attack, though it was of course true that the Germans there would resist desperately.

* * * * *

Though invited to speak earlier, I had hitherto said nothing. I now stated the British position.

It had long been agreed, I said, with the United States that we should invade North or North-West France across the Channel. The enterprise was absorbing most of our preparations and resources. A long dissertation on facts and figures would be necessary to show why it had been impossible to carry out this operation in 1943, but we were resolved to do it in 1944. Instead of the cross-Channel invasion of 1943 a series of operations had been launched in the Mediterranean. This had been done with full recognition that they were of a secondary character; but we had felt that they were the best contribution we could make in

1943, having regard to our resources and to transportation. The British and American Governments had now set themselves the task of carrying out a cross-Channel invasion in the late spring or summer of 1944. The forces which could be accumulated by that time amounted to about sixteen British and nineteen United States divisions—a total of thirty-five divisions. These divisions were much stronger both in numbers and equipment than the German divisions.

Stalin here observed that he never regarded the operations in the Mediterranean as being of a secondary character. They were of the first importance, but not from the point of view of invading Germany.

I replied that none the less the President and I had both regarded them as stepping-stones to the decisive cross-Channel operation. Having regard to the British forces engaged in the Mediterranean and India, the sixteen British divisions which were being put into the cross-Channel operation were the most that could be provided by a country with a total population of forty-five millions. These divisions could be kept up to strength in the line, but the number could not be increased. It would have to be left to the United States, who had a large number of reserve divisions, to broaden the front and nourish the battle. The early spring and summer of 1944 were still six months away however, and the President and I had been asking ourselves what could be done during these six months with the resources available in the Mediterranean that would best take the weight off Russia, without postponing "Overlord" for more than perhaps a month or two. Seven of the best Anglo-American divisions and a certain number of landing-craft had already been, or were being, moved from the Mediterranean to the United Kingdom. The result had been a weakening of effort on the Italian front. The weather had been bad, and it had not yet been possible to take Rome; but it was hoped to take it by January; and General Alexander, who, under General Eisenhower, was commanding the Fifteenth Army Group in Italy, aimed not only at taking Rome, but at destroying or capturing ten or eleven German divisions.

I explained that we had not contemplated going into the broad part of the leg of Italy, still less invading Germany across the Alps. The general plan was first to capture Rome and seize the airfields north of it, which would enable us to bomb Southern

Germany, and then to establish ourselves on a line towards Pisa-Rimini. After that the possibility of establishing a Third Front in conformity with, but not in substitution for, the cross-Channel operation would have to be planned. One of the possibilities was to move into Southern France, and the second, suggested by the President, was to move from the head of the Adriatic north-east towards the Danube.

Meanwhile what should be done in the next six months? There was much to be said for supporting Tito, who was holding a number of German divisions and doing much more for the Allied cause than the Chetniks under Mihailović. There would clearly be great advantage in supporting him with supplies and guerrilla activities, and the Balkan theatre was one of the areas where we could stretch the enemy to the utmost. This brought us to the biggest problem which would have to be decided after consideration by the military staffs, namely, how to bring Turkey into the war and open communications through the Ægean to the Dardanelles and thence to the Black Sea. Once Turkey was in the war and we had the use of her air bases we could capture the islands in the Ægean with comparatively small forces, say two or three divisions, and the air forces already in that theatre. If we had access to the Black Sea ports convoys could be run continuously. At present we had had to limit ourselves to four convoys by the Northern route, as the escorts were required for "Overlord"; but once the Dardanelles were open the escort vessels already in the Mediterranean could keep up a ceaseless flow of supplies to the Soviet Black Sea ports.

How could we persuade Turkey to come into the war? If she came in, what should she be asked to do? Should she merely give us her bases, or should she attack Bulgaria and declare war on Germany? Should she move forward or should she stay on the Thracian frontier? What would be the effect on Bulgaria, who owed a profound debt to Russia for rescuing her in former days from the Turkish yoke? How would Roumania react? They were already putting out genuine peace-feelers for unconditional surrender. Then there was Hungary. Which way would she go? There might well be a political landslide among the satellite States which would enable the Greeks to revolt and hustle the Germans out of Greece. All these were questions on which the Soviets had a special point of view and special knowledge. It would be invaluable to know what they thought about it all. Would these plans in the Eastern Mediterranean be of sufficient interest to the Soviet Government to make them wish us to go ahead, even if it meant a delay of one to two months from May 1 in launching "Overlord"? The British and American Governments had deliberately kept their minds open on the subject until they knew what the Soviet Government felt about these problems.

The President here reminded me of the further project of moving up to the Northern Adriatic and then north-east to the Danube. I agreed and said that once we had taken Rome and destroyed the German armies south of the Apennines in the narrow part of Italy the Anglo-American armies would advance far enough to make contact with the enemy. We could then hold the line with the minimum forces and keep the option to strike with the remainder either in the South of France or, in accordance with the President's idea, north-east from the head of the Adriatic. Neither of these problems had been considered in detail, but if Stalin should look upon them with favour a technical sub-committee could be set up to examine ways and means and facts and figures and to report to the Conference.

The discussion now came to a crucial point. The record says:

Marshal Stalin addressed the following questions to the Prime Minister:

Question: "Am I right in thinking that the invasion of France is to be undertaken by thirty-five divisions?"

Answer: "Yes. Particularly strong divisions."

Question: "Is it intended that this operation should be carried out by the forces now in Italy?"

Answer: "No. Seven divisions have already been, or are in process of being, withdrawn from Italy and North Africa to take part in 'Overlord'. These seven divisions are required to make up the thirty-five divisions mentioned in your first question. After they have been withdrawn about twenty-two divisions will be left in the Mediterranean for Italy or other objectives. Some of these could be used either for an operation against Southern France or for moving from the head of the Adriatic towards the Danube. Both these operations will be timed in conformity with 'Overlord'. Meanwhile it should not be difficult to spare two or three divisions to take the islands in the Ægean."

* * * * *

I then explained that it would be quite impossible to transfer any divisions from the Mediterranean to the United Kingdom over and above the seven mentioned. Shipping would not run to it. Thirty-five Anglo-American divisions would be assembled in the United Kingdom for the initial assault. Thereafter the British could do no more than maintain in Northern France their sixteen divisions, but the United States would continue to pump in further troops until the Expeditionary Force in Northern France amounted all told to fifty or sixty divisions. Both the British and American divisions, if line of communication troops, corps troops, flak, etc., were taken into account, amounted gross to about 40,000 men each. There were already very considerable Anglo-American air forces in the United Kingdom, but even so the United States Air Force was going to be doubled, or perhaps trebled, in the next six months. Thus there would be a tremendous weight of air-power concentrated in an area from which the enemy could be easily reached. All the forces and equipment were being built up according to a prearranged schedule, which would be shown to the Soviet authorities if they so desired.

Stalin asked me about the operation against the South of France. I said it had not yet been planned in detail, but the idea was that it might be done in conformity or simultaneously with "Overlord". The assault force would consist of troops now in Italy. I added that it would also be necessary to examine the President's idea of moving north-east from the head of the Adriatic.

Stalin next asked how many Anglo-American troops would have to be allotted if Turkey came into the war.

Observing that I spoke for myself alone, I said that two or three divisions at the most would be required to take the islands in the Ægean, and that, in addition, we should probably have to give Turkey about twenty squadrons of air forces and several regiments of flak to defend herself. Both the air forces and the flak could be provided without prejudice to other operations.

Stalin thought it would be a mistake to send part of our forces to Turkey and elsewhere and part to Southern France. The best course would be to make "Overlord" the basic operation for 1944, and, once Rome had been captured, to send all available forces in Italy to Southern France. These forces could then join hands with the "Overlord" forces when the invasion was launched. France was the weakest spot on the German front. He did not himself expect Turkey to agree to enter the war.

I asked whether the Soviet Government was not very anxious to get Turkey into the war. We had tried once and had failed, but was it not intended that we should renew the effort?

"I am all in favour of trying again," said Stalin. "We ought to take them by the scruff of the neck if necessary."

I then said that I entirely agreed with Marshal Stalin's observations about the undesirability of dispersion, but all that I suggested was that a handful of divisions—say two or three—would be very well employed in making contact with Turkey, while the air forces which would come into play were those which were already defending Egypt and would merely be advancing their line. Thus there was no appreciable diversion of effort, either from the Italian front or from "Overlord".

Stalin thought it would be well worth while to take the islands if this could be done with three or four divisions.

What I particularly dreaded, I said, was an interval of six months' inactivity between the capture of Rome and "Overlord". We ought to be fighting the enemy all the time, and the operations which I had suggested, although admittedly of a secondary character, should be the subject of careful consideration.

Stalin repeated that "Overlord" was a very serious operation, and that it was better to help it by invading the South of France. He would even prefer to assume a defensive rôle in Italy and forgo the capture of Rome for the present if this would admit the invasion of Southern France by, say, ten divisions. Two months later "Overlord" would follow, and the two invasions could then join hands.

I replied that we should be no stronger if we pulled out of the advance on Rome, and once we had taken the city we should be in a much stronger position through having destroyed or badly mutilated ten or eleven German divisions. Moreover, we required the airfields north of Rome for the bombing of Germany. It would be impossible for us to forgo the capture of Rome. To do so would be regarded on all sides as a crushing defeat, and the British Parliament would not tolerate the idea for a moment.

★　★　★　★　★

314

The President now suggested that the timing of operations required the most careful consideration. Any operation undertaken in the Eastern Mediterranean would probably put off "Overlord" until June or July. He himself was opposed to such a delay if it could possibly be avoided. He therefore suggested that the military experts should examine the possibility of operations against Southern France on the timing put forward by Stalin, *i.e.*, two months before "Overlord", the governing factor being that "Overlord" should be launched at the prescribed time.

Stalin said that the experience gained by the Soviets during the last two years of fighting was that a big offensive, if undertaken from only one direction, rarely yielded results. The better course was to launch offensives from two or more directions simultaneously. This compelled the enemy to disperse his forces, and at the same time gave an opportunity for the attacks, provided they were close enough to each other, to make contact and increase the power of the offensive as a whole. He suggested that this principle might well be applied to the problem under discussion.

I did not disagree in principle with these views. The suggestions that I had made for minor help to Yugoslavia and Turkey did not, I said, conflict in any way with that general conception. At the same time, I wished it to be placed on record that I could not in any circumstances agree to sacrifice the activities of the armies in the Mediterranean, which included twenty British and British-controlled divisions, merely in order to keep the exact date of May 1 for "Overlord". If Turkey refused to come into the war it could not be helped. I earnestly hoped that I should not be asked to agree to any such rigid timing of operations as the President had suggested. Would it not be right for the Conference to meditate over all that had been said and to continue their discussions on the following day? The President agreed, and suggested that the Staffs should set to work the following morning.

Stalin then observed that he had not expected that military questions would be discussed at the Conference, and he had not brought his military experts with him. Nevertheless Marshal Voroshilov would do his best.

I asked how it was proposed to discuss the question of Turkey. The problem was probably as much political as military. The questions to which the Conference should address itself were as follows:

(a) What do we want Turkey to do?

(b) What are we prepared to offer her to bring her into the war?

(c) What will be the consequences of any such offer?

Stalin agreed. Turkey was an ally of England and on terms of friendship with the United States. It was for them to persuade her to take the proper course. When I said that Turkey would be mad if she declined Russia's invitation to come in on the winning side, and at the same time lost the sympathy of Great Britain, Stalin rejoined that a number of people preferred to be mad, and all neutrals regarded those who were waging war as fools to fight when they might be doing nothing.

I concluded the meeting by saying that, although we were all great friends, it would be idle for us to delude ourselves that we saw eye to eye on all matters. Time and patience were necessary.

Here ended our first talk.

CHAPTER XX

CONVERSATIONS AND CONFERENCES

A Talk with Stalin about Germany – Poland and Her Frontiers – Roosevelt's Plan for the "Four Policemen" – I Present the Stalingrad Sword of Honour by the King's Command – Our Second Plenary Session – Stalin Asks Who Will Command "Overlord" – I State the British View about "Overlord" and Italy – Thirty Enemy Divisions Held in the Balkans – How to Persuade Turkey to Enter the War – The Position of Bulgaria – Argument about the Date of Crossing the Channel – The Importance of Not Wrecking the Italian Campaign – The Issue of Turkey – Stalin's Direct Question to Me about "Overlord" – I Declare Against Mass Executions of Germans.

THE formal conferences were interspersed with what may be thought to be even more important talks between Roosevelt, Stalin, and myself at luncheons and dinners. Here there were very few things that could not be said and received in good-humour. On Sunday night the 28th the President was our host for dinner. We were a party of ten or eleven, including the interpreters, and conversation soon became general and serious.

After dinner on this first evening, when we were strolling about the room, I led Stalin to a sofa and suggested that we talk for a little on what was to happen after the war was won. He assented, and we sat down. Eden joined us. "Let us," said the Marshal, "first consider the worst that might happen." He thought that Germany had every possibility of recovering from this war, and might start on a new one within a comparatively short time. He feared the revival of German nationalism. After Versailles peace had seemed assured, but Germany had recovered very quickly. We must therefore establish a strong body to prevent Germany starting a new war. He was convinced that she would recover. When I asked, "How soon?" he replied, "Within fifteen to twenty years." I said that the world must be made safe for at least fifty years. If it was only for fifteen to twenty years then we should have betrayed our soldiers.

Stalin thought we should consider restraints on Germany's manufacturing capacity. The Germans were an able people, very industrious and resourceful, and they would recover quickly. I replied that there would have to be certain measures of control. I would forbid them all aviation, civil and military, and I would forbid the General Staff system. "Would you," asked Stalin, "also forbid the existence of watchmakers' and furniture factories for making parts of shells? The Germans produced toy rifles which were used for teaching hundreds of thousands of men how to shoot."

"Nothing," I said, "is final. The world rolls on. We have now learnt something. Our duty is to make the world safe for at least fifty years by German disarmament, by preventing re-armament, by supervision of German factories, by forbidding all aviation, and by territorial changes of a far-reaching character. It all comes back to the question whether Great Britain, the United States, and the U.S.S.R. can keep a close friendship and supervise Germany in their mutual interest. We ought not to be afraid to give orders as soon as we see any danger."

"There was control after the last war," said Stalin, "but it failed."

"We were inexperienced then," I replied. "The last war was not to the same extent a national war, and Russia was not a party at the Peace Conference. It will be different this time." I had a feeling that Prussia should be isolated and reduced, that Bavaria, Austria, and Hungary might form a broad, peaceful, unaggressive confederation. I thought Prussia should be dealt with more sternly than the other parts of the Reich, which might thus be influenced against throwing in their lot with her. It must be remembered that these were war-time moods.

"All very good, but insufficient," was Stalin's comment.

Russia, I continued, would have her Army, Great Britain and the United States their Navies and Air Forces. In addition, all three Powers would have their other resources. All would be strongly armed, and must not assume any obligation to disarm. "We are the trustees for the peace of the world. If we fail there will be perhaps a hundred years of chaos. If we are strong we can carry out our trusteeship. There is more," I went on, "than merely keeping the peace. The three Powers should guide the future of the world. I do not want to enforce any system on other nations. I ask for freedom and for the right of all nations to develop as they like. We three must remain friends in order to ensure happy homes in all countries."

Stalin asked again what was to happen to Germany.

I replied that I was not against the toilers in Germany, but only against the leaders and against dangerous combinations. He said that there were many toilers in the German divisions who fought under orders. When he asked German prisoners who came from the labouring classes (such is the record, but he probably meant "Communist Party") why they fought for Hitler they replied that they were carrying out orders. He shot such prisoners.

*　*　*　*　*

I suggested that we should discuss the Polish question. He agreed and invited me to begin. I said that we had declared war on account of Poland. Poland was therefore important to us. Nothing was more important than the security of the Russian western frontier. But I had given no pledges about frontiers. I wanted heart-to-heart talks with the Russians about this. When Marshal Stalin felt like telling us what he thought about it the matter could be discussed and we could reach some agreement, and the Marshal should tell me what was necessary for the defence of the western frontiers of Russia. After this war in Europe, which might end in 1944, the Soviet Union would be overwhelmingly strong and Russia would have a great responsibility in any decision she took with regard to Poland. Personally I thought Poland might move westwards, like soldiers taking two steps "left close". If Poland trod on some German toes that could not be helped, but there must be a strong Poland. Poland was an instrument needed in the orchestra of Europe.

Stalin said the Polish people had their culture and their language, which must exist. They could not be extirpated.

"Are we to try," I asked, "to draw frontier lines?"

"Yes."

"I have no power from Parliament, nor, I believe, has the President, to define any frontier lines. But we might now, in Teheran, see if the three heads of Governments, working in agreement, could form some sort of policy which we could recommend to the Poles and advise them to accept."

We agreed to look at the problem. Stalin asked whether it would be without Polish participation. I said "Yes", and that when this was all informally agreed between ourselves we could go to the Poles later. Mr. Eden here remarked that he had been much struck by Stalin's statement that afternoon that the Poles could go as far west as the Oder. He saw hope in that and was much encouraged. Stalin asked whether we thought he was going to swallow Poland up. Eden said he did not know how much the Russians were going to eat. How much would they leave undigested? Stalin said the Russians did not want anything belonging to other people, although they might have a bite at Germany. Eden said that what Poland lost in the east she might gain in the west. Stalin replied that possibly she might, but he did not know. I then demonstrated with the help of three matches my idea of Poland moving westwards. This pleased Stalin, and on this note our group parted for the moment.

* * * * *

The morning of the 29th was occupied by a conference of the British, Soviet, and American military chiefs. As I knew that Stalin and Roosevelt had already had a private conversation, and were of course staying at the same Embassy, I suggested that the President and I might lunch together before the second plenary meeting that afternoon. Roosevelt however declined, and sent Harriman to me to explain that he did not want Stalin to know that he and I were meeting privately. I was surprised at this, for I thought we all three should treat each other with equal confidence. The President after luncheon had a further interview with Stalin and Molotov, at which many important matters were discussed, including particularly Mr. Roosevelt's plan for the government of the post-war world. This should be carried out by the "Four Policemen", namely, the U.S.S.R., the United States, Great Britain, and China. Stalin did not react favourably to this. He said the "Four Policemen" would not be welcomed by the small nations of Europe. He did not believe that China would be very powerful when the war ended, and even if she were European States would resent having China as an enforcement authority for themselves. In this the Soviet leader certainly showed himself more prescient and possessed of a truer sense of values than the President. When Stalin proposed as an alternative that there should be one committee for Europe and another for the Far East—the European committee to consist of Britain, Russia, the United States, and possibly one other European nation—the President replied that this was somewhat similar to my idea of regional committees, one for Europe, one for the Far East, and one for the Americas. He does not seem to have made it clear that I also contemplated a Supreme United Nations Council, of which the three regional committees would be the components. As I was not informed till much later of what had taken place I was not able to correct this erroneous presentation.

* * * * *

Before our second plenary session began at four o'clock I presented, by the King's command, the Sword of Honour which His Majesty had had specially designed and wrought to commemorate the glorious defence of Stalingrad. The large outer hall was filled with Russian officers and soldiers. When, after a few sentences of explanation, I handed the splendid weapon to Marshal Stalin he raised it in a most impressive gesture to his lips and kissed the scabbard. He then passed it to Voroshilov, who dropped it. It was carried from the room in great solemnity, escorted by a Russian guard of honour. As this procession moved away I saw the President sitting at the side of the room, obviously stirred by the ceremony. We then moved to the conference chamber and took our seats again at the round table, this time with all the Chiefs of Staff, who were now to report the result of their morning's labours.

The C.I.G.S. said that they had surveyed various operations, and they realised that unless something was done in the Mediterranean between now and the launching of "Overlord" the Germans would be able to transfer troops from Italy to Russia or Northern France. They had considered carrying the advance up the leg of the Italian peninsula, strengthening the Partisans in Yugoslavia so that they could hold German divisions in the Balkans, and getting Turkey into the war. They had also discussed a landing in Southern France to coincide with "Overlord". Portal had reviewed our bombing offensive and Marshall the United States build-up in Britain.

General Marshall said that the problem confronting the Western Allies in Europe was not one of troops or material, but of ships and landing-craft and getting fighter airfields close enough to the scene of operations. Landing-craft were particularly short, and the most vital need was for the L.S.T.s, which carried forty tanks apiece. So far as "Overlord" was concerned, the flow of troops and supplies was proceeding according to schedule. The variable and questionable factor in almost every one of the problems facing the Allies was landing-craft. The building programme had been accelerated both in the United Kingdom and in the United States, with two objects: first, to increase the scale of the initial assault for "Overlord", and, secondly, to enable us to undertake the operations which we thought right in the Mediterranean.

⋆   ⋆   ⋆   ⋆   ⋆

Stalin then put the crucial question, "Who will command 'Overlord'?" The President replied that this had not yet been decided. Stalin said bluntly that the operation would come to nought unless one man was placed in charge of all the preparations for it. Roosevelt explained that this had already been done. General Morgan, a British officer, had been given a combined Anglo-American staff and had been planning the operation for some considerable time. Everything, in fact, had already been decided, except the name of the Supreme Commander. Stalin declared it essential that a man should be appointed at once to be responsible not only for the planning, but also for the execution. Otherwise, although General Morgan might say that everything was ready, the Supreme Commander, when appointed, might have very different ideas and wish to alter everything.

I said that General Morgan had been appointed some months before by the Combined Chiefs of Staff, with the approval of the President and myself, to be Chief Staff Officer to the Supreme Commander (Designate). His Majesty's Government had expressed their willingness to serve under a United States Commander, since the United States would be responsible for the build-up of the invasion force and would have the proponderance in numbers. In the Mediterranean, on the other hand, practically all the naval forces were British and we had also a considerable preponderance in Army forces. We therefore felt that the command of this theatre should properly go to the British. I suggested that the appointment of a Supreme Commander was more appropriate for discussion by the three heads of Governments than in a somewhat large conference. Stalin said that the Soviet Government laid no claim to a voice in the appointment. They merely wanted to know who it would be. It was vital that this appointment should be made as soon as possible and that the general chosen should be responsible not only for the preparation of the plan, but also for carrying it out. I agreed that the decision who was to command "Overlord" was one of the most important points to be dealt with, and said it would be settled within the next fortnight at latest.

$$\star \quad \star \quad \star \quad \star \quad \star$$

I then set out the British case. I said that I was somewhat concerned at the number and complexity of the problems which confronted us. The Conference represented some twelve to fourteen hundred millions of the human race, who depended upon our reaching right conclusions. It was therefore imperative that we should not separate until the great military, political, and moral problems confronting us had been firmly resolved; but I proposed to confine myself to a few specific points which might be studied by a military sub-committee.

First, what help could be given to "Overlord" by the large forces already assembled in the Mediterranean? In particular, what was the scale of operations which could be launched against Southern France by the troops in Italy? This project had been mentioned by both the President and Stalin, but it had not yet been studied in sufficient detail for anyone to express a final view. Stalin had very rightly stressed the value of pincers operations, but it was obviously useless to attack with a small force which could be annihilated before the main body came on the scene. Speaking entirely for myself, I said I thought that sufficient landing-craft to transport at least two divisions should be retained in the Mediterranean. With a landing-craft force of this size we could help forward the advance up the leg of Italy by seaborne outflanking movements, and thus avoid the slow, laborious methods of frontal attack. Secondly, these landing-craft would enable us to take Rhodes and open the Ægean simultaneously with the entry of Turkey into the war. This same force of landing-craft would enable us five or six months hence to make a descent upon Southern France in concert with "Overlord".

Clearly, all these operations would require the most careful timing and study, but there seemed to be a good hope that all those I had mentioned could be carried through. On the other hand, it was obvious that landing-craft sufficient to transport two divisions could not be kept in the Mediterranean without setting back the date of "Overlord" for perhaps six to eight weeks, or, alternatively, without recalling from the East the assault craft and ships which had been sent there for operations against the Japanese. This placed us in a dilemma. It was a case of balancing one problem against the other. I said I should be grateful to hear the views of Marshal Stalin and Marshal Voroshilov on these points, since their military record inspired their British Allies with so much admiration and respect.

The second main point was the question of Yugoslavia and the Dalmatian coast. No fewer than twenty-one German divisions were held in the Balkans by Partisan forces. There were, in addition, nine Bulgarian divisions in Greece and Yugoslavia. Thus thirty enemy divisions were being contained by these gallant guerrillas. Surely therefore the Balkan theatre was one of the areas in which we could stretch the enemy to the utmost and give ourselves relief in the heavy battles which lay ahead. We ourselves had no ambitions in the Balkans. All we wanted to do was to nail down these thirty hostile divisions. M. Molotov, Mr. Eden, and a representative of the President should meet together and advise the Conference on all the political points at issue. For example, did our Soviet friends and Allies see any political difficulty in the course advocated? If so, what? We were determined to work harmoniously with them. From the military point of view there was no question of using large forces in this area. All that was required was to help the Partisans with supplies and equipment and Commando operations.

The third and last point was Turkey. Great Britain was Turkey's ally, and had accepted the task of trying to persuade or induce Turkey to enter the war before Christmas. If the President was prepared to come in at this point and take the lead the British Government would be entirely happy to leave it to him. I said I was prepared, on behalf of His Majesty's Government, to give an assurance that Great Britain would go a long way towards bringing Turkey into the war. From the military point of view the entry of Turkey into the war would not mean the diversion of more than two or three Allied divisions at most.

I then asked what the Soviet Government felt about Bulgaria. Would they be prepared to tell Bulgaria that if Turkey found herself at war with Germany and Bulgaria were to attack Turkey the Soviets would at once regard Bulgaria as an enemy? I suggested that Molotov and Eden and a representative of the President might meet to advise the Conference on the best way of getting Turkey into the war. If we could only bring this about it would be a terrible blow to Germany. Bulgaria would be weakened, Roumania was already trying desperately hard to surrender unconditionally, and the effects on Hungary would be considerable. The object of all the operations in the Mediterranean which I had contemplated was to take the weight off Russia and to give the best possible chance to "Overlord".

* * * * *

I had spoken for about ten minutes. There was a pause. Stalin then said: "The Soviet Government will consider themselves at war with Bulgaria if, as a result of Turkey's entry into the war, Bulgaria threatens Turkey." I thanked him for this assurance, and inquired whether I could inform the Turks. Stalin said that he was quite agreeable to this. He then proceeded to give his own ideas on the Balkans. He said there seemed to be no difference of opinion, and he was all in favour of help being given to the Partisans. But he added bluntly that the entry of Turkey into the war, the support of Yugoslavia, and the capture of Rome were, to the Russian way of thinking, relatively unimportant. If the Conference had been convened to discuss military matters "Overlord" must come first.

If a military commission was to be set up as had been suggested it would clearly have to be given precise instructions as to the task it was required to perform. The Russians needed help, and urgent help, in their great struggle against the German Army. This could best be given by the early and vigorous prosecution of Operation "Overlord". There were three main matters to be decided. First, the date. This should be some time in May and no later. Secondly, it should be supported by a landing in the South of France. If this could be carried out two or three months before

"Overlord" so much the better, but, if not, it might coincide with it, and, if it could not coincide, it would still help if it took place a little after it. The assault on the South of France as a supporting operation would be definitely helpful to "Overlord". The capture of Rome and other operations in the Mediterranean could only be regarded as diversions.

The third matter to be decided was the appointment of a Commander-in-Chief for "Overlord". He said he would like to see this made before the Conference ended, or at least within a week thereafter. Preparations for "Overlord" could not be carried on successfully unless there was a Supreme Commander. Choosing the man was of course a matter for the British and American Governments, but the Soviet Government would be glad to know his name.

★　★　★　★　★

The President said that we were all agreed on the importance of "Overlord", but not about its date. If "Overlord" was to be carried out during May one at least of the Mediterranean operations would have to go by the board. If however landing-craft and other equipment were retained in the Mediterranean, then it would have to be postponed till June or July. There were obvious dangers in delaying "Overlord". If we launched expeditions in the Eastern Mediterranean, even with only two or three divisions, there was always the possibility of their developing into bigger commitments involving the dispatch of larger forces. If this happened even the later date of "Overlord" would be prejudiced.

Mr. Roosevelt then referred to my point about the thirty German and Bulgarian divisions which were contained in the Balkans. He recommended that we should intensify the process of keeping them pinned down by Commando forces. It was important to hold them in this area and prevent them from doing harm elsewhere. There was clearly general agreement that Tito should be supported, but that this should be done without subtracting from the "Overlord" operation.

Stalin said that, according to his information, the Germans had eight divisions in Yugoslavia, five in Greece, and three in Bulgaria, and twenty-five divisions in France. He was not prepared to agree to any delay in "Overlord" beyond the month of May.

I said I could not agree to give any such undertaking. Nevertheless I did not think there was any fundamental divergence in the views so far expressed. I was willing to do everything in the power of His Majesty's Government to begin "Overlord" at the earliest possible moment, but I did not consider that the very great possibilities in the Mediterranean should be ruthlessly sacrificed and cast aside as if they were of no value, merely to save a month or so in the launching of "Overlord". There was a large British army in the Mediterranean, and I could not agree that it should stand idle for nearly six months. It should be fighting the enemy with the greatest vigour alongside its American Allies. I had every hope that, together, British and American forces would destroy a large force of Germans in Italy, and, having advanced northward of Rome, would hold a considerable German army on the Italian front. To be quiescent in Italy and remain inert for nearly six months would be an improper use of our forces and lay us open to the reproach that the Russians were bearing almost the entire burden of the land war.

Stalin said that he had never contemplated a complete cessation of all operations in Italy during the winter.

I explained that if landing-craft were taken away from the Mediterranean this would mean a definite curtailment of our operations there. I reminded Stalin of the three conditions on which the success of "Overlord" depended. First, there must be a satisfactory reduction in the strength of the German fighter force in North-West Europe between now and the assault. Secondly, German reserves in France and the Low Countries must not be more on the day of the assault than about twelve full-strength first-quality mobile divisions. Thirdly, it must not be possible for the Germans to transfer from other fronts more than fifteen first-quality divisions during the first sixty days of the operation. To obtain these conditions we should have to hold as many Germans as possible in Italy and Yugoslavia. If Turkey entered the war, this would be an added help, but not an essential condition. The Germans now in Italy had for the most part come from France. If we slackened off our pressure in Italy they would go back again. We must continue to engage the enemy on the only front where at present we could fight them. If we engaged them as fiercely as possible during the winter months in the Mediterranean this would make the best possible contribution towards creating the conditions needed for a successful "Overlord".

Stalin asked what would happen if there were thirteen or fourteen mobile German divisions in France and more than fifteen available from other fronts. Would this rule out "Overlord"? I said, "No, certainly not."

* * * * *

I then turned the discussion back to Turkey. We had agreed to press her to enter the war by the end of the year. If she did, the only military operations needed would be to establish our planes on the Turkish airfields in Anatolia and capture the island of Rhodes. One assault division and some garrison troops would suffice. Once in possession of Rhodes and the Turkish air bases we could starve out all the other Ægean islands at our leisure. These operations would not involve us in an unlimited liability, and could be regarded as a commitment of a strictly limited character. If our efforts to bring Turkey in were unsuccessful, that would be the end of the matter. Nevertheless, failure to bring Turkey in would also be a relief to the Germans. There was a further point about Turkey. If she came in and we captured Rhodes and subsequently turned the Germans out of the other Ægean islands our troops and air forces in Egypt could all move forward into action to the northward instead of remaining in their present defensive rôle.

The issue of Turkey should not be lightly turned aside. As the President and General Marshall had stated, the scale, nature, and timing of our operations all turned upon the availability of landing-craft and transportation of forces across the sea. I said I was prepared to go into this question at any time and at any length and in any detail, but if the small number of landing-craft involved could not be retained in the Mediterranean or found from some other theatre no operations on any scale would be possible in the Mediterranean area, and this ban included an assault on the South of France. These arguments should be very carefully weighed before decisions were taken. I told Stalin that I agreed with him that a definite reference should be given to the Technical Military Committee, and I suggested that the terms of reference should be drawn up severally by the heads of the three Governments.

Stalin said that, on thinking it over, he did not feel that a Military Committee was necessary. In order to take decisions it was not necessary to go into detail. The issues at stake were the date of "Overlord", the appointment of the Commander-in-Chief, and whether any supporting operations could be carried out in the South of France. All this had to be decided by the plenary Conference. Nor did he see any necessity for a Committee of the Foreign Secretaries. The appointment of these committees would delay the completion of the Conference, and he, for his part, could not extend his visit to Teheran beyond December 1, or at the latest December 2.

The President said that he had drawn up tentative terms of reference in simple form for the Military Committee, if it was decided that this body should get to work. The terms were in two sentences, namely: "Paragraph 1: The Committee of three Staffs will assume that Operation 'Overlord' is the dominating operation in 1944. Paragraph 2: The Committee will make recommendations as to subsidiary operations to be carried out, taking into most careful account any delay on Operation 'Overlord'." This was agreed.

Stalin said that the Soviet Government was vitally concerned with the date of "Overlord", particularly because of the need for co-ordinating operations on the Russian front. The President observed that the "Overlord" date had been fixed at the Quebec Conference, and it was only the important developments which had occurred since then that had caused any change to be contemplated.

Before we separated Stalin looked at me across the table and said, "I wish to pose a very direct question to the Prime Minister about 'Overlord'. Do the Prime Minister and the British Staff really believe in 'Overlord'?" I replied, "Provided the conditions previously stated for 'Overlord' are established when the time comes, it will be our stern duty to hurl across the Channel against the Germans every sinew of our strength." On this we separated.

* * * * *

Stalin was our host at dinner. The company was strictly limited—Stalin and Molotov, the President, Hopkins, Harriman, and Clark Kerr, myself and Eden, and our interpreters. After the labours of the Conference there was a good deal of gaiety, and many toasts were proposed. Presently Elliott Roosevelt, who had flown out to join his father, appeared at the door and somebody beckoned him to come in. He therefore took his seat at the table. He even intervened in the conversation, and has since given a highly coloured and extremely misleading account of what he heard. Stalin, as Hopkins recounts, indulged in a great deal of "teasing" of me, which I did not at all resent until the Marshal entered in a genial manner upon a serious and even deadly aspect of the punishment to be inflicted upon the Germans. The German General Staff, he said, must be liquidated. The whole force of Hitler's mighty armies depended upon about fifty thousand officers and technicians. If these were rounded up and shot at the end of the war German military strength would be extirpated. On this I thought it right to say, "The British Parliament and public will never tolerate mass executions. Even if in war passion they allowed them to begin they would turn violently against those responsible after the first butchery had taken place. The Soviets must be under no delusion on this point."

Stalin however, perhaps only in mischief, pursued the subject. "Fifty thousand," he said, "must be shot." I was deeply angered. "I would rather," I said, "be taken out into the garden here and now and be shot myself than sully my own and my country's honour by such infamy."

At this point the President intervened. He had a compromise to propose. Not fifty thousand should be shot, but only forty-nine thousand. By this he hoped, no doubt, to reduce the whole matter to ridicule. Eden also made signs and gestures intended to reassure me that it was all a joke. But now Elliott Roosevelt rose in his place at the end of the table and made a speech, saying how cordially he agreed with Marshal Stalin's plan and how sure he was that the United States Army would support it. At this intrusion I got up and left the table, walking off into the next room, which was in semi-darkness. I had not been there a minute before hands were clapped upon my shoulders from behind, and there was Stalin, with Molotov at his side, both grinning broadly, and eagerly declaring that they were only playing, and that nothing of a serious character had entered their heads. Stalin has a very captivating manner when he chooses to use it, and I never saw him do so to such an extent as at this moment. Although I was not then, and am not now, fully convinced that all was chaff and there was no serious intent lurking behind, I consented to return, and the rest of the evening passed pleasantly.

CHAPTER XXI

TEHERAN: THE CRUX

*My Sixty-ninth Birthday – I See Stalin Alone – Earnestness of Our
Preparations for "Overlord" – The Effect in the Mediterranean - The
Supreme Command – Everything Turns on Landing-craft – The Forces
Gathered for "Overlord" – A Great Battle Impending in Italy –
Stalin Emphasises the Need for "Overlord" – He Offers a Russian
Offensive in May or June – The President's Luncheon for "Three
Only" – Russia's Claim to Warm-Water Ports – The Third Plenary
Session, November 30 – The Main Military Decisions Taken – A
Communiqué Agreed – Dinner at the British Legation – Compliments
All Round and Many Speeches – General Brooke's Rejoinder to
Stalin.*

OVEMBER 30 was for me a crowded and memorable
day. It was my sixty-ninth birthday, and was passed
almost entirely in transacting some of the most important
business with which I have ever been concerned. The fact that
the President was in private contact with Marshal Stalin and
dwelling at the Soviet Embassy, and that he had avoided ever
seeing me alone since we left Cairo, in spite of our hitherto
intimate relations and the way in which our vital affairs were
interwoven, led me to seek a direct personal interview with
Stalin. I felt that the Russian leader was not deriving a true
impression of the British attitude. The false idea was forming in
his mind that, to put it shortly, "Churchill and the British Staffs
mean to stop 'Overlord' if they can, because they want to invade
the Balkans instead." It was my duty to remove this double
misconception.

The exact date of "Overlord" depended upon the movements
of a comparatively small number of landing-craft. These landing-
craft were not required for any operation in the Balkans. The

President had committed us to an operation in the Bay of Bengal. If this were cancelled there would be enough landing-craft for all I wanted, namely, the amphibious power to land against opposition two divisions at a time on the coasts of Italy or Southern France, and also to carry out "Overlord" as planned in May. I had agreed with the President that May should be the month, and he had, for his part, given up the specific date of May I. This would give me the time I needed. If I could persuade the President to obtain relief from his promise to Chiang Kai-shek and drop the Bay of Bengal plan, which had never been mentioned in our Teheran conferences, there would be enough landing-craft both for the Mediterranean and for a punctual "Overlord". In the event the great landings began on June 6, but this date was decided much later on, not by any requirements of mine, but by the moon and the weather. I also succeeded when we returned to Cairo, as will be seen, in persuading the President to abandon the enterprise in the Bay of Bengal. I therefore consider that I got what I deemed imperative. But this was far from certain at Teheran on this November morning. I was determined that Stalin should know the main facts. I did not feel entitled to tell him that the President and I had agreed upon May for "Overlord". I knew that Roosevelt wanted to tell him this himself at our luncheon which was to follow my conversation with the Marshal.

The following is founded upon the record made by Major Birse, my trusted interpreter, of my private talk with Stalin.

* * * * *

I began by reminding the Marshal that I was half American and had a great affection for the American people. What I was going to say was not to be understood as disparaging to the Americans, and I would be perfectly loyal towards them, but there were things which it was better to say outright between two persons.

We had a preponderance of troops over the Americans in the Mediterranean. There were two or three times more British troops than American there. That was why I was anxious that the armies in the Mediterranean should not be hamstrung if it could be avoided. I wanted to use them all the time. In Italy there were some thirteen to fourteen divisions, of which nine or ten were British. There were two armies, the Fifth Anglo-American Army, and the Eighth Army, which was entirely British. The choice had been represented as keeping to the date of "Overlord" or pressing on with the operations in the Mediterranean. But that was not the whole story. The Americans wanted me to undertake an amphibious operation in the Bay of Bengal against the Japanese in March. I was not keen about it. If we had the landing-craft needed for the Bay of Bengal in the Mediterranean we should have enough to do all we wanted there and still be able to keep to an early date for "Overlord". It was not a choice between the Mediterranean and the date of "Overlord", but between the Bay of Bengal and the date of "Overlord". However, the Americans had pinned us down to a date for "Overlord" and operations in the Mediterranean had suffered in the last two months. Our army in Italy was somewhat disheartened by the removal of seven divisions. We had sent home three divisions, and the Americans were sending four of theirs, all in preparation for "Overlord". That was why we had not been able to take full advantage of the Italian collapse. But it also proved the earnestness of our preparations for "Overlord".

It was vital to get an early decision on the appointment of the Commander-in-Chief. Up till August we British were to have had the Supreme Command in "Overlord", but at Quebec I had told the President that I would agree to the appointment of an American, while we should have the Supreme Command in the Mediterranean. I was content with this because the Americans, although equal in numbers to the British when we landed, would soon have a preponderance, and their stake would be greater after the first few months. On the other hand, as the British had the preponderance in the Mediterranean and I had my own ideas about the war there I considered it right that we should have the Supreme Command in that theatre. The President had accepted this arrangement, and it now rested with him to nominate the Commander-in-Chief for "Overlord". As soon as the President did so I would nominate the Mediterranean Commander-in-Chief and other commanders. The President had delayed the appointment for domestic reasons connected with high personages, but I had urged him to decide before we all left Teheran. Stalin said that was good.

I then turned to the question of landing-craft, and explained once again how and why they were the bottle-neck. We had plenty of troops in the Mediterranean, even after the removal of the seven divisions, and there would be an adequate invading British and American army in the United Kingdom. All turned on landing-craft. When the Marshal had made his momentous announcement two days before about Russia's coming into the war against Japan after Hitler's surrender I had immediately suggested to the Americans that they might find more landing-craft for the operations we had been asked to carry out in the Indian Ocean, or that they might send some landing-craft from the Pacific to help the first lift of "Overlord". In that case there might be enough for all. But the Americans were very touchy about the Pacific. I had pointed out to them that Japan would be beaten much sooner if Russia joined in the war against her, and that they could therefore afford to give us more help.

The issue between myself and the Americans was in fact a very narrow one. It was not that I was in any way lukewarm about "Overlord". I wanted to get what I needed for the Mediterranean and at the same time keep to the date for "Overlord". The details had to be hammered out between the Staffs, and I had hoped that this might be done in Cairo. Unfortunately Chiang Kai-shek had been there and Chinese questions had taken up nearly all the time. But I was sure that in the end enough landing-craft would be found for all.

Now about "Overlord". The British would have ready by the date fixed in May or June nearly sixteen divisions, with their corps troops, landing-craft troops, anti-aircraft, and services, a total of slightly over half a million men. These would consist of some of our best troops, including battle-trained men from the Mediterranean. In addition the British would have all that was needed from the Royal Navy to handle transportation and to protect the Army, and there would be the metropolitan Air Forces of about 4,000 first-line British aircraft in continuous action. The American import of troops was now beginning. Up till now they had sent mainly air troops and stores for the Army, but in the next four or five months I thought 150,000 men or more would come every month, making a total of seven to eight hundred thousand men by May. The defeat of the submarines in the Atlantic had made this movement possible. I was in favour of launching the operation in the South of France about the same

time as "Overlord" or at whatever moment was found correct.
We should be holding enemy troops in Italy, and of the twenty-
two or twenty-three divisions in the Mediterranean as many as
possible would go to the South of France and the rest would
remain in Italy.

A great battle was impending in Italy. General Alexander
had about half a million men under him. There were thirteen
or fourteen Allied divisions against nine to ten German. The
weather had been bad and bridges had been swept away, but in
December we intended to push on, with General Montgomery
leading the Eighth Army. The amphibious landing would be
made near the Tiber. At the same time the Fifth Army would be
fiercely engaged holding the enemy. It might turn into a minia-
ture Stalingrad. We did not intend to push into the wide part of
Italy, but to hold the narrow leg.

Stalin said he must warn me that the Red Army was depending
on the success of our invasion of Northern France. If there were
no operations in May 1944 then the Red Army would think
that there would be no operations at all that year. The weather
would be bad and there would be transport difficulties. If the
operation did not take place he did not want the Red Army to be
disappointed. Disappointment could only create bad feeling. If
there was no big change in the European war in 1944 it would be
very difficult for the Russians to carry on. They were war-weary.
He feared that a feeling of isolation might develop in the Red
Army. That was why he had tried to find out whether "Overlord" would be undertaken on time as promised. If not, he would
have to take steps to prevent bad feeling in the Red Army. It was
most important.

I said "Overlord" would certainly take place, provided the
enemy did not bring into France larger forces than the Americans
and British could gather there. If the Germans had thirty to
forty divisions in France I did not think the force we were going
to put across the Channel would be able to hold on. I was not
afraid of going on shore, but of what would happen on the
thirtieth, fortieth, or fiftieth day. However, if the Red Army
engaged the enemy and we held them in Italy, and possibly the
Turks came into the war, then I thought we could win.

Stalin said that the first steps of "Overlord" would have a good
effect on the Red Army, and if he knew that it was going to take

M

place in May or June he could already prepare blows against Germany. The spring was the best time. March and April were months of slackness, during which he could concentrate troops and material, and in May and June he could attack. Germany would have no troops for France. The transfer of German divisions to the east was continuing. The Germans were afraid of their Eastern Front, because it had no Channel which had to be crossed and there was no France to be entered. The Germans were afraid of the Red Army advance. The Red Army would advance if it saw that help was coming from the Allies. He asked when "Overlord" would begin.

I said that I could not disclose the date for "Overlord" without the President's agreement, but the answer would be given at lunch-time, and I thought he would be satisfied.

*   *   *   *   *

After a short interval the Marshal and I separately proceeded to the President's quarters for the luncheon of "Three Only" (with our interpreters) to which he had invited us. Roosevelt then told Stalin that we were both agreed that "Overlord" should be launched during the month of May. The Marshal was evidently greatly pleased and relieved by this solemn and direct engagement which we both made. The conversation turned on lighter subjects, and the only part of which I have a record was the question of Russia's outlet upon the seas and oceans. I had always thought it was a wrong thing, capable of breeding disastrous quarrels, that a mighty land-mass like the Russian Empire, with its population of nearly two hundred millions, should be denied during the winter months all effective access to the broad waters.

When Marshal Stalin raised this question of warm-water ports for Russia I said there were no obstacles. He also asked about the Dardanelles and the revision of the Treaty of Sèvres. I said that I wanted to get Turkey into the war, and this was an awkward moment for raising the question. Stalin replied that the time would come later. I said I expected Russia would sail the oceans with her Navy and merchant fleet, and we would welcome her ships. At this Stalin remarked that Lord Curzon had had other ideas. I said that in those days we did not see eye to eye with Russia.

The President said that the Baltic should be free to all nations for merchant shipping. There should be free zones in the ports, and trustees should be appointed for the Kiel Canal, while the Dardanelles ought to be free to the commerce of the world. Stalin asked whether this would apply to Russian commerce, and we assured him that it would.

Stalin then asked what could be done for Russia in the Far East. I replied that Russia had Vladivostok, but he pointed out that the port was ice-bound, and also depended on the Straits of Tsushima. At present the only exit that the Russians had was Murmansk. I answered that I wished to meet the Russian grievance, because the government of the world must be entrusted to satisfied nations, who wished nothing more for themselves than what they had. If the world-government were in the hands of hungry nations there would always be danger. But none of us had any reason to seek for anything more. The peace would be kept by peoples who lived in their own way and were not ambitious. Our power placed us above the rest. We were like rich men dwelling at peace within their habitations.

* * * * *

After a brief interval the third plenary session began as before in the Russian Embassy at four o'clock. There was a full attendance and we numbered nearly thirty.

The President said he was very happy to inform the Conference that agreement had been reached on the main military problems.

Sir Alan Brooke said that, after sitting in combined session, the United States and British Chiefs of Staff had recommended us to launch "Overlord" in May, "in conjunction with a supporting operation against the South of France, on the largest scale permitted by the landing-craft available at that time."

I then emphasised the need for the combined United States and British Staffs to keep in closest touch with the Soviet military authorities, so that all operations on the Eastern as well as the Western and Mediterranean Fronts were concerted. By this means the three Great Powers would close in on the wild beast so that he was engaged on all sides at the same moment. Very detailed Staff work would be necessary to launch "Overlord", which was the biggest combined operation ever planned.

Stalin said that he understood the importance of the decision taken by the Staffs and the difficulties inherent in carrying it out. The danger period for "Overlord" would be at the time of deployment from the landings. At this point the Germans might transfer troops from the east in order to create the maximum difficulties for "Overlord". In order to prevent any movement from the east of any considerable German forces he undertook to organise a large-scale Russian offensive in May.*

The President remarked on the importance of the timing of operations in all theatres. Now that the three Staffs had got together he hoped they would keep together. He had already informed Marshal Stalin that the next step was to appoint the Commander for "Overlord". After consultation with his own Staffs and with me, it should be possible to make a decision within three or four days. Now that the main military decisions had been taken, it seemed right for the British and American Staffs to return to Cairo as soon as possible to work out the details. To this Stalin and I agreed.

I added that now that the supreme decisions had been taken every effort must be bent to find the ways and means to get more landing-craft. With five months still to go before the launching of "Overlord", and with all the resources of America and Great Britain at our disposal, it should be possible to do this. If "Overlord" was to be done it must be done with smashing force, and I hoped that the Staffs would find ways and means of increasing the initial assault forces.

I asked if there would be any difficulty in the three Staffs concerting cover plans. Stalin explained that the Russians had made considerable use of deception by means of dummy tanks, aircraft, and airfields. Radio deception had also proved effective. He was entirely agreeable to the Staffs collaborating with the object of devising joint cover and deception schemes. "In wartime," I said, "truth is so precious that she should always be attended by a bodyguard of lies." Stalin and his comrades greatly appreciated this remark when it was translated, and upon this note our formal conference ended gaily.

I then suggested that the Staffs should draft a short communiqué to cover the military talks for submission to the President, Marshal Stalin, and myself. The note to be sounded was brevity, mystery, and a foretaste of impending doom for Germany. The following communiqué was therefore framed and agreed to by all:

* The main Russian attack began on June 23.

. . . Our Military Staffs have joined in our round table discussions, and we have concerted our plans for the destruction of the German forces. We have reached complete agreement as to the scope and timing of the operations which will be undertaken from the east, west, and south.

* * * * *

Hitherto we had assembled for our conferences or meals in the Soviet Embassy. I had claimed however that I should be the host at the third dinner, which should be held in the British Legation. This could not well be disputed. Great Britain and I myself both came first alphabetically, and in seniority I was four or five years older than Roosevelt or Stalin. We were by centuries the longest established of the three Governments; I might have added, but did not, that we had been the longest in the war; and, finally, November 30 was my birthday. These arguments, particularly the last one, were conclusive, and all preparations were made by our Minister for a dinner of nearly forty persons, including not only the political and military chiefs, but some of their higher staffs. The Soviet Political Police, the N.K.V.D., insisted on searching the British Legation from top to bottom, looking behind every door and under every cushion, before Stalin appeared; and about fifty armed Russian policemen, under their own general, posted themselves near all the doors and windows. The American Security men were also much in evidence. Everything however passed off agreeably. Stalin, arriving under heavy guard, was in the best of tempers, and the President, from his wheeled chair, beamed on us all in pleasure and goodwill.

This was a memorable occasion in my life. On my right sat the President of the United States, on my left the master of Russia. Together we controlled a large preponderance of the naval and three-quarters of all the air forces in the world, and could direct armies of nearly twenty millions of men, engaged in the most terrible of wars that had yet occurred in human history. I could not help rejoicing at the long way we had come on the road to victory since the summer of 1940, when we had been alone, and, apart from the Navy and the Air, practically unarmed, against the triumphant and unbroken might of Germany and Italy, with almost all Europe and its resources in their grasp. Mr. Roosevelt gave me for a birthday present a beautiful Persian porcelain vase, which, although it was broken into fragments on the homeward journey, has been marvellously reconstructed and is one of my treasures.

During dinner I had a most pleasant conversation with both my august guests. Stalin repeated the question he had posed at the Conference, "Who will command 'Overlord'?" I said that the President had not yet finally made up his mind, but that I was almost certain it would be General Marshall, who sat opposite us at no great distance, and that was how it had stood hitherto. He was evidently very pleased at this. He then spoke about General Brooke. He thought that he did not like the Russians. He had been very abrupt and rough with them at our first Moscow meeting in August 1942. I reassured him, remarking that military men were apt to be blunt and hard-cut when dealing with war problems with their professional colleagues. Stalin said that he liked them all the better for that. He gazed at Brooke intently across the room.

When the time came I proposed the health of our illustrious guests, and the President proposed my health and wished me many happy returns of the day. He was followed by Stalin, who spoke in a similar strain.

* * * * *

Many informal toasts were then proposed, according to the Russian custom, which is certainly very well suited to banquets of this kind. Hopkins made a speech couched in a happy vein, in the course of which he said that he had made "a very long and thorough study of the British Constitution, which is unwritten, and of the War Cabinet, whose authority and composition are not specifically defined". As the result of this study, he said, "I have learnt that the provisions of the British Constitution and the powers of the War Cabinet are just whatever Winston Churchill wants them to be at any given moment." This caused general laughter. The reader of these volumes will know how little foundation there was in this jocular assertion. It is true that I received a measure of loyal support in the direction of the war from Parliament and my Cabinet colleagues which may well be unprecedented, and that there were very few large issues upon which I was overruled; but it was with some pride that I reminded my two great comrades on more than one occasion that I was the only one of our trinity who could at any moment be dismissed from power by the vote of a House of Commons freely elected on universal franchise, or could be controlled from day to day by the opinion of a War Cabinet representing all parties in the State. The President's term of office was fixed, and his powers not only as President but as Commander-in-Chief were almost absolute under the American Constitution. Stalin appeared to be, and at this moment certainly was, all-powerful in Russia. They could order; I had to convince and persuade. I was glad that this should be so. The process was laborious, but I had no reason to complain of the way it worked.

*   *   *   *   *

As the dinner proceeded there were many speeches, and most of the principal figures, including Molotov and General Marshall, made their contribution. But the speech which stands out in my memory came from General Brooke. I quote the account he was good enough to write for me.

"Half-way through the dinner," he says, "the President very kindly proposed my health, referring to the time when my father had visited his father at Hyde Park. Just as he was finishing, and I was thinking what an easy time I should have replying to such kind words, Stalin got up and said he would finish the toast. He then proceeded to imply that I had failed to show real feelings of friendship towards the Red Army, that I was lacking in a true appreciation of its fine qualities, and that he hoped in future I should be able to show greater comradeship towards the soldiers of the Red Army!

"I was very much surprised by these accusations, as I could not think what they were based on. I had however seen enough of Stalin by then to know that if I sat down under these insults I should lose any respect he might ever have had for me, and that he would continue such attacks in the future.

"I therefore rose to thank the President most profusely for his very kind expressions, and then turned to Stalin in approximately the following words:

"'Now, Marshal, may I deal with your toast. I am surprised that you should have found it necessary to raise accusations against me that are entirely unfounded. You will remember that this morning while we were discussing cover plans Mr. Churchill said that "in war truth must have an escort of lies". You will also remember that you yourself told us that in all your great offensives your real intentions were always kept concealed from the outer world. You told us that all your dummy tanks and dummy aeroplanes were always massed on those fronts that were of an immediate interest, while your true intentions were covered by a cloak of complete secrecy.

" 'Well, Marshal, you have been misled by dummy tanks and dummy aeroplanes, and you have failed to observe those feelings of true friendship which I have for the Red Army, nor have you seen the feelings of genuine comradeship which I bear towards all its members.' "

As this was translated by Pavlov, sentence by sentence, to Stalin I watched his expression carefully. It was inscrutable. But at the end he turned to me and said with evident relish, "I like that man. He rings true. I must have a talk with him afterwards."

At length we moved into the ante-chamber, and here everyone moved about in changing groups. I felt that there was a greater sense of solidarity and good-comradeship than we had ever reached before in the Grand Alliance. I had not invited Randolph and Sarah to the dinner, though they came in while my birthday toast was being proposed, but now Stalin singled them out and greeted them most warmly, and of course the President knew them well.

As I moved around I saw Stalin in a small circle face to face with "Brookie", as I call him. The General's account continues: "As we walked out of the room the Prime Minister told me that he had felt somewhat nervous as to what I should say next when I had referred to 'truth' and 'lies'. He comforted me however by telling me that my reply to the toast had had the right effect on Stalin. I therefore decided to return to the attack in the ante-room. I went up to Stalin and told him how surprised I was, and grieved, that he should have found it necessary to raise such accusations against me in his toast. He replied at once through Pavlov, 'The best friendships are those founded on misunderstandings,' and he shook me warmly by the hand."

It seemed to me that all the clouds had passed away, and in fact Stalin's confidence in my friend was established on a foundation of respect and goodwill which was never shaken while we all worked together.

It must have been after two in the morning when we finally separated. The Marshal resigned himself to his escort and departed, and the President was conveyed to his quarters in the Soviet Embassy. I went to bed tired out but content, feeling sure that nothing but good had been done. It certainly was a happy birthday for me.

CHAPTER XXII

TEHERAN: CONCLUSIONS

Conversation at Luncheon, December 1 – How to Gain Turkey – The Russian Share of Italian Ships – The Frontiers of Poland – The "Curzon Line" and the Line of the Oder – A Frank Talk – Finland – "No Annexations and No Indemnities" – Final Accord – The Question of Germany – Partition? – President Roosevelt's Suggestion – I Unfold a Personal View – Marshal Stalin's Standpoint – More About Poland – Broad Agreement on Military Policy – Political Aspects Remote and Speculative – Deep Fear of German Might at this War Climax – The Present Partition: "It Cannot Last."

SEVERAL of our gravest political issues stood out before and after the main decision on strategy had been reached. The Three lunched together again at the President's table in the Soviet Embassy on December 1. In addition on this occasion Molotov, Hopkins, Eden, Clark Kerr, and Harriman were present. The question of inducing Turkey to enter the war was our first topic.

Hopkins asked what support we should have to give Turkey if she came in. Roosevelt said that Inönü would ask what we could do. Until the landing-craft situation had been studied we should be careful in making promises. I said that we had seventeen British squadrons in Egypt which were not under the Anglo-American command, and Air Marshal Tedder had three more squadrons which we could spare. They were chiefly fighters and could be used to protect Turkey. In addition we had three regiments of anti-aircraft guns. This was all we had promised. We had not promised Turkey any troops. She had fifty divisions equipped, and there was no need to send any troops.

Stalin said that if Turkey entered the war she would make part of her territory available. I agreed, and said Ploesti would be

344

vulnerable. We British were not offering Turkey anything that was not ours to give, and we were only giving three squadrons from the Central Mediterranean to make up the number from seventeen to twenty. Perhaps the Americans could add a few bomber squadrons. We had said that we would only give air protection. We had no army available. The landing-craft required in March for taking Rhodes could be sandwiched in between Italy and "Overlord". The President hoped this could be done, but said that casualties among landing-craft were very heavy and we should want all we could get for "Overlord". I replied that I saw no difficulty. We had made no offers to Turkey, nor did I know if Inönü would accept any. The President would be in Cairo and could see what his Staffs would have to say. We British could only offer our twenty squadrons. The Turks did not need any army; they needed air protection. In addition, Inönü might not come to Cairo.

"He might fall ill," interjected Stalin.

I said that if he refused to come and the President had to leave I proposed to go in a cruiser and see him in Adana. Inönü would come there. Landing-craft were the bottle-neck for all our operations. Some might be forthcoming from the Indian Ocean or the Pacific, or more could be built. If this could not be done we should have to give up something, but it was agreed that "Overlord" was not to suffer.

Roosevelt then said that my suggestion that landing-craft should be provided from the Pacific was impossible. Distances were too great, and every day the Americans were proceeding north in the Gilbert and Marshall Islands to attack Japanese supply lines. They needed all the landing-craft they had.

Hopkins asked how many landing-craft would be needed for taking Rhodes. I replied that there was no commitment to Turkey about Rhodes or any other island, and there was no commitment in landing-craft. Roosevelt said that if he were Inönü he would ask for Crete and other islands to be taken.

I said: "What I want is air bases in the region of Smyrna and Badrun. Those airfields have been constructed by us. When we get them and put in squadrons we can drive the Germans out of the air. It pays us anyhow to lose one aircraft for every German machine shot down. We must starve out the German garrisons on the islands. If Turkey takes an active part the islands will fall of themselves. It would not be necessary in that case to attack even Rhodes. The islands have to be supplied by Germany, and if we have air cover from Turkey our destroyers can cut down German convoys, which they cannot do at present because Germany commands the air. Turkish bases will give us continued pressure against the Germans, and that will be a preparation for 'Overlord'."

Stalin agreed, and the President consented to go forward on the basis of twenty squadrons and some bombers, but no amphibious operations.

I then summed up. We were offering Turkey only limited air protection and anti-aircraft guns, but the winter was approaching and Germany would not invade Turkey. We would continue to supply her with arms. There was the priceless opportunity for Turkey of accepting the Soviet invitation to sit beside us at the Peace Conference. There was the assurance that if Bulgaria attacked Turkey because the latter had declared war on Germany the Soviet Union would retaliate on Bulgaria, a thing which had never happened before. Then there was the offer of association with the victorious Powers and our good offices and friendship.

"What measures," asked Stalin, "does Mr. Churchill expect from the Soviet Union in case Turkey declares war on Germany, as a result of which Bulgaria attacks Turkey and the Soviet declares war on Bulgaria?"

I said I was not asking for anything specific, but as the Soviet armies advanced through Odessa they would create a great effect among the population in Bulgaria. The Turkish Army had rifles, brave infantry, fairly good artillery, but no A.A. guns, no aircraft, and very few tanks. We had established military schools, but they were not attended regularly. The Turks were not quick to learn. Their Army was brave, but not modern. Twenty-five million pounds had been spent on weapons, mainly American, and we had shipped them.

Stalin said it was possible Turkey would not have to fight. They would give us their air bases; that might be the course of events, and it would be good.

The President then asked Mr. Eden to tell us what the Turks had said in Cairo. Mr. Eden said he had asked the Turkish Foreign Minister to give us air bases and told him that Germany would not attack Turkey. The Foreign Minister had refused, saying that Germany would react against Turkish provocation. Turkey would rather come in by agreement than be brought in indirectly as a result of such action as had been suggested.

I observed that when we asked the Turks to strain their neutrality by giving us their air bases they replied, "Oh, no, we cannot play a passive rôle," but if we asked them to start war in earnest they answered, "Oh, no, we are not sufficiently armed." I proposed, if necessary, to try other methods. If Turkey refused she would forfeit her chance to sit at the Peace Conference. She would be treated like other neutrals. We would say that Great Britain had no further interest in her affairs and we would stop the supply of arms.

Mr. Eden said he would like to get quite clear in his mind the demands that were to be made on Turkey. Was it understood that Turkey should go to war with Germany and no one else? If as a result the Germans made Bulgaria join them in a war against Turkey would the Soviet Government go to war with Bulgaria? Stalin agreed on both points. I said that, for myself, I would be satisfied with strained neutrality from Turkey. There was thus a very great measure of agreement on the limited steps for which I asked in order to win the great prize of bringing Turkey into the war, and it was settled that President Inönü should be invited to come to Cairo and talk it all over with me and the President. Although I felt how deeply Turkish minds had been affected by our failure to attack Rhodes, by the loss of Cos and Leros, and the consequent German command of the air in the Ægean, I left the subject, having got all I had thought it right to ask, and with fair hopes that it would not be insufficient.

*   *   *   *   *

Molotov now asked whether the Soviet Government could not be given an answer about the Italian ships. Roosevelt's reply was very simple. A large number of merchant ships and a smaller number of warships could be used by the three nations during the war, and could then be distributed by title. It would be best until then that those should use these ships who could use them best. Molotov said that Russia would be able to make good use of them. I asked where the Soviet Government would like them delivered. Stalin said in the Black Sea, and, if this were not possible, then in the North. If Turkey did not come into the war the Black Sea would be impossible, but use could be made of them in the North.

I said that this was a very small thing after all the efforts that Russia was making or had made. We only asked for a little time to handle the matter with the Italians. I said I should like to see the ships go to the Black Sea, and that perhaps I might at the same time send some of His Majesty's ships with them. The President and I needed time to arrange the matter with the Italians, who were already helping with some of their smaller ships in patrol work, and some Italian submarines were carrying important supplies. There must be no mutiny in the Italian Fleet and no scuttling of ships. A couple of months should be enough for me and the President to arrange with the Italians. The ships could pass under Russian orders by that date, after refitting. I went on to say that I should like to put four or five British submarines into the Black Sea. This was one of the things which might be asked of Turkey if she accepted only "strained neutrality". But we would abide by Marshal Stalin's wishes. We had no ambitions in the Black Sea.

Stalin replied that he would be grateful for any help.

* * * * *

After an interval, when luncheon was over, we moved into another room, and took our seats at a conference table. Our discussions continued all through the afternoon. Poland was the next important subject.

The President began by saying that he hoped the Polish and Soviet Governments would resume relations, so that any decision taken could be accepted by the Polish Government. But he admitted there were difficulties. Stalin asked with what Government he would have to negotiate. The Polish Government and their friends in Poland were in contact with the Germans. They killed the Partisans. Neither the President nor I could have any idea of what was now going on there.

I said that the Polish question was important for us in the United Kingdom, because we had declared war on Germany for invading Poland. Although Great Britain had been unprepared the German attack on Poland had launched us into the war. I reverted to my illustration of the three matches—Germany, Poland, and the Soviet Union. One of the main objects of the

Allies was to achieve the security of the Soviet western frontier, and so to prevent an attack by Germany in the future. Here I reminded Stalin of his mention of the line of the Oder in the West.

Stalin, interrupting, said that previously there had been no mention of re-establishing relations with the Polish Government, but only of determining Poland's frontiers. To-day the matter had been put quite differently. Russia, even more than other States, was interested in good relations with Poland, because for her it was a question of the security of her frontiers. Russia was in favour of the reconstruction, development, and expansion of Poland mainly at the expense of Germany. But he separated Poland from the Polish Government in exile. He had broken off relations with the Polish Government in exile, not on account of caprice, but because it had joined with Hitler in slanderous propaganda against Russia. What guarantee was there that this would not happen again? He would like to have a guarantee that the Polish Government in exile would not kill Partisans, but, on the contrary, would urge the Poles to fight the Germans and not concern themselves with any machinations. He would welcome any Polish Government which would take such active measures, and he would be glad to renew relations with them. But he was by no means sure that the Polish Government in exile was ever likely to become the kind of Government it ought to be.

Here I said that it would be a great help if round that very table we could learn what were the Russian ideas about the frontiers. I should then put the matter before the Poles and say frankly if I thought the conditions fair. His Majesty's Government, for whom alone I spoke, would like to be able to tell the Poles that the plan was a good one and the best that they were likely to get and that His Majesty's Government would not argue against it at the peace table. Then we could get on with the President's idea of resuming relations. What we wanted was a strong and independent Poland, friendly to Russia.

Stalin said that that was true, but that the Poles could not be allowed to seize the Ukraine and White Russian territory. That was not fair. According to the 1939 frontier, the soil of the Ukraine and White Russia was returned to the Ukraine and to White Russia. Soviet Russia adhered to the frontiers of 1939, for they appeared to be ethnologically the right ones.

Eden asked if this meant the Ribbentrop-Molotov Line.

"Call it whatever you like," said Stalin.

Molotov remarked that it was generally called the Curzon Line.

"No," said Eden, "there are important differences."

Molotov said there were none.

I then produced a map and showed the Curzon Line and the 1939 line, and indicated also the line of the Oder. Eden said that the south end of the Curzon Line had never been defined in terms.

At this point the meeting broke into groups. There was a general gathering round my map and round a map which was produced by the Americans, and it was difficult for the interpreters to take notes.

Eden suggested that the Curzon Line was intended to pass to the east of Lvov.

Stalin replied that the line on my map had not been drawn right. Lvov should be left on the Russian side and the line should go westwards towards Przemysl. Molotov would get a map of the Curzon Line and a description of it. He said that he did not want any Polish population, and that if he found any district inhabited by Poles he would gladly give it up.

I suggested that the value of the German land was much greater than the Pripet Marshes. It was industrial and it would make a much better Poland. We should like to be able to say to the Poles that the Russians were right, and to tell the Poles that they must agree that they had had a fair deal. If the Poles did not accept we could not help it. Here I made it clear that I was speaking for the British alone, adding that the President had many Poles in the United States who were his fellow-citizens.

Stalin said again that if it were proved to him that any district were Polish he would not claim it, and here he made some shadowing on the map west of the Curzon Line and south of Vilna, which he admitted to be mainly Polish.

At this point the meeting again separated into groups, and there was a prolonged study of the Oder Line on a map. When this came to an end I said that I liked the picture, and that I would say to the Poles that if they did not accept it they would be foolish, and I would remind them that but for the Red Army they would have been utterly destroyed. I would point out to them that they had been given a fine place to live in, more than three hundred miles each way.

Stalin said that it would indeed be a large, industrial State.

"And friendly to Russia," I interjected.

Stalin replied that Russia wanted a friendly Poland.

I then, runs the record, said to Mr. Eden, with some emphasis, that I was not going to break my heart about this cession of part of Germany to Poland or about Lvov. Eden said that if Marshal Stalin would take the Curzon and Oder Lines as a basis on which to argue that might provide a beginning.

At this point Molotov produced the Russian version of the Curzon Line, and the text of a wireless telegram from Lord Curzon giving all the place-names. I asked whether Molotov would object to the Poles getting the Oppeln district. He said he did not think so.

I said that the Poles would be wise to take our advice. I was not prepared to make a great squawk about Lvov. Turning to Marshal Stalin, I added that I did not think we were very far apart in principle. Roosevelt asked Stalin whether he thought a transfer of population on a voluntary basis would be possible. The Marshal said that probably it would be.

On this we left the Polish discussion.

*   *   *   *   *

The President next asked Stalin whether he was ready to discuss Finland. Could the United States Government do anything to help to get Finland out of the war?

Stalin said that recently the Swedish Vice-Minister for Foreign Affairs had told Madame Kollontay (the Soviet Ambassadress) that the Finns were afraid that Russia wanted to turn Finland into a Russian province. The Soviet Government had replied that they had no wish to make Finland a Russian province unless the Finns forced them to do so. Madame Kollontay had then been instructed to tell the Finns that the Soviet Government would have no objection to receiving a Finnish delegation in Moscow; but they wished the Finns to state their views about dropping out of the war. In Teheran he had just received the gist of the Finnish reply, which was conveyed to him through M. Boheman. The reply did not make any mention of Finland's desire to dissociate herself from Germany. It raised the question of frontiers. The

Finns suggested that as a basis of discussion the 1939 frontier should be adopted, with some corrections in favour of the Soviet Union. Stalin believed that the Finns were not really anxious to conduct serious negotiations. Their conditions were unacceptable, and the Finns well knew it. The Finns still hoped for a German victory; and some of them at any rate had a strong belief that the Germans were going to win.

Roosevelt asked if it would help if the United States Government advised the Finns to go to Moscow. Stalin replied they were ready enough to go to Moscow, but it would not do much good if they went with their present programme.

I said that in the days of the Russo-Finnish War I had been sympathetic to Finland, but I had turned against her when she came into the war against the Soviets. Russia must have security for Leningrad and its approaches. The position of the Soviet Union as a permanent naval and air Power in the Baltic must be assured. But people in the United Kingdom would be unhappy if the Finns were incorporated in the Soviet Union against their will. I had therefore been glad to hear what Marshal Stalin had said. I did not think it useful to ask for indemnities. The Finns might cut down a few trees, but that would not do much good.

Stalin said that he did not want money, but within, say, five or eight years the Finns would be well able to make good the damage they had done to Russia by supplying her with paper, wood, and many other things. He thought the Finns should be given a lesson, and he was determined to get compensation.

I said I imagined that the harm the Finns did to Russia by their improper attack far exceeded what a poor country like Finland could supply. I added, "There is still ringing in my ears the famous slogan, 'No annexations and no indemnities.' Perhaps Marshal Stalin will not be pleased with me for saying that."

Stalin, with a broad grin, replied, "I have told you that I am becoming a Conservative."

I then asked what it was he wanted. We had "Overlord" coming. I should like to have Sweden with us in the war and Finland out of the war by the spring. Stalin said that would be good.

The conversation then turned to territorial detail—Viborg ("Nothing doing about Viborg," said Stalin), the Karelian Isthmus, Hangö. "If the cession of Hangö presents a difficulty," said Stalin, "I am willing to take Petsamo instead." "A fair exchange," said Roosevelt.

I said the British wanted two things: first, that Russia should be satisfied with her frontiers; second, that the Finns should be free and independent and live as well as they could in those very uncomfortable regions. But we did not want to put any pressure on Russia. Stalin said that, after all, allies could squeeze each other if they wanted to from time to time. But let the Finns live. It would be all right so long as half the damage they had done was made good. Roosevelt asked whether it would be any use if the Finns were to go to Moscow without any conditions. Stalin said that if there were no assurances that an agreement would be concluded, then an expedition to Moscow would help Germany, who would make capital out of any failure, and also the aggressive elements in Finland, who would say that the Russians did not really want peace.

I said that would be a lie, and that we would all say so loudly.

"All right," said Stalin, "let them come if you insist."

Roosevelt said that the present Finnish leaders were pro-German; if there were others we might get somewhere. Stalin thought it would be better to have others, but he did not object even to Ryti. Anyone, even the devil, might come. He was not afraid of devils.

I said I hoped Marshal Stalin would handle the question of Finland with due regard to the possibility of Sweden coming into the war in time for our general offensive in May.

Stalin agreed, but said that he could not diverge from several conditions:

(1) Restoration of the 1940 treaty.
(2) Hangö or Petsamo. (Here he added that Hangö was leased to the Soviet Union, but he would propose to take Petsamo.)
(3) Compensation in kind as to 50 per cent. for damage. Quantities could be discussed later.
(4) A breach with Germany.
(5) The expulsion of all Germans.
(6) Demobilisation.

I replied about compensation that it was easy enough to do damage, but very hard to repair it, and that it was bad for any one country to fall into tribute to another. I said, "Experience shows that large indemnities do not work." Stalin proposed to occupy part of Finland if the Finns did not pay, but if they did pay the Russians would withdraw within the year.

"I have not yet," I said, "been elected a Soviet commissar, but if I were I would advise against this. There are much bigger things to think about." We were behind the Russians and ready to help them at every turn, but we must think of the May battle. President Roosevelt said that he was ready to stand behind all that had been said (against large indemnities).

$$\star \quad \star \quad \star \quad \star \quad \star$$

Stalin now asked, "Are there any other questions?" The President replied, "There is the question of Germany." Stalin said that he would like to see Germany split up. The President agreed, but Stalin suggested that I would object.

I said I did not object in principle. Roosevelt said that, so that there could be some discussion, he and his advisers had had a shot at a plan some three months before. This involved the dividing of Germany into five parts. Stalin, with a grin, suggested that I was not listening because I was not inclined to see Germany split up. I said that I considered that the root of the evil lay in Prussia, in the Prussian Army and the General Staff.

Roosevelt then explained his plan for splitting Germany into five parts:

(1) Prussia.
(2) Hanover and the north-west part of Germany.
(3) Saxony and the Leipzig area.
(4) Hesse-Darmstadt, Hesse-Cassel, and the section south of the Rhine.
(5) Bavaria, Baden, and Württemberg.

These five sections would be self-governing, but there were two more that would be governed by the United Nations:

(1) Kiel and its canal and Hamburg.
(2) The Ruhr and the Saar.

These would be under the control of the United Nations as trustees. He was only throwing this out as an idea which might be talked over.

"If," I said, "I might use the American idiom, I would say that the President has 'said a mouthful'. Mr. Roosevelt's plan is a new one to me. In my opinion there are two things, one destructive and the other constructive. I have two clear ideas in mind. First the isolation of Prussia. What is to be done to Prussia after that is only secondary. Then I would like to detach Bavaria, Württemberg, the Palatinate, Saxony, and Baden. Whereas I would treat Prussia sternly, I would make things easier for the second group, which I should like to see work in with what I would call a Danubian Confederation. The people of those parts of Germany are not the most ferocious, and I should like to see them live tolerably, and in a generation they would feel differently. South Germans are not going to start another war, and we would have to make it worth their while to forget Prussia. I do not much mind whether there are one or two groups."

I asked Marshal Stalin whether he would be prepared to go into action on this front. Stalin said he would, but he preferred a plan for the partition of Germany—something like the President's plan, which was more likely to weaken Germany. When one had to deal with large masses of German troops one found them all fighting like devils, as the British and American Armies would soon learn. The Austrians by themselves were different, and he described the way they surrendered. All Germans were the same. It was the Prussian officers that provided the cement. But fundamentally there was no difference between North Germans and South Germans, for all Germans fought like fierce beasts. We should be careful not to include the Austrians in any kind of combination. Austria had existed independently, and could do so again. So also must Hungary exist independently. After breaking up Germany it would be most unwise to create new combinations, Danubian or otherwise.

President Roosevelt agreed warmly. There was no difference between Germans. The Bavarians had no officer class; otherwise they were exactly like the Prussians, as the American troops had already discovered.

I said that if Germany were divided into a number of parts as suggested by the President, and these parts were not attached to other combinations, they would reunite. It was not a question of dividing Germany so much as giving a life to the cut-off bits and making them content not to be dependent on the

Greater Reich. Even if this were achieved for fifty years that would be a lot.

Stalin said that a Danubian combination would not be able to live, and the Germans would take advantage of this by putting flesh on something that was only a skeleton and thus creating a new great State. He asked whether Hungary and Roumania would be members of any such combination. He then reiterated the advantages which it would present to Germany in the future. It was far better to break up and scatter the German tribes. Of course they would want to unite, no matter how much they were split up. They would always want to reunite. In this he saw great danger, which would have to be neutralised by various economic measures, and in the long run by force if necessary. That was the only way to keep the peace. But if we were to make a large combination with Germans in it trouble was bound to come. We had to see to it that they were kept separate, and that Hungary and Germany were not coupled. There were no measures possible to exclude a movement towards reunion. Germans would always want to reunite and to take their revenge. It would be necessary to keep ourselves strong enough to beat them if they ever let loose another war.

I asked Stalin if he contemplated a Europe of little States, all disjointed, with no larger units at all.

He replied that he was speaking of Germany, not Europe. Poland and France were large States. Roumania and Bulgaria were small States. But Germany should at all costs be broken up so that she could not reunite. The President pointed out that his plan was a way of doing this. I said that I must make it clear that we could now only take a preliminary survey of a vast historical problem. Stalin said that it was certainly very preliminary.

*　　*　　*　　*　　*

I then brought the discussion back to Poland. I said I did not ask for any agreement, nor was I convinced on the matter myself, but I would rather like to get something down on paper. I then produced the following formula: "It is thought in principle that the home of the Polish State and nation should be between the so-called Curzon Line and the line of the Oder,* including for

* No question as to whether it should be the Eastern or Western Neisse had yet arisen.

Poland East Prussia (as defined) and Oppeln; but the actual tracing of the frontier line requires careful study, and possibly disentanglement of population at some points." Why not a formula on which I could say something like this to the Poles: "I do not know if the Russians would approve, but I think that I might get it for you. You see, you are being well looked after." I added that we should never get the Poles to say that they were satisfied. Nothing would satisfy the Poles.

Stalin then said that the Russians would like to have the warm-water port of Königsberg, and he sketched a possible line on the map. This would put Russia on the neck of Germany. If he got this he would be ready enough to agree to my formula about Poland. I asked what about Lvov. Stalin said he would accept the Curzon Line.

* * * * *

The same evening Roosevelt, Stalin, and I initialled the following document, which sets forth the military conclusions of our Triple Conference.

The Conference:

(1) Agreed that the Partisans in Yugoslavia should be supported by supplies and equipment to the greatest possible extent, and also by Commando operations.

(2) Agreed that, from the military point of view, it was most desirable that Turkey should come into the war on the side of the Allies before the end of the year.

(3) Took note of Marshal Stalin's statement that if Turkey found herself at war with Germany, and as a result Bulgaria declared war on Turkey or attacked her, the Soviet would immediately be at war with Bulgaria. The Conference further took note that this fact would be explicitly stated in the forthcoming negotiations to bring Turkey into the war.

(4) Took note that Operation "Overlord" would be launched during May 1944, in conjunction with an operation against Southern France. The latter operation would be undertaken in as great a strength as availability of landing-craft permitted. The Conference further took note of Marshal Stalin's statement that the Soviet forces would launch an offensive at about the same time with the object of preventing the German forces from transferring from the Eastern to the Western Front.

(5) Agreed that the military Staffs of the three Powers should

henceforward keep in close touch with each other in regard to the impending operations in Europe. In particular it was agreed that a cover plan to mystify and mislead the enemy as regards these operations should be concerted between the Staffs concerned.

* * * * *

Thus our long and hard discussions at Teheran reached their end. The military conclusions governed in the main the future of the war. The cross-Channel invasion was fixed for May, subject naturally to tides and the moon. It was to be aided by a renewed major Russian offensive. At first sight I liked the proposed descent upon the French southern shore by part of the Allied Armies in Italy. The project had not been examined in detail, but the fact that both the Americans and the Russians favoured it made it easier to secure the landing-craft necessary for the success of our Italian campaign and the capture of Rome, without which it would have been a failure. I was of course more attracted by the President's alternative suggestion of a right-handed move from Italy by Istria and Trieste, with ultimate designs for reaching Vienna through the Ljubljana Gap. All this lay five or six months ahead. There would be plenty of time to make a final choice as the general war shaped itself, if only the life of our armies in Italy was not paralysed by depriving them of their modest requirements in landing-craft. Many amphibious or semi-amphibious schemes were open. I expected that the seaborne operations in the Bay of Bengal would be abandoned, and this, as the next chapter will show, proved correct. I was glad to feel that several important options were still preserved. Our strong efforts were to be renewed to bring Turkey into the war, with all that might accompany this in the Ægean, and follow from it in the Black Sea. In this we were to be disappointed. Surveying the whole military scene, as we separated in an atmosphere of friendship and unity of immediate purpose, I personally was well content.

* * * * *

The political aspects were at once more remote and speculative. Obviously they depended upon the results of the great battles yet to be fought, and after that upon the mood of each of the Allies when victory was gained. It would not have been right at Teheran for the Western democracies to found their plans upon suspicions of the Russian attitude in the hour of triumph and when all her dangers were removed. Stalin's promise to enter the war against Japan as soon as Hitler was overthrown and his armies defeated was of the highest importance. The hope of the future lay in the most speedy ending of the war and the establishment of a World Instrument to prevent another war, founded upon the combined strength of the three Great Powers, whose leaders had joined hands in friendship around the table.

We had procured a mitigation for Finland, which on the whole is operative to-day. The frontiers of the new Poland had been broadly outlined both in the east and in the west. The Curzon Line, subject to interpretation in the east, and the line of the Oder, in the west, seemed to afford a true and lasting home for the Polish nation after all its sufferings. At the time the question between the Eastern and Western Neisse, which flow together to form the Oder river, had not arisen. When in July 1945 it arose in a violent form and under totally different conditions at the Potsdam Conference I at once declared that Great Britain adhered only to the eastern tributary. And this is still our position.

*　*　*　*　*

The supreme question of the treatment to be accorded to Germany by the victors could at this milestone only be the subject of "a preliminary survey of a vast political problem", and, as Stalin described it, "certainly very preliminary." It must be remembered that we were in the midst of a fearful struggle with the mighty Nazi Power. All the hazards of war lay around us, and all its passions of comradeship among Allies, of retribution upon the common foe, dominated our minds. The President's tentative projects for the partition of Germany into five self-governing states and two territories, of vital consequence, under the United Nations, were of course far more acceptable to Marshal Stalin than the proposal which I made for the isolation of Prussia and the constitution of a Danubian Confederation, or of a South Germany and also a Danubian Confederation. This was only my personal view. But I do not at all repent having put it forward in the circumstances which lay about us at Teheran.

We all deeply feared the might of a united Germany. Prussia had a great history of her own. It would be possible, I thought, to make a stern but honourable peace with her, and at the same time to recreate in modern forms what had been in general outline the Austro-Hungarian Empire, of which it has been well said, "If it did not exist it would have to be invented." Here would be a great area in which not only peace but friendship might reign at a far earlier date than in any other solution. Thus a United Europe might be formed in which all the victors and vanquished might find a sure foundation for the life and freedom of all their tormented millions.

I do not feel any break in the continuity of my thought in this immense sphere. But vast and disastrous changes have fallen upon us in the realm of fact. The Polish frontiers exist only in name, and Poland lies quivering in the Russian-Communist grip. Germany has indeed been partitioned, but only by a hideous division into zones of military occupation. About this tragedy it can only be said IT CANNOT LAST.

CHAPTER XXIII

CAIRO AGAIN. THE HIGH COMMAND

*Anglo-American Discussions in Cairo – The Andaman Islands Plan –
No Agreement on This at Our First Plenary Meeting, December 4 –
The President Decides to Abandon the Plan – Our Joint Telegram to
Premier Stalin, December 6 – Question about the Number of Troops
Asked for by Mountbatten – Staff Discussion on the Strategy to be
Pursued against Japan – Our Conference with the Turks at Cairo –
Outline Plan for Aiding Turkey – The Turks Will Not Commit
Themselves – President Roosevelt Appoints General Eisenhower to
Command "Overlord" – The President and I Visit the Sphinx.*

ON December 2 I got back to Cairo from Teheran, and
was once more installed in the villa near the Pyramids.
The President arrived the same evening, and we resumed
our intimate discussions on the whole scene of the war and on
the results of our talks with Stalin. Meanwhile the Combined
Chiefs of Staff, who had refreshed themselves by a visit to
Jerusalem on their way back from Teheran, were to carry forward
their discussions on all their great business the next day. Admiral
Mountbatten had returned to India, whence he had submitted
the revised plan he had been instructed to make for an amphibious
attack on the Andaman Islands (Operation "Buccaneer"). This
would absorb the vitally needed landing-craft already sent to him
from the Mediterranean. I wished to make a final attempt to win
the Americans to the alternative enterprise against Rhodes.

The next evening I dined again with the President. Eden was
with me. We remained at the table until after midnight, still
discussing our points of difference. I shared the views of our
Chiefs of Staff, who were much worried by the promise which
the President had made to Generalissimo Chiang Kai-shek before
Teheran to launch an early attack across the Bay of Bengal. This

would have swept away my hopes and plans for taking Rhodes, on which I believed the entry of Turkey into the war largely depended. But Mr. Roosevelt's heart was set upon it. When our Chiefs of Staff raised it in the military conferences the United States Staffs simply declined to discuss the matter. The President, they said, had taken his decision and they had no choice but to obey.

On the afternoon of December 4 we held our first plenary meeting since Teheran, but made little headway. The President began by saying that he must leave on December 6, and that all reports should be ready for the final agreement of both parties by the evening of Sunday, December 5. Apart from the question of the entry of Turkey into the war, the only outstanding point seemed to be the comparatively small one of the use to be made of a score of landing-craft and their equipment. It was unthinkable that one could be beaten by a petty item like that, and he felt bound to say that the detail *must* be disposed of.

I said that I did not wish to leave the Conference in any doubt that the British delegation viewed our early dispersal with great apprehension. There were still many questions of first-class importance to be settled. Two decisive events had taken place in the last few days. In the first place, Marshal Stalin had voluntarily proclaimed that the Soviet would declare war on Japan the moment Germany was defeated. This would give us better bases than we could ever find in China, and made it all the more important that we should concentrate on making "Overlord" a success. It would be necessary for the Staffs to examine how this new fact would affect operations in the Pacific and South-East Asia.

The second event of first-class importance was the decision to cross the Channel during May. I myself would have preferred a July date, but I was determined nevertheless to do all in my power to make a May date a complete success. It was a task transcending all others. A million Americans were to be thrown in eventually, and five or six hundred thousand British. Terrific battles were to be expected, on a scale far greater than anything that we had experienced before. In order to give "Overlord" the greatest chance of success, it was thought necessary that the descent on the Riviera ("Anvil") should be as strong as possible. It seemed to me that the crisis for the invading armies would come at about the thirtieth day, and it was essential that every possible step should be taken by action elsewhere to prevent the Germans from concentrating a superior force against our beach-heads. As soon as the "Overlord" and "Anvil" forces got into the same zone they would come under the same commander.

The President, summing up the discussion, asked whether he was correct in thinking that there was general agreement on the following points:

(a) Nothing should be done to hinder "Overlord".

(b) Nothing should be done to hinder "Anvil".

(c) By hook or by crook we should scrape up sufficient landing-craft to operate in the Eastern Mediterranean if Turkey came into the war.

(d) Admiral Mountbatten should be told to go ahead and do his best [in the Bay of Bengal] with what had already been allocated to him.

On this last point I suggested that it might be necessary to withdraw resources from Mountbatten in order to strengthen "Overlord" and "Anvil". The President said that he could not agree with this. We had a moral obligation to do something for China, and he would not be prepared to forgo the amphibious operation except for some very good and readily apparent reason. I replied that this "very good reason" might be provided by our supreme adventure in France. At present the "Overlord" assault was only on a three-division basis, whereas we had put nine divisions ashore in Sicily on the first day. The main operation was at present on a very narrow margin.

Reverting to the Riviera attack, I expressed the view that it should be planned on the basis of an assault force of at least two divisions. This would provide enough landing-craft to do the outflanking operations in Italy, and also, if Turkey came into the war soon, to capture Rhodes. I then pointed out that operations in South-East Asia must be judged in their relation to the predominating importance of "Overlord". I said that I was surprised at the demands for taking the Andamans which had reached me from Admiral Mountbatten. In the face of Marshal Stalin's promise that Russia would come into the war operations in the South-East Asia Command had lost a good deal of their value, while, on the other hand, their cost had been put up to a prohibitive extent.

The discussion continued on whether or not to persist in the

Andamans project. The President resisted the British wish to drop it. No conclusion was reached, except that the Chiefs of Staff were directed to go into details.

* * * * *

On December 5 we met again, and the report of the Combined Staffs on operations in the European theatre was read out by the President and agreed. Everything was now narrowed down to the Far Eastern operation. Rhodes had receded in the picture, and I concentrated on getting the landing-craft for "Anvil" and the Mediterranean. A new factor had presented itself. The estimates of the South-East Asia Command of the force needed to storm the Andamans had been startling. The President said that 14,000 should be sufficient. Anyhow, the 50,000 men proposed certainly broke the back of the Andamans expedition so far as this meeting was concerned. It was agreed for the moment that Mountbatten should be asked what amphibious operations he could undertake on a smaller scale, on the assumption that most of the landing-craft and assault shipping were withdrawn from South-East Asia during the next few weeks. Thus we parted, leaving Mr. Roosevelt much distressed.

Before anything further could be done the deadlock in Cairo was broken. In the afternoon the President, in consultation with his advisers, decided to abandon the Andaman Islands plan. He sent me a laconic private message: "'Buccaneer' is off." General Ismay reminds me that when I told him the welcome news cryptically on the telephone that the President had changed his mind and was so informing Chiang Kai-shek I said, "He is a better man that ruleth his spirit than he that taketh a city." We all met together at 7.30 p.m. the next evening at the Kirk villa to go over the final report of the Conference. The Southern France assault operation was formally approved, and the President read out his signal to Generalissimo Chiang Kai-shek, informing him of the decision to abandon the Andamans plan.

* * * * *

I now worked out with the President a joint summary of our decisions to be sent to Stalin.

Prime Minister and President Roosevelt to   6 Dec 43
Premier Stalin

In the Cairo Conference just concluded we have arrived at following decisions as to the conduct of war in 1944 against Germany additional to the agreement reached by the three of us at Teheran.

The bomber offensive against Germany, with the objective of destroying German air combat strength, the German military, industrial, and economic system, and preparing the way for a cross-Channel operation, will be given the highest strategical priority.

We have reduced the scale of operations scheduled for March in the Bay of Bengal to permit the reinforcement of amphibious craft for the operation against Southern France.

We have ordered the utmost endeavours to increase the production of landing-craft in U.K. and the U.S.A. for the reinforcement of "Overlord", and further orders have been issued to divert certain landing-craft from the Pacific for the same purpose.

*   *   *   *   *

In informing the South-East Asia Command of our decisions I did not conceal from Mountbatten the shock which the estimates of his advisers which he had endorsed had been to me.

Prime Minister to Admiral Mountbatten (Delhi)   9 Dec 43

You will have seen the President's telegram to the Generalissimo about the abandonment of "Buccaneer", with which, as you know, I am in entire agreement. This arises from the decision at Teheran to concentrate everything on "Overlord" and a simultaneous operation against the South of France.

Everyone here has been unpleasantly affected by your request to use 50,000 British and Imperial troops, of which 33,700 are combatant, against 5,000 Japanese. I was astounded to hear of such a requirement, and I cannot feel sure you are getting competent military advice. The Americans have been taking their islands on the basis of two and a half to one, and that your generals should ask for six and a half to one has produced a very bad impression. Even the detailed figures with which I have been furnished do not remove it.

I hope that preparations will now go forward for Sumatra after the monsoon. However, while such standards as those you have accepted for the Andamans prevail there is not much hope of making any form of amphibious war.

Mountbatten replied that the United States in their recent landings had deployed a superiority of troops varying from between three to one to over six to one. The larger figure applied when cover from shore-based aircraft was not possible. For taking the Andamans he would have carrier-borne and not shore-based aircraft, and their effort was likely to be expended after four days. It was therefore essential to capture the Andamans airfield within that time. The resources already allotted to him would enable him to carry the 50,000 men proposed. Of these however only 9,000 could be landed by the first two waves. He did not therefore feel he was asking for an undue superiority in order to ensure quick success. He cited the American landing at Munda, where with an even higher ratio of superiority only very slow progress had been made.

I remained unconvinced. But the following post-war comment from the War Office should be printed in order that the point at issue may be fairly presented.

Operation "Buccaneer", an assault on the Andaman Islands, involved transporting our forces 1,000 miles from the nearest base, and the force included all troops required for the development of facilities, the building of airfield and strips, and for work in the docks. It was estimated that 16,000 would be non-fighting troops, and included in the balance of "fighting" troops were all headquarters, engineers, and anti-aircraft units. The enemy was considered to have air superiority in the area. Admittedly the "teeth" part of the force outnumbered the estimated Japanese garrison by about four to one, but this was not much greater than what was at that time accepted as a desirable preponderance for an assault landing. It cannot be overlooked that we had been uniformly unsuccessful against the Japanese for the previous twelve months. Lord Mountbatten undoubtedly wished to make his first assault a success, if only for the sake of theatre morale.

* * * * *

The Combined Chiefs of Staff also discussed among themselves the British share in the strategy to be pursued against Japan, and presented their recommendations to the President and me in their final report of the Cairo Conference. In summary, they proposed that the main effort of the South-East Asia Command should be in Burma. After the defeat of Germany an Army and air contingent, with air resources all based on Australia, should be sent to co-operate with General MacArthur. The British effort by sea should be mainly in the Pacific, and not in the Bay of Bengal. The British Chiefs of Staff, like myself, recoiled from the idea of a strenuous and wasteful campaign in North Burma for the sake of building a road to China of doubtful value. On the other hand, they accepted the fact that Admiral Mountbatten could not carry out any large-scale amphibious operations until six months after a

German collapse. The plan of reinforcing the Pacific could be begun much sooner. They therefore endorsed the American view. In their final report both Staffs stated that they "had agreed in principle as a basis for further investigation and preparation" the overall plan for the defeat of Japan. This plan contemplated the dispatch of a detachment of the British Fleet which was provisionally scheduled to become active in the Pacific in June 1944. The President and I both initialled this document, but in the pressure of more urgent business and of the President's imperative need to return to the United States no occasion was found when we could discuss these long-term schemes either with our own advisers or between ourselves. We however felt sure there would be time to review the whole position later.

*　　*　　*　　*　　*

One of the main purposes of our Cairo meeting had been to resume talks with the Turkish leaders. I had telegraphed President Inönü on December 1 from Teheran suggesting that he should join the President and myself in Cairo. It was arranged that Vyshinsky should also be present. These conversations arose out of the exchange of views between Mr. Eden and the Turkish Foreign Minister in Cairo at the beginning of November on the former's journey home from Moscow. The Turks now came again to Cairo on December 4, and the following evening I entertained the Turkish President to dinner. My guest displayed great caution, and in subsequent meetings showed to what extent his advisers were still impressed by the German military machine. I pressed the case hard. With Italy out of the war the advantages of Turkey's entry were manifestly increased and her risks lessened.

On December 6 I drafted a memorandum to the British Chiefs of Staff setting forth in detail the policy and action which would be necessary if, after all, Turkey came in on our side.

Prime Minister to General Ismay, for C.O.S. Committee　　　6 Dec 43
OPERATION "SATURN"

After the Cairo Conference the Turkish Government will state that their policy is unchanged, and use all precautionary measures to allay enemy suspicions.

2. Nevertheless it is necessary that the preparation and protection of the Turkish airfields should proceed at full speed without a day's delay, and that all necessary personnel, in mufti, and materials should

be sent in. A period of six or seven weeks should suffice for this, the British squadrons being ready to fly in to the airfields at any time after February 1, the exact date to be fixed in consultation with the Turkish Government and in relation to the move of the enemy. A margin of a fortnight may be allowed for this, during which time further supplies and personnel will be introduced at full speed.

3. In the lull following the expected capture of Rome in January it is desirable that three groups of medium bombers should be placed under the command of the A.O.C.-in-C. Middle East and posted in Cyrenaica for "softening" action against enemy airfields and shipping and to cover the fly-in of the British fighter squadrons. The action of these bombers can begin irrespective of any decision taken about the fly-in. But if the enemy are quiescent it would be better to reserve their action to cover the fly-in and the events immediately following it. The details of the employment and timing of the movement of this force should be worked out by the Commander-in-Chief.

4. By February 15 the fly-in should be completed, and from that moment onwards a very considerable degree of protection against air attack will have been secured to Turkey.

5. Once established in the airfields the British squadrons, in consultation with the Turkish Government, will begin their operations in the Ægean, being supported at the same time by the medium bomber groups from Cyrenaica. Under this air cover British naval forces in the Levant, strengthened as may be necessary, will attack enemy shipping and convoys engaged in supplying the islands.

6. All preparations should meanwhile be made for Rhodes. For this purpose a first-class British division should be used for the assault, a lower category division being held ready to garrison the island, thereby setting free the British division for further operations in Italy. Rhodes of course depends upon the landing-craft being available. This operation should take place before the end of February, all landing-craft thereafter being prepared for "Anvil".

7. What action should be expected from the enemy? Evidently it is the Allied interest to delay this as long as possible. Therefore the Turkish Government should continue to the last moment in relations with Germany and Bulgaria, and should reply diplomatically to any protest they may make, while continuing their preparations. If Bulgaria adopts a threatening attitude to Turkey she should be notified by the Russians that if she delivers an attack at Germany's orders the Russian Soviet Union will immediately declare war on Bulgaria. It is for consideration whether the Bulgarians should not also be told that for every ton of bombs dropped by the Germans or by them upon Constantinople or Smyrna two or three tons will be dropped on Sofia.

Should the Russian armies be continuing their victorious advance in South Russia and should the Anglo-American armies prosper in the Battle of Rome it seems most unlikely that Bulgaria will attempt to invade Turkey. She may however withdraw her nine divisions from Greece and Yugoslavia and make a concentration opposite the Turkish front in Thrace.

8. Meanwhile it is also possible that, under the increasing pressure of events, Bulgaria will endeavour to make a separate peace with the three Great Allies. It is not suggested that Turkey should declare war at any stage; she should continue her protective re-equipment and await the enemy's actions.

9. Meanwhile, as soon as the sea passage from Egypt to Turkey has been opened by the British and naval domination of the Ægean achieved every effort will be made to pass supplies and support into Smyrna, and if possible through the Dardanelles, so that the further equipment of the Turkish Army and the feeding of Constantinople can proceed as fast as possible.

10. After the fly-in of the British squadrons has been completed the Turkish Government should facilitate the secret passage into the Black Sea of six or eight British submarines, together with the necessary stores. As no depot ship can be made available base facilities should, if possible, be arranged at Ismet. These submarines should suffice to take a heavy toll of any Roumanian and German evacuations from the Crimea, and also assist any Russian descent on the Roumanian shore which the Roumanian political attitude might render possible. Such a movement would however be dependent on Russian wishes.

The Turks departed to report to their Parliament, and it was agreed that in the meantime British specialists should be assembled to implement the first stages of Operation "Saturn". And there the matter rested.

★　　★　　★　　★　　★

In all our many talks at Cairo the President never referred to the vital and urgent issue of the command of "Overlord", and I was under the impression that our original arrangement and agreement held good. But on the day before his departure from Cairo he told me his final decision. We were driving in his motor-car from Cairo to the Pyramids. He then said, almost casually, that he could not spare General Marshall, whose great influence at the head of military affairs and of the war direction, under the President, was invaluable, and indispensable to the successful conduct of the war. He therefore proposed to nominate

Eisenhower to "Overlord", and asked me for my opinion. I said it was for him to decide, but that we had also the warmest regard for General Eisenhower, and would trust our fortunes to his direction with hearty goodwill.

Up to this time I had thought Eisenhower was to go to Washington as Military Chief of Staff, while Marshall commanded "Overlord". Eisenhower had heard of this too, and was very unhappy at the prospect of leaving the Mediterranean for Washington. Now it was all settled: Eisenhower for "Overlord", Marshall to stay at Washington, and a British commander for the Mediterranean.

The full story of the President's long delay and hesitations and of his final decision is referred to by Mr. Hopkins' biographer, who says that Roosevelt made the decision on Sunday, December 5, "against the almost impassioned advice of Hopkins and Stimson, against the known preference of both Stalin and Churchill, against his own proclaimed inclination." Then Mr. Sherwood quotes the following extract from a note which he had from General Marshall after the war. "If I recall," said Marshall, "the President stated, in completing our conversation, 'I feel I could not sleep at night with you out of the country.'"[*] There can be little doubt that the President felt that the command only of "Overlord" was not sufficient to justify General Marshall's departure from Washington.

* * * * *

At last our labours were finished. I gave a dinner at the villa to the Combined Chiefs of Staff, Mr. Eden, Mr. Casey, and one or two others. I remember being struck by the optimism which prevailed in high Service circles. The idea was mooted that Hitler would not be strong enough to face the spring campaign, and might collapse even before "Overlord" was launched in the summer. I was so much impressed by the current of opinion that I asked everybody to give his view in succession round the table. All the professional authorities were inclined to think that the German collapse was imminent. The three politicians present took the opposite view. Of course, on these vast matters on which so many lives depend there is always a great deal of guesswork. So much is unknown and immeasurable. Who can tell how weak

[*] Sherwood, *Roosevelt and Hopkins*, pp. 802–3.

the enemy may be behind his flaming fronts and brazen mask? At what moment will his will-power break? At what moment will he be beaten down?

★   ★   ★   ★   ★

The President had found no time for sightseeing, but I could not bear his leaving without seeing the Sphinx. One day after tea I said, "You must come now." We motored there forthwith, and examined this wonder of the world from every angle. Roosevelt and I gazed at her for some minutes in silence as the evening shadows fell. She told us nothing and maintained her inscrutable smile. There was no use waiting longer.

On December 7 I bade farewell to my great friend when he flew off from the airfield beyond the Pyramids.

CHAPTER XXIV

IN CARTHAGE RUINS

ANZIO

Our Air Journey to Tunis – I Have Pneumonia – Choice of Commanders for "Overlord" and in the Mediterranean – The President Agrees with the Appointments – My Wife Arrives from England – A Climax of the War – How to Break the Deadlock in Italy – The Genesis of "Anzio" – The British Chiefs of Staff Agree to the Operation – The Problem of Landing-craft – Our Conference on Christmas Day – Anxieties at Home – I Report to the President.

I HAD not been at all well during this journey and Conference. Soon after I started I had a temperature. After several days this was succeeded by a cold and sore throat, which made me keep to my bed most of the time I was in Malta. I arrived voiceless at Teheran, but this did not last long, and I was able to carry on sufficiently. All these symptoms had disappeared when I got back to Cairo. As the Conference drew to its close I became conscious of being very tired. For instance, I noticed that I no longer dried myself after my bath, but lay on the bed wrapped in my towel till I dried naturally.

A little after midnight on December 11 I and my personal party left in our York machine for Tunis. I had planned to spend one night there at General Eisenhower's villa, and to fly next day to Alexander's and then Montgomery's headquarters in Italy, where the weather was reported to be absolutely vile and all advances were fitful.

Morning saw us over the Tunis airfields. We were directed by a signal not to land where we had been told, and were shifted to another field some forty miles away. We all got out, and they began to unload the luggage. It would be an hour before motorcars could come, and then a long drive. As I sat on my official boxes near the machines I certainly did feel completely worn out. Now however came a telephone message from General Eisenhower, who was waiting at the first airfield, that we had been wrongly transferred and that landing was quite possible there. So we scrambled back into our York, and in ten minutes were with him, quite close to his villa. Ike, always the soul of hospitality, had waited two hours with imperturbable good-humour. I got into his car, and after we had driven for a little while I said, "I am afraid I shall have to stay with you longer than I had planned. I am completely at the end of my tether, and I cannot go on to the front until I have recovered some strength."

All that day I slept, and the next day came fever and symptoms at the base of my lung which were adjudged to portend pneumonia. So here I was at this pregnant moment on the broad of my back amid the ruins of ancient Carthage.

*   *   *   *   *

When the X-ray photographs showed that there was a shadow on one of my lungs I found that everything had been diagnosed and foreseen by Lord Moran. Dr. Bedford and other high medical authorities in the Mediterranean and excellent nurses arrived from all quarters as if by magic. The admirable M and B, from which I did not suffer any inconvenience, was used at the earliest moment, and after a week's fever the intruders were repulsed. Although Lord Moran records that he judged that the issue was at one time in doubt, I did not share his view. I did not feel so ill in this attack as I had the previous February. The M and B, which I also called Moran and Bedford, did the work most effectively. There is no doubt that pneumonia is a very different illness from what it was before this marvellous drug was discovered. I did not at any time relinquish my part in the direction of affairs, and there was not the slightest delay in giving the decisions which were required from me.

Prime Minister to Foreign Secretary   13 Dec 43
I am caught amid these ancient ruins with a temperature and must wait till I am normal. Future movements uncertain.

Angora must be left under no illusions that failure to comply when request is made on February 15 is the virtual end of the alliance, and that making impossible demands is only another way of saying no.

You should ask the Staffs to report upon the possibilities of the

Germans being able to gather enough forces for a further separate invasion of Turkey. I believe this to be absolute rubbish.

Prime Minister to President Roosevelt   15 Dec 43

Am stranded amid the ruins of Carthage, where you stayed, with fever which has ripened into pneumonia. All your people are doing everything possible, but I do not pretend I am enjoying myself. I hope soon to send you some of the suggestions for the new commands. I hope you had a pleasant voyage and are fit. Love to Harry.

President Roosevelt to Prime Minister   17 Dec 43

I am distressed about the pneumonia, and both Harry and I plead with you to be good and throw it off rapidly. I have just left the *Iowa* and am on my way up the Potomac. The Bible says you must do just what Moran orders, but at this moment I cannot put my finger on the verse and the chapter. . . . Nothing further seems to be imminent, so do what Sarah says, and give her my love and take it easy.

*   *   *   *   *

It now fell to me, as British Minister of Defence responsible to the War Cabinet, to propose a British Supreme Commander for the Mediterranean. This post we confided to General Wilson, it being also settled that General Alexander should command the whole campaign in Italy, as he had done under General Eisenhower. It was also arranged that General Devers, of the U.S. Army, should become General Wilson's Deputy in the Mediterranean, and Air Chief Marshal Tedder General Eisenhower's Deputy in "Overlord", and that General Montgomery should actually command the whole cross-Channel invasion force until such time as the Supreme Commander could transfer his headquarters to France and assume the direct operational control. All this was carried out with the utmost smoothness in perfect agreement by the President and by me, with Cabinet approval, and worked in good comradeship and friendship by all concerned.

I should add that when in November 1944 General Alexander was nominated to succeed General Wilson as Supreme Commander in the Mediterranean I myself proposed, on behalf of His Majesty's Government, that United States General Mark Clark should take command under him of the whole of the forces in Italy, three-quarters of which were British, Imperial, or British-controlled. This he did with marked distinction and success.

The operative telegrams were:

374

Prime Minister to President Roosevelt   18 Dec 43

Thank you so much for your telegram. I have hearkened unto the voice of Moran and made good progress, but I am fixed here for another week.

2. Since our last talk on the subject I have given much thought to the remodelling of the commands, and have had discussions with Eisenhower, Alexander, and Tedder. I have also consulted my colleagues at home, and have to-day had a long conversation with the C.I.G.S. on his return from a visit to Italy. As a result I am able to place before you the following proposals, which, if you approve them, will, I am satisfied, be generally accepted.

3. I had always thought that Alexander would succeed Eisenhower, but am convinced by the arguments of the C.I.G.S., Eisenhower, and others that it would be impossible for him or Montgomery to act as Supreme Commander and at the same time fight the battles which will take place in Italy after the conquest of Rome. Alexander himself quite saw this.

4. I therefore propose General Wilson as Supreme Commander, *vice* Eisenhower. Under him will be:

(*a*) General Commanding, Algiers: a United States officer. We have heard that it might be convenient to you to transfer General Devers from his present post.

(*b*) Commander-in-Chief of the Armies in Italy: Alexander.

(*c*) General in charge of Operation "Anvil": Clark. We understand that this was what you and General Marshall had in mind. If so, we concur.

(*d*) A British major-general in charge of the Yugoslav assistance measures, Tito, Greeks, etc.

(*e*) Commander-in-Chief Mid-East, for operational purposes within the Mediterranean theatre, and also in charge of the Turkish operations: Paget (now commanding British Home Forces).

5. The Air Officer Commanding-in-Chief should be an American, appointed by you. Arnold when passing through here spoke of Brereton or Eaker. We would agree to either, but we should miss the latter from the bombing and "Overlord" build-up. Sholto Douglas will be Deputy Air Officer Commanding-in-Chief, and also Commander-in-Chief of all the R.A.F. in the Mediterranean theatre.

6. Political assistance will be provided for the Supreme Commander:

(*a*) by Messrs. Murphy and Macmillan, who work hand-in-hand;

(*b*) from the French angle by Duff Cooper and Wilson;

(*c*) from the Middle Eastern area by the Minister of State or his successor.

7. Bedell Smith will accompany Eisenhower after a few weeks and become his Chief of Staff in England, being replaced here by a British Chief of Staff. We leave it to you to decide whether you would like to have a Deputy Supreme Commander, who would of course be an American.

8. You will understand that I have given most careful consideration to the appointment of Sir Henry Maitland Wilson, and I am satisfied that for the great co-ordination task which will be entrusted to him he has all the qualifications and the necessary vigour. This is also the opinion of the C.I.G.S. When I mentioned this idea to you at Cairo you seemed to like it.

9. Turning to the "Overlord" theatre, I propose to you that Tedder shall be Eisenhower's Deputy Supreme Commander, on account of the great part the air will play in this operation, and this is most agreeable to Eisenhower. The War Cabinet desires that Montgomery should command the first expeditionary group of armies. I feel the Cabinet are right, as Montgomery is a public hero and will give confidence among our people, not unshared by yours.

10. I beg most earnestly that I may soon have your reply on these proposals, or at least upon the key ones, as the Commander of "Overlord" is urgently required, and I should like to arrange for Wilson to take over from Eisenhower at an early date, and to come to him even sooner in order to settle the many consequential details.

President Roosevelt to Prime Minister   20 Dec 43

I am agreeable to an announcement on January 1 of selection of Eisenhower to command "Overlord", Tedder to be Eisenhower's Deputy Supreme Commander, Wilson to relieve Eisenhower as Supreme Commander Mediterranean (this change to be made when Eisenhower reports that conditions in Italy justify the change), Eaker to command Allied Air Force Mediterranean.

2. I prefer to delay announcement of changes in subordinate commands until after the first of the year, because I want to have opportunity to discuss it with Marshall, who will return to Washington in a few days.

3. I am delighted that you are really so much better, and I wish I could be with you at Marrakesh. I hope you have sent for your brushes.

★ ★ ★ ★ ★

The days passed in much discomfort. Fever flickered in and out. I lived on my theme of the war, and it was like being transported out of oneself. The doctors tried to keep the work away from my bedside, but I defied them. They all kept on saying, "Don't work, don't worry," to such an extent that I decided to read a novel. I had long ago read Jane Austen's *Sense and Sensibility*, and now I thought I would have *Pride and Prejudice*. Sarah read it to me beautifully from the foot of the bed. I had always thought it would be better than its rival. What calm lives they had, those people! No worries about the French Revolution, or the crashing struggle of the Napoleonic wars. Only manners controlling natural passion so far as they could, together with cultured explanations of any mischances. All this seemed to go very well with M and B.

One morning Sarah was absent from her chair at the foot of my bed, and I was about to ask for my box of telegrams in the prohibited hours when in she walked with her mother. I had no idea that my wife was flying out from England to join me. She had hurried to the airport to fly in a two-engined Dakota. The weather was bad, but Lord Beaverbrook was vigilant. He got to the airport first, and stopped her flight until a four-engined plane could be procured. (I always think it better to have four engines when flying long distances across the sea.) Now she had arrived after a very rough journey in an unheated plane in mid-winter. Jock Colville had escorted her, and was a welcome addition to my hard-pressed personal staff, through whom so much business was being directed. "My love to Clemmie," cabled the President. "I feel relieved that she is with you as your superior officer."

*   *   *   *   *

As I lay prostrate I felt we were at one of the climaxes of the war. The mounting of "Overlord" was the greatest event and duty in the world. But must we sabotage everything we could have in Italy, where the main strength overseas of our country was involved? Were we to leave it a stagnant pool from which we had drawn every fish we wanted? As I saw the problem, the campaign in Italy, in which a million or more of our British, British-controlled, and Allied troops were engaged, was the faithful and indispensable comrade and counterpart to the main cross-Channel operation. Here the American clear-cut, logical, large-scale, mass production style of thought was formidable. In life people have first to be taught "Concentrate on essentials". This is no doubt the first step out of confusion and fatuity; but it is only the first step. The second stage in war is a general harmony

377

of war effort by making everything fit together, and every scrap of fighting strength play its full part all the time. I was sure that a vigorous campaign in Italy during the first half of 1944 would be the greatest help to the supreme operation of crossing the Channel, on which all minds were set and all engagements made. But every item which any Staff officer could claim as "essential" or "vital", to use these hard-worked words, had to be argued out as if it carried with it the success or failure of our main purpose. Twenty or a dozen vehicle landing-craft had to be fought for as if the major issue turned upon them.

The case seemed to me brutally simple. All the ships we had would be used to carry to England everything the United States could produce in arms and men. Surely the enormous forces we could not possibly move by sea from the Italian theatre should play their part. Either they would gain Italy easily and immediately bite upon the German inner front, or they would draw large German forces from the front which we were to attack across the Channel in the last days of May, or the early days of June, as the moon and the tides prescribed.

*   *   *   *   *

The deadlock to which our armies in Italy had been brought by the stubborn German resistance on the eighty-mile front from sea to sea had already led General Eisenhower to contemplate an amphibious flanking attack. He had planned to land with one division south of the Tiber and make a dart for Rome, in conjunction with an attack by the main armies. The arrest of these armies and the distance of the landing point from them made everyone feel that more than one division was required. I had of course always been a partisan of the "end run", as the Americans call it, or "cat-claw", which was my term. I had never succeeded in getting this manœuvre open to sea-power included in any of our Desert advances. In Sicily however General Patton had twice used the command of the sea flank as he advanced along the northern coast of the island with great effect. Both at Carthage and at Marrakesh I was near enough to the scene of action to convene meetings of all the chief commanders.

There was a great deal of professional support. Eisenhower was already committed in principle, though his new appointment to the command of "Overlord" now gave him a different sense

378

of values and a new horizon. Alexander, Deputy Supreme Commander and commanding the armies in Italy, thought the operation right and necessary; Bedell Smith was ardent and helpful in every direction. This was also true of Admiral John Cunningham, who held all the naval cards, and of Air Marshal Tedder. I had therefore a powerful array of Mediterranean authorities. Moreover, I felt sure the British Chiefs of Staff would like the plan, and that with their agreement I could obtain the approval of the War Cabinet. When you cannot give orders hard and lengthy toils must be faced.

"Overlord" in May was sacrosanct. We had pledged ourselves at Teheran only a month before. Nothing could be considered which prevented our keeping our supreme engagement. In this case troops, air-power, and sea-power presented no obstacles. All turned upon L.S.T.s (Landing-ships, Tanks). This included "Landing-ships, Vehicles", because landing tanks was only a small proportion of their indispensable work. A lengthy correspondence conducted in cipher between me and Whitehall and Washington arose. The military student may some day be interested to read the details of this tense and clear-cut argument, of which only a skeleton is here printed. The L.S.T.s must, in the name of "Overlord", be in England at certain dates. These dates had been calculated with extreme precision, and of course with all the margins for accident which, at every stage, enter into military planning, and would make almost all action impossible if they were not controlled from the top. Everyone claims his margin at every stage, and the sum of the margins is usually "No".

I began my effort on December 19, when the C.I.G.S. arrived at Carthage to see me on his way home from Montgomery's headquarters in Italy. We had hoped to go there together, but my illness had prevented me. We had a full discussion, and I found that General Brooke had by a separate route of thought arrived at the same conclusion as I had. We agreed on the policy, and also that while I should deal with the commanders on the spot he would do his best to overcome all difficulties at home. General Brooke then left by air for London. I telegraphed:

Prime Minister to Chiefs of Staff   19 Dec 43

I am anxiously awaiting a full list of all landing-craft of all types in the Mediterranean now, showing their condition and employment, and especially whether it is true that a large number are absorbed in purely supply work to the prevention of their amphibious duties. There is no doubt that the stagnation of the whole campaign on the Italian front is becoming scandalous. The C.I.G.S.'s visit confirmed my worst forebodings. The total neglect to provide amphibious action on the Adriatic side and the failure to strike any similar blow on the west have been disastrous.

None of the landing-craft in the Mediterranean have been put to the slightest use [for assault purposes] for three months, neither coming home in preparation for "Overlord", nor for the Ægean islands, nor in the Italian battle. There are few instances, even in this war, of such valuable forces being so completely wasted.

The Chiefs of Staff had evidently been thinking on the same lines, and, after hearing General Brooke's account, replied on the 22nd:

We are in full agreement with you that the present stagnation cannot be allowed to continue. For every reason it is essential that something should be done to speed things up. The solution, as you say, clearly lies in making use of our amphibious power to strike round on the enemy's flank and open up the way for a rapid advance on Rome.

After the L.S.T.s are withdrawn for "Overlord" on January 15 General Eisenhower should have at his disposal an amphibious lift sufficient for a little more than one division, and he has a plan to make a landing behind the enemy just south of Rome. The weakness of this plan is that the assault in that strength on the coast cannot be launched until the Fifth Army is within supporting distance of the force to be landed. If the available lift could be increased however a stronger force could be landed without waiting for the main army to arrive within immediate supporting distance. Such a landing moreover would have a more far-reaching effect on the whole progress of the campaign, and would be much more likely to open the way for a rapid advance. We think the aim should be to provide a lift for at least two divisions.

We have telegraphed to the Commander-in-Chief Mediterranean for the information you ask for on landing-craft. We have every hope that it will be possible to make some economy in this direction, but we must look farther afield if we are to give General Eisenhower the two-divisional lift.

A possible source of supply is the craft already on their way back from South-East Asia to the Mediterranean. . . . A small number of craft have also been left in South-East Asia.

After explaining that the new plan would involve giving up

both the capture of Rhodes and also a minor amphibious operation on the Arakan coast of Burma, they ended:

If you approve the above line of thought we propose to take the
matter up with the Combined Chiefs of Staff with a view to action
being taken on these lines at once.

*   *   *   *   *

This led to a hard scrutiny of our resources. Some landing-
craft for the cancelled operation against the Andamans were on
their way to the Mediterranean across the Indian Ocean. Others
were due to return home for "Overlord". All were in extreme
demand.

I had been reluctant to agree to the abandonment of the attack
on Rhodes we had talked of to President Inönü. A far greater
effort must be made with the Turks, as well as to expedite the
operation and the subsequent return of landing-craft for "Anvil"
(the assault on Southern France). By December 23 however I
was becoming resigned to Turkish neutrality, and I replied from
Carthage:

You will observe that whereas you are thinking of a decision in
Italy Ike is looking forward to "Anvil", which is now very much part
of his main interest. I recognise that if the Turks will not play we
may have to sacrifice the Ægean policy, especially if it is marked up
so high and so slow. I hope however that this decision will not be
taken till after full exploration of the whole scene. I hope to see
Eisenhower to-day, and Alexander is visiting me. Thereafter I shall
ask Jumbo [General Wilson] to come here on his way home. I wish
to keep all the issues open for the next three or four days. Supposing
Turkey jibs and Rhodes is shut out, we must have the big Rome
amphibious operation, and also have some clearing up on the Dalmatian coast, especially Argostoli and Corfu. In no case can we sacrifice
Rome for the Riviera. We must have both.

Meanwhile I had had a long talk with Alexander. He demurred
to the suggestion that he was not very keen on the Anzio landing.
He wanted a two-division lift, and the problem was how this
could be supplied. Bedell Smith, who had also arrived, thought
he could make up pretty nearly a two-division lift provided that
airborne troops were counted as well. If this were supplied and
decision taken on the morrow or the next day Alexander could
strike in the last week of January. The question was, how to find

381

the landing-craft. When I asked Bedell Smith why we should not delay the "Overlord" L.S.T.s, etc., till February 15 he replied he just could not bear asking for a third extension. I had no such compunction.

There were 104 L.S.T.s in the Mediterranean, but most of them were due to return home for "Overlord". By the middle of January we should only have thirty-six, with another fifteen arriving from the Indian Ocean about that time. To carry two divisions it was said we needed eighty-eight. No more could arrive till April. The only solution was to hold most of those in the Mediterranean for another three weeks. There were good hopes that this could be done without injury to "Overlord" or to the landing on the Riviera.

* * * * *

On the 24th the Chiefs of Staff sent me a detailed statement of their ideas, and a draft which they proposed to send to their Washington colleagues. They favoured the plan, but feared we should never win American consent.

Their conclusions were:

We ask the Combined Chiefs of Staff to agree:

(a) That the remainder of the Andamans assault shipping and craft should be ordered to the Mediterranean.

(b) That such resources as can reach the Central Mediterranean in time should be employed by the Supreme Allied Commander Mediterranean Theatre for the launching of a two-divisional amphibious assault designed to enable Rome to be captured and the armies to advance to the Pisa–Rimini line, and that instructions to this effect should be issued forthwith. There will be sufficient time for the subsequent withdrawal of these resources for the South of France attack.

(c) That our negotiations with Turkey should continue on the present basis, but that amphibious operations in the Ægean should be ruled out.

(d) That Admiral Mountbatten should be informed of these decisions, and instructed to make his final recommendations for operations to be carried out in his theatre with the resources remaining to him.

* * * * *

I had with me at this tense period from my Defence Office only General Hollis, but he proved a tower of strength. I was also greatly aided by Captain Power, R.N., who was Admiral John Cunningham's Deputy Chief of Staff (Plans). He cleared away a mass of argument which obstructed the decision. He said in his able paper, which the Admiral fully approved:

The L.S.T.s now in the Mediterranean are thoroughly trained. They have all taken part in at least two assault operations, and have done a great deal of additional work on ferrying, continually loading and unloading over beaches, yards, or quays. They are well manned and accustomed to steaming and manœuvring in close company. They should require no further naval training prior to "Overlord", except that they are unaccustomed to problems of tide and the technique of beaching and unbeaching in tidal waters. Being good seamen, however, they should require but very brief instruction and training before they master the new problem. . . . Mediterranean experience shows that there is no need to marry the L.S.T.s and the troops concerned until eleven days before calling for the operation—three days for initial loading, six days for rehearsal, two days for reloading. . . .

I should estimate that seven days' allowance for tide training would be more than adequate for these well-trained ships.

Total training allowance should therefore be approximately three weeks. . . . They therefore have ample time before "Overlord", except that they cannot all refit at once.

* * * * *

As a result of detailed discussion with the assembled commanders I sent home the following proposals after midnight on the 24th:

Prime Minister to Chiefs of Staff and   25 Dec 43 (12.30 a.m.)
First Sea Lord

I have had talks to-night with General Wilson and General Alexander and Air Chief Marshal Tedder and their staffs about Anzio.

We are all agreed that it must be carried out on sufficient scale to ensure success, namely, at least a two-divisional assault. Target date will be about January 20. Assumption is that Rhodes is not on. We feel strongly that the only right course is to delay for not more than one month departure from Mediterranean of all British L.S.T.s now due to leave in January and on February 1 (totalling fifty-six L.S.T.s). The fifteen L.S.T.s from the Bay of Bengal would not arrive in time for Anzio, but would play their part in repayment of "Overlord" a little later. . . .

I wish Chiefs of Staff to give earliest attention to the paper prepared at my request by Captain Power. This sets out the economies in time which might be effected in the preparation of L.S.T.s for "Overlord". All present to-night considered that Captain Power's paper showed a firm grasp of the situation, and his proposals should be capable of achievement. . . .

The Chiefs of Staff were not at first convinced. They mentioned various points of detail; and details were decisive. They also "earnestly hoped" I would agree to their draft note explaining the situation to the Combined Chiefs of Staff. I was sure that we must be agreed among ourselves on all essentials first, and I replied as follows:

Prime Minister to Chiefs of Staff   26 Dec 43
I have been into the facts most thoroughly with the Admiral and with General Gale and their staffs. There is not the slightest chance of mounting Anzio on a two-division basis unless the whole fifty-six L.S.T.s are held back another three weeks—*i.e.*, until February 5. They know a good deal about training for assault landings in the Mediterranean. Pray let me know the argument as between three weeks and a month, and let me know exactly each day's employment prescribed for vessels on return. . . . You are expected to organise dockyards so as to refit twenty-five a month.

The success of Anzio depends on the strength of the initial landing. If this is two full divisions plus paratroops it should be decisive, as it cuts the communications of the whole of the enemy forces facing the Fifth Army. The enemy must therefore annihilate the landing force by withdrawals from the Fifth Army front or immediately retreat. Nothing less than two divisions will serve. Weather uncertainties make it necessary to put them ashore with at least four days' supplies. It is not intended to maintain these divisions for long over the beaches, but rather to bring the battle to a climax in a week or ten days. . . .

It is no use your telegraphing to the Combined Chiefs of Staff until we are in agreement on the one vital matter, namely, the delay of three weeks in the return of the fifty-six L.S.T.s. On this depends the success or ruin of our Italian campaign.

The Chiefs of Staff gave many solid reasons for their anxieties in their reply of December 27, and added, "We feel we should not conceal from you the difficulty we expect with the United States Chiefs of Staff if we tell them frankly the true position as we see it."

*   *   *   *   *

All the morning of Christmas Day our conference at Carthage continued. Eisenhower, Alexander, Bedell Smith, General

Wilson, Tedder, Admiral John Cunningham, and other high officers were present. The only one not there was General Mark Clark, of the Fifth Army. This was an oversight which I regret, as it was to his army that the operation was eventually entrusted and he ought to have had the background in his mind. We were all agreed that nothing less than a two-division lift would suffice. At this time I contemplated an assault by two British divisions from the Eighth Army, in which Montgomery was about to be succeeded by General Leese. I thought the amphibious operation involved potential mortal risks to the landed forces, and I preferred to run them with British troops, because it was to Britain that I was responsible. Moreover, the striking force would then have been homogeneous instead of half and half.

Everything turned on landing-craft, which held for some weeks all our strategy in the tightest ligature. What with the rigid date prescribed for "Overlord" and the movement, repair, and refitting of less than a hundred of these small vessels, all plans were in a strait-jacket. The telegrams which passed show how we escaped, though mauled, from this predicament. But I must also admit that I was so much occupied in fighting for the principle that I did not succeed in getting, and indeed did not dare to demand, the necessary weight and volume for the "cat-claw". Actually there were enough L.S.T.s for the operation as planned, and in my opinion, if the extravagant demands of the military machine had been reduced, we could, without prejudice to any other pledge or commitment, have flung ashore south of the Tiber a still larger force with full mobility. However, the issue was fought out in terms of routine Army requirements and the exact dates when L.S.T.s could be free for "Overlord", making of course all allowances for their return home in winter Biscay weather, and with the time-margins for their refits stated at their maximum. If I had asked for a three-division lift I should not have got anything. How often in life must one be content with what one can get! Still, it would be better to do it right.

★   ★   ★   ★   ★

The brute fact of delaying the return to England of the fifty-six L.S.T.s for three weeks had to be faced. Against this towered up the date of "Overlord"—MAY. The reader will note in the following telegram the first appearance of JUNE 6.

Prime Minister to Chiefs of Staff   26 Dec 43

I am proceeding entirely on the basis of keeping to the May "Overlord". I am sure this can be done and problem solved by persevering energetically. I may however say in strictest secrecy that both Eisenhower and Montgomery have expressed themselves entirely dissatisfied with what they have heard of the present plan for "Overlord", and I gather they will demand a far larger first flight. I should think it very likely that when they have examined the plan they will propose a delay. Our contract is "during May", but I do not know whether if responsible commanders required the June moon around June 6, and could show much better prospects then, the extra week might not have to be conceded. Preliminary air bombardment would begin anyhow in May.

Beware therefore that we do not sacrifice our vital task in Italy in order to achieve a date which anyhow may be postponed on other and larger grounds. Eisenhower even spoke of telegraphing himself to Stalin, once he had assumed effective command and was master of the problem, demanding a reasonable measure of delay. I did not lend myself to this at all, as I am fighting the case on the Teheran [agreement] line. All the more do I expect you to help me. Be careful this is kept to yourselves and the three War Cabinet Ministers on Defence Committee, Mr. Attlee, Mr. Eden, and Mr. Lyttelton.

At the close of this decisive Christmas Day conference at Carthage I sent the following to the President, and a similar telegram home. I was careful to state the root fact bluntly.

         25 Dec 43

I held a conference to-day with Eisenhower, and all his high officers. Report as follows:

General Alexander is prepared to execute the landing at Anzio about January 20 if he can get a lift of two divisions. This should decide the Battle of Rome, and possibly achieve the destruction of a substantial part of enemy's army. To strike with less than two divisions would be to court disaster, having regard to the positions likely to be achieved by that date by Fifth and Eighth Armies.

For this purpose eighty-eight L.S.T.s are required. These can only be obtained by delaying the return home of fifty-six L.S.T.s due to leave the Mediterranean from January 15 onward, sending them home by convoys starting February 5. Nothing less than this will suffice. The fifteen L.S.T.s from India cannot arrive in time, though they would be invaluable to replace casualties and for the building up of "Anvil".

By various expedients it is believed that the lost three weeks can be recovered and the existing prescribed build-up for "Overlord" maintained.

Having kept these fifty-six L.S.T.s in the Mediterranean so long, it would seem irrational to remove them for the very week when they can render decisive service. What, also, could be more dangerous than to let the Italian battle stagnate and fester on for another three months? We cannot afford to go forward leaving a vast half-finished job behind us. It therefore seemed to those present that every effort should be made to bring off Anzio on a two-division basis around January 20, and orders have been issued to General Alexander to prepare accordingly. If this opportunity is not grasped we must expect the ruin of the Mediterranean campaign of 1944. I earnestly hope therefore that you may agree to the three weeks' delay in return of the fifty-six landing-craft, and that all the authorities will be instructed to make sure that the May "Overlord" is not prejudiced thereby.

I recognise with regret that Rhodes and the Ægean policy must be side-tracked in these higher interests, and it may well be that "Pig-stick" [the attack on the Arakan, west of Burma] will require to be moderated into "Pigstuck" in order to build up three divisions for the landing in the South of France. This has been most painful to me, but I could not face the Italian stalemate and disaster which will otherwise ensue.

It was at this point, while all hung in suspense, that I flew from Carthage to Marrakesh, bearing my burdens with me.

CHAPTER XXV

AT MARRAKESH

CONVALESCENCE

By Air to Marrakesh – Joyful News: The President's Telegram of December 28 – June 3 versus May 5 as the Date for "Overlord" – The American Parachute Regiment – Montgomery's Visit – New Year Correspondence with the President – Conferences at Marrakesh on the Anzio Expedition, January 7 and 8 – Generals Eisenhower and Montgomery Incline to the Moon Period of June 3 for "Overlord" – The President's View – The Polish Question Again – Visit of President Beneš – A Tribute to Beneš – Friendly Contacts with General de Gaulle – Russia's Share in the Italian Fleet – A Compromise – Home Before Anzio.

LORD MORAN thought it possible for me to leave Carthage after Christmas, but insisted that I must have three weeks' convalescence somewhere. And where could be better than the lovely villa at Marrakesh, where the President and I had stayed after Casablanca a year before? All plans had been made during the past few days. I was to be the guest of the United States Army at Marrakesh. It was also thought that I had been long enough at Carthage to be located. Small vessels had ceaselessly to patrol the bay in front of the villa in case some U-boat turned up for a surprise raid. There might also be a long-range air attack. I had my own protection in a battalion of the Coldstream Guards. I was too ill, or too busy, to be consulted about all this, but I saw in my beloved Marrakesh a haven where I could regain my strength. Tedder had planned out the flight with great care. The doctors did not want me to fly above six thousand feet, and he had arranged our route through the Atlas Mountains on this basis. I was delighted when the morning of December 27 came and I dressed for the first time again in my uniform. As I was leaving the door a telegram was put in my hand, giving the fateful news of the sinking of the *Scharnhorst*.★ I stopped to dictate the following telegram to Stalin:

Prime Minister to Premier Stalin   27 Dec 43
    The Arctic convoys to Russia have brought us luck. Yesterday enemy attempted to intercept with battle-cruiser *Scharnhorst*. Commander-in-Chief Admiral Fraser with the *Duke of York* (35,000-ton battleship) cut off *Scharnhorst's* retreat, and after an action sunk her.
    2. Am much better, and off to the south for convalescence.

A very cordial reply to this was received a few days later, ending, "I shake your hand firmly."

Outside the villa a magnificent guard of the Coldstream was drawn up. I had not realised how much I had been weakened by my illness. I found it quite a difficulty to walk along the ranks and climb into the motor-car. The flight at six thousand feet had been planned on the weather forecast that the skies would be clear. However, as we sailed on and the uplands of Tunisia began to rise about us I saw a lot of large fleecy and presently blackish clouds gathering around, and after a couple of hours we were more often in mist than in sunlight. I have always had a great objection to what are called "stuffed clouds"—*i.e.*, clouds with mountains inside them—and flying an intricate route through the various valleys before us in order to keep under six thousand feet seemed to me an unfair proposition for the others in the plane. I therefore sent for the pilot and told him to fly at least two thousand feet above the highest mountain within a hundred miles of his route. Lord Moran agreed. Oxygen was brought by a skilled administrator, specially provided for the journey. We sailed up into the blue. I got along all right, and we made a perfect landing at about four o'clock on the Marrakesh airfield. Our second plane, which had adhered strictly to its instructions, had a very severe and dangerous flight through the various gorges and passes, many of which were traversed with only fleeting glimpses of the towering mountains. At this low height the weather was by no means good. The plane arrived safely an hour behind us with one of its doors blown off and nearly everybody very sick. I was sorry indeed they should have been put to so much discomfort

★ See pp. 244-5.

and risk on my account. They could have flown it all out comfortably under blue skies at twelve or even eleven thousand feet.

Nothing could exceed the comfort, and even luxury, of my new abode, or the kindness of everyone concerned. But one thing rose above all others in my mind—what answer would the President give to my telegram? When I thought of the dull, dead-weight resistance, taking no account of timing and proportion, that I had encountered about all Mediterranean projects I awaited the answer with deep anxiety. What I asked for was a hazardous enterprise on the Italian coast, and a possible delay of three weeks from May 1—four if the moon phase was to be observed—in the date of the Channel crossing. I had gained the agreement of the commanders on the spot. The British Chiefs of Staff had always agreed in principle, and were now satisfied in detail. But what would the Americans say to a four weeks' postponement of "Overlord"? However, when one is thoroughly tired out the blessing of sleep is not usually denied.

* * * * *

It was with joy, not, I confess, unmingled with surprise, that the next day I received the following:

President Roosevelt to Prime Minister　　　　　　　　28 Dec 43
It is agreed to delay the departure of fifty-six L.S.T.s scheduled for "Overlord" for mounting Anzio on January 20, and on the basis that "Overlord" remains the paramount operation and will be carried out on the date agreed to at Cairo and Teheran. All possible expedients should be undertaken to overcome probable effect on "Overlord" preparation, to which end the other twelve L.S.T.s for "Overlord" should depart as now scheduled and the fifteen L.S.T.s *ex* Andamans arriving in Mediterranean on January 14 should proceed directly to United Kingdom. I agree that Rhodes and the Ægean must be side-tracked and that we cannot give further consideration to launching Rhodes prior to "Anvil" [Riviera]. In view of the Soviet-British-American agreement reached in Teheran I cannot agree without Stalin's approval to any use of forces or equipment elsewhere that might delay or hazard the success of "Overlord" or "Anvil".

I replied:

Prime Minister to President Roosevelt　　　　　　　　28 Dec 43
I thank God for this fine decision, which engages us once again in wholehearted unity upon a great enterprise.

I have heard from the British Chiefs of Staff that the Admiralty can conform to the conditions provided the releases are made from the Anzio plan of the number which are agreed upon. The Chiefs of Staff will be telegraphing to-day in full detail to the Combined Chiefs of Staff. Meanwhile here the word is "Full steam ahead".

After travelling quite unaffected at 13,000 feet I arrived yesterday at our villa, where I am indeed in the lap of luxury, thanks to overflowing American hospitality. Max [Beaverbrook] has just flown in from London. I propose to stay here in the sunshine till I am quite strong again.

Great efforts had indeed been made by the Staffs at home, and especially by the Admiralty, to accomplish the "cat-claw", and I hastened to congratulate them. General Alexander had asked for eighty-eight landing-craft; they promised him all but one. The President's telegram was a marvel. I was sure that I owed it not only to his goodwill, but to Marshall's balance of mind, to Eisenhower's loyalty to the show he was about to quit, and to Bedell Smith's active, knowledgeable, fact-armed diplomacy.

On the same day Alexander sent us his plan. After conferring with General Mark Clark and General Brian Robertson, Chief Administrative Officer and son of the C.I.G.S. of the First World War, he had decided to use an American and a British division. Armour, paratroops, and Commandos would be on a fifty-fifty basis, and the whole would be under an American corps commander. The attack would go in about January 20. Ten days beforehand he would launch a big offensive against Cassino to draw off the German reserves. The forward plunge of the main armies would follow. I was well content. So far so good.

* * * * *

I had however another small margin on which to draw. I wired to the Chiefs of Staff:

I am fighting the issue [of the date of "Overlord"] entirely on the Teheran basis. This assumed May 20 rather than May 5, which is an altogether new date. Our contract with Stalin would be fulfilled by any date up to May 31. It seems to me from what I have heard from Eisenhower that June 3, which is the corresponding moon phase, would be perfectly permissible, especially if it were asked for by the commanders now nominated for the operation. There is no need to discuss such matters now, but here is something to veer and haul on.

Pray let me have the alternative build-up comparing May 5 with

June 3. I repeat this is not to be considered as anything in the nature of a decision for delay, and is not to go to anyone outside our circle.

The Chiefs of Staff replied:

To fulfil the conditions of the plan made by existing commanders the "Overlord" assault should take place about May 5. However, this date cannot be regarded as final, and even if delays occur in the return and refitting programme of the L.S.T.s so that all have not joined their assault forces by April 13, this should not rule out a May date for the "Overlord" assault.

The arrangements proposed certainly do not preclude the achievement of a May assault, but the programme is tightly stretched. No violation of the agreement reached at Teheran is however involved, and we do not think it necessary at this stage to consult the Russians.

I commented on this as follows:

30 Dec 43

Our contract would be fulfilled by May 31. In my opinion it would be a *bona fide* execution of it if we fixed June 3, which is the corresponding moon phase to May 5, for the actual assault. It is however better to work to May 5, and thus have a month to spare.

★　★　★　★　★

Now a new point of importance arose.

Prime Minister to Field-Marshal Dill, Washington　　　3 Jan 44

Alexander signals as follows:

"Clark is planning Anzio, and the usual difficulties are coming to light. For example, it appears that we shall not be able to keep the 504th American Parachute Regiment, and Eisenhower is reluctant to press for their retention. The British Parachute Brigade is in the line and engaged. I have nothing immediately available to relieve them with, and we cannot afford the delay in getting them out and across to the Naples area. Further, they are not operationally experienced and badly need training."

2. Eisenhower is now with Marshall. Will you appeal to them to let this 504th American Regiment do this one fine and critical job before they come home for "Overlord"? It is so rarely that opportunities for decisive air action by paratroops present themselves, and it seems improvident to take them from the decisive point just when they might render exemplary and outstanding service. They can be sent home immediately afterwards in time for "Overlord", observing that we have already [at home] about double as many parachute and airborne troops for "Overlord" as there are transport aircraft to lift. Let me know what happens.

General Marshall agreed.   We shall see later how this sacrifice was wasted.

*   *   *   *   *

I had asked Montgomery to visit me on his way home from Italy to take up his new command in "Overlord". I had offered him this task so full of hazard. Of course in the absence of special reasons a general should accept any duty to which he is called by national authority. At the same time nothing in the unwritten law obliges enthusiasm. In the Grenadier Guards, with whom I once had the honour to serve, all orders are received with the one word "Sir".   However, all kinds of inflections may be given to this monosyllable. I was gratified and also relieved to find that Montgomery was delighted and eager for what I had always regarded as a majestic, inevitable, but terrible task. When he arrived at Marrakesh we had a two hours' drive out to our picnic at the foot of the Atlas. I had given him early in the morning the plan prepared over so many months by General Morgan and the Anglo-American Joint Staffs in London. After he had read it in summary he said at once, "This will not do. I must have more in the initial punch." After considerable argument a whole set of arrangements was made in consequence of his opinion, and proved right. Evidently he was a firm believer in the operation, and I was very pleased at this.

The ladies had now come up, and we all lunched by the side of a dazzling stream in fresh air and brilliant sunshine. It was indeed an oasis in the vast desert of human conflict through which we had to toil. Presently I pushed forward into the mountains and our cars zigzagged slowly up the road to a viewpoint which I knew. But the General would have none of this. He got out of the car and walked straight up the hill, "to keep himself in training," as he put it. I warned him not to waste his vigour, considering what was coming. I emphasised the truths that energy of mind does not depend on energy of body; that energy should be exercised and not exhausted; that athletics are one thing and strategy another. These admonitions were in vain. The General was in the highest spirits; he leaped about the rocks like an antelope, and I felt a strong reassurance that all would be well.

*   *   *   *   *

393

The New Year opened for me in agreeable correspondence with the President.

Prime Minister (Marrakesh) to President Roosevelt　　　30 Dec 43

I have now received from my brother Jack full accounts of the Christmas tree at Chequers.★ All my grandchildren were there, and a number of other children, and a good time was had by all. Winant, who was present, has promised to write to you about it. Thank you so much for sending me this token. I have also to thank you for the wonderful map case which has arrived from you for me, and which I am longing to see. We are indeed in comfort at this beautiful villa, and I am making good progress. The sun is shining to-day, but nothing did me the same good as your telegram showing how easily our minds work together on the grimly simple issues of this vast war. Alexander reports he has arranged satisfactory plans with Clark for Anzio. He is using the British 1st and the American 3rd Divisions, with paratroops and armour. I am glad of this. It is fitting that we should share equally in suffering, risk, and honour.

I received on the same day congratulations on my recovery from Franco and Tito. So what?

Sarah thanks you for your message and sends her love.

Unhappily the President was himself laid up with influenza.

President Roosevelt to Prime Minister　　　31 Dec 43

I am in bed for two or three days with a mild case of the 'flu, which, in a mild form, has become epidemic throughout the country.

I am delighted that you are safely at the villa. I suggest that on New Year's Day you invite the two gentlemen who congratulated you, then lock them in the top of the tower where we saw the sunset, and tell them you will stay at the bottom to see whether the black or the red throws the other one over the battlements.

Prime Minister to President Roosevelt　　　1 Jan 44

I am so sorry about your influenza. I earnestly hope you will defer to Dr. McIntyre's advice and show that attitude of submission to the medical faculty which you have so sedulously enjoined on me.

The villa is perfect. The doctors want me to stay here for the next three weeks. The weather is bright, though cool. The cook is a marvel. We go for picnics to the mountains. Last night Eisenhower was with us on his way to you, and I had long talks with him. Montgomery is here now on his way to England. I think we have a fine team, and they certainly mean to pull together.

★ Mr. Roosevelt grew Christmas trees at Hyde Park, and prided himself on this. He had sent me one.

I have not yet been able to arrange the contest in the tower. The Red is in better training than the Black.

Accept all my best wishes for a New Year which will not only be marked by triumph but will open wider doors to our future work together.

Clemmie and Sarah also send their salutations.

*   *   *   *   *

Although the main issue about the landing-craft for Anzio had been settled many details of their employment raised serious discussion.

General Alexander to Prime Minister   4 Jan 44

I have just returned from conference with General Clark on my way back from Tunis, and certain factors have come to light which are causing me grave concern, and I must therefore ask for your help and assistance. The facts are these. The removal of all but six of the L.S.T.s after the initial landing will not allow us to put the two divisions ashore complete with their essential fighting vehicles. . . . My experience of combined operations is that the initial assault to get ashore can be effected, but the success of the operation depends on whether the full fighting strength of the expedition can be concentrated in time to withstand the inevitable counter-attack. For Anzio two divisions are the minimum force to put ashore in face of likely German resistance. Yet we are willing to accept this if the two divisions can be concentrated on land in strength and in time. . . . We are willing to accept any risks to achieve our object, but if the two divisions get sealed off by the Germans we obviously cannot leave them there without any support when there will be L.S.T.s somewhere in the Mediterranean sufficient for that purpose. . . . Clark and I are confident that we have a great chance of pulling off something big if given the means with which to do it. The means required are fourteen L.S.T.s for maintenance until such time as the Anzio force and the Fifth Army join hands, and a further ten L.S.T.s for a period of fifteen days from the landing to build up the two divisions in guns, tanks, and other supporting arms to a strength sufficient to fight on level terms with the Germans. Even if this does interfere with preparations for "Anvil" to some extent, surely the prize is worth it.

I therefore summoned the authorities concerned to Marrakesh, and held two conferences on January 7 and 8, attended by Lord Beaverbrook, General Wilson, Admiral John Cunningham, General Alexander, General Devers, General Bedell Smith, and others. Captain Power had just returned from London after

395

clearing up many intricate points about the landing-craft with the Chiefs of Staff, and now, with the full support of his admiral, rendered us similar services. I was able to report to the President on the 8th as follows:

A unanimous agreement for action as proposed was reached by the responsible officers of both countries and of all Services as a result of our two conferences. Everyone is in good heart and the resources seem sufficient. Every aspect was thrashed out in full detail by subcommittees in the interval between the two conferences. . . . Intention is to land a corps of two divisions for the assault, and to follow up with a mobile striking force based on the elements of a third division to cut enemy's communications.

It should be possible to do this, barring accident, without conflicting with requirements of "Overlord" or "Anvil", and still have sufficiency of landing-craft to maintain the force up till the end of February, weather permitting and God being with us.

General Wilson, who to-day assumes duty as Supreme Allied Commander-in-Chief Mediterranean, has issued instructions to subordinate commanders to give effect to the above. He is also informing Combined Chiefs of Staff.

All these calculations were based upon the May (or X) date being maintained for "Overlord", though I myself had always thought that the moon period of June 3 (Y date) would probably be found most suitable, and I was glad to learn from General Eisenhower on his passage through Marrakesh that he was inclining towards this solution, which gave him and Montgomery more time to arrange for the larger forces it was now proposed to use in the first descent. I had telegraphed to the President setting out the whole question, and reminding him of our talks and agreements at Teheran.

Prime Minister to President Roosevelt 6 Jan 44

Bedell Smith and Devers came through here morning of 5th. Bedell told me that he and Montgomery are convinced that it is better to put in a much heavier and broader "Overlord" than to expand the landing on the Riviera above our pre-Teheran conception, and that he is putting this to Eisenhower and your Chiefs of Staff. I have always expected that when the commanders took the matter into their hands they would make alterations in the plans, which nevertheless have proved invaluable as a basis for future decisions. As you know, I have always hoped that the initial assault at "Overlord" could be with heavier forces than we have hitherto mentioned.

It also seems to me, from what I heard, very probable that the June moon will be the earliest practicable date. I do not see why we should resist this if the commanders feel they have a better chance then. At Teheran the Chiefs of Staff's recommendation was June 1 or one day earlier, which you and I agreed to express more agreeably as "during May". In conversation with Uncle Joe we never mentioned such a date as May 5, or even May 8, but always spoke to him [of] around the 20th. Neither did we at any time dwell upon the exact phase of the operation which should fall on any particular day. If now the June date is accepted as final I do not feel that we shall in any way have broken faith with him. The operation will anyhow begin in May with feints and softening bombardments, and I do not think U.J. is the kind of man to be unreasonable over forty-eight hours.

On the other hand, the ground will be drier for U.J.'s great operations by June. We shall make a much heavier attack, and with much better chances of success. I am making you suggestions through Leathers for running another Arctic convoy, for which we can provide the escorts if you can provide the ships and cargoes, we having practically finished our quotas.

I do not think it necessary to make any communication to U.J. at the present time, but in a few weeks, after Eisenhower has presented his final conclusions to us, we should no doubt tell him all the story in all its strength, including any modification of "Anvil", with the authority of the responsible commanders behind our statement.

The President answered this important telegram, the facts of which were not in dispute between us, a week later. He had by then also received full reports of the conclusions of our meetings about the Anzio operation, which were all on the basis that the earlier date could be maintained for "Overlord" if desired.

President Roosevelt to Prime Minister   14 Jan 44

It is my understanding that in Teheran Uncle J. was given a promise that "Overlord" would be launched during May and supported by strongest practicable landing in the South of France at about the same time, and that he agreed to plan for simultaneous Russian attack on Eastern Front.

I do not believe that we should make any decision now to defer the operations, certainly not until the responsible commanders, Eisenhower and Wilson, have had full opportunity to explore all possibilities and make factual reports. In the meantime no communication should be sent to Uncle J. on this subject.

I think the psychology of bringing this thing up at this time would be very bad, in view of the fact that it is only a little over a month since the three of us agreed on the statement in Teheran.

"I am very glad," I replied, on the 16th, "to see that we are in complete agreement."

*   *   *   *   *

Physical weakness oppressed me at Marrakesh following my illness at Carthage. All my painting tackle had been sent out, but I could not face it. I could hardly walk at all. Even tottering from the motor-car to a picnic luncheon in lovely weather amid the foothills of the Atlas was limited to eighty or a hundred yards. I passed eighteen hours out of the twenty-four prone. I never remember such extreme fatigue and weakness in body. On the other hand, every temptation, inducement, exhortation, and to some extent compulsion, to relax and lie down presented itself in the most seductive form. The Taylor villa was a perfect haven, lacking nothing that comfort could require or luxury suggest. I was utterly tired out, and here was the most attractive bed of repose, not only offered by gracious hosts, but enjoined by Lord Moran, the President, and the War Cabinet. However, events continued to offer irresistible distraction.

*   *   *   *   *

The Polish question, which had played so great a part at Teheran, had led me to cable Eden from Carthage.

Prime Minister to Foreign Secretary   20 Dec 43

I think you should now open the Polish frontiers question with the Poles, stating it is at my personal wish, and that I would have done it myself but for my temporary incapacitation. You should show them the formula and the rough line on the map on the eastern side, and the line of the Oder, including the Oppeln district, on the west. This gives them a magnificent piece of country three or four hundred miles across each way, and with over 250 miles of seaboard, even on the basis that they do not begin till west of Königsberg. The Poles should understand of course that these are only very broad, tentative suggestions, but that they would be most unwise to let them fall to the ground. Even if they do not get Lvov, I should still advise their acceptance, and that they put themselves in the hands of British and American friends to try to turn this plan into reality. You should put it to them that by taking over and holding firmly the present German territories up to the Oder they will be rendering a service to Europe as a whole by

making the basis of a friendly policy towards Russia and close association with Czechoslovakia. This would give a chance for the rebirth
of the Polish nation brighter than any yet seen.

Once we know that they will accept and endorse these proposals
we will address ourselves to the Russians and endeavour to make
matters firm and precise. On the other hand, if they cast it all aside I
do not see how His Majesty's Government can press for anything
more for them. The Russian armies may in a few months be crossing
the frontiers of pre-war Poland, and it seems of the utmost consequence
to have friendly recognition by Russia of the Polish Government and a
broad understanding of the post-war frontiers settlement agreed before
then. I shall be most interested to hear what their reaction is.

★   ★   ★   ★   ★

President Beneš was now on his way from Moscow to London.
As these volumes show, I had had a long contact with him. It will
be remembered that he had played perhaps a decisive part in
warning Stalin of the pro-German conspiracy against him in
1936.★ At any rate, his relations with the Soviets were of the most
friendly and intimate character. I asked him to look in on me at
Marrakesh on his way back. His profound knowledge of the
Eastern European scene made his views on Poland and on what
the Russians would do for Poland most important. For twenty
years or more Beneš, as Foreign Secretary or President of
Czechoslovakia, had been the faithful ally of France and friend
of the Western Powers, while at the same time maintaining a
unique association with Stalin. When France and Britain sacrificed Czechoslovakia, and later when, on the eve of the war,
Ribbentrop made his agreement with Molotov, Beneš was a very
lonely man. But then, after a lengthy interval, came Hitler's
attack on Russia, and all Beneš's common stock with the Soviets
came again into full validity. Russia might well have fought
Germany about Czechoslovakia in 1938. Anyhow, both were
now under the same cruel lash.

It was very pleasant to me to talk in the sunshine and amid the
flowers of my Marrakesh abode to this old political associate and
mature European statesman, whom I had first met in 1918, in
company with the great Masaryk, the founder of his country and
the father of a son who died faithfully in her cause. Beneš was
of course at this time optimistic.

★ See Volume I, p. 258 (Cassell's 2nd edition).

I gave the following account of our talk to the President.

6 Jan 44

Beneš has been here, and is very hopeful about the Russian situation. He may be most useful in trying to make the Poles see reason and in reconciling them to the Russians, whose confidence he has long possessed. He brought a new map with pencil marks by U.J. showing the eastern frontier from Königsberg to the Curzon Line, giving the Poles Lomza and Bialystok regions in the north, but not Lemberg [Lvov] at the southern end. For their western frontier he offers the line of the Oder, including the major part of Oppeln. This gives the Poles a fine place to live in, more than 300 miles square, and with 250 miles of seaboard on the Baltic. As soon as I get home I shall go all out with the Polish Government to close with this or something like it, and, having closed, they must proclaim themselves as ready to accept the duty of guarding the bulwark of the Oder against further German aggression upon Russia, and also they must back the settlement to the limit. This will be their duty to the Powers of Europe, who will twice have rescued them. If I can get this tidied up early in February a visit from them to you would clinch matters.

The Russians are quite agreeable to Beneš having his old pre-Munich frontier back, with a slight military adjustment along the northern crests of the mountains and a little territory to the eastward linking them with Russia.

As this was the last time I ever saw President Beneš I will record my tribute to him. In all his thought and aims he consistently sustained the main principles on which Western civilisation is founded, and was ever true to the cause of his native land, over which he presided for more than twenty years. He was a master of administration and diplomacy. He knew how to endure with patience and fortitude long periods of adverse fortune. Where he failed—and it cost him and his country much—was in not taking violent decisions at the supreme moment. He was too experienced a diplomatist, too astute a year-to-year politician, to realise the moment and to stake all on victory or death. Had he told his cannons to fire at Munich time the Second World War would have begun under conditions far less favourable to Hitler, who needed many months to make his army and his armour.

* * * * *

In spite of the tension with General de Gaulle about Peyrouton, Boisson, and Flandin, all of whom had been arrested by the Free

French authorities in December, I determined to make an effort to renew friendly relations with him before returning home. On New Year's Day I asked him to dine and sleep at the villa on January 3. "This," I said, "would give us an opportunity of long-needed talks. My wife is with me here, and if Madame de Gaulle would care to accompany you it would give us both much pleasure." The General evidently thought the notice too short. I ought to have known that he would not sleep anywhere in North Africa but in a French official residence. He pleaded the pressure of his other engagements. So I let it alone. However, having learnt later that he would arrive in Marrakesh on January 12, I invited him to luncheon that day, and he accepted. Mr. Duff Cooper and Lady Diana, Lord Beaverbrook, Mr. Nairn the Consul and his wife, were also our guests. The General arrived in the best of humour, greeted Mrs. Churchill in English, and spoke it throughout the meal. To make things equal I spoke French.

After luncheon the ladies went off to visit the bazaars, and de Gaulle and I and the other men settled down in the garden for a long talk. I had a lot of awkward subjects to deal with, and I thought my speaking French would add a lighter touch to them. Mr. Nairn, who made a few notes afterwards, records, "I heard Mr. Churchill say to Mr. Duff Cooper in English in a very audible whisper, 'I'm doing rather well, aren't I? Now that the General speaks English so well he understands my French perfectly.' Then everyone, General de Gaulle setting the example, burst out laughing. The Prime Minister continued in French, but the super-sensitive General was completely disarmed and ready to accept Mr. Churchill's comments in a friendly and helpful spirit."

The comments were numerous and serious. Why was he pursuing this vendetta against the French notabilities who had fallen into his power? Did he not realise how much difficulty he made for himself in the United States? How angry the President was with him? How much we all depended on American aid and goodwill? Why should he complicate his own task by this and all sorts of other needless friction? Why should he always try to offend these powerful Governments, without whose help he could not live? Upon a smaller point, why had he driven General Georges, whom I had specially brought from France to make things easier, off the Committee? At this de Gaulle said he had offered General Georges the Chancellorship of the Legion of

Honour. I asked what reply he had received. "I received no reply," he answered. I said I was not surprised. Had he the Chancellorship to bestow? But all ended pleasantly, and the General proposed that I should attend a review he would hold in my honour the next morning, which I agreed to do. And accordingly de Gaulle and I stood on a small platform while quite a large array of French and Moroccan troops marched past for an hour amid the cheers of the inhabitants of the Marrakesh oasis.

* * * * *

Another question arising out of Teheran raised considerable difficulty. We have seen how Stalin had asked for a share in the Italian Fleet, and the President was under the impression that he himself had mentioned in conversation one-third. The British Chiefs of Staff did not like this, and had always spoken to their Russian colleagues on a different basis. The President was worried about his personal remark "one-third", and set the whole position out to me with great frankness.

President Roosevelt to Prime Minister   9 Jan 44

As I told you, Harriman requested information on the action we were taking to carry out our commitments to turn over Italian ships to the Soviet by February 1 so that he could discuss the matter with Molotov if he were queried. I told him it was my intention to allocate one-third of the captured Italian ships to the Soviet war effort, beginning February 1, as rapidly as they could be made available.

Harriman then reminded me that Stalin's request at Teheran was a reiteration of the Soviet request originally made at Moscow in October [namely, for one battleship, one cruiser, eight destroyers, and four submarines for North Russia, and 40,000 tons of merchant shipping for the Black Sea], and that no mention was made at Moscow or Teheran of the Russians getting additional ships up to one-third of those captured. Accordingly, Harriman regarded my cable of December 21 as being for his information, and he has not discussed the question of one-third with Molotov.

Harriman also emphasised the very great importance of fulfilling our pledge to yield these ships. For us to fail or to delay would, in his opinion, only arouse suspicion in Stalin and in his associates as to the firmness of other commitments made at Teheran.

On the other hand, the Chiefs of Staff have raised numerous objections to the transfer, based on probable effects that this course would have on pending operations. They fear a loss of Italian naval and military co-operation, and the scuttling or sabotage of valuable ships which we need for "Anvil" and "Overlord". They foresee no material benefit to the Russian war effort at this time, since the warships are presently quite unsuited for Northern waters and the Black Sea is closed to merchant vessels.

The very wise provisions of the modified agreement [negotiated by Admiral Cunningham] give the United Nations the right to make disposition of any or all Italian ships as they may think fit. It is of importance that we should acquire and maintain the confidence of our Ally, and I feel that every practicable effort should be made to arrive at a solution whereby the Italian ships requested by the Soviet be turned over to them, beginning about February 1.

Do you believe it wise to present to Uncle J. the possible effect on "Overlord-Anvil" as expressed by our Staffs, and suggest a delay in assigning Italian ships to him until after the launching of "Overlord-Anvil"? I am particularly desirous of having an expression of your opinion in view of the present British command of the Mediterranean theatre and in order that we may reach a complete agreement as to the action to be taken. It is patently impracticable for either of us to act singly in this matter, but I think you will agree that we must not go back on what we told Uncle J.

This message was not entirely clear. I agreed to the ships mentioned in our agreement of October, but not to the more general terms of "one-third". I therefore replied:

Prime Minister to President Roosevelt   9 Jan 44
I entirely agree with you that we must not break faith with Stalin about the ships. I have been for a week in correspondence with Anthony on the subject, and hope to submit a proposal to you for a joint communication from you and me in a day or two.

I was myself in full accord with the Chiefs of Staff on both sides of the Atlantic. I felt that the immediate transfer of these Italian warships, which had so resolutely made their way to Malta and placed themselves in our hands, might have most damaging results to Italian co-operation with the Allies. Throughout the year 1943 my aim had been not only to make Italy surrender, but to bring her in on our side, with all that that meant to the progress of the war and to the future settlement of Europe. I was therefore prepared to press the War Cabinet and the Admiralty to make a substantial British sacrifice and to supply a number of British ships to the Russians, instead of breaking Italian hearts at this moment, so pregnant, as it seemed to me, with consequences for the future. Various messages passed between us, and I was very glad indeed to find how closely my colleagues at home and the Chiefs of Staff agreed. One could not expect the United States, with the whole burden of war in the Pacific weighing upon them, to make any large contribution. We, on the other hand, had certainly at this time an ample margin of naval power, both in the Mediterranean and, now that the *Scharnhorst* was at the bottom, in home and Arctic waters as well. As soon as I had reached an agreement with my friends at home I sent the following proposals to the President:

Prime Minister to President Roosevelt   16 Jan 44

My recollection is clear that nothing was said at Teheran about "one-third", but that a promise was made to meet the Russian claim put forward at Moscow to have transferred to them one battleship, one cruiser, eight destroyers, four submarines, and 40,000 tons of merchant shipping.

2. On the other hand, the main difficulties raised by the Chiefs of Staff are solid, and I think it very likely that once Stalin is convinced of our intentions and our good faith he will leave us to handle the matter in the smoothest and swiftest way possible.

3. I suggest therefore that we now signal him jointly to the following effect.

"(i) . . . The Combined Chiefs of Staff . . . think it would be dangerous to our triple interests actually to carry out any transfer or to say anything about it to the Italians at present. Nevertheless if after full consideration you desire us to proceed we will make a secret approach to Badoglio with a view to concluding the necessary arrangements. . . . These would have to be on the lines that Italian ships selected should be sailed to a suitable Allied port, where they would be collected by Russian crews, who would sail them into Russian Northern ports, which are the only ones now open where any refitting necessary could be undertaken.

"(ii) We are however very conscious of the dangers of this course, and have therefore decided to propose the following alternative:

"The British battleship *Royal Sovereign* has recently completed refit in the United States. She is fitted with Radar for all types of armament. Great Britain has also a cruiser available. His Majesty's Government are willing, for their part, that these vessels should be taken over during February at British ports by Soviet crews and sailed to North Russian ports. You could then make such alterations as you find necessary for Arctic conditions. These vessels would be temporarily transferred on loan to the Soviet Government, and would fly the Soviet flag until, without prejudice to the military operations, the necessary transfer of Italian vessels could be arranged.

"If events should take a favourable turn with Turks and the Straits become open the vessels would be ready to operate if desired in the Black Sea. We hope you will very carefully consider this alternative, which we think is in every way superior to first proposal."

4. If you could find the cruiser instead of our having to do so we should be relieved. We cannot do anything about the eight destroyers, but perhaps you may be able to supply this need. Otherwise we must say we have absolutely not got them until after "Overlord" and "Anvil". As to the 40,000 tons of merchant shipping, I should think that with your great supply and vastly improved sinkings you might supply these, but we should be willing to share fifty-fifty.

5. I hope, my dear friend, you will consider all these possibilities and let me know how you feel. In my opinion Stalin will be moved in a favourable manner by this handsome proposal. At any rate, it shows our faith and our goodwill. I doubt whether, having this alternative before him, he will press for the premature raising of the Italian problem, but we shall have done the right thing.

* * * * *

This alternative was accepted by the President. The Americans undertook themselves to furnish a cruiser, and the whole matter was presented to Stalin substantially in the form I suggested in a joint telegram from the President and me on January 23. Stalin's reply, when it came later, was as follows:

Premier Stalin to Prime Minister and President Roosevelt 29 Jan 44

I received on January 23 both your joint messages, signed by you, Mr. Prime Minister, and you, Mr. President, regarding the question of the handing over of Italian shipping for the use of the Soviet Union.

I must say that, after your joint affirmative reply at Teheran to the question which I raised of the handing over to the Soviet Union of Italian shipping by the end of January 1944, I considered this question settled, and the thought never entered my mind of the possibility of any kind of reconsideration of this decision, which was taken and agreed between the three of us. All the more so since, as we agreed at the time, this question was to be completely settled with the Italians.

Now I see that this is not so, and that nothing has even been mentioned to the Italians on the subject.

In order however not to complicate this question, which is of such great importance for our common struggle against Germany, the Soviet Government is prepared to accept your proposal regarding the dispatch from British ports to the U.S.S.R. of the battleship *Royal Sovereign* and one cruiser, and regarding the temporary use of these vessels by the Naval High Command of the U.S.S.R. until such time as the appropriate Italian shipping is made available to the Soviet Union. Similarly, we shall be prepared to accept from the U.S.A. and Great Britain 40,000 tons of merchant shipping, which will also be used by us until such time as a similar tonnage of Italian shipping is handed over to us. It is important that there should be no delays now regarding the matter, and that all the shipping indicated should be handed over to us during the month of February.

In your reply however there is no mention of the handing over to the Soviet Union of eight Italian destroyers and four submarines, to the handing over of which to the Soviet Union at the end of January you, Mr. Prime Minister, and you, Mr. President, agreed in Teheran. Meanwhile, for the Soviet Union this very question of destroyers and submarines, without which the handing over of one battleship and one cruiser has no significance, is of capital importance. You understand yourselves that a cruiser and a battleship are powerless without escorting destroyers. Since the whole of Italy's Fleet is under your control, to carry out the decision which was taken at Teheran to hand over for the use of the Soviet Union eight destroyers and four submarines out of that Fleet should present no difficulties. I am agreeable [literally, "I agree"] that, instead of Italian destroyers and submarines, a similar number of American or British destroyers and submarines should be handed over to the Soviet Union for our use. Moreover, the question of the handing over of destroyers and submarines cannot be postponed, but must be settled at one and the same time with the handing over of the battleship and cruiser, as was definitely agreed between us at Teheran.

Eventually the matter was settled as I hoped, although there was a good deal of correspondence, not all of a pleasant character, about it with our Soviet Ally. The *Royal Sovereign* and the American cruiser were handed over as proposed. There was an inevitable delay about the destroyers till after the "Overlord" operation was complete. The Admiralty sweetened this pill by lending Russia four of our modern submarines. As is well known, the Soviets after the war faithfully returned the ships, and arrangements were made to transfer vessels from the Italian Fleet in a manner acceptable to all concerned.

⋆   ⋆   ⋆   ⋆   ⋆

Much as I should have liked, and much as I was pressed, to recuperate for another fortnight in this delectable asylum, I determined to be at home before the shock of Anzio occurred. On January 14 therefore we all flew in beautiful weather to Gibraltar, where the *King George V* awaited me. I arrived early in the afternoon, and repaired again to the Convent.⋆ General Wilson, who had assumed his duties as Supreme Commander in the Mediterranean, and Admiral John Cunningham, the Naval Commander-in-Chief, had both arrived by air from Algiers, and we had an anxious but hopeful talk about the momentous operation for which we were all working. On the 15th I joined the rest of my party, who were already on board the *King George V*. She made her way out of Algeciras Bay wide into the Atlantic, and thence to Plymouth. After a restful voyage we were welcomed by the War Cabinet and Chiefs of Staff, who really seemed quite glad to see me back. I had been more than two months away from England, and they had been through a lot of worry on account both of my illness and my activities. It was indeed a homecoming, and I felt deeply grateful to all these trusty friends and fellow-workers.

⋆ See Vol. IV, p. 728.

CHAPTER XXVI

MARSHAL TITO AND YUGOSLAVIA

Mihailović and Tito – Importance of the Balkan Struggle – The Deakin and Maclean Missions – Growth of Partisan Strength after the Italian Surrender – My Telegram to Roosevelt of October 23, 1943 – Bitter Quarrels between Mihailović and Tito – Three New Factors in Our Policy – Randolph Joins Maclean – Difficult Position of King Peter – My Letter to Tito of January 8, 1944 – His Reply – Further Correspondence – We Withdraw Our Liaison Officers from Mihailović – My Account to Parliament of February 22, 1944 – King Peter Dismisses the Purić Government.

T*HE* reader must now go back to a fierce and sombre tale, which the main narrative has outstripped. Yugoslavia since Hitler's invasion and conquest in April 1941 had been the scene of fearful events. The spirited boy King took refuge in England with such of Prince Paul's ministers and other members of the Government as had defied the German assault. In the mountains there began again the fierce guerrilla with which the Serbs had resisted the Turks for centuries. General Mihailović was its first and foremost champion, and round him rallied the surviving *élite* of Yugoslavia. In the vortex of world affairs their struggle was hardly noticeable. It belongs to the "unestimated sum of human pain". Mihailović suffered as a guerrilla leader from the fact that many of his followers were well-known people with relations and friends in Serbia, and property and recognisable connections elsewhere. The Germans pursued a policy of murderous blackmail. They retaliated for guerrilla activities by shooting batches of four or five hundred selected people in Belgrade. Under this pressure Mihailović drifted gradually into a posture where some of his commanders made accommodations with the German and Italian troops to be left alone in certain mountain areas in return for doing little or nothing against the enemy. Those who have triumphantly withstood such strains may brand his name, but history, more discriminating, should not erase it from the scroll of Serbian patriots. By the autumn of 1941 Serbian resistance to the German terror had become only a shadow. The national struggle could only be sustained by the innate valour of the common people. This however was not lacking

A wild and furious war for existence against the Germans broke into flame among the Partisans. Among these Tito stood forth, pre-eminent and soon dominant. Tito, as he called himself, was a Soviet-trained Communist who, until Russia was invaded by Hitler, and after Yugoslavia had been assailed, had fomented political strikes along the Dalmatian coast, in accordance with the general Comintern policy. But once he united in his breast and brain his Communist doctrine with his burning ardour for his native land in her extreme torment he became a leader, with adherents who had little to lose but their lives, who were ready to die, and if to die to kill. This confronted the Germans with a problem which could not be solved by the mass executions of notables or persons of substance. They found themselves confronted by desperate men who had to be hunted down in their lairs. The Partisans under Tito wrested weapons from German hands. They grew rapidly in numbers. No reprisals, however bloody, upon hostages or villages deterred them. For them it was death or freedom. Soon they began to inflict heavy injury upon the Germans and became masters of wide regions.

It was inevitable that the Partisan movement should also come into savage quarrels with their fellow-countrymen who were resisting half-heartedly or making bargains for immunity with the common foe. The Partisans deliberately violated any agreements made with the enemy by the Cetniks—as the followers of General Mihailović were called. The Germans then shot Cetnik hostages, and in revenge Cetniks gave the Germans information about the Partisans. All this happened sporadically and uncontrollably in these wild mountain regions. It was a tragedy within a tragedy.

$$\star \quad \star \quad \star \quad \star \quad \star$$

I had followed these events amid other preoccupations so far as was possible. Except for a trickle of supplies dropped from aircraft, we were not able to help. Our headquarters in the Middle

East was responsible for all operations in this theatre, and maintained a system of agents and liaison officers with the followers of Mihailović. When in the summer of 1943 we broke into Sicily and Italy, the Balkans, and especially Yugoslavia, never left my thoughts. Up to this point our missions had only gone to the bands under Mihailović, who represented the official resistance to the Germans and the Yugoslav Government in Cairo. In May 1943 we took a new departure. It was decided to send small parties of British officers and N.C.O.s to establish contact with the Yugoslav Partisans, in spite of the fact that cruel strife was proceeding between them and the Cetniks, and that Tito was waging war as a Communist not only against the German invaders but against the Serbian monarchy and Mihailović. At the end of that month Captain Deakin, an Oxford don who had helped me for five years before the war in my literary work, was dropped by parachute to set up a mission with Tito. Other British missions followed, and by June much evidence had accumulated. The Chiefs of Staff reported on June 6: "It is clear from information available to the War Office that the Cetniks are hopelessly compromised in their relations with the Axis in Herzegovina and Montenegro. During the recent fighting in the latter area it has been the well-organised Partisans rather than the Cetniks who have been holding down the Axis forces."

Towards the end of the month my attention was drawn to the question of obtaining the best results from local resistance to the Axis in Yugoslavia. Having called for full information, I presided at a Chiefs of Staff conference at Downing Street on June 23. In the course of the discussion I emphasised the very great value of giving all possible support to the Yugoslav anti-Axis movement, which was containing about thirty-three Axis divisions in that area. This matter was of such importance that I directed that the small number of additional aircraft required to increase our aid must be provided, if necessary at the expense of the bombing of Germany and of the U-boat war,

On July 7, the eve of our landing in Sicily, I drew General Alexander's attention to these possibilities.

Prime Minister to General Alexander   7 July 43

I presume you have read about the recent heavy fighting in Yugoslavia and the widespread sabotage and guerrilla beginning in Greece. Albania also should be a fertile field. All this has grown up with no more aid from Britain than the dropping of a few bundles by parachute. If we can get hold of the mouth of the Adriatic so as to be able to run even a few ships into Dalmatian or Greek ports the whole of the Western Balkans might flare up, with far-reaching results. All this is however hunting in the next field.

A fortnight later I elaborated my thought on the essential connection between the Italian and Balkan theatres in the following important telegram:

Prime Minister to General Alexander   22 July 43

I am going with the Staffs to meet the President before August 15 in Canada. Thus we shall all be on the spot at the time when Sicily may very likely be cleaned up. . . .

I am sending you by an officer a full account which I have had prepared of the marvellous resistance put up by the so-called Partisan followers of Tito in Bosnia and the powerful cold-blooded manœuvres of Mihailović in Serbia. Besides this there are the resistances of the guerrillas in Albania and recently in Greece. The Germans have not only been reinforcing the Balkan peninsula with divisions, but they have been continually improving the quality and mobility of these divisions and have been stiffening up the local Italians. The enemy cannot spare these forces, and if Italy collapses the Germans could not bear the weight themselves. Great prizes lie in the Balkan direction.

No objective can compete with the capture of Rome, which in its turn gives a stage later all the advantages hoped for from the Balkan liberation. . . . The fall of Italy, the effect upon the other German satellites, and the subsequent utter loneliness of Germany may conceivably produce decisive results in Europe, especially in view of the vast strength evinced by the Russian armies.

This message is sent to give you my whole mind, which is, I believe, in full harmony with the Chiefs of Staff.

★   ★   ★   ★   ★

Before leaving for Quebec I decided to pave the way for further action in the Balkans by appointing a senior officer to lead a larger mission to the Partisans in the field, and with authority to make direct recommendations to me about our future action towards them.

Prime Minister to Foreign Secretary   28 July 43

Mr. Fitzroy Maclean, M.P., is a man of daring character, with Parliamentary status and Foreign Office training. He is to go to Yugoslavia and work with Tito. The idea is that a brigadier should be

sent out to take command later on. In my view we should plump for
Maclean and make him the head of any mission now contemplated,
and give him a good military staff officer under his authority. What
we want is a daring Ambassador-leader with these hardy and hunted
guerrillas.

This mission landed in Yugoslavia by parachute in September
1943, to find the situation revolutionised. The news of the Italian
surrender had reached Yugoslavia only with the official broadcast
announcements. But, in spite of complete absence of any warning by us, Tito took quick and fruitful action. Within a few weeks
six Italian divisions had been disarmed by the Partisan forces, and
another two went over to fight with them against the Germans.
With Italian equipment the Yugoslavs were now able to arm
80,000 more men, and to occupy for the moment most of the
Adriatic coastline. There was now a good chance of strengthening our general position in the Adriatic in relation to the Italian
front. The Yugoslav Partisan army, now totalling 200,000 men,
although fighting primarily as guerrillas, was now engaged in
widespread action against the Germans, who continued their
violent reprisals with increasing fury.

One effect of this increased activity in Yugoslavia was to
exacerbate the conflict between Tito and Mihailović. Tito's
growing military strength raised in an increasingly acute form
the ultimate position of the Yugoslav monarchy and the exiled
Government. Till the end of the war sincere and prolonged efforts
were made both in London and within Yugoslavia to reach a
working compromise between both sides. I had hoped that the
Russians would use their good offices in this matter. When Mr.
Eden went to Moscow in October 1943 the subject of Yugoslavia
was placed on the Conference agenda. At the meeting of October 23 he made a frank and fair statement of our attitude in the
hope of securing a common Allied policy towards Yugoslavia,
but the Russians displayed no wish either to pool information or
to discuss a plan of action.

Even after many weeks I saw little prospect of any working
arrangement between the hostile factions in Yugoslavia.

Former Naval Person to President Roosevelt   23 Oct 43

In spite of the vexatious broils between the followers of Tito and
Mihailović in Yugoslavia and those that have broken out between

the two sets of Greek guerrillas, the situation in the Balkan peninsula is grievous for the enemy. . . . We British have about eighty separate missions under General Wilson's control working with Partisans and Patriot bands scattered over these immense mountainous regions, 900 miles by about 300 miles in extent. Some of our officers there of brigadier's rank are very capable, and have in numerous cases been there for two years. . . .

The fighting is of the most cruel and bloody character, with merciless reprisals and executions of hostages by the Huns. But the enemy also is suffering heavily, and is now consuming not less than twenty-five German and eight Bulgarian divisions in the theatre, without being able to control more than key points and with increasing difficulty in maintaining railway traffic. We hope soon to compose the Greek quarrels, but the differences between Tito's Partisans and Mihailović's Serbs are very deep-seated.

My gloomy forecast proved true. At the end of November Tito summoned a political congress of his movement at Jajce, in Bosnia, and not only set up a Provisional Government, "with sole authority to represent the Yugoslav nation," but also formally deprived the Royal Yugoslav Government in Cairo of all its rights. The King was forbidden to return to the country until after the liberation. The Partisans had established themselves without question as the leading elements of resistance in Yugoslavia, particularly since the Italian surrender. But it was important that no irrevocable political decisions about the future régime in Yugoslavia should be made in the atmosphere of occupation, civil war, and *émigré* politics. The tragic figure of Mihailović had become the major obstacle. We had to maintain close military contact with the Partisans, and therefore to persuade the King to dismiss Mihailović from his post as Minister of War. Early in December we withdrew official support from Mihailović and recalled the British missions operating in his territory.

*   *   *   *   *

Yugoslav affairs were considered at the Teheran Conference against this background. Although it was decided by the three Allied Powers to give the maximum support to the Partisans, the rôle of Yugoslavia in the war was dismissed by Stalin as of minor importance, and the Russians even disputed our figures of the number of Axis divisions in the Balkans. The Soviet Government however agreed to send a Russian mission to Tito as a result of

Mr. Eden's initiative. They also wished to keep contact with Mihailović.

On my return from Teheran to Cairo I saw King Peter, and told him about the strength and significance of the Partisan movement and that it might be necessary for him to dismiss Mihailović from his Cabinet. The only hope which the King possessed of returning to his country would be, with our mediation, to reach some provisional arrangement with Tito without delay and before the Partisans further extended their hold upon the country. The Russians too professed their willingness to work for some kind of compromise. On December 21 the Soviet Ambassador handed the following message to Mr. Eden:

The Soviet Government is aware that at the present time very strained relations exist between Marshal Tito and the National Committee of Liberation of Yugoslavia on the one hand and King Peter and his Government on the other. Mutual attacks and hard accusations on both sides, especially those which have recently taken place, have led to open hostilities, which hamper the cause of the struggle for the liberation of Yugoslavia. The Soviet Government shares the view of the British Government that in the interests of the fight of the Yugoslavian people against the German invaders it is necessary to make efforts to find a basis for collaboration between the two sides. The Soviet Government sees the great difficulties standing in the way of the realisation of this task, but it is ready to do everything possible to find a compromise between the two sides, with the purpose of uniting all the forces of the Yugoslavian people in the interests of the common struggle of the Allies.

I received almost unanimous advice as to what course to pursue in this disagreeable situation. Officers who had served with Tito and the commanders of missions to Mihailović presented similar pictures. The British Ambassador to the Royal Yugoslav Government, Mr. Stevenson, was equally convinced. He telegraphed to the Foreign Office on December 25: "Our policy must be based on three new factors: The Partisans will be the rulers of Yugoslavia. They are of such value to us militarily that we must back them to the full, subordinating political considerations to military. It is extremely doubtful whether we can any longer regard the monarchy as a unifying element in Yugoslavia."

* * * * *

414

This crisis in Yugoslav affairs pressed on me as I lay ill at Marrakesh. Maclean, who had been with me in Cairo, was now due to return to Yugoslavia. He was anxious to have my son with him, and it was arranged that Randolph should join the mission by parachute.

Prime Minister to Foreign Secretary 29 Dec 43

Randolph, who is now waiting for a drop into Yugoslavia, left behind the following note for me, dated 25th instant. It seems to me sound, and to represent to a large extent your point of view and mine. He will be going in a few days.

"1. Three weeks ago in Cairo Stevenson made no attempt to resist the arguments of Maclean and Deakin that the condition precedent for any useful political action in Yugoslavia was the repudiation of General Mihailović. Despite the polemics indulged in by both sides, this is as true to-day as it was three weeks ago, though perhaps, owing to the procrastination of the King, we shall only gain a military and not a political advantage.

"2. Maclean stressed in Cairo that no *quid pro quo* could be obtained for the King by the dismissal of Mihailović, but that this gesture might create an atmosphere in which the King's fortunes could be advanced. This position has been prejudiced, but is still true, with limitations, to-day.

"3. Two things are surely therefore required:

(i) The immediate repudiation of Mihailović by His Majesty's Government and if possible by King Peter.

(ii) The immediate return to Tito's headquarters of Maclean to try (*a*) to obtain the maximum military advantage from the situation, and (*b*) to explore what advantage may be gained for the King from the new situation that will be created upon the dismissal of Mihailović."

I added my own views, and a draft reply to Tito.

Prime Minister to Foreign Secretary 30 Dec 43

There is no possibility now of getting Tito to accept King Peter as a *quid pro quo* for repudiating Mihailović. Once Mihailović is gone the King's chances will be greatly improved and we can plead his case at Tito's headquarters. I thought we were all agreed in Cairo to advise Peter to dismiss Mihailović before the end of the year. Everything Deakin and Maclean said and all the reports received show that he had been in active collaboration with the Germans. We shall never bring the parties together till he has been disowned not only by us, but by the King.

Pray let me know whether I shall send the following message, or whether I shall merely give a friendly acknowledgment, in which latter case I fear we shall have lost a good opportunity of my establishing a personal relationship with this important man.

I do not wish to hawk this private message around to the United States and Stalin, with the inevitable delays involved. Unless you disagree I propose to send it, as a letter, by air courier to Maclean at Bari, who will deliver it. He and Randolph will be dropping in a few days. Let me know also the form in which you will repudiate Mihailović, and invite the King to do so. It is, in my opinion, Peter's only chance.

And on January 2:

I have been convinced by the arguments of men I know and trust that Mihailović is a millstone tied round the neck of the little King, and he has no chance till he gets rid of him.

The Foreign Secretary agreed, and I now wrote to Tito, who had sent me congratulations on my recovery:

AFRICA: *January* 8, 1944

I thank you very much for your kind message about my health from yourself and the heroic Patriot and Partisan army of Yugoslavia. From Major Deakin, who is a friend of mine, I learnt all about your valiant efforts. It is my most earnest desire to give you all aid in human power by sea supplies, by air support, and by Commandos helping you in the island fighting. Brigadier Maclean is also a friend of mine, and a colleague in the House of Commons. With him at your headquarters will soon be serving my son, Major Randolph Churchill, who is also a Member of Parliament.

One supreme object stands before us, namely, to cleanse the soil of Europe from the filthy Nazi-Fascist taint. You may be sure that we British have no desire to dictate the future government of Yugoslavia. At the same time we hope that all will pull together as much as possible for the defeat of the common foe, and afterwards settle the form of government in accordance with the will of the people.

I am resolved that the British Government shall give no further military support to Mihailović and will only give help to you, and we should be glad if the Royal Yugoslavian Government would dismiss him from their councils. King Peter the Second however escaped as a boy from the treacherous clutches of the Regent Prince Paul, and came to us as the representative of Yugoslavia and as a young prince in distress. It would not be chivalrous or honourable for Great Britain

416

to cast him aside. Nor can we ask him to cut all his existing contacts with his country. I hope therefore that you will understand we shall in any case remain in official relations with him, while at the same time giving you all possible military support. I hope also that there may be an end to polemics on either side, for these only help the Germans.

You may be sure I shall work in the closest contact with my friends Marshal Stalin and President Roosevelt; and I earnestly hope that the Military Mission which the Soviet Government are sending to your headquarters will work in similar harmony with the Anglo-American Mission under Brigadier Maclean. Please correspond with me through Brigadier Maclean, and let me know of anything you think I can do to help, for I will certainly try my best.

Looking forward to the end of your sufferings and to the liberation of all Europe from tyranny . . .

It took nearly a month to get an answer.

Marshal Tito to Prime Minister [received February 3, 1944]
Your Excellency,

Your message brought by Brigadier Maclean is valuable proof that our people have in their superhuman struggle for freedom and independence a true friend and Ally at their side who deeply comprehends our needs and our aspirations. For me personally your message is an honour, for it expresses your high acknowledgment of our struggle and the efforts of our National Liberation Army. I thank you heartily for your photographs from the Teheran Conference, with your dedication. Your Excellency may be sure that we will endeavour to keep your friendship, won in a most difficult hour of our people's history, and which is extremely dear to us. The devastation of the country, and the people exhausted with suffering, need, and will need in future, the help of our great Allies not only during the war but also in peace to enable us to heal the terrible wounds inflicted on us by the ignoble Fascist invader. It is our wish to fulfil to the utmost our duty as an Ally in the common military effort against our common enemy. Aid tendered to us by our Allies very much contributes to ease our situation on the battlefield. We also hope, with your help, to obtain heavy armament (tanks and aircraft), which in the present phase of the war and owing to the present strength of our National Liberation Army is indispensable to us.

2. I quite understand your engagements towards King Peter II and his Government, and I will contrive as far as the interests of our peoples permit to avoid unnecessary politics and not cause inconvenience to our Allies in this matter. I assure you however, Your

Excellency, that the internal political situation created in this arduous struggle for liberation is not only a machine for the strivings of individuals or some political group, but it is the irresistible desire of all patriots, of all those who are fighting and long connected with this struggle, and these are the enormous majority of the peoples of Yugoslavia. Therefore the people have set [themselves] difficult tasks, and we are bound to accomplish them.

3. At the present moment all our efforts turn to one direction, and that is, (1) to assemble all patriotic and honourable elements so as to render our struggle against the invader as efficient as possible; (2) to create union and brotherhood of the Yugoslav nations, which did not exist before this war, and the absence of which caused the catastrophe in our country; (3) to create conditions for the establishment of a State in which all nations of Yugoslavia would feel happy, and that is a truly democratic Yugoslavia, a federative Yugoslavia. I am convinced that you understand us, and that we will have your valuable support in these strivings of our people.

> Yours very sincerely,
> TITO
> *Marshal of Yugoslavia*

I replied at once.

Prime Minister to Marshal Tito (Yugoslavia)   5 Feb 44

I am very glad my letter has reached you safely, and I have received your message with pleasure. I can understand the position of reserve which you adopt towards King Peter. I have for several months past been in favour of advising him to dismiss Mihailović and to face the consequent resignation of all his present advisers. I have been deterred from doing this by the argument that I should thus be advising him to cast away his only adherents. You will understand I feel a personal responsibility towards him. I should be obliged if you would let me know whether his dismissal of Mihailović would pave the way for friendly relations with you and your Movement, and, later on, for his joining you in the field, it being understood that the future question of the monarchy is reserved until Yugoslavia has been entirely liberated. There is no doubt that a working arrangement between you and the King would consolidate many forces, especially Serbian elements, now estranged, and that it would invest your Government and Movement with added authority and provide them with numerous resources. Yugoslavia would then be able to speak with a united voice in the councils of the Allies during this formative period, when so much is in flux. I much hope that you will feel able to give me the answer you can see I want.

2. His Britannic Majesty's Government desire to assemble all patriotic and honourable elements so as to render your struggle against the invader as efficient as possible; secondly, to create union and brotherhood of the Yugoslav nations; and, thirdly, to create conditions for a truly democratic and federative Yugoslavia. You will certainly have the support of His Majesty's Government in all this.

3. I have asked the Supreme Allied Commander in the Mediterranean to form immediately an amphibious force of Commandos, supported by air and flotillas, to attack, with your aid, the garrisons which the Germans have left in the islands they have taken along the Dalmatian coast. There is no reason why these garrisons should not be exterminated with forces which will shortly be available. Secondly, we must try to get a through line of communication with you from the sea, even if we have to move it from time to time. This alone will enable tanks and anti-tank guns and other heavy munitions, together with other necessary supplies, to be brought in in the quantities which your armies require. You should talk all this over with Brigadier Maclean, who has my entire confidence and immediate access to me, as well as to the Supreme Commander.

Tito replied:

9 Feb 44

I was obliged to consult the members of the National Committee of Liberation of Yugoslavia and members of the Anti-Fascist Council of National Liberation on the points raised in your messages. The analysis of these points led to the following conclusions:

(1) The Anti-Fascist Council of National Liberation of Yugoslavia, as you know, confirmed at their second session on November 29, 1943, that they firmly stand for the Union of Yugoslav Nations. However, as long as there are two Governments, one in Yugoslavia and the other in Cairo, there can be no complete union. Therefore the Government in Cairo must be suppressed, and with them Draza Mihailović. That Government must account to the Government of A.C.N.L.Y. for having squandered enormous sums of the nation's money.

(2) The National Committee of Liberation of Yugoslavia should be acknowledged by the Allies as the only Government of Yugoslavia, and King Peter II, in support, should submit to the laws of A.C.N.L.Y.

(3) If King Peter accepts all these conditions the Anti-Fascist Council of National Liberation will not refuse to co-operate with him, on condition that the question of the monarchy in

Yugoslavia be decided after the liberation of Yugoslavia by the free will of the people.

(4) King Peter II should issue a declaration to the effect that he has only the interests of his fatherland at heart, which he wishes to be free and organised as the people themselves decide after the war is over by their free will, and until then he will do all in his power to support the arduous struggle of the peoples of Yugoslavia. . . .

Prime Minister to Marshal Tito   25 Feb 44

I fully comprehend your difficulties, and I welcome the spirit in which you approach them. I thank you for understanding mine. The first step for us is to withdraw our liaison officers safely from Mihailović. Orders have been issued accordingly, but may take a few weeks to fulfil. Meanwhile, can you not assure me that if King Peter frees himself from Mihailović and other bad advisers he will be invited by you to join his countrymen in the field, provided always that the Yugoslav nations are free to settle their own constitution after the war? If I judge this boy aright, he has no dearer wish than to stand at the side of all those Yugoslavs who are fighting the common foe, but you can understand that I cannot press him to dismiss Mihailović, throw over his Government, and cut off all contact with Serbia before knowing whether he can count on your support and co-operation.

I have suggested to King Peter that he should return to London to discuss these matters with me. I hope therefore that you will on reflection be ready to modify your demands, and thus enable us both to work for the unification of Yugoslavia against the common enemy. Do not hesitate to make me precise and specific requests. If meanwhile I cannot do all you wish, be sure it is not from lack of goodwill to you or your country.

*   *   *   *   *

When I was able to explain all this to Parliament on February 22, 1944, I told the following tale:

"Led with great skill, organised on the guerrilla principle, the Partisans were at once elusive and deadly. They were here, they were there, they were everywhere. Large-scale offensives have been launched against them by the Germans, but in every case the Partisans, even when surrounded, have escaped, after inflicting great losses and toil upon the enemy. The Partisan movement soon outstripped in numbers the forces of General Mihailović. Not only Croats and Slovenes, but large numbers of Serbians, joined with Marshal Tito, and he has at this moment more than a quarter of a million men with him, and large quantities of arms taken from the enemy or from the Italians, and these men are organised into a considerable number of divisions and corps.

"The whole movement has taken shape and form, without losing the guerrilla quality without which it could not possibly succeed. Around and within these heroic forces a national and unifying movement has developed. The Communist element had the honour of being the beginners, but as the movement increased in strength and numbers a modifying and unifying process has taken place and national conceptions have supervened. In Marshal Tito the Partisans have found an outstanding leader, glorious in the fight for freedom. Unhappily, perhaps inevitably, these new forces came into collision with those under General Mihailović. Their activities upset his commanders' accommodations with the enemy. He endeavoured to repress them, and many tragic fights took place and bitter feuds sprang up between men of the same race and country, whose misfortunes were due only to the common foe.

"For a long time past I have taken a particular interest in Marshal Tito's movement, and have tried, and am trying, by every available means to bring him help. A young friend of mine, an Oxford don, Captain Deakin, now Lieut.-Colonel Deakin, D.S.O., entered Yugoslavia by parachute nearly a year ago, and was for eight months at Marshal Tito's headquarters. On one occasion both were wounded by the same bomb. They became friends. Certainly it is a bond between people, but a bond which, I trust, we shall not have to institute in our own personal relationships. From Colonel Deakin's reports we derived a lively picture of the whole struggle and its personalities."

* * * * *

For two months longer the political wrangle over Yugoslav affairs continued in *émigré* circles in London. Each day lost diminished the chances of a balanced arrangement.

Prime Minister to Foreign Secretary   1 Apr 44

I consider that the King should be pressed to the utmost limit to get rid of his present fatal millstone advisers. As you know, I thought this would have been accomplished before the end of last year. I do not know what has been gained by all the spinning out that has gone on. . . . My idea throughout has been that the King should dissociate himself from Mihailović, that he should accept the resignation of the Purić Government or dismiss them, and that it would not do any great harm if he remained without a Government for a few weeks. . . . I agree that King Peter should make a suitable declaration. I fear we must leave things at this for the time being.

. . . I have seen somewhere that three German divisions have been recalled out of Yugoslavia to hold down Hungary, and of course it will be of the greatest importance for Tito's forces to make contact with the Hungarian Partisans and take the fullest possible advantage of the situation now opening to his northward.

All these developments help us and help Tito, but they certainly do not help the King and his bedraggled Government. Unless he acts promptly, as the sense of your minute indicates, his chances of regaining his throne will, in my opinion, be lost. Since we discussed these matters in Cairo we have seen the entry of a grandiose Russian Mission to Tito's headquarters, and there is little doubt that the Russians will drive straight ahead for a Communist Tito-governed Yugoslavia, and will denounce everything done to the contrary as "undemocratic".

I hope therefore you will act most promptly now, draft the King a good declaration, make him dismiss Purić and Co., repudiate all contact with Mihailović, and make him form a stop-gap Government not obnoxious to Tito. Thus we may have a forlorn hope of making a bridge between them in the next five or six weeks. We are not justified in withholding military forces that wish or can be induced to fight with the Partisans because of the complexities of Serbian politics.

It was not until nearly the end of May that Mihailović was dismissed, and a moderate politician, Dr. Subašić, the former Governor of Croatia and member of Dr. Maček's Peasant Party, was asked to form a new Administration.

Prime Minister to Marshal Tito (Yugoslavia)　　　　　17 May 44
This morning, as the result of British advice, King Peter II dismissed M. Purić's Administration, which included General Mihailović as Minister of War. He is now about to form an Administration or found a Council of State under the Ban of Croatia (Dr. Ivan Subašić). This of course has the strong approval of His Britannic Majesty's Government.

We do not know what will happen in the Serbian part of Yugoslavia. Mihailović certainly holds a powerful position locally as Commander-in-Chief, and it does not follow that his ceasing to be Minister of War will rob him of his influence. We cannot predict what he will do. There is also a very large body, amounting perhaps to 200,000, of Serbian peasant proprietary who are anti-German but strongly

Serbian, and who naturally hold the views of a peasants' ownership community, contrary to the Karl Marx theory. My object is that these forces may be made to work with you for a united, independent Yugoslavia, which will expel from the soil of Yugoslavia the filthy Hitlerite murderers and invaders till not one remains.

It is of importance to the common cause and to our relations with you that these changes should be given a fair chance to develop in a favourable way to the main object. I should greatly regret it if you were at all in a hurry to denounce them in public. Crucial events impend in Europe. The battle in Italy goes in our favour. General Wilson assures me of his resolve to aid you to the very utmost. I feel therefore that I have a right to ask you to forbear from any utterances adverse to this new event, at least for a few weeks till we can have exchanged telegrams upon it.

Brigadier Maclean, who is with me now, will be with you in less than three weeks, with all the views he has gathered here, and I hope that at the very least you will await his return.

Meanwhile I congratulate you once more upon the number of enemy divisions which you are holding gripped on your various fronts. You will realise, Marshal Tito, that the war will soon come to a very high pitch of intensity, and that British, American, and Russian forces will all hurl themselves on the common foe. You must be at your strongest during this climax. While I cannot guarantee a speedy breakdown of the enemy's power, there is certainly a chance of it.

And on the 24th:

The King has sacked Purić and Co., and I think the Ban of Croatia will rally a certain force round him. My idea is that this Government should lie quiet for a bit and let events flow on their course. This, I think, was rather in accord with your idea in the first telegrams we exchanged. I am keeping the Russians and Americans informed of all that goes on between us.

Give my love to Randolph should he come into your sphere. Maclean will be coming back soon. I wish I could come myself, but I am too old and heavy to jump out on a parachute.

Here then we may leave this scene for others not less convulsive but larger.

CHAPTER XXVII

THE ANZIO STROKE

*Bitter Fighting on the Cassino Front – The Anzio Surprise Landing
– The Disastrous Pause – Kesselring's Critical Position – Delay at
the Beach-head – Renewed Attacks at Cassino – Frustration at Anzio
– My Questions to General Wilson of February 6 – My Telegram to
Field-Marshal Dill, February 8 – Immense Number of Vehicles in
the Beach-head – Disappointment and Casualties – German Effort to
Drive Us into the Sea, February 16 – The Deadly Battle Won –
Kesselring Accepts Failure, March 1 – I Tell the Story to Parlia-
ment, February 22 – Smuts' Message of February 23 – My Reply –
Important German Forces Diverted from France to Italy.*

THE first weeks of January were spent in intensive preparations
for Operation "Shingle", as Anzio was called in our codes,
and preliminary operations by the Fifth Army to draw the
enemy's attention and reserves away from the beach-head. To
that end the Army carried out a series of attacks which, it was
hoped, would take them across the rivers Garigliano and Rapido,
while the French Corps on the right swung round to threaten
the high ground north of Cassino. Fighting was bitter, for the
Germans clearly meant to prevent us from breaking into the
Gustav Line, which, with Cassino as its central feature, was the
rearmost position of their deep defensive zone. In these rocky
mountains a great fortified system had been created, with lavish
use of concrete and steel. From their observation posts on the
heights the enemy could direct their guns on all movements in
the valleys below.

After preliminary attacks in severe winter weather the Fifth
Army opened their main offensive on January 12, with the French
Corps making a ten-mile advance on the northern flank. Three
days later the IInd U.S. Corps occupied Monte Trocchio, the last

barrier before the river Liri, across which they formed, but could not retain, a bridgehead. Then the Xth British Corps crossed the lower Garigliano, and captured Minturno and the outskirts of Castelforte, but were held in their further attempts to advance northwards. Nor could their right wing take Sant' Ambrogio.

All this however had the desired effect on the enemy. It distracted their attention from the approaching threat to their vulnerable seaward flank and caused them to bring up three good divisions from reserve to restore the situation. They attacked the Xth British Corps, but failed to throw it back. By the afternoon of the 21st the convoys for Anzio were well out to sea, covered by our aircraft. The weather was well suited to a concealed approach. Our heavy attacks on enemy airfields, and especially at Perugia, the German air reconnaissance base, kept many of their aircraft grounded. General Westphal, who was Kesselring's Chief of Staff, gives a vivid picture of the position at German headquarters during these days.

On January 21 Admiral Canaris, Chief of the German Intelligence, visited Army Group headquarters, where he was pressed to communicate any information he might have about the enemy intentions in regard to a landing. In particular we wanted to know about the positions of aircraft-carriers, battleships, and landing-craft. Canaris was unable to give us any details, but thought that there was no need to fear a new landing in the near future. This was certainly his view. Not only air reconnaissance, but also the German counter-espionage, was almost completely out of action at this time. A few hours after the departure of Canaris the enemy landed at Anzio.*

*   *   *   *   *

It was with tense, but I trust suppressed, excitement that I awaited the outcome of this considerable stroke.

To Stalin I telegraphed:

21 Jan 44

We have launched the big attack against the German armies defending Rome which I told you about at Teheran. The weather conditions seem favourable. I hope to have good news for you before long.

Presently I learned that the VIth Corps, under the American General Lucas, had landed on the Anzio beaches at 2 a.m. on the 22nd, the 3rd United States Division south of the town, and the 1st British Division north of it. There was very little opposition

---

* Westphal, *Heer in Fesseln*, p. 240.

and practically no casualties. By midnight 36,000 men and over 3,000 vehicles were ashore. "We appear," signalled Alexander, who was on the spot, "to have got almost complete surprise. I have stressed the importance of strong-hitting mobile patrols being boldly pushed out to gain contact with the enemy, but so far have not received reports of their activities." I was in full agreement with this, and replied: "Thank you for all your messages. Am very glad you are pegging out claims rather than digging in beach-heads."

* * * * *

But now came disaster, and the ruin in its prime purpose of the enterprise. General Lucas confined himself to occupying his beach-head and having equipment and vehicles brought ashore. General Penney, commanding the British 1st Division, was anxious to push inland. His reserve brigade was however held back with the corps. Minor probing attacks towards Cisterna and Campoleone occupied the 22nd and 23rd. No general attempt to advance was made by the commander of the expedition. By the evening of the 23rd the whole of the two divisions and their attached troops, including two British Commandos, the United States Rangers, and parachutists, had been landed, with masses of impedimenta. The defences of the beach-head were growing, but the opportunity for which great exertions had been made was gone.

Kesselring reacted quickly to his critical situation. The bulk of his reserves were already committed against us on the Cassino front, but he pulled in whatever units were available, and in forty-eight hours the equivalent of about two divisions was assembled to resist our further advance.

The German General Westphal's comments on the way in which this was done are illuminating.

At the moment of the landing south of Rome, apart from certain coastal batteries standing by, there were only two battalions. . . . There was nothing else in the neighbourhood which could be thrown against the enemy on that same day. The road to Rome was open. No one could have stopped a bold advance-guard entering the Holy City. The breath-taking situation continued for the first two days after the landing. It was only then that German counter-measures were effective. What was their nature? In December 1943 the

ANZIO

[German] Army Group had issued a comprehensive plan of emergency for the whole of Italy. In it was laid down what troops and columns should move against the possible landing-points, on what roads and at what times, and what tasks they should undertake. It was only necessary to issue the code-word "Case Richard" to put into effect these prearranged plans. In fact, most of the troops, in spite of icy roads over the Apennines, arrived before schedule. The German High Command helped by sending troops from France, Yugoslavia, and the homeland. . . . The enemy kept surprisingly quiet. They were apparently engaged in building up a bridgehead. It was thus possible to build up a new front opposite them. The command of this sector was taken over by the general headquarters of the Fourteenth Army, up to now based in Northern Italy and under General von Mackensen.★

The threat to his flank did not weaken Kesselring's determination to withstand our assaults at Cassino. The German intentions were made crystal-clear by an order from Hitler captured on the 24th:

★ *Heer in Fesseln,* p. 242.

427

The Gustav Line must be held at all costs for the sake of the political consequences which would follow a completely successful defence. The Fuehrer expects the bitterest struggle for every yard.

He was certainly obeyed.

★   ★   ★   ★   ★

On the 25th Alexander reported that the beach-head was reasonably secure. The 3rd United States Division was four miles from Cisterna and the British 1st Division two miles from Campeoleone, and contact was continuous along the entire front. On the 27th serious news arrived. Neither place had been taken. The Guards Brigade had beaten off a counter-attack of infantry and tanks and had gone forward, but they were still about a mile and a half short of Campoleone, and the Americans were still south of Cisterna. Alexander said that neither he nor General Clark was satisfied with the speed of the advance, and that Clark was going to the beach-head at once. I replied:

Prime Minister to General Alexander   28 Jan 44

I am glad to learn that Clark is going to visit the beach-head. It would be unpleasant if your troops were sealed off there and the main army could not advance up from the south.

This however was exactly what was going to happen.

★   ★   ★   ★   ★

Meanwhile our attacks on the Germans in the Cassino positions continued. The Xth British Corps having drawn to its front most of the enemy reinforcements, it was decided to attack farther north so as to seize the high ground above Cassino and envelop the position from that side. Good progress was made. The IInd U.S. Corps crossed the river Rapido above Cassino town, with the French Corps on their right keeping abreast of them, and took Monte Castellone and Colle Majola. Thence they attacked southwards against Monastery Hill; but the Germans had reinforced and held on fanatically. By early February the IInd Corps had expended its strength. General Alexander decided that fresh troops would be needed to restore impetus to the assault. He had already ordered a New Zealand Corps to be formed, under General Freyberg, composed of three divisions brought over from the Eighth Army on the Adriatic. Indeed, that army, which had attempted to pin the enemy on their front by offensive action,

428

had had to send no fewer than five divisions to sustain the heavy fighting on the west coast, and for the next few months had to remain on the defensive.

Further severe battles obviously impended on both fronts, and it was necessary to find more troops. The 3rd Polish Carpathian Division was due to arrive on the main front at the beginning of February. General Wilson had ready the 18th Infantry and the 1st Guards Brigade in North Africa. By January 30 the 1st U.S. Armoured Division had landed at Anzio and the 45th U.S. Division was on its way. All this had to be done over the difficult beaches or through the tiny fishing port. "The situation as it now stands," signalled Admiral John Cunningham, "bears little relation to the lightning thrust by two or three divisions envisaged at Marrakesh, but you may rest assured that no effort will be spared by the Navies to provide the sinews of victory." This promise, as will be seen, was amply redeemed.

*   *   *   *   *

While the fighting at Cassino was at its zenith, on January 30 the VIth Corps at Anzio made its first attack in strength. Some ground was gained, but the 3rd U.S. Division failed to take Cisterna and the 1st British Division Campoleone. More than four divisions were already ashore in the beach-head. But the Germans, despite our air action against their communications, had reinforced quickly and strongly. Elements of eight divisions faced us in positions which they had now had time to fortify. Galling artillery fire harassed the crowded lodgments we had gained, and our shipping lying off the beaches suffered damage from air attacks by night. On February 2 Alexander again visited the battle-front, and sent me a full report. German resistance had increased, and was especially strong opposite the 3rd U.S. Division at Cisterna and the 1st British Division at Campoleone. No further offensive was possible until these points were captured. The 3rd Division had fought hard for Cisterna during the last two or three days. The men were tired and were still about a mile from the town. A brigade of the 1st Division was holding Campoleone railway station, but they were in a very long and narrow salient and were being shot at "by everything from three sides". Alexander concluded: "We shall presently be in a position to carry out a properly co-ordinated thrust in full strength to achieve our object of cutting the enemy's main line of supply, for which I have ordered plans to be prepared."

Before effect could be given to Alexander's orders the enemy launched a counter-attack on February 3 which drove in the salient of the 1st British Division and was clearly only a prelude to harder things to come. In the words of General Wilson's report, "the perimeter was sealed off and our forces therein are not capable of advancing."

I had been much troubled at several features of the Anzio operation, as the following telegrams will show.

Prime Minister to General Wilson (Algiers) and C.-in-C.   6 Feb 44
Mediterranean

I do not want to worry General Alexander in the height of the battle, but I am not at all surprised at the inquiry from the United States Chiefs of Staff. There are three points on which you should touch. First, why was the 504th Regiment of paratroops not used at Anzio as proposed, and why is the existing British Parachute Brigade used as ordinary infantry in the line? Secondly, why was no attempt made to occupy the high ground and at least the towns of Velletri, Campoleone, and Cisterna twelve or twenty-four hours after the unopposed landing? Thirdly, the question asked by the United States Chiefs of Staff: why has there been no heavily mounted aggressive offensive on the main front to coincide with the withdrawal of troops by the Germans to face the landing?

2. In my early telegrams to General Alexander I raised all these points in a suggestive form, and particularly deprecated a continuance of the multiplicity of small attacks in battalion, company, and even platoon strength. I repeat however that I do not wish General Alexander's attention to be diverted from the battle, which is at its height, in order to answer questions or write explanations about the past.

General Wilson replied that the 504th Paratroop Regiment was seaborne and not airborne because of a last-minute decision by General Clark. The British paratroops were employed in the line because of infantry shortage. On my second question he said there was no lack of urging from above, and that both Alexander and Clark went to the beach-head during the first forty-eight hours to hasten the offensive. Though General Lucas had achieved surprise he had failed to take advantage of it. This was due to his "Salerno complex"—that as a prelude to success the first task was to repel the inevitable enemy counter-attack. He did not feel sure of achieving this before the arrival of the 1st U.S. Armoured

Division combat team. The assault, said Wilson, was only geared to function at a slow speed. He also explained the difficulties of forcing the main front on the Rapido river and around Cassino.

General Marshall shared my concern, and I passed this report to Washington with the following comment:

Prime Minister to Field-Marshal Dill (Washington)   8 Feb 44
You should impart this report to General Marshall at your discretion. . . . My comment is that senior commanders should not "urge", but "order".

All this has been a disappointment to me. Nevertheless it is a great advantage that the enemy should come in strength and fight in South Italy, thus being drawn far from other battlefields. Moreover, we have a great need to keep continually engaging them, and even a battle of attrition is better than standing by and watching the Russians fight. We should also learn a good many lessons about how not to do it which will be valuable in "Overlord".

* * * * *

The Admiral had been even better than his word about the landing-craft. I now put a direct question to him.

Prime Minister to Commander-in-Chief Mediterranean   8 Feb 44
Let me know the number of vehicles landed at Anzio by the seventh and fourteenth days respectively. I should be glad, if it were possible without too much trouble or delay, to distinguish trucks, cannon, and tanks.

The reply was both prompt and startling. By the seventh day 12,350 vehicles had been landed, including 356 tanks; by the fourteenth day 21,940 vehicles, including 380 tanks. This represented a total of 315 L.S.T. shipments. It was interesting to notice that, apart from 4,000 trucks which went to and fro in the ships, nearly 18,000 vehicles were landed in the Anzio beach-head by the fourteenth day in order to serve a total force of 70,000 men, including of course the drivers and those who did the repair and maintenance of the vehicles.

I replied on February 10:

Thank you for information.
How many of our men are driving or looking after 18,000 vehicles in this narrow space? We must have a great superiority of chauffeurs. I am shocked that the enemy have more infantry than we. Let me have our latest ration strength in the bridgehead.

Later the same day further reports came in. General Wilson said that the weather had spoilt our air attacks. The 1st British Division was under severe pressure and had had to give ground and Alexander was arranging to relieve it.

All this was a great disappointment at home and in the United States. I did not of course know what orders had been given to General Lucas, but it is a root principle to push out and join issue with the enemy, and it would seem that his judgment was against it from the beginning. As I said at the time, I had hoped that we were hurling a wild cat on to the shore, but all we had got was a stranded whale. The spectacle of 18,000 vehicles accumulated ashore by the fourteenth day for only 70,000 men, or less than four men to a vehicle, including drivers and attendants, though they did not move more than twelve or fourteen miles, was astonishing. We were apparently still stronger than the Germans in fighting power. The ease with which they moved their pieces about on the board and the rapidity with which they adjusted the perilous gaps they had to make on their southern front was most impressive. It all seemed to give us very adverse data for "Overlord".

I cabled to Alexander:

. . . I have a feeling that you may have hesitated to assert your authority because you were dealing so largely with Americans and therefore *urged* an advance instead of *ordering* it. You are however quite entitled to give them orders, and I have it from the highest American authorities that it is their wish that their troops should receive direct orders. They say their Army has been framed more on Prussian lines than on the more smooth British lines, and that American commanders expect to receive positive orders, which they will immediately obey. Do not hesitate therefore to give orders just as you would to our own men. The Americans are very good to work with, and quite prepared to take the rough with the smooth.

Alexander replied on February 11:

The first phase of operations, which started so full of promise, has now just passed, owing to the enemy's ability to concentrate so quickly sufficient force to stabilise what was to him a very serious situation. The battle has now reached the second phase, in which we must now at all costs crush his counter-attacks, and then, with our own forces regrouped, resume offensive to break inland and get astride his communications leading from Rome to the south. This I have every intention of doing. Out of the thirty-five battalions of the VIth Corps casualties are as follows: British, up to February 6, killed, 285; wounded, 1,371; missing, 1,048. American, up to February 9, killed, 597; wounded, 2,506; missing, 1,116. These losses include those of nine Ranger battalions. Total casualties, 6,923. I am very grateful for your kind message at the end of your telegram. I well realise the disappointment to you and all at home. I have every hope and intention of reaching the goal we set out to gain.

* * * * *

The expected major effort to drive us back into the sea at Anzio opened on February 16, when the enemy employed over four divisions, supported by 450 guns, in a direct thrust southwards from Campoleone. Hitler's special order of the day was read out to the troops before the attack. He demanded that our beach-head "abscess" be eliminated in three days. The attack fell at an awkward moment, as the 45th U.S. and 56th British Divisions, transferred from the Cassino front, were just relieving our gallant 1st Division, who soon found themselves in full action again. A deep, dangerous wedge was driven into our line, which was forced back here to the original beach-head. The artillery fire, which had embarrassed all the occupants of the beach-head since they landed, reached a new intensity. All hung in the balance. No further retreat was possible. Even a short advance would have given the enemy the power to use not merely their long-range guns in harassing fire upon the landing stages and shipping, but to put down a proper field artillery barrage upon all intakes or departures. I had no illusions about the issue. It was life or death.

But fortune, hitherto baffling, rewarded the desperate valour of the British and American armies. Before Hitler's stipulated three days the German attack was stopped. Then their own salient was counter-attacked in flank and cut out under fire from all our artillery and bombardment by every aircraft we could fly. The fighting was intense, losses on both sides were heavy, but the deadly battle was won.

One more attempt was made by Hitler—for his was the will-power at work—at the end of February. The 3rd U.S. Division, on the eastern flank, was attacked by three German divisions. These were weakened and shaken by their previous failure. The Americans held stubbornly, and the attack was broken in a day, when the Germans had suffered more than 2,500 casualties. On

March 1 Kesselring accepted his failure. He had frustrated the Anzio expedition. He could not destroy it. I cabled to the President:

I must send you my warmest congratulations on the grand fighting of your troops, particularly the United States 3rd Division, in the Anzio beach-head. I am always deeply moved to think of our men fighting side by side in so many fierce battles and of the inspiring additions to our history which these famous episodes will make. Of course I have been very anxious about the beach-head, where we have so little ground to give. The stakes are very high on both sides now, and the suspense is long-drawn. I feel sure we shall win both here and at Cassino.

* * * * *

In my report to Parliament on February 22, 1944,* Anzio was presented in its proportion. I told the story as far as was then possible.

"It was certainly no light matter to launch this considerable army upon the seas—40,000 or 50,000 men in the first instance—with all the uncertainty of winter weather and all the unknowable strength of enemy fortifications. The operation itself was a model of combined work. The landing was virtually unopposed. Subsequent events did not however take the course which had been hoped or planned. In the upshot we got a great army ashore, equipped with masses of artillery, tanks, and very many thousands of vehicles, and our troops moving inland came into contact with the enemy.

"The German reactions to this descent have been remarkable. Hitler has apparently resolved to defend Rome with the same obstinacy which he showed at Stalingrad, in Tunisia, and, recently, in the Dnieper Bend. No fewer than seven extra German divisions were brought rapidly down from France, Northern Italy, and Yugoslavia, and a determined attempt has been made to destroy the bridgehead and drive us into the sea. Battles of prolonged and intense fierceness and fury have been fought. At the same time the American and British Fifth Army to the southward is pressing forward with all its strength. Another battle is raging there.

"On broad grounds of strategy, Hitler's decision to send into the south of Italy as many as eighteen divisions, involving, with

* See p. 420.

their maintenance troops, probably something like half a million Germans, and to make a large secondary front in Italy, is not unwelcome to the Allies. We must fight the Germans somewhere, unless we are to stand still and watch the Russians. This wearing battle in Italy occupies troops who could not be employed in other greater operations, and it is an effective prelude to them."

* * * * *

General Smuts telegraphed to me next day in terms which illustrate so well his breadth of vision.

General Smuts to Prime Minister 23 Feb 44

Your very effective recital of British war effort will greatly impress world public opinion. It gives vast number of new facts not generally known, which form the proper pendant to Russia's magnificent effort. It will also counterbalance the one-sided impression given by our propaganda of our own ineffectiveness in Burma and at Anzio in comparison with vast sweep of Russian victories. I myself have not followed our strategy in the Anzio beach-head, which I had thought would link up with the Cassino front with the object of breaking resistance of Germans in the mountains in the south. An isolated pocket has now been created, which is unconnected with enemy's main southern front, and which is itself besieged instead of giving relief to the pressure against us in the south.

The position is once more restored to its right proportions by your emphasis on our vast air effort, which destroys Germany's war effort at its source and prepares for the coming Western Front in the best possible way. But I would not myself give undue publicity to this front, since it may hold unpleasant surprises for us. The retreat of the German armies in the East is not only due to Russian prowess and our attraction of Luftwaffe from that front, but probably also to the Germans withdrawing large strategic reserves to counter our threat in the West. In a theatre where enemy is fully prepared for us serious delays, if not setbacks, may be met with, and we may have to face grave disappointments. The German plan may be to halt us effectively in the West, and then hasten back to the East to stop the penetration of Russian armies into Germany, which he must mortally fear. If this is not the German plan, I do not understand their strategy of fighting stubbornly against us for every inch of ground in Italy, while letting Russia achieve such successes on the Eastern Front.

Instead of giving undue publicity to our Western Front, our propaganda should for the present be concentrated on our air offensive against Germany. I do believe that this has had even more far-reaching effects than the Russian land victories.

If any reserves are called for, remember our now well-trained South African 6th Armoured Division, which is in Egypt. They only need some added transport to give a good account of themselves in a suitable theatre.

To this I replied, expressing views which I hold to this day:

Prime Minister to Field-Marshal Smuts   27 Feb 44

Thank you for your telegram. During the Conferences at Carthage and at Marrakesh I was able to clear difficulties out of the way and get this big amphibious operation at Anzio soundly organised. My personal efforts did not extend to the conduct of the battle, which of course I left altogether to the commanders, once they were landed safely at the right place, as they were. In all his talks with me Alexander envisaged that the essence of the battle was the seizure of the Alban Hills with the utmost speed, and to this end I was able to obtain from the United States their 504th Parachute Regiment, although at the time it was under orders to return for "Overlord". But at the last moment General Clark cancelled the use of this regiment, and the American General Lucas, a man of fifty-five, who at Salerno had distinguished himself in command of a corps, seems to have had the idea in his mind that at all costs he must be prepared for a counterattack. As a result, although directly I learnt the landing was successful I sent Alexander injunctions that he should peg out claims rather than consolidate bridgeheads, the whole operation became stagnant. Needless to say, the logistic calculations all turned out to be on the overgenerous side and there were very large margins in hand. No one can deny that this was lucky, seeing that plans originally made for 50,000 men are now comfortably supporting 170,000.

Naturally I am very disappointed at what has appeared to be the frittering away of a brilliant opening in which both fortune and design had played their part. I do not in any way however repent of what has been done. As a result the Germans have now transferred into the south of Italy at least eight more divisions, so that in all there are eighteen south of Rome. It is vital to the success of "Overlord" that we keep away from that theatre and hold elsewhere as many German divisions as possible, and hard fighting in Italy throughout the spring will provide for the main operation a perfect prelude and accompaniment.

We had hoped that a big thrust would be launched northwards from the Cassino front to correspond with the landing. This was indeed planned, but it did not take place because apparently it proved immensely difficult to debouch past Cassino up the Liri valley. Naturally we are striving with might and main to join up the two forces, and at any moment the curtain may go up on the next act of the drama.

Truscott, a young American Divisional Commander, whom everyone speaks of most highly, has now superseded Lucas. My confidence in Alexander remains undiminished.

Here at home all goes fairly well, though the little folk are more active. However, their chirrupings will be stilled before long by the thunder of the cannonade.

Most earnestly do I look forward to seeing you, and I rejoice that you will be at my side in momentous times.

* * * * *

Such is the story of the struggle of Anzio; a story of high opportunity and shattered hopes, of skilful inception on our part and swift recovery by the enemy, of valour shared by both. We now know that early in January the German High Command had intended to transfer five of their best divisions from Italy to North-West Europe. Kesselring protested that in such an event he could no longer carry out his orders to fight south of Rome and he would have to withdraw. Just as the argument was at its height the Anzio landing took place. The High Command dropped the idea, and instead of the Italian front contributing forces to North-West Europe the reverse took place. Hitler was enraged at the failure of his Fourteenth Army to drive the Allies into the sea. After their offensive of February 16 he ordered a selected group of twenty officers of all arms and ranks fighting in Italy to report to him personally about conditions at the front. This was the first and only time that this happened during the war. "He would have done much better," comments General Westphal, "to visit the front himself and been convinced of Allied superiority in planes and guns."

We knew nothing of all these changes of plan at the time, but it proves that the aggressive action of our armies in Italy, and specifically the Anzio stroke, made its full contribution towards the success of "Overlord". We shall see later on the part it played in the liberation of Rome.

CHAPTER XXVIII

ITALY: CASSINO

Mussolini and Ciano – Marshal Badoglio's Harassed Government – Correspondence with President Roosevelt on This – My Statement on Italian Political Affairs in the House of Commons, February 22 – Bombing of the Monastery at Cassino – The Weather Brings a Deadlock – Discussion with Roosevelt on the Italian Political Situation – The Russians Recognise the Badoglio Government – The Campaign in Italy Drags – Alexander's Convincing Explanation – Anglo-American Argument about "Overlord", "Anvil", and the Italian Campaign – Views of General Eisenhower and General Wilson – My Telegram to General Marshall of April 16 on the Military Position – The Crown Prince Umberto Becomes Lieutenant-Governor of the Realm – Prelude to the New Allied Offensive.

THE bitterness and confusion of the Italian scene were heightened in the New Year. Mussolini's phantom republic came under mounting pressure from the Germans. The governing circles around Badoglio in the south were assailed by intrigues in Italy and despised by public opinion in Britain and the United States. Mussolini was the first to react.

When he arrived in Munich after his escape he found there his daughter Edda and her husband, Count Ciano. These two had fled from Rome at the time of the surrender, and, although Ciano had voted against his father-in-law at the fateful meeting of the Grand Council, he hoped, thanks to the influence of his wife, for a reconciliation. During these days in Munich this in fact happened. This aroused the indignation of Hitler, who had already placed the Ciano family under house arrest on their arrival. The reluctance of the Duce to punish the traitors to Fascism, and particularly Ciano, was perhaps the main reason why Hitler formed such a low opinion of his colleague at this critical time.

It was not until the declining strength of the "Republic of Salo" had fallen far, and the impatience of its German masters had sharpened, that Mussolini agreed to let loose a wave of calculated vengeance. All those leaders of the old Fascist régime who had voted against him in July and who could be caught in German-occupied Italy were brought to trial at the end of 1943, in the medieval fortress at Verona. Among them was Ciano. Without exception they received the death sentence. In spite of the entreaties and threats of Edda, the Duce could not relent. In January 1944 the group, which included not only Ciano but also the seventy-eight-year-old Marshal de Bono, a colleague in the march on Rome, were taken out to die a traitor's death—to be shot in the back tied to a chair. They all died bravely.

The end of Ciano was in keeping with all the elements of Renaissance tragedy. Mussolini's submission to Hitler's vengeful demands brought him only shame, and the miserable neo-Fascist republic dragged on by Lake Garda—a relic of the Broken Axis.

* * * * *

In the south Badoglio was continually harassed by the remnants of the opposition to Fascism in its early days, and which had sprung up in political groupings since the previous summer. They not only pressed for a broader Administration in which they would share, but also sought to destroy the monarchy, which they declared to be compromised by prolonged acquiescence in Mussolini's rule. There was growing public support for their activities, both in America and in England. In January a congress of the six Italian parties was held in Bari, and resolutions in this sense were passed.

I therefore telegraphed to the President:

Prime Minister to President Roosevelt 3 Feb 44
I earnestly hope that the existing régime in Italy will be allowed to function at least until the great battles now being fought by the soldiers of our two countries have resulted in our capture of Rome. I am sure that a disturbance now of such authority as remains in the Italian State and the attempt to create a new authority out of political groups with no real backing will add greatly to our difficulties. Moreover, these groups, when formed into a Government, in order to win credit from the Italian people, would feel it essential to assert Italian interests in a much stronger form than the King and Badoglio dare to do. I feel it would be a great pity if Badoglio threw in his hand, and

our reports show that the Italian Navy might be powerfully affected by action against the King. Much British and American blood is flowing, and I plead that military considerations should carry weight.

His reply was reassuring.

President Roosevelt to Prime Minister   11 Feb 44

I have directed the Department of State to take no action toward effecting any change in the existing Government of Italy at the present time, and until our military situation in the Italian campaign is sufficiently improved to warrant risking the disaffection of those Italians who are now assisting the Allied forces.

I think, though, that you and I should regard this only as a temporary reprieve for the two old gentlemen.

I elaborated my view.

Prime Minister to President Roosevelt   13 Feb 44

I fully agree we should review the whole scene after we are settled in Rome. We have not got there yet, and Lincoln's birthday celebrations remind me about not crossing the Fox River till you get to it.

The present régime is the lawful Government of Italy, with whom we have concluded an armistice, in consequence of which the Italian Navy came over, and, with some of the Italian Army and Air Force, are fighting on our side. This Italian Government will obey our directions far more than any other that we may laboriously constitute. On the other hand, it has more power over the Fleet, Army officials, etc., than anything else which can be set up out of the worn-out débris of political parties, none of whom have the slightest title by election or prescription. A new Italian Government will have to make its reputation with the Italian people by standing up to us. They will very likely try to wriggle out of the armistice terms. As for being instrumental in handing over without a mutiny part of the Italian Fleet to Russia, I cannot conceive that they would do so, or that if they did their writ would run with the Italian Navy. I hope therefore that when the time comes we shall consult together. I gave strong support to the State Department over Darlan. They seem rueful about that episode now. Looking back upon it, I consider it was right. Several thousand British and American soldiers are alive to-day because of it, and it got us Dakar at a time when we could ill have spared the large forces needed for its capture. . . .

I have had a letter from Harry. He is an indomitable spirit. I cannot help feeling very anxious about his frail body and another operation. I should always be grateful for any news about him, for I rate him high among the Paladins. I have just heard that his son has been killed in the Marshall Islands battle. As I do not know whether his state of health will have permitted him to receive this news, I am sending him a message through you.

As the President and myself were at one on the main issue, I made a statement on Italian political affairs in my speech of February 22 in the House of Commons.

"The battle in Italy will be hard and long. I am not yet convinced that any other Government can be formed at the present time in Italy which could command the same obedience from the Italian armed forces. Should we succeed in the present battle and enter Rome, as I trust and believe we shall, we shall be free to discuss the whole Italian political situation, and we shall do so with many advantages that we do not possess at the present time. It is from Rome that a more broadly based Italian Government can best be formed. Whether a Government thus formed will be so helpful to the Allies as the present dispensation I cannot tell. It might of course be a Government which would try to make its position good with the Italian people by resisting, as much as it dared, the demands made on them in the interests of the Allied armies. I should be sorry however to see an unsettling change made at a time when the battle is at its climax, swaying to and fro. When you have to hold a hot coffee-pot it is better not to break the handle off until you are sure that you will get another equally convenient and serviceable, or at any rate until there is a dishcloth handy.

"The representatives of the various Italian parties who assembled a fortnight ago at Bari are of course eager to become the Government of Italy. They will have no elective authority, and certainly no constitutional authority, until either the present King abdicates or his successor invites them to take office. It is by no means certain that they would have any effective authority over the Italian armed forces now fighting with us. Italy lies prostrate under her miseries and disasters. Food is scarce; shipping to bring it is voraciously absorbed by our ever-expanding military operations. I think we have gained this year 12,000,000 tons increase to the Allies, yet the shortage continues, because our great operations absorb every ship as it comes, and the movement of food is difficult.

"It would be a mistake to suppose that the kind of political conditions or forces exist in Italy which work so healthily in unbeaten lands, or in countries which have not been shattered by war or stifled by a long period of Fascist rule. We shall see more clearly how to proceed and have more varied resources at our disposal if and when we are in possession of the capital city. The policy therefore which His Majesty's Government have agreed provisionally with the Government of the United States is to win the battle for Rome and take a new view when we are there."

$\star$ $\star$ $\star$ $\star$ $\star$

The second major attack at Cassino began on February 15 with the bombing of the monastery.* The height on which the monastery stood surveyed the junction of the rivers Rapido and Liri and was the pivot of the whole German defence. It had already proved itself a formidable, strongly defended obstacle. Its steep sides, swept by fire, were crowned by the famous building, which several times in previous wars had been pillaged, destroyed, and rebuilt. There is controversy about whether it should have been destroyed once again. The monastery did not contain German troops, but the enemy fortifications were hardly separate from the building itself. The monastery dominated the whole battlefield, and naturally General Freyberg, the Corps Commander concerned, wished to have it heavily bombarded from the air before he launched the infantry attack. The Army Commander, General Mark Clark, unwillingly sought and obtained permission from General Alexander, who accepted the responsibility. On February 15 therefore, after the monks had been given full warning, over 450 tons of bombs were dropped, and heavy damage was done. The great outer walls and gateway still stood. The result was not good. The Germans had now every excuse for making whatever use they could of the rubble of the ruins, and this gave them even better opportunities for defence than when the building was intact.

It fell to the 4th Indian Division, which had recently relieved the Americans on the ridges north of the monastery, to make the attack. On two successive nights they tried in vain to seize a knoll that lay between their position and Monastery Hill. On the night of February 18 a third attempt was made. The fighting was desperate, and all our men who reached the knoll were killed. Later that night a brigade by-passed the knoll and moved directly at the monastery, only to encounter a concealed ravine heavily

* See map, facing p. 526.

mined and covered by enemy machine-guns at shortest range. Here they lost heavily and were stopped. While this fierce conflict was raging on the heights above them the New Zealand Division succeeded in crossing the river Rapido just below Cassino town; but they were counter-attacked by tanks before their bridgehead was secure and forced back again. The direct attack on Cassino had failed.

At the beginning of March the weather brought about a deadlock. Napoleon's fifth element—mud—bogged down both sides. We could not break the main front at Cassino, and the Germans had equally failed to drive us into the sea at Anzio. In numbers there was little to choose between the combatants. By now we had twenty divisions in Italy, but both Americans and French had had very heavy losses. The enemy had eighteen or nineteen divisions south of Rome, and five more in Northern Italy, but they too were tired and worn.

There could be no hope now of a break-out from the Anzio beach-head and no prospect of an early link-up between our two separated forces until the Cassino front was broken. The prime need therefore was to make the beach-head really firm, to relieve and reinforce the troops, and to pack in stores to withstand a virtual siege and nourish a subsequent sortie. Time was short, since many of the landing-craft had to leave for "Overlord" in the middle of the month. Their move had so far been rightly postponed, but no further delay was possible. The Navies put all their strength into the effort, with admirable results. The previous average daily tonnage landed had been 3,000; in the first ten days of March this was more than doubled. I followed this process with attention.

On March 12 I asked, "What is the ration strength in the bridgehead at present? How many vehicles have been landed there from the beginning? How many days' reserve supplies of food and ammunition have been built up, and what is the basis of this calculation?"

General Alexander replied that the ration strength was 90,200 United States and 35,500 British. Nearly 25,000 vehicles of all kinds had been landed. He gave full details of the supplies of food, ammunition, and petrol. The margins were not large, but improving.

A few days later Vesuvius was in violent eruption. For several days traffic from the Naples airfields was partially interrupted, but the work in the ports went on. On March 24 a report to the Naval Commander-in-Chief stated: "The Naples group of ports is now discharging at the rate of twelve million tons a year, while Vesuvius is estimated to be doing thirty millions a day. We can but admire this gesture of the gods."

* * * * *

While the battles I have described were going on politics raged around Badoglio. Roosevelt was being clamorously pressed to support major changes in the Italian Government. He suggested that we might yield to the pressure of opinion.

I telegraphed to him:

Prime Minister to President Roosevelt   8 Mar 44

Your cable causes me concern. It is a departure from your agreement with me of February 11, which you kindly reaffirmed in your [later] cable as "finished business". On the strength of the first assurances I made my statement to Parliament.

My advices do not lead me to believe that any new facts of importance have arisen or that the Allied forces are not capable of maintaining order in the regions they have occupied as the result of the "unconditional surrender" of Italy. It would be a very serious mistake to give way to [local] agitation, especially when accompanied by threats on the part of groups of office-seeking politicians. We should then be liable to set up in Italy an Administration which might not command the allegiance of the armed forces, but which would endeavour to make its position with the Italian people by standing up to the Allies. In fact, we should have another but more intractable version of the de Gaullist Committee. Meanwhile, in the midst of a heart-shaking battle we are to get rid of the helpful Government of the King and Badoglio, which is doing its utmost to work its passage and aid us in every way.

I readily admit that the course you recommend would be the more popular and would have at least a transitory success. But I am sure that for the victorious conquerors to have their hands forced in this way by sections of the defeated population would be unfortunate. So also would be the obvious open division between you and me and between our two Governments. I gave you and the State Department loyal and vigorous support over the Darlan affair. Unity of action between our two Governments was never more necessary than at the present time, considering the great battles in which we are engaged and which lie ahead.

His reply on the same day encouraged me to believe that we were in agreement. "It is my strongest wish," he said, "that you and I should continue to work in complete harmony in this matter as in all others. We may differ on timing, but things like that can be worked out, and on the big objectives like self-determination we are as one."

The pressures however continued. The idea of making a bargain with the six Italian Opposition parties gained support in the Supreme Headquarters at Algiers, and General Wilson telegraphed in this sense to the Combined Chiefs of Staff in Washington and London. This he was entitled to do as he served both countries. Nevertheless my views remained unchanged, and my colleagues in the War Cabinet, who saw all that was passing, were in broad agreement with them.

Prime Minister to President Roosevelt   13 Mar 44
I fear that if we drive out the King and Badoglio at this stage we shall only have complicated the task of the Armies. I see that this is also the Soviet view. They are certainly realistic, but of course their aim may be a Communist Italy, and it may suit them to use the King and Badoglio till everything is ready for an extreme solution. I can assure you that this danger is also in my mind. My idea remains that we should try to construct a broadly based Government, taking into account the opinion of the democratic North of Italy and seeking representatives from there. Of course if we cannot get Rome for several months we shall have to act earlier, but without the favourable conditions which will be open to us once we are in possession of the capital. We shall then have much better chances of finding a really representative footing.

The President's reply disappointed me.

President Roosevelt to Prime Minister   13 Mar 44
I am sorry if earlier messages were not clear. I did not at any time intend to convey to you agreement that we postpone all political decisions until after Rome had been taken. The political situation in Italy has developed rapidly since our earlier messages; the military situation has not kept pace. The capture of Rome is still remote and major political decisions must be taken.
I do not like having to use stern measures against our friends in Italy, except for good reason. In the present situation the Commander-in-Chief and his political advisers, both British and American, have recommended that we give immediate support to the programme of

the six Opposition parties. Thus we have, happily, for once, our political and military considerations entirely in harmony.

We do not need to intervene beyond informing the executive junta of our support of their programme and confirming this to the King if necessary. The Italians can present the solution to the King and work out the programme among themselves.

I cannot for the life of me understand why we should hesitate any longer in supporting a policy so admirably suited to our common military and political aims. American public opinion would never understand our continued tolerance and apparent support of Victor Emmanuel.

The Russians now complicated the position by sending an official representative to the Badoglio Government without consulting us.

Prime Minister to President Roosevelt 14 Mar 44

The Russians have announced that they have sent a fully accredited Ambassador to the present Italian Government, with whom we are still technically at war. I do not think it would be wise, without further consideration, to accept the programme of the so-called Six Parties and demand forthwith the abdication of the King and installation of Signor Croce as Lieutenant of the Realm. I will however consult the War Cabinet upon what you justly call a "major political decision". Our war with Italy has lasted since June 1940, and the British Empire has suffered 232,000 casualties in men, as well as our losses in ships. I feel sure that in this matter our view will receive consideration from you. We ought to make every effort to act together. Pray remember that I have committed myself in public, and that any divergence will certainly become known.

The War Cabinet considered these messages, and I reported their conclusions to the President.

15 Mar 44

I consulted the War Cabinet this morning on the proposal that the British and American Governments should accept the Six Party programme without further delay. The War Cabinet asked me to assure you that they agree fully with your wish to establish a more broadly based Government in Italy, and that the future form of government of the Italian people can only be settled by self-determination. They also agree with you that the point to consider is the timing. On this they have no doubt that it would be far better to wait till we are masters of Rome before parting company with the King and Badoglio, because from Rome a more representative and solidly based Administration can be constructed than is possible now. They feel that nothing could be worse for our joint interests and for the future of Italy than to set up a weak democratic Government which flopped. Even a settlement reached at Rome could not be final, because it would be necessary to review it when the northern provinces and great industrial centres favourable to us and essential to a democratic solution, like Milan and Turin, have been liberated. They do not consider that the Six Parties are representative in any true sense of the Italian democracy or Italian nation, or that they could at the present time replace the existing Italian Government, which has loyally and effectively worked in our interests.

In reaching these conclusions the War Cabinet have of course had before them the telegrams sent by the Allied Commander-in-Chief [General Wilson], whose views on this subject they do not share. Meanwhile we should be quite ready to discuss the suggestions put to the State Department by the Foreign Secretary. It is also of course recognised that should the capture of Rome be unduly protracted, say for two or three months, the question of timing would have to be reviewed.

Finally, they ask me to emphasise the great importance of not exposing to the world any divergences of view which may exist between our two Governments, especially in face of the independent action taken by Russia in entering into diplomatic relations with the Badoglio Government without consultation with other Allies. It would be a great pity if our respective viewpoints had to be argued out in Parliament and the Press, when waiting a few months may make it possible for all three Governments to take united action.

This was the end of the matter for the moment.

★　　★　　★　　★　　★

Although Anzio was now no longer an anxiety the campaign in Italy as a whole had dragged. We had hoped that by this time the Germans would have been driven north of Rome and that a substantial part of our armies would have been set free for a strong landing on the Riviera coast to help the main cross-Channel invasion. This operation, called "Anvil", had been agreed in principle at Teheran. It was soon to become a cause of contention between ourselves and our American Allies. The campaign in Italy had obviously to be carried forward a long way before this issue arose, and the immediate need was to break the deadlock on the Cassino front. Preparations for the third Battle of Cassino were begun soon after the February failure, but the bad weather delayed it until March 15.

This time Cassino town was the primary objective. After a heavy bombardment, in which nearly 1,000 tons of bombs and 1,200 tons of shells were expended, our infantry advanced. "It seemed to me inconceivable," said Alexander, "that any troops should be left alive after eight hours of such terrific hammering." But they were. The 1st German Parachute Division, probably the toughest fighters in all their Army, fought it out amid the heaps of rubble with the New Zealanders and Indians. By nightfall the greater part of the town was in our hands, while the 4th Indian Division, coming down from the north, made equally good progress and next day were two-thirds of the way up Monastery Hill. Then the battle swung against us. Our tanks could not cross the large craters made by the bombardment and follow up the infantry assault. Nearly two days passed before they could help. The enemy filtered in reinforcements. The weather broke in storm and rain. Our attacks gained ground, but the early success was not repeated, and the enemy were not to be overborne in the slogging match.

I wondered why we did not make flank attacks to dislodge the enemy from positions which had twice already proved so strong.

Prime Minister to General Alexander   20 Mar 44

I wish you would explain to me why this passage by Cassino Monastery Hill, etc., all on a front of two or three miles, is the only place which you must keep butting at. About five or six divisions have been worn out going into these jaws. Of course I do not know the ground or the battle conditions, but, looking at it from afar, it is puzzling why, if the enemy can be held and dominated at this point, no attacks can be made on the flanks. It seems very hard to understand why this most strongly defended point is the only passage forward, or why, when it is saturated [in a military sense], ground cannot be gained on one side or the other. I have the greatest confidence in you and will back you up through thick and thin, but do try to explain to me why no flanking movements can be made.

His answer was lucid and convincing. It explained the situation in words written at the moment, and is of high value to the military historian.

General Alexander to Prime Minister   20 Mar 44

I reply to your telegram of March 20. Along whole main battlefront from Adriatic to south coast there is only Liri valley leading direct to Rome which is suitable terrain for development of our superiority in artillery and armour. The main highway, known as Route Six, is the only road, except cart-tracks, which leads from the mountains where we are into Liri valley over Rapido river. This exit into the plain is blocked and dominated by Monte Cassino, on which stands the monastery. Repeated attempts have been made to outflank Monastery Hill from the north, but all these attacks have been unsuccessful, owing to deep ravines, rocky escarpments, and knife-edges, which limit movements to anything except comparatively small parties of infantry, who can only be maintained by porters and to a limited extent by mules where we have managed under great difficulties to make some mule-tracks.

Further, Monastery Hill is cut off almost completely from north by a ravine so steep and deep that so far it has proved impossible to cross it. A wider turning movement is even more difficult, as it has to cross Mount Cairo, which is a precipitous peak now deep in snow. The Americans tried to outflank this Cassino bastion from the south by an attack across the Rapido river, but this, as you know, failed, with heavy losses to the 34th and 36th Divisions. The Rapido is difficult to cross south of Cassino owing to flood-water at this time of year, soft, marshy ground which adds to problems of bridging, lack of any roads to bring up bridging material, and to the strength of enemy's positions on far bank. Again, a crossing of the Rapido river south of Cassino, as already proved, comes under very heavy enfilade artillery fire from German gun positions tucked away at foot of the mountains immediately behind or west of Cassino, and also from foothills of mountains on south of Liri valley.

Freyberg's attack was designed as a direct assault on this bastion, success depending on crushing enemy resistance by surprise and an overwhelming concentration of fire-power. The plan was to rush Cassino town and then to flow round the east and southern slopes of Monastery Hill and take the bastion by storm from a direction where enemy's artillery could not seriously interfere with our movement. It very nearly succeeded in its initial stages, with negligible losses to us. We got, and still have, two bridges over the Rapido river, one on Highway Six and the other over railway bridge; both are fit for tanks. The Gurkhas got and are still within 200 to 300 yards of monastery. That we have not succeeded in taking our objective within first forty-eight hours may be summarised as follows:

The destruction caused in Cassino to roads and movement by bombing was so terrific that the employment of tanks or any other fighting vehicles has been seriously hampered. The tenacity of these German paratroops is quite remarkable, considering that they were subjected to the whole Mediterranean Air Force plus the better part of 800 guns under greatest concentration of fire-power which has ever been put down and lasting for six hours. I doubt if there are any other troops in the world who could have stood up to it and then gone on fighting with the ferocity they have. I am meeting Freyberg and the Army Commanders to-morrow to discuss the situation.

If we call it off we shall hold on to the two bridges and adjust our positions so as to hold the advantageous key points already gained. The Eighth Army's plan for entering the Liri valley in force will be undertaken when regrouping is completed. The plan must envisage an attack on a wider front and with greater forces than Freyberg has been able to have for this operation. A little later, when the snow goes off mountains, the rivers drop, and the ground hardens, movement will be possible over terrain which at present is impassable.

Prime Minister to General Alexander   21 Mar 44

Thank you very much for your full explanation. I hope you will not have to "call it off" when you have gone so far. Surely the enemy is very hard pressed too. Every good wish.

The war weighs very heavy on us all just now.

The struggle in the ruins of Cassino town continued until the 23rd, with hard fighting in attacks and counter-attacks. The New Zealanders and the Indians could do no more. We kept hold of a large part of the town, but the Gurkhas had to be withdrawn from their perch high up the Monastery Hill, where supplies could not reach them even by air because of the steep hillside.

★　　★　　★　　★　　★

In reply to my request General Wilson reported the casualties suffered by the New Zealand Corps during the battle. They totalled:

2nd New Zealand Division			1,050
4th Indian Division: British	401	} 1,160	
Indian	759		
78th British Division			190
		Total	2,400

This was a heavy price to pay for what might seem small gains. We had however established a firm bridgehead at Cassino over the river Rapido, which, with the deep bulge made by the Xth Corps across the lower Garigliano in January, was of great value when the final, successful battle came. Here and at the Anzio bridgehead we had pinned down in Central Italy nearly twenty good German divisions. Many of them might have gone to France.

Before the Gustav Line could be assaulted again with any hope of success our troops had to be rested and regrouped. Most of the Eighth Army had to be brought over from the Adriatic side and two armies concentrated for the next battle, the British Eighth on the Cassino front, the American Fifth on the lower Garigliano. For this General Alexander needed nearly two months.

This meant that the Mediterranean could only help the cross-Channel assault in early June, by fighting south of Rome. The United States Chiefs of Staff still strove for a subsidiary landing in Southern France, and for some weeks there was much argument between us about what orders should be given to General Wilson.

*   *   *   *   *

The story must here be told of the Anglo-American argument, first as between "Overlord" and "Anvil", and then as between "Anvil" and the Italian campaign. It will be recalled that in my talk with Montgomery at Marrakesh on December 31 he said that he must have more in the initial punch across the Channel, and that on January 6 I telegraphed to the President that Bedell Smith and Montgomery were convinced that it was better to put in a much heavier and broader "Overlord" than to expand "Anvil" beyond what we had planned in outline before Teheran.

This was keenly debated at a conference held by General Eisenhower on January 21, shortly after his arrival in England. Eisenhower himself firmly believed in the vital importance of "Anvil", and thought it would be a mistake to impoverish it for the sake of strengthening "Overlord". As a result of this conference however he sent a telegram to the Combined Chiefs of Staff in Washington, in which he said:

"Overlord" and "Anvil" must be viewed as one whole. If sufficient resources could be made available the ideal would be a five-divisional "Overlord" and a three-divisional "Anvil". If insufficient forces are available for this however I am driven to the conclusion that we should adopt a five-divisional "Overlord" and a one-divisional "Anvil", the latter being maintained as a threat until enemy weakness justifies its active employment.

On this telegram the British Chiefs of Staff presented their own views to Washington, namely:

(a) That the first onfall of "Overlord" should be increased to five divisions, whatever the cost to "Anvil".

(b) That every effort should be made to undertake "Anvil" by using two divisions or more in the assault.

(c) That if these divisions could not be carried landing-craft in the Mediterranean should be reduced to the requirements for a lift of one division.

The American Chiefs of Staff were unable to agree. They considered that a threat in lieu of an actual operation was inadequate and insisted on a two-divisional assault. On this telegram I minuted, "Apparently the two-division lift for 'Anvil' is given priority over 'Overlord'. This is directly counter to the views of Generals Eisenhower and Montgomery."

On February 4 the British Chiefs of Staff, in full consultation with me, sent a lengthy telegram to their American colleagues, in which they emphasised that the paramount consideration was that "Overlord" should succeed, and that the right solution was to build up "Overlord" to the strength required by the Supreme Commander and then to allocate to the Mediterranean whatever additional resources could be found. They questioned the wisdom of undertaking "Anvil" at all, in view of the way things were going in Italy, and pointed out that when "Anvil" first found favour at Teheran we expected that the Germans would withdraw to a line north of Rome. But now it was clear beyond all doubt that the Germans intended to resist our advance in Italy to the utmost. They also pointed out that the distance between the South of France and the beaches of Normandy was nearly five hundred miles, and that a diversion could be created from Italy or other points just as well as through the Rhone valley. "Anvil" in fact was too far away to help "Overlord".

On this the United States Chiefs of Staff proposed that the issue should be decided at a conference between General Eisenhower, who would be their representative, and the British Chiefs of Staff. To this we readily assented, but several weeks were to pass before agreement was reached. General Eisenhower was still reluctant to abandon "Anvil", but he was beginning to doubt whether it would still be possible to withdraw trained divisions from Italy. On March 21 General Wilson was asked for his opinion. He said he was strongly opposed to withdrawing troops from Italy until Rome had been captured, and he advised that "Anvil" should be cancelled and that we should only land in the South of France if the Germans cracked.

This turned the scale. The British Chiefs of Staff telegraphed to Washington that it was clear that "Anvil" could not be carried out on the prescribed date, since it was impossible to withdraw either troops from the battle in Italy or landing-craft from the Anzio bridgehead. The American Chiefs of Staff assented, and agreed that General Wilson should prepare to land in the South of France in July, and also to contain and destroy as many German troops in Italy as possible if it were decided to fight it out there. It was thought that early June would be time enough to decide which plan should be carried out.

That I myself was strongly in favour of maintaining the thrust in Italy can be seen from this telegram:

Prime Minister to General Marshall (*Washington*)   16 Apr 44
It is of course very painful to us to forgo the invaluable addition to our landing-craft in the Mediterranean which you so kindly offered under certain conditions and had no doubt great trouble to obtain. What I cannot bear is to agree beforehand to starve a battle or have to break it off just at the moment when success, after long efforts and heavy losses, may be in view. Our forces in Italy are not much larger than those of the enemy. They comprise seven or eight different races, while the enemy is all German. The wet weather has hitherto restricted the full use of our superiority in artillery, in armour, and in the air. Alexander tells me that he strikes out *north-east*, not south-east, from the Anzio beach-head shortly after his main thrust across the Rapido. Thus there will not necessarily be a moment when we shall pause and say, "Halt here. Go over to the defensive. All aboard for 'Anvil'." Nor will there necessarily be an exact moment when the cutting of supplies for the Italian battle for the sake of "Anvil" can be fixed beforehand in imagination. A half-hearted undercurrent sets in with an army which has a divided objective, part to the front and part to the rear. This infects all the rearward services, who cannot help knowing. Remember the terrible bleeding the armies in Italy got when their seven best divisions were taken for "Overlord".

2. Of course, if the battle goes wrong early and we are hung up before other enemy lines of defence and forced to go over to a general defensive no doubt strong forces could then be spared, but the drain

of feeding the bridgehead would continue to press on our landing-craft, and without your Pacific landing-craft there will be no two-division lift for any amphibious operations, "Anvil" or other.

3. Therefore it seems to me we must throw our hearts into this battle, for the sake of which so many American and British lives have already been sacrificed, and make it, like "Overlord", an all-out conquer or die. It may well be that by May 31 we shall see many things which are now veiled from us. I regret having to forgo such an hour of choice.

4. Dill tells me that you had expected me to support "Anvil" more vigorously in view of my enthusiasm for it when it was first proposed by you at Teheran. Please do me the justice to remember that the situation is vastly changed. In November we hoped to take Rome in January, and there were many signs that the enemy was ready to [retire] northwards up the Italian peninsula. Instead of this, in spite of our great amphibious expedition, we are stuck where we are, and the enemy has brought down to the battle south of Rome the eight mobile divisions we should have hoped a full-scale "Anvil" would have contained. Thus there has been cause for rejoicing as well as bitter disappointment.

5. The whole of this difficult question only arises out of the absurd shortage of the L.S.T.s. How it is that the plans of two great empires like Britain and the United States should be so much hamstrung and limited by a hundred or two of these particular vessels will never be understood by history. I am deeply concerned at the strong dis-inclination of the American Government even to keep the manufacture of L.S.T.s at its full height so as to have a sufficient number to give to us to help you in the war against Japan. The absence of these special vessels may limit our whole war effort on your left flank, and I fear we shall be accused unjustly of not doing our best, as we are resolved to do.

The instructions Wilson received reflected my views, and in a telegram to the President on April 24 I said:

I am very glad at what has happened in Italy. It seems to me that we have both succeeded in gaining what we sought. The only thing now lacking is a victory. I had long talks with Alexander when he was here for a few days' consultation. He defended his actions, or inactions, with much force, pointing out the small plurality of his army, its mixed character, there being no fewer than seven separate nationalities against the homogeneous Germans, the vileness of the weather, and the extremely awkward nature of the ground. At latest by May 14 he will attack and push everything in as hard as possible.

If this battle were successful, or even raging at full blast, it would fit in very well with other plans.

* * * * *

Political events in Southern Italy again came to a head. A constitutional compromise was reached whereby the King would hand over his powers to his son, the Crown Prince Umberto, as Lieutenant-Governor of the Realm. The fate of the monarchy would then await a plebiscite after the ultimate victory. The royal decree was signed on April 12, and was to take effect at the moment when the Allies entered Rome. At the end of the month Badoglio reconstructed his Government to include leading political figures in the South, of whom Croce and Sforza were the most prominent.

* * * * *

While our armies were preparing to attack General Wilson used all his air-power to impede and injure the enemy, who, like us, were using the pause for reorganising and replenishing themselves for further battle. The potent Allied Air joined in attacking enemy land communications in the hope that these could be kept cut and their troops forced to withdraw for lack of supplies. This operation, optimistically called "Strangle", aimed at blocking the three main railway lines from Northern Italy, the principal targets being bridges, viaducts, and other bottle-necks. They tried to starve the Germans out of Central Italy.

The effort lasted more than six weeks, and did great damage. Railway movement was consistently stopped far north of Rome, but it failed to attain all that we hoped. By working their coastal shipping to full capacity, transferring loads to motor transport, and making full use of the hours of darkness the enemy contrived to maintain themselves. But they could not build enough reserve stocks for protracted and heavy fighting, and in the severe land battles at the end of May they were much weakened. The junction of our separated armies and their capture of Rome took place more rapidly than we had forecast. The German Air Force suffered severely in trying to defend its communications. By early May it could muster only a bare seven hundred against our thousand combat aircraft.

Here then we may leave the Italian theatre, where much was ripening, for the supreme operation across the Channel.

CHAPTER XXIX

THE MOUNTING AIR OFFENSIVE

Our Progress in Bomber Expansion – Early Failures in the Accuracy of Our Bombing – Radar Aids to Target-Finding – The Germans Forced to Turn to Fighter Production – The Americans Join in the Bombing of Axis Europe in 1943 – The Casablanca Directive – British Night Bombing of the Ruhr – The Air Battle at Hamburg – The Onslaught on Berlin – Heavy American Losses at Schweinfurt, October 14, and Their Sequel – British Losses in the Attack on Nuremberg – American Fortresses At Last Provided with Long-Range Fighters – Increase in the Power of British Bombs – Lord Cherwell's Inquiry – Aluminised Explosives – Effect of Our Air Offensive on German War Economy – Part to be Played by the Allied Air Force in "Overlord" – British War Cabinet's Distress at Heavy French Civilian Casualties – We Accept President Roosevelt's Decision – The Valour and Devotion of British and American Bomber Crews.

BOMBER Command played an ever-growing part in all our war plans, and eventually made a decisive contribution to victory. Some review of its activities is required at this point in the story.

It was not till 1943 that we possessed sufficient and suitable aircraft for striking heavy and continuous blows, and in the same year the bombers of the American Eighth Air Force joined in our strategic air offensive. Ever since 1940 I had encouraged the expansion of our bomber strength. The difficulties were numerous. Production lagged behind forecasts; other theatres of war and the campaign against the U-boats made heavy demands; and when the Americans came into the war their output was of course at first largely diverted to their own needs. Although growth in numbers had been slow, our new four-engined planes carried a far heavier weight of bombs. In the opening months of

1942 the average load per aircraft was 2,800 lb.; by the end of that year it was 4,400 lb.; during 1943 it rose to 7,500 lb.

Early in the war both we and the Germans had found that bombers, even in close formation, could not fight their way in daylight through an efficient fighter defence without over-heavy casualties. Like the enemy we had had to turn to night attacks. We were too confident at first about the accuracy of our bombing, and our attempts in the winter of 1940–41 to destroy German oil plants, paramount but small targets, proved a failure. In the spring of 1941 Bomber Command was called to join in the Battle of the Atlantic, and not till July was the offensive against Germany resumed. The targets now chosen were industrial cities and their railway centres, especially the Ruhr, and Hamburg, Bremen, Hanover, Frankfurt, and Stuttgart. However, neither our means nor our methods sufficed. Our losses mounted, and during the winter months we had to reduce our effort. In February 1942 "Gee", the new position-finder already described,* was brought into use, and with its help the Ruhr became our primary goal. Under the vigorous leadership of Air Marshal Harris dramatic results were achieved. His operations included fire-raising attacks on Lübeck and Rostock, the thousand-bomber assault on Cologne in May, and the daylight attack on the submarine Diesel engine works at Augsburg, when Squadron-Leader Nettleton won the Victoria Cross.

In August the Pathfinder Force was formed, under Air Commodore Bennett. Radar aids were playing a growing part in navigation and target-finding, and it was a wise measure to entrust the scarce and complicated apparatus to specialists whose duty was to find the way and point the target to others.

Although accurate night bombing, denied so long, thus came gradually into being, the bomber offensive of 1942 did not lower Germany's war production or civilian morale. The strength of her economy had been under-estimated. Productive capacity and labour were drawn extensively from the occupied countries, and German armament production seems to have actually increased. Under the iron discipline imposed by Goebbels, who was in charge of relief measures, civilian morale stood firm and local disasters were prevented from having a national effect. But the

* Details of the several devices mentioned in this chapter are given in Vol. IV, Chapter XVI.

German leaders had become deeply alarmed and were forced on to the defensive in the air. German aircraft production was increasingly devoted to fighters rather than bombers. This was the beginning of defeat for the Luftwaffe, and a turning-point in our struggle for the air supremacy which we gained in 1944, without which we could not have won the war. Second only in importance to this moral victory over the minds of Hitler and his air commanders was the dangerous Third Air Front created for Germany in the West, to the advantage of the Russians, and of ourselves in the Mediterranean.

Thus we come to the year 1943, when the Americans joined in the bombing of Axis Europe. They had different ideas about method. Whereas we had adopted and were now bringing to efficiency our night-bombing technique, they were convinced that their heavily armed Fortress bombers in close formation could penetrate deeply into Germany by daylight without fighter escort. I was doubtful whether this was a practicable system, and have recorded in a previous volume how at Casablanca I discussed my misgivings with General Eaker, commanding the U.S. air forces in England, and withdrew my opposition.* The Casablanca directive, issued to the British and American Bomber Commands in the United Kingdom on February 4, 1943, gave them their task in the following terms:

Your primary object will be the progressive destruction and dislocation of the German military, industrial, and economic system, and the undermining of the morale of the German people to a point where their capacity for armed resistance is fatally weakened.

Within that general concept your primary objectives . . . will for the present be in the following priority:

    (a) German submarine yards.
    (b) The German aircraft industry.
    (c) Transportation.
    (d) Oil plants.
    (e) Other targets in enemy war industry.

General Eaker, with the American Eighth Air Force, aimed at destroying six groups of targets by daylight precision bombing. He did not receive the reinforcements for which he had asked, but made many gallant and costly attacks. Air Marshal Harris,

* Vol. IV, pp. 608–9.

bombing only at night, concentrated from March to July 1943 mainly upon the Ruhr, beginning on the night of March 5–6 with the heavily defended town of Essen. Eight Mosquitoes dropped target indicators, using the blind-bombing device of "Oboe"; then twenty-two heavy bombers of the Pathfinder Force further illuminated the target for an intense attack by 392 aircraft. Essen was severely damaged for the first time in the war. As the power and activities of Bomber Command developed Goebbels became more and more despairing of the outcome, and his diaries bitterly reproach the Luftwaffe for its failure to stop the British bombers. Speer, the most capable of German Ministers of Production, in an address to Gauleiters in June 1943, referred to the serious losses in production of coal and iron and crank-shafts, and to the decision to double the anti-aircraft defences of the Ruhr and draft in 100,000 men for repair duties.

While the British were at last succeeding in wrecking the Ruhr munitions centres the American Fortresses were meeting with serious opposition from German day fighters, and General Eaker soon realised that if his plan was to succeed he must first defeat the German Air Force. In the greatly improved state of the U-boat war a change in the priorities of targets was accepted by the Combined Chiefs of Staff. In a directive known as "Point-blank", issued on June 10, 1943, they amended the Casablanca decisions so as to give first emphasis to the attack on the German fighter forces and the German aircraft industry.

On July 24–25 the very heavy British attacks on Hamburg began. Hamburg was beyond the range of "Oboe", and the fullest use was made of the blind-bombing device of H_2S, which was carried in the aeroplane and did not depend on signals from home. This instrument gave an outline of the main ground features on a screen in the aircraft which resembled a television screen of to-day. The picture was particularly good where the land was broken up by water, as it is in the dock area of Hamburg. Bomber Command had been gaining experience of H_2S since its first use in January, and for the assault on Hamburg an additional device called "Window", which we had long held in reserve, was used for the first time. As is explained in Volume IV, this simply consisted of strips of metallised paper dropped by the bombers. A cloud of such strips, tuned to the German wave-length and weighing only a few pounds, looked like an aircraft on the enemy's Radar screens, and thus made it very difficult for either their night fighters to be guided to our bombers or for the A.A. guns and searchlights to be aimed at them.*

The four attacks against Hamburg from July 24 to August 3 caused greater destruction than had ever been suffered by so large a city in so short a time. The second attack delivered such a concentration of incendiary bombs mixed with high explosive that there arose a fire tornado which raged through the city with a terrifying howl and defied all human counter-measures. The Air Battle of Hamburg has been described by many Germans as "the great catastrophe". Speer himself admitted after the war that he had calculated that if similar attacks had been delivered in quick succession against six other major German cities it would have led to a breakdown of war production. Germany was saved from this fate in 1943 partly because H_2S was found to be difficult to use, even for area bombing, if there were no prominent water features within the target, and partly because of the resolute defence put up by Germany's ever-resourceful night fighters.

Our third great air onslaught of 1943 was upon Berlin. It lasted from November 1943 to March 1944. If this great industrial centre could have been paralysed like Hamburg German war production as well as morale might have been given a mortal blow.

Bomber Command pressed home its attacks with undaunted courage and determination in the face of fearful difficulties. The weather was appalling, and most of the bombing had to rely on the Radar eye of H_2S. The night photographs taken by the bombers at the moment of bomb release showed nothing but clouds. The same disappointment befell the daylight flights over Berlin of the Photographic Reconnaissance Unit. We knew from the admissions of Germans themselves that great destruction was being caused, but we could not judge the relative success of our sixteen major attacks by comparing the photographic evidence of each. We had to wait until March 1944 to obtain photographs clear enough for the damage to be assessed. It fell short of what had been achieved at Hamburg.

Meanwhile the U.S. Eighth Air Force in its assault on the enemy's fighter forces and aircraft industry in accordance with the "Point-blank" directive was enduring increasing losses at the

* See Vol. IV, pp. 257–9.

hands of the German day fighters, which met them with mounting strength and efficiency. The culmination was reached on October 14, 1943. In their attack on the ball-bearing plants at Schweinfurt, which were vital to the German aircraft industry, the Americans had sixty of their large Fortress aircraft destroyed out of 291. It was thereafter accepted that unescorted daylight bombers could not gain air superiority over Germany, and their offensive was suspended until long-range fighters could be produced to cover them in sufficient strength.

Something very like a dispute arose upon whether British Bomber Command should attack Schweinfurt by their own methods. In the end it was decided that the attack should be made by both Air Forces in daylight and in darkness. The American Eighth Air Force, aided at last by the long-range fighters for which they had waited a long time, attacked with 266 bombers by daylight on February 24, 1944, and on the same night Bomber Command sent 734 aircraft. Here was a really combined offensive directed towards the common aim. Unfortunately, the discussion had lasted so long that this tremendous attack was robbed of much of its effectiveness. Warned by the American daylight attack four months earlier, Speer had dispersed Schweinfurt's industry.

*   *   *   *   *

Prolonged and obstinate technical argument on the policy of night or day bombing, and generous rivalry in trying out the opposing theories with the utmost sacrifice and heroism by both the British and American Air Forces, reached its climax after the last attack on Berlin. On March 30–31, 1944, out of 795 aircraft dispatched by British Bomber Command against Nuremberg ninety-four did not return. This was our heaviest loss in one raid, and caused Bomber Command to re-examine its tactics before launching further deep-penetration attacks by night into Germany. This was proof of the power which the enemy's night fighter force, strengthened by the best crews from other vital fronts, had developed under our relentless offensive. But by forcing the enemy to concentrate his strength on defending inner Germany the Western Allies gained the complete air superiority which they needed for the approaching cross-Channel invasion.

*   *   *   *   *

All this time the Americans were intent on bringing their Fortress bombers into action by day as soon as they could be protected by fighters of sufficiently long range to seek out and destroy the enemy's fighters in the air or go down and attack them on their airfields. After long delay this vital need was met. First the Thunderbolt, then the Lightning, and finally the Mustang gave them day fighters which had auxiliary fuel tanks and a radius of action which was increased from 475 miles to 850. On February 23, 1944, there began a week of concentrated bomber attacks by day on the German aircraft industry. The American long-range fighters at last mastered the enemy's, and the day bombers delivered precision attacks without undue interference or loss.

This was a turning-point in the air war against Germany. From now onwards the U.S. Eighth Air Force was able to bomb targets in Germany by day with high accuracy and ever-increasing freedom. Germany, through her loss of air superiority by day, exposed her vitals to our strategic offensive. The German night fighters, with the cream of their pilots, remained formidable till the end of the war; but this, by lowering the standard of the day fighters, aided the new developments in the American Air Force, and in 1944 daylight air superiority over Germany was gained. By April new measures of deception and new tactics to confuse the enemy's defences enabled the British to resume their full-scale night offensive against German cities. The U.S. Eighth Air Force, having got the measure of the enemy's day fighters, was ready to complete this offensive "round the clock". Such was the position at the advent of "Overlord".

* * * * *

The ever-growing preponderance of our air attack on Germany received an appreciable reinforcement from the new explosive power given to our bombs. This arose as an incident in our anxious discussions in 1943 about the threat of the rockets and the "doodle-bugs". Those experts who were taking the more gloomy view of our danger made a number of pessimistic assumptions in comparing the effect of our bombs in Germany with the expected effects of rockets in England. German houses, they said, were very much stronger than English houses, so that we might expect twice as many to be destroyed per ton of explosives in England as in

Germany. In stating this case they incidentally took for granted that the enemy bombs were nearly twice as powerful as the British, since the Germans mixed aluminium powder with the high explosive. Lord Cherwell pointed out this statement to me, and I ordered a searching inquiry to be conducted under his guidance. The results astonished everyone concerned.

Prime Minister to Minister of Production 12 Oct 43

I recently invited Lord Cherwell to inquire into and report on the relative efficiency of the high explosives used by the German and British forces respectively. His preliminary report had shown the undoubted superiority of the German explosive charges.

The Chiefs of Staff strongly recommend that we should change over to aluminised explosives without waiting for the result of further trials. I agree. Pray let me have a report of what this change will involve in the course of the next week.

The question of how this state of affairs has been allowed to arise should be the subject of an inquiry held under the authority of the Minister of Defence. Pray propose three members, with reference. The whole matter is to be kept most secret.

Action was taken accordingly. It appeared that in the early days when aluminium was scarce it had been decided to use all the aluminium powder which could be spared for making depth-charges, and that this custom had persisted, although aluminium had now become more plentiful. Orders were immediately given to improve our explosive—in the first place in our heavy bombs—by adding aluminium powder, and their efficiency during the whole latter half of the war was thus increased by about half as much again. I thought these revelations deserved the attention of my colleagues, and sent out the following in February 1944:

ALUMINISED EXPLOSIVES 17 Feb 44

At the end of September 1943, during discussions about the German long-range rocket, doubts were expressed about the efficiency of our high explosives as compared with those of the Germans. The Paymaster-General immediately discussed the matter with the Chief of the Air Staff, and the latter proposed to the Chiefs of Staff Committee, who supported his proposals strongly, that urgent action should be taken to establish the true facts, and that if a substantial inferiority was revealed the competent authorities should be called upon to give an explanation and a proposed remedy.

2. At the suggestion of the Chiefs of Staff Committee the Paymaster-

General undertook the inquiry suggested, and on October 6 submitted a report to the Chiefs of Staff Committee which clearly established that our explosives were inferior to the Germans' and that an improvement estimated by various authorities as between 40 per cent. and 100 per cent. could be made if aluminised explosives were used instead of the existing types. Lord Cherwell recommended that the most urgent possible preparations to change over should be made without waiting for the result of further trials. With this recommendation the Chiefs of Staff Committee and I agreed, and immediate action was taken to effect the change-over.

3. I also appointed a committee consisting of Sir Walter Monckton (chairman), Sir Alan Barlow, and Sir Robert Robertson "to consider the report on the efficiency of our blast bombs, to examine the course of our experimental and development work on this subject during the present war, and to report whether, and if so why, there has been any failure to prosecute research to a successful conclusion or to apply the results of that research in practice".

Briefly, an unfortunate experiment in 1941 gave a misleading result, chiefly owing to the unsatisfactory methods of measuring blast pressures in use at that time. In addition, the impression that in any event no aluminium could be obtained discouraged those in charge from repeating the experiment until midsummer 1943. It was only when the Paymaster-General's attention was drawn to an alleged superiority of German explosives, as stated above, that the necessary impetus was given to turn the lessons of fresh experiments to account.

4. There is no doubt that the power of aluminised explosives is very much greater than that of the types which were being used earlier, and I have thought it right to bring to the notice of my colleagues the important service rendered by the Paymaster-General in calling attention to a most unsatisfactory state of affairs, which might have continued for some time, with serious detriment to our war effort, unless he had intervened.

This episode shows how useful it is in great organisations to have a roving eye.

★　　★　　★　　★　　★

It is difficult to say to what extent German war economy and armaments production had so far been damaged by the Anglo-American bomber offensive. Bomber Command's three great area battles of 1943—the Ruhr, Hamburg, and Berlin—had created widespread havoc and caused consternation and alarm throughout Germany, and especially in the minds of the German leaders. But they were able to use factories and forced labour from the occupied countries, and under the brilliant control of Speer these were mobilised with extraordinary speed and efficiency. The morale of the people in the bombed cities, though severely shaken, was not allowed to degenerate into a nation-wide panic.

In the reports submitted to Hitler, which must of course be taken with reserve, it was claimed that German armament production was doubled in 1942. Remembering our own loss of output under much less severe bombing, this assertion is difficult to credit. The Germans admitted that production was almost stationary in 1943, and this is evidence of the increasing power of Bomber Command. In the spring of 1944 the Allied strategic bombers were required for "Overlord", and the weight of attack on Germany itself was inevitably reduced. But by now we were the masters in the air. The bitterness of the struggle had thrown a greater strain on the Luftwaffe than it was able to bear. By being forced to concentrate on building fighters it had lost all power of strategic counter-attack by bombing back at us. Unbalanced and exhausted, it was henceforth unable to defend either itself or Germany from our grievous blows. For our air superiority, which by the end of 1944 was to become air supremacy, full tribute must be paid to the U.S. Eighth Air Force, once it gained its long-range fighters.

* * * * *

As "Overlord" approached a momentous question confronted us. What part was the mighty weapon of the air to play in the supreme operation? After prolonged technical controversy among the air authorities of both countries, the plan which prevailed was to destroy German railway communications in France, Belgium, and Western Germany by discharging 66,000 tons of bombs during the three months before D Day, thus creating a "railway desert" around the German troops in Normandy. This plan had already entered its early stages. The principal targets were the repair and maintenance depots and the locomotives in ninety-three key railway centres on the many approaches to Normandy. The tactical air forces assisted in this general plan, and were given in addition the special task as D Day drew near of destroying bridges and rolling-stock.

I wrote to General Eisenhower on April 3:

The Cabinet to-day took rather a grave and on the whole an adverse view of the proposal to bomb so many French railway centres, in view of the fact that scores of thousands of French civilians, men, women, and children, would lose their lives or be injured. Considering that they are all our friends, this might be held to be an act of very great severity, bringing much hatred on the Allied Air Forces. It was decided that the Defence Committee should consider the matter during this week, and that thereafter the Foreign Office should address the State Department and I should myself send a personal telegram to the President.

The argument for concentration on these particular targets is very nicely balanced on military grounds.

General Eisenhower replied on the 5th:

We must never forget that one of the fundamental factors leading to the decision for undertaking "Overlord" was the conviction that our overpowering Air Force would make feasible an operation which might otherwise be considered extremely hazardous, if not foolhardy. . . . The weight of the argument that has been brought against the bombing of transportation centres in occupied territories is heavy indeed; but I and my military advisers have become convinced that the bombing of these centres will increase our chances for success in the critical battle. . . . I personally believe that estimates of probable casualties have been grossly exaggerated.

* * * * *

As the air offensive against the railways developed the losses among French and Belgian civilians, though far less than the prior estimates, caused the British War Cabinet distress and anxiety.

Prime Minister to President Roosevelt   7 May 44

The War Cabinet have been much concerned during the last three weeks about the number of Frenchmen killed in the raids on the railway centres in France. We have had numerous Staff meetings with our own officers, and I have discussed the matter with Generals Eisenhower and Bedell Smith. There were and are great differences of opinion in the two Air Forces—not between them, but criss-cross—about the efficacy of the "railway plan" as a short-term project. In the end Eisenhower, Tedder, Bedell Smith, and Portal all declare themselves converted. I am personally by no means convinced that this is the best way to use our Air Forces in the preliminary period, and still think that the German Air Force should be the main target. . . .

2. When this project was first put forward a loss of 80,000 French civilian casualties, including injured, say 20,000 killed, was mentioned.

The War Cabinet could not view this figure without grave dismay on account of the apparently ruthless use of the Air Forces, particularly of the Royal Air Force, on whom the brunt of this kind of work necessarily falls, and the reproaches that would be made upon the inaccuracy of night bombing. The results of the first, say, three-sevenths of the bombing have however shown that the casualties to French civil life are very much less than was expected by the commanders. . . .

3. I am satisfied that all possible care will be taken to minimise this slaughter of friendly civilian life. Nevertheless the War Cabinet share my apprehensions of the bad effect which will be produced upon the French civilian population by these slaughters, all taking place so long before "Overlord" D Day. They may easily bring about a great revulsion in French feeling towards their approaching United States and British liberators. They may leave a legacy of hate behind them. It may well be that the French losses will grow heavier on and after D Day, but in the heat of battle, when British and United States troops will probably be losing at a much higher rate, a new proportion establishes itself in men's minds. It is the intervening period that causes me most anxiety. . . .

4. The Cabinet ask me to invite you to consider the matter from the highest political standpoint and to give us your opinion as a matter between Governments. It must be remembered, on the one hand, that this slaughter is among a friendly people who have committed no crimes against us, and not among the German foe, with all their record of cruelty and ruthlessness. On the other hand, we naturally feel the hazardous nature of Operation "Overlord" and are in deadly earnest about making it a success. I have been careful in stating this case to you to use only the most moderate terms, but I ought to let you know that the War Cabinet is unanimous in its anxiety about these French slaughters, even reduced as they have been, and also in its doubts as to whether almost as good military results could not be produced by other methods. Whatever is settled between us, we are quite willing to share responsibilities with you.

The President replied on the 11th:

I share fully with you your distress at the loss of life among the French population incident to our air preparations for "Overlord".

I share also with you a satisfaction that every possible care is being and will be taken to minimise civilian casualties. No possibility of alleviating adverse French opinion should be overlooked, always provided that there is no reduction of our effectiveness against the enemy at this crucial time.

However regrettable the attendant loss of civilian lives is, I am not prepared to impose from this distance any restriction on military action by the responsible commanders that in their opinion might militate against the success of "Overlord" or cause additional loss of life to our Allied forces of invasion.

This was decisive. Meanwhile the rate of the casualties to French civilians continued to be less than had been feared. The sealing off of the Normandy battlefield from reinforcements by rail may well have been the greatest direct contribution that the bomber forces could make to "Overlord". The price was paid.

★　　★　　★　　★　　★

This chapter has been dominated by technical matters. The British and United States rival themes of air attack by night or day have been shown under the hard test of results. The improvements in our explosives and the intricacies of Radar and all its variants have been presented, I trust, in a form intelligible to the lay reader. But it would be wrong to end without paying our tribute of respect and admiration to the officers and men who fought and died in this fearful battle of the air, the like of which had never before been known, or even with any precision imagined. The moral tests to which the crew of a bomber were subjected reached the extreme limits of human valour and sacrifice. Here chance was carried to its most extreme and violent degree above all else. There was a rule that no one should go on more than thirty raids without a break. But many who entered on their last dozen wild adventures felt that the odds against them were increasing. How can one be lucky thirty times running in a world of averages and machinery? Detective-Constable McSweeney, one of the Scotland Yard officers who looked after me in the early days of the war, was determined to fight in a bomber. I saw him several times during his training and his fighting. One day, gay and jaunty as ever, but with a thoughtful look, he said, "My next will be my twenty-ninth." It was his last. Not only our hearts and admiration but our minds in strong comprehension of these ordeals must go out to these heroic men, whose duty to their country and their cause sustained them in superhuman trials.

I have mentioned facts like "the Americans had sixty of their large Fortress aircraft destroyed out of 291", and on another occasion "out of 795 aircraft dispatched by British Bomber Command against Nuremberg ninety-four did not return". The American Fortresses carried a crew of ten men, and the British night bombers seven. Here we have each time six or seven hundred of these skilled, highly trained warriors lost in an hour. This was indeed ordeal by fire. In the British and American bombing of Germany and Italy during the war the casualties were over a hundred and forty thousand, and in the period with which this chapter deals there were more British and American air-crew casualties than there were killed and wounded in the great operation of crossing the Channel. They never flinched or failed. It is to their devotion that in no small measure we owe our victory. Let us give them our salute.

CHAPTER XXX

THE GREEK TORMENT

*Greek and Jewish Inspiration – Greece under German Occupation –
Formation of E.A.M. and E.L.A.S. – Our Missions to Greece –
Political Designs of the Communist Guerrilla Bands – General Smuts'
Advice – Danger of a Communist Coup d'État – The Question of the
Monarchy – Our Ambassador's Views on the Situation – M. Tsouderos
Tenders His Resignation – King George's Decision to Return to
Cairo – My Telegrams to Mr. Leeper of April 7 and 8 – Mutiny in
the Greek Navy and of the Greek Brigade in Egypt – Our Policy
Towards the Greeks – The Mutinous Brigade Surrounded – Arrival
of the King in Cairo – My Telegram to President Roosevelt of
April 16 – His Most Helpful Message – Climax of the Greek Mutinies
– General Paget's Skilful Methods – Surrender of the Mutineers –
Formation of a New Greek Government under M. Papandreou – My
Statement to the House, May 24.*

*T*HE Greeks rival the Jews in being the most politically-minded
race in the world. No matter how forlorn their circumstances
or how grave the peril to their country, they are always
divided into many parties, with many leaders who fight among
themselves with desperate vigour. It has been well said that
wherever there are three Jews it will be found that there are two
Prime Ministers and one leader of the Opposition. The same is
true of this other famous ancient race, whose stormy and endless
struggle for life stretches back to the fountain springs of human
thought. No two races have set such a mark upon the world.
Both have shown a capacity for survival, in spite of unending
perils and sufferings from external oppressors, matched only by
their own ceaseless feuds, quarrels, and convulsions. The passage
of several thousand years sees no change in their characteristics
and no diminution of their trials or their vitality. They have sur-

vived in spite of all that the world could do against them, and all
they could do against themselves, and each of them from angles so
different have left us the inheritance of their genius and wisdom.
No two cities have counted more with mankind than Athens and
Jerusalem. Their messages in religion, philosophy, and art have
been the main guiding lights of modern faith and culture. Centuries of foreign rule and indescribable, endless oppression leave
them still living, active communities and forces in the modern
world, quarrelling among themselves with insatiable vivacity.
Personally I have always been on the side of both, and believed
in their invincible power to survive internal strife and the world
tides threatening their extinction.

* * * * *

After the withdrawal of the Allies in April 1941 Greece was
occupied by the Axis Powers. The collapse of the Army and the
retirement of the King and his Government into exile revived the
bitter controversies of Greek politics. Both in the country and in
Greek circles abroad there was hard criticism of the monarchy,
which had sanctioned the dictatorship of General Metaxas, and
thereby directly associated itself with the régime which had now
been defeated. When King George II left Crete in May 1941 he
took with him a Government which was mainly Royalist, headed
by M. Tsouderos. Their long journey by Cairo and South Africa
to London provided ample time for political discussion among
Greek communities abroad. The constitution had been suspended
in 1936, and the debate upon the future régime when Greece
would finally be liberated had to be conducted among refugees
on Allied soil.

I had long realised the importance of this issue, and in October
1941 addressed a letter to the Greek Prime Minister, congratulat-
ing him on his first broadcast from London to occupied Greece,
and expressing my gratification that Greece had been declared to
be a democratic country under a constitutional monarchy. The
King himself broadcast in the New Year to his country on the
same lines. If a united nation was to rise out of the war it was
essential that links should be maintained between the exiles and
Greek opinion at home.

During the first winter of Axis occupation Greece suffered
severely from famine, partially relieved by Red Cross shipments,

R*

and also from the exhaustion of the fighting which had ended in the destruction of her Army. But at the time of the surrender arms were hidden in the mountains, and in sporadic fashion, and on a minor scale, resistance to the enemy was planned. In the towns of Central Greece starvation provided plenty of recruits. In April 1942 the body calling itself the National Liberation Front (known by its initials in Greek as E.A.M.), which had come into being in the previous autumn, announced the formation of the People's Liberation Army (E.L.A.S.). Small fighting groups were recruited during the following year, particularly in Central and Northern Greece, while in Epirus and the mountains of the north-west remnants of the Greek Army and local mountaineers gathered round the person of Colonel Napoleon Zervas. The E.A.M.-E.L.A.S. organisation was dominated by a hard core of Communist leaders. The adherents of Zervas, originally Republican in sympathy, became as time passed exclusively anti-Communist. Around these two centres Greek resistance to the Germans gathered. Neither of them had any direct contact with the Greek Government in London, nor any sympathy for its position.

On the eve of Alamein we decided to attack the German supply lines leading down through Greece to the Piræus, the port of Athens and an important base on the German route to North Africa. In the autumn of 1942 the first British Military Mission, under Lieut.-Colonel Myers, was accordingly dropped by parachute into Greece and made contact with the guerrillas. With their aid a vital viaduct on the main Athens railway line was destroyed. Simultaneously brilliant and daring sabotage operations were carried out by Greek agents against Axis shipping in the Piræus. The success of these operations encouraged Middle East Headquarters to send more British parties with supplies of explosives and arms. Thus direct contact with occupied Greece was established.

During the summer of 1943 the British missions were strengthened. We had an added motive for stimulating activities in this area as a cover for our pending operations in Sicily. Special efforts were made to convince the enemy that, following on their defeat in Tunisia, the Allies were planning a major landing on Greek soil. Combined Anglo-Greek parties blew another railway bridge on the main Athens line, and other sabotage operations were successful. The result was that two German divisions were moved into Greece which might have been used in Sicily. This however was the last direct military contribution which the Greek guerrillas made to the war, and henceforward the scene was dominated by the struggle to gain political power at the end of hostilities.

Political quarrels hampered guerrilla warfare, and we soon found ourselves in a complicated and disagreeable situation. It was becoming clear that there were three divergent elements: E.L.A.S., now numbering 20,000 men, and predominantly under Communist control; the Zervas bands, known as E.D.E.S., totalling 5,000; and the Royalist politicians, grouped in Cairo or in London round the King, to whom we had a special obligation as the head of a State which had fought as our Ally in 1941. All now thought that the Allies would probably win the war, and the struggle among them for political power began in earnest, to the advantage of the common foe. In March 1943 a group of prominent politicians in Athens signed a manifesto enjoining the King not to return after the war until a plebiscite had been held. It was important that the King should make clear where he stood. On July 4 he therefore made a conciliatory broadcast to the Greek people promising that a General Election would be held as soon as the country was liberated and that the Greek Government abroad would resign when it arrived in Athens in order that a broadly based Administration could be formed. But opinion inside Greece sought more immediate action. Shortly afterwards a minor mutiny took place in the small Greek forces which we had assembled in the Middle East, where E.A.M. propaganda was now spreading. In August a delegation of six leaders from the main resistance groups in Greece was brought to Cairo, and they too urged that a plebiscite should be held before the King returned, and that three places in the exiled Government should be held by politicians inside Greece. Neither the King nor his Prime Minister would agree.

While I was in Quebec I had received the following message from King George about these developments.

King of Greece (Cairo) to Prime Minister and President   19 Aug 43
Roosevelt

On July 4 I declared to my people that after their liberation they will be invited to determine by means of free election the form of their Government.

I am now suddenly faced by the most curious situation, of the unexpected arrival of certain individuals from Greece who are supposed to represent various guerrilla bands; in addition, a representative of certain old political parties, who wish to press me to declare that I should only return after a plebiscite which would decide the form of the future régime. . . . In these circumstances I would much appreciate your advice as to the policy which would at this time best serve the cause of Greece and the United Nations.

My present personal inclination is to continue the policy agreed between us before I left England. I feel very strongly that I should return to Greece with my troops, even if I left my country after a short period to work for its national interests among our Allies, should subsequent developments make it politic for me to do so.

I had minuted on this:

Prime Minister to Foreign Secretary   19 Aug 43
If substantial British forces take part in the liberation of Greece the King should go back with the Anglo-Greek Army. This is much the more probable alternative. If however the Greeks are strong enough to drive out the Germans themselves we shall have a good deal less to say in the matter. It follows that the King should demand equal Royalist representation with the Republicans now proposed. In any case he would make a great mistake to agree in any way to remain outside Greece while the fighting for the liberation is going on and while conditions preclude the holding of a peaceful plebiscite.

Smuts, who followed Greek fortunes attentively, also sent a prescient comment.

General Smuts to Prime Minister   20 Aug 43
There appears to be strong suspicion that British Intelligence agents who brought Greek Patriots and other party representatives to Cairo are anti-Royalist, and that Patriot representatives even have Communist leanings. King George has always been strongly pro-Ally, and sacrificed much for Allied cause, and we have every good reason to stand by him in this crisis. It seems to me sound policy that you should once more make it quite clear to the Greek Government that the United Kingdom Government stands by the King, at least until such time as Greek people, under proper conditions of public tranquillity, are able to decide on their future régime. A plebiscite or General Election on the régime immediately on the Allied occupation of Greece should be ruled out as likely to lead to civil strife, if not to civil war, in the existing bitterness of feeling. Allied administration under military occupation should be continued until public opinion

has settled down and safe conditions of public tranquillity have been established. During this interim period of Allied administration King George and Royal Family might well return to Greece to lend their moral support and authority to the Allied administration.

I very much fear that, in the inflamed conditions of public feeling, not only in Greece but also in other Balkan countries, chaos may ensue after the Allied occupation unless a strong hand is kept on the local situation. With politics let loose among those peoples we may have a wave of disorder and wholesale Communism set going all over those parts of Europe. This may even be the danger in Italy, but certainly in Greece and the Balkans. It should therefore be made plain at this stage that we mean to maintain public order and authority under Allied control until the situation is safe for local self-determination. The Greek situation brings matters to a head, and you may now consider it proper to raise this matter with the President, as a very important question of future policy is involved. The Bolshevisation of a broken and ruined Europe remains a definite possibility, to be guarded against by supply of food and work and interim Allied control.

$$\star \quad \star \quad \star \quad \star \quad \star$$

The Italian surrender in September 1943 affected the whole balance of forces in Greece. E.L.A.S. was able to acquire most of the Italian equipment, including the weapons of an entire division, and thus gained military supremacy. The danger of a Communist *coup d'état* in the event of German withdrawal, which now became a practical possibility, needed careful attention. On September 29 I sent a minute to the Chiefs of Staff:

Prime Minister to General Ismay, for C.O.S. Committee　　29 Sept 43
I am in full agreement with the Foreign Secretary in this essentially political question. Should the Germans evacuate Greece we must certainly be able to send 5,000 British troops with armoured cars and Bren gun carriers into Athens. They need have no transport or artillery. The Greek troops in Egypt would accompany them. Their duty would be to give support at the centre to the restored lawful Greek Government. The Greeks would not know how many were coming behind them. There may be some bickering between the Greek guerrilla bands, but great respect will be paid to the British, more especially as the saving of the country from famine depends entirely on our exertions in the early months of liberation. The troops need not be organised to contend with more than rioting in the capital or incursion into the capital from the countryside. . . .

Once a stable Government is set up we should take our departure.

This was the first suggestion that we might be forced to intervene in Greek internal affairs at the moment of liberation.

The pace of events now increased as E.L.A.S. developed its plans to take over political power as soon as the Germans withdrew and before an ordered constitutional Government could be established. During the winter there was little activity against the enemy. In October E.L.A.S. forces attacked E.D.E.S. (Zervas), and the British Headquarters in Cairo suspended all shipments of arms to the former. Every effort was made by our missions on the spot to limit and bring to an end the civil war which had now broken out in the ruined and occupied country.

*　　*　　*　　*　　*

The decisions of the Conferences in Cairo and in Teheran indirectly affected the position in Greece. There would never be a major Allied landing there, nor was it likely that any considerable British forces would follow a German retreat. The arrangements to prevent anarchy had therefore to be considered. The one figure presented to us as above party rancour was Damaskinos, Archbishop of Athens. While in Cairo Mr. Eden had impressed on the King the advantages of a temporary Regency. At the same time we hoped by sending the Greek Brigade in the Middle East to fight in Italy to raise the prestige of the exiled Government, and also to have loyal troops to send into Western Greece if need be.

The King would not agree to a Regency and returned to London. By now E.A.M., with its military component E.L.A.S., had formed a State within a State in the mountains of Central and Northern Greece. In February 1944 British officers succeeded in establishing an uneasy truce between E.L.A.S. and E.D.E.S. But the Soviet armies were now on the borders of Roumania. The chances of a German evacuation of the Balkans increased, and with them the possibilities of a return of the Royal Government, with British support. Assuming that both these events might take place in April, the E.A.M. leaders decided to act.

On March 26 a Political Committee of National Liberation was set up in the mountains, and the news broadcast to the world. This was a direct challenge to the future authority of the Tsouderos Government. An alternative Communist-controlled Administration was thus formed as a rallying-point for all Greeks.

This was the signal for trouble in the Greek armed forces in the Middle East and in Greek Government circles abroad. On March 31 a group of officers from the Army, Navy, and Air Force called on Tsouderos in Cairo to demand his resignation. Matters had now come to a head, but the Greek King in London did not appreciate their urgency. Mr. Leeper, our Ambassador to the Greek Government located in Cairo, telegraphed on April 6: "I feel I must express myself with some bluntness. The King of Greece is playing with fire. He is endangering not only the interests of the monarchy but those of his country by not realising in time the rapid trend of events. . . . E.A.M. have realised the danger to them of a united front between politicians in Athens and the Greek Government in Cairo. They have realised that the outcome of an agreement would be the reinforcement of the Government here and the end of their experiment to set up a separate Government in the mountains. They have therefore used the interval to strike at the Greek Government by subverting the Greek forces. Their agitation has had some success, and within the next few days it may have more." "M. Tsouderos," wrote the Ambassador, "finds himself in a dilemma. He had secured a good basis of collaboration with his colleagues as a result of messages of support from the Archbishop and politicians in Athens, but this agreement was based on his being able to induce the King to sign a Constitutional Act appointing the Archbishop as Regent. Some weeks have now passed, during which time M. Tsouderos has received no final reply from the King, but merely a preliminary view from him of a negative character. This he concealed from his colleagues in order to avoid an explosion. . . . The situation could have been held but for recent E.A.M. agitation in the Army."

Later in the day M. Tsouderos resigned, and recommended M. Venizelos, the Minister of Marine in his Government, as his successor. On April 4 disorders broke out in the Greek Army, the 1st Brigade of which I was hoping could take part in the Italian campaign. On the 5th the office of the Greek Provost-Marshal in Cairo was occupied by a hundred mutineers, who had to be surrounded by British troops and Egyptian police and were removed without trouble in lorries to an isolation camp. At Alexandria a leader of the Greek seamen's union had barricaded himself in his house with thirty supporters, and was defying the police. Five ships of the Royal Hellenic Navy declared themselves in favour of a republic and demanded the resignation of every member of the existing Government. All the members of the Greek Government tendered their resignations to the King, but agreed to remain in office pending acceptance.

*   *   *   *   *

I was at this time in charge of the Foreign Office, owing to Mr. Eden's absence. I thus had all the threads directly in my hands.

I had sent the following to the Supreme Allied Commander in the Mediterranean:

Prime Minister to General Wilson; repeated to General   5 Apr 44
Alexander

It is now more than three months since we agreed that a Greek Brigade, if necessary without its vehicular equipment, should be sent from Egypt to Italy to take part in the Allied offensive. I am told that one company has already got there, and that the others will be there during the month. Why is there all this delay and difficulty in moving this handful of men? They are very liable in Egypt to be contaminated by revolutionary and Communist elements there. Satan finds some mischief still for idle hands to do. Now do please try to get them shipped off out of Egypt as soon as possible and assembled in some suitable town in Southern Italy. I feel this small matter, which has large political significance, ought not to have hung fire so long.

I also sent the following message to M. Tsouderos on April 7:

I was much shocked to hear of your resignation, which seems to leave Greece forlorn at a moment of peril for her national life. The King, whom I have just seen, tells me he has not accepted your resignation. He is coming out to Alexandria next week. Surely you can await his arrival.

The situation in the Greek Army and Navy had by now further deteriorated, and Venizelos announced that he could no longer accept office. M. Tsouderos replied on April 7: "I shall remain at my post as the laws of Greece require and as you desire until this present crisis has found lawful solution. If the King waits until he returns to Egypt before he resolves this crisis I fear that by that time there may be no longer any opportunity of resolving it."

Mr. Leeper telegraphed to the Foreign Office on April 7:

"What is happening here among the Greeks is nothing less than a revolution. It is under such conditions that a makeshift Greek Government in exile, suffering from all the weakness which that implies, has been trying to cope with the situation. It has failed completely, but has been handicapped by being able to make no legal change without the sanction of the King at a distance. . . ."

Our Ambassador hoped however that the situation could be settled in Cairo without the King's presence. "The King of Greece's return here at present would certainly provoke fresh trouble. Tsouderos and all his colleagues are strongly of this opinion. He would find himself isolated and unable to do anything, and would be a grave embarrassment to us." He asked the Foreign Office to do everything in their power to stop his return. "In the circumstances in which we are living here at the moment the advice of people on the spot should, I submit, be accepted. My views are shared by everybody here."

* * * * *

The King of Greece came to luncheon with me in London on this day. I showed him the Ambassador's telegram without comment. He said he would go to Cairo at once. I thought he was quite right.

Prime Minister to Mr. Leeper   7 Apr 44

I have discussed the situation with the King. He is resolved to return to Cairo, leaving by air Sunday evening, and notwithstanding your telegram (which I have shown the King) I consider he is right to do so. If, as you say, what is happening in Cairo is a Greek revolution, I cannot advise him to stay away and allow the issue to be decided in his absence. . . . All local Greek politicians and agitators should at the same time be warned that we shall not hesitate to take adequate measures of security to prevent agitation and demonstrations which might threaten law and order in Egypt and the position and authority of the King and the Greek Government. . . . You should inform M. Tsouderos that I count on him to remain at his post until the present crisis has found a lawful solution. . . .

This is an occasion for you to show those qualities of imperturbability and command which are associated with the British Diplomatic Service.

And the next day I added:

Prime Minister to Mr. Leeper   8 Apr 44

Weather permitting, the King will leave Sunday night. Meanwhile it is M. Tsouderos's duty to stand to his post. Of course if he can get M. Sophocles Venizelos to stay with him all the better. When the King arrives the British Security Service must ensure his personal safety. He may require a few days to make up his mind, and must on no account be hustled. I am asking the military commanders to move the Greek Brigade as fast as possible to Italy. They will of course weed out recalcitrant elements. In the same way the Admiral is expected to preserve the discipline of all ships under his command, using no more force than is necessary.

For you yourself there is a great opportunity. You should stick to the line I have marked out and not be worried about the consequences. You speak of living on the lid of a volcano. Wherever else do you expect to live in times like these? Please however be careful to follow very exactly the instructions you are receiving from me, namely, first in priority, order and discipline to be maintained in the armed forces; secondly, the safety of the King's person to be ensured; thirdly, every effort to be made to induce Tsouderos to hold office till the King returns and has had time to look around; fourthly, try to get Venizelos to remain with Tsouderos; fifthly, celebrate Easter Sunday in a manner pious and becoming.

*   *   *   *   *

On April 8 a Greek destroyer refused to obey orders to proceed to sea unless a Government was formed which would include E.A.M. representatives. The mutinous Greek Brigade had taken up defensive positions round their camp, and trouble was expected in the small Greek Air Force units as well. I was forced to give up my hopes of getting the Greek Brigade sent to Italy. Later I telegraphed to General Paget, who commanded the British forces in Egypt:

Prime Minister to General Paget   8 Apr 44

A mutinous brigade threatening its officers should certainly be surrounded and forced to surrender by stoppage of all supplies. Why do you leave out water? Will this not bring the desired result quicker? Obviously these troops should be disarmed. I agree that the hope of getting them to Italy may have to be abandoned. Keep me fully informed of plans for disarming. We cannot tolerate political revolutions carried out by foreign military formations for which we are ultimately responsible. In all cases large numbers of British troops should be used so as to overawe, and thus minimise bloodshed.

I also sent Mr. Leeper a full statement of our policy for use with the Greeks.

9 Apr 44

Our relations are definitely established with the lawfully constituted Greek Government headed by the King, who is the ally of Britain and cannot be discarded to suit a momentary surge of appetite among ambitious *émigré* nonentities. Neither can Greece find constitutional expression in particular sets of guerrillas, in many cases indistinguishable from banditti, who are masquerading as the saviours of their country while living on the local villagers. If necessary I shall denounce these elements and tendencies publicly in order to emphasise the love Great Britain has for Greece, whose sufferings she shared in a small measure, being, alas, not then armed as we are now. Our only desire and interest is to see Greece a glorious, free nation in the Eastern Mediterranean, the honoured friend and ally of the victorious Powers. Let all therefore work for this objective, and make it quite clear that any failure in good conduct will not be overlooked.

I had been working very hard to arrange the movement of the Greek Brigade to Italy. Here they might still take part in the entry into Rome which is to be expected during the summer. This Brigade, the 1st Greek Brigade, representatives of the army which had beaten back the Italian invader and were only felled by the treacherous and brutal intervention of the German hordes, had and still has the chance of raising the name of Greece high in the world. It is a lamentable fact that they should have signalised this opportunity by an undignified, even squalid, exhibition of indiscipline, which many will attribute to an unworthy fear of being sent to the front.

In the same way the Greek Navy, which is full of daring seamen and is playing a worthy part upholding its country's good name, should not suddenly have tried to meddle with politics and presume to dictate a constitution to the Greek people. I believe that both of these two forces can be brought back to a high sense of national honour and duty if courageous leadership is forthcoming, backed by overwhelming force in reserve.

All the time I have been planning to place Greece back high in the councils of the victorious nations. Witness how we have included them in the Italian Advisory Council and tried to send a brigade to take part in the impending victories in Italy. Greeks who are in safety in Egypt under our protection, equipped with our vessels or armed with our weapons or otherwise in security under the military authority of the British Commander-in-Chief Middle East, will place themselves in an abject and shameful position before all history if they allow their domestic feuds to mar their performance of the solemn duties to their country of which they have become the heirs. They may easily, by selfish, excitable behaviour, reduce Greece to a country without expression either at home or abroad, and their names will be stained as long as history is written.

The King is the servant of his people. He makes no claim to rule them. He submits himself freely to the judgment of the people as soon as normal conditions are restored. He places himself and his Royal House entirely at the disposition of the Greek nation. Once the German invader has been driven out Greece can be a republic or a monarchy, entirely as the people wish. Why then cannot the Greeks keep their hatreds for the common enemy, who has wrought them such cruel injuries and would obliterate them as a free people, were it not for the resolute exertions of the Great Allies?

* * * * *

General Paget now reported to me that as the 1st Greek Brigade had mutinied against its officers and refused to hand in its arms under specific orders from him he proposed to take direct action to carry out such orders. I telegraphed on April 9: "These small-scale events are developing rapidly, and I fully concur with the action you are taking. . . . *You will have achieved success if you bring the Brigade under control without bloodshed. But brought under control it must be. Count on my support.*"

The Greek Brigade was now surrounded by superior British forces. Its strength was 4,500 men, with over fifty guns, which were all deployed in defensive positions against us. On April 12 I sent further directions to Mr. Leeper and all others concerned: "There can be no question of making terms with mutineers about political matters. They must return to their duty unconditionally. They must submit to be disarmed unconditionally. It would be a great pity to give any assurances about the non-punishment of ringleaders. . . . The question of clemency would rest with the King. Let me know how this stands before taking any decisive action."

And further:

Prime Minister to Mr. Leeper and all Principals concerned   14 Apr 44
(*Cairo*)

Surely you should let lack of supplies work its part both in the camp and the harbour before resorting to firing. You should use the weapon of blockade to the full and defend yourselves against attempts to break out. Do not worry too much about the external effects. Do not show yourself over-eager to parley. Simply keep them rounded up by artillery and superior force and let hunger play its part. On no account accept any assistance from American or Russian sources, otherwise than as specially enjoined by me. You have ample force at your disposal and plenty of time. It is much more important that the [mutineers] should be reduced to proper discipline than that any particular Greek Government should be set up. It would even be harmful if a brigade and a flotilla had been permitted to meddle in political issues.

My latest information reports that the situation of the Greek Brigade shows signs of improving and that they have finished their rations. You should take full advantage of these tendencies and keep me informed.

And the next day:

Prime Minister to Mr. Leeper   15 Apr 44
Do not be influenced by possible anti-British sentiment among the local Greeks. It would be a great mistake to end this grave business up in a pleasant kiss all round. That might come later as an act of clemency from the King and his new Government. We have got to get these men into our hands disarmed, without conditions, and I trust without bloodshed.

* * * * *

Meanwhile the King had arrived in Cairo, and on April 12 had issued a proclamation stating that a representative Government composed largely of Greeks from within Greece would be formed. The next day Venizelos took office in succession to Tsouderos, and steps were taken in secret to bring out representatives from metropolitan Greece.

I now reported the whole position to the President, who was sympathetic to my view and to King George of Greece.

Prime Minister to President Roosevelt   16 Apr 44
The outbreak in the Greek Army and Navy followed closely on the establishment in the mountains of Greece of the Political Committee sponsored by E.A.M., and there is little doubt that the extremist elements who have long been working to subvert the allegiance of the Greek forces to their legitimate King and Government seized on this as a heaven-sent opportunity for open and violent action. The dissident elements are undoubtedly opposed to the King and in favour of a republic, but throughout the disturbances there have been almost no direct attacks on the King's personal position, and the only specific demand put forward is that the Greek Government should take

immediate and effective steps to recognise and associate with themselves the Political Committee in Greece.

This crisis came at a particularly unfortunate moment, since M. Tsouderos had already sent an invitation to a number of moderate politicians in Athens urging them to come to Cairo to join the Government. He had also invited representatives of E.A.M., the Communist-controlled organisation which has created and now dominates the Political Committee. Tsouderos was thus doing everything in his power to create a truly representative Greek Government.

In this programme he had the support of his colleagues, and they appear to have had no hand in provoking the disturbances in the Greek forces. But they were extremely jealous of Tsouderos's position, and used the trouble in the Greek Army, which was at first on a small scale, to get rid of him. Feeling that he had lost control of the situation, Tsouderos resigned and proposed Venizelos for the Premiership. The trouble in the Greek Army rapidly spread to the Navy, and assumed the proportions of a full-scale mutiny in both forces. The politicians in Cairo realised that the matter had gone beyond one of personal rivalries or ambitions, and their only thought was to find some candidate for the Premiership sufficiently notorious for his Left Wing views to be acceptable to the mutinous elements in the forces.

The King of Greece was reluctant to accept a new Government whose composition was in effect dictated by the mutineers. He considered that order in the Greek armed forces must be restored before any lawful reconstruction of the Government could be undertaken. I entirely agreed with him, and instructed our Ambassador to the Greek Government to do his utmost to induce the Greek Ministers to remain at their posts until the King could get back to Cairo and take stock of the situation. This, I am glad to say, they agreed to do. I also gave instructions to the military authorities in the Middle East to deal firmly with indiscipline in the Greece forces under their command. Order in the Greek Army and Navy has not been completely re-established, but the dissident elements are being isolated, and once the ringleaders are under arrest the mutiny should rapidly subside.

The King of Greece has now reached Cairo, and, after studying the position for himself, has formed a Government under M. Venizelos.

The President sent me the following most helpful message:

President Roosevelt to Prime Minister   18 Apr 44

Thank you for the information regarding recent difficulties encountered in Greek participation in our Allied effort.

I join with you in a hope that your line of action toward the problem may succeed in bringing the Greeks back into the Allied camp and to a participation against the barbarians that will be worthy of traditions established by the heroes of Greek history. Frankly, as one whose family and who personally has contributed by personal help to Greek independence for over a century, I am unhappy over the present situation, and hope that Greeks everywhere will set aside pettiness and regain their sense of proportion. Let every Greek think of their glorious past and show a personal unselfishness which is so necessary now. You can quote me if you want to in the above sense.

Prime Minister to President Roosevelt   18 Apr 44
Thank you so much. I have told our people to make use of your message to the King and his new Ministers, and to read it to the mutinous brigade and recalcitrant ships. It may have a most salutary effect.

* * * * *

As matters reached a climax at Alexandria I telegraphed to the Naval Commander-in-Chief:

                                                       17 Apr 44
You should leave the senior member of the *Averoff* * in no doubt that his guarantee that the use of firearms will be avoided will not be reciprocated by us. We shall fire on mutineers whenever it is necessary. No officers or sailors of the Greek Navy have the slightest right to meddle in the formation of the new Government. Their duty is to obey the orders they receive from the Greek Government recognised by the Great Allies.

The mutiny in the Greek Brigade was also approaching a crisis.

Prime Minister to General Paget   22 Apr 44
If you find it necessary to open fire on the mutineers' camp you should consider whether you might not start with a few ranging shots directed on their batteries which are aiming at you. If they make no reply, after an appropriate interval let them have a stiffer dose, and at the same time tell them the weight of fire which you are ready to direct on them if they persist. We are prepared to use the utmost force, but let us avoid slaughter if possible. It is proposed that the onus should lie to the account of the British rather than of the slender, tottering Greek Government.

I received by return the following reply:

General Paget to Prime Minister   23 Apr 44
My plan is in line with your suggestions. In order to get close observation of their camp we must first capture two Greek posts on

* Greek cruiser.

high ground. This will be done, by infantry only, just before dawn. When it is light we will lay a smoke-screen over their camp for ten minutes. Then there will be a pause for the smoke to clear away, after which leaflets will be dropped. They will state that there will be a further smoke-screen for half an hour, under cover of which all who wish should leave camp and come over to our lines. If mutineers are still holding out after this a few shells will be fired at one of their batteries, followed by a further pause to allow for surrender. We shall continue this process until all their guns are knocked out. If the mutineers still will not surrender it will be necessary to make an infantry assault on the camp under covering fire from artillery and tanks; but tanks will be used in sniping rôle and will not advance into the camp, as the mutineers are known to be well supplied with anti-tank weapons. They are undoubtedly now very short of food, but they have managed to get some from the local Arabs. It has not proved possible to invest the camp closely enough to stop this.

On the evening of the same day the mutinous Greek ships were boarded by loyal Greek sailors, and with about fifty casualties the mutineers were collected and sent ashore. General Paget now hoped to obtain the surrender of the Greek Brigade by parley and without bloodshed. The handling of the affair was completely successful, and I was able to inform the President the next day that British troops had occupied key positions on the ridge overlooking the Greek camp after slight opposition. There were no Greek casualties, but one British officer was killed. The Greek Brigade surrendered and laid down its arms, and was evacuated to a prisoner-of-war cage, where the ringleaders were arrested. The naval mutineers had surrendered unconditionally twenty-four hours earlier.

To General Paget I said: "I congratulate you on the satisfactory outcome of your firm and well-devised action."

The President shared my relief.

President Roosevelt to Prime Minister   26 Apr 44

I am very pleased indeed by your success in handling the Greek naval and military mutiny. I will hope for a similar success in your efforts with the Egyptian political problem. Our prospects of assisting "Overlord" by vigorous action in Italy do look much better with a fixed date upon which we may expect all our pressure against the enemy. In view of our postponement of "Anvil" a real success in Italy now seems essential.

Everything goes well here in my vacation residence. The doctor agrees with me that I am better.

* * * * *

We had also kept the Russians informed of these events, both by messages to Molotov and through the Soviet Embassy in Cairo. The Soviet Government confined itself to criticism of our actions, and when on May 5 a formal request to Russia for co-operation in Greek affairs was made in Moscow the reply was that it would be improper to join in any public pronouncement on political matters in Greece.

* * * * *

With the end of the mutiny the question of the formation of a Greek Government became acute. It was not felt that Venizelos was suitable for this task, and the leader of the Greek Social Democratic Party, Papandreou, who had been specially brought out of Greece, took office on April 26. The following day he issued a proclamation which was to form the agenda for a conference of all parties, including leaders from the Greek mountains. These delegates met at a mountain resort in the Lebanon on May 17, where it was agreed, after a fierce debate lasting three days, to set up an Administration in Cairo in which all groups would be represented under the Premiership of Papandreou, while in the mountains of Greece a united military organisation would continue to struggle against the Germans. This arrangement held promise for the future.

On May 24 came the announcement of the new Greek Government. I reported these events to the House of Commons on the same day.

After prolonged discussion complete unity was reached at the Lebanon conference, and all parties will be represented in the new Government, which will devote itself to what is after all the only purpose worthy of consideration, namely, the formation of a national Army in which all the guerrilla bands will be incorporated, and the driving, with this Army, of the enemy from the country, or, better still, destroying him where he stands.

On Monday there was published in the newspapers the very agreeable letter which I received from the leaders of the [Greek] Communists and the extreme Left Wing party. There is published to-day in the papers the letter I have received from M. Papandreou expressing the hopes which he has for the future of his Government, and thanks for the assistance we have given in getting round these troubles—what I call the diseases of defeat, which Greece has now a chance of shaking off. I believe that the present situation—I hope and pray that it may be so—indicates that a new and fair start will come to Greece in her struggle to cleanse her native soil from the foreign invader. I have therefore to report to the House that a very marked and beneficial change has occurred in the situation in Greece, which is more than I could say when I last spoke upon this subject.

Thus this dangerous episode, which, although on a small scale compared with the vast movement of the war, might have been the cause of endless discussions detrimental to our affairs, came to a satisfactory conclusion. I have recorded it in detail because of the very direct personal responsibility which I assumed. I circulated all my telegrams to the War Cabinet as they were sent, and my colleagues in no way hampered my freedom of action. It was certainly an achievement that our military commanders were able by overwhelming force, firmness, and patience to quell these political mutinies among such fiery troops without bloodshed, except for the loss of a single British officer, Major J. R. Copeland, of the 2nd Battalion Rifle Brigade, who certainly did not die in vain.

The difficulties and struggles which lay before us all in this nerve-centre of Europe and the world will be recounted in their proper place. I consider however that, taken by and large, my policy was vindicated by events; and this is true not only of the period of the war, but up to the present time of writing.

CHAPTER XXXI

BURMA AND BEYOND

A Retrospect – The United States and Australian Advance in the Pacific – Allied Ascendancy on the Sea and in the Air – A Year of Immense Progress Against Japan – The American Air-lift over "the Hump" – Our Divergence of View – The President's Telegram of February 25 – Successful Opening of the Burma Campaign of 1944 – Japanese Plan to Invade India – Wingate's Famous Chindits Operation – He is Killed – The Japanese Attack on Imphal Begins – Defence of Kohima – The Climax of the Battle – All Depends on the Air – General Stilwell's Success at Myitkyina – The Struggle Around Imphal – Defeat of the Japanese Bid for India.

T HE reader must now be asked to hark back nearly a year in order that a summary may be presented to him of the war against Japan in the Pacific, which was at this time the main effort of the United States and of the Commonwealth of Australia.

By the latter half of 1943 the Japanese had lost the eastern end of New Guinea. Before he could attack the Philippines General MacArthur had first to reoccupy all its northern shore. Part of the 41st U.S. Division worked their way towards Salamaua, and at the end of June other troops landed near it from the sea. They were joined by the 3rd Australian Division from Wau, and began their attack on Salamaua. It was purposely deliberate, so as to draw reinforcements from Lae, the next major objective. The attack on Lae began on September 4, 1943, when the 9th Australian Division, of Alamein fame, landed on the coast ten miles east of the town. Next day American parachutists dropped on Nadzap, in the Markham valley, and, with the help of Australian pioneers, rapidly made an airfield. The 7th Australian Division flew in, and immediately advanced. Attacked from two sides, Lae was taken on September 16. Salamaua had fallen a few days before, and Finschhafen fell on October 2. All were fiercely defended. The Markham valley, running north-west from Lae, had many potential airfields, and the 7th Australian Division, swift to exploit success, occupied its length in a series of airborne assaults. All the operations were well conceived and skilfully executed, and the co-operation of all three fighting Services was brought to a high pitch.

The Australian capture of Finschhafen was followed by fierce Japanese counter-attacks, and there was much fighting during the last fortnight of October. By mid-November the 5th Australian Division was moving forward through the mountains of the Huon peninsula, overcoming a series of strongly held positions, while the 9th Australian Division was clearing the heights overlooking the Markham valley. Part of the 32nd U.S. Division made an amphibious landing at Saidor early in January 1944, where they were joined on February 11 by the 5th Australian Division. It had taken five months to clear the Huon peninsula. Out of 12,000 Japanese who had been engaged there not more than 4,200 survived.

In April General MacArthur made an amphibious leap of four hundred miles. He by-passed 50,000 Japanese around Wewak, and landed an American division at Aitape and two more near Hollandia. The Japanese Air Force had been thoroughly pounded, and 380 machines were found destroyed. Allied superiority by sea and air was henceforward so decisive that MacArthur could select whatever objectives suited him best and leave behind him large pockets of Japanese to be dealt with later. His final bound was to Biak Island, where the 41st U.S. Division had a fierce struggle against an enemy garrison nearly ten thousand strong. A convoy of a dozen Japanese warships was destroyed or crippled by air attack as they tried to bring reinforcements, and the island was effectively in American possession before the end of June 1944. This marked the end of the two-year struggle in New Guinea, where the stubborn resistance of the enemy, the physical difficulties of the country, the ravages of disease, and the absence of communications made the campaign as arduous as any in history.

* * * * *

Farther east, at the beginning of July 1943, and simultaneously with General MacArthur's attack on Salamaua, Admiral Halsey

NEW GUINEA

0   100   200   300   400   500 MILES

had struck in New Georgia. After several weeks of severe fighting both this and the adjacent islands were won. Air fighting again dominated the scene, and the ascendancy of the American airmen soon proved decisive. Japanese losses in the air now exceeded those of the Americans by four or five to one.

In July and August a series of naval actions gave the Americans command of the sea. By September the backbone of Japanese resistance had been broken, and although severe fighting continued at Bougainville and other islands the campaign in the Solomons was ended by December 1943. Such positions as remained in enemy hands had been neutralised and could now be safely by-passed and left to wilt.

Rabaul itself, in New Britain, became the next centre of attack. During November and December it was heavily and repeatedly struck by Allied air forces, and in the last days of 1943 General MacArthur's amphibious forces landed on the western extremity of New Britain at Cape Gloucester. It was now decided to by-pass Rabaul. An alternative base was therefore needed to sustain the advance to the Philippines, and this was within MacArthur's grasp at Manus Island, in the Admiralty Group. In February 1944 the first stage of this envelopment was accomplished by the seizure of Green Island, 120 miles east of Rabaul. This was followed by the brilliant capture of the whole Admiralty Group, to the westward. In March Emirau Island, immediately to the north, was taken by Admiral Halsey, and the isolation of Rabaul was complete. The air and sea surrounding these islands thus passed entirely under American control.

* * * * *

Meanwhile the main American maritime forces, under Admiral Nimitz, began to concentrate for his drive through the island groups near the equator, which were the outposts defending the Japanese fleet base at Truk, in the Carolines. The most easterly of these groups, the Gilberts, seized from the British in 1941, was chosen for the first attack. In October 1943 Admiral Spruance, who had gained fame at Midway, was appointed to command the Central Pacific force. In November, while Halsey was attacking Bougainville, Spruance struck at Tarawa, in the Gilberts. The island was strongly fortified, and was held by about 3,500 Japanese troops. The landing by the 2nd Marine Division was bitterly contested, in spite of heavy preliminary air attacks. After four fierce days, in which casualties were severe, the island was captured.

With Tarawa eliminated the way was clear for attack on the Marshall Group, to the north and west of the Gilberts. In February 1944 they were the object of amphibious operations on the greatest scale yet attempted in the Pacific, and by the end of the month the Americans were victorious. Without pause Spruance began the next phase of his advance, the softening by air attack of Japanese defences in the Carolines and Marianas. The flexibility of seaborne attack in an ocean area is the most remarkable feature of these operations. While we in Europe were making our final preparations for "Overlord" with immense concentration of force in the narrow waters of the Channel, Spruance's carriers were ranging over huge areas, striking at islands in the Marianas, the Palau group, and the Carolines, deep within the Japanese defensive perimeter, and at the same time helping MacArthur in his attack on Hollandia. On the eve of "Overlord" Japan's strength was everywhere on the wane; her defence system in the Central Pacific had been breached at many points and was ripe for disruption.

Summing up these operations in the South-West Pacific, General Marshall could report that in a little over twelve months the Allies had "pushed 1,300 miles closer to the heart of the Japanese Empire, cutting off more than 135,000 enemy troops beyond hope of rescue".

✴   ✴   ✴   ✴   ✴

The curtain must now rise on a widely different scene in South-East Asia. For more than eighteen months the Japanese had been masters of a vast defensive arc covering their early conquests. This stretched from the jungle-covered mountains of Northern and Western Burma, where our British and Indian troops were at close grips with them, across the sea to the Andamans and the great Dutch dependencies of Sumatra and Java, and thence in an easterly bend along the string of lesser islands to New Guinea.

The Americans had established a bomber force in China which was doing good work against the enemy's sea communications between the mainland and the Philippines. They wanted to extend this effort by basing long-range aircraft in China to attack

Japan itself. The Burma Road was cut, and they were carrying all supplies for them and the Chinese armies by air over the southern spurs of the Himalayas, which they called "the Hump". This was a stupendous task. I had always advocated air aid to China and the improvement of the air route and protection of the airfields, but I hoped this might be done by forces essentially airborne and air-sustained on the Wingate model, but on a larger scale. The American wish to succour China not only by an ever-increasing air-lift, but also by land, led to heavy demands upon Britain and the Indian Empire. They pressed as a matter of the highest urgency and importance the making of a motor road from the existing roadhead at Ledo through five hundred miles of jungles and mountains into Chinese territory. Only one metre-gauge, single-line railway ran through Assam to Ledo. It was already in constant use for many other needs, including the supply of the troops who held the frontier positions; but in order to build the road to China the Americans wanted us to reconquer Northern Burma first and quickly.

Certainly we favoured keeping China in the war and operating air forces from her territory, but a sense of proportion and the study of alternatives were needed. I disliked intensely the prospect of a large-scale campaign in Northern Burma. One could not choose a worse place for fighting the Japanese. Making a road from Ledo to China was also an immense, laborious task, unlikely to be finished until the need for it had passed. Even if it were done in time to replenish the Chinese armies while they were still engaged it would make little difference to their fighting capacity. The need to strengthen the American air bases in China would also, in our view, diminish as Allied advances in the Pacific and from Australia gained us airfields closer to Japan. On both counts therefore we argued that the enormous expenditure of man-power and material would not be worth while. But we never succeeded in deflecting the Americans from their purpose. Their national psychology is such that the bigger the Idea the more wholeheartedly and obstinately do they throw themselves into making it a success. It is an admirable characteristic provided the Idea is good.

We of course wanted to recapture Burma, but we did not want to have to do it by land advances from slender communications and across the most forbidding fighting country imaginable. The south of Burma, with its port of Rangoon, was far more valuable than the north. But all of it was remote from Japan, and for our forces to become side-tracked and entangled there would deny us our rightful share in a Far Eastern victory. I wished, on the contrary, to contain the Japanese in Burma, and break into or through the great arc of islands forming the outer fringe of the Dutch East Indies. Our whole British-Indian Imperial front would thus advance across the Bay of Bengal into close contact with the enemy, by using amphibious power at every stage. This divergence of opinion, albeit honestly held and frankly discussed, and with decisions loyally executed, continued. It is against this permanent background of geography, limited resources, and clash of policies that the story of the campaign should be read.

* * * * *

The Washington standpoint was clearly set forth to me by the President.

President Roosevelt to Prime Minister   25 Feb 44
My Chiefs of Staff are agreed that the primary intermediate objective of our advance across the Pacific lies in the Formosa–China coast–Luzon area. The success of recent operations in the Gilberts and Marshalls indicates that we can accelerate our movements westward. There appears to be a possibility that we can reach the Formosa–China–Luzon area before the summer of 1945. From the time we enter this vital zone until we gain a firm lodgment in this area it is essential that our operations be supported by the maximum air-power that can be brought to bear. This necessitates the greatest expansion possible of the air strength based in China.

I have always advocated the development of China as a base for the support of our Pacific advances, and now that the war has taken a greater turn in our favour time is all too short to provide the support we should have from that direction.

It is mandatory therefore that we make every effort to increase the flow of supplies into China. This can only be done by increasing the air tonnage or by opening a road through Burma.

Our occupation of Myitkyina will enable us immediately to increase the air-lift to China, by providing an intermediate air transport base, as well as by increasing the protection of the air route.

General Stilwell is confident that his Chinese-American force can seize Myitkyina by the end of this dry season, and, once there, can hold it, provided Mountbatten's IVth Corps from Imphal secures the Shwebo Monywa area. I realise this imposes a most difficult task, but

I feel that with your energetic encouragement Mountbatten's commanders are capable of overcoming the many difficulties involved.

The continued build-up of Japanese strength in Burma requires us to undertake the most aggressive action within our power to retain the initiative and prevent them from launching an offensive that may carry them over the borders into India. . . . I most urgently hope therefore that you back to the maximum a vigorous and immediate campaign in Upper Burma.

* * * * *

The campaign had been opened in December, when General Stilwell, with two Chinese divisions, organised and trained by himself in India, crossed the watershed from Ledo into the jungles below the main mountain ranges. He was opposed by the renowned Japanese 18th Division, but forged ahead steadily, and by early January had penetrated forty miles, while the road-makers toiled behind him. In the south the British XVth Corps, under General Christison, began their advance down the Arakan coast on January 19. At the same time the Allied air forces redoubled their efforts, and, with the aid of newly arrived Spitfires, gained a degree of air superiority which was shortly to prove invaluable.

On February 4 our advance was suddenly halted. The Japanese also had a plan. Since November they had increased their strength in Burma from five divisions to eight, and they proposed to invade Eastern India and raise the flag of rebellion against the British. Their first stroke was a counter-offensive in the Arakan towards the port of Chittagong, which would draw our attention and our reserves to that front. Holding our 5th Division frontally on the coast, they passed the better part of a division through the jungle and round the flank of the 7th Division, which was farther inland. Within a few days it was surrounded and the enemy threatened to cut the coastal road behind the 5th Division. They fully expected both divisions to withdraw, but they had reckoned without one factor, supply by air. The 7th Division grouped themselves into perimeters, stood their ground, and fought it out. For a fortnight food, water, and ammunition were delivered to them, like manna, from above. The enemy had no such facilities; they had taken with them only ten days' supply, and the obstinacy of the 7th Division prevented more reaching them. Unable to overwhelm our forward troops, pressed from the north by our 26th Division, which had been brought from reserve, they broke up into small parties to fight their way back through the jungle, leaving five thousand dead behind.

The XVth Corps resumed their advance, proud of an achievement which put an end to the legend of Japanese invincibility in the jungle.

Prime Minister to Admiral Mountbatten   1 Mar 44

I sent you to-day my public congratulations on the Arakan fighting. I am so glad this measure of success has attended it. It is a sign of the new spirit in your forces, and will, I trust, urge everyone to keep closer to the enemy. Looking at the maps from here, I do not see why you should not continue your advance along the coast in the direction of Akyab.

*   *   *   *   *

In February there were sure signs that the enemy were also preparing an attack on the central front against Imphal, thereby forestalling our own projected advance to the Chindwin. The now famous Chindits* operation was a part of our offensive plan. Although it was clear that the Japanese would get their blow in first, it was decided that Wingate's brigades should carry on with their task. This was principally to cut the enemy's communications near Indaw, thereby dislocating their supply system, and notably that of the Japanese 18th Division, with whom Stilwell was at close grips. The enemy would moreover be forced to detach troops to deal with the menace behind his fighting front. One Chindits brigade, the 16th British, had already started on February 5 from Ledo. They marched across 450 miles of mountain and jungle and were supplied solely from the air.

On March 5, sustained by an American "Air Commando" of 250 machines, the fly-in of the 77th and 111th Brigades, British and Gurkha troops, began. After assembly at their rallying-point they set out upon their task and cut the railway north of Indaw.

I sent a full account of all this to the President.

14 Mar 44

I feel you will be interested to hear about the flying in of two of Wingate's Long-Range Penetration brigades. Landing strips in two areas were selected from which the brigades could advance westwards primarily to interrupt the Japanese lines of communication, and so assist the American-Chinese operations taking place farther north. The strips were 100 miles inside enemy territory and 260 miles from the transport base.

* "Chindits," the familiar name for Wingate's Long-Range Penetration Force.

The first landings were made by gliders, whose occupants then prepared the strips to receive transport aircraft. Between March 6 and March 11 seven thousand five hundred men, with all their gear and with mules, were successfully landed. The only losses were a number of the gliders, and some of these should be repairable. The brigades have now started their advance, but a small holding party has been left at one of the strips to receive a flight of Spitfires and a squadron of Hurricane fighter-bombers which were to fly in to protect the base and provide air support.

The only serious mishap occurred on the first night. One of the strips in the northern area was found to have been obstructed by the Japanese, and the surface of the remaining strip was much worse than was expected, causing crashes which blocked the strip and prevented further landings that night. A few of the gliders had to be turned back in the air, and failed to reach our territory. Another strip was immediately prepared in this area, and was ready for landing two days later. The total of killed, wounded, and missing is at most 145.

The operation appears to have been a complete surprise for the Japanese. There has been no enemy air action against the strips in the northern area, and the one in the south was only bombed on March 10 after our men had left it. As it happened, the enemy were concentrating aircraft at airfields in the Mandalay area as part of their own plans. In consequence the strong air forces we had collected to protect the landings had a very good bag, and in two days destroyed sixty-one enemy aircraft for the loss of only three of our own.

We are all very well pleased that Wingate's venture has started so well, and the success of this flying-in operation augurs well for the future. Your men have played an important part both in the transport squadrons and in the supporting air operations.

"I am thrilled," replied Roosevelt the next day, "by the news of our success under Wingate. If you wire him please give him my hearty good wishes. May the good work go on. This marks an epic achievement for the airborne troops, not forgetting the mules."

Wingate did not live long to enjoy this first success or to reap its fruits. On March 24, to my great distress, he was killed in the air. He insisted on starting. The facts are unknown. Probably the pilot lost his way in thick weather. The aircraft crashed into a hillside, and it was long before it was discovered. With him a bright flame was extinguished.

* * * * *

British advance in Arakan
Stilwell's advance on Myitkyina
Chindits' northward march
Japanese attack on Imphal
and Kohima

Himalaya Mts.

H i m a l a y a

I
N
D
I
A

R. Brahmaputra

Ledo

Gauhati

Maingkwan

CHINA

Dimapur Walawbum
Kohima

NASSAM

Kamaing

Myitkyina

Imphal

Mogaung

TO KUNMING
& CHUNGKING

Silchar

Mawlu
Indaw

Bhamo

YUNNAN

Tamu

Katha

Tiddim

Kunlong

Kalewa

Lashio

Chittagong

Shwebo

Monywa

Mandalay

B U R M A

Arakan
Hills

R. Irrawaddy

Akyab

R. Salween

Prome

S I A M

B A Y

O F

B E N G A L

Rangoon
Moulmein

0   50   100   150 MILES

B U R M A

On March 8 three Japanese divisions began their expected attack on our central front. General Scoones withdrew his IVth Corps, also of three divisions, to the Imphal plateau, so as to fight concentrated on ground of his own choosing. If the enemy cut the road to the railhead at Dimapur he would have to depend upon the air until the battle was won. The Japanese repeated the tactics they had used with misfortune in the Arakan. They counted on capturing our stores at Imphal to feed themselves. They also intended to cut not only the road to Dimapur, but also the railway there, and thus sever the supply route maintaining Stilwell's force and the United States air-lift to China. Important issues were therefore at stake.

The key lay again in transport aircraft. Mountbatten's resources, though considerable, were not nearly enough. He sought to retain twenty United States aircraft already borrowed from "the Hump" traffic, and asked for seventy more. This was a hard requirement to make or to procure. In the anxious weeks that followed I gave him my strongest support. "Chiefs of Staff and I," I told him, "are backing you up to the full. I have telegraphed to the President. In my view nothing matters but the battle. Be sure you win." In the end Mountbatten's needs were largely met by the temporary loan of seventy-nine aircraft from the Mediterranean.

By the end of March the Japanese had cut the road to Dimapur and were pressing hard on the fringes of the Imphal plain from three sides. The 5th Indian Division was flown into Imphal from the Arakan front, where operations were halted, and the 7th Indian Division was flown into Dimapur. Thither by rail came the headquarters of the XXXIIIrd Corps, under General Stopford, the 2nd British Division, an independent Indian brigade, and also the last remaining brigade of Wingate's force.

At Kohima, a roadside township that commanded the pass to the Assam valley, the Japanese northern attack was held. Here the garrison consisted of a battalion of the Royal West Kent, a Nepalese battalion, and a battalion of the Assam Rifles, with every man, and even convalescents from the hospital, who could bear arms. They were attacked on April 4 by the Japanese 31st Division, slowly forced back into a diminishing area, and finally on to a single hill. They had no supplies except what was dropped on them by parachutes. Attacked on every side, they held on steadfastly, supported by bombing and cannon-fire from the air, until they were relieved on the 20th by the 161st Indian Brigade, which, with the 2nd British Division, was fighting its way up from Dimapur. Four thousand Japanese were killed. The valiant defence of Kohima against enormous odds was a fine episode.

*   *   *   *   *

We had the command of the air, but we depended upon having enough transport planes. The climax came in May. Sixty thousand British and Indian soldiers, with all their modern equipment, were confined in a circle on the Imphal plain. I could feel the stress amid all other business. On the principle "Nothing matters but the battle" I used my authority.

Prime Minister to Admiral Mountbatten (South-East Asia)   4 May 44
Let nothing go from the battle that you need for victory. I will not accept denial of this from any quarter, and will back you to the full.

Prime Minister to General Ismay, for C.O.S. Committee   9 May 44
The gap must be filled at all costs, either by delaying the return of the seventy-nine transport aircraft to the Mediterranean, or by drawing twenty plus fifty-nine from "the Hump", or by a combination of both. We cannot on any account throw away this battle. I am quite willing to telegraph to the President pointing out to him the disastrous consequences to his own plans for helping China which would follow the casting away of this battle.

Prime Minister to General Ismay and General Hollis, for   14 May 44
C.O.S. Committee
Whatever happens Admiral Mountbatten is not to send away the seventy-nine aircraft to the Mediterranean except as they are replaced in his command by suitable American aircraft either from United States or "the Hump". His argument seems to me unanswerable.

I have not been given any sufficient reasons to show that Genera Alexander's battle will be hampered if the date of the arrival of these aircraft in the Mediterranean is postponed. General Wilson has already an overwhelming superiority in the air, and these aircraft are not needed so much for the battle as for amphibious operations following its success, whereas they are vital to the operations proceeding in Burma.

General Hollis should therefore prepare me a short note which I will discuss with him at midnight to-night. Meanwhile this minute should be brought to the attention of the Chiefs of Staff. I am determined that Mountbatten's battle shall not be ruined by the folly of flying 150 aircraft 5,000 miles in opposite directions, and I will appeal to the President to-morrow unless I am satisfied that the needs are met.

*　　*　　*　　*　　*

Meanwhile on the northern front Stilwell was making good progress towards the line Mogaung–Myitkyina, against the stubborn resistance of the Japanese 18th Division. He was anxious about his eastern flank, where their 56th Division, along the Chinese frontier, might turn upon him. The President persuaded Chiang Kai-shek to send Stilwell another Chinese division, but it was not till April 21 that the Generalissimo agreed to order his troops in Yunnan to advance into Burma. On May 10 four Chinese divisions crossed the Salween at and above Kunlong, thus worrying the Japanese flank.

The Chindits, operating on the enemy communications, had been reinforced in early April by two more brigades, so that five were now in action. They worked northwards up the railway, preventing the passage of reinforcements and destroying dumps as they went. Despite the havoc they caused, the Japanese withdrew nothing from the Imphal front and only one battalion from Stilwell's. They brought their 53rd Division from Siam and tried, at the cost of over 5,400 killed, but without success, to quell the nuisance.

On May 17 Stilwell sprung a surprise both on the Japanese and ourselves by capturing the airfield at Myitkyina by a swift advance of General Merrill's U.S. brigade. Reinforcements were flown in to assault the town, but the Japanese held it obstinately till early August. At the end of May Mogaung, Stilwell's other main objective, was invested by the leading Chindits brigade, the 77th, and finally fell to them on June 26. These successes were largely due to Stilwell's leadership, energy, and pertinacity; but his troops were exhausted by their efforts and many had to be withdrawn.

*　　*　　*　　*　　*

Around Imphal the situation was still at full strain. Our Air Force was dominant, but the monsoon was hindering the air supply, on which our success depended. All our four divisions were slowly pushing outwards from their encirclement. Along the Kohima road the relieving force and the besieged were fighting their way towards each other. It was a race against time. We marked their progress with tense feelings.

Prime Minister to Admiral Mountbatten (South-East Asia)   22 June 44

The Chiefs of Staff have expressed anxiety about the situation in Imphal, particularly in respect of reserves of supplies and ammunition. You are absolutely entitled to ask for all aircraft necessary to maintain the situation, whether they come from "the Hump" or any other source. "The Hump" must be considered the current reserve, and should be drawn upon whenever necessary. The Americans have by a brilliant feat of arms landed us in Myitkyina, but neither Myitkyina nor Imphal can be held without drawing on "the Hump". If you fail to make your demands in good time, invoking me if necessary to help from here, it will be no good complaining afterwards if it is not a success. Keep your hand close on the job, which seems to me both serious and critical. Every good wish.

The finale came while this message was on the way. I quote Admiral Mountbatten's report:

In the third week in June the situation was critical, and it seemed possible, after all the efforts of the previous two months, that early in July the IVth Corps would finally run out of reserves. But on June 22, with a week and a half in hand, the 2nd British and 5th Indian Divisions met at a point twenty-nine miles north of Imphal and the road to the plain was open. On the same day the convoys began to roll in.

Mountbatten was justified in adding, "The Japanese bid for India was virtually over, and ahead lay the prospect of the first major British victory in Burma."

CHAPTER XXXII

STRATEGY AGAINST JAPAN

The Choice Before Us – My Minute of January 24, 1944 – Arrival of Admiral Mountbatten's Mission – The New Plan – United States Objections – A Powerful Japanese Fleet Moves to Singapore – Prevention of Amphibious Operations – We Lose Local Naval Superiority – My Telegram to the President of March 10 – The President's Reply – I Give a Ruling to the Chiefs of Staff, March 20 – The "Middle Strategy"

WHILE the fierce and critical fighting by land and air described in the last chapter was raging in Burma and the Pacific the whole future policy of the conduct of the war against Japan was being hotly debated among ourselves in London, among the Americans in Washington, and between London and Washington. I have already mentioned the report of the Combined Chiefs of Staff at the Cairo Conference on the long-term policy in the Pacific, and the British share in it, and how this had been initialled by the President and me without our being able in the pressure of events to study it, or discuss it together or with our advisers. It was only when at Marrakesh I received a request to transmit a dispatch on the subject to the Dominions that I became aware how far the British Chiefs of Staff had developed their opinions. I found myself immediately in disagreement, and thus arose the only considerable difference which I and the War Cabinet had with our trusted military colleagues.

Briefly the following choice lay before us. Should we send our naval forces and any troops or air-power we could spare or transport to act with the left flank of the United States forces in the South-West Pacific, basing ourselves upon Australia? Our Chiefs of Staff thought we should, and they had had no difficulty in reaching agreement with their American comrades in Cairo. I, on the other hand, and my colleagues, held that we should advance eastwards to the Malay peninsula and the Dutch islands, using India as our base. The Chiefs of Staff contended that whereas Mountbatten could not carry out amphibious operations on a major scale until six months after a German defeat, their Pacific reinforcement plan, to which they suggested we were committed, could be begun much sooner.

As soon as I got home I convened a meeting of the Defence Committee, where the whole subject was for the first time effectively examined and thrashed out between us.

A few days later I wrote the following minute:

Prime Minister to General Ismay, for C.O.S. Committee   24 Jan 44

All my Ministerial colleagues who were present at the meeting on the 19th have spoken to me about the projects then expounded by the Planners in a strongly adverse sense. I myself am not in agreement with these plans, and the issue will have to be debated as between Governments. It must also be remembered that this plan is entirely different from that expounded to us by General MacArthur's Chief of Staff, so that evidently there is a great difference of opinion even among the Americans themselves upon it.

2. No one would object to sending the handful of ships proposed to work with the American Fleet in any June operation they may have in view, and of course we should always be ready to build up a fleet in the Pacific. But no plan of war in these theatres could be considered satisfactory which provided no outlet in 1944–45, before Hitler is defeated, for the very large air and military forces we have standing in India and around the Bay of Bengal.

3. For these forces the only effectual operation is Sumatra ["Culverin"]. I have long been convinced that this is the most practicable manner of drawing off very large numbers of Japanese aircraft, and possibly of troops, or, in the alternative, of regaining important territory and securing bases from which we may strike equally at Singapore, at Bangkok, in the Malacca Straits, and along the Japanese communications with Burma. My colleagues agree with me in thinking that it is upon this that we should concentrate our efforts, making it clear to the Americans that if we help them in the Pacific, as we shall do, we shall expect them to assist us with a proper supply of landing-craft in time to attack Sumatra in October, November, or December. This they can perfectly well do from the immense new construction of L.S.T.s, which will be continuous throughout the year. . . .

4. We must await the arrival of the officers whom Admiral Mountbatten is sending, to go into the matter fully with them, and we
cannot send any telegrams to the Dominions until we have at least
formed our own view.

In mid-February 1944 Mountbatten's mission arrived, headed
by his able American Deputy Chief of Staff, General Wedemeyer.
Mountbatten did not believe the American project for a through
road from Northern Assam to China could be completed for
two-way traffic before June 1946. He therefore advised dropping
it and expanding the existing air route instead. If this were done
he would not have to capture so large a part of Northern Burma.
With the resources thus released he wished to penetrate the
enemy perimeter of Malaya and the Dutch East Indies, and push
rapidly north-eastwards from base to base along the Asiatic coast.
This would open better communication with China by sea, and
would be a direct help to the American advances on Japan from
the Central Pacific and New Guinea. Sumatra would have to be
captured first, and he proposed to do this as soon as amphibious
resources were released from North-West Europe. "Culverin"
was thus revived.

This strategy was however opposed to the recommendations
which the Combined Chiefs of Staff had agreed upon at Cairo.
It raised our differences about long-term policy in an immediate
and practical form. Having long been an advocate of the Sumatra
enterprise, I liked Mountbatten's new plan. I still believed that
the size of the forces considered necessary for Sumatra was excessive, but nevertheless there would be a surplus over the needs
of the Burma land campaign, as proposed by Mountbatten, and
I was against sending them to play a minor part in MacArthur's
operations. In this I was fully supported by the Foreign Office,
who thought that the British rôle in the Far East should not be a
mere minor contribution to the Americans; this was not likely to
appeal to the British people. Moreover, the peoples of Asia were
little interested in the Pacific islands as compared with the wide
regions which meant most to them. In contrast, the strategy
advocated by South-East Asia Command would have immediate
psychological and political effects which would hasten the defeat
of Japan.

I was quite sure that American minds would move in a different direction. I was not therefore surprised at a passage in President Roosevelt's telegram to me of February 25, 1944:

I am gravely concerned over the recent trends in strategy that favour an operation toward Sumatra and Malaya in the future rather than face the immediate obstacles that confront us in Burma. I fail to see how an operation against Sumatra and Malaya, requiring tremendous resources and forces, can possibly be mounted until after the conclusion of the war in Europe. Lucrative as a successful "Culverin" might be, there appears much more to be gained by employing all the resources we now have available in an all-out drive into Upper Burma, so that we can build up our air strength in China and ensure the essential support for our westward advance to the Formosa–China–Luzon area.

This did not augur well for the success of Wedemeyer's mission. They presented themselves in Washington in March to the American Chiefs of Staff. They were not the first in the field. Admiral Mountbatten's Commanders-in-Chief had fully supported his plans, but not so his Deputy, the American General Stilwell. This was understandable, as Stilwell combined the office of Deputy with several others, notably that of Chief of Staff to Chiang Kai-shek. It was not a good arrangement on the part of the Americans, but we had had no option but to consent. Stilwell favoured every measure which might conceivably aid China, and believed that supply by road could begin sooner than South-East Asia Command expected. He was entitled to urge his views on Admiral Mountbatten, and when they were not accepted to represent them, with Mountbatten's consent, to his superiors in Washington. But he also permitted himself, without Mountbatten's knowledge, to send a mission to Washington to state his case there.

The American Chiefs of Staff had recently decided that though General MacArthur's advance towards the Philippines should continue the main attack should be made by Admiral Nimitz from the Central Pacific against Formosa. They therefore thought the strategic value of liberating Malaya and the Dutch East Indies would be small and tardy. They saw no need for any attack on Sumatra. Their hearts were still set on flying more supplies to China over "the Hump" and building the Burma Road. They also had a new plan for basing long-range bombers in China to attack Japan, which would need more supply tonnage than they had so far required. Wedemeyer marshalled the arguments for Mountbatten's proposals with great skill, but he failed to convince his auditors and masters.

$$\star \quad \star \quad \star \quad \star \quad \star$$

However, at this very time an unexpected event of the first importance occurred. A powerful Japanese fleet, including seven battleships, moved from the Central Pacific to Singapore. Their purpose was uncertain, but we now know that it was partly to seek temporary shelter from American air attack, and also to bring them nearer to their oil supplies in the Dutch East Indies. None the less, they might break into the Bay of Bengal, and this possibility put a stop for the time being to "Culverin" or other amphibious adventures in Indian waters. We no longer had even local naval superiority. I immediately recognised this unpleasant fact.

Prime Minister to General Ismay, for C.O.S. Committee   7 Mar 44

The plan for Sumatra was made on the assumption that no considerable detachment would be made from the Japanese main Fleet. This was of course pure assumption, based on what it would be reasonable for the enemy to do, and there never could be any guarantee that the enemy would not do unreasonable things. However, at that time the Japanese were believed to be concerned in defending Truk and Rabaul and other outposts against the United States and in holding themselves in readiness for the possibilities of a fleet action. They have now abandoned any such intentions, if they had them, and, falling back from their outpost line, are able to make defensive dispositions of their Fleet, which includes the stationing of a strong force at Singapore. While that Fleet is there it is evident that we could not do Sumatra, or anything like it, unless our own naval forces were built up to the point where we should welcome a fleet action. It is very much to the advantage of the United States that the Japanese should be held at Singapore. The longer they are there the greater the opportunities for Admiral Nimitz to act with freedom and advance with rapidity. How long the Japanese can afford to remain at Singapore depends upon the progress of the American advance. It seems quite certain they will have to reunite their Fleet, and, having reunited it, will have again to contemplate the idea of a general engagement for the sake of the Philippines or nearer home. The probabilities of their coming back to Singapore, should they leave it, can only be assessed in relation to the situation prevailing at the time. The longer we can detain them in their present position at Singapore the greater the help we can give the United States. This will be achieved by continued preparations for large amphibious attacks the moment they are forced by the United States' main advance to reunite their Fleet and withdraw into the Pacific.

2. Make sure this minute is put before the Joint Planners.

★　　★　　★　　★　　★

Meanwhile our discussions with our Chiefs of Staff were long and sometimes tense. The policy of helping General MacArthur or Admiral Nimitz depended on what size of force could be based on Australia, and whether on the east or north and west coasts. We had insufficient information, and further investigation was admittedly needed. It would obviously be a very great strain on our shipping. In March we seemed to have reached a deadlock among ourselves at home. The Chiefs of Staff felt that the Americans were expecting us to send a fleet to the Pacific for operations which might occur in June. I therefore thought it necessary to clear up this point with the President, and also to inform him of the whole position.

Prime Minister to President Roosevelt　　　　　　　　　　10 Mar 44
In the final report of the Cairo Conference the Combined Chiefs of Staff reported that they had "approved in principle as a basis for further investigation and preparation" an overall plan for the defeat of Japan. This plan contemplated the dispatch to the Pacific of a detachment of the British Fleet which was provisionally scheduled to become operational in the Pacific in June 1944. Although you and I both initialled the final report neither of us had had the opportunity of going into these matters personally, as we were concerned with affairs of more immediate urgency. Since then the War Cabinet and Chiefs of Staff have been "investigating", and we have not so far reached united conclusions. Meanwhile the Japanese Fleet has arrived at Singapore, which constitutes in my mind a new major fact.

2. After the surrender of the Italian Fleet in September 1943 I was very keen on sending a detachment of our Fleet as quickly as possible to the Pacific, but when I opened this to Admiral King he explained to me how very strong the United States Navy was already in those waters compared with the Japanese, and I formed the impression that he did not need us very much. I have also seen several telegrams from our naval representatives in Washington which tend to confirm the above impression. On the other hand, I am told that Admiral King has informed the First Sea Lord that he would like to have our detachment, provided it did not arrive until August or September, when its

logistic requirements could more easily be met. I am, in the upshot, left in doubt about whether we are really needed this year.

3. Accordingly I should be very grateful if you could let me know whether there is any specific American operation in the Pacific (*a*) before the end of 1944 or (*b*) before the summer of 1945 which would be hindered or prevented by the absence of a British Fleet detachment.

4. On the other hand, the movement of the Japanese Fleet to Singapore, which coincided, *inter alia*, with their knowledge of the movement of our battleship squadron into the Indian Ocean, seems to show their sensitiveness about the Andamans, Nicobars, and Sumatra. It would surely be an advantage to you if, by keeping up the threat in the Bay of Bengal, we could detain the Japanese Fleet or a large portion of it at Singapore, and thus secure you a clear field in the Pacific to enable your by-passing process and advance to develop at full speed.

5. General Wedemeyer is able to unfold all Mountbatten's plans in the Indian theatre and the Bay of Bengal. They certainly seem to fit in with the kind of requests which Chiang Kai-shek was making, which you favoured, but which we were unable to make good before the monsoon on account of the Mediterranean and "Overlord" operations. I am personally still of opinion that amphibious action across the Bay of Bengal will enable all our forces and establishments in India to play their highest part in the next eighteen months in the war against Japan. We are examining now the logistics in detail, and, *prima facie*, it seems that we could attack with two or three times the strength the islands across the Bay of Bengal, and thereafter the Malay peninsula, than we could by prolonging our communications about 9,000 miles round the south of Australia and operating from the Pacific side and on your southern flank. There is also the objection of dividing our Fleet and our effort between the Pacific and Indian Oceans and throwing out of gear so many of our existing establishments from Calcutta to Ceylon and way back in the Suez Canal zone.

6. Before however reaching any final conclusions in my mind about this matter I should like to know what answer you would give to the question I posed in paragraph 3, namely, would your Pacific operations be hindered if, for the present at any rate and while the Japanese Fleet is at Singapore, we kept our centre of gravity in the Indian Ocean and the Bay of Bengal and planned amphibious operations there as resources came to hand?

The President's reply to my direct question was conclusive.

President Roosevelt to Prime Minister   13 Mar 44
(*a*) There will be no specific operation in the Pacific during 1944 that would be adversely affected by the absence of a British Fleet

detachment. (*b*) It is not at the present time possible to anticipate with sufficient accuracy future developments in the Pacific to be certain that a British Fleet detachment will not be needed there during the year of 1945, but it does not now appear that such a reinforcement will be needed before the summer of 1945.

In consideration of recent enemy dispositions it is my personal opinion that unless we have unexpected bad luck in the Pacific your naval force will be of more value to our common effort by remaining in the Indian Ocean.

All of the above estimates are of course based on current conditions, and are therefore subject to change if the circumstances change.

* * * *

Thus fortified upon the distressing controversy in which I and my Cabinet colleagues were engaged with the Chiefs of Staff, I felt it my duty to give a ruling. In this case I addressed myself to each of the Chiefs of Staff personally, and not collectively to them as a committee.

Prime Minister to First Sea Lord, C.I.G.S., and C.A.S.   20 Mar 44

I have addressed the attached minute to each of the Chiefs of Staff personally.

1. My question and the President's reply are directed . . . solely to the point as to whether there is any obligation to the American authorities that we should send a detachment of the British Fleet to the Pacific before the summer of 1945, and whether their operations would be hampered if we stood out. We now know that there is no obligation and that their operations will not be hampered, also that they will not in any case require our assistance (barring some catastrophe) before the autumn of 1945. We are therefore free to consider the matter among ourselves and from the point of view of British interests only. . . .

3. The serious nature of the present position has been brought home to me by the reluctance of the Chiefs of Staff to meet with their American counterparts for fear of revealing to the United States their differences from me and my Cabinet colleagues. The Ministers on the Defence Committee are convinced, and I am sure that the War Cabinet would agree if the matter were brought before them, that it is in the interest of Britain to pursue what may be termed the "Bay of Bengal strategy", at any rate for the next twelve months. I therefore feel it my duty, as Prime Minister and Minister of Defence, to give the following rulings:

(*a*) Unless unforeseen events occur, the Indian theatre and the Bay of Bengal will remain, until the summer of 1945, the centre of gravity for the British and Imperial war effort against Japan.

(*b*) All preparations will be made for amphibious action across the Bay of Bengal against the Malay peninsula and the various island outposts by which it is defended, the ultimate objective being the reconquest of Singapore.

(*c*) A powerful British fleet will be built up, based on Ceylon, Addu Atoll, and East Indian ports, under the shield of our strong shore-based aircraft. The fleet train for this Eastern Fleet must be developed as fast as possible, subject to the priority needs of "Overlord" and the Mediterranean, and the necessary feeding of this country on its present rations.

(*d*) The plans of South-East Asia Command for amphibious action across the Bay of Bengal will be examined, corrected, and improved, with the desire of engaging the enemy as closely and as soon as possible.

(*e*) The Reconnaissance Mission to Australia should be sent as soon as I have approved the personnel. They should report promptly upon the existing facilities in Australia and on the recaptured islands to the north of it, and propose measures for carrying the Eastern Fleet and its fleet train, with any additions that may be required, into the South-West Pacific and basing it on Australian ports should we at any time wish to adopt that policy.

4. I should be very ready to discuss the above rulings with the Chiefs of Staff in order that we may be clear in our minds as to the line we are going to take in discussions with our American friends. Meanwhile, with this difference on long-term plans settled, we may bend ourselves to the tremendous and urgent tasks which are now so near, and in which we shall have need of all our comradeship and mutual confidence.

Nevertheless the scene was melting and reshaping so rapidly that I preferred to keep the options open, and we continued to study other plans. As the Japanese Fleet might stop us attacking across the Bay of Bengal, and we could not mount any large amphibious operation in the East until six months after Germany had been defeated, a middle course was considered. This "middle strategy", as it was termed in our circle, was to advance northwards from Australia, help General MacArthur to liberate Borneo, and then strike either at Singapore and Malaya or at Hong Kong and the China coast. This could be done by forming a British and Australian force under an Australian commander, who would be subordinate to MacArthur.

The disadvantages were obvious. The "middle strategy" would do little to help the Americans in the Central Pacific. If their plans went well we should not reach Borneo in time to take part even in the assault against Hong Kong, and we should probably find ourselves shut out from the main fighting in the Pacific, in which we were determined to share. The Australians welcomed the idea of establishing an Imperial Command which would relieve American predominance over the whole zone, but the bases on their east coast were already fully engaged. A new organisation to meet British needs might cause dislocation. Moreover, it was a much longer sea voyage to Australia than to India, and this would be a heavy strain on our shipping.

At the time the answers to most of these puzzles were unknown, but the broad problems were laid before a conference of Dominion Premiers which assembled in London on May 1. The Australian and New Zealand Prime Ministers were assured that their own countries would not be expected to increase the sum of their war effort, and pronounced themselves in favour of the "middle strategy". They also agreed to find the troops and most of the aircraft. The proposal offered a useful opportunity for Dominion effort. However, in the end these plans did not mature. The course of events soon changed fundamentally the conditions which prevailed or could be foreshadowed at the Cairo Conference or in the months which followed; and anyhow the war with Japan ended in a manner and at a date which no one dreamed of at the time of the discussion.

CHAPTER XXXIII

PREPARATIONS FOR "OVERLORD"

*Hard Memories – The Cross-Channel Plan – The Commanders –
Increased Weight of the Assault – The Mulberry Harbours – Plans for
the Airborne Attack – "Waterproofing" of Vehicles – Fire Plan of the
Naval Bombardment – My Telegram to General Marshall of March 11
– Training the Troops in Amphibious Operations – D Day and
H Hour – Final Dispositions and First Objectives – The Navy's Task
– The Air Offensive – Deception Devices – The Germans Misled –
All Southern England One Vast Camp.*

THOUGHT arising from factual experience may be a bridle
or a spur. The reader of these volumes will be aware that
while I was always willing to join with the United States in
a direct assault across the Channel on the German sea-front in
France, I was not convinced that this was the only way of winning
the war, and I knew that it would be a very heavy and hazardous
adventure. The fearful price we had had to pay in human life and
blood for the great offensives of the First World War was graven
in my mind. Memories of the Somme and Passchendaele and
many lesser frontal attacks upon the Germans were not to be
blotted out by time or reflection. It still seemed to me, after a
quarter of a century, that fortifications of concrete and steel armed
with modern fire-power, and fully manned by trained, resolute
men, could only be overcome by surprise in time or place by
turning their flanks, or by some new and mechanical device like
the tank. Superiority of bombardment, terrific as it may be, was
no final answer. The defenders could easily have ready other lines
behind their first, and the intervening ground which the artillery
could conquer would become impassable crater-fields. These
were the fruits of knowledge which the French and British had
bought so dearly from 1915 to 1917.

THE COAST OF NORTH-WEST EUROPE

Since then new factors had appeared, but they did not all tell the same way. The fire-power of the defence had vastly increased. The development of minefields both on land and in the sea was enormous. On the other hand, we, the attackers, held air supremacy, and could land large numbers of paratroops behind the enemy's front, and above all block and paralyse the communications by which he could bring reinforcements for a counter-attack.

Throughout the summer months of 1943 General Morgan and his Allied Inter-Service Staff had laboured at the plan. In a previous chapter I have described how it was presented to me during my voyage to Quebec for the "Quadrant" Conference. There the scheme was generally approved, but there was one feature of it which requires comment. The size and scope of the first assault on the Normandy beaches was necessarily limited by the numbers of landing-craft available. General Morgan's instructions were to plan an assault by three divisions, with two divisions as an immediate follow-up. He accordingly proposed to land the three divisions on the coast between Caen and Carentan. He would have liked to land part of the force north of Carentan, nearer to Cherbourg, but he thought it unwise to divide so small a force. The estuary of the river Vire at Carentan was marshy and it would have been difficult for the two wings of the attack to keep in touch. No doubt he was right. I would certainly have preferred a stronger attack on a broader front, but at that time, ten months before the event, we could not be sure of having enough landing-craft.

It was the absence of important harbours in all this stretch of coast which had impelled Mountbatten's staff to propose the synthetic harbours. The decisions at Quebec confirmed the need and clarified the issues. I kept in touch with the development of this project, which was pressed forward by a committee of experts and Service representatives, summoned by Brigadier Bruce White of the War Office, himself an eminent civil engineer. It was a tremendous undertaking, and high credit is due to many, not least to Major-General Sir Harold Wernher, whose task it was to co-ordinate the many interests concerned.

Here too should be mentioned "Pluto", the submarine pipe-lines which carried petrol from the Isle of Wight to Normandy and later from Dungeness to Calais. This idea and many others owed much to Mountbatten's staff. Space forbids description of the many contrivances devised to overcome the formidable obstacles and minefields guarding the beaches. Some were fitted to our tanks to protect their crews; others served the landing-craft. All these matters aroused my personal interest, and, when it seemed necessary, my intervention.

*   *   *   *   *

General Morgan and his staff were well content with the approval given at Quebec to their proposals. The troops could now begin their training and their special equipment could be made. For this Morgan had been given powers greater than a Staff officer usually wields.

The discussions which led to the appointment of General

Eisenhower to the Supreme Command and of General Montgomery to command the expeditionary army have already been related. Eisenhower's Deputy was Air Chief Marshal Tedder. Air Marshal Leigh-Mallory was appointed to the Air and Admiral Ramsay to the Naval Command. General Eisenhower brought with him General Bedell Smith as his Chief of Staff, to whom General Morgan was appointed Deputy.

Eisenhower and Montgomery disagreed with one important feature of the plan. They wanted an assault in greater strength and on a wider front, so as to gain quickly a good-sized bridgehead in which to build up their forces for the break-out. Also it was important to capture the docks at Cherbourg earlier than had been planned. They wanted a first assault by five divisions instead of three. Of course this was perfectly right. General Morgan himself had advocated an extension of the initial landing, but had not been given enough resources. But where were the extra landing-craft to come from? South-East Asia had already been stripped. There were sufficient in the Mediterranean to carry two divisions, but these were needed for "Anvil", the seaborne assault on Southern France which was to take place at the same time as "Overlord" and draw German troops away from the North. If "Anvil" were to be reduced it would be too weak to be helpful. It was not until March that General Eisenhower, in conference with the British Chiefs of Staff, made his final decision. The American Chiefs of Staff had agreed that he should speak for them. Having recently come from the Mediterranean, he knew all about "Anvil", and now as Supreme Commander of "Overlord" he could best judge the needs of both. It was agreed to take the ships of one division from "Anvil" and to use them for "Overlord". The ships for a second division could be found by postponing "Overlord" till the June moon period. The output of new landing-craft in that month would fill the gap. As for the additional troops, Britain and the United States would each contribute one division to bring the total up to five. The United States also agreed to provide naval support for their extra division. Thus the naval forces allocated to the operation were roughly 80 per cent. British and 20 per cent. American. Planning now went ahead on this revised and greatly improved foundation.

* * * * *

As soon as I returned from Marrakesh I busied myself with the many technical matters of the "Overlord" preparations. Across the Channel the whole front bristled with obstacles; defences had been built and manned. The enemy expected us, but did they know *where* or *when* or *how*? They had no flanks that could be turned, at any rate within the range of our fighter air cover. Ships were more vulnerable than ever to shore batteries, which could aim by Radar. Once our troops were landed they still had to be supplied and the enemy's air and tank counter-attacks beaten off. I never ceased to search for means to overcome the perils which lay before us.

Prime Minister to General Ismay and Sir Edward Bridges   23 Jan 44

In view of the many repercussions which "Overlord" preparations will make on our life, and in order to keep the whole matter under constant survey, I propose to set up a weekly committee, over which I will preside myself. This committee will be a substitute for the Anti-U-boat Warfare Committee, which can now be put on a two-monthly basis.

Pray let me have your suggestions for the personnel of this new committee.

★   ★   ★   ★   ★

The "Mulberry" harbours, I now heard, were meeting with difficulties. I therefore summoned a conference on January 24. It was intended to plant a breakwater ("Gooseberry") in each divisional assault area. This now meant a total of five "Gooseberries", two of which would in due course be absorbed into the "Mulberries". On the suggestion of Admiral Tennant, who was in charge of the operational side of the "Mulberry" plan, it was agreed that all the "Gooseberries" should be composed of blockships, although this meant using many more vessels. Moving under their own power, they could quickly reach the scene and be sunk in the right place, thus providing a certain amount of shelter almost at once. All could be laid in four or five days. The "Phœnix" concrete caissons to complete the "Mulberries" would be towed over by instalments, but this would take at least a fortnight. There was a shortage of tugs, and I gave instructions for a census. The Admiralty needed eight thousand yards of blockships. Nearly all were provided by using seventy old merchant ships and four obsolete warships. As the British were building most of the "Mulberries" I thought we could reasonably expect the Americans to help with the blockships. At my suggestion they did so, contributing nearly half. For the rest, the twenty-three "Whale" floating pier units were progressing well, but the steel "Bombardons", for the outer breakwaters, were meeting technical troubles, which the Admiralty had to solve.

* * * * *

The plans for airborne attack seemed to me to deserve special attention and support.

Prime Minister to General Ismay, for C.O.S. Committee   28 Jan 44

I am not at all satisfied with the provision that, on existing plans, is being made for the carriage of airborne troops for "Overlord". There are four airborne divisions available, but I am told that there are only sufficient aircraft to lift one of these divisions. This is not on account of lack of production, but because the date by which everything must be ready has been set at March 15. The production of Stirlings and Albemarles between March 15 and May 15 will be 110 aircraft— seventy Stirlings and forty Albemarles. All these should be available for the battle. I have also asked you to examine how many aircraft can be made available from Coastal Command. It is clear to me that if strenuous effort is made much more ample resources could be secured for General Eisenhower.

2. General Eisenhower should be asked to state the maximum airborne forces he desires to launch simultaneously at the opening of "Overlord". At the same time I should be glad to receive a statement of what we are giving him under present plans. I will preside at a meeting next week to review the position and see how we can meet General Eisenhower's requirements.

* * * * *

The appointment of the commanders gave a fresh impetus. "D.D." tanks which could swim ashore had already been successfully used in the Mediterranean, and would certainly be wanted again. There was also a process of "waterproofing" ordinary tracked and wheeled vehicles to enable them to drive ashore under their own power through several feet of water. But, as usual, the Army's demands for vehicles of all kinds seemed wildly extravagant.

Prime Minister to Minister of Production and Minister   25 Jan 44
of Supply

Pray let me have the report upon the possibilities of producing 300 D.D. tanks by the end of April.

2. What is the position of waterproofing material?

3. I understand that General Montgomery has given a list of some of his priorities to the Ministry of Supply. Let me see this list, with comments upon the possibility of meeting his wishes.

Prime Minister to General Montgomery   31 Jan 44

You spoke to me about waterproofing materials, and every effort is being made to produce what is necessary. Surely however the whole 200,000 vehicles with their one hundred varieties, each of which is a separate proposition, do not require to be waterproofed. Many of these vehicles will not come in till three or four months after the landing has begun, and we hope that by that time the troops will not have to wade ashore. It is very necessary that selective processes and refinements should play their part in the preparations for "Overlord" at this stage in the war, when one need can usually be met only at the expense of another. I know you will bear this in mind.

2. I am most anxious that you should have, if possible, a two-division lift for your airborne force. This would be helped if a firm date could be fixed. The Air Ministry and Ministry of Aircraft Production have been given target dates—for instance, March 15 as the date for providing certain aircraft, such as Albemarles, etc., of which 180 are to be available. If however without prejudice to the above a two-months later date were acceptable, then in this batch alone instead of 180 there would be 270 by May 15. I cannot doubt that similar expansions could be obtained in the case of many other requisites. I am well aware of the arguments about training, but it is the crews and not the machines which need training. If highly skilled crews can be obtained (from, say, the Fleet Air Arm) they can practise on the existing stock of machines so as to have a redundancy of troops to be taken, up till zero hour, over the outflow of machines. Talk to me about this when we meet.

I was most interested in the fire plan of the opening bombardment, particularly its naval aspect.

Prime Minister to First Sea Lord   20 Feb 44

As you will remember, I have several times stressed in my minutes to the Chiefs of Staff the great importance of a bombarding squadron or fleet in Operation "Overlord". Once the air shield has been established the power of the warships is liberated. High-velocity guns are particularly suited for the smashing of concrete pill-boxes. You have told me of the arrangements that you are making, and I consider they should be pressed to the fullest possible extreme.

2. I had a talk yesterday with Admiral Cooke [U.S.N.], who showed me photographs of the Kwaijalein attack in the Marshalls.

He also stressed the great value of short-range bombardment, at, say, 2,000 yards. The beaches in our case will not be convenient for that, I presume. Nevertheless the greater the power that can be brought to bear the better. Here is the time to use the *Ramillies* class; and, as I have said, men can be taken off other ships in order to work up a bombardment for the actual event of the landing, after which they can return to their duties.

3. I propose to have a Defence Committee meeting on Monday week, February 28, to discuss this aspect of "Overlord". Meanwhile I shall be glad to have a paper from you.

In the event naval bombarding forces included six battle-ships, two large monitors, and twenty-two cruisers, besides large numbers of destroyers and smaller vessels. Two-thirds of these were British.

* * * * *

I was anxious that General Marshall should realise the efforts I was making to sustain the plan he had so long desired. I accordingly telegraphed:

Prime Minister to General Marshall (Washington)   11 Mar 44

Since I got home from Marrakesh I have looked carefully into the following aspects of "Overlord", namely:

(i) "Mulberry" and all connected with it;
(ii) airborne assault lift, including method of glider attack;
(iii) inshore bombarding squadrons; and
(iv) Air Command arrangements.

I have presided at a series of meetings at which either Ike or Bedell has been present, and I am satisfied that everything is going on well. Ike and Bedell will probably tell you they are well pleased. I am hardening very much on this operation as the time approaches, *in the sense of wishing to strike if humanly possible, even if the limiting conditions we laid down at Moscow are not exactly fulfilled.** I hope a chance may come for us to have a talk before long. Every good wish.

* * * * *

Once the size of the expedition had been determined it was possible to go ahead with intensive training. Not the least of our difficulties was to find enough room. A broad partition was arranged between British and American forces, whereby the British occupied the south-eastern and the Americans the south-western parts of England. The inhabitants of coastal areas

* Author's subsequent italics.

accepted all the inconveniences in good part. One British division with its naval counterpart did all its earlier training in the Moray Firth area in Scotland. The winter storms prepared them for the rough-and-tumble of D Day.

The theory and practice of amphibious operations had long been established by the Combined Operations Staff, under Admiral Mountbatten, who had been succeeded by General Laycock. It had now to be taught to all concerned, in addition to the thorough general training needed for modern warfare. This of course had long been going on in Britain and America in exercises great and small with live ammunition. Many officers and men entered into battle for the first time, but all bore themselves like seasoned troops.

Lessons from previous large-scale exercises, and of course from our hard experience at Dieppe, were applied in final rehearsals by all three Services, which culminated in early May. All this activity did not pass unnoticed by the enemy. We did not object, and special pains were taken that they should be remarked by watchers in the Pas de Calais, where we wanted the Germans to believe we were coming.

Our plans had to be altered and kept up to date as fresh information came in about the enemy. We knew the general layout of his troops and his principal defences, the gun positions, the strong-points and entrenchments along the coast, but after Rommel took command in late January great additions and refinements began to appear. In particular we had to discover any new types of obstacle that might be installed, and contrive the antidote

Constant air reconnaissance kept us informed of what was going on across the Channel. And of course there were other ways of finding out. Many trips were made by parties in small craft to resolve some doubtful point, to take soundings inshore, to examine new obstacles, or to test the slope and nature of a beach. All this had to be done in darkness, with silent approach, stealthy reconnaissance, and timely withdrawal.

★   ★   ★   ★   ★

An intricate decision was the choice of D Day and H Hour, the moment at which the leading assault craft should hit the beach. From this many other timings had to be worked backwards. It

NORMANDY

was agreed to approach the enemy coast by moonlight, because this would help both our ships and our airborne troops. A short period of daylight before H Hour was also needed to give order to the deployment of the small craft and accuracy to the covering bombardment. But if the interval between first light and H Hour was too long the enemy would have more time to recover from their surprise and fire on our troops in the act of landing.

Then there were the tides. If we landed at high tide the under-water obstacles would obstruct the approach; if at low tide the troops would have far to go across the exposed beaches. Many other factors had to be considered, and it was finally decided to land about three hours before high water. But this was not all. The tides varied by forty minutes between the eastern and western beaches, and there was a submerged reef in one of the British sectors. Each sector had to have a different H Hour, which varied from one place to another by as much as eighty-five minutes.

Only on three days in each lunar month were all the desired conditions fulfilled. The first three-day period after May 31, General Eisenhower's target date, was June 5, 6, and 7. Thus was June 5 chosen. If the weather were not propitious on any of those three days the whole operation would have to be postponed at least a fortnight—indeed, a whole month if we waited for the moon.

*　*　*　*

By April our plans were taking final shape. The Second British Army, under General Dempsey, was to land three divisions on beaches north and north-west of Caen. One airborne division was to be dropped, a few hours before, north-east of Caen to capture the bridges over the lower Orne and protect the eastern flank. On the British right the First U.S. Army, under General Omar Bradley, was to land one division on the coast east of the Vire estuary and one division north of it. The latter would be aided by a previous drop of two airborne divisions a few miles inland. Each Army had one division in ships for immediate reinforcement.

The first objectives of the attack included Caen, Bayeux, Isigny, and Carentan. When these were gained the Americans would advance across the Cotentin peninsula, and also drive northward to capture Cherbourg. The British would protect the American flank from counter-attack from the east, gaining ground south and south-east of Caen, where we could create airfields and use our armour. It was hoped to reach the line Falaise–Avranches three weeks after the landing, and, with the strong reinforcements by that time ashore, to break out eastwards towards Paris, north-eastwards towards the Seine, and westwards to capture the Brittany ports.

These plans depended on our ability to maintain a rapid build-up over the beaches. To co-ordinate all the intricate shipping movements a special organisation was established at the Supreme Commander's headquarters at Portsmouth, with subordinate inter-Service bodies at the embarkation ports. This enabled the commanders on the far shore to control the flow of supplies to their beaches. A similar organisation controlled supplies from the air. The nourishing and expanding of the numerous organisations on the beaches of France was a prime feature. They would soon be as busy as a major port.

The Navy's task would be to carry the Army safely across the Channel and support the landing with all available means; thereafter to ensure the timely arrival of reinforcements and supplies, despite all the hazards of the sea and the enemy. Admiral

Ramsay commanded two Task Forces, one British and the other American. The Eastern Task Force, under Admiral Vian, would control all naval operations in the British sector. Admiral Kirk, U.S.N., operated similarly for the American First Army. These two commands contained five assault forces, each carrying the fighting elements of a division and each having its own specialised craft to give close support to the troops in the landings. Here was the hard core of the attack. Surrounding and protecting the assault forces would be the powerful Allied Navies and Air Forces.

From the embarkation ports, stretching from Felixstowe on the east to the Bristol Channel on the west, shipping would be brought coastwise in convoy to a rendezvous near the Isle of Wight. From here the vast armada would sail to Normandy. Because of the great congestion in our southern ports and to help our deception plans, the heavy naval bombarding forces would assemble in the Clyde and at Belfast.

Mines were the chief danger during the approach, although U-boats and light surface craft would also present a threat, and minesweeping was of vital concern. A mine barrier extended across our line of approach, and we could not tell what more the enemy might do at the last moment in the assault area itself. Ten separate channels through the barrier must be swept for the assault convoys, and thereafter the whole area must be searched. Twenty-nine flotillas of minesweepers were assembled, amounting to about three hundred and fifty craft.

The mighty offensive assigned to Bomber Command and described in an earlier chapter had already been in progress for many weeks. The Allied tactical air forces, under Air Chief Marshal Leigh-Mallory, not only helped the heavy bombers to destroy enemy communications and isolate the battle area, but also had to defeat the enemy's Air Force before the battle began on land. German airfields and installations were attacked for three weeks before D Day in growing weight of bombardment, while fighter sweeps tempted the reluctant enemy to battle. For the assault itself the initial task was to protect our naval forces and convoys from attack by sea or air; then to neutralise the enemy's Radar installations, and, while joining in the joint bombardment plan, additionally to provide fighter cover over the anchorages and beaches. Three airborne divisions were to be delivered safely and in darkness on to their objectives, together with a number of special parties to stir and encourage the seething Resistance Movement.

* * * * *

The bombardment to cover the first landing was a prime factor. Before D Day preliminary air attacks had been delivered on many coastal batteries, not merely those covering the invasion beaches, but, for the sake of deception, all along the French shore. On the night before D Day a great force of British heavy bombers would attack the ten most important batteries that might oppose the landings. At dawn their place was to be taken by medium bombers and ships' gunfire, directed by spotting aircraft. About half an hour after first light the full weight of the U.S. heavy and medium bombers would fall upon the enemy defences. A great variety of guns and rockets mounted in naval assault craft would join in a crescendo of fire.

* * * * *

Of course we had not only to plan for what we were really going to do. The enemy were bound to know that a great invasion was being prepared; we had to conceal the place and time of attack and make him think we were landing somewhere else and at a different moment. This alone involved an immense amount of thought and action. Coastal areas were banned to visitors; censorship was tightened; letters after a certain date were held back from delivery; foreign embassies were forbidden to send cipher telegrams, and even their diplomatic bags were delayed.

Our major deception was to pretend that we were coming across the Straits of Dover. It would not be proper even now to describe all the methods employed to mislead the enemy, but the obvious ones of simulated concentrations of troops in Kent and Sussex, of fleets of dummy ships collected in the Cinque Ports, of landing exercises on the near-by beaches, of increased wireless activity, were all used. More reconnaissances were made at or over the places we were *not* going to than at the places we were. The final result was admirable. The German High Command firmly believed the evidence we put at their disposal. Rundstedt, the Commander-in-Chief on the Western Front, was convinced that the Pas de Calais was our objective.

* * * * *

The concentration of the assaulting forces—176,000 men, 20,000 vehicles, and many thousand tons of stores, all to be shipped in the first two days—was in itself an enormous task. It was handled principally by the War Office and the railway authorities, and with great success. From their normal stations all over Britain the troops were brought to the southern counties, into areas stretching from Ipswich round to Cornwall and the Bristol Channel. The three airborne divisions which were to drop on Normandy before the sea assault were assembled close to the airfields whence they would set out. From their concentration areas in rear troops were brought forward for embarkation in assigned priority to camps in marshalling areas near the coast. At the marshalling camps they were divided up into detachments corresponding to the ship- or boat-loads in which they would be embarked. Here every man received his orders. Once briefed, none were permitted to leave camp. The camps themselves were situated near to the embarkation points. These were ports or "hards"—i.e., stretches of beach concreted to allow of easy embarkation on smaller craft. Here they were to be met by the naval ships.

It seemed most improbable that all this movement by sea and land would escape the attentions of the enemy. There were many tempting targets for their Air, and full precautions were taken. Nearly seven thousand guns and rockets and over a thousand balloons protected the great masses of men and vehicles. But there was no sign of the Luftwaffe. How different things were four years before! The Home Guard, who had so patiently waited for a worth-while job all those years, now found it. Not only were they manning sections of anti-aircraft and coast defences, but they also took over many routine and security duties, thus releasing other soldiers for battle.

All Southern England thus became a vast military camp, filled with men trained, instructed, and eager to come to grips with the Germans across the water.

CHAPTER XXXIV

ROME

May 11—June 9

The Regrouping of the Allied Armies – Alexander's Great Offensive Begins, May 11 – General Juin Takes Ausonia – The Poles Capture the Cassino Monastery – General Advance of the Allies – My Telegram to Alexander of May 17, and His Reply – Report from General Wilson – The Climax Approaches – The Canadian Corps in the Liri Valley – Capture of Cisterna – Alexander's Report, May 24 – The Anzio Army under General Truscott Advances to the Alban Hills, but Fails to Take Valmontone – My Telegrams of May 28 to Alexander – Stubborn German Resistance – Alexander's Telegram of May 30, and My Reply – Valmontone Captured by the Americans, June 2 – The Allied Entry into Rome, June 4 – The War Cabinet Send Congratulations to All – I Send the Good Tidings to Stalin – The Magnificent Achievements of the Russian Armies – Hitler Faces Impending Doom on Three Fronts.

THE regrouping of our forces in Italy was undertaken in great secrecy. Everything possible was done to conceal the movements from the enemy and to mislead him. By the time they were completed General Clark, of the Fifth Army, had over seven divisions, four of them French, on the front from the sea to the river Liri; thence the Eighth Army, now under General Leese, continued the line through Cassino into the mountains with the equivalent of nearly twelve. Six divisions had been packed into the Anzio beach-head ready to sally forth at the best moment; the equivalent of only three remained in the Adriatic sector. In all the Allies mustered over twenty-eight divisions.

Opposed to them were twenty-three German divisions, but our deception arrangements, which included the threat of a landing at Civitavecchia, the seaport of Rome, had puzzled

German meteorological officers informed their High Command that invasion on the 5th or 6th of June would not be possible owing to stormy weather, which might last for several days. The fact that such a complex series of movements could be accomplished without detection by a wary and determined enemy is a remarkable tribute to the work of the Allied Air Forces and the excellence of our deception plans.

* * * * *

All day on June 5 the convoys bearing the spearhead of the invasion converged on the rendezvous south of the Isle of Wight. Thence, in an endless stream, led by the minesweepers on a wide front and protected on all sides by the might of the Allied Navies and Air Forces, the greatest armada that ever left our shores set out for the coast of France. The rough conditions at sea were a severe trial to troops on the eve of battle, particularly in the terrible discomfort of the smaller craft. Yet, in spite of all, the vast movement was carried through with almost the precision of a parade, and, although not wholly without loss, such casualties and delays as did occur, mostly to small craft in tow, had no appreciable effect on events.

Round all our coasts the network of defence was keyed to the highest pitch of activity. The Home Fleet was alert against any move by German surface ships, while air patrols watched the enemy coast from Norway to the Channel. Far out at sea, in the Western Approaches and in the Bay of Biscay, aircraft of Coastal Command, in great strength, supported by flotillas of destroyers, kept watch for possible enemy reactions. Our intelligence told us that over fifty U-boats were concentrated in the French Biscay ports, ready to intervene when the moment came. The hour was now striking.

* * * * *

Here then we reach what the Western Powers may justly regard as the supreme climax of the war. Nor, though the road might be long and hard, could we doubt that decisive victory would be gained. Africa was cleared. India had been defended from invasion. Japan, over-strained and disillusioned, was recoiling on her homeland. All danger to Australia and New Zealand had passed away. Italy was fighting on our side. The Russian armies had driven the German invaders from their country. All the gains Hitler had acquired so swiftly from the Soviets three years before had vanished, with staggering losses of men and equipment. The Crimea had been cleared. The Polish frontiers had been reached. Roumania and Bulgaria were desperately seeking to escape the vengeance of their Eastern conquerors. Russia's new offensive, timed with our Continental landing, was about to break. While I sat in my chair in the Map Room of the Annexe the thrilling news of the capture of Rome arrived. The immense cross-Channel enterprise for the liberation of France had begun. All the ships were at sea. We had the mastery of the oceans and of the air. The Hitler tyranny was doomed.

Here then we might pause in thankfulness and take hope, not only for victory on all fronts and in all three elements, but also for a safe and happy future for tormented mankind.

APPENDICES

APPENDIX A

LIST OF ABBREVIATIONS

A.A. guns	Anti-aircraft guns, or ack-ack guns
A.D.G.B.	Air Defence of Great Britain
A.F.V.s	Armoured fighting vehicles
A.T. rifles	Anti-tank rifles
A.T.S.	(Women's) Auxiliary Territorial Service
C.A.S.	Chief of the Air Staff
C.I.G.S.	Chief of the Imperial General Staff
C.-in-C.	Commander-in-Chief
C.O.S.	Chiefs of Staff
F.O.	Foreign Office
G.H.Q.	General Headquarters
G.O.C.	General Officer Commanding
H.M.G.	His Majesty's Government
M.A.P.	Ministry of Aircraft Production
M.E.W.	Ministry of Economic Warfare
M.O.I.	Ministry of Information
M. OF L.	Ministry of Labour
M. OF S.	Ministry of Supply
P.M.	Prime Minister
V.C.A.S.	Vice-Chief of the Air Staff
V.C.I.G.S.	Vice-Chief of the Imperial General Staff
V.C.N.S.	Vice-Chief of the Naval Staff
W.A.A.F.	Women's Auxiliary Air Force
W.R.N.S.	Women's Royal Naval Service ("Wrens")

APPENDIX B

LIST OF CODE-NAMES

ACCOLADE: Operations in the Ægean.

ADMIRAL Q: President Roosevelt.

ANAKIM: Recapture of Burma.

ANVIL: Allied landings in the South of France, 1944.

AVALANCHE: Amphibious assault on Naples (Salerno).

BAYTOWN: Attack across the Straits of Messina.

BOMBARDON: Steel outer breakwater used in artificial harbours

BUCCANEER: Operation against the Andaman Islands.

CAIRO THREE: The Teheran Conference, 1943.

CALIPH: Operation to assist "Overlord" by an invasion of Southern and Central France.

COLONEL WARDEN: The Prime Minister.

CULVERIN: Operations against Northern Sumatra.

EUREKA: The Teheran Conference, 1943.

GEE: Radar aid to bomber navigation.

GOOSEBERRY: Breakwater used in artificial harbours.

HABAKKUK: Floating seadrome made of ice.

HERCULES: The capture of Rhodes.

HUSKY: The capture of Sicily.

JUPITER: Operations in Northern Norway.

LILO: Breakwater used in artificial harbours.

MULBERRY: Artificial harbour.

OBOE: Blind-bombing device.

OVERLORD: The liberation of France in 1944.

PENITENT: Operations against the Dalmatian coast.

PHŒNIX: Concrete caisson used in artificial harbours.

PIGSTICK: Landings behind the Japanese positions south of Mayu peninsula, on the Arakan coast of Burma.

PLOUGH FORCE: Special Combined Operations Force.

PLUTO: Oil pipe-line across the English Channel.

POINT-BLANK: Directive issued by the Combined Chiefs of Staff amending the Casablanca decisions.

QUADRANT: The Quebec Conference, 1943.

ROUND-UP: Plan for liberation of France in 1943.

SATURN: Establishment of an Allied force in Turkey in 1943.

SEXTANT: The Cairo Conference, 1943.

SHINGLE: Amphibious operation south of Rome at Anzio.

SLEDGEHAMMER: Plan for attack on Brest or Cherbourg in 1942.

STRANGLE: Air attack on railway lines in Northern Italy.

TENTACLE: Floating airfield, constructed mainly of concrete.

TORCH: Allied invasion of French North Africa in 1942.

TRIDENT: The Washington Conference, 1943.

TUBE ALLOYS: Atom bomb research.

WHALE: Floating pier used in artificial harbours.

WINDOW: Tinfoil strips used to confuse German Radar.

ZIP: Signal used by Commanders-in-Chief to denote the start of an operation.

APPENDIX C

PRIME MINISTER'S PERSONAL MINUTES AND TELEGRAMS

JUNE 1943 – MAY 1944

JUNE

Prime Minister to Minister of War Transport and   6 June 43
First Sea Lord

I should be obliged if you would let me have a note on the ships that have passed through the Mediterranean in the different convoys, the character of the cargoes, and what stores have been carried for the British Red Cross to Russia.

Let me also know what is proposed in the future.

Prime Minister to Secretary of State for Air and   8 June 43
Minister of Home Security

Please let me have a report setting out what is being done to protect our reservoirs from attacks like those we have made recently in Germany [on the Möhne Dam].

Prime Minister to Lord Cherwell   10 June 43

POST-WAR CIVIL AVIATION

A Preliminary Note

My ideas about post-war civil aviation are based on the principle of "a fair field and no favour". All the airports of the world should be open to the through traffic of all nations (except the guilty nations) on the payment of reasonable expenses for maintenance and service. No country would however have *the right* to operate an air company, State or private, inside the territory of another. If possible no subsidies should be paid by any Governments. If the traffic proved unremunerative the necessary support should be given on a schedule agreed by the countries concerned, and in part on the basis of air mail contracts. Subject to the above, any company or corporation, State, or individual would be free to operate throughout the world.

2. After the war it is proposed that a World Organisation responsible for maintaining peace should be set up. Air-power resulting from civil aviation would necessarily be subject to the control of this body. A sub-committee of the World Council or sub-committees of the Continental councils (if any) would regulate disputes and supervise

or control quasi-military developments and implications. Subject to this, nations would be encouraged and afforded all facilities to render the best service from the point of view of safety, comfort, and speed of which they were capable.

3. The difficulty of getting agreement among the Dominions at this stage should not prevent the formulation of British policy after consultation with them. At the same time it is of the utmost importance and urgency to ascertain the views and wishes of the United States. Everything will be much easier if agreement is reached with them. . . .

Prime Minister to Major Morton   11 June 43

What is the truth about the tales I hear of applications by various bodies for the leading captured generals to visit some of our education centres and generally to be taken about the country to see things? There was an idea, for instance, that [the Italian] General Jesse should visit Eton. I should be opposed to any of this nonsense. These generals are not to be moved out of their places of internment without my being informed beforehand in each case.

Prime Minister to Sir Edward Bridges   13 June 43

Please draft for me a further warning to all Ministers, high officials, Parliamentary Private Secretaries, etc., about speaking with extreme caution and reticence to foreign [neutral] diplomatic representatives in this country. Although these are very often quite friendly and sincerely wish us to win the war, they do not hesitate to magnify their own positions with their Governments by reporting anything they can pick up, and the Governments may trade this to the enemy in return for other items. Only those who have the duty and authority, either general or special, to impart information should discuss war matters with them or in their presence.

2. Even general war matters and items appearing in the newspapers should not be discussed, because confirmation of these is obtained by these foreigners when they come into contact with persons who have secret knowledge. Lunches and dinners of an informal character with members of the diplomatic staffs should be avoided. You should be consulted in any particular case, and you have my authority to advise. Personal intimacy with foreigners should be reduced to a minimum.

Prime Minister to First Lord   13 June 43

Admiral Cunningham expressed the opinion to me that our light naval craft could have achieved even more in the Mediterranean if the engines of the motor torpedo-boats had been more reliable. Let me have a report on this, and let me know whether this is a local problem connected with the maintenance of these craft or whether there is a basic weakness in the design.

APPENDIX C

Prime Minister to Foreign Secretary and   13 June 43
Minister of Information

I have read the report on German morale in Tunisia. It is hardly possible to pay a higher tribute to the fighting qualities of the German soldier, and the introduction of words like "brutish" in no way detracts from the formidable impression this account gives. Their "extraordinary stupidity" certainly does not extend to the use of their arms or to their seizing of tactical opportunities.

Prime Minister to General Ismay and   15 June 43
Sir Edward Bridges

Will you please make the following terminology effective in all British official correspondence:

For "aeroplane" the word "aircraft" should be used; for "aerodrome" either "airfield" or "airport". The expression "airdrome" should not be used by us.

It is a good thing to have a rule and stick to it.

Prime Minister to Minister of Aircraft Production   15 June 43
[Sir Stafford Cripps]

I am very pleased to see that you are keeping so well up to your programme. You are quite right about the harm that is done by over-calling the hand. Promises which cannot be fulfilled lead to a large waste of effort by the Air Ministry in training, buildings, etc., quite apart from the effect on your own factories.

What I am not quite clear about is your labour situation. I note that you have received a very much smaller quota than was allocated to you. Had you discounted this when you made the programme, or does the fact that you could fulfil it mean that efficiency has increased beyond your expectations? These matters will all have to be considered most carefully in view of the constantly increasing labour stringency. You certainly seem to have received a smaller fraction than any other department so far.

I approve of your list of aircraft with special priorities. As you say, anything that can be done to exceed the programme would be particularly valuable for these types.

I am very pleased that you are pushing ahead with new types of fighters. I am particularly interested in the jet-propelled type of aircraft, of which you showed me a model the other day. Please report progress from time to time, and let me know when we may expect these machines to become available for operations.

Prime Minister to Director of Military Intelligence   15 June 43

What is your present most detailed estimate of the strength in Sicily? First, the Germans: we know the strength in detail of the division which is forming. It is under 7,000. What oddments are there, including air groundsmen? What reinforcements have reached them, or are on the way?

Secondly, give me an analysis of the Italians there. There was a story about eighty-four battalions for coastal garrison purposes; also, another estimate said seven or eight divisions. How are they divided? The easy surrender of the 15,000 men on Pantelleria and the four or five thousand on Lampedusa shows the temper of these Italian masses.

Prime Minister to Chief of the Air Staff   16 June 43

The air forces in Egypt, etc., are very large indeed. Pray let me know how they are to play their part in the next few months. They seem to be doing very little at present. What state of preparation have the plans for reinforcing Turkey reached? What proportion of the air forces in Egypt, etc., are employed in helping in Sicily? We cannot afford to have any part of the Air Force standing idle.

Prime Minister to General Ismay   17 June 43

I am strongly of the opinion that wound stripes should be issued as in the last war. Pray bring this to the notice of the three departments. The War Office are of course the principal party concerned. I wish to make a submission to the King by Monday. The matter must have been previously considered. Let me have any papers on the subject. There must be no further delay in this, on account of the "Purple Hearts" which the Americans are giving to their own soldiers and are distressed not to give to ours.

2. The second question is the issue of chevrons for every year of service abroad, which I think also would be greatly appreciated by the soldiers.

Prime Minister to General Ismay, for C.O.S. Committee   17 June 43

I am anxious about deception plans for Sicily, and therefore asked last night for a special report. The newspapers all seem to be pointing to Sicily, and, to judge by the maps and cartoons that are published in so many organs here, and, I have no doubt, in the United States, this objective would seem to be proclaimed and common property.

2. Safety lies in multiplication and confusion of objectives. A helpful note seems to have been struck this morning in some papers in saying that we have sufficient forces to attack several objectives at once. This should be stressed. Mr. Bracken is seeing the Press representatives this afternoon. Also, surely Greece requires some prominence?

Prime Minister to General Ismay, for C.O.S. Committee   18 June 43

Why cannot we fit some of these Fijian Commandos into the Burma fighting or elsewhere?

Prime Minister to Chief of the Air Staff　　　　　　　19 June 43

I quite understand the relief given to Takoradi by the new route through Casablanca, and by the opening of the Mediterranean. Indeed, the time has come to consider economies of personnel on the Takoradi route, and I shall be glad to receive your proposals to this end.

Prime Minister to Secretary of State for India　　　　20 June 43

I entirely agree with the Deputy Prime Minister that the pay of the Indian Army should be increased. Broadly speaking, I should make a 25 per cent. reduction in the numbers and spread the saving over the pay of the rest.

Prime Minister to Lord President　　　　　　　　　20 June 43

Would it not be well to instruct the Minister of Works and Buildings to use his compulsory powers for land acquisition and to build these 3,000 cottages [for agricultural labourers] exactly as if they were airfields or war factories, and to fit them in as best possible with the necessary war requirements, assigning them a reasonable priority? To ask local authorities all over the country, unarmed with the necessary powers, to get a move on in respect of this handful of cottages and to make their way through the inevitable correspondence with all the public departments engaged in war activities would lead to an immense amount of futile effort. It seems to me that everybody is being disturbed and that we are becoming involved in discredit through this comparatively small job. Broadly speaking, my view is, either do it or don't do it.

Prime Minister to Brigadier Jacob　　　　　　　　22 June 43

Please make out the table about the coast defences of Tripoli, showing the contrast between the pre-war estimates and what was actually found. Naturally, as the war progressed we learnt through frequent contacts more about the defence armaments of Tripoli. We shall now however be attacking a number of new places with which we have not been in contact, and for these the inflated pre-war estimates may exercise an undue influence. This was the whole point of my inquiry.

Prime Minister to C.I.G.S.　　　　　　　　　　　25 June 43

What is the position about the increased proportion of rifle strength in an infantry battalion? It was agreed that it should be increased by thirty-six, and I hoped that it might be by seventy-two.

Prime Minister to Secretary of State for War　　　　26 June 43

I am glad to see that large receipts of .300 ball ammunition are expected by the end of July. In view of these, and having regard to the existing stocks, it should be possible to make extra issnes to the

Home Guard for training at once, so as to take advantage of the remaining summer months.

Prime Minister to Chiefs of Staff Committee   30 June 43
I note that 95 per cent. of the Army and R.A.F. vehicles shipped in May to theatres other than North Africa were boxed. This is most satisfactory, and a considerable contribution to the war effort.

I trust you will aim at a similarly high standard in the remaining theatres. Every month gained in getting adequate assembly plant running is a real saving.*

Prime Minister to Minister of Production and   30 June 43
President of the Board of Trade
I am still anxious about the leather position. Are you satisfied that there will not be a run on the shops when the new ration books become valid? Cannot anything be done to ease the shoe repair position?

In view of the seriousness of the civilian situation, could any relief be obtained from the Services, either in boots or in leather? I note that stocks of boots for the 2½ million men in the Army are higher than civilian stocks for 14 million men.

What are you doing about the long-term outlook? Would it not be desirable to work out with the Americans a picture of world supply and demand over, say, the next twelve months?

Prime Minister to C.I.G.S.   30 June 43
I understand that seventy-five cargo ships are said to be required to carry the equipment of the British troops who will return from North Africa in the winter. This presumably means that they will bring back most of their vehicles with them.

As we are still sending out considerable numbers of vehicles to North Africa, could we not make a saving of shipping in both directions if the returning divisions left most of their vehicles in Africa and were given new ones in England?

JULY

Prime Minister to General Ismay, for C.O.S. Committee 2 July 43
The North African Headquarters seem to be getting more than ever "sicklied o'er with the pale cast of thought". It is quite right for Planning Staffs to explore mentally all possible hypotheses, but happily human affairs are simpler than that.

2. We must first fight the battle which is in the hands of Alexander and Montgomery. Supposing that all goes well, or that there is even

* See Vol. IV, pp. 779, 784, 796.

a collapse, the next step will show itself quite clearly. If, on the other hand, we do not succeed in Sicily no question of the next step arises.

3. We cannot allow the Americans to prevent our powerful armies from having full employment. Their Staffs seem now to be wriggling away to [the idea of] Sardinia. We must stiffen them all up and allow no weakness. I trust the Chiefs of Staff will once again prevent through the Combined Chiefs of Staff this weak shuffling away from the issue.

4. Above all we must preserve to ourselves the full power to judge and launch once we know what Sicily tastes like.

5. I should be very glad to discuss this with you this afternoon at 3 p.m. I do not like the present attitude. Strong guidance must be given.

Prime Minister to Lord Cherwell   3 July 43
MAN-POWER
Please divide the subject into seven or eight main claimants—Army, Navy, Air, Ministry of Aircraft Production, etc. How many did they have, and what did they ask for in the January review? What did they get, and how many have they got now? How many more are they asking for now?

It is on this table that I propose to work.

Let me have it to-night.

Prime Minister to Lord President and Sir E. Bridges   3 July 43
What is the exact situation now about these cottages for agricultural labourers? Who is in charge of building them, and when are they going to get built? The Minister of Works and Buildings led me to understand that he has the whole matter in his hands now. Is this so?

Prime Minister to Lord President   5 July 43
You may remember my note last December about the increase in short-term sickness, shown in figures compiled by the Government Actuary.

It is disquieting to find that the rising trend has continued during the winter. The addition thus revealed to the numbers normally kept away from work by sickness is quite an appreciable fraction of our total labour force; and the effect on the war effort is the same if a large proportion of them are war-weary rather than genuinely ill.

Prime Minister to Secretary of State for Air and   5 July 43
Chief of the Air Staff
In view of all the assurances given about the comparative impotence of enemy bombing, I am of the opinion that the time has come to review the question of the black-out so far as night work in industrial establishments is concerned.

The need for saving labour in every direction in order to speed up the aircraft programme makes it indispensable that night work is not hampered by black-out restrictions.

I should like an assurance that the Air Ministry is not insisting on any restrictions of this character which hamper production.

Prime Minister to Secretary of State for War   5 July 43

I am glad to note that your requirements of crude rubber are no higher than in 1942, and that the Army is helping to conserve our supplies of vital raw materials. Since the number of Army vehicles will be greater this year the result is satisfactory.

Prime Minister to Minister of Economic Warfare   5 July 43

I do not view the situation in France as you do, and I do not agree with your sweeping generalisations, taken from much too narrow a base. If the [French] Liberation Committee so conduct themselves as to win the confidence of the British and United States Governments, we could no doubt transfer to them the responsibility of financing the Resistance movements in France. It is however the Committee, and not General de Gaulle, with whom we should work. We are now endeavouring to build up the collective and impersonal strength of the Committee and to elevate the civilian influences as much as possible.

Prime Minister to Sir Edward Bridges   11 July 43

I am very much interested in the question of Basic English. The widespread use of this would be a gain to us far more durable and fruitful than the annexation of great provinces. It would also fit in with my ideas of closer union with the United States by making it even more worth while to belong to the English-speaking club.

2. I propose to raise this to-morrow at the Cabinet with a view to setting up a committee of Ministers to examine the matter, and, if the result is favourable, to advise how best to proceed. The Minister of Information, the Colonial Secretary, the President of the Board of Education, and perhaps Mr. Law, representing the Foreign Office, would all seem suitable.

3. I contemplate that the B.B.C. should teach Basic English every day as part of their propaganda, and generally make a big push to propagate this method of interchange of thought.

4. Let me know your ideas about the committee, and put the matter on the agenda for to-morrow.

Prime Minister to Foreign Secretary   11 July 43

About King Peter's marriage, we should recur to first principles. The whole tradition of military Europe has been in favour of *les noces de guerre*, and nothing could be more natural and nothing could be more becoming than that a young king should marry a highly suitable princess on the eve of his departure for the war. Thus he has a chance of perpetuating his dynasty, and anyhow of giving effect to those primary instincts to which the humblest of human beings have a right.

2. Against this we have some tale, which I disbelieve of a martial race, that the Serb principle is that no one must get married in war-time. *Prima facie* this would seem to condone extra-marital relations. Then a bundle of Ministers that has been flung out of Yugoslavia are rolling over each other to obtain the shadow offices of an *émigré* Government. Some are in favour of the marriage, some are not. The King and the Princess are strongly in favour of it, and in my view in this tangle they are the only ones whose opinions should weigh with us.

3. The Foreign Office should discard eighteenth-century politics and take a simple and straightforward view. Let us tell the King and tell his Ministers we think the marriage should take place, and if the King is worthy of his hazardous throne we may leave the rest to him.

4. I may add that I am prepared to go into action in the House of Commons or on any democratic platform in Great Britain or the United States on the principles set forth above; and I think the Cabinet ought to have a chance of expressing its own views. We might be back in the refinements of Louis XIV instead of the lusty squalor of the twentieth century. Are we not fighting this war for liberty and democracy? My advice to the King, if you wish me to see him, will be to go to the nearest Registry Office and take a chance. So what?

Prime Minister to Secretary of State for Air and   12 July 43
Chief of the Air Staff

AIRCRAFT FOR AUSTRALIA

It is of high importance for the future of the British Commonwealth and Empire that we should be represented in the defence of Australia and the war in the Pacific. From this point of view the single squadron of the Royal Air Force which we have sent has played a part out of all proportion to the size of the unit. The fact that Australia has over here 8,100 Australian air crews, including some of their very best airmen, and the share they have taken in the Empire Training Scheme, certainly leaves us heavily in their debt so far as the air is concerned.

2. It is not merely a question of Spitfires or other fighter aircraft, but of British squadrons capable of doing full justice to the Royal Air Force. I should therefore like to send three Spitfire fighter squadrons to Australia during the present year, and persuade the Americans to give us the fighter aircraft they would otherwise have sent to Australia. I have little doubt that I can explain all this quite satisfactorily to the President. You will note however that I am not proposing to mount Australian airmen on British machines, but to send complete British

units. I note from my last return that you have 945 more fighter pilots on effective strength than fighter machines serviceable, and therefore it seems to me that forty or fifty could easily be spared out of these. It is my duty to preserve goodwill between the Mother Country and this vast continent of Australia, inhabited by six million people of our race and tongue.

3. Pray let me have your comments and proposals.

(Action this Day.)
Prime Minister to General Ismay, for C.O.S. Committee   13 July 43

The time has come to bring the Polish troops from Persia into the Mediterranean theatre. Politically this is highly desirable, as the men wish to fight, and once engaged will worry less about their own affairs, which are tragic. The whole corps should move from Persia to Port Said and Alexandria. The intention is to use them in Italy.

2. We have five months in hand to use all our strength against Italy. Let me have a list of the British-controlled [Allied] troops available which are not yet committed to the Sicilian battle and are capable of active field operations.

Prime Minister to First Sea Lord   13 July 43

I am shocked to see the destruction of the *Duchess of York* convoy. Will you let me have a copy of the signal from the C.-in-C. Mediterranean about ten days ago, warning us of the "intolerable" (I think that was the word) dangers of the air attack on this route too near the Spanish coast? The loss of these large ships will spoil our monthly record, which anyhow is burdened with operational casualties. Pray let me know what will be done to avoid this form of air attack in the future. Surely it is worth while going farther out beyond the range of Focke-Wulfs.

2. I see that *Port Fairy* was damaged west of Cape St. Vincent. Where did the aircraft come from, and how far out was she? If the enemy could reach her why could not Gibraltar air give her protection?

Prime Minister to Sir Edward Bridges   14 July 43

The Public Relations Officers are becoming a scandal, and the whole system requires searching scrutiny and drastic pruning. Pray advise me how to proceed. A small Cabinet committee with a suitable reference would seem to be indicated.

(Action this Day.)
Prime Minister to Secretary of State for War and   16 July 43
C.I.G.S.

I learn with great concern from C.I.G.S. that our 1st Armoured Division, a unit of exceptional quality and experience, on which years of training have been lavished, is now being used to guard prisoners of war. As an emergency measure for, say, a month this might be tolerated. It must now immediately be brought to an end. Rifle-armed formations, not incorporated in divisional units, to the number of at least 10,000 must be sent to North Africa either from this country or the Delta to guard prisoners. Lord Leathers should regard the shipping for any from this country as a high priority.

2. At the earliest moment the 1st Armoured Division is to be re-constituted with its vehicles and brought up to full strength. The necessary training to restore its efficiency cannot be delayed. Let me have a programme and time-table. I understand that C.I.G.S. has already protested to General Eisenhower. Let me know exactly what happened, and what the answer was.

3. Are there any more units in this condition? Let me have a list of all divisional and separate brigade formations (a) in North-West Africa and (b) in the Middle East, stating the condition of each and the task on which it is employed. What is the state of the South African Division? What has happened to the 201st Guards Brigade? Where is the 7th Armoured Division? Where is the 4th Indian Division? Is the New Zealand Division progressing to schedule? What stage has been reached in the movement of the Polish Division to Syria? How far are these divisions complete and equipped?

Prime Minister to Chief of the Air Staff   16 July 43

I still do not understand why it is necessary to have 2,946 crews on effective strength [in Fighter Command] in order to man 1,732 serviceable aircraft, or indeed a total initial equipment of 1,966.

See how different are the figures of Bomber Command, who are far more heavily engaged than the fighters, and who have only 1,353 crews to an initial establishment of 1,072 aircraft, and only 1,095 crews operational for 1,039 aircraft serviceable.

The losses in Fighter Command are not comparable to those endured by the bombers, and yet it has this enormous surplus of crews. How far does this personnel surplus extend into the ground staff?

Prime Minister to Lord President of the Council   17 July 43

I have promised Lord Winterton a further communication about the building of the agricultural cottages. I now feel however that as I should like him to have a fuller explanation of the position than could conveniently be contained in a letter it would be helpful if you could see Lord Winterton yourself.*

(*Action this Day.*)

Prime Minister to C.I.G.S.   19 July 43

I do not feel very comfortable about the strength of the Dover

* See minute of July 3 to Lord President.

Garrison, which I visited on Saturday. There is only one battalion in Dover, and another at St. Margaret's Bay. These can be reinforced by a brigade after some hours. There are of course plenty of troops farther back.

2. There is of course no question of invasion, but when I asked General Swayne what would happen if three or four thousand Storm Troopers of the Commando type came across one night he was not able to give me a very reassuring answer. He said they would certainly get ashore, but would be turned out afterwards, and he also emphasised the shortness of the warning that would be received. This is not good enough. Dover is so near that perhaps half an hour is all the notice you would get by Radar. I do not think the Germans are likely to try, but it would be a tremendous score if they did have possession of part of Dover for even three or four hours. It would produce an effect on public opinion ten times as bad as the *Scharnhorst* and *Gneisenau* incident.

3. I should be much against locking up too many troops even at this point on the coast, but it seems to me we have gone to the other extreme and are exposing ourselves to what might be a most vexatious affront. In my opinion, at least another brigade should be actually in the coast defences or the strong-points, and available for immediate action should a landing be attempted. We should all look very silly if some of our valuable guns were blown up.

Pray go into this matter anew.

Prime Minister to Secretary of State for War and   19 July 43
Minister of Information

In difficult cases about releases from military service it is important that the rules should not be broken or relaxed. Nevertheless the Secretary of State has a discretionary power, where the public service may be advantaged, to make exceptions in respect of high-class personnel whose contributions to the war effort may be greater in their civilian employment. In using this discretion he would naturally have regard to the fact that only a very small part of the Army is engaged in actual fighting, and that many transferences from civil life to the Army merely involve a change of non-combatant job.

2. It is the duty of Ministers to settle such matters by personal arrangement, and not to let them come to a point where either departmental antagonisms arise on small points or I am called upon to intervene.

Prime Minister to Minister of Information   19 July 43

I saw again yesterday the two American Army films *Divide and Conquer* and *The Battle of Britain*. I think they are the best propaganda yet seen in this country. Moreover, they teach people about what happened in 1940, which few realised completely at the time and which is already beginning to fade in memory. I consider that these films should have the widest possible showing. Is there any difficulty in our picture-houses taking them? What terms, broadly, would you arrange with them? If there is any monopolistic refusal do not hesitate to come to me. I would ask for legislation if necessary.

2. Where are the other four films? Two have certainly been mentioned by name. I wish to see them. Why is there this long delay? Are the film companies making underground resistance? Please let me have a report on these second two films. What is holding them up?

3. As you know, I am willing to make a short statement introducing the films and praising the attitude of the Americans. But I wish to see the other two films first. I take much interest in this business, and I hope you will press it forward strongly.

Prime Minister to Chief of the Air Staff 21 July 43

I am disposed to sanction this proposal of the Secretary for Petroleum. You know I attach the greatest importance to the creation of a sufficiency of landing-grounds specially adapted to meet fog conditions. I hope this is fully realised.

Prime Minister to First Lord 23 July 43

I think it is rather a pregnant fact that out of 45,000 officers and ratings [in the Fleet Air Arm], of whom over 4,000 are officers, only thirty should have been killed, are missing, or have been taken prisoners during the three months ending April 30. I am very glad of course that they have not suffered, but the whole question of the scale of the Fleet Air Arm is raised by this clear proof of how very rarely it is brought into contact with the enemy. When such immense demands are made upon us by the Fleet Air Arm in respect of men and machines, one is bound, however ungrateful the task may seem, to scrutinise its actual employment against the enemy. I am sure it is not the fault of the officers and men that they have not had more opportunity, and it may be the period in question was exceptional. We cannot however keep such a large mass of high-class personnel of the highest fighting quality in a condition of non-activity so far as actual contact with the enemy is concerned.

Pray give this matter your careful consideration, because I shall be returning to it in the near future.

Prime Minister to General Ismay, for C.O.S. Committee 24 July 43

See now how all these difficulties [in Burma] are mounting up, and what a vast expenditure of force is required for these trumpery gains. All the commanders on the spot seem to be competing with one another to magnify their demands and the obstacles they have to overcome.

2. All this shows how necessary it is to decide on a commander. I still consider he should be a determined and competent soldier, in the prime of life, and with the latest experience in the field. General Oliver Leese is, I believe, the right man, and as soon as the fighting in Sicily is over he should come back to this country for consultation. I consider Wingate should command the army against Burma. He is a man of genius and audacity, and has rightly been discerned by all eyes as a figure quite above the ordinary level. The expression "the Clive of Burma" has already gained currency. There is no doubt that in the welter of inefficiency and lassitude which has characterised our operations on the Indian front this man, his force and his achievements, stand out, and no mere question of seniority must obstruct the advance of real personalities to their proper stations in war. He too should come home for discussion here at an early date.

Prime Minister to General Ismay, for C.O.S. Committee　　　25 July 43

See the various telegrams about the ill-treatment of our people in North Russia. The only way to deal with this kind of thing is for ostentatious preparations to be made to withdraw the whole of our personnel without saying anything to the Russian authorities. Let a plan be made for this. As soon as the local Russians see that we are off they will report to Moscow, and will of course realise that the departure of our personnel means the end of the Arctic convoys. If anything will bring them to their senses this will. If not, anyway we had better be out of it, as it only causes friction. Experience has taught me that it is not worth while arguing with Soviet people. One simply has to confront them with the new fact and await their reactions.

Prime Minister to C.I.G.S.　　　25 July 43

I am obliged to you for reviewing the strength of the Dover Garrison. I had not taken into consideration the important forces mentioned by you. Are you sure that all these, especially the Royal Navy and Royal Air Force, are organised for immediate action at the shortest notice? Of course it could only be by night.

The possibility I had in mind was a smash-and-grab raid by about 2,000 Storm Troopers brought across in fast motor-boats. Provided you are satisfied that there is no danger of this, that the cliffs are unscalable and that the landing-points and defences are adequately garrisoned, I am content.*

Prime Minister to General Ismay, for C.O.S. Committee　　　26 July 43

It is vital and urgent to appoint a young, competent soldier, well

---

* See minute of July 19 to C.I.G.S.

trained in war, to become Supreme Commander [in the Burma theatre], and to re-examine the whole problem of the war on this front so as to infuse vigour and audacity into the operations.

2. I know the Chiefs of Staff fully realise what a foolish thing it now looks to go and concentrate precious resources from the Mediterranean in order to attack the one speck of land in the whole of this theatre, namely, Akyab, which the enemy are making a kind of Gibraltar and are capable of reinforcing up to an entire Japanese division. For this petty purpose, now rightly stripped of its consequential attempt upon Rangoon, we are to utilise the whole amphibious resources available in the Bay of Bengal for the whole of the year 1944. Even Ramree is to be left over until after the 1944 monsoon. A more silly way of waging war by a nation possessing overwhelming sea-power and air-power can hardly be conceived, and I should certainly not be prepared to take responsibility for such a waste of effort, and above all of time.

3. The proper course for the campaign of 1944 is as follows:

(a) Maximum air aid to China; improvement of the air route and protection of the airfields.

(b) Maximum pressure by operations similar to those conducted by General Wingate in Assam, and, wherever [else] contact can be made on land, with the Japanese forces.

(c) The far-flung amphibious operation hitherto called "Second Anakim", which can be launched in regions where fighting is not interrupted by the monsoon season and where our naval and air powers can be brought into the fullest play. It is on this that the most urgent and intense study should now be concentrated by the Staffs.

4. The matter must now be brought up before the Defence Committee, in order that their views in principle may be ascertained before our Conference at Quebec.

Prime Minister to President of the Board of Trade   26 July 43

I am told that in spite of contributions from civilian supplies there is at present a shortage of playing-cards for use by the forces and workers in industry. The importance of providing amusement for the forces in their leisure hours and in long periods of waiting and monotony in out-of-the-way places, and for the sailors penned up in their ships for months together, cannot be overstated. Nothing is more handy, more portable, or more capable of prolonged usage than a pack of cards.

Let me have a report on this subject, and show me how you can remedy this deficiency. It ought to mean only a microscopic drain on our resources to make a few hundred thousand packs.

Prime Minister to Secretary of State for War (to see)   26 July 43
and C.I.G.S.

I am willing not to send a personal telegram to Eisenhower on the state of the 1st Armoured Division in order that he may not think you were pressing me to do so. However, I can only agree to this if prompt and drastic action is taken, for I am determined that this fine unit shall be immediately brought to the highest state of efficiency and equipment. We shall need it all the more if large distances have to be covered rapidly in Italy, and especially if our front broadens out into the northern part of Italy and the valley of the Po.

2. Will you therefore inform General Eisenhower that I am deeply concerned in this matter, and procure a prompt and satisfactory settlement with him.

3. Will you also give me a programme of the re-equipment of the division, and thereafter let me have reports fortnightly on the progress made towards its becoming in all ways fit for action.*

Prime Minister to Minister of Agriculture   30 July 43

I shall be much obliged if you will give me a brief report on the harvest, both hay and corn.

Prime Minister to Colonel Price   31 July 43

I do not consider that the date 1948 should now be mentioned as the hypothetical date for the ending of the war with Japan. This matter can be discussed between us during our Conference at Quebec and on the way to it. . . . Obviously the long-term projects of the Admiralty must be before us at the time of taking any such decisions.

Prime Minister to Minister of Aircraft Production   31 July 43

I am concerned that you hold out such slender hopes of our getting jet-propelled aircraft soon. I have heard that there is considerable diffusion of effort, and that even the air frames, which should not present any difficulty, are apt to be behindhand.

Would it not be a good thing to examine the numerous engines which it seems are under development and to concentrate our efforts on the two or three [types] which we may hope to get into production quickly? There are numerous reports of German jet-propelled aircraft, and we cannot afford to be left behind.

AUGUST

Prime Minister to President of the Board of Trade   1 Aug 43

Thank you for your note about shortages of playing-cards. What happened to the 1,950,000 produced over and above the 1,300,000 issued in the last twelve months?

* See minute of July 16 to Secretary of State for War.

2. As to the future twelve months, the demands appear to be well under 2,000,000 packs, against which you propose to make 2,250,000 packs. I should be very willing to support you in getting the twenty more workers and hundred tons of paper necessary to make an additional million, but first I must know what has happened to the 1,950,000 surplus in the last twelve months, and, secondly, what is the reserve you consider necessary to have "in hand for emergency". The important thing is to have the cards freely forthcoming when called for, and although the soldiers should have priority civilian workers need them too.*

Prime Minister to First Sea Lord   1 Aug 43

I have suggested to the President that we issue from Hyde Park during "Quadrant" our monthly statement about the anti-U-boat warfare. This will mean it will come out on the 13th or 14th, instead of on the 10th.

2. I am anxious to strike a strong and heavy blow this time on German hopes, and I should like to press the President to agree to the following items:

> (a) In the first half of 1942 1.6 ships; in the second half of 1942 .8 of a ship; in the first half of 1943 .4 of a ship.
>
> (b) In the ninety-two days of May, June, and July eighty-seven, or whatever is the figure, U-boats are known to have been destroyed, in addition to the many which have been damaged.
>
> (c) The losses of Allied merchant shipping all over the world were greater in July than in June, which was a record month, but they are substantially less than the average of, say, the period January 1942 to June 1943, inclusive, or January 1943 to June 1943, inclusive, whichever you like. The operational losses in the capture of Sicily do not exceed, say, 70,000 tons.
>
> (d) During the present year—i.e., to the end of July—the new ships completed by the United States, Great Britain, and Canada exceeded all sinkings in the shipping of the United Nations by upwards of, say, three million tons—i.e., the nearest million under the true figure.

Pray let these points be considered before we leave, so that I can discuss the whole matter with the President.

P.S. How many of them were sunk by the British?

Prime Minister to General Ismay   2 Aug 43

Make sure that no code-names are approved without my seeing them first.

* See minute of July 26 to President of the Board of Trade.

Prime Minister to C.I.G.S.   2 Aug 43

Eisenhower's telegram about relief of the 1st Armoured Division from garrison duties.

1. Please let me know what can be done, consulting Lord Leathers about shipping, to meet the further requirements of guards for prisoners of war.*

2. I do not understand why it was necessary to strip all other armoured units in the Middle East in order to provide the very limited armoured forces taking part in "Husky". Let me have a report showing the exact number of tanks held by each of the various units in Africa, and also the last tank report, which showed, I think, nearly 3,000 tanks in possession of Middle East Command.

3. We should not hesitate to take Shermans from a British armoured division in this country to send out at once by special ships in order to get the 1st Armoured Division rapidly re-equipped.

4. Let me also have a return showing the number of tanks available in Great Britain, and the number expected from America and from supply in the next three months.

Prime Minister to C.I.G.S.   2 Aug 43

I am counting on you to make sure that these prime units of our Army which we have had so much trouble and delay in making are not melted down into slush by uncomprehending hands.

We are getting a mass of tanks of all kinds in the Middle East, and also at the same time a litter of bits and pieces of personnel, where once stood perfectly organised veteran armoured divisions and brigades.

Nothing must stand in the way of rehabilitation.

Prime Minister to Lord President of the Council   2 Aug 43

I am much obliged to you for all the trouble you have taken, and I welcome the further inquiries you are to make into the Army Bureau of Current Affairs.

Every effort should be used to prevent extra time, money, and military personnel being absorbed in these activities, which, although admirable in themselves, must not be allowed unduly to cumber the military machine and increase the heavy disproportion of non-combatant services. Above all, no man fit to fight should be drawn into this organisation, and the utmost vigilance must be used to correct the tendency of all such bodies to magnify themselves and their numbers.

Prime Minister to Minister of Aircraft Production   3 Aug 43

The fall in engine production is very painful. I quite realise that it

---

* See minutes of July 16 and 26.

is the holiday season, but the fall in new production seems to have been much greater this year than last.

Prime Minister to Deputy Prime Minister   6 Aug 43

Your committee on Air Force establishments should certainly probe the enormous surpluses of crews compared with serviceable aircraft in the fighter squadrons.* 3,038 crews are maintained to man 1,725 aircraft. The reason given is that they have to be standing about waiting to take off at any moment, but this reason is good only over certain areas and under certain conditions. The fighter aircraft have not had heavy losses since the Battle of Britain, and it looks to me as if substantial economies could be made here. One wonders whether everything is on a similarly lavish scale. Bomber Command, although in far more continuous heavy action, works on a much smaller margin. Coastal Command are however remarkably well supplied with surplus crews. Here however the need to have as many aircraft as possible out on the long patrols is paramount, and may be only satisfiable by practical duplication of crews. This, I repeat, does not apply to fighter aircraft.

2. Another point which requires searching is the accumulation of Hurricanes and Spitfires at Takoradi. In the latest return, dated July 30, there are 183, of which forty-three are Spitfires. Considering that this route is falling into abeyance on account of a much better route becoming open through the Mediterranean, we should scrutinise narrowly the personnel employed on the route, as well as this habit of keeping a mass of invaluable aircraft additional to all Middle East reserves in the tank at Takoradi.

Prime Minister to Foreign Secretary   6 Aug 43

I do not think that the Russians have any anxieties about the rearmament of Turkey on its present scale. The Russians' preponderance of strength is so great that the trifling improvements we are making in the Turkish forces need not, and I believe will not, disturb them.

2. No doubt they would be annoyed by Turkey complicating the situation in the Balkans without doing anything effective to help Russia defeat Germany.

3. Obviously however the Russians will not remain contented with the present state of the Straits, and I do not suppose they have forgotten that we offered them Constantinople in the earlier part of the late war. Turkey's greatest safety lies in the active association with the United Nations. As you know, the time may come very soon when we shall ask her to admit our air squadrons and certain other forces to protect them in order to bomb Ploesti and gradually secure the control of the

---

* See minute of July 16 to Chief of the Air Staff.

Straits and the Black Sea. There is not much basis of real conversation with Russia about Turkey till we know what line Turkey takes.

Prime Minister to General Ismay   8 Aug 43

I have crossed out on the attached paper many unsuitable names. Operations in which large numbers of men may lose their lives ought not to be described by code-words which imply a boastful and over-confident sentiment, such as "Triumphant", or, conversely, which are calculated to invest the plan with an air of despondency, such as "Woe-betide", "Massacre", "Jumble", "Trouble", "Fidget", "Flimsy", "Pathetic", and "Jaundice". They ought not to be names of a frivol-ous character, such as "Bunnyhug", "Billingsgate", "Aperitif", and "Ballyhoo". They should not be ordinary words often used in other connections, such as "Flood", "Smooth", "Sudden", "Supreme", "Fullforce", and "Fullspeed". Names of living people—Ministers or commanders—should be avoided; *e.g.*, "Bracken."

2. After all, the world is wide, and intelligent thought will readily supply an unlimited number of well-sounding names which do not suggest the character of the operation or disparage it in any way and do not enable some widow or mother to say that her son was killed in an operation called "Bunnyhug" or "Ballyhoo".

3. Proper names are good in this field. The heroes of antiquity, figures from Greek and Roman mythology, the constellations and stars, famous racehorses, names of British and American war heroes, could be used, provided they fall within the rules above. There are no doubt many other themes that could be suggested.

4. Care should be taken in all this process. An efficient and a successful administration manifests itself equally in small as in great matters.*

Prime Minister to General Ismay, for C.O.S. Committee   10 Aug 43

Please see this telegram.† There is no objection to the employment of Commandos, which are in fact regular troops of the highest order and the only ones we are likely to be able to spare for the Balkans this year. Fully accredited British military or diplomatic officers can of course accompany the Commandos to negotiate any surrender that may be asked for. The Middle East Commanders-in-Chief must not be encouraged to take conventional reactionary views.

Prime Minister to Minister of Production and   11 Aug 43
Minister of Supply

I am shocked at the appallingly low output of thirty-nine tanks for

* See minute of August 2 to General Ismay.

† From Middle East Defence Committee, deprecating the employment of Com-mandos in the Dodecanese, etc., as the Italians and Germans were unlikely to surrender to them.

the week ending July 31. I do not feel that the explanation of summer holidays is sufficient, and I shall be glad if you will let me have a full report. How does this figure compare with forecasts, and are your forecasts being realised, especially in the modern type of tanks? I shall require to be fully convinced on this matter, which has an important bearing on our policy regarding acceptance of American tanks.

Prime Minister to Foreign Secretary   14 Aug 43

All this is quite true, but it might better have been left unsaid. The displacement of Ribbentrop by von Papen would be a milestone of importance, and would probably lead to further disintegration in the Nazi machine. There is no need for us to discourage this process by continually uttering the slogan "Unconditional Surrender". As long as we do not have to commit ourselves to dealing with any particular new figure or new Government our advantage is clear. We certainly do not want, if we can help it, to get them all fused together in a solid desperate block for whom there is no hope. I am sure you will agree with me that a gradual break-up in Germany must mean a weakening of their resistance, and consequently the saving of hundreds of thousands of British and American lives.

Prime Minister to First Sea Lord   15 Aug 43

I hope you will consider whether it is not possible to arrest the traffic in the Cape area by turning your ships into Simonstown and Kilindini until the anti-U-boat reinforcements now on the way have arrived. I have asked Lord Leathers to give me the proportion of ships sunk to the total sailed. Nineteen is however a very heavy loss on a small and severely rationed traffic.

SEPTEMBER

Prime Minister (Washington) to Sir Ronald Campbell   13 Sept 43

I have drafted the following message, as you desire, for our Consuls in the Middle West.

Before sending it out you should consult Mr. Harry Hopkins privately as to whether he thinks it would be a suitable intervention for me to make.

"British Consuls in the Middle West should let everyone there know how much we in Britain admire and value the tremendous war effort made by so many of these States, which, though a thousand miles from the sea, are making their weight tell on all the battle-fronts and hastening the triumph of the good cause.

"I wish indeed I could have come to some of these great cities to express myself our British thanks for the splendid exertions which are being made."

Prime Minister to Mr. President   13 Sept 43

CIVIL AVIATION

I have told our Government that you made no objection when I said that we intended to hold a preliminary Commonwealth meeting in London or Canada, and that this would be only to focus our own British Commonwealth ideas for subsequent discussion with the United States Government.

2. I said that, about the proposed International Conference, you thought it might wait till the matter had been discussed at the forth-coming tripartite Anglo-Soviet-American meetings.

3. I mentioned that your preliminary view comprised the following:

  (i) There should be private ownership.

  (ii) Key points should be available for international use on a reciprocal basis.

  (iii) Internal traffic should be reserved to internal companies.

  (iv) Government support may be required on an international basis for certain non-paying routes.

Prime Minister to Lord President of the Council   16 Sept 43

The Italians have not been able to comply with the conditions specified in General Eisenhower's broadcast of July 29, and in my view we may therefore consider our hands free in the matter. We should proceed with all arrangements now made for the further importation of Italian prisoners. Where are the great mass that we have taken? Over 250,000 were captured by General Wavell alone. It would be rather difficult to move to England men taken after the armistice, who in many cases have done their best to help us or have not resisted at all, but we have these larger pools to draw on, and work in the United Kingdom is more important than in India or South Africa. There should be a certain amount of return shipping from India. The War Office should supply the exact location of all Italian prisoners belonging to us, wherever they may be.

2. An arrangement could no doubt be made with the Badoglio Government, whom we have many ways of helping, in respect of further supplies of Italian labour. As a result of an arrangement with the Italian Government by which we get more labour, I see no reason why the status of Italian prisoners now in Great Britain should not be modified and they be placed on the basis of civilian Pioneer Corps internees, or something like that. I certainly look

forward to getting 100,000 more Italians into England for work purposes during 1944.

Prime Minister to First Lord and V.C.N.S.   26 Sept 43

What is being done to equip our submarines with an acoustic torpedo for their own defence when submerged and attacked by enemy anti-submarine craft?

Prime Minister to Minister of Food and   27 Sept 43
Minister of War Transport

I think we should certainly use some of the shipping space in vessels returning from North Africa for bringing over oranges and lemons from the Mediterranean area to this country. Pray consult together and let me have a note setting out what is being done and what is possible.

Prime Minister to First Lord   27 Sept 43

Please see that Lord Cherwell is kept informed about the German glider bomb, and also about the foxing devices, so that he can keep me in touch with all developments.

Prime Minister to Minister of War Transport   29 Sept 43

It is indispensable to diminish the queues for the buses and provide a better service for workers returning home, especially in the London area. This is certainly possible in view of the greatly improved oil position. Pray make proposals for immediate action in good time before the winter comes. You should aim at a 25 per cent. increase in the evening services. War efficiency is lost when people are tired out before they get home.

Prime Minister to C.I.G.S.   30 Sept 43

Let me have a short return of the present garrison at Cyprus. They ought to be able to find seven or eight thousand men in case the opportunity comes for an unopposed re-entry into Greece. There would be no question of occupying the country, but only giving a political support to a lawful restored Government.

Prime Minister to President of the Board of Trade and   30 Sept 43
Minister of Food

It seems clear that there may be a world shortage of many important foodstuffs after the liberation of Europe. I am anxious lest we should be committed to any estimates of relief requirements, which might prejudice our own supplies, before the Cabinet has had an opportunity of discussing the whole question.

Pray let me have a note on this as soon as possible.

OCTOBER

Prime Minister to Admiral Mountbatten, and to   2 Oct 43
General Ismay, for C.O.S. Committee

It seems to me that this draft Order of the Day would be a very good text for Admiral Mountbatten to use when visiting detachments of his forces. I deprecate however at this stage any general publication of such a document. The only consequence of it will be to draw more Japanese to this theatre. I cannot too strongly emphasise the importance of damping down all publicity about this theatre for at least three months. If it is communicated to any portion of the troops the strictest censorship should be used to prevent it being printed either in the Indian or world Press. I shall myself be referring to the South-East Asia theatre when I next speak in the House of Commons, in terms like these:

"The climatic conditions, the famine and the floods, have greatly set back all possibilities in this theatre. The new Commander-in-Chief will require to survey the whole situation on the spot and to visit many parts of the great regions with which he is concerned. Further prolonged periods of training are necessary for the troops. It would be very foolish to base expectations of large-scale action upon the fact that a new Commander-in-Chief has been appointed and that the Command is undergoing a very complete reorganisation."

This is much the best way to get through these next three or four months. It need in no way prevent the animation of the Army by visits of Admiral Mountbatten to the various widely separated centres of the Command or his infusing into all officers and men the sense of great days coming. The opposite impression should however be given to the world public and to the enemy.

> The sower went forth sowing,
> The seed in secret slept
> Through months of faith and patience,
> Till out the red blade leapt.

Prime Minister to Secretary of State for India   3 Oct 43

BASIC ENGLISH

I was shocked to find on my return to this country that the Cabinet committee appointed on July 12, 1943, had never once met. You volunteered to undertake this task, and I certainly thought you would be admirably qualified for it. Pray let me have a report of your progress up to date.

I have received a letter from Mr. Ogden suggesting that a special investigator should be sent to spend a week with him to learn all about Basic English, and I think it would be very wise to accept this invitation, so that your committee can be advised on details at an early date. The matter has become of great importance, as Premier Stalin is also interested. If you feel the pressure of your other duties is too heavy on you I will myself take on the duty of presiding over the committee, but I hope you will be able to relieve me of this.*

Prime Minister to First Lord   4 Oct 43
I should be obliged if you would let Lord Cherwell make me a short report on acoustic homing torpedoes, as he will be able to explain them to me very briefly.†

Prime Minister to Minister of War Transport   4 Oct 43
Surely we ought to get hold of this 24,000-ton ship [Italian merchant ship *Saturnia*] and put her on the Atlantic route at the earliest moment for the build-up for "Overlord".

Prime Minister to Minister of Labour and   6 Oct 43
National Service
I am glad to see you have managed to get 17,800 new workers into M.A.P.'s labour force in August, apart from increases in the additional work done for M.A.P. in other factories. If you can keep up this excellent rate we should achieve the target set on July 23 by the end of the year.

Prime Minister to Chief of the Air Staff   6 Oct 43
Recent evidence shows that the Germans are working hard on jet-propelled aircraft, and accentuates the need for the utmost pressure to be put on their development here.

Prime Minister to Foreign Secretary   6 Oct 43
It should be remembered that the reason why we sheered off making this agreement about the western frontiers of Russia and substituted the Twenty Years Treaty was the perfectly clear menace of very considerable division of opinion in the House of Commons. I know of no reason for supposing that this same opposition might not manifest itself again, perhaps in an even stronger form. The opponents would have the advantage of invoking very large principles against us.

At a Peace Conference the position can be viewed as a whole, and adjustments in one direction balanced by those in another. There is therefore the greatest need to reserve territorial questions for the general settlement. This is even more true of the United States' position, especially in an election year. It would be well therefore to have the American attitude clearly deployed before we adopt a new position in advance of the Twenty Years Treaty.

* See minute of July 11 to Sir Edward Bridges.
† See minute of September 26.

2. I think we should do everything in our power to persuade the Poles to agree with the Russians about their eastern frontier, in return for gains in East Prussia and Silesia. We could certainly promise to use our influence in this respect.

Prime Minister to Chief of the Air Staff   7 Oct 43

Fog Dispersal

Lord Cherwell tells me he had seen the installation working at Graveley, although not in fog, and that he was much impressed by it. Although it burns several tons of oil per minute, this will probably be improved. If the installations allow us to operate on nights which have hitherto been barred because there is a risk of fog a lot will be gained even if the burners never have to be turned on. And of course the saving of bombers, if and when fog occurs, is worth many tons of oil, of which we now happily have a good stock.

I hope that the rate of progress with the installations will be maintained and that all eight will be operational by December.

Prime Minister to Foreign Secretary and   7 Oct 43
Minister of War Transport

What is this report from Washington so widely quoted in to-day's newspapers, on the Allied shipping position, stating that at least 2,500,000 Americans can be sent over here before Christmas and that the invasion of the Continent can be advanced by at least six months? This nonsense is said to emanate from the Senate Sub-Committee on War Mobilisation.

I shall certainly be asked questions about this when the House meets.

Prime Minister to Secretary of State for War   11 Oct 43
and C.I.G.S.

Confusion is caused by the attempt to calculate Allied and enemy strength in "divisions". The word "division" is no common standard. For instance, the establishment of a German standard division is 20,000. The average standard strength on the Russian front is probably not more than 7,000 or 8,000. We had a case the other day of a German division of no more than 1,800 infantry and eighteen guns. What is the establishment and strength of the Russian divisions opposite to them? Let me have a list of the German divisions south of Rome, showing their estimated battle strength. What are the estimated battle strengths of all British divisions in Italy and in North Africa in men and guns, including anti-tank and anti-aircraft? What is the believed strength of the United States divisions in Italy and in Africa? What is the strength of each British division in the Expeditionary Force—*i.e.*, the number of men who will actually go overseas as a unit?

It is said that a British division with its share of corps troops and L. of C. is 42,000, yet when they are moved abroad 15,000 seems to be the maximum. I have been told that the United States divisions being built up for "Overlord" have an overall strength of 51,000. How many of these per division will actually proceed overseas?

2. A report showing the effective strengths of all divisions in the West should be prepared, and I should like to have this return kept up to date every month, according to the best information or estimates possible.

3. Let me have the best analysis you can make of the British forces in Italy, showing the number of divisions and their battle strengths, and also, separately, the ration strength of the British army now landed in Italy.

Prime Minister to Minister of War Transport　　　　　　　11 Oct 43
Let me have a report on bus queues in London and other great cities, and what measures you are taking to reduce them.*

Prime Minister to Minister of Production　　　　　　　12 Oct 43
I recently invited Lord Cherwell to inquire into and report on the relative efficiency of the high explosives used by the German and British forces respectively. A copy of his preliminary report is attached.

The Chiefs of Staff strongly recommend that we should change over to aluminised explosives without waiting for the result of further trials. I agree. Pray let me have a report of what this change will involve in the course of the next week.

The question of how this state of affairs has been allowed to arise should be the subject of an inquiry held under the authority of the Minister of Defence. Pray propose three members, with reference. The whole matter is to be kept most secret.

Prime Minister to Foreign Office, Lord President of the　　　13 Oct 43
Council, and Chancellor of the Exchequer
Field-Marshal Smuts tells me that he has about 80,000 Italian prisoners in South Africa, and that he would be very glad to let us have a large number of them—he mentioned up to 40,000—for work in the United Kingdom.

This seems to me very important, and should be considered.†

Prime Minister to Brigadier Jacob　　　　　　　　　　16 Oct 43
Let me have the most detailed analysis possible, without undue delay, of the base troops [in Egypt], amounting to 241,000. What are they the base of now the war has moved away from the Middle East and

* See minutes of September 29 and October 16.
† See minute of September 16 to Lord President.

the armies remain based on North-West Africa to a large extent? It seems to me that this figure of 241,000 men, including 116,000 British, requires most searching examination, and I propose that a special committee shall be appointed on that subject. Let me first of all however have the facts immediately available.

Prime Minister to Minister of War Transport   16 Oct 43

BUS QUEUES

I am glad you are taking steps to improve the position. In the London Passenger Transport Board region about 5½ million bus journeys are made daily. An extra minute wasted per journey every day is equivalent to 10,000 persons working a nine-hour day over the year in this area alone.*

PLANS FOR THE TRANSITION PERIOD
                                                                 23 Oct 43

At their meeting on October 21 the War Cabinet approved generally the line of approach set out in my memorandum of October 19, and I undertook to circulate a further note setting out the procedure for ensuring the completion of plans for the transition period.

I

2. The first step is to obtain a list of all the action which has to be taken, the schemes which must be prepared, and the administrative arrangements which must be planned and organised in advance, so that when hostilities with Germany cease the country as a whole will find that the new emergency has been foreseen and the necessary preliminary action has been taken.

3. For this purpose each department is called upon to submit to the Secretary of the War Cabinet not later than November 10 a schedule showing all the action which they will have to take and the measures required,

  (*a*) in the period immediately after hostilities with Germany end;
  (*b*) so far as can reasonably be foreseen, during the rest of the transition period, which may be taken as a working basis as two years from the defeat of Germany.

4. The returns should cover all matters for which each department is primarily responsible. There are however numerous questions of common concern to many departments which have been remitted for examination to special organisations or committees. In these cases returns should be submitted by the head of the organisation or the chairman of the committee concerned.

* See minutes of September 29 and October 11.

5. The returns should include the following particulars:

(a) The state of preparedness of the schemes—*i.e.*, whether they are ready now or how long they will take to complete.

(b) Points of principle on which decisions are necessary before further work can be carried out.

(c) Whether legislation by statute, Order in Council, or Defence Regulation is called for, whether such legislation has been prepared, and whether it needs to be enacted before the defeat of Germany.

6. An important part of the plan will be a careful survey of the whole field of legislation (including Defence Regulations and other subordinate legislation) to determine which war-time powers must be retained and which can be dispensed with in the transitional period. This examination is already being carried out by the committee on emergency legislation, under the chairmanship of Sir Claud Schuster.

7. The second stage will be for a general survey to be framed showing the whole range of preparations for the transition period. At this stage we must make sure that there are no gaps or contradictions between the different parts of the plan. I will myself supervise this process.

8. While the transition from peace to war differs in many respects from the transition from war to peace, and War Book procedure is not altogether appropriate, it will probably be convenient that all departments should have a copy of this survey to assist them in understanding how their preparations fit in with the general scheme.

An officer of high rank should be designated in each department who should be personally responsible for seeing that the schedule of the preparations for which his department is primarily responsible is kept continuously up to date.

III

9. The third stage will be to make sure that the whole scheme is brought to a state of readiness and is so maintained. It may be found, in the first instance, that preparatory action on a number of important matters is being delayed because decisions have not been reached on points of principle. I propose, when the general plan has been drawn up, to preside over a series of meetings at which the various parts will be reviewed, and decisions thereafter obtained from the War Cabinet on any matters which hamper the progress of preparations.*

* See Chapter IX, pp. 151–2.

Prime Minister to Home Secretary 24 Oct 43

Once we are sure that we have a plan for food, work, and homes ready in case Hitler collapses it will be quite possible to refine it.

Prime Minister to Brigadier Hollis, for C.O.S. Committee 24 Oct 43

This paper about directives to Supreme Commanders looks very simple from a distance and appeals to the American sense of logic. However, in practice it is found not sufficient for a Government to give a general a directive to beat the enemy and wait to see what happens. The matter is much more complicated. The general may well be below the level of his task, and has often been found so. A definite measure of guidance and control is required from the Staffs and from the high Government authorities. It would not be in accordance with the British view that any such element should be ruled out.

Prime Minister to First Lord 24 Oct 43

I do not consider you have any right to strike off these forty vessels from the escort and fleet destroyer strength. They may, if you will, be left unmanned in material reserve and only brought out in case of serious emergency.

It is quite impossible for us to take up so much of the war effort of the country in building up such enormous new programmes if you do not make full use of your material. Considering that you are now building destroyers which take two years to build, we must consider whether these older ones cannot be repaired and kept going. This failure, coupled with the immense demands for aircraft-carriers, causes me a great deal of concern now that the Italian Fleet and the German Navy are practically extinct. Future naval programmes must be subjected to a very strict scrutiny, not only by me but by the War Cabinet.

Prime Minister to Brigadier Hollis 27 Oct 43

Why has it been decided to abandon the rubber Lilo? Let me have photographs showing the cruciform Lilo, and explain how it produces the desired effect. It seems to me that a complete change of plan has been made.

What is the difference between this concrete and steel structure and ordinary breakwaters? What time would it take to put down? How many ships would it require to carry, and so on?

It would be a pity to spoil a promising plan by magnifying the demands on material and labour to an excessive degree.

Prime Minister to Chancellor of the Duchy of Lancaster 27 Oct 43

I am not in favour of the appointment to high military rank of, or of the wearing of uniform by, civilians holding civilian or quasi-civilian posts unless this is clearly necessary to the successful performance of their duties. In this light, pray inquire into the principles adopted in the Security Service for gazetting its officers to commissions and as regards their wearing uniform. Let me have a short report.

Prime Minister to Brigadier Hollis   31 Oct 43

Let me have a return showing the present development of the British forces for "Overlord"; also a statement of what formations will be left here at home apart from the above.

NOVEMBER

Prime Minister to C.I.G.S.   1 Nov 43

Thank you for your information, which still however leaves me mystified on various points. I entirely agree that we must have a "yardstick", and that is exactly what I am in search of. A yardstick is a common measure, and it is just by this test that the use of the word "division", which may mean a German 20,000 or a Russian 15,000, or a British and American 42,000, so lamentably fails.

2. Please let me have the best analysis the Intelligence Department can make of a gross British and a full German division, showing of what elements the additional British 22,000 consists. . . .*

4. Let us take the 5th British Infantry Division, which has newly arrived in Italy, as an example. It has 18,480 men on its strength. Where are the other 23,000 odd? When do they come into Italy? What proportion of these 23,000 are combatant troops in the sense of taking their places in the fighting line at some time or other?

5. Could I also have a list of the corps and army formations in Italy, with their estimated ration strength attached? Of course I quite understand these estimates may not be exactly up to date.

6. In the British Expeditionary Force what part is played by the Polish Armoured Division, which I see has no fewer than 400 tanks? It does not appear to be included either in the Twenty-first Army Group or the Home Field Army. Are there any other units of this kind? What happens to all the Army tank brigades, of which there are eight on my latest return? It is absolutely necessary for me to form an opinion on these matters.

7. My impression is that the Germans get about 12,000 men who actually fight out of divisions of 20,000 gross, and we get about 15,000 or 16,000 out of divisions of 42,000. If so the result is not very encouraging, considering that the Germans fight at least as well as we

* See minute of October 11 to Secretary of State for War.

do and move over great distances with much rapidity. On the other hand, the British corps and army commanders have larger proportions of artillery, engineers, signals, etc., in their hands than the Germans, and can therefore support their divisions more powerfully as circumstances require.

8. As far as possible, when giving me returns, pray let me have ration strength, number of battalions, number of tanks, and number of guns. I take a grave view of the increasing sedentary and non-combatant tail which we are acquiring. For an operation like "Overlord", where every man has to have his place in the boat and be fed over beaches, the most thorough analysis must be made of the rearward services, especially in the opening phases. I hope to find time shortly to go into this in some detail at the Defence Committee or Staff meeting.

Prime Minister to First Lord   1 Nov 43

I am at first sight wholly in favour of your view about the light fleet carriers, and I shall be glad to discuss the matter with you and the First Sea Lord and Controller some time this week. I cannot see that there is any need for such great numbers in 1945 and 1946.

2. The whole question of our naval strength must however now be raised. The Admiralty are demanding 288,000 more men for the Fleet in 1944 and 71,000 for the shipyards; total, about 360,000. This is at a time when the man-power shortage enforces heavy cuts on every form of national war activity. The question arises, why does the Admiralty require more men in 1944 than in 1943, observing that the new facts are:

(a) The decisive defeat of the U-boats, largely through the air assistance.

(b) The surrender of the Italian Fleet.

(c) The accession of the *Richelieu* and many lesser French units to active service.

(d) The establishment by the United States of two-to-one strength over the Japanese in the Pacific.

(e) The immobilisation for a good many months to come of the *Tirpitz*, the only hostile capital unit in the Western world (unless the new German carrier is ready).

3. One would expect that in view of these immense new facts it would be possible to make very sensible reductions even in the existing personnel of the Navy and to lay up old vessels in care and maintenance without hesitation as new ones come out. It is for Cabinet consideration whether a very large programme of laying up old vessels and also of slowing down or suspending the more distant units now under

construction should not be adopted. All this would be in answer to the question, Why should you ask for so much more when your opponents' force is so much less and your Allies' so much stronger? The Admiralty would not render the best service to the country at this crisis if it kept in commission a single vessel that was not needed against the enemy.

4. With regard to the forty odd destroyers which it is proposed to lay up, I think the right course would be to keep them all in care and maintenance after refitting them and to slow down or suspend the long-range fleet destroyers, which we shall not get for two years.

5. Let me now have a list of all warships which you propose to keep in commission in 1944, compared with those which existed at the time when Italy and Germany were both our enemies, say January 1, 1941, together with their complements. The destroyers and smaller craft may be stated in categories with the complements aggregated. Let me have the estimate as it stood at January 1, 1941, as it stands to-day, and as you propose it for January 1, 1945, distinguishing between afloat and ashore and including the Fleet Air Arm.

6. I note that the United States have definitely diminished their programme of anti-U-boat craft in order to develop landing-craft. Hitherto I have perpetually pressed for the ceaseless construction of anti-U-boat vessels as each slip became vacant, but our growing numbers, and many signs of weakness in the enemy's production and in the morale of their crews, require that the whole of this section should be reviewed.

Prime Minister to Minister of Aircraft Production   6 Nov 43

I am impressed by the large number of man-hours which your minute of October 27 shows to be consumed in modifications to Service aircraft. I hope the modifications are confined to those strictly necessary to improve the fighting value of our aircraft.

Looking at the tables attached to your minute, the disquieting fact emerges that we have no really heavy bomber under development. The Vickers Windsor will not really be much larger—though we must trust it will be better—than the improved Lancaster, which will be coming into production at the end of next year. In the meanwhile the Americans have the Boeing B.29 already in production, with an all-up weight of 120,000 lb., stated to carry nine tons of bombs with a range of 3,000 miles. I understand they also have projected a six-engine aircraft, the B.36, with an all-up weight of over 250,000 lb., designed to carry a load of over thirty tons with a range of 4,600 miles. Ought we not to be looking forward to making aircraft of similar performance?

Prime Minister to Secretary of State for War and C.I.G.S.   6 Nov 43

As I understand it, the plan is that on D Day the Americans will have fifteen divisions in "Overlord" and we twelve. Now it seems to me a great pity that we cannot make our quota equal, or if possible one better. So much depends upon the interpretation given to the word "division".* I should like to be able to tell them [the Americans], "We will match you man for man and gun for gun on the battle-front," and also that we have made extra exertions for this. In this way we should maintain our right to be effectively consulted in operations which are of such capital consequence.

2. For the above purpose I would run considerable risks with what is left in the Island. If necessary the Home Guard could be largely mobilised during the period when all the Regular troops have left the country, and the resulting decline in the factory munitions output accepted.

3. We have carried the recent trouble about the Italian campaign entirely by mentioning that we had preponderance on the battle-front. We ought to have at least equality in this other most critical task. Moreover, the announcement of the fact that we had lifted [*i.e.,* increased] our contribution would sweeten all the discussions which are now proceeding, and might well enable us to secure any necessary retardation of D Day. Pray think this over and let us talk together.

Prime Minister to Lord President of the Council   11 Nov 43

I hope that out of the present surplus of grain you will manage to do a little more for the domestic poultry-keeper. He can usually provide or collect scrap to balance the grain, so that we get more eggs for a given amount than if it were handed to the commercial producer. It costs no labour, and the extra eggs are not an undue reward for the enterprise and initiative of the owner. Moreover, it gives him an interest and something to talk about. The present miserably small allowance of one ration per ration card frequently does not allow enough hens to be kept in a small household to justify putting up the poultry run, etc. I feel sure that if it were increased a good many more people would produce their own eggs, and thus save shipping and labour.

Prime Minister to President of the Board of Education   11 Nov 43

Thank you for your report of September 16 about the use of the cinema in schools. I have read it with interest, and I am glad to know that you are giving your personal attention to this matter.

2. There must be a number of children whose talents would remain undeveloped, or at any rate under-developed, if the written and spoken

---

* See minutes of October 11 and November 1.

word was not supplemented by visual aids of this kind. In addition, really good films should benefit all school-children. The films produced might possibly fall into two main categories:

(a) films designed to fit in with and illustrate the ordinary curriculum; and

(b) films to show children the proud inheritance to which they are the heirs, and of which they will become in time the guardians.

3. You will not expect me to enter into any commitment on the financial side. The additional costs of the educational proposals shown in the appendix to your White Paper are considerable, and no doubt this particular aspect will be assessed in relation to the various other parts of your programme. I note however that in Germany a fee used to be charged to the parents to finance the provision of films and projectors. I am not clear how this would fit in with your proposals, more especially if the film becomes a part of the regular curriculum, at which the children's attendance is compulsory, but if there were voluntary shows presumably some form of charge could be made. Perhaps you would kindly develop this point for me in rather more detail.

Prime Minister to General Ismay, for C.O.S. Committee   16 Nov 43

The reasons which led us to supply a more substantial garrison to the Falkland Islands were serious, and I should like to know in what way they have been altered by the course of events before any reduction is authorised. It would be a pity if a Japanese cruiser took over these islands, including the new defences which we are to leave unmanned. This is not a likely contingency, but it exists none the less. What would you propose to do with the 1,500 men? What regiments do they belong to?

Prime Minister to First Sea Lord, and to General Ismay,   21 Nov 43
for C.O.S. Committee

The centre point of my thought is the capture of Rome at the beginning of January and the capture of Rhodes at the end. The former is already provided for. For the latter two requisites are necessary: first, a declaration of war by Turkey and the use of the Turkish bases; second, a good British division to be landed at the first wave, to be backed up and followed by the 10th Indian as the second wave. Landing-ships and craft will be required therefore on the scale of a division. These divisions need not be fully equipped with transport, etc., on account of the small distances over which they have to operate and the fact that the 8,000 Germans will be pinned down to key points. How much landing-craft will be needed? Where can it be obtained? The First Sea Lord has in mind that some landing-ships now in South-East Asia Command should come to the Mediterranean for this job and then return in time for "Culverin" [Sumatra] or any other operation there.

2. If it be true that Admiral Mountbatten has abandoned "Culverin" there really cannot be much hurry. The capture of the Andamans is a trivial prize compared with Rhodes, and also it can be undertaken at any time later in the year. In addition to the capture of Rhodes and all that follows from it, the surrender or destruction of 8,000 or 9,000 Germans will give us three times the [German] prisoners we have so far taken during all our operations in Italy.

DECEMBER

Prime Minister to Secretary of State for War   13 Dec 43

While in the Middle East my attention was drawn by the 4th Hussars to Army Council Instruction 1408, published on November 26, about the wearing of unauthorised headdresses. According to this, authorised headdress for all units of the Royal Armoured Corps (except 11th Hussars) is described as "black beret to be worn both with battle-dress and with Service dress", although permission is given for officers to wear Service dress caps if in their possession until replacement becomes necessary.

2. The 4th Hussars are concerned lest after the war this ruling will continue and they, like the Tank Corps, will have no hat they can wear except the black beret.

3. As Colonel of the regiment, I should like to be able to assure them that, so far as the 4th Hussars are concerned, this is only a wartime measure, and that when supplies are more plentiful they will once more be allowed to purchase and wear Service dress caps.

4. I should like this assurance to be given. Pray let me know your views.

JANUARY

Prime Minister (Marrakesh) to Secretary of State for War   7 Jan 44

We should make every effort to ease the lot of the Home Guard, whose duties are more exhausting than those of any form of Civil Defence. Most of the men are now proficient, and should not be compelled to attend parades merely to complete forty-eight hours of duty a month. Anti-aircraft Home Guard are credited with twelve hours for each night's duty, whether there is an "Alert" or not, but the ordinary Home Guard's parades are in the evenings and every week-end. Many of these men have had little free time for more than three years, and compulsory parades, with fines, sometimes ending in imprisonment, for non-attendance, can cause considerable industrial unrest.

At this stage in the war Home Guard hours of duty should be officially reduced and not left to the discretion of the unit commander. Guards and strenuous exercises should be cut to a minimum, and parades for those holding proficiency badges limited to weapon maintenance.

Prime Minister to First Lord and First Sea Lord   10 Jan 44

RADIO PROXIMITY FUZE

Are you content with the situation in which the American Navy will have a good supply of fuzes, even for 4-inch guns, by the spring, whereas we shall have no such facilities during the war? I consider this point is a serious one and should be faced by the Admiralty.

2. Is there any possibility of our obtaining an allocation from the United States, or are you satisfied that our methods are good enough?

Prime Minister to General Ismay, for C.O.S. Committee   17 Jan 44

This report [by the Joint Intelligence Staff on Japanese intentions in the South-East Asia area] confirms the view I have held for some time that the danger of invasion of India by Japan has passed. During the next few months the Eastern Fleet will come into being, and will soon grow to a strength superior to any detachment which it would be worth while for the Japanese to make, having regard to the preoccupations in the Pacific. The air defence of India has also become very strong.

2. All the above brings me again to the conclusion that there ought to be a continuous reduction in the vast mass of low-grade troops now maintained under arms in India. Nearly two million men are on our pay-lists and ration strength, apart from the British troops in the country and on the frontier. The Viceroy and General Auchinleck should be instructed to reduce the numbers by at least half a million during the course of the present year. In this process, which will no doubt largely take place by uncompensated wastage, the greatest care should be taken to improve the quality of the remaining units and to rely as much as possible upon the martial races. An effort should be made to get back to the high efficiency and standard of the pre-war Indian troops. The officers and skilled personnel from the disbanded battalions should be concentrated on these units, thus increasing the officer, and particularly the white officer, cadre. The standards of recruiting should everywhere be stiffened, and the intake reduced to the limits of the really trustworthy fighting recruits.

3. Meanwhile I should like to have a financial statement from the India Office showing the cost of the military establishments in India (exclusive of British troops) for every year since the outbreak of war, together with the average bearing of man-power.

Prime Minister to General Ismay   19 Jan 44

It would seem to be about time that the circular sent to generals and other high commanders about making speeches should be renewed. Let me see the text of it. There seem to have been a lot of speeches and interviews lately.

Prime Minister to General Ismay, for C.O.S. Committee   19 Jan 44

We ought to assert domination of the Dalmatian coast. It is within easy reach of our commanding Air Force in Italy. We have large naval superiority. After Anzio is over it ought to be easy to organise a circus of, say, 2,000 Commando men and a dozen or so light tanks, and go round and clean up every single island the Germans have occupied, killing or capturing their garrisons. A plan should be made for this which we could consider and then present to the Supreme Commander for his consideration.

Pray let work be begun upon this at once. We are letting the whole of this Dalmatian coast be sealed off from us by an enemy who has neither the command of the air nor the sea. How can he garrison the islands in any strength to resist a concentrated attack?

Prime Minister to Dominions Secretary   23 Jan 44

I have always wanted the New Zealand Division to take part in the Battle of Rome, more as a symbol than because we cannot find other troops. This they are now very likely to do. It would be a pity for them to quit the European scene.

I should prefer to let the numbers of the division fall until they became a brigade group. Even so they could be called a division and some other brigade be attached to them. I like to have them there, and they will be proud of it in future years.

I should not ask Mr. Fraser to run into any serious difficulties about the return of particular individuals.

Prime Minister to General Ismay   25 Jan 44

General Montgomery speaks of his need to have ten Commando units for "Overlord" and has only seven. Pray let me know whether this request could be met. What arrangements have been made for bringing home some of the specialised personnel for teaching purposes of the 2nd Special Air Service Regiment? It is not intended to bring the regiment home, but I agreed that some of the special personnel should come as instructors.

Prime Minister to General Ismay, for C.O.S. Committee   25 Jan 44

I have now read this paper about "British Strategic Needs in the Levant States". The Chiefs of Staff seem to assume that partition [of Palestine] will arouse Jewish resentment. It is, on the contrary, the White Paper policy that arouses the Jewish resentment. The opposition to partition will come from the Arabs, and any violence by the Arabs will be countered by the Jews. It must be remembered that Lord Wavell has stated that, left to themselves, the Jews would beat the Arabs. There cannot therefore be any great danger in our joining with the Jews to enforce the kind of proposals about partition which are set forth in the Ministerial paper. I therefore cannot accept in any way the requirements for internal security set out in the table, which proceeds upon the assumption that both the Jews and the Arabs would join together to fight us. Obviously we shall not proceed with any plan of partition which the Jews do not support.

Prime Minister to Dominions Secretary   25 Jan 44

It is to my mind very unwise to make plans on the basis of Hitler being defeated in 1944. The possibility of his gaining a victory in France cannot be excluded. The hazards of battle are very great. The reserves of the enemy are capable of being thrown from point to point with great facility. All my information from the interior of Germany goes to show that Hitler and his Government are still in the fullest control, and that there is no sign of revolt as a result of the bombings. In all our contacts with the German troops, such as we see in Italy, their quality, discipline, and skill are apparent.

Prime Minister to Secretary of State for War and C.I.G.S.   25 Jan 44

I do not approve of the title "Allied Central Mediterranean Force", and it should not have been made public without my having been previously consulted.

2. An army which will amount to upwards of twenty divisions should not be described as a "Force". The activities of this army are not coextensive with the Central Mediterranean. For instance, Malta and Tunis are both in the Central Mediterranean; likewise Corsica and Sardinia. Furthermore, Yugoslavia, which is specially reserved to the Supreme Commander, is not—except possibly for purely operational purposes—placed under General Alexander. The title is therefore from every point of view a misnomer.

3. The appointment which I offered General Alexander and which he accepted was "Commander of the Allied Armies in Italy". This follows the precedent of the last war, when "British Expeditionary Force" was changed as the armies grew to "British Armies in France and Flanders". The change should therefore be made, and a con-

venient moment to do so would be when the Battle of Rome has decided itself, assuming the decision is satisfactory.

Prime Minister to General Montgomery   27 Jan 44

Herewith is an interim answer from the Minister of Production about D.D. tanks. It does not look too bad.

2. I shall have a further report presently about waterproofing material. 200,000 vehicles seems a vast outfit to attach to an army which, at thirty divisions of 20,000 men apiece, would only have 600,000 men, of which less than three-quarters would actually fight. As each vehicle takes at least a man and a half to drive and look after it, here are 300,000 men already absorbed. One hopes there will be enough infantry with rifles and bayonets to protect this great mass of vehicles from falling into the hands of the enemy.*

Prime Minister to Major-General Hollis   28 Jan 44

It would not be a good thing for the main headquarters in the Mediterranean to be set up in Italy. General Wilson's sphere comprises the entire North African front, and he should not be located in any one particular area. General Alexander should have the command in Italy without being overshadowed by the presence of the Supreme Commander's headquarters. I do not feel enough effort has been made to overcome the difficulties of a move [of these headquarters] to the Tunis area. Has Malta been investigated? If nothing else will serve, it would be better for him to remain at Algiers, after conducting a proper purge of the excessive officers who have accumulated there.

Prime Minister to Home Secretary   30 Jan 44

Your minute to me of January 24 about the employment of Communists on secret Government work.

I agree that the existence of the panel must be a secret. All members should be specially warned. Final decision whether action is to be taken against a Communist sympathiser must rest with the department employing him, whose Ministerial head is responsible to Parliament.

There are three degrees of responsibility in this business.

M.I.5 is responsible for the evidence produced before the panel. The panel is responsible for weighing that evidence and deciding whether to proceed with the department concerned. The department is responsible for deciding what action to take, if any.

I agree that the panel should include a senior representative of the Treasury experienced in handling staff questions, but am against compelling the panel to include a representative of the interested department. If the panel rejects a case it would be unfair that a member of the suspect's department should know it had ever been brought up.

* See pp. 519-20.

The chairman of the panel should have discretion to co-opt a member of the interested department according to circumstances.

Prime Minister to Foreign Secretary　　　　　　　　　　30 Jan 44

I think Sir Owen O'Malley should be asked very secretly to express his opinion on the Katyn Wood inquiry. How does the argument about the length of time the birch-trees had grown over the graves fit in with this new tale? Did anybody look at the birch-trees?

Prime Minister to First Lord and First Sea Lord　　　　31 Jan 44

I am willing that four of the fast improved carriers should be included in the forthcoming Admiralty programme; but I consider that the first two should have a considerable lead over the second two, in order that advantage may be taken of any possible improvements noticeable during construction. I also consider that the four battleships sanctioned by Parliament but not proceeded with during the war, namely, *Lion*, *Temeraire*, *Conqueror*, and *Thunderer*, should also remain in the naval programme, it being understood that no work is done upon them other than designing. Efforts should be made to finish *Vanguard* by the summer of '45. Let me know what is involved in this.

2. I wonder whether you are not ordering far more warships than we can even lay down during the war. In 1943 888,000 tons displacement were ordered, only 402,000 tons laid down, and 337,000 tons were completed. Thus, unless ships are laid down much faster than in 1943 it would take two and a quarter years even to lay down last year's orders. Hitherto we have been having at least two programmes a year, with the result that you have an immense amount of sanctioned shipbuilding, far more than you can possibly carry out or digest. It is not in the interest of the Navy to present such an aspect to critical eyes. This should certainly govern the whole of the new programme, and I do not think any vessel should be included in it which either obstructs the completion of a similar vessel already ordered or cannot itself be laid down during the calendar year 1944—or, if you will, the financial year 1944–45.

3. We spoke of the War Fleet against Japan in 1945. I consider we should have the four *King George V's*, the *Renown*, *Nelson*, *Queen Elizabeth*, and *Warspite*, in all eight battleships, together with as many armoured carriers and auxiliary carriers as have come to hand, the above being supported as necessary by cruiser squadrons and flotillas. A programme for developing the Fleet train* stage by stage should be submitted. I hope the *Vanguard* will be able to join during the autumn. The question of fitting the *Littorios* for this service should also be considered. Let me know what it involves in time, labour, and money.

---

* An organisation for supplying the Fleet with fuel, stores, etc.

4. I agree that in June 1944 we should furnish the contingent you have already prepared, provided always that the United States desire it. Above all, we must be careful not to prejudice Operation "Culverin" [Sumatra], which is the only means of bringing the large military and air forces we have around the Bay of Bengal into effective action against the enemy in 1944–45. The disposition of the Fleet between the Bay of Bengal and the Pacific must provide for the execution of "Culverin" if other difficulties are surmounted and unless unexpected developments occur.

5. We must ask the United States Chiefs of Staff to lend us a proper supply of landing-craft for November or December at "Culverin", and in view of the help we are to give them with the Fleet they should not deny these to us. This matter however awaits the arrival of Admiral Mountbatten's officers.

6. For the post-war Fleet we should aim at survivors of the four *K.G.V.s*, one modernised *Nelson*, *Vanguard*, four 16-inch battleships, which will be kept on our lists and proceeded with as may be possible, and we should claim the two *Littorios*, a potential total of twelve battleships. This of course depends upon whether the battleship is not rendered obsolete by new inventions. So far this has certainly not been the case. On the contrary, the U-boat danger to battleships has been largely mastered and the air menace to them is under much better control than ever before. I hold strongly that we have an overwhelming claim on the *Littorios* because of the preponderance of our efforts in the Mediterranean and the fact that we have sacrificed new construction of heavy ships to the immediate needs of the war. Perhaps you will let me have your sketch of a post-war Fleet—say in 1947—balanced on this sort of scale, in order that I may consider the whole picture more maturely.

7. I approve the policy of using the *Warspite*, and I hope also the *Rodney*, as part of our bombarding fleet for "Overlord". What other vessels have you available for this purpose? I presume measures are being taken to provide the proper gunnery complements, training of the latest kind, and the necessary spotters, and that there is no lack of ammunition, both anti-personnel and for destroying concrete defences. Under the air shield the bombarding squadrons should have great scope.

8. I will send you my comments on your man-power proposals later. I should think you [now] have at least 100,000 men in the training establishments, harbour services, and bases, men in transit, etc., on which you can draw during the next two years before trenching upon our limited pools. This will require a very sensible reduction of the training establishments and plants.

FEBRUARY

Prime Minister to General Ismay, for C.O.S. Committee   2 Feb 44

All experience shows that once a great offensive has been launched quiescence and comparative unpreparedness prevail on other parts of the front not affected. The battle draws everything into itself, and there are moments when gains of priceless value in other quarters can be gathered cheaply or perhaps for nothing.

2. Pray have the following examined with the utmost secrecy.

(a) During March, April, and May move the 1st and 6th British Armoured and the 6th South African Armoured Divisions into Morocco. Cover would be perhaps local unrest, or anyhow reinforcements for "Overlord".

(b) On D plus say twenty or thirty, when everyone is all out, bring these divisions to Bordeaux with a minimum of landing-craft, after seizing the place by *coup de main*. This should be possible, as the Air would all have been drawn into the northward. A force of this character let loose in the south and centre of France would instantly arouse widespread revolt and would be of measureless assistance to the main battle.

3. Examine also the possibilities of the move overland quietly of these troops to Morocco, embarkation in great secrecy, and a [sea] move by a wide curve to the point of attack.

4. The above is without prejudice to "Anvil", in which none of these forces would be involved.

5. Should the operation, which may be called "Caliph", prosper, a follow-up by the United States with infantry divisions brought directly across the Atlantic to the new base could be arranged.

6. Arising from the above, how many ships would be wanted to convey the three armoured divisions? How many landing-craft would be required for, say, 5,000 Commandos to make sure of the entries (it is of course intended to land the divisions at regular quays)? How could the shipping be found and brought to Casablanca without attracting undue notice? How long would the embarkation, the voyage, and, if all went well, the disembarkation take? A carrier force would have to be provided to cover the landing, but this should not be difficult if by then we have got shore bases established in the north. It is silly to go on as we are, butting at only one place, without trying to reap the immense opportunities which will be open almost everywhere else.

Prime Minister to Dominions Secretary   2 Feb 44

I could have a special Cabinet meeting on Friday, if desired, to consider the presence in Dublin of Axis diplomatic missions. Otherwise it can be brought up on Monday at the full meeting.

2. Much more dangerous even than the information betrayed about the movements of Anglo-American troop convoys is what will certainly be passing in a stream about our preparations for "Overlord". If the German and Japanese Ministers remain at their posts in Dublin it may be necessary on military grounds to sever all contacts between Ireland and the Continent in the near future for a period of months. At present anyone can get in an Irish ship to Spain and give the latest news he has picked up in England about British and American preparations. Even if complete severance by sea was instituted it would not prevent the German Ambassador from sending a wireless warning of Zero, even though that was the last he was able to send.

3. I am preparing a telegram for the President, bringing to his notice some of these dangers, which I think very grave; and I am asking also that it should be considered by the C.O.S. Committee.

Prime Minister to Foreign Secretary 5 Feb 44

Your minute about raising certain legations to the status of embassies.

I must say I think Cuba has as good a claim as some of the other places—*la perla de las Antillas*. Great offence will be given if all the others have it and this large, rich, beautiful island, the home of the cigar, is denied. Surely Cuba has much more claim than Venezuela. You will make a bitter enemy if you leave them out, and after a bit you will be forced to give them what you have given to the others.

Prime Minister to General Ismay 7 Feb 44

Where is the report on "Caliph"? You should also tell the Planners, if they have not finished their work, that the assembly area of Morocco should be used for at least three French divisions to follow up the inroad of the British armour at "Caliph".*

Prime Minister to Sir Edward Bridges 12 Feb 44

I have no intention of moving from the Cabinet War Room until after we have had at least one Blitz which is altogether out of relation to anything we have previously experienced. I do not think the new forms of bombardment make any difference to this. You should provide reasonable accommodation for the Lord Privy Seal. The other Ministers' rooms can stay as at present.

Prime Minister to Sir Edward Bridges 19 Feb 44

The principle enunciated in Lord Selborne's note about housing in the transitional period after the war seems to me unanswerable. To peg land prices at the 1939 level without relation to any alteration in

* See minute of February 2 to General Ismay.

the value of money would be a confiscatory act applied only to one class of property. Provision must be inserted in any legislation that the value shall be the same as it was in 1939—i.e., the same in real value.

Prime Minister to General Ismay, for C.O.S. Committee　　19 Feb 44

The object of Plough Force was to operate in Norway during the snow period, and much depended in essence upon small tanks being carried by aircraft in which the men could fight and move and, to some extent, find shelter. Since then "Plough" has been taken for ordinary duties as Commandos. How far has the flying tank principle been made effective? What are the numbers of the Plough Force? Whereabouts in Italy is it actually at the present moment? How has it acquitted itself?

2. I do not myself think it wise to rule out "Jupiter" finally from the operations of this war. We ought of course to have liberated Norway during the campaign of 1943, but our American Allies would probably not have consented to such strategy, and it would not have been possible to obtain the necessary support here. In the event of "Overlord" not being successful or Hitler accumulating forces there quite beyond our power to tackle it would perhaps be necessary to adopt the flanking movements both in Norway and from Turkey and the Ægean in the winter of 1944–45. In view of such contingencies I am reluctant to liquidate this Force. It could surely meanwhile be employed in the Balkans or in exterminating the German garrisons in the islands off the Dalmatian coast.

3. Pray let me have your views upon the above.

Prime Minister to Home Secretary　　22 Feb 44

It would be a great mistake to have a national day of prayer for "Overlord". In my view there is no need for another day of prayer or thanksgiving at the present time.

Prime Minister to Foreign Secretary　　25 Feb 44

We "invade" all countries with whom we are at war.

2. We "enter" all subjugated Allied lands we wish to "liberate".

3. With regard to a country like Italy, with whose Government we have signed an armistice, we "invaded" in the first instance, but, in view of the Italian co-operation, we must consider all further advances by us in Italy to be in the nature of "liberation".

Prime Minister to Foreign Secretary　　27 Feb 44

I entirely agree that we should pay out of hand all civil claims against members of the United States forces over the five-thousand-dollar limit, which the Americans are apparently constitutionally unable to settle.

2. The remedy for the reckless driving which is causing so much trouble is a conversation between me and Eisenhower. I am sure that if the case is put to him he will exercise a controlling and effective authority. At any rate, we ought to try this first.

3. Surely it is not necessary to make all this long statement in Parliament, which seems to me to be likely to cause a lot of ill-feeling in the United States; and I was not aware that you were subjected to much pressure in the House on this matter. I should greatly prefer to let Eisenhower put his screw on and see what happens, meanwhile confining your statement to the fact that we will pay the claims over five thousand dollars pending further discussion by His Majesty's Government with that of the United States.

Prime Minister to General Ismay and General Pile　　　28 Feb 44
There is no doubt that the blast effect of the new German bombs has increased. In these circumstances, and indeed on general grounds, would it not be well to provide, so far as possible, slit trenches and blast or splinter cover for anti-aircraft personnel not on duty during the air raids? Each raid is likely to be short on account of the enemy's reliance on "Window", and the anti-aircraft personnel, a large proportion of whom are women, should be directed to use the slit trenches when not otherwise employed during the raids. In most cases the batteries should be able to do the bulk of the work themselves if materials are provided. Where outside assistance is required priority should be given to the most exposed positions.

MARCH

Prime Minister to Minister of Aircraft Production　　　1 Mar 44
My congratulations upon the output of aircraft for February, and upon beating the programme. Pray convey to all those who have achieved or exceeded their programme my best thanks.

Prime Minister to President Roosevelt　　　2 Mar 44
Here is a suggested item for your draft of our monthly anti-U-boat war statement, provided later information about sinkings in February 1944 does not considerably increase the figure shown below:
"February 1944 was the best month since the United States entered the war. The total sinkings of all Allied shipping in February by enemy action only were less than one-fifth of the sinkings in February 1943, and less than one-ninth of the sinkings in February 1942."
The figures in British notation are: February 1944, 70,000 tons; February 1943, 378,000; February 1942, 659,500. We have a very good haul of U-boats too.

Prime Minister to Minister of Home Security　　　　　2 Mar 44

Thank you for the analysis of the returns of the civilian respirator inspections which you sent to me. I see that about nine out of every ten people have a serviceable mask. This seems an adequate insurance against the risk of the enemy's starting gas warfare at a period when we are dropping more than thirty times the tonnage of bombs on Germany that she is dropping on us.

Prime Minister to Sir Alan Lascelles　　　　　4 Mar 44

You should see the Home Secretary's minute about a national day of prayer for "Overlord". I think there are serious dangers in drawing attention to the coming shock in this way, especially as no one can know when it is going to be. We have to be very much on our guard against unduly depressing the troops.*

Prime Minister to Minister of Aircraft Production　　　　　5 Mar 44

I am informed that American aircraft are now being produced without paint, and that, apart from economies in time and material, as much as twenty miles an hour may thus be added to the speed of certain types. Pray let me know whether it is intended to adopt a similar policy with regard to British aircraft.

Prime Minister to Minister of Supply　　　　　7 Mar 44

Just off the main road between Amersham and Uxbridge, at a place called Chalfont St. Giles, there is a rubbish heap or salvage dump where for the last three years work has been going on. I pass it every time I go to Chequers. Are tins and metal objects being recovered from what was a dump in past years, or are they being thrown down there together with other rubbish? Is it being sifted or extended? It is impossible to see as one passes. The one thing that is evident is that the work is endless, and apparently makes no progress.

Prime Minister to Lord Portal　　　　　7 Mar 44

Just below the Foreign Office, on the grass opposite St. James's Park lake, there is a very untidy sack with holes in it and sand leaking out, a sandbag structure, and some kind of obstacle formerly used as a practice ground by the local Home Guard. It does not seem to have been used for a very long time. Such a conspicuous place ought not to look untidy, unless there is some real need which can be satisfied in no other way.

Prime Minister to Chancellor of the Exchequer, First Lord　　　7 Mar 44
of the Admiralty, Secretary of State for War, and Secretary
of State for Air

I understand that you are considering the best means of making

* See minute of February 22.

minor improvements in the allowances of the Forces. I am quite firm about changes in basic pay. But the war has now been going on a long time, and this, together with the arrival of large numbers of better-paid American Service personnel, does justify some concession to our own forces. Without having gone into the matter deeply, I consider that it would not be unreasonable if the concessions made involved an additional expenditure at the rate of £20,000,000 per annum. Furthermore, I think that special consideration should be given to married personnel, and in this category especially to the lowest paid classes.

I should be glad if you would take the above into account in framing your proposals, which you will no doubt submit to me.

Prime Minister to Secretary of State for War   8 Mar 44
(Minister of War Transport to see)

Except for combat landings we cannot afford to ship vehicles on wheels.

I understand there were about 200,000 Army vehicles of all types in the Mediterranean area on December 31, and some 1,000 have been shipped from the United Kingdom and North America in January. Is not this shipment equivalent to about four months' wastage at the September-December rate?

With this large stock in hand, would it not be possible to stop shipment of vehicles going in the next three or four months, when shipping space will be so urgently needed for other purposes?

Prime Minister to President Roosevelt   9 Mar 44

Gold and dollar holdings in the United States.

1. You will remember that we discussed the dollar balances in Cairo on December 8, and that I gave a memorandum to Harry. I certainly understood that you felt we ought not to be treated worse than France or Russia in these matters. France has at least two billions, and no overseas liabilities against them. So has Russia. These dollar balances are not, as your telegram might suggest, a particular part of our assets which is available in the United States, but our total reserves. Against these reserves we have incurred for the common cause liabilities of at least ten billions on the other side of the account.

2. Since our talk Lord Halifax met Mr. Hull and Mr. Morgenthau as recently as January 8, when the matters mentioned in the first paragraph of your telegram under reply were discussed. Lord Halifax reported to us that Mr. Morgenthau stated to him that it was not at present intended to reduce our dollar balances in any other way, and in reliance on this personal assurance to Lord Halifax we agreed to the exclusion of the politically difficult items from Lend-Lease.

3. Will you allow me to say that the suggestion of reducing our dollar balances, which constitute our sole liquid reserve, to one billion dollars would really not be consistent either with equal treatment of Allies or with any conception of equal sacrifice or pooling of resources? We have not shirked our duty or indulged in an easy way of living. We have already spent practically all our convertible foreign investments in the struggle. We alone of the Allies will emerge from the war with great overseas war debts. I do not know what would happen if we were now asked to disperse our last liquid reserves required to meet pressing needs, or how I could put my case to Parliament without its affecting public sentiment in the most painful manner, and that at a time when British and American blood will be flowing in broad and equal streams and when the shortening of the war even by a month would far exceed the sums under consideration.

4. I venture to put these arguments before you in order that you may be fully armed with our case, for my confidence in your sense of justice, and, I may add, in that of the American people, is unshakable.

5. But see also my immediately following.

Prime Minister to President Roosevelt						9 Mar 44

Further to my telegram, I have laid before you our case about dollar balances in its full strength, but I have wondered whether you might be meaning only that we should search for some arrangement to enable us to put a portion of our balance less conspicuously in the limelight. If this is so, and if you desire it, we will go into this very carefully with Stettinius when he visits us.

2. Since we received your telegram we now learn that Mr. Crowley on March 8 promised to give Congress the amount of our dollar balances now and at the outbreak of war. This raises serious dangers. I am confident in the justice of our case if it could be stated as a whole, and of course if the matter becomes public property we shall have to justify ourselves in public. The disclosure of the vast debit balance which is growing up against us outside the United States would certainly have most injurious effects upon our sterling position, and consequently upon the whole strength of the Allies at this period. We therefore ask that there shall be no disclosure; if this is not possible, that the disclosure shall be in strict confidence, and also that the substance of our case should be stated to the body to whom the disclosure is made.

Prime Minister to Minister of Supply						9 Mar 44

I am told that the demand for the new insecticide, D.D.T., is urgent and increasing. Pray let me know what output is to be expected, whether this is completely adequate, and, if not, whether anything can be done to expand and accelerate it. It is most important, especially for the South-East Asia Command, that ample supplies should be made available at the earliest possible moment.

Please try to get a move on on a large scale.

Prime Minister to President Roosevelt   10 Mar 44

I am sending you to-day by courier an inscription I have had drawn up for Harry about his boy who was killed. It would be very kind of you to have it sent him wherever he is recuperating. How does his operation stand now?

Prime Minister to General Giraud (Algiers)   10 Mar 44

Pray accept my profound sympathy with you in the death of your daughter, who was captured in Tunisia and carried off into Germany with her four children.

Prime Minister to Mr. Duff Cooper (Algiers)   10 Mar 44

You may let General de Gaulle know privately that I am much in favour of the Leclerc division fighting with us in the main battle here, and from my talks with General Eisenhower I gather he has the same view. I am therefore working in this sense to overcome the difficulties of transportation, etc., and I am pretty confident I shall succeed.

Prime Minister to First Lord and First Sea Lord   11 Mar 44

Let me have a short report on the character and quality of the U-boat prisoners now being taken, compared with any other significant period of the war.

Prime Minister to Foreign Secretary   11 Mar 44

It seems to me a pity to move Mallet from Stockholm at this critical time. I always deprecate military men being moved from employments or commands where they have gained a great mass of special information and are pursuing a definite theme, because of promotion in ordinary Service routine. In war-time the convenience of the State ranks above the careers of individuals. An Ambassador has to be given time to take root. The first year he is probably not much use. The second he begins to function effectively. He is nearly always brought away in the third. Mallet must be in the midst of all this Stockholm tangle. I am most anxious that Sweden shall eventually come into the war, which I think there is quite a chance of her doing.

Prime Minister to C.I.G.S.   13 Mar 44

What is all this about, and what are these troops that are taking part and have lost thirty lives in these vigorous manœuvres?* Surely these

* Military exercises in Transjordan.

forces should be brought into battle somewhere or other instead of losing their lives in exercises. How many are engaged?

Prime Minister to Lord President, Chancellor of the   14 Mar 44
Exchequer, Minister of Works and Buildings, and
Minister of Health

General Bedell Smith mentioned to me yesterday the very high and extortionate prices now being charged to American officers over here for flats and small houses. A medium-sized flat, he said, was £28 a week, and the small house that he occupied was £35 a week. There is no reason why the Americans should not pay a fair and equitable price for accommodation, which they are quite willing to do, but I do not think extortion or profiteering should be allowed.

I am not certain who deals with this, but would you very kindly give it your attention and let me know, first, about the facts, and, secondly, whether there is any remedy.

Prime Minister to C.A.S. and General Ismay   18 Mar 44

What air authority in Italy was responsible for ordering low-level machine-gunning attacks on civilians in the streets? I can quite understand bombing the marshalling yards in Rome, but I trust it was not a British airman who committed the offence here described.

Let me have a special report.

Prime Minister to President Roosevelt   19 Mar 44

We have followed Gray's* lead in Ireland, and it is early days to start reassuring de Valera. There is not much sense in a doctor telling a patient that the medicine he has just prescribed for his nerve troubles is only coloured water. I think it would be much better to keep them guessing for a while.

2. I do not propose to stop the necessary trade between Britain and Ireland or to prevent anything going into Ireland. I do propose to stop ships going from Ireland to Spain and Portugal and other foreign ports until "Overlord" is launched. One must remember that a ship may start out in one direction and turn off in another. There is no difficulty in stopping ships. The above also applies to outward-bound airplanes, which we shall try to stop by every means in our power. The object of these measures is not spite against the Irish, but preservation of British and American soldiers' lives and against our plans being betrayed by emissaries sent by sea or air from the German Minister in Dublin. Since the beginning of 1943 only nineteen Irish ships have left Irish ports, some several times, so the evil is not very great. We are also cutting off telephones and restricting communications to the

_____
* The U.S. representative in Dublin.

614

utmost, and also stopping the Anglo-Irish air line from running. I repeat, all our actions will be taken from motives of self-preservation and none from those of spite.

3. If however the Irish retaliate by doing something which in no way helps them but merely annoys us, such as stopping the Foynes airport facilities, I should feel free to retaliate on their cross-Channel trade. They would have opened a new chapter and economic measures of retaliation would be considered. I would tell you about these before we took them.

4. It seems to me that so far from allaying alarm in de Valera's circles we should let fear work its healthy process. Thereby we shall get behind the scenes a continued stiffening up of the Irish measures to prevent leakages, which even now are not so bad.

5. I gather that the State Department will probably not disagree with the above, for Mr. Hull says in his message: "I am inclined to believe however that for the time being at least we should not make any statement to the Press or commit ourselves to the Irish Government that we have no intention of instituting economic sanctions." And I hope this may also be your view.

Prime Minister to General Ismay, for C.O.S. Committee   19 Mar 44

The difference between a Chief of Staff and a Commander-in-Chief in the field is more apparent than real. Both are office workers. Both may make periodical trips to the front. Both are subject to air raids. Indeed, in many cases the similarity might be extended to Army Group Commanders, and even to Army Commanders. The conditions under which the military art is practised nowadays are not at all similar to those of former generations. There is therefore no reason why General Marshall should not receive the Soviet military decoration.

Prime Minister to First Lord and First Sea Lord   19 Mar 44

This is a serious disaster. Who were the 1,055 drowned? Were they troops outward or homeward bound? British or American?

How is it that in a convoy of this kind more could not be rescued?*

Prime Minister to Director of Military Intelligence   19 Mar 44

Why must you write "intensive" here? "Intense" is the right word. You should read Fowler's *Modern English Usage* on the use of the two words.

---

* The British transport *Khedive Ismail*, proceeding in convoy from East Africa to Ceylon, was torpedoed by a Japanese U-boat near Addu Atoll on February 12, and sank in two minutes. She carried 1,947 passengers, including British, American, and African troops and members of the Women's Services. The U-boat was sunk soon afterwards by British destroyers.

Prime Minister to Foreign Secretary   19 Mar 44

It seems to me most improvident in time of war to take a man away from a post where he has gained great influence and knowledge and to send him to some entirely different atmosphere where he has to begin all over again. I gather you now propose to move two Ambassadors. Surely we are in an extraordinary period in our lives and history, and procuring the highest service for the public during this crisis should be our only aim.

All the great Ambassadors who have exercised influence have remained long at their posts. Maisky was here for about ten years. Monsieur de Staël, whom I remember as a boy, was a tradition. Soveral [Portuguese Ambassador] was here, I think, for fifteen years or more. I could quote many other examples.

The departmental view is no doubt opposed to long tenures and the doctrine of "Buggins's turn" is very powerful. I agreed to your moving Sir Noel Charles from Rio because of the very great need there is in Italy for a competent diplomatist. You have yourself told me how many regrets this move has caused in Brazil. I certainly did not expect it would lead to a kind of "general post" among the Ambassadors, each moving into a field about which he knows nothing, and I should greatly deplore this. In my opinion, and I speak from long experience, the natural term of an Ambassador's mission should be six years, unless he is guilty of incompetence or divergence from the Government's policy, when of course he cannot be recalled too soon.

Prime Minister to Leader of the House and   29 Mar 44
Secretary of State for War

It seems to me that the Army annual bill should be the occasion for making the following amendments in our present practice:

(a) It should be made clear that every reasonable facility will be given for serving officers and men of all ranks to be adopted as candidates for constituencies either for by-elections or General Elections.

(b) No serving officers or men of any party, other than Members of Parliament, must take part in political demonstrations or in political agitation. They may attend meetings, but they must not appear on public platforms during the period of their service.

(c) In the event of a by-election occurring involving a Service candidate, he should be given leave from the issue of his address or other formal opening of his candidature till the declaration of the poll, after which his rights as a Member of Parliament are valid.

(d) The regulation against Regular officers not being eligible to stand for constituencies must be deemed henceforward to have lapsed till the end of the war, during which period Regulars and "Hostilities Only" men will be treated equally.

(e) Members of Parliament serving with the forces must be free to speak in any constituency, and not merely in their own.

Will you please concert this together and arrange with the Admiralty and Air Ministry, who must conform.

APRIL

Prime Minister to Mr. Geoffrey Lloyd, Secretary for   1 Apr 44
Petroleum

I was most interested to hear of the successful use of the fog-dispersal equipment at Fiskerton on March 18, when it increased the visibility from 200 yards to 1,500 yards and enabled five bombers to land safely. I am delighted to know that this equipment is giving so good an account of itself. It is a fine reward to you and your department that your labours have already resulted in the saving of valuable lives and equipment. You have my full support in further developing this project.

Prime Minister to Lord Cherwell   1 Apr 44

Pray let me have the figures of our casualties since the beginning of the campaign on the Italian mainland analysed, first of all in relation to the numbers of fighting troops engaged in the theatre, then in relation to the proportions of killed and wounded to missing. It must be remembered that "missing" includes prisoners who give themselves up. The lower the proportion of missing the more creditable.

Prime Minister to General Ismay, for Chiefs of Staff   2 Apr 44
and Vice-Chiefs of Staff

By all means dispose of the anti-aircraft defences in the United Kingdom as may be necessary to sustain the "Overlord" ports. You are answerable that reasonable, though reduced, security is provided elsewhere. It is quite understood that the British public will take their share of anything that is going.

Prime Minister to General Ismay, for Chiefs of Staff   2 Apr 44

I should think we have such good supplies of poison gas now that there could be a definite reduction in the personnel employed by 40 per cent., including the 10 per cent. already accomplished—*i.e.*, 30 per cent. more. Let me have your views after consulting with the Ministry of Supply.

Prime Minister to Secretary of State for War and   2 Apr 44
Secretary of State for Air

I hear that the new insecticide D.D.T. has proved extremely success-ful. As it takes some time to produce, it would be well to make sure the demands stated to the Ministry of Supply will really meet all your needs, especially in the Asiatic theatre.

Pray let me know what the position is.*

Prime Minister to Deputy Prime Minister   2 Apr 44

I am sure Bedell Smith would not have mentioned the matter to me if the charges were not excessive. £28 a week for a medium-sized flat and £35 a week for a small house seem outside the bounds of reason. Perhaps these few cases could be examined by Lord Portal himself. Anyhow, if he got into touch with General Bedell Smith I should have done my bit.†

Prime Minister to Minister of Food   2 Apr 44

Good. You will gain much credit by stamping on these little trashy prosecutions [against a baker], and also by purging the regulations from petty, meticulous, arrogant officialism, which tends to affect the reputation of a great and successful department.

Prime Minister to Minister of Works   2 Apr 44

I agree with all your comments on my paper about Emergency Housing. Pray let me have my print amended to suit them, and then submit the proof in print.

In addition we must have a better word than "prefabricated". Why not "ready-made"?

Prime Minister to Home Secretary   3 Apr 44

Let me have a report on why the Witchcraft Act, 1735, was used in a modern court of justice.

What was the cost of this trial to the State?—observing that witnesses were brought from Portsmouth and maintained here in this crowded London for a fortnight, and the Recorder kept busy with all this obso-lete tomfoolery, to the detriment of necessary work in the courts.

Prime Minister to General Montgomery   4 Apr 44

You spoke to me the other night about the 6th Guards Army Tank Brigade. I have given a good deal of thought to this matter, which I am prepared to discuss with you as well as with the War Office at any time. Meanwhile I have said no action to destroy this brigade is to be taken.

* See minute of March 9 to Minister of Supply.
† See minute of March 14.

Prime Minister to Secretary of State for War and C.I.G.S.   4 Apr 44

There is the 6th Guards Army Tank Brigade, equipped with the latest Churchills. For over two years these men have been trained together with one object and purpose. It seems to me a disastrous procedure to disband them now and fling the men into the general pool, either of any particular armoured division or of the Foot Guards or infantry of the Line. No action should be taken on this point until it has been thoroughly discussed between us.

2. I had an idea, which I should like examined, of letting the two brigades of the Guards Armoured Division and the 6th Guards Army Tank Brigade, three brigades in all, go into action together, and fold up as casualties occur to men and vehicles until they come down to the ordinary divisional strength. Thus we should have more punch at the outset and fold up out of the carefully prepared material, instead of dissipating a portion of this material and destroying all the unities that have been so laboriously evolved. I trust I may have your help in this.

Prime Minister to Secretary of State for War and C.I.G.S.   9 Apr 44
(General Montgomery to see)

I have carefully considered the points you put to me. Instead of melting down the Guards, why do we not keep them up at the expense of the Line? The Russians are doing this; they make Guards divisions on a very large scale. The Germans also gear upwards; for instance, creating Panzer Grenadier divisions which actually cost them less men than infantry divisions, and calling a lot of determined youngsters, gathered largely from the airfields, "paratroops". There is no doubt these special terms raise *esprit de corps*. No one doubts that the performances of the Guards fully justify the prestige which attaches to them.

2. Therefore I wish that the Guards should draw upon the Line, and that the existing Guards formations shall be maintained not only from Guards recruits, but where necessary from Line recruits. This does not affect the pooling of the two brigades in Italy, for which I have already given approval.

3. Subject to the above writing up of the Guards at the expense of the Line:

(*a*) I agree to the running down of the six lower establishment divisions and the reorganisation of the residues into two cadre divisions.

(*b*) I do not agree to the abolition of the 6th Guards Tank Brigade.*

* See minutes of April 4.

(c) I agree to the dispersal of the headquarters and divisional troops of the 10th Armoured Division, retaining the Armoured Brigade of this division.

(d) The largest possible block of the R.A.F. Regiment should be scraped off the airfields and incorporated in the general pool of infantry of the Army. Some may be fitted direct into the reinforcements of the Guards. At least 25,000 men should be extracted from the Royal Air Force Regiment.

Prime Minister to Minister of State and   13 Apr 44
Sir Alexander Cadogan

You will remember that we are purging all our secret establishments of Communists because we know they owe no allegiance to us or to our cause and will always betray secrets to the Soviet, even while we are working together. The fact of the two Communists being on the French Committee requires extremely careful treatment of the question of imparting secret information to them.

Prime Minister to Secretary of State for Air and   18 Apr 44
Secretary of State for War

The serious reductions which we now have to face in the formations of the Army make it necessary to examine all possible means of economy. I do not think we can afford to continue to maintain a special body of troops purely for the defence of airfields. The R.A.F. Regiment was established at a time when invasion of this country was likely, and when our life depended upon the security of our fighter airfields. Since then it has been reduced, but the time has now come to consider whether the greater part of it should not be taken to reinforce the field formations of the Army. Pray examine this proposal in consultation. The largest possible block of the R.A.F. Regiment should be incorporated in the general pool of infantry of the Army. I consider that at least 25,000 men should be so transferred.*

2. The matter is urgent, so I should like to have your definite proposals as soon as possible.

Prime Minister to Secretary of State for War and C.I.G.S.   19 Apr 44

I think we ought to do something for Martel.† You cannot blame him for his ill success in Russia. They treat all our people like dogs. Martel fought a good fight with his tanks about Armentières, in France. He gave a very far-sighted account of the Russian Army when he visited it two years before the war. I do not agree with him in some ways about tanks, but I am sure he is an officer of exceptional

---

* See minute of April 9.
† Lieut.-General Sir Giffard Martel.

quality. It should certainly be possible to find him a job. Let me know what you will do.

Prime Minister to Sir Alexander Cadogan   19 Apr 44
"Unconditional Surrender"

I have pointed out to the Cabinet that the actual terms contemplated for Germany are not of a character to reassure them at all, if stated in detail. Both President Roosevelt and Marshal Stalin at Teheran wished to cut Germany into smaller pieces than I had in mind. Stalin spoke of very large mass executions of over 50,000 of the staffs and military experts. Whether he was joking or not could not be ascertained. The atmosphere was jovial, but also grim. He certainly said that he would require 4,000,000 German males to work for an indefinite period to rebuild Russia. We have promised the Poles that they shall have compensation both in East Prussia and, if they like, up to the line of the Oder. There are a lot of other terms implying the German ruin and indefinite prevention of their rising again as an armed Power. . . .

On the other hand, they know that "unconditional surrender" was interpreted in a very favourable manner in the case of the Italians, and we see now what the Roumanians are offered if they will come over.

Prime Minister to Foreign Secretary and   23 Apr 44
Sir Alexander Cadogan

Our supreme object is that the Russians should declare war on the Japanese as soon as possible. You will remember Stalin's declaration at Teheran. From this point of view it is difficult to see why an agreement which shows the Russians' eagerness to prevent the breaking of the Russo-Japanese neutrality pact of April 1941 is "good" for us. The mere fact that the Japanese are prepared to make substantial sacrifices for it shows what they think about it, and that they hope to delay a Russian breach. This is very natural on their part. Why is it "good" for us?

2. The Japanese motives are clear, but as to the Russian motives, personally I thought the business looked rather suspicious. They are cashing in on the fact that Britain and the United States are at war with Japan, which causes Japan embarrassment. They are getting their own quarrels with Japan settled. This will put them in a better position to drive a hard bargain with us when Hitler is defeated before they embark upon hostilities with Japan. It may of course be part of a deception scheme to lull the Japanese into a false sense of security. Personally I do not like it.

Prime Minister to Foreign Secretary   29 Apr 44

I agree with your minute [on negotiations with Germany about food relief for occupied countries]. There can be no question at present of interfering with the sink-at-sight zones, which have been increasingly established by the Admiralty to facilitate operations.

2. There is no question of our approaching the Swiss or any other Government on a policy we do not accept.

3. It should be made clear that in any relief of Europe we shall certainly subject our population to any levels of rationing or dieting for which the United States sets an example.

Prime Minister to First Lord and First Sea Lord   29 Apr 44

Admiral James Somerville has added new claims to our confidence by his brilliant attack at Sabang while the main Japanese fleet was at Singapore. Why do we want to make a change here at all?

It seems to me he knows the theatre, has right ideas about it, and is capable of daring action. Does he want to go to Washington and give up his fighting command?

Prime Minister to Minister of Food   29 Apr 44

None of the papers you have sent me touch the question of the excessive demands of the United States for meat. I consented to delay putting the facts before the President because you said you would raise the matter. So far as I can make out, your Ministry take the line that provided the Americans meet our requirements then we should agree to their demands from Australia and New Zealand. But it is surely necessary for the Governments concerned, including our own, to be satisfied about the scale of provision.

2. Invaluable meat is being wasted, and at the same time the Americans are complaining that the Australians and New Zealanders are withdrawing men from the front, while the Australians blithely retort that they have all come back to grow meat for the American Army.

Unless your reply to me is of a satisfactory character I shall have to telegraph to the President. I ought to have done it weeks ago.

Prime Minister to Lord Cherwell   30 Apr 44

Before I approve the Admiralty's paper [on the German acoustic torpedo ("Gnat")] let me know whether there is anything in the following idea:

Fire a mechanism from a depth-charge projector, which would be called a "Squawker". This might either lie (floating or submerged) where it fell, and "squawk", or it might be given a motion likely to intercept a "Gnat". There seems to be no reason why fifteen or twenty of these, fired at the right time and on a reasonable judgment of the enemy's attack, might not attract him.

Alternatively, "Squawkers" might circle round our own ships at moments of danger. They would do them no harm if they hit them but they might cover their tails very effectively.

Is there anything in this?

MAY

Prime Minister to Foreign Secretary, and to General Hollis, 1 May 44 for C.O.S. Committee

I am all for getting the Brazilian division into Italy as soon as possible. Every effort should be made, subject to battle exigencies, to bring this into Italy. There should be no talk of a token force. The above also applies to the air squadron.

Prime Minister to Foreign Secretary 4 May 44

A paper should be drafted for the Cabinet, and possibly for the Imperial Conference, setting forth shortly—for that is essential—the brute issues between us and the Soviet Government which are developing in Italy, in Roumania, in Bulgaria, in Yugoslavia, and above all in Greece. It ought to be possible to get this on one page.

Broadly speaking the issue is, are we going to acquiesce in the Communisation of the Balkans and perhaps of Italy? Mr. Curtin touched upon this to-day, and I am of opinion on the whole that we ought to come to a definite conclusion about it, and that if our conclusion is that we resist the Communist infusion and invasion we should put it to them pretty plainly at the best moment that military events permit. We should of course have to consult the United States first.

Prime Minister to Foreign Secretary 4 May 44

Pray consider whether it might not be wise for us to recall our Ambassador from Moscow for consultation. We should like to have a talk with him. It would make a good gap with the Russians at the present time. Averell Harriman has already departed for the United States.

2. Let me know how you feel about this. I am not very clear on it myself, but evidently we are approaching a showdown with the Russians about their Communist intrigues in Italy, Yugoslavia, and Greece, and I do not think they would like very much a period in which they had neither a British nor an American Ambassador in Moscow. I must say I think their attitude becomes more difficult every day. I hope you have had a talk with Harriman. Take some opportunity of telling me about all this.

Prime Minister to General Ismay 7 May 44

I do not like Press conferences, even off the record, on the eve of an important battle. Once zero hour has struck the principles desired by General Alexander should be inculcated upon the Press, who should be allowed to mingle in the fighting. I have recently been perturbed at reported statements from Naples, one in the *Corriere*, explaining that we are about to attack. Is it really necessary to tell the enemy this? Of course, he may possibly think we are such fools that it is an obvious blind, but this is a dangerous chance to take.

Prime Minister to General Hollis   7 May 44

I certainly expressed myself strongly against these military missions to Algiers, from what I heard about them at the Gibraltar conference, and I greatly regret that they should have piled themselves up and ensconced themselves at Algiers, where they are not needed in any way, but only add to the horribly bloated staffs which are lurking there, most of them away from all participation in the war. I certainly wish this matter to be taken up with a view to recalling and putting to some useful work these highly paid and no doubt highly skilled and experienced officers. The best thing would be to form a Sacred Legion of about 1,000 Staff officers and let them set an example to the troops in leading some particularly desperate attack. Anyhow, the missions should be liquidated.

Prime Minister to Director of Military Intelligence   7 May 44

Please let me have the best return possible of killed, wounded, and prisoners in Italy, by nationalities, including Germans, together with the ratio in all cases as far as possible between (*a*) killed and missing and (*b*) killed, wounded, and missing. We seem to have lost 38,000 in killed, missing, and prisoners of war; whereas we have taken about 35,000 prisoners of war, to which should perhaps be added 20,000 killed, making a total missing and killed of, say, 55,000 Germans to our overall figure of 38,000, of whom 19,000 were killed. This is upon the fronts of armies where the enemy is on the whole considerably the smaller. It seems to me that very satisfactory figures might emerge from this final calculation, even though on the whole fronts our ratio of killed to missing is less satisfactory than the Americans'.

Prime Minister to Foreign Secretary   7 May 44

I am puzzled at the procedure which Ambassador Clark Kerr uses in Moscow. Apparently he takes every telegram and delivers it personally to Molotov or Stalin, whichever he can get at, and waits sometimes for several days if these potentates are away or do not choose to give audience. Now there are some telegrams which certainly he should deliver himself, but should not others be sent by an officer and be presented? I wish you would let me know what is the proper usage about all this. It seems to me that it would be much better, for instance when we send a very stiff message, not to have our man waiting about to be bulldozed, and afterwards sometimes offer deprecatory observations which weaken the force of what it has been decided to say.

Prime Minister to Lord Privy Seal   7 May 44

I feel sure you cannot have looked into the extraordinary consequences of our coming out of this war owing India a bigger debt, after having defended her, than we owed to the United States at the end of the last war. Your note does not seem at all to take into consideration these frightful consequences.

Prime Minister to First Lord of the Admiralty   10 May 44

Thank you for your report of April 5 about the "Gnat". It occurred to me that if fifteen or twenty noise-makers (which might be called "Squawkers") could be fired overboard from a depth-charge or other projector at the right time they might attract and distract the "Gnats". This would have the great advantage of avoiding any towing gear and the other demerits of "foxers".

I am glad to learn that you are thinking and working on these lines, and I hope you will be able to get these "Squawkers" into operation soon.*

Prime Minister to Lord Portal   14 May 44

It is now some months since I begged you to have some more samples made of your prefabricated house.† I hear that each one takes about six weeks' labour to prepare, and that in addition to the house at the Tate Gallery another has been constructed and is on its way to Scotland for exhibition, and two others are shortly to be built, with all the improvements. I am very glad to hear of this, although it is less than I had hoped. You must give your house a chance to be seen by working women and people of all classes. Please see that the ones you are making are pressed on.

Prime Minister to Secretary of State for Air   20 May 44

You have been asked to supply 25,000 men from the R.A.F. Regiment, which was built up in quite different circumstances from those which now exist.‡ These men are vitally needed for the support of the Army in the forthcoming battle. I was willing to go into this in detail with you at an early date, but as I have to make a speech in the House on Wednesday of this week I could not find the time beforehand. Meanwhile I have asked that you supply 2,000 good men for the

---

* See minute of April 30 to Lord Cherwell.
† See minute of April 2 to Minister of Works.
‡ See minute of April 9.

upkeep of the Guards. They will be much better employed there than loafing around overcrowded airfields warding off dangers which have ceased to threaten. I must ask you to comply with this request. Otherwise it will be necessary to bring the matter before the War Cabinet on Tuesday next at a special meeting, for immediate decision. I must make it clear that this is without prejudice to the further demands that will be made upon you by a committee which will be set up for the purpose of extracting the necessary men.

2. The Army have already had a very considerable comb-out from their anti-aircraft regiments of men suitable for infantry, and it is quite wrong at the present stage in the war to retain many of the first-class men in the R.A.F. Regiment in a purely passive rôle.

3. There is of course no difficulty in effecting the transfer. This was clearly shown when both the Army and the R.A.F. transferred men to the Navy at the end of last year, when there was an urgent need for landing-craft crews. I have little doubt that many would volunteer, but everyone well understands in these days that men must be directed to where their services can best be used in the common task.

4. I therefore ask you to help me by carrying out my request for the 2,000 men. Time is short and the need urgent.★

Prime Minister to C.I.G.S.   21 May 44

Why are we told that the 1st Polish Armoured Division cannot function because there are not sufficient rear administrative units available to maintain it? Surely a reasonable effort at adjustment could be made to enable this fine division to strengthen our already too slender forces on the Continent. Pray let me have an account of the deficiencies.

Prime Minister to Minister of Production   21 May 44

Thank you for your minute of May 11 about penicillin. By all means try to get as large an allocation from America as you can, but do not let anything stand in the way of increasing our output here. It does not seem as if we shall produce much this year.

Prime Minister to Mr. Sandys   21 May 44

You might read this report [from General O'Connor, about the armour protection and escape arrangements of the Cromwell tank], and make any remarks you like about it to-morrow in writing. I had rather gathered the idea that the difficulty about the lower man escaping would become extreme if the cordite or the petrol in the compartment above him caught fire. Perhaps you can reassure me on this.

★ 2,000 men were transferred on June 27, 1944.

Prime Minister to Foreign Secretary 22 May 44

It is said about Foreign Office minutes that if you read the odd paragraph numbers and the even paragraph numbers in series you get both sides of the case fully stated. Why would it not be sufficient to say both to the United States and Russia, "We are not in favour of giving Italy Allied status at this stage"?

2. I have read this telegram through, and it states very well all the arguments for and against every course, with a highly questionable and unexpected conclusion that "a partial Peace Treaty should be arranged with Italy as soon as conditions permit". It may well be that even when all the Governments meet together there will be no Peace Treaty after the fall of Hitler, but only a prolonged armistice.

3. I am sure you would find that a shorter, simple indication of our position would carry more weight and would be more likely to reach the highest quarters. Pray speak to me about this, especially if you do not like my comments.

Prime Minister to Foreign Secretary, Minister of 23 May 44
War Transport, Minister of Production, and
Minister of Food

All this matter [reduction of imports on account of "Overlord"] is left between Lord Leathers and General Eisenhower, but I have said that I would sacrifice 500,000 tons additional imports into this country for the next four months, provided that the United States guarantee this amount shall be made up in the two or three months following. Twenty-four millions a year is our absolute minimum.

Prime Minister to Foreign Secretary 23 May 44

I saw in one of the papers that Russia was about to recognise the Provisional Government of France. I approved of your telegram to Sir A. Clark Kerr. This has not perhaps reached Stalin, but the matter is very important, because I am determined not to sever myself from the President on this and be found lining up with Russia against him. It would be very bad if we had to say that Russia did not consult us on this matter and that we are now in consultation with the United States. But even that would be better than a line-up by Britain and Russia against the President. In fact, I would have nothing to do with it on this subject. Russia has no right to take this step without consultation with her two Allies, who are doing all the fighting in the West.

Prime Minister to General Ismay, for C.O.S. Committee 25 May 44

Obviously garrisons must be provided by the British Empire for redeemed territories. The problem will become insoluble if it is to be expressed in the usual jargon of divisions. Once the enemy has been driven out, battalions and armoured car companies, with occasional assignments of artillery and tanks, all fitted to the particular districts concerned, are all that is needed. There must be a mass of troops in India who could be drawn upon for this.

2. A division is a kind of athletic entity, capable of the highest operations of war. It has nothing whatever to do with the particular static or mobile police forces which are required to hold down doubtful countries. These should always have a large admixture of local people, and they have never got to consider the question of bringing seventy guns into action at one time.

Prime Minister to Foreign Secretary   25 May 44

As I see it, the Big Three or Big Four will be the trustees or steering committee of the whole body in respect of the use of force to prevent war; but I think much larger bodies, and possibly functional bodies, would deal with the economic side. You should make it clear that we have no idea of three or four Great Powers ruling the world. On the contrary, their victory will entitle them to serve the world in the supreme respect of preventing the outbreak of more wars. We should certainly not be prepared ourselves to submit to an economic, financial, and monetary system laid down by, say, Russia, or the United States with her faggot-vote China.

The Supreme World Council or Executive is not to rule the nations. It is only to prevent them tearing each other in pieces. I feel I could argue this very strongly from the point of view of derogation of national sovereignties.

Prime Minister to Minister of Food   26 May 44

I am glad to hear all you say about better rations, and think what you are doing very wise. Try to cut out petty annoyances, whether in the hotels, the little shops, or the private lives of ordinary people. Nothing should be done for spite's sake. The great work of rationing in this country, which has given so much confidence and absence of class feeling, should not be prejudiced by little trumpery regulations which when enforced make hard cases. Let me have some of your ideas on this.

Prime Minister to Foreign Secretary   27 May 44

It is a great pity, when an important message agreed upon between us has been sent to Stalin from me, that it should not be delivered as fast as possible. There would always be an opportunity for the Ambassador to give a warning if he thought it would do extreme harm, and in exceptional cases he might use his discretion. But the idea that the message should be left hanging about in Moscow for four, five, or six days to find time for Stalin to see him, or until he returns from the front, cannot be necessary. An officer in uniform should be given facilities to deliver the message as a letter.

Sometimes misunderstandings arise because one sends a message and waits a long time for an answer. After it comes one finds it is quite a nice answer, but meanwhile one has been thinking the worse of the silence. Nothing should stand in the way of prompt communication.*

Prime Minister to C.I.G.S.   27 May 44
Please do not on any account let the Polish Division be kept out of the battle-front. Not only is it a magnificent fighting force, but its exploits will help to keep alive the soul of Poland, on which much turns in the future. Could I kindly have a list of the rearward services which it lacks, showing the number of vehicles, officers, personnel, etc.?
P.S. General Bedell Smith says he can help in getting some drafts for this division by flying them from Africa and the United States.†

Prime Minister to Minister of Aircraft Production   27 May 44
Many congratulations on the record flight of 506 miles per hour set up by De Havilland's jet aircraft. Please pass this on to those concerned.
I am a little perturbed to hear that you are proposing to centralise jet-propulsion development in your new Government company. There is a great deal to be said for encouraging overlapping in research and development rather than putting all the eggs in one basket. I quite appreciate that the many delays in jet-propulsion development may have led you to consider that some new organisation is required, but I wonder whether it is wise to remove work on jet-propulsion from Farnborough, where I understand much solid work has been done, and where it is so easy for engine and aircraft development to proceed hand-in-hand.‡

Prime Minister to Minister of Fuel and Power   27 May 44
I hope you will put a stop to nonsense like this [report in the *Yorkshire Post* that a householder was fined £1, with two guineas costs, for having borrowed coal from a neighbour]. Nothing makes departments so unpopular as these acts of petty bureaucratic folly which come to light from time to time, and are, I fear, only typical of a vast amount of silly wrongdoing by small officials or committees.
You should make an example of the people concerned with this.

Prime Minister to First Lord and First Sea Lord   28 May 44
Do not hesitate to be blunt with these Russians when they become unduly truculent. This is better done by manner and attitude than by

* See minute of May 7 to Foreign Secretary.
† See minute of May 21 to C.I.G.S.
‡ See minutes of July 31 and October 6, 1943.

actual words, which can be reported, and also by neglect of certain civilities to the superior people when they have been intolerably offensive. They should certainly be given a feeling that we are not afraid of them.

2. On the other hand, any ceremonial they may wish in regard to the handing over of the vessels [British warships in lieu of Italian] should be staged with the utmost formality and made a public success. I am certainly not going to communicate with Marshal Stalin about any of this. It is for the Russians to show gratitude rather than for us to show deference. All friendly relations between the junior officers should be cultivated. Not one word of thanks has ever been expressed to us for this transfer of ships. We have borne the brunt of meeting their requests for shipping. There are all sorts of ways of making people feel that you resent their insults.

3. If however their conduct improves you should neglect nothing which will encourage this amendment.

Prime Minister to Deputy Supreme Commander,   29 May 44
Allied Expeditionary Force

Thank you for your minute of May 11 about Mailly-le-Camp [German tank training depot]. There is no doubt that the attack on this compact target was a great success. It would seem right, as we urged, to continue to give a high priority to operations of this sort, which contribute directly towards the disorganisation of the German armies and involve no French casualties.

Have you exceeded the 10,000 limit [of French civilian casualties]?

Prime Minister to First Lord   29 May 44

The reason why this Communist newspaper has not been allowed to send war correspondents to operational theatres or to occasions where security has to be maintained is because Communists do not hesitate to betray any British or American secrets they may find to the Communist Party, no doubt for transmission to Russia. In this case any betrayal they may make to their masters will not do any harm. They should however be told that the Russian Government have stipulated that not a word is to get out about these ships until they have safely made their way to Russia. They will certainly obey this injunction once it is proved to them. Their treason and their loyalties only work on single tracks. In these circumstances I approve of their being invited, after having been made acquainted with the fact that the Russians have stipulated that the secret is to be kept till the ships are safely in Russian hands.

APPENDIX D

MONTHLY TOTALS OF SHIPPING LOSSES, BRITISH, ALLIED, AND NEUTRAL, BY ENEMY ACTION

Month	British		Allied		Neutral		Total	
	No. of Ships	Gross Tons	No. of Ships	Gross Tons	No. of Ships	Gross Tons	No. of Ships	Gross Tons
January 1943	19	98,096	24	143,358	7	19,905	50	261,359
February ..	29	166,947	39	232,235	5	3,880	73	403,062
March.. ..	62	384,914	53	303,284	5	5,191	120	693,389
April	33	194,252	27	137,081	4	13,347	64	344,680
May	31	146,496	26	151,299	1	1,633	58	299,428
June	12	44,975	13	75,854	3	2,996	28	123,825
July	30	187,759	26	166,231	5	11,408	61	365,398
August ..	14	62,900	9	56,578	2	323	25	119,801
September ..	12	60,541	15	94,010	2	1,868	29	156,419
October ..	11	57,565	17	81,631	1	665	29	139,861
November ..	15	61,593	12	82,696	2	102	29	144,391
December ..	10	55,611	21	112,913	—	—	31	168,524
TOTALS ..	278	1,521,649	282	1,637,170	37	61,318	597	3,220,137
January 1944	16	67,112	9	62,115	1	1,408	26	130,635
February ..	12	63,411	8	53,244	3	200	23	116,855
March.. ..	10	49,637	14	104,964	1	3,359	25	157,960
April	3	21,439	10	60,933	—	—	13	82,372
May	5	27,297	—	—	—	—	5	27,297
TOTALS ..	46	228,896	41	281,256	5	4,967	92	515,119

APPENDIX E

SUMMARY OF
ORDER OF BATTLE, GERMAN AND ITALIAN
DIVISIONS, ON SEPTEMBER 8, 1943*

(Source: *Come Arrivammo all'Armistizio*, by General Francesco Rossi)

Divisions marked with a "dagger" are recorded as being weak or of low category.

	Italian	*German*
North Italy	5 infantry †5 infantry	6⅓ infantry 2 motor and armoured
Central Italy	3 infantry 2 motor and armoured †2 infantry	2 motor and armoured
Southern Italy	3 infantry †1 infantry	2 infantry 4 motor and armoured
Sardinia	4 infantry	1 motor
Southern France	4 infantry (under relief by German troops, strength unknown, from Rundstedt's command)	
Corsica	2 infantry	⅓ infantry
Slovenia, Croatia, Dalmatia	8 infantry	9 infantry 6 brigades (Croat Alpine troops)
Herzegovina, Montenegro	6 infantry	2 infantry 1 motor and armoured 2 brigades (Croat Alpine troops)

* See Chapter VIII.

Albania	5 infantry 1 motor	Nil (but a call on 2 German and 2 Bulgarian divisions in Serbia and Macedonia)
Greece	7 infantry	6 infantry 1 armoured
Crete Ægean	1 infantry 2 infantry	1 infantry 1 infantry with A.F.V.s

TOTALS

	Italian	German
Italian mainland	21 divisions, of which 8 are weak or of low category	16⅓
Sardinia	4	1
"Overseas"	36	21⅓
GRAND TOTALS	61 Italian divisions, of which 8 are weak or of low category	38⅔ German divisions

---

GERMAN DISPOSITIONS IN DETAIL, SEPTEMBER 8, 1943

ARMY GROUP – ROMMEL

Northern Italy	24 Armd. Div. } Hitler S.S. Armd. Div. }	*Area* Parma–Bologna
	44 Inf. Div. } One inf. bde. }	Alto Adige
	71 Inf. Div.	Tarvisio–Piedicolle–Postumia
	65 Inf. Div. } 76 Inf. Div. } 94 Inf. Div. } 305 Inf. Div. }	Sestri Levante–Val Taro– Pontremoli–Apuania

633

w★★

GERMAN SOUTHERN COMMAND – KESSELRING

Central Italy	3 Pz. Gr. Mot./Armd.	Lake Bolsena–
	2 Pz. Gr. Parachute	Viterbo
Southern Italy	15 Inf. Div.	Formia
	H. Goering Armd. Div.	Naples
	16 Armd. Div.	Salerno
	1 Parachute Div.	Puglia Basilicata
	26 Armd. Div.	Calabria
	29 Pz. Gr. Mot. Div.	Calabria
Sardinia	90 Inf. Mot. Div.	
Corsica	One brigade "Reich Fuehrer", Mot./Armd.	

GERMAN SOUTH-EAST COMMAND – LOHR

Slovenia, Croatia, Dalmatia	114 Inf. Div. 373 (German-Croat) Inf. Div.	} Bihac
	187 Inf. Div. 369 (German-Croat) Inf. Div. 173 Inf. Div.	} Sava
	Two (?) inf. divs. One S.S. div.	} Zagreb
	One (Croat) Mtn. Div. Six (Croat) Mtn. Bdes.	} Various
Herzegovina, Montenegro	Prinz Eugen S.S. Mot./Armd. Div.	Mostar
	118 (?108) Inf. Div.	Prijepolie Plevlja
	297 Inf. Div.	Ibar Valley
	Two (Croat) Mtn. Bdes.	Various
Greece	One Mtn. Div.	Janina
	One L. of C. div.	Salonica
	One inf. div.	Larissa
	104 Inf. Div.	Agrinion
	11 Inf. Div.	Piræus
	117 Inf. Div. One armd. div.	} Peloponnese
Crete	22 Inf. Div.	
Rhodes	One 55 mot./armd. div.	

APPENDIX F

THE RELEASE OF THE MOSLEYS
CONSTITUTIONAL ISSUES

WHILE we were in conference at Cairo and Teheran a domestic issue of constitutional importance which had been before us since the beginning of October came to a head. It is recounted here in order not to break the general narrative.

Prime Minister to Home Secretary   6 Oct 43
Let me know what is the report of the Medical Commissioners upon Sir Oswald Mosley's state of health. I have received privately some rather serious medical reports about him, but they are of course unofficial.

Mr. Morrison's reports confirmed this information, and he decided to release Sir Oswald and his wife. I was sure this would raise controversy.

Prime Minister to Home Secretary   21 Nov 43
I expect you will be questioned about the release of the Mosleys. No doubt the pith of your case is health and humanity. You might however consider whether you should not unfold as a background the great principle of *habeas corpus* and trial by jury, which are the supreme protection invented by the British people for ordinary individuals against the State. The power of the Executive to cast a man into prison without formulating any charge known to the law, and particularly to deny him judgment by his peers for an indefinite period, is in the highest degree odious, and is the foundation of all totalitarian Governments, whether Nazi or Communist. It is only when extreme danger to the State can be pleaded that this power may be temporarily assumed by the Executive, and even so its working must be interpreted with the utmost vigilance by a Free Parliament. As the danger passes, persons so imprisoned, against whom there is no charge which courts and juries would accept, should be released, as you have been steadily doing, until hardly any are left. Extraordinary powers assumed by the Executive with the consent of Parliament in emergencies should be yielded up when and as the emergency declines. Nothing can be more abhorrent to democracy than to imprison a person or keep him in prison because he is unpopular. This is really the test of civilisation.

Differences arose between Ministers on the step the Home Secretary proposed to take. I assured him of my full support, though I should have preferred to deal with the question as a whole, rather than in a particular case.

Prime Minister (Cairo) to Home Secretary   25 Nov 43
I am convinced 18B should be completely abolished, as the national emergency no longer justifies abrogation of individual rights of *habeas corpus* and

trial by jury on definite charges. I doubt very much whether any serious resistance would be made to this. There are of course a number of totalitarian-minded people who like to keep their political opponents in prison on *lettres de cachet*, but I do not think they constitute a majority. I have already on more than one occasion expressed in Parliament my distaste for these exceptional powers, and my hope that success and security would enable us to dispense with them. However, as these views conflict with the line you have adopted I shall not press them at this stage.

Any unpopularity you have incurred through correct and humane exercise of your functions will be repaid in a few months by public respect.

Prime Minister (Cairo) to Deputy Prime Minister and   25 Nov 43
Home Secretary

In case there is a debate on an amendment to the Address to terminate 18B, I would strongly counsel the line that we very much regret having to be responsible for such powers, which we fully admit are contrary to the whole spirit of British public life and British history. These powers were conferred on us by Parliament because of the dire peril of the State, and we have to administer them in accordance with the principles of humanity, but all the time we desire to give back these powers from the Executive to Parliament. The fact that we have gained great victories and are in a much safer position makes the Government the more desirous of parting with exceptional powers. The time has not yet come when these can be fully dispensed with, but we can look forward to that day.

2. On no account should we lend any countenance to the totalitarian idea of the right of the Executive to lock up its political opponents or unpopular people. The door should be kept open for the full restoration of the fundamental British rights of *habeas corpus* and trial by jury on charges known to the law. I must warn you that departure from these broad principles because the Home Office have a few people they like to keep under control by exceptional means may become a source of very grave difference between us and the totalitarian-minded folk. In such a quarrel I am sure I could carry the majority in the House of Commons and the mass of the nation. Anyhow, I would try. It seems to me you have a perfectly good line in deploring the fact that such powers are thrust on you and in proclaiming your resolve to use them with the utmost circumspection and humanity. Do not quit the heights.

Mr. Attlee now reported to me that the Cabinet had decided to support the Home Secretary in releasing the Mosleys from prison. There was, I learned, considerable Parliamentary agitation against this step.

Prime Minister (Teheran) to Home Secretary   29 Nov 43

Considering you are supported by the Cabinet, and by me as Prime Minister, you have no choice whatever but to fight the matter through, and you will no doubt be supported in any direct issue by a very large majority.

2. There is no hurry about the general question of 18B. I certainly recommend however that you express your distaste for such powers and your regret

that dangers of the country have forced you to assume them, and your earnest desire to return to normal. This is a becoming attitude in a democratic Minister.

Mr. Morrison showed firmness and courage in resisting the storm that threatened him, and, as is often the case, it dispersed. People who are not prepared to do unpopular things and to defy clamour are not fit to be Ministers in times of stress.

Prime Minister (Teheran) to Home Secretary   2 Dec 43
I congratulate you on the strong support given to you by the House of Commons. Your courageous and humane discharge of your most difficult and disagreeable functions will gain its reward in the respect of the British nation.

APPENDIX G

MINISTERIAL APPOINTMENTS, JUNE 1943 – MAY 1944

(Members of the War Cabinet are shown in italics)

PRIME MINISTER AND FIRST LORD OF THE TREASURY, MINISTER OF DEFENCE	*Mr. Winston S. Churchill*
ADMIRALTY, FIRST LORD OF THE	MR. A. V. ALEXANDER
AGRICULTURE AND FISHERIES, MINISTER OF	MR. R. S. HUDSON
AIR, SECRETARY OF STATE FOR	SIR ARCHIBALD SINCLAIR
AIRCRAFT PRODUCTION, MINISTER OF	SIR STAFFORD CRIPPS
BURMA, SECRETARY OF STATE FOR	MR. L. S. AMERY
CHANCELLOR OF THE DUCHY OF LANCASTER	(a) MR. A. DUFF COOPER (b) MR. ERNEST BROWN (appointed November 17, 1943)
CHANCELLOR OF THE EXCHEQUER	(a) SIR KINGSLEY WOOD (b) *Sir John Anderson* (appointed September 28, 1943)
COLONIES, SECRETARY OF STATE FOR THE	COLONEL OLIVER STANLEY
DOMINION AFFAIRS, SECRETARY OF STATE FOR	(a) *Mr. Clement Attlee* (b) VISCOUNT CRANBORNE (appointed September 28, 1943)
ECONOMIC WARFARE, MINISTER OF	THE EARL OF SELBORNE
EDUCATION, PRESIDENT OF THE BOARD OF	MR. R. A. BUTLER (By the Education Act, 1944, the title of the office was changed to "Minister of Education")
FOOD, MINISTER OF	(a) LORD WOOLTON (b) COLONEL J. J. LLEWELLIN (appointed November 12, 1943)

FOREIGN AFFAIRS, SECRETARY OF STATE FOR	*Mr. Anthony Eden*
FUEL AND POWER, MINISTER OF	MAJOR G. LLOYD GEORGE
HEALTH, MINISTER OF	(*a*) MR. ERNEST BROWN
	(*b*) MR. H. U. WILLINK (appointed November 17, 1943)
HOME DEPARTMENT, SECRETARY OF STATE FOR THE	*Mr. Herbert Morrison*
INDIA, SECRETARY OF STATE FOR	MR. L. S. AMERY
INFORMATION, MINISTER OF	MR. BRENDAN BRACKEN
LABOUR AND NATIONAL SERVICE, MINISTER OF	*Mr. Ernest Bevin*
LAW OFFICERS:	
ATTORNEY-GENERAL	SIR DONALD SOMERVELL
LORD ADVOCATE	MR. J. S. C. REID
SOLICITOR-GENERAL	SIR DAVID MAXWELL FYFE
SOLICITOR-GENERAL FOR SCOTLAND	SIR DAVID KING MURRAY
LORD CHANCELLOR	VISCOUNT SIMON
LORD PRESIDENT OF THE COUNCIL	(*a*) *Sir John Anderson*
	(*b*) *Mr. Clement Attlee* (appointed September 28, 1943)
LORD PRIVY SEAL	(*a*) VISCOUNT CRANBORNE
	(*b*) LORD BEAVERBROOK (appointed September 28, 1943)
MINISTER OF STATE	MR. R. K. LAW (appointed September 25, 1943)
MINISTER WITHOUT PORTFOLIO	SIR WILLIAM JOWITT
PAYMASTER-GENERAL	LORD CHERWELL
PENSIONS, MINISTER OF	SIR WALTER WOMERSLEY
POSTMASTER-GENERAL	CAPTAIN H. F. C. CROOKSHANK
PRODUCTION, MINISTER OF	*Mr. Oliver Lyttelton*
RECONSTRUCTION, MINISTER OF	*Lord Woolton* (appointed November 12)
SCOTLAND, SECRETARY OF STATE FOR	MR. THOMAS JOHNSTON

SUPPLY, MINISTER OF	SIR ANDREW DUNCAN
TOWN AND COUNTRY PLANNING, MINISTER OF	MR. W. S. MORRISON (appointed February 5, 1943)
TRADE, PRESIDENT OF THE BOARD OF	MR. HUGH DALTON
WAR, SECRETARY OF STATE FOR	SIR JAMES GRIGG
WAR TRANSPORT, MINISTER OF	LORD LEATHERS
WORKS AND BUILDINGS, MINISTER OF	LORD PORTAL
MINISTERS OVERSEAS:	
MIDDLE EAST, MINISTER OF STATE RESIDENT IN THE	(a) *Mr. R. G. Casey* (until December 23, 1943) (b) LORD MOYNE (appointed January 29, 1944) (c) SIR EDWARD GRIGG (appointed November 22, 1944)
WASHINGTON, MINISTER RESIDENT FOR SUPPLY IN	(a) COLONEL J. J. LLEWELLIN (b) MR. BEN SMITH (appointed November 12, 1943)
ALLIED FORCE HEADQUARTERS, MEDITERRANEAN COMMAND, MINISTER RESIDENT AT	MR. HAROLD MACMILLAN
WEST AFRICA, MINISTER RESIDENT IN	VISCOUNT SWINTON
MIDDLE EAST, DEPUTY MINISTER OF STATE RESIDENT IN THE	LORD MOYNE (until January 29, 1944. when office lapsed)
HOUSE OF LORDS, LEADER OF THE	VISCOUNT CRANBORNE
HOUSE OF COMMONS, LEADER OF THE	*Mr. Anthony Eden*

INDEX

ment on campaign in, 494–6, 506–8;
command of air in, 496, 501–2; British
success in, on Arakan coast, 496–7;
Chindits in, 497–8; battle in, for Imphal
plain, 497, 500–3; Mountbatten's views
as to operation in, 506; question of command in, 577–8

Burma Road, opening of, 308; making of,
494–6, 506–7

Bus queues, 586, 590–1

Butler, Rt. Hon. R. A., minute to, 597;
President of Board of Education, 638

Cadogan, Rt. Hon. Sir Alexander, in
Washington, 84; minutes to, 620–1

Caen, 516, 524

Cairo, diversionary preparations at, before
Teheran meeting, 272–3; Eden's talks
with Turks at, 295–6, 346–7; Thanksgiving Day party at, 300–1; Greek
Government crisis in, 477–80; mutiny
of Greek troops in, 477–8; King of
Hellenes returns to, 479–80

Cairo Conferences, difficulties over arrangements for, 279–84, 288; protection
for, 288–9; journey to Cairo, 287–9, 291;
Chinese business at, 289–91; meetings
of, 294–6, 362–4; question of one overall
Supreme Command raised at, 296–300;
talks with Turks at, 345, 367, 369; summary of decisions arrived at, 364–5;
influence of, on Greek affairs, 476;
dollar balances discussed at, 611

Calabria, descents on coast of, 85; progress
through, 86, 117, 218; German troops
in, 216

"Caliph", Operation, 606–7

Caltagirone, 33

Cameron, Lieutenant Donald, R.N.R., 234

Campbell, Rt. Hon. Sir Ronald, Ambassador at Lisbon, 88–9; minute to, 584

Campoleone, 426, 428–30

Canada, takes joint responsibility for North
Atlantic convoys, 7; work on Pykrete in,
69; Churchill greeted in, 72; Churchill
sworn Privy Counsellor of Cabinet of,
106; his broadcast to, 107–9; war contributions of, 107–8

Canadian Air Force, in Battle of Atlantic, 8

Canadian Army, in Sicily, 28, 37; protects
Britain, 107; in Italy, 116, 131, 224, 530,
534–5, 537

Canaris, Admiral, 425

Canberra, H.M.A.S., loss of, 17, 20

Cape Orlando, 37

Careless talk, precautions against, 565

Carentan, 524

Caroline Islands, Japanese base in, 16, 113,
492; U.S. air attacks on, 493

Carthage, Churchill at, 373–9; Christmas
Day conference at, 384–6; protection of,
388

Carton de Wiart, Lieut.-General Sir Adrian,
liaison officer with Chiang Kai-shek, 84;
accompanies Italian emissary to Lisbon,
96–7

Casablanca, 568

Casablanca Conference, Sicilian campaign
decided upon by, 23; "Overlord" planning arranged at, 65; directive issued to
Allied Air Forces at, 458–9

Casey, Rt. Hon. R. G., Minister of State
Resident in Middle East, 132, 370, 640;
Cairo villa of, 280, 289

Cassino, Monastery Hill at, 224–5, 428,
448–50, 529–30, 582; first offensive
against, 391, 424, 428–9, 435–6; second
offensive against, 442–3; bombing of
monastery, 442; third offensive against,
447–51; fighting in streets of, 448; the
terrain at, 448–50; casualties at, 450;
fourth offensive against, 528–30, 532;
capture of, 530, 532, 534

Castelforte, 425

Castellano, General, proposes Italian co-
operation against Germans, 92; discussions on peace terms with, 94–8; signs
armistice, 99

Castellone, Monte, 428

Castelrossa island, 184

Catania, 26, 33, 37–8

Catapult-aircraft merchant ships, 11

Catroux, General Georges, on French
Committee of National Liberation, 154–
155, 160; in Levant, 165

Caviglia, Marshal, 101

Ceccano, 537

Centuripe, 37

Cephalonia, 170

Ceprano, 534

Cesaro, 37

Chalfont St. Giles, 610

Charles, Sir Noel, 616

Cherbourg, objective in "Overlord", 66,
516–17, 524; flying-bomb launching
sites near, 210, 212; German naval reinforcements at, 546

Cherwell, Lord, on danger from rockets,
206, 212–13; on aluminised explosives,
463–4, 590; minutes to, 564, 570, 617,
622; and glider bombs, 586; Paymaster-
General, 588, 639; on fog dispersal apparatus, 589

Chetniks, 311; make accommodations with
Germans, 408–10; Partisan strife with,
409–10, 421

Chevrons for service abroad, 567

Chiang Kai-shek, Generalissimo, British
liaison officer with, 84; at Cairo Con-

Messina, Straits of, Germans escape across,
38, 85; British attack across, 85-6, 99,
116-17
Metaxas, General, 471
M.I.5, and Communists on Government
work, 603
Middle East, convoys through Mediterranean to, 4; use of forces in, 121, 574
Middle East Command, plans campaign in
Ægean, 181; ordered to send shipping
to India, 181, 189-90; stripping of, for
Eisenhower, 184, 192, 195, 199; Air
Forces of, needed in Dodecanese, 187,
195-6; unoccupied troops and aircraft
of, 305-6, 314; Paget for, 375; sends
missions to Greece, 472; suspends shipments of arms to E.L.A.S., 476; tanks in
possession of, 581
Mihailović, General Draga, Chetniks of,
311; Resistance movement of, 408, 411;
relations of, with Germans, 408-9, 415;
Allied support of, 410; antagonism be-
tween Tito and, 412-13, 419, 421;
British support withdrawn from, 413,
416, 420; King Peter asked to dismiss,
413-16, 418, 420-2; dismissal of, 420-1;
following of, in Serbia, 422-3
Mikoyan, M., 261
Milan, Communist demonstrations in, 89
Military service, releases from, 575
Minesweepers, in "Overlord", 525, 557
Minturno, 425
Mogaung, 502
Mogilev, 232
Möhne Dam, destruction of, 63
Molotov, Vyacheslav, asks for resumption
of Arctic convoys, 232, 234; demands
limitation of British Service personnel in
North Russia, 235; on value of Arctic
convoys, 242; present at Eden's talks
with Stalin, 243-4, 259; at Conference
of Foreign Secretaries, 249, 253-6, 261;
elected chairman, 253; conciliatory atti-
tude of, 261; and Cairo Conference, 279,
282-4; at Teheran, 303, 306, 320, 324-5,
329-30, 341, 344; asks for Italian ships,
347; on Curzon Line, 350-1
Monckton, Sir Walter, 464
Monnet, M., 160
Montecorvino airfield, 85, 125
Montenegro, "Garibaldi Divisions" in, 170
Montgomery, Field-Marshal Sir Bernard
(Viscount), in Sicily, 25-6; brings Eighth
Army up to link with Fifth at Salerno,
125, 130, 134-6; minutes to, 135, 520,
618; minute from, 136; position of, in
"Overlord", 269, 374, 376, 393; in
Italy, 335, 375; successor to, 385; dis-
satisfied with plan for "Overlord", 386,
393, 451, 517; at Marrakesh, 393-4;

vehicles required by, 520, 543-4, 603; at
final "Overlord" conference, 542-3;
Churchill writes in private book of, 544;
wants Commandos for "Overlord", 601
Monywa, 495
Moore, Admiral Sir H. R., minute to, 586
Moran, Lord, 303, 373-4, 388-9
Moray Firth, 522
Morgan, Lieut.-General Sir F. E., goes to
Quebec, 62; "Cossac", 65, 322; plan
of, for "Overlord", 75, 393, 515-16;
Deputy to Bedell Smith, 517
Morgenthau, Henry, 611
Moroccan division, in Italy, 224
Morocco, 606-7
Morrison, Rt. Hon. Herbert S., and
London's danger from rockets, 206;
minutes to, as Minister of Home
Security, 564, 593, 610; minutes to, as
Home Secretary, 603, 608, 618, 635-7;
and release of Mosleys, 635-7; Home
Secretary, 639
Morrison, Rt. Hon. W. S., Minister of
Town and Country Planning, 640
Morton, Major Sir Desmond, 565
Moscow, Conference of Foreign Secre-
taries in, 237, 241, 247-66; Stalin agrees
to seeing Finnish delegation in, 351-3
Mosley, Sir Oswald, release of, 635-7
Mosquito aircraft, over Berlin, 207; use of
"Oboe" by, 459
Mountbatten, Vice-Admiral Lord Louis
(Earl), Chief of Combined Operations,
64-6, 516, 522; minutes to, 66, 365, 497,
501, 503, 587; for S.E. Asia Command,
70, 73, 79, 109, 115, 307, 587; demon-
strates strength of Pykrete, 81; U.S.
Press criticisms of, 269-70; at Cairo Conference, 294; plans of, for amphibious
operation on Andaman Islands, 361,
364-6, 599; limited resources of, 382;
Burma objective of, 495-6; needs aircraft to supply army, 500-3; reports
British victory, 503; discussion on operations for, 505-8
Moyne, Lord, 640
"Mulberry" harbours, 66-8, 516, 518-19,
562
Munda, 366
Murmansk, 337
Murphy, Robert, and French Committee,
155, 157, 160; political assistant, Mediterranean, 375
Murray, Rt. Hon. Sir David King, Solici-
tor-General for Scotland, 639
Mussolini, Benito, difficult position of, 30,
40-1; fall of, 37, 40-9; blamed for war,
40, 43, 47; convenes Grand Council, 41;
meets Hitler, 44-5, 169-70; sees the
King, 45-7; defeated at Grand Council,

support given to, 292, 411; Bulgarian troops in, 295, 324, 369; German divisions held in, 324, 410, 423; Resistance movements in, 408-9; civil factions in, 409-10, 412-13, 421; British missions to, 410-13, 415-17; Russian attitude to, 412-14; position of monarchy in, 412-414, 419-20; Provisional Government in, 413; attempts to obtain collaboration between rival Governments of, 414-20;

Tito's aims for unity in, 418; Communisation of. 623; enemy divisions in, September 8, 1943, 632, 634

Yunnan, 79

Zanussi, General, 96-7
Zervas, Colonel Napoleon, 472-3
Zionists, 62
"Zip", 563